Walt Disney World® Resort, Universal Orlando®

Also Includes SeaWorld® and Central Florida

ECONOGUIDE.COM | 2002

Corey Sandler

Contemporary Books

Chicago New York San Francisco Lisbon London Madrid Mexico City Milan New Delhi San Juan Seoul Singapore Sydney Toronto

Contemporary Books
*A Division of The **McGraw-Hill** Companies*

1 2 3 4 5 6 7 8 9 0 LBM/LBM 0 9 8 7 6 5 4 3 2 1

ISBN 0-8092-2628-6
ISSN 1521-9267

This book was set in Stone Serif by Word Association, Inc.
Printed and bound by Lake Book Manufacturing

This book is printed on acid-free paper.

To Willie and Tessa
May their lives always be a magical theme park

Contents

Acknowledgments

Dozens of hard-working and creative people helped move my words from the keyboard to the place where you read this book now.

Among the many to thank are Adam Miller and Julia Anderson of Contemporary Books.

Our appreciation extends to Walt Disney World, Universal Orlando, SeaWorld Orlando, and Busch Gardens Tampa for their assistance. Thanks, too, to the hotels, restaurants, and attractions that offered discount coupons to our readers.

Thanks to Andrea Boucher who polished my words with skill and good humor. As always, thanks to Janice Keefe who ran the office—and the author—so well.

And finally, thanks to you for buying this book. We all hope you find it of value; please let us know how we can improve the book in future editions. (Enclose a stamped envelope if you'd like a reply; no phone calls, please.)

You can send me E-mail at: csandler@econoguide.com.

And you can check out information about all the books in the *Econoguide* travel book series on our website, at www.econoguide.com.

Corey Sandler
Econoguide Travel Books
P.O. Box 2779
Nantucket, MA 02584

About the Author

Corey Sandler is a former newsman and editor for the Associated Press, Gannett Newspapers, IDG, and Ziff-Davis Publishing. He has written more than 160 books on travel, video game, and computer topics; his titles have been translated into French, Spanish, German, Italian, Portuguese, Polish, and Chinese. When he's not traveling, he lives with his wife and two children on Nantucket island, thirty miles off the coast of Massachusetts.

We hope you'll look for these other *Econoguide* titles by Corey Sandler, also from Contemporary Books:

Econoguide Disneyland Resort, Universal Studios Hollywood
Econoguide Las Vegas
Econoguide Washington, D.C., Williamsburg
Econoguide Pacific Northwest
Econoguide Canada
Econoguide London
Econoguide Paris
Econoguide Cruises
Golf U.S.A.

The books are available at your local bookstore, on the Web, and through our website, www.econoguide.com.

Introduction to the 2002 Edition

Thirty years ago there was just a single major theme park in Orlando. In 1971 the Magic Kingdom opened in the reclaimed swamp and forests of what was in the process of becoming Walt Disney World.

Today there are four theme parks on Disney property, three water parks, a circus, a baseball stadium, a race track, ninety-nine holes of golf, and much more. About fifteen minutes away is Universal Orlando with two theme parks, and SeaWorld with two more.

And the next millennium of theme park excitement is underway in Florida's theme park mecca.

At Epcot Center, construction is underway on Mission: SPACE, an "astronaut experience." Universal Orlando has gotten the bugs out of its high-tech Universal Studios Islands of Adventure park, while it gets the bugs in at Men in Black at the Universal Studios Florida park.

SeaWorld, renowned for its devotion to things natural, is now the home of the most unnatural thrill in Orlando: Kraken, the highest, fastest, and longest roller coaster in town. Across the road is Discovery Cove, an ultra-exclusive marine park with some of the best facilities (and absolutely the highest prices) anywhere.

The *Econoguide* Best of Orlando and Central Florida

Walt Disney World	Universal Orlando	Other Attractions
Magic Kingdom	Universal Studios Florida	SeaWorld Orlando
Disney's Animal Kingdom	Universal Studios Islands of Adventure	Discovery Cove
Disney–MGM Studios	Universal CityWalk Orlando	Kennedy Space Center Visitor Center
Epcot Center		Wet 'n Wild
Downtown Disney		Gatorland
Cirque du Soleil		Busch Gardens Tampa Bay
Blizzard Beach		
Typhoon Lagoon		

The technological and storytelling marvel known as Islands of Adventure includes Spider-Man, by most opinions the most advanced theme park ride in town, as well as a pair of roller coasters (The Hulk and Dueling Dragons) that seem several steps beyond the laws of physics. Nearby, Universal CityWalk, is an entertainment and dining magnet by night.

Top draws at Walt Disney World include several recent additions: the wild GM Test Track at Epcot, the fabulous *Fantasmic!* show and the thrilling Rock 'n' Roller Coaster at Disney–MGM Studios, and a state-of-the-art old-fashioned dark ride, The Many Adventures of Winnie the Pooh, at the Magic Kingdom.

At Downtown Disney the weird and wonderful Cirque du Soleil is in residence in a permanent circus tent. Across the way Disney Quest is an indoor virtual reality theme park.

The Kennedy Space Center Visitor Complex continues to expand its peek into the world of the Space Shuttle and the International Space Station.

In Tampa Bay, Busch Gardens made a big splash with Rhino Rally, an unusual safari ride into the midst of its animals, which begins as a truck ride and ends as a river raft adventure.

And we're all keeping an eye on rumors such as these: a fifth major theme park at Walt Disney World, perhaps with a science fiction theme, and another water park at Disney.

Universal Studios owns two thousand acres on the other side of I-4, and there's some deep thinking going on about a few more theme parks and other entertainments.

How in the world can you keep track of everything worth knowing about in Central Florida? Here's a humble suggestion: *Econoguide 2002 Walt Disney World Resort, Universal Orlando.*

An Insider's Guide

I'm a huge fan of Orlando. I've been there enough times that I'm on a first-name basis with flight attendants, car rental clerks, and hotel check-in staff. And I swear that the ghoul in charge of the Tower of Terror saves me the front row in the soon-to-be-out-of-control elevator.

I don't know of many other places with so much to do, so many interesting places to visit . . . and so many ways to spend hard-earned dollars.

My goal in the *Econoguide* series is to help you get the most for your money and make the best use of your time. This is not a guide for cheapskates; you will, though, learn how to travel well—considerably better than the folks in front and behind you in line. (Oh, and I'll offer some tips on how to reduce the chances of finding long lines.)

Once again I've gone back and walked every mile of every major park and attraction and looked everywhere for changes and new features. There are thousands of changes, minor and major, from last year's edition of the book.

And, of course, you'll also find a selection of money-saving coupons. Pardon me for saying so, but buying this book is a no-brainer: you'll save many times the cover price by using just a few of the coupons, including ticket discounts at Universal Studios, SeaWorld, travel agencies, hotels, and much more.

About Walt Disney World and Orlando

Walt Disney World is a magical kingdom of fantastic delights for children of all ages; I recommend it highly.

I also love Universal Studios Florida, Universal Studios Islands of Adventure, SeaWorld, and dozens of other excellent attractions and recreational opportunities in the Orlando and Central Florida region.

But let's get something straight here: as wonderful an entertainment opportunity as they are, Walt Disney World, Universal Orlando, SeaWorld, and all the rest are basically gigantic vacuum cleaners aimed at your wallet.

Disney's greatest accomplishment in Orlando was the creation of an entire world of entertainment: four theme parks, three water parks, half a dozen golf courses, a baseball stadium, a world-class automobile racetrack, dozens of hotels, hundreds of restaurants, and thousands of major and minor diversions from tennis to horseback riding to boating to bicycling to cartooning lessons. There's a whole island of restaurants and nightclubs, a gigantic movie theater complex, and a permanent circus. For many guests, a week's visit to Orlando can be spent entirely within the boundaries of the Walt Disney World resort.

But now, for the first time, Disney has serious competition for multi-day visits. Universal Orlando has two parks on its property, the Wet 'n Wild water park nearby, a huge rock and roll club, its own island of restaurants and clubs, and the first of five planned hotel complexes.

Not Too Cute

After visits that have totaled months at Walt Disney World, the Disneyland Resort, Disneyland Paris, and Tokyo Disneyland, I've come up with my All-Purpose Disney Attraction Classification Guide. I've decided that Disney attractions can be divided into "Disney Cute," "Disney Smart," and "Disney Wow."

Disney Cute is Mickey Mouse, Winnie the Pooh, Aladdin, It's a Small World, Tiki Birds, Snow White, Cinderella, and Dumbo. That's where they set the hook with young children and their parents.

Disney Smart is Disney's Animal Kingdom, Epcot's Future World, Epcot's World Showcase, Epcot's Innoventions, the Hall of Presidents, the Carousel of Progress, and the Special Effects and Production Tour. This is where Disney magic helps us learn.

Disney Wow is the GM Test Track, Rock 'n' Roller Coaster, Dinosaur, Space Mountain, Tower of Terror II, Star Tours, The Great Movie Ride, Thunder Mountain Railroad, and Splash Mountain. These are the things that make us say, "Ooh."

One reason for Disney's success is that they have learned to mix Cute, Smart, and Wow. It's the reason children come back as adolescents and then as parents; it's the reason adults can enjoy accompanying their youngsters.

Add to this Disney's impressive devotion to expanding its attraction to adults with things such as water parks, golf courses, tennis courts, nightclubs, and spectacularly sybaritic hotels, and it's only just begun: Disney's Wide World of Sports, the spring training baseball facilities for the Atlanta Braves, the national

Theme park top ten. According to the trade magazine *Amusement Business*, Walt Disney World included four of the top six theme parks in North America in 2000. Universal Studios Florida, Universal's Islands of Adventure, SeaWorld Orlando, and Busch Gardens Tampa are also in the top ten. Here are the magazine's estimates:

1. The Magic Kingdom at Walt Disney World, Orlando. 15.4 million visitors.
2. Disneyland, Anaheim. 13.9 million.
3. Epcot at Walt Disney World. 10.6 million.
4. Disney–MGM Studios at Walt Disney World. 8.9 million.
5. Disney's Animal Kingdom at Walt Disney World. 8.3 million.
6. Universal Studios Florida, 8.1 million.
7. Universal's Islands of Adventure, Orlando. 6 million.
8. Universal Studios Hollywood, 5.2 million.
9. SeaWorld Orlando. 5.2 million.
10. Busch Gardens Tampa Bay. 5 million.

headquarters of the Amateur Athletic Union, and much more.

Call those "Disney for Adults," and they will be the reason this place will continue to be a lure for us all once we are too jaded for Cute, too educated for Smart, and (alas) too old for Wow.

Why This Book?

Now, don't get me wrong: Walt Disney World and Universal Orlando may be the best-designed, best-run, and most overall satisfying tourist attractions on this planet. But you also have the right to spend your time and money as carefully as possible. That's what this book is all about.

This book is aimed at helping you get the very most from your time and money as you travel to Orlando and visit the parks and attractions there.

About Independence

That other guidebook about Walt Disney World, the one with "The Official Guide" stamped on its cover, offers an impressive batch of material. But, in my humble opinion, it suffers from a fatal closeness to its subject: it is prepared with the Walt Disney Company (and published by a Disney corporate cousin).

That would explains why it finds very little that is anything less than wonderful within the boundaries of Walt Disney World, and why it almost ignores the world outside.

In that official book there is hardly a mention of Universal Orlando, SeaWorld, or Busch Gardens, for example. This is not because they are unworthy of mention or because visitors to Walt Disney World don't visit those attractions and others. The reason for their absence is the fact that the Walt Disney Company does not profit from them.

So let me state again our independence: the author and publisher of this book have no connection with Walt Disney World, Universal Orlando, SeaWorld, Busch Gardens, or any of the other attractions written about here. Similarly, there is no financial interest in any of the discount coupons published within the book.

Our profit comes from you, the readers of this book, and it is you we hope to serve as best we can.

Part I
On the Road to Orlando

Chapter 1
When: The Seasons of Central Florida

Here are two hypothetical days from a vacation trip to Orlando:

July 4. It wasn't exactly the flight you wanted. However, you're grateful for the privilege of forking over $840 for a coach seat in the jammed cabin of the jet. All of the rooms inside the park—at $240 per night—are sold out, but you were lucky enough to pay just $150 for a very ordinary hotel room that is a twenty-minute bumper-to-bumper drive from the parking lots.

According to the driver of the tram you are parked near the Magic Kingdom, although you're not sure you're in the same county. When you get to the ticket booths there's a thirty-minute wait just to get on the monorail to the entrance. Once inside you sprint to Tomorrowland to find that the line for Space Mountain includes what seems to be the occupants of every car you passed on the long, long ride through the gigantic parking lot.

Or perhaps you've set as your goal the thrilling GM Test Track at Epcot. In your mind's eye you imagine zipping around the fifty-degree curves at 65 miles per hour; when you get there you find a traffic jam with people in line all the way back to the airport.

At Disney–MGM Studios you want to be a millionaire, but all the money in your pockets is not enough to get you into *Who Wants to Be a Millionaire—Play It!*

At Universal's Islands of Adventure the lines for the Incredible Hulk Coaster are incredible, for Dr. Doom's Fearfall they're fearsome, and the only way you're going to get into Back to the Future is to go back to the past.

And you'd better plan on showing up for lunch at 10:45 A.M. and dinner at 4:30 P.M. if you hope to find a table at the lowliest overpriced burger stop. But there are always the cooling thrills at Blizzard Beach, right? True, but the line for Florida's only ski resort stretches back to Philadelphia.

March 20. It seems like it's just your family and a crew of flight attendants, stretched out at thirty thousand feet. Even nicer, you were able to grab a deep-discount excursion fare ticket for $188. Your hotel room outside the parks cost $29.95, and the road to the kingdom is empty.

The sleek monorail stands empty and waiting for you at the transportation center. Your leisurely walk to Space Mountain puts you into a ten-minute queue; later in the day you drop into a rocket car without breaking stride. At Epcot your private vehicle waits your arrival at the GM Test Track.

Over at Universal's Islands of Adventure, Spider-Man senses your arrival personally and The Cat in the Hat is looking for company.

Take your pick of restaurants, and feel free to take a break in the afternoon and run over to Typhoon Lagoon; temperatures often reach eighty degrees, and the lagoon is like the beach on a semiprivate tropical island.

Do I have to point out which trip is likely to be more enjoyable?

Our Guiding Rule

The basic *Econoguide* strategy to getting the most out of your trip is this: *Go when most people don't; stay home when everyone else is standing in line.*

Specifically, I suggest you try to make your visit to Florida when school is in session and in the weeks between holidays: between Labor Day and Thanksgiving, between Thanksgiving and Christmas, between New Year's Day and Presidents' Week, between Presidents' Week and spring break or Easter, between Easter and Memorial Day.

I'm not just talking about crowds at Walt Disney World, Universal Studios Orlando, SeaWorld, and elsewhere in Central Florida. There's also the availability of discount airline tickets, off-season motel rates, and restaurant specials to consider.

You'll find lower prices when businesses are anxious for your patronage. The best deals can be found in low-season or what travel agents call the "shoulder-season," midway between the slowest and busiest times.

But this doesn't mean you can't have a good time if your schedule (or your children's) requires you to visit at high-season. I'll show you ways to save money and time, any time of the year.

A Walt Disney World Vacation Calendar

Walt Disney World is, and probably always will be, the number one attraction in Orlando; the crowd estimates in this calendar are based on the history of that four-theme-park resort. However, the same relative crowd levels can be expected at Universal Studios Orlando's theme parks and at other attractions in Florida.

New Year's Eve and New Year's Day

Second week of January through end of the month

Disney World Indy 200 Weekend

Warm and semiprivate. Room rates at low-season level, except during special events such as the Disney World Indy 200 Weekend.

New Year's Day and a few days afterward are the crowded aftermath of the

Christmas rush. But when the kids go back to school and most of the adults return to work after the Christmas–New Year's holiday, the population at the parks drops off very sharply. The second week of January through the first week of February is usually the second least crowded period of the year, with daily attendance averaging about twenty-five thousand visitors at the Magic Kingdom. Watch out, though, for the late-January weekend when an Indy 200 race is held at the track near the Magic Kingdom; the race draws as many as fifty thousand visitors, and many of them spill over to the parks after the race. The Walt Disney World Marathon is held in mid-January, drawing more than ten thousand participants and their supporters.

Key to calendar

= Semiprivate

= Moderate crowds

= Heavy crowds

= Elbow-to-elbow

During this time the parks close early and do not offer nighttime parades or fireworks, but you'll be able to walk right onto most major rides and attractions; room rates are at their lowest level.

February

First ten days of February

Moderate crowds. Warm but not hot. Room rates lower than at peak-season levels.

Early February is a period of average attendance, reaching thirty thousand to thirty-five thousand visitors daily. The parks generally close early except for weekends, and there are no nighttime parades or fireworks.

Presidents' Week holiday period

Heavy crowds for holiday week. Room rates at high-season level.

Presidents' Week (celebrated in many school districts in and around the period from February 12 to February 22) is a time of fairly heavy attendance, up to about forty-five thousand visitors daily. Watch out for Race Week in Daytona, too. The parks are open late, with nightly parades and fireworks.

Late February

A quiet time. Rooms drop to shoulder-season levels.

March

Entire month

March comes in like a lamb. Back to moderate attendance. Thermometer nudges into the eighties. Room rates at shoulder-season level.

Attendance falls off to moderate from the end of February through the first week of April, averaging about thirty-five thousand visitors. There are days in early March when you will have the parks to yourself, but at other times you will join thousands of college kids on early spring break or baseball fans drawn south for Spring Training. Weatherwise, though, this is not a bad time to come to Florida—with luck you will run into eighty-degree water park days. The parks generally close early and there are no nighttime parades or fireworks in the first half of the month; during spring break the parks are open later.

April

First and fourth week of April

Usually a lovely time, with moderate attendance and room rates below peak-season levels.

Sneak in before or after the spring break rush. The parks generally close early, and there are no nighttime parades or fireworks.

Second and third week of April

The Easter Parade can attract a lot of bunnies and college breakers. Consistent eighty-degree weather. Room rates at high-season levels.

The second and third weeks of April are among the most crowded times, as Easter visitors and spring break students clog the turnstiles at rates of up to sixty thousand per day. The parks are open late, with parades and fireworks.

May

Entire month of May

Moderate attendance, swimming weather, and shoulder-season rates.

Another relatively quiet period, from the end of April through the first week of June. Expect average attendance of about thirty thousand per day. The parks generally close early, and there are no nighttime parades or fireworks.

June to August

The crazy days of summer

Hot sun, lots and lots of company, and high-season rates.

Just after Memorial Day the throngs of people come—and stay. Crowds of about sixty thousand per day can be expected from the first week of June through the third week of August. Room rates are at high-season. Temperatures average in the nineties; and you can expect a few heavy downpours or steady rains. Parks are open late, with nighttime parades and fireworks.

And just to make things even more crowded, sometimes it seems as if half of Brazil comes north for warm weather in August.

September to Mid-November

The post-summer doldrums

Theme park heaven: no lines, no crowds, and low, low rates. Watch out for Golf Classic weekend, though. Temperatures still high.

Where have all the tourists gone? On the day after Labor Day the turnstiles slow to a crawl, averaging about twenty thousand visitors per day. Room rates reach bottom, too. The weather is quite good, although the occasional tropical storm or hurricane can dampen a few days here and there. The parks generally close at 6 P.M. or 7 P.M., but the lack of lines should allow you to see everything you want. There are some late hours on weekends, with parades or fireworks.

In recent years the Golf Classic has occupied a weekend in late October, bringing thousands of PGA fans to hotels and the parks.

November

🚶🚶🚶 ***Thanksgiving for what?***

Airlines, hotels, and restaurants give thanks for the huge crowds at Thanksgiving. Rates at high-season level.

The one-week period around Thanksgiving brings the brief return of "No vacancy" signs at motels and in attraction lines. Average attendance is about fifty-five thousand visitors. The parks generally close early, except for the holiday week and weekends surrounding it.

December

🚶 ***First through third weeks***

This is it: the secret season. Mickey can get lonely at times like these, and hotels will almost pay you to come and stay.

From after Thanksgiving until the day Christmas vacation starts is the quietest time of the year for a visit. Attendance levels average fifteen thousand to twenty thousand per day, and lines are rare. Room rates are rock-bottom, too. The parks generally close early, and there are no nighttime parades or fireworks, except for on weekends.

🚶🚶🚶🚶 ***Christmas Holiday***

The not-at-all-secret season. Your sisters and cousins and aunts will all be in line, in front of you. You may need a loan for the super-high-season room rates.

The Christmas–New Year's holiday is the most crowded, least time-efficient time to visit Central Florida. You'll be shoulder to shoulder with an average of seventy-five thousand to eighty thousand other visitors each day at Walt Disney World, with large crowds and long lines at Universal Studios, SeaWorld, and other area attractions. Parks are open late, a full schedule of parades by day and night, capped off by fireworks.

The crowds can become so large that some of the parks actually close the gates by mid-morning. Don't feel too bad if you're shut out. It could be worse: you could be inside . . . in line.

You cannot count on air temperatures warm enough for swimming, either. Room rates are at their highest levels, too.

It's a festive, happy time, but frankly, we'd rather be alone or close to it. If you must go be sure to arrive at the park early and follow the Power Trip plan for your best chance.

Special events at Walt Disney World

February: Chinese New Year at Epcot.

Mid-February: Pleasure Island Mardi Gras.

Mid-March: St. Patrick's Day Celebration at Pleasure Island.

Easter: Walt Disney World Easter Parade at the Magic Kingdom.

Spring (Mid-April through early June): Epcot International Flower & Garden Festival.

Memorial Day Weekend: Special late-night entertainment and late hours at all parks.

Late October: Walt Disney World Golf Classic.

Holiday Special Events

The "Walt Disney World Happy Easter Parade," marches down Main Street in the Magic Kingdom and is broadcast nationally; check with Disney reservations before you visit to find out if the parade will be taped a few days ahead of Easter itself; it usually is.

The lovely Epcot International Flower & Garden Festival takes place within the gates of Epcot from mid-April through June 1.

At the end of October, the park celebrates Mickey's Not-So-Scary Halloween Party, which is just what it sounds like. Guests are invited to dress in costumes and trick-or-treat throughout the park from 7 P.M. to midnight over a three-day weekend. The party also includes parades, live music, and storytelling, culminating in a special fireworks display.

In recent years, special tickets for the Halloween party were priced at about $26 plus tax for general admission and $20 plus tax for children (ages 3–9). A small discount was offered for advance purchase. For information, contact any Walt Disney World ticket location or Ticketmaster.

Just how powerful is Disney? How's this: The Magic Kingdom predicts a 100 percent chance of snow flurries in balmy central Florida for Mickey's Very Merry Christmas Party each year.

Of course, this is Disney and it's not really snow. But then again, that's not really a mouse wearing those size 48 shoes, either. (Sorry to disillusion you.) Instead, there's a phalanx of artificial snow machines set up behind Main Street U.S.A. to blanket the crowds at the end of the nightly "Mickey's Very Merry Christmas Parade." And there are also special stage shows and fireworks shows with a holiday theme.

The Christmas party requires a separate admission ticket; in recent years the park was cleared at the end of each day and then reopened at 8 P.M., remaining open until 1 A.M. Certain length-of-stay ticket packages included the extra night's admission.

At Disney–MGM Studios the park looks like a hardware store gone crazy with the "Osborne Family Light Extravaganza." Epcot celebrates "Holidays Around the World" and World Showcase pavilions.

At Universal Studios Florida big annual events include a monstrous Halloween party and an extended Mardi Gras celebration in late winter.

The Best Day to Go to the Park

When Mommy, Daddy, Willie, and Tessa arrive in Orlando on Sunday (the most common arrival date) for a week's visit (the most common length of vacation), the first place they will go is the Magic Kingdom on Monday. Epcot comes next, then the Disney–MGM Studios. The remainder of the week is usually given over to other area parks and attractions.

But we believe the best plan for your visit is to adopt what we call a "Contrarian View." In other words, go against the common logic of others that says, "We came here for the Magic Kingdom and that's where we'll go first."

Disney's Animal Kingdom, the newest park at Walt Disney World will be the first stop for many visitors because it is the newest park at Walt Disney World.

So, too, Universal's Islands of Adventure will be a major draw for years to come; you can expect long lines there during holiday periods and much of the rest of the year as well. The good news is that the new park may reduce the crowds a bit at the neighboring Universal Studios Florida. But most visitors come to Orlando for Disney and will head there first; a contrarian approach says head to Universal early in the week instead of later.

	GO	DON'T GO
Magic Kingdom	Sunday Thursday Friday	Monday Tuesday Wednesday Saturday
Disney's Animal Kingdom	Sunday Thursday Friday Saturday	Monday Tuesday Wednesday
Epcot	Sunday Monday Thursday Friday	Tuesday Wednesday Saturday
Disney–MGM Studios	Sunday Monday Friday Saturday	Tuesday Wednesday Thursday
Universal Studios Florida, Universal Studios Islands of Adventure and other area attractions	Sunday Monday Tuesday Friday	Wednesday Thursday Saturday
SeaWorld	Weekdays	Weekends

By the way, it should be obvious that seven days is not enough time to come close to sampling all that Orlando and Central Florida have to offer; if time and money are no object I'd suggest a ten-day to two-week visit with about half of the time devoted to Disney World and the other days for Universal Studios Florida, SeaWorld, Busch Gardens, and all the other attractions in the area.

Here is one schedule you might want to consider if you are visiting Central Florida during one of the busy times of the year. It starts with arrival on Saturday, which is a bit against the tide; if you get to Orlando early enough you may be able to visit a water park or other attraction (other than the Magic Kingdom) that night.

The *Econoguide* Contrarian Schedule

SATURDAY
Arrive in Orlando. Visit water parks, smaller attractions, dinner theaters, or Pleasure Island

SUNDAY
Magic Kingdom, Animal Kingdom, Disney–MGM Studios, Universal Studios Florida, or Universal's Islands of Adventures

MONDAY
Universal's Islands of Adventure or Disney–MGM Studios

TUESDAY
SeaWorld, beach, golf, water parks, or other attractions

WEDNESDAY
Busch Gardens, Space Center, Cypress Gardens, or Splendid China

THURSDAY
Epcot Center

FRIDAY
Magic Kingdom, Animal Kingdom

SATURDAY
A second chance at the park of your choice (avoid Magic Kingdom, Animal Kingdom, and SeaWorld)

CENTRAL FLORIDA WEATHER AVERAGES

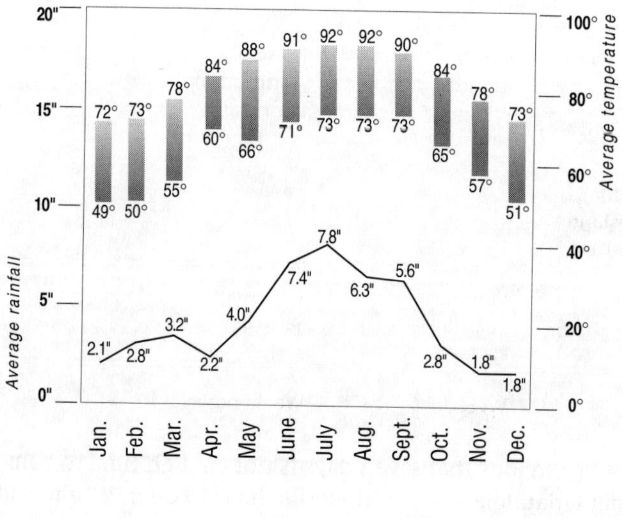

Chapter 2
How: Planes, Trains, and Automobiles

I love to travel, but I hate to waste time and money. It all but kills me to know that I spent $200 more than I should have for an airline ticket, or that the next guy over has a nicer hotel room at a better price. Put another way, my goal is to take more vacations and spend more time in wondrous places than most people, and to have a better time while I'm at it.

Let's get something straight here, though: This is not a guide for the cheapskate who wants a $10-a-night tour of dreadful dives and uninspiring but free sights.

I'm perfectly willing to spend money for value received. Our joint goal will be to find the very best for our time and money.

Air Travel

The way I figure it, one major airline is pretty much like another. Sure, one company may offer a larger bag of peanuts while the other promises its flight attendants have more accommodating smiles. Me, I'm much more interested in other things:

1. Safety
2. The most convenient schedule
3. The lowest price

Though I'm sometimes willing to trade price for convenience, I'll never risk my neck for a few dollars.

But that doesn't mean I don't try my hardest to get the very best price on airline tickets. I watch the newspapers for seasonal sales and price wars, clip coupons from the usual and not-so-usual sources, consult the burgeoning world of Internet travel agencies, and happily play one airline against the other.

Alice in Airlineland

There are three golden rules to saving hundreds of dollars on travel: be flexible, be flexible, and be flexible.

- Be flexible about when you choose to travel. Go, if you can, in seasons when airlines, hotels, and attractions offer substantial discounts.

Checking in again. Having a boarding pass issued by a travel agent is not the same as checking in at the airport; you'll still need to show your ticket at the counter so the agent knows you're there.

• Be flexible about the day of the week you travel. You can often save hundreds of dollars by changing your departure date one or two days. Ask your travel agent or airline reservationist for current fare rules and restrictions.

The lightest air travel days are generally Tuesday through Thursday, Saturday afternoons, and Sunday mornings. The busiest times are Sunday evenings, Monday mornings, and all day Friday.

In general you'll receive the lowest possible fare if you include a Saturday in your trip, buying what is known as an "excursion fare." Airlines use this as a way to exclude business travelers from the cheapest fares, assuming that they will want to be home by Friday night.

• Be flexible when you choose the hour of your departure. There is generally lower demand—and therefore lower prices—for flights that leave in the middle of the day or very late at night.

• Be flexible on the route you'll take, or your willingness to put up with a change of plane or stopover. Once again, you're putting the law of supply and demand in your favor. A direct flight from Chicago to Orlando for a family of four may cost hundreds of dollars more than a flight from Chicago to Orlando that includes a change of planes in Raleigh-Durham or Atlanta, for example.

• Don't overlook the possibility of flying out of a different airport, either. For example, residents of metropolitan New York can find domestic flights from La Guardia, Newark, or White Plains. Suburbanites of Boston might want to consider flights from Worcester or Providence as possibly cheaper alternatives to Logan Airport. Most visitors will fly into Orlando, although some super-discount flights and charters use Sanford airport, which is just a bit less convenient.

Look for airports where there is competition—especially if one of the carriers is a discount airline—rather than places where one airline all but owns the terminal.

For a family of four, it's easy to save a few hundred dollars with careful shopping, enough to pay for a chauffeured limousine or a nice meal.

• Plan way ahead of time and purchase the most deeply discounted advance tickets, which are usually noncancelable. Most carriers limit the number of discount tickets on any particular flight; although there may be plenty of seats left on the day you want to travel, they are usually priced at higher rates.

In a significant change in recent years, most airlines have modified "nonrefundable" fares to become "noncancelable." What this means is that if you're forced to cancel or change your trip, your tickets retain their value and can be applied against another trip, usually for a fee of about $75 per ticket; in 2001 some airlines boosted the change fee to $100.

• Conversely, you can take a chance and wait for the last possible moment, keeping in contact with charter tour operators and accepting a bargain price on a "leftover" seat and hotel reservation. You *may* also find that some airlines will reduce the prices on leftover seats within a few weeks of your date of departure; check regularly with the airline or ask your travel agent to do it for you. In fact some travel agencies use computer programs that keep a constant electronic eagle eye on available seats and fares.

• Some websites feature "last minute" fares. The prices may be very attractive, but the tickets are almost certain to be accompanied by restrictions making it impossible or expensive to make any changes once they have been issued.

Double indemnity. Your homeowner's or renter's insurance policy may include coverage for theft of your possessions while you travel, making it unnecessary to purchase a special policy. Check with your insurance agent.

• Take advantage of special discount programs such as senior citizens' clubs, military discounts, or offerings from organizations to which you may belong. If you're in the over-sixties category you may not even have to belong to a group such as the American Association of Retired Persons (AARP); simply ask the airline reservationist if there is a discount available. You may have to prove your age when you pick up your ticket.

• The day of the week on which you buy your tickets may also make a price difference. Airlines often test out higher fares over the relatively quiet weekends. They're looking to see if their competitors will match their higher rates; if the other carriers don't bite, the fares often float back down by Monday morning. Shop during the week.

Other Money-Saving Strategies

Airlines are forever weeping and gnashing their teeth about huge losses due to cutthroat competition. And then they regularly turn around and drop their prices radically with major sales. I don't waste time worrying about the bottom line of the airlines; it's my own wallet I want to keep full. Therefore, the savvy traveler keeps an eye out for airline fare wars all the time. Read the ads in newspapers and keep an ear open for news broadcasts that often cover the outbreak of price drops. If you have a good relationship with a travel agent you can ask to be notified of any fare sales.

The most common times for airfare wars are in the weeks leading up to the quietest seasons for carriers, including the period from mid-May to mid-June (except the Memorial Day weekend), between Labor Day and Thanksgiving, and again in the winter with the exception of Christmas, New Year's, and President's Day holiday periods.

Don't be afraid to ask for a refund on previously purchased tickets if fares go down for the period of your travel. The airline may refund the difference, or you may be able to re-ticket your itinerary at the new fare, paying a $100 penalty for cashing in the old tickets. Be persistent: if the difference in fare is significant it may be worth making a visit to the airport to meet with a supervisor at the ticket counter.

Study the fine print on discount coupons from airlines or third parties such as supermarkets, catalog companies, and direct marketers. In most cases, I have found these coupons are often less valuable than they seem. Read the fine print

Finding a bucket shop. Look for ads for ticket brokers and bucket shops in the classified ads in *USA Today*, the "Mart" section of the *Wall Street Journal* or in specialty travel magazines.

carefully and be sure to ask the reservationist if the price you are quoted under the terms of the coupon is higher than another available fare.

Consider buying from discounters known as "consolidators" or, less kindly, as "bucket shops." These companies buy slow-to-sell tickets from airlines in volume and resell them at rock-bottom prices. Look for ads in Sunday newspaper travel sections and on websites posted by consolidators.

You can also find ticket broker and bucket shop ads on-line and in the classified ads in *USA Today*, the "Mart" section of *The Wall Street Journal*, and the back pages of *The Village Voice*. Some travel agencies can also offer consolidator tickets.

Just be sure to weigh the savings on the ticket price against any restrictions; for example, they may not be changeable, and they usually don't accrue frequent flyer mileage.

Beating the Airlines at Their Own Game

In my opinion the airlines deserve all the headaches we travelers can give them because of the illogical and costly pricing schemes they throw at us—deals such as a fare of $350 to fly ninety miles between two cities where they hold a monopoly, and $198 bargain fares to travel three thousand miles across the nation. Or round-trip fares of $300 if you leave on a Thursday and return on a Monday, and $1,200 if you leave on Monday and return the next Thursday.

But a creative traveler can find ways to work around most of these roadblocks. Nothing I'm going to suggest here is against the law; some of the tips, though, are against the rules of some airlines. Here are a couple of strategies.

Nested tickets. This scheme generally works in either of two situations: when regular fares are more than twice as high as excursion fares that include a Saturday night stay over, or when you plan to fly between two locations twice in less than a year.

Let's say you want to fly from Boston to Orlando. Buy two sets of tickets in your name. The first is from Boston to Orlando and back. This set has the return date for when you want to come back from your second trip. The other set of tickets is from Orlando to Boston and back to Orlando, this time making the first leg of the ticket for the date you want to come back from the first trip, and the second leg of the trip the date you want to depart for the second trip.

If this sounds complicated that's because it is. It will be up to you to keep your tickets straight when you travel. Some airlines have threatened to crack down on such practices by searching their computer databases for multiple reservations. That doesn't mean you can't buy such tickets. Check with a travel agent for advice. One solution: buy one set of tickets on one airline and the other set on another carrier.

Split tickets. Fare wars sometimes result in super-cheap fares through a connecting city. For example, an airline seeking to boost traffic through a hub in Atlanta might set up a situation in which it is less expensive to get from

Chicago to Orlando by buying a round-trip ticket from Chicago to Atlanta, and then a separate round-trip ticket from Atlanta to Orlando.

Be sure to book a schedule that allows enough time between flights; if you miss your connection you could end up losing time and money.

Standing Up for Standing By

One of the little-known secrets of air travel on most airlines and most types of tickets is the fact that travelers who have valid tickets are allowed to stand by for flights other than the ones for which they have reservations; if there are empty seats on the flight, standby ticket holders are permitted to board.

Here's what I do know: if I can't get the exact flight I want for a trip I make the closest acceptable reservations available and then show up early at the airport and head for the check-in counter for the flight I really want to take. Unless you're seeking to travel during an impossibly overbooked holiday period or arrive on a bad-weather day when flights have been canceled, your chances of successfully standing by for a flight are usually pretty good.

Overbooking

"Overbooking" is a polite industry term that refers to the legal practice of selling more than an airline can deliver. It all stems, alas, from the unpleasant habit of many travelers who neglect to cancel flight reservations that will not be used. Airlines study the patterns on various flight and city pairs and apply a formula that allows them to sell more tickets than there are seats, with the expectation that a certain percentage will not show up at the airport.

But what happens if all passengers holding reservations show up? Obviously, the result will be more travelers than seats, and some will have to be left behind.

The involuntary bump list will begin with the names of passengers who are late to check in. Airlines must ask for volunteers before bumping any passengers who have followed the rules on check-in.

Now, assuming no one is willing to give up his seat just for the fun of it, the airline will offer some sort of compensation—either a free ticket or cash, or both. It is up to the passenger and the airline to negotiate an acceptable deal. The U.S. Department of Transportation's consumer protection regulations set minimum levels of compensation for passengers who are bumped from a flight as a result of overbooking.

It isn't considered "bumping" if a flight is canceled because of problems with equipment, bad weather, or the lack of a flight crew.

You're also not eligible for compensation if the airline substitutes a smaller aircraft for operational or safety reasons, or if the flight involves an aircraft with sixty seats or less.

How to Get Bumped

Why in the world would you *want* to be bumped? Well, perhaps you'd like to look at missing your plane as an opportunity to earn a little money for your time rather than as an annoyance. Is a two-hour delay worth $100 an hour?

How about $800 for a family of four to wait a few hours on the way home—that should pay for a week's hotel stay on your next trip.

If you're not in a rush to get to Florida—or to get home—you might want to volunteer to be bumped. I wouldn't recommend this on the busiest travel days of the year or if you're booked on the last flight of the day, unless you're also looking forward to a free night in an airport motel.

My very best haul: on a flight home from London, my family of four was bought off with a free night's stay in a luxury hotel, $1,000 each in vouchers for future tickets, and an upgrade on our flight home the next day.

Bad Weather, Bad Planes, Strikes, and Other Headaches

You don't want pilots to fly into weather they consider unsafe, of course. You also don't want them to take up a plane with a mechanical problem. No matter how you feel about unions, you probably don't want to cross a picket line to board a plane piloted by strikebreakers. And so, you should accept an airline's cancellation of a flight for any of these legitimate reasons.

Here's the bad news, though: if a flight is canceled for an "act of God," such as bad weather, an earthquake, or a plague of locusts, or because of a labor dispute, the airline isn't required to do anything except refund your money. In practice, though, carriers will usually make a good effort to find another way to get you to your destination more or less on time, which could mean rebooking on another flight on the same airline or on a different carrier. But you could be facing a delay of a day or more in the worst situations, such as a major snowstorm that delays interconnecting flights around the nation.

Here is a summary of your rather limited rights as an air passenger:

- An airline is required to compensate you above the cost of your ticket only if you're bumped from an oversold flight against your will.
- If you volunteer to be bumped, you can negotiate for the best deal with the ticket agent or a supervisor; for your inconvenience, you can usually expect to be offered a free round-trip ticket on the airline.
- If your scheduled flight is unable to deliver you directly to the destination on your ticket, and alternate transportation such as a bus or limousine is provided, the airline is required to pay you twice the amount of your one-way fare if arrival at your destination will be more than two hours later than the original ticket promised.
- If you purchased your ticket with a credit card, the airline must credit your account within seven days of receiving an application for a refund.

All that said, in many cases you will be able to convince an agent or a supervisor to go beyond the letter of the law. I've found that the best strategy is to politely but firmly stand your ground. Ask the ticket clerk for another flight, for a free night in a hotel and a flight in the morning, or for any other reasonable accommodation. Don't take no for an answer, but remain polite and ask for a supervisor if necessary. Sooner or later they'll do something to get you out of the way.

And then there are labor problems such as those that faced companies like

American Airlines and USAirways in recent years. Your best defense against a strike is to anticipate it before it happens; keep your ears open for labor disputes when you make a reservation. Then keep in touch with your travel agent or with the airline itself in the days leading up to a strike deadline.

It is often easier to make alternate plans or seek a refund in the days immediately before a strike; if you wait until the deadline arrives you're going to be somewhere in a very long line of upset people.

In the instance of a strike a major airline will attempt to reroute you on another airline if possible; if you buy your own ticket on another carrier you're unlikely to be reimbursed. If your flight is canceled you'll certainly be able to claim a full refund of your fare or obtain a voucher in its value without paying any penalties.

Airline Safety

There are no guarantees in life, but in general, flying aboard an airplane is considerably safer than driving to the airport. All major carriers have very good safety records; some are better than others. I pay attention to news reports of Federal Aviation Administration (FAA) inspections and rulings and then I consider making adjustments to my plans.

And though I love to squeeze George Washington until he yelps, I make it a point to avoid start-up and super-cut-rate airlines because I have my doubts about how much money they can afford to devote to maintenance. Many of these airlines also have a fleet of elderly or outdated planes.

Among major air carriers, the fatal accident rate over the course of the last twenty-five years stands somewhere between 0.3 and 0.74 incidents per 1 million flights. Not included in these calculations are small commuter airlines (except those that are affiliated with major carriers).

The very low numbers over such a long period of time, experts say, make them poor predictors of future incidents. Instead, you should pay more attention to reports of FAA or National Transportation Safety Board (NTSB) rulings on maintenance and training problems.

The best policy. Consider buying trip cancelation insurance from a travel agency, tour operator, or directly from an insurance company (ask your insurance agent for advice).

The policies are intended to reimburse you for any lost deposits or prepayments if you must cancel a trip because you or certain members of your family become ill. Read the policy carefully to understand the circumstances under which the company will pay.

Take care not to purchase more coverage than you need; if your tour package costs $5,000 but you would lose only $1,000 in the event of a cancelation, then the amount of insurance required is just $1,000. Some policies will cover you for health and accident benefits while on vacation, excluding any pre-existing conditions.

Be sure you understand your contract with your airline; you may be able to reschedule a flight or even receive a refund after payment of a service charge; some airlines give full refunds or free rescheduling if you can prove a medical reason for the change.

Don't wait to drop a card. Keep in touch with your travel agent or tour operator. In many cases they can anticipate major changes before departure time and will let you know. And many operators will try hard to keep you from demanding a refund if you find a major change unacceptable.

They may offer a discount or an upgrade on a substitute trip or adjust the final price of the changed tour.

About Travel Agencies

Do you need a travel agent? My advice: Get a good one, or go it alone. Good travel agents are those who remember who they work for: you.

Remember that there is a built-in conflict of interest between an agent and a traveler, because the agent is in most cases paid by someone else.

Agents receive a commission on airline tickets, hotel reservations, car rentals, and other services they sell you. The more they sell (or the higher the price), the more they earn.

I would recommend you start planning for any trip by calling the airlines and a few hotels and finding the best package you can put together for yourself. *Then* call your travel agent and ask him or her to do better.

If your agent contributes knowledge or experience, comes up with dollar-saving alternatives to your own package, or offers some other kind of convenience, then go ahead and book through the agency. If, as I often find, you know a lot more about your destination and are willing to spend a lot more time to save money than is the agent, do it yourself.

A number of large agencies offer rebates on part of their commissions to travelers. Some of these companies cater only to frequent flyers who will bring in a lot of business; other rebate agencies offer only limited services to clients.

You can find discount travel agencies through many major credit card companies (Citibank and American Express among them) or through associations and clubs. Some warehouse shopping clubs have rebate travel agencies.

And if you establish a regular relationship with your travel agency and bring them enough business to make them glad to hear from you, don't be afraid to ask them for a discount equal to a few percentage points.

Another important new tool for travelers is the Internet where you'll find computerized travel agencies that offer airline, hotel, car, cruise, and package reservations. You won't receive personalized assistance, but you will be able to make as many price checks and itinerary routings as you'd like without apology.

Several of the services feature special deals, including companion fares and rebates you won't find offered elsewhere.

Some of the best Internet agencies include:

Atevo	www.atevo.com
Microsoft Expedia	www.expedia.com
Travelocity	www.travelocity.com
The Trip	www.thetrip.com

You can also book directly with a number of major airlines, sometimes taking advantage of special Internet prices or bonus frequent flyer mileage. Airlines have figured out that they can make millions by cutting the travel agent out of the equation; most share some of their new profit with direct buyers.

Among the airlines that offer on-line booking are:

American Airlines	www.aa.com
Continental Airlines	www.continental.com
Delta Airlines	www.delta.com
Northwest Airlines	www.nwa.com
Southwest	www.southwest.com
United Airlines	www.united.com
USAirways	www.usairways.com

Tour Packages and Charter Flights

Tour packages and flights sold by tour operators or travel agents may look similar, but the consumer may end up with significantly different rights.

What you end up with all depends on whether the flight is a scheduled or nonscheduled flight. A "scheduled flight" is one that is published in the *Official Airline Guide* and is available to the general public through a travel agent or from the airline. This doesn't mean a scheduled flight will be on a major carrier or that you'll be flying on a 747 jumbo jet; it could just as easily be the propeller-driven pride of Hayseed Airlines. Every scheduled flight, though, does have to meet stringent federal government certification requirements.

A "nonscheduled flight" is commonly known as a "charter flight." The term is sometimes also applied to a package that includes a nonscheduled flight, hotel rooms, ground transportation, and other elements. Charter flights are generally put together by a tour operator who purchases all the seats on a specific flight to a specific destination or rents an airplane and crew from an air carrier.

Charter flights and charter tours are regulated by federal agencies, but your rights as a consumer are much more limited than those given to buyers of tickets on a scheduled flight.

You wouldn't purchase a hamburger without knowing the price and specifications (two all-beef patties on a sesame seed bun, etc.). Why, then, would you spend hundreds or even thousands of dollars on a tour and not understand the contract that underlies the transaction?

When you purchase a charter flight or a tour package, you should review a contract that spells out your rights. This document is sometimes referred to as the "Operator Participant Contract"

Lug-it-yourself. If you are using a scheduled airline to connect with a charter flight, or the other way around, your baggage will not be automatically transferred. You must make the transfer yourself.

Charter and tour flights operate independently of other flights. If you are on a trip that combines scheduled and nonscheduled flights, or two unrelated charter flights, you may end up losing your money and flight because of delays.

It may make sense to avoid such combinations for that reason, or to leave extra hours or even days between connections. Some tour operators offer travel delay insurance that pays for accommodations or alternative travel arrangements necessitated by certain types of delays.

or the "Terms and Conditions." Look for this contract in the booklet or brochure that describes the packages; ask for it if one is not offered. Remember that the contract is designed mostly to benefit the tour operator, and each contract may be different from others you have agreed to in the past. The rule here is: *if you don't understand it, don't sign it.*

How to Book a Package or Charter Flight

For charter flights and packages consider using a travel agent, preferably one you know and trust from prior experience. In general the tour operator pays the travel agent's commission. Some tour packages, however, are available only from the operator who organized the tour; in certain cases you may be able to negotiate a better price by dealing directly with the operator, although you are giving up one layer of protection for your rights.

Pay for your ticket with a credit card; this is a cardinal rule for almost any situation in which you're prepaying for a service or product. If you end up in a dispute with the travel company or the agency, you should be able to enlist the assistance of the credit card issuer on your behalf.

Realize that charter airlines don't have large fleets of planes available to substitute in the event of a mechanical problem or an extensive weather delay. They may not be able to arrange for a substitute plane from another carrier.

If you're still willing to try a charter after all of these warnings, make one more check of the bottom line before you sign the contract.

- First of all, is the air travel significantly less expensive than the lowest nonrefundable fare from a scheduled carrier? (Remember that you are, in effect, buying a nonrefundable fare with most charter flight contracts.)
- Have you included taxes, service charges, baggage transfer fees, or other charges the tour operator may put into the contract?
- Are the savings significantly more than the 10 percent the charter operator may (typically) boost the price without your permission? Do any savings come at a cost of time? Put a value on your time.
- Finally, don't buy a complete package until you have compared it to the a la carte cost of such a trip. Call the hotels offered by the tour operator, or similar ones in the same area, and ask them a simple question: "What is your best price for a room?" Be sure to mention any discount programs that are applicable, including the American Automobile Association (AAA) or other organizations. Do the same for car rental agencies, and place a call to any attractions you plan to visit to get current prices.

Accident and Sickness Insurance

The idea of falling ill or suffering an injury while hundreds of miles away from home and your family doctor can be a terrifying thought.

But before you sign on the bottom line for an accident and sickness insurance policy, be sure to consult with your own insurance agent or your company's personnel office to see how far your personal medical insurance policy will reach. Does the policy cover vacation trips and exclude business travel? Can you purchase a "rider," or extension, to your personal policy?

The only reason to purchase an accident and sickness policy is to fill in any gaps in coverage you already have. If you don't have health insurance a travel policy is certainly valuable, but perhaps you should consider whether you should spend the money on a year-round policy instead of taking a vacation.

Also be aware that nearly every kind of health insurance has an exclusionary period for preexisting conditions. If you are sick before you set out on a trip you may find the policy will not pay for treating the problem.

Orlando International Airport

Orlando's airport has grown from a backwater strip to one of the busiest—and most efficiently operated—terminals in the country. Located about thirty minutes west of Walt Disney World, it is served by several major highways as well as bus and limousine service.

There are three main clusters of gates at the airport; each cluster is connected to the single ticketing and baggage claim area by an automated monorail; you won't be the first to observe that the first semi–thrill ride of your vacation is at the airport.

Here are the gate assignments as they existed in mid-2001; be sure to check with your airline on arrival for any changes:

Gates 1–29 "A" Side of Terminal. Aeropostal, Aerolineas Argentinas, Air Jamaica, Air Transat, Allegro, America West Airlines, American Airlines, American Eagle, ATA, Aviateca, Bahamasair, Britannia, Canada 3000, Champion Air, Continental Airlines, Copa Airlines, El Al, Falcon Air Express, First Air, Flair, Grupo Taca, Gulfstream International, Iberia, Lacsa, Mexicana, Miami Air, Omni Air International, Planet Airways, Royal, Ryan International, Southwest Airlines, Sunworld, Transmeridian Airlines, TWA

Gates 30–59 "B" Side of Terminal. ANA, Air Canada, MetroJet, Midwest Express, Northwest, United, USAirways, USAirways Express

Gates 60–99 "B" Side of Terminal. Aero Mexico, Balair, British Airways, Cayman Airways, Comair, Delta, Delta Express, Frontier, Icelandair, LTU, Martinair, Saudi Arabian Airlines, TransBrasil, Virgin Atlantic

Gates 100–129 "B" Side of Terminal. AirTran, Jet Blue, Midway Air, Southwest Airlines, Sun Country Airlines

The Virgin connection. Virgin Atlantic Airways has made Orlando its largest gateway in the United States, with more than twenty flights from there each week. Guests heading for a Virgin Atlantic flight can check their bags at a facility alongside the Virgin Megastore in Downtown Disney and spend the day at Walt Disney World before their night flight to London or Manchester.

Orlando Sanford Airport

Sanford's airport is located about twenty-five miles northeast of Orlando, off Route 4. In recent years Pan Am has offered scheduled service from a handful of destinations; a number of charter airlines, including some international carriers, also use the airport. For information, call ☎ (407) 585-4000 or consult 💻 www.orlandosanfordairport.com.

Area Transportation Information

Orlando International Airport Visitor Information. (407) 825-2352. www.state.fl.us/goaa.

I-Ride. (407) 248-9590. www.Iridetrolley.com. A bus service along International Drive, connecting hotels, attractions, and restaurants. The trolley-like bus runs from SeaWorld to Belz Factory Outlet seven days a week from 7 A.M. to midnight, about fifteen minutes apart, making more than fifty scheduled stops between SeaWorld Orlando and the Belz Factory Outlet World.

The service carries more than a million passengers a year. A single adult fare is 75 cents; children twelve and younger ride free when accompanied by a paying adult. One-day passes are $2; multi-day passes are also available.

The Mercado has its own shuttle serving hotels on International Drive.

LYNX/Tri-County Regional Transportation Authority. (407) 841-8240. www.golynx.com. Public transportation in Orlando and nearby.

Amtrak. (407) 843-7611 or (800) 872-7245. www.amtrak.com. Daily train service to Orlando from New York, Tampa, and Miami. Stops include downtown Orlando, Winter Park, and Sanford. The Auto Train transports passengers and their cars from Lorton, Virginia, each day, departing in the afternoon and arriving about 9 A.M. of the next day in Sanford, twenty-five miles northeast of downtown Orlando.

Greyhound Bus Lines. (407) 292-3424. www.greyhound.com. The Kissimmee station is located at 16 North Orlando Avenue. Shuttle vans and taxis are available from the station.

Mears Transportation. (407) 423-5566. www.mearstransportation.com. Shuttle van, town car, and limousine service from Orlando International Airport to hotels and attractions.

Drive?, He Said

Everyone's conception of the perfect vacation is different, but for me, I draw a distinction between getting there and being there. I want the getting there part to be as quick and simple as possible, and the being there part to be as long as I can manage and afford. Therefore, I fly to most any destination more than a few hundred miles from my home. The cost of driving, hotels, meals en route, and general physical and mental wear and tear rarely equals a deeply discounted excursion fare.

If you do drive, though, you can save a few dollars by using the services of AAA or another automobile club. And before you head out make certain your vehicle is in traveling shape: a tune-up and fully inflated, inspected tires will save gas, money, and headaches.

If you plan to travel by bus or train be aware that the national carriers generally have the same sort of peak and off-peak pricing as the airlines. The cheapest time to buy tickets is when the fewest people want them.

Extra miles. Don't let it force you to pay too much for a rental car, but all things being equal, use a rental agency that awards frequent flyer mileage in a program you use.

Renting a Car for a Florida Trip

If you are planning to stay at a hotel within Walt Disney World you may be able to do without renting a car, although you will not be able to get to attractions and restaurants outside the Disney boundaries without calling a cab or car service.

If you are staying outside Walt Disney World you may be able to use a hotel shuttle bus to the parks; but you will find your options limited by the bus schedule.

You should consider renting a car. The good news is that Orlando is one of the most competitive markets anywhere in the country. Except during peak periods, rental rates for a small car are as low as $150 to $250 per week; a larger or more luxurious car rents for about twice that amount.

Your travel agent may be of assistance in finding the best rates; you can make a few phone calls by yourself, too. Rental rates generally follow the same low-shoulder–high-season structure. I have paid as little as $59 a week for a tiny subcompact (a convertible, no less) in low season.

Fast food. One advantage to bringing a car to the park is the chance to save a bit of money and get a more relaxed, better meal by ducking out of the park at lunch and visiting a decent buffet or menu restaurant; come back to the park for some evening rides and the fireworks. (Get your hand stamped when you leave the park *and* hold on to your ticket stub—both are needed for readmission on the same day. Your parking receipt is also valid for reentry to any of the parking lots.)

Every major car rental agency, and many not-so-major ones, has operations in Orlando. Consider the value of your time in choosing among rental companies with locations at the Orlando airport—including Avis, Budget, Dollar, and National—and those who conduct their business a few miles away. The lowest rates are generally offered by companies that put you on a bus and take you to their lot; you'll have to wait for a bus in both directions, adding as much as thirty minutes to each end of your transaction. Alamo, perhaps the biggest operator in Orlando, is one of the farthest away and often features one of the slowest counters; on one recent trip, in the relatively slow month of May, I lost a full hour in line at Alamo. They earned this special mention.

Car Rental Gotchas

Car rental companies will try—with varying levels of pressure—to convince you to purchase special insurance coverage. They'll tell you it's "only" $7 or $9 per day. What a deal! But that works out to about $2,500 or $3,330 per year for a set of rental wheels. The coverage is intended primarily to protect the rental company, not you.

Check with your insurance agent to determine how well your personal automobile policy covers a rental car and its contents. We strongly recommend you use a credit card that offers rental car insurance; such insurance usually covers the deductible below your personal policy. The extra auto insurance by itself is usually worth an upgrade to a "gold card" or other extra-service credit card.

The only sticky area comes for those visitors who have a driver's license but no car, and therefore no insurance. Again consult your credit card company and your insurance agent to see what kind of coverage you have or need.

Although it is theoretically possible to rent a car without a credit card, you will find it to be a rather inconvenient process. If they cannot hold your credit card account hostage most agencies will require a large cash deposit—perhaps as much as several thousand dollars—before they will give you the keys.

Pay attention, too, when the rental agent explains the gas tank policy. The most common plan says you must return the car with a full tank; if the agency must refill the tank you will be billed a service charge plus what is usually a very high per-gallon rate.

Other optional plans include one where the rental agency sells you a full tank when you first drive away and takes no note of how much gas remains when you return the car. Unless you somehow manage to return the car with the engine running on fumes, you are in effect making a gift to the agency with every gallon you bring back.

I prefer the first option, refilling the tank on the way to the airport on getaway day.

Super Rental Deals

If you can figure out a way to get to Florida inexpensively in the spring, you can take advantage of the glut of rental vehicles of all description that agencies wish were elsewhere—mostly up north.

Companies including Avis, Budget, Hertz, and National offer cars for as little as $6 a day, provided you drop off the car in one of a few dozen northeast cities. Under most plans you can hold on to the car for as long as two weeks.

The situation is reversed in the fall, when car agencies want to send vehicles down south for the snowbirds.

Interstate 4 Exits in Kissimmee/Orlando Area

25A	US 192 East. Motel strip toward downtown Kissimmee. Water Mania, Old Town, Medieval Times.
25B	US 192 West. Main gate of Walt Disney World. Motel strip, Splendid China.
26A/B	Epcot Center, Disney–MGM Studios, Typhoon Lagoon, Epcot Resorts, Disney Village, Pleasure Island.
27	SR 535 to Kissimmee and Lake Buena Vista. Hotel Plaza Resorts, Disney Village Resorts, Fort Wilderness, River Country.
27A	SeaWorld. Central Florida Parkway Eastbound (toward Orlando) only.
28	528 East (Beeline) to SeaWorld, Orlando International Airport and Kennedy Space Center. (Toll road.)
29	SR 482 (Sand Lake Road) to Orlando, Orlando International Airport, and International Drive.
30A/B	Highway 435 (Kirkman Road). Universal Studios.
31	Florida Turnpike south to Miami or north to Wildwood.
33A	Hwy. 441, 17-92 (South Orange Blossom Trail).

MAJOR ROADS NEAR WALT DISNEY WORLD

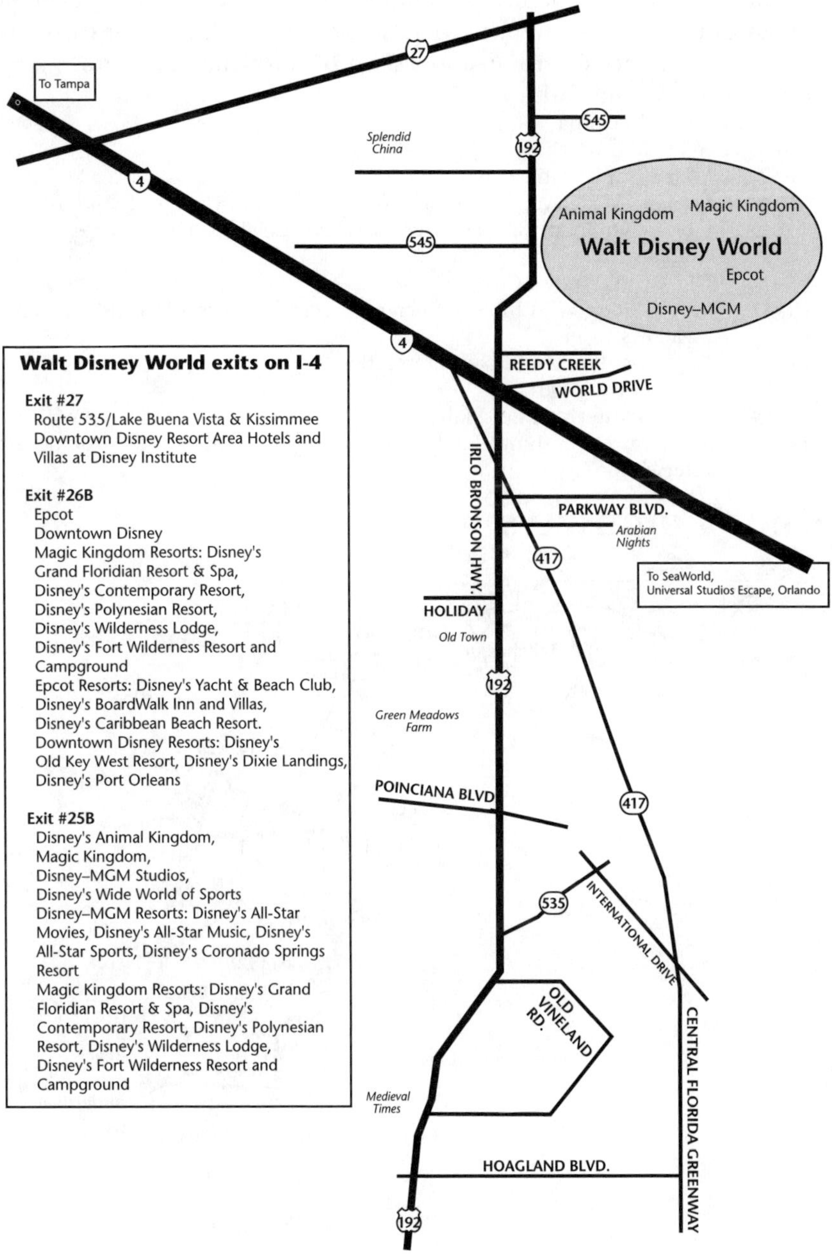

A Guide to Highway 192

A new road sign system helps demark a twelve-mile stretch of the confusing U.S. Highway 192, also known as Irlo Bronson Highway.

In the initial project, markers are numbered from 4 at the western end near Splendid China and the entrance to Walt Disney World, to 15 at the eastern end of the Kissimmee tourist area just short of Hoagland Boulevard.

Here are a few landmarks:

4	Splendid China
5–6	A World of Orchids
6–7	Walt Disney World main gate
7–8	Disney's Wide World of Sports. I-4 to SeaWorld, Universal Studios Florida, Orlando, Church Street, Disney's Celebration
8–9	Arabian Nights, Water Mania
9–10	Old Town, Pirate's Cove
10–11	Movie Rider, Wild Bill's, Poinciana Boulevard crosses U.S. 192, Green Meadows Farm
11–12	Capone's, Vineland Road intersection
12–13	Congo River Golf
13–14	Manufacturer's Outlet Mall
14–15	Medieval Times, Jungleland, River Adventure Golf, Hoagland Boulevard intersection

FLORIDA HIGHWAYS

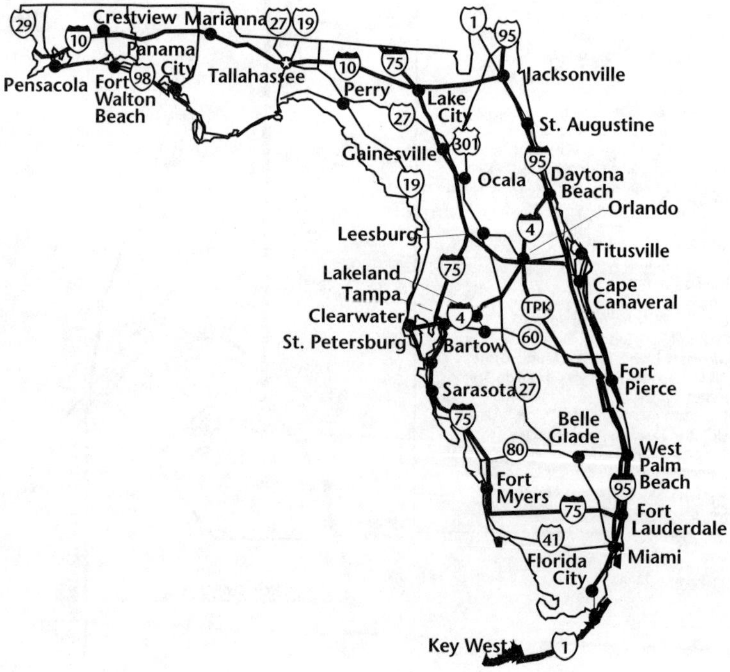

Chapter 3
Where: Sleeping and Eating for Less

Everybody's got to sleep and eat. But no two people seem to place the same value on a bed and a meal.

When I travel I usually spend as little time as possible in my room—I collapse into bed much too late to visit the pool or stroll the lobby, and I'm off on my next adventure at sunrise. So I'm looking for something quiet, clean, safe, and convenient to my next day's plans. Others, though, get all wrought up about glass elevators, room service, retail shops, and the number of channels on the television set in the room.

On the other hand, when I travel to a theme park, my main gustatory goal is to find a place to eat where there are cloth napkins and the butter does not come in the shape of mouse ears. For some of you, that's exactly the goal.

In this chapter we'll take an *Econoguide* tour through the many options for sleeping and eating in and around Walt Disney World. I'll begin with the hotels and restaurants within the boundaries of the park.

(Coverage of restaurants within the theme parks can be found in the chapters on the Magic Kingdom, Epcot, Disney–MGM Studios, Disney's Animal Kingdom, Universal Studios Orlando, Universal's Islands of Adventure, SeaWorld, and Busch Gardens Tampa.)

At Walt Disney World the newest place to stay is Disney's Animal Kingdom Lodge, opened in 2001. A year later the first half of the mammoth 5,760-room Disney's Pop Century Resort will open between Disney's Wide World of Sports and Disney's Caribbean Beach Resort.

When the current projects are completed, the total number of guest rooms at Walt Disney World will exceed thirty-three thousand, at nineteen resorts.

At Universal Orlando the lovely Portofino resort and the Hard Rock Hotel are open. In 2002 the **Royal Pacific Resort at Universal Orlando** joins them.

Negotiating for a Room

Notice the title of this section: it's *not* called "buying" a room. Hotel rooms, like almost everything else, can be negotiated by the savvy traveler.

Here is how to pay the highest possible price for a hotel room: walk up to the front desk without a reservation and say, "I'd like a room." If there any rooms available, you may be charged the "rack rate," which is the published maximum nightly charge.

Here are a few ways to pay the lowest possible price:

1. Before you head for your vacation, spend an hour on the phone and call directly to a half dozen hotels that seem to be in the price range you'd like to spend. (We recommend membership in AAA and use of their annual tour books as starting points for your research.)

Start by asking for the "room rate." Then ask them for their "best rate." Does that sound unnecessary? Trust me, it's not: I can't begin to count the number of times the rates have dropped substantially when I have asked again.

True story: I once called the reservation desk of a major hotel chain and asked for the rates for a night at a Chicago location. "That will be $149 per night," I was told. "Ouch," I said. "Oh, would you like to spend less?" the reservationist answered. I admitted that I would, and she punched a few keys on her keyboard. "They have a special promotion going on. How about $109 per night?" she asked.

Not bad for a city hotel, I reasoned, but still I hadn't asked the big question. "What is your best rate?" I asked. "Oh, our best rate? That would be $79," said the agent.

But, wait: "OK, I'll take it. I'm a AAA member, by the way." Another pause. "That's fine, Mr. Sandler. The nightly room rate will be $71.10. Have a nice day."

When you feel you've negotiated the best deal you can obtain over the phone, make a reservation at the hotel of your choice. Be sure to go over the dates and prices one more time, and obtain the name of the person you spoke with and get a confirmation number if available.

2. But wait: when you show up at your hotel on the first night, stop and look at the marquee outside and see if the hotel is advertising a discount rate. Most of the hotels in the Walt Disney World area adjust their prices based on attendance levels at the park. It is not uncommon to see prices change by $10 or more over the course of a day.

Here's where you need to be bold. Walk up to the desk as if you *did not* have a reservation, and ask the clerk: "What is your best room rate for tonight?" If the rate they quote you is less than the rate in your reservation, you are now properly armed to ask for a reduction in your room rate.

Similarly, if the room rate advertised out front on the marquee drops during your stay, don't be shy about asking that your charges be reduced. Just be sure to ask for the reduction *before* you spend another night at the old rate, and obtain the name of the clerk who promises a change. If the hotel tries a lame excuse, such as "That's only for new check-ins," you can offer to check out and then check back in again. That will usually work; you can always check out and go to the hotel across the road that will usually match the rates of its competitor.

3. And here is the way to make the most flexible choice, in the low-season only. Come down without a reservation, and then cruise one of the motel strips such as I-192 (Bronson) or International Drive. Check the outdoor marquees for

discount prices and make notes. Find a phone, and make a few calls to the ones you found attractive. Once again, be sure to ask for the best price. The later in the day you search for a room, the more likely you are to find a hotel ready to make a deal.

Wrong numbers. Be sure you understand the telephone billing policy at the motel. Some establishments allow free local calls, while others charge as much as $1 for such calls. (I'm especially unhappy with service charges for 800 numbers.) Be sure to examine your bill carefully at checkout and make sure it is correct. We strongly suggest you obtain a telephone credit card and use it when you travel; nearly all motels tack high service charges on long distance calls and there is no reason to pay it.

Dialing for Dollars

As I cited in my "True Story," you must be aggressive in guarding your checkbook in dealing with a reservation agent. Sometimes you will also need to be persistent.

The fact is that a single room may be offered at four different prices by four different agents: you may find the lowest price by calling directly to the hotel; in some cases, a chain's toll-free central reservations service may have some special deals. Occasionally travel agents are offered special promotional rates.

If you're doing your own booking call the central reservations number for a chain and follow up with a direct call to the hotel. If you use a travel agent request that the agent verify the lowest rate indicated on the agency's computer with a direct call to the hotel.

Think of it this way: if you can save $20 a night on a week's stay, your first few meals are free.

Here's my card. Membership in AAA brings some important benefits for the traveler, although you may not be able to apply the club's usual 10 percent discount on top of whatever hotel rate you negotiate. (It doesn't hurt to ask, though.) Be sure to request a tour book as well as Florida and Orlando maps from AAA, even if you plan to fly to Florida; they are much better than the maps given by car rental agencies.

Where Should You Stay?

Except during the most busy holiday travel times of the year—Christmas through New Year's, spring break, and the Fourth of July through mid-August, among them—you're not going to have *any* trouble locating a decent place to stay in the Orlando and Kissimmee area. In fact, the biggest problem is choosing among the various options.

In this chapter, I'll offer a tour of the main hotel areas in and around Walt Disney World.

How should you choose a place to stay? I'd suggest you start by deciding on a price range you'd be willing to pay. Then decide what sort of accommodations fit your needs—in the Kissimmee-Orlando area you can find single rooms and spacious suites in nearly every price range. At the extremes—the least expensive and the most expensive—the difference in quality can be substantial. In the middle price ranges the difference among rooms is often mostly related to location.

Safety first. The small safes available in some hotels can be valuable to the traveler; be sure to inquire whether there is a service charge for their use. We've been in hotels that apply the charge regardless of whether we used the safe or not; look over your bill at check-out and object to any charges that are not proper. In any case, we'd suggest that any objects that are so valuable you feel it necessary to lock them up should probably be left home.

Weekly, not weakly. Are you staying a full week? Ask for the weekly rate. If the room clerk says there is no such rate, ask to speak to the manager: he or she should be willing to shave the price for a long-term stay.

If you're traveling with a family do you want a luxury multi-bedroom suite or a set of connecting single rooms? Do you need a refrigerator or kitchen? (You can easily save $20 per day for a family of four by eating breakfast in your room; but if a room with a refrigerator costs $25 more per day, it's no deal at all.)

Are you willing to drive fifteen minutes in the morning and at the end of the day to save money or obtain a better room for the same price?

Few would argue with the statement that some of the most exciting and most convenient hotels are to be found within the Walt Disney World park boundaries, but they come at a not insignificant premium.

Following are ranges for low-season rooms; high-season rates can be as much as double:

$25 to $60 per night. East and west of I-4 on I-192, also known as Irlo Bronson Highway. The farther east or west you go on Bronson, up to about eight miles from I-4, the lower the prices.

You'll also find budget motels in the South Orange Blossom Trail area and in some downtown Orlando districts, about twenty to thirty minutes away from Walt Disney World.

$50 to $100 per night. Walt Disney World budget hotels, including the very basic All-Star Sports, Music, Movies, and Pop Century Resorts. Other moderately priced places are on International Drive; resort motels can be found on I-192 and in the Apopka Vineland Road area. Half an hour away, rooms in this range can be found in downtown Orlando and near Orlando International Airport.

$100 to $300 per night. Walt Disney World premium hotels, first-class hotels in Lake Buena Vista, and better establishments along International Drive and within Universal Orlando.

As you can see, the room rates are pretty self-selecting for location and, to a large extent, the quality of the room. Next you can make decisions on extras, including special recreational facilities.

Hotels Within Walt Disney World

Within Walt Disney World are five clusters of hotels and resorts. Reservations can be made through travel agencies or through the Disney central travel desk at ☎ (407) 934-7639 or consult 🖳 www.disneyworld.com/vacation.html.

Hotels accept American Express, MasterCard, Visa, and the Disney Credit Card. In most cases reservations must be cancelled more than seventy-two hours prior to the arrival date; check-in time is 3 P.M. and checkout 11 A.M.

Disney World Resorts Price Ranges

Rates are per night, vary by season, and are subject to change. Hotels within the resort start at the Value level; lower-priced accommodations are available outside the Disney border.

$$ Value (About $77 to $104)
- Disney's All-Star Sports Resort
- Disney's All-Star Music Resort
- Disney's All-Star Movies Resort
- Disney's Pop Century Resort *(opens in 2002)*

$$$ Moderate (About $124 to $179)
- Disney's Caribbean Beach Resort
- Disney's Dixie Landings Resort
- Disney's Port Orleans Resort
- Disney's Coronado Springs Resort

$$$$ Deluxe
- Disney's Animal Kingdom Lodge ($199 to $510)
- Disney's Beach Club Resort ($264 to $540)
- Disney's Contemporary Resort ($190 to $750)
- Disney's Wilderness Lodge ($185 to $390)
- Disney's Polynesian Resort ($185 to $600)
- Disney's BoardWalk Inn ($184 to $580, suites to $1,540)
- Disney's Yacht and Beach Club Resort ($264 to $975)
- Disney's Grand Floridian Resort & Spa ($299 to $645)
- Dolphin and Swan Resorts ($295 to $490; suites $610 to $2,850)
- Disney's Old Key West Resort ($229 to $300, suites to $790)

Housekeeping Villas
- Disney's Old Key West Resort ($305 to $1,050)
- Disney's Fort Wilderness Homes ($180 to $254)
  - Cabins ($204 to $275)
  - Camp sites ($35 to $74)
- Disney's BoardWalk Villas ($254 to $1,540)
- Villas at Disney Institute ($204 to $510)

Children younger than eighteen stay free with their parents; an additional charge of $8 to $15 per adult is added for more than two adults in a room. All Disney hotels offer free rollaway beds, up to the room's limit on occupancy.

Disney hotels have as many as four "seasons" for room prices. Super Value rates are generally in effect in January and September. Value rates are offered in early February, post-Easter to early June, the end of August, and from October 1 through mid-December. Regular rates are generally in effect from mid-February through mid-April, and from mid-June through mid-August. Top Holiday rates are charged from mid-December through New Year's Eve.

Magic Kingdom Resort Area

★★★Disney's Wilderness Lodge. $$$$. 901 Timberline Drive, Lake Buena Vista. ☎ (407) 824-3200. A rustic, 728-room lodge patterned after the famed Old Faithful Inn at Yellowstone National Park. The lodge includes massive log columns, totem poles, and stone fireplaces—just the sort of thing you'd expect in Central Florida, right? But wait: there's also a twelve-story geyser, a waterfall, and a rocky swimming pool that begins in the lobby as a hot spring and works its way outside.

The resort, located between the Contemporary Resort and Fort Wilderness, offers a view of the Electrical Water Pageant, with launch service to the parks.

The **Cub's Den** offers a supervised dining and Western-theme entertainment club for children ages four to twelve, including movies and video games. The club is open from 5 P.M. to midnight, at a charge of $6 per hour.

Artist Point ($$$) celebrates the flavors of the Pacific Northwest with items such as maple-glazed king salmon, elk sausage, and pan-seared rainbow trout at dinner, served from 5:30 to 10 P.M. The gourmet eatery is transformed in the early morning from 7:30 to 11:15 A.M. as the site of a character breakfast with Pocahontas, John Smith, Meeko, and more.

The Whispering **Canyon Cafe** ($$) features all-you-can-eat buffets for breakfast and dinner and a family-style cookout each evening. At lunchtime, an a la carte menu includes sandwiches, burgers, and chili.

Roaring Forks ($) offers counter-service burgers, sandwiches, salads, and other basic fare.

Transportation to the Magic Kingdom includes boat service from the hotel dock, and buses to the other theme parks and elsewhere in Walt Disney World.

★★Disney Contemporary Resort. $$$$. 4600 North World Drive, Lake Buena Vista. ☎ (407) 824-1000. Is it a hotel that has a monorail running through the middle, or a monorail station with a hotel surrounding it? Either way, it's a most unusual setting and just a mouse trot from the main gate of Walt Disney World. It's a great place to view the nightly Electrical Water Pageant in season, especially if your room faces the lagoon. The resort includes 1,052 rooms, a health club, and a marina.

Note that not all of the rooms are in the fifteen-story, A-shaped main building with the monorail station but may be located in the more ordinary annex buildings along the lake. There are suites on the hotel's fourteenth floor that include private concierge and special services.

The **Concourse Steakhouse** has trellised ceilings that allow peeks through to the ninety-foot-high atrium lobby and the monorail trains passing through. Breakfast, lunch, and dinner are offered from 7 A.M. through 10 P.M., with dinner entrees starting at about $15. Specialties include charbroiled steak, oven-roasted chicken, pasta dishes, and seafood.

The **Contemporary Cafe** offers a breakfast and dinner buffet.

High above it all, on the fifteenth floor, is by most accounts Disney's best (and among the priciest) gourmet eatery. The **California Grill** ($$$) has offerings ranging from sushi and lemon grass soup to spicy braised lamb shank with Thai red curried lentils, Atlantic salmon baked under a black-olive crust with grilled vegetable ratatouille, and pan-seared yellowfin tuna with black beans. Dinner is served from 5:30 to 10 P.M. You can watch specialties being prepared within the exhibition kitchen, or catch a view of the fireworks or water parade from the windows.

Disney hotels and restaurants

★★	Better hotels
★★★	Superior hotels
★★★★	*Econoguide* Best
$	Budget room rates
$$	Moderate room rates
$$$	Deluxe room rates
$$$$	Premium room rates

Hotel restaurant price ranges

Entrée prices at dinner. Prices are approximate and subject to change.

$	$10 and less
$$	$10 to $19
$$$	$20 to $34
$$$$	$35 and more

Chef Mickey's Restaurant ($$) offers breakfast or dinner with the majordomo mouse himself. Dinner selections include shrimp, prime rib, carved meats, and a salad bar. Breakfast is served from 7:30 to 11:30 A.M., priced at about $13.95 for adults and $7.95 for children ages three to eleven. Dinner is available from 5 to 9:30 P.M., priced at $17.95 for adults and $7.95 for children ages three to eleven.

Sports facilities include a white sand beach, six clay tennis courts, two heated outdoor swimming pools with a water slide, and a toney fitness center. Guests can rent Water Sprites from the marina, or a waterskiing boat with driver and skis.

The **Mouseketeer Clubhouse** is open from 4:30 P.M. to midnight for children ages four to twelve; rates are about $8 per hour per child. For reservations call ☎ (407) 824-3038. Two movies (Disney titles, of course) are shown each night in the theater at the Fiesta Fun Center, which is also the home of a large collection of video arcade machines.

Transportation to the parks is by monorail, water taxi, and bus. You can also catch a water taxi to Discovery Island.

★★★★Disney's Grand Floridian Resort & Spa. $$$$. 4401 Grand Floridian Way, Lake Buena Vista. ☎ (407) 824-3000. An opulent resort along the shores of Seven Seas Lagoon with its own monorail station. A mixture of Victorian elegance and modernity in white and coral trim; in typical Disney fashion it is much prettier than the real thing probably ever was. The hotel drew its design from some of the grand old hotels of Palm Beach at the turn of the century, including the Royal Poinciana.

The spectacular five-story Grand Lobby is topped by stained-glass skylights and lit in the evening by grand chandeliers. A Big Band entertains nightly. Some of the rooms include quirky dormers and turrets, as well as balconies that offer close-up views of the Magic Kingdom.

There are fifteen honeymoon suites and other suites with as many as three bedrooms. The resort includes 901 rooms, a health club, tennis courts, a marina with Water Sprites and sailboats, and a white sand beach fronting Seven Seas Lagoon.

The **Mouseketeer Club** for children ages four to twelve is open 4:30 P.M. to midnight. Rates are $8 per hour, with dinner included. Call ☎ (407) 824-2985 for reservations.

The prime restaurant is **Victoria and Albert's** ($$$$), with just sixty-five seats and a most refined atmosphere where you'll be attended by a butler and maid in Victorian dress. The prix-fixe menu, which usually includes meat, fish, and poultry offerings, is priced at about $80 per person before orders from the

Babysitter club. Guests at hotels at Walt Disney World can hire an in-room babysitter by consulting with Guest Services or the In-Room KinderCare Learning Center.

extensive and expensive wine list. Some samples: salmon sautéed in olive oil with olives, capers, and tomato; roasted rack of lamb with Madeira almond sauce; and Bailey's Irish Cream soufflé. The restaurant is one of the few in Walt Disney World that require men to wear jackets. Depending on the season there may be just one or two seatings per evening; reservations are a must. And for the ultimate in up-close dining, you can attempt to reserve The Chef's Table, located right in the kitchen; you and your guests can watch and interact with the chef and his team as they prepare a dinner based on your preferences. The Chef's table seats up to six and is often booked up to six months in advance.

Citricos ($$$), a posh eatery featuring Mediterranean, Caribbean, Italian, and South Florida cuisine, is a mix of New and Old World design and menu with an "on-stage" kitchen. Specialties include Florida lobster ratatouille with lamb loin, and a citrus soufflé. Most dishes are prepared without butter or cream sauces, emphasizing oils infused with herbs and spices. Decadent desserts include chocolate ravioli with licorice ice cream.

Other changes at the Grand Floridian Resort & Spa include deluxe concierge services and the addition of a forty-four-foot yacht available for private parties on the lake right outside its doors.

1900 Park Fare ($$) offers buffet breakfasts and dinners in an attractive room that features carousel horses, a one-hundred-year-old band organ named Big Bertha, and Disney characters. There's a breakfast buffet with Mary Poppins and friends featuring pancakes and waffles, and dinner with Mickey and Minnie from 5:30 to 9 P.M.

The showplace seafood and steak eatery is **Narcoossee's** ($$$), with diners surrounding an open kitchen in a building that is built out into Seven Seas Lagoon. Open for lunch 11:30 A.M. to 3 P.M., and dinner from 5 to 10 P.M.; entrees start at about $15 and climb sharply. The chef calls the menu "Floribbean," with specialties such as oven-roasted Caicos baby conch and roasted grouper with crabmeat crust. *Narcoosee*, by the way, is a Native American word meaning "little bear."

Afternoon tea and light fare is served at the **Garden View Lounge** ($$). The **Grand Floridian Cafe** ($$) offers a coffee-shop menu all day, including Pasta Havana with garlic, cilantro, white wine, lemon juice, and cream sauce served with your choice of vegetables, chicken, or shrimp; mango chicken; and filet mignon. Informal meals, including pizza, burgers, and sandwiches, are available at Gasparilla Grill and Games ($).

There are two clay tennis courts and a heated swimming pool; the marina at the white sand beach offers watercraft for rent.

Transportation to the parks is by monorail, water taxi, and bus. The parking lot is across the road; at the end of a long day, it can feel like the next county.

★★★Disney's Polynesian Resort. $$$$. 1600 Seven Seas Drive, Lake Buena Vista. ☎ (407) 824-2000. A Disneyfied version of Hawaiian Island architecture and landscaping, including palm-lined, torch-lit walkways, tropical gardens, two exotic swimming pools (one with a slide built into a volcano), and a station on the monorail. Oh, and did I mention the indoor waterfall in the lobby? This place is especially magical at night.

Dancers perform at the nightly **Polynesian Revue** dinner show; there are four other restaurants in the complex. The resort includes 855 rooms in two- and three-story island-style longhouses, plus a marina, pools, and a kid's club. You can rent Water Sprites, sailboats, and other watercraft at the marina.

Every room has a patio, with most offering a view of the lagoon or one of the swimming pools. Special suites that include King Kamehameha concierge services are on the lagoon side of several of the longhouses.

The **'Ohana Feast** ($$$), served nightly from 5 to 10 P.M., includes fire-grilled meats, fowl, and shrimp, and stir-fried vegetables and noodles. A character breakfast ($$) is served from 7:30 to 11 A.M., hosted by Minnie.

Kona Cafe is an energetic casual restaurant that mixes Pacific Rim spices and American classics for breakfast, lunch, and dinner. Pots of Kona coffee are ground to order all day. In the evening Luau Cove is home to a **Polynesian Luau** ($$$), including hula and fire dancers.

Kids have their own club at **Neverland**, for guests ages four to twelve. Open from 5 P.M. to midnight, with a three-hour minimum at $8 per hour; there's even a special buffet for the kids served from 6 to 8 P.M. Call for reservations at ☎ (407) 824-2170.

The resort includes two heated outdoor swimming pools, a sand volleyball court, and a white sand beach. Watercraft are available for rent at the marina.

Transportation to the parks is by monorail, water taxi, and bus. You can also see the nightly Electrical Water Pageant from the resort.

★Fort Wilderness Resort and Campground. $$–$$$$. 4510 North Fort Wilderness Trail, Lake Buena Vista. ☎ (407) 824-2900. Park your camper, pitch a tent, or rent one of Disney's Fleetwood Trailer Homes, complete with air-conditioning, television, telephone, kitchen, and daily housekeeping service. All of the 784 campsites at the secluded 780-acre site include electrical hookups, water, and a charcoal grill; most have sanitary hookups. The sites are intended for tent or trailer campers up to sixty-five feet. Comfort stations, a trading post, and shower and laundry facilities are nearby.

Pay attention to the campsite number you are assigned; a savvy visitor may be able to improve on the location. Numbers from 100 to 599 are near the beach and Pioneer Hall. The high numbers, from 1,500, are quiet and remote.

Inside one of the 408 wilderness homes you'll probably have a hard time remembering you are within the woods; the one-bedroom units include a double or bunk bed, and a double Murphy bed in the sitting area. There's a full kitchen, daily maid service, and air-conditioning, too.

Disney's Fort Wilderness Resort and Campground also offers **wilderness cabins**. Yes, they're cabins, but they also feature daily maid service, cable television, and air conditioning, with sleeping space for six and a full kitchen and outdoor grill. Nightly rental rates range from $199 to $234 per night.

The **Tri-Circle D Petting Farm** is located between Pioneer Hall and Horse

Barn, open to children of all ages, for free. Kids weighing less than eighty pounds can also ride a pony at the farm.

The resort includes horseback riding, fishing, canoeing, and biking. There are two heated swimming pools and a large beach on Bay Lake. Nearby are the Osprey Ridge and Eagle Pines golf courses, and the **River Country** water park. There's a nightly campfire gathering near the Meadow Trading Post, including free Disney movies and sing-alongs with Chip 'n Dale. Fort Wilderness is also a good place to watch the nightly Electrical Water Pageant.

In the center of the resort is **Pioneer Hall**, which includes the **Hoop-Dee-Doo Musical Revue** ($$$), an all-you-can-eat hoedown dinner show presented three times a night in peak season and featuring fried chicken, spare ribs, corn on the cob, and strawberry shortcake. Reservations are essential most nights.

Crockett's Tavern ($) is open for dinner only, from 4 to 11 P.M., featuring snacks and fast food.

The **Trail's End Buffet** ($), which features a dramatic high-beamed ceiling, offers meals all day. Breakfast is offered 7:30 to 11 A.M., lunch from 11:30 A.M. to 3:30 P.M., and dinner from 4 to 10 P.M. The dish du jour becomes pizza from 9:30 to 11 P.M. nightly.

You can purchase groceries at the **Crossroads of Lake Buena Vista** shopping center just outside of the Walt Disney World park or bring them in your own vehicle. Transportation to the parks is by bus, tram, and water taxi.

A limited number of tents are available for rent if you don't want to bring your own equipment.

★★Shades of Green on Walt Disney Resort—U.S. Armed Forces Recreation Center. ☎ (407) 824-3600. The former Disney Inn, situated between two PGA tour golf courses (probably the only ones in the world with sand traps shaped like Mickey Mouse), this 288-room rustic resort is offered to vacationing servicemen and -women from all branches of the armed forces, as well as civilian employees of the Department of Defense and certain other present and former employees and spouses of military branches.

Epcot and Disney–MGM Resort Area

★★★Disney's Yacht and Beach Club Resorts. $$$$. 1800 Epcot Resorts Boulevard, Lake Buena Vista. ☎ (407) 934-8000. A pair of attractive resorts nearby to Epcot Center and the Disney–MGM Studios Theme Park and set around their own lake. The Yacht Club is the more formal of the two, made to appear like a New England grand hotel with its own small lighthouse. Both hotels share **Stormalong Bay**, a fantasy lagoon filled with pools and water activities, including water slides, bubble jets, and a whirlpool. A fleet of boats is available for rent, too.

The **Yacht Club** includes 635 rooms and the **Beach Club** an additional 580; it also has a health club, tennis courts, a marina, a beach, and a pool. The **Sandcastle Club** is for kids ages four to twelve, open from 5 P.M. to midnight with a charge of about $4 per hour for the first child and $2 per hour for additional kids. Dinner is available for an additional charge. Call ☎ (407) 934-6290 for information.

The **Cape May Cafe** ($$) offers a nightly indoor New England–style clambake with clams, mussels, chicken, chowders, and more, served buffet style from 5:30 to 9:30 P.M. The breakfast buffet ($), served from 7:30 to 11 A.M., stars Goofy, Chip 'n Dale.

At the Yacht Club, there's the **Yachtsman Steakhouse** ($$$) from 5:30 to 10 P.M., where you can dine on Chateaubriand, steak, fish, or poultry.

The **Yacht Club Galley** ($) features a buffet breakfast and menu items all day, including pot roast, barbecue pork ribs, Pasta Primavera, and Seafood Sunrise, which is a dish of shrimp, scallops, crab cake, and rice pilaf with saffron dijon and spicy tomato sauce.

Down by the beach shared by both clubs is **Hurricane Hanna's Grill** ($), open for lunch and dinner for burgers and dogs, and **Beaches and Cream** ($), serving all-American hot dogs and ice cream.

The resorts are within walking or quick tram distance of the International Gateway entrance to Epcot Center; you can also catch a water taxi to the Disney–MGM Studios or a bus to the Magic Kingdom.

★★★Walt Disney World Dolphin. $$$$. 1500 Epcot Resorts Boulevard, Lake Buena Vista. ☎ (407) 934-4000. **★★★Walt Disney World. Swan $$$$.** 1200 Epcot Resorts Boulevard, Lake Buena Vista. ☎ (407) 934-3000. 🖳 www.swandolphin.com. Why not a triangular hotel with a huge dolphin's head on top, or a rounded building graced by a pair of tremendous swans? This is Walt Disney World, after all. Two of the most distinctive hotels of the park face off across a grotto pool that has a waterfall and whirlpools.

The **Dolphin**, operated by Sheraton, offers 1,509 rooms and includes several interesting eateries. **Shula's Steak House**, partly owned by former Miami Dolphins Coach Don Shula, is one of the best beeferies in town. **Juan & Only's Cantina** ($$) is known for its Mexican specialties, including a fajita bar. **Palio** ($$) is a casual Italian bistro that features strolling musicians and a wood-fired oven.

Next door at the **Swan** (operated by Westin Hotels and Resorts) you will find the **Garden Grove Cafe** ($$) in a greenhouse, and **Kimono's** ($$), an Oriental lounge and sushi bar. At night, the Garden Grove becomes **Gulliver's** ($$$), serving prime rib and fresh seafood in a fanciful setting. The room is also used for character breakfasts and dinners.

The resorts include a health club, tennis courts, a marina, a beach, and **Camp Dolphin** and **Camp Swan** for kids ages four to twelve; the camps are generally open evenings from about 4 P.M. to midnight; call to check hours and make reservations.

Disney's Fantasia Gardens and **Fantasia Fairways Miniature Golf** are located across the road from the Swan and Dolphin.

Both hotels are within walking distance of, or a short tram ride to the International Gateway entrance of Epcot near the France Pavilion. Water taxis run to Disney–MGM Studios. Buses head to the Magic Kingdom and other parts of Walt Disney World.

★★Disney's Caribbean Beach Resort. $$$. 900 Cayman Way, Lake Buena Vista. ☎ (407) 934-3400. One of the best bargains within the park, the sprawling 2,112-room resort spreads across five "villages" named after Caribbean islands (Aruba, Barbados, Jamaica, Martinique, and Trinidad). Each colorful village has its own pool and beach, with rooms in two-story buildings.

In addition, the five communities are linked to the **Old Port Royale** ($) food court along **Barefoot Bay**. You'll find a wide range of fast-food choices, including **Wok Shop** (for basic Chinese fare), **Cinnamon Bay Bakery, Montego's Deli, Port Royale Hamburger Shop, Bridgetown Broiler** (grilled chicken and fajitas), and **Royale Pizza & Pasta Shop**; outside is a large swimming pool that includes a fort with water slides and water cannon.

The **Captain's Tavern** ($$) includes Aruba scallops blackened with herbs, Cayman Paella, Trinidad Chicken, pork chops, and rib eye steak.

Guests can rent a bike or boat at the marina, and there is a lovely 1.5-mile walking or jogging path around the lake at the resort. And there is **Parrot Cay**, a children's playground on a small island.

Transportation to the parks is by bus.

★★Disney's All-Star Sports Resort. $$. 1701 West Buena Vista Drive, Lake Buena Vista. ☎ (407) 939-5000. Together with the All-Star Music and All-Star Movies resorts, this is Disney's "economy" zone; the hotels are spiffed-up motels with comparatively small rooms.

The 246-acre site is just southwest of the Disney–MGM Studios and near the **Blizzard Beach** water park. Transportation to the theme parks is by bus.

The 1,920-room All-Star Sports Resort focuses on five sports themes: football, baseball, basketball, tennis, and surfing. All around are unusual sports scenes, including palm trees arranged to look like a basketball team at tip-off, an interior courtyard that resembles a football field, a quiet pool in the shape of a baseball infield, and wild sports icons.

At the **Surf's Up** building, bold colors glisten on thirty-eight-foot-tall surfboards, and nearly a thousand colorful fish appear to be swimming along a wavy balcony; two giant shark fins encircle a free-form pool surrounded by swaying palms. At the **Hoops Hotel**, huge pennants from favorite college teams cover the roof line, and five-foot basketballs hang from the railings. The baseball-theme **Home Run Hotel** features stadium lights, scoreboards, and an outfield fence. Footballs and helmets big enough for Godzilla welcome guests to the **Touchdown Hotel**. And stairwells shaped like cans of tennis balls decorate the **Center Court** hotel.

The central check-in is at **Stadium Hall**, which features red, white, and blue seats, caged basketball court lighting, and red lockers. At the **End Zone** ($) food court, open from 6 A.M. to 11 P.M., giant sports figures perch atop brightly colored dining booths.

The scheme carries over to the guest rooms, too, which offer sports bedspreads, megaphone light fixtures, and bold artwork.

★★Disney's All-Star Music Resort. $$. 1801 West Buena Vista Drive, Lake Buena Vista. ☎ (407) 939-6000. The 1,920-room All-Star Music Resort features country, rock, Broadway, calypso, and jazz themes.

Top hats, musical notes, and an oversized Broadway show marquee complete with "chorus line" dancers add to the facade at **Broadway**. Giant amplifiers, speakers, microphones and a neon-lit, oversized juke box rock on at the **Rock Inn**.

Check-in for the music-theme hotel is in **Melody Hall**, where you'll also find the **Intermission** food court ($), open from 6 A.M. to 11 P.M.

Guests can cool off at one of two themed pools, one in the shape of a guitar, the other a grand piano.

★★Disney's All-Star Movies Resort. $$. The third installment in the All-Star group features giant icons from favorite Disney movies, including *101 Dalmatians, Toy Story, Fantasia, The Mighty Ducks, Fantasia 2000*, and *The Love Bug*. There are 1,920 more rooms plus a hockey-rink swimming pool and a Fantasia pool where Sorcerer Mickey directs a liquid symphony.

Pongo and Perdita from *101 Dalmatians* and Buzz Lightyear from *Toy Story* tower more than thirty-five feet tall. Giant sorcerer's hats, spell books, brooms, and buckets decorate the Fantasia area, and the Mighty Ducks section scores points with giant hockey sticks, goalie nets, and duck-shaped hockey masks.

Also at the resort is an area that salutes a segment from *Fantasia 2000* named "The Steadfast Tin Soldier," with larger-than-life icons that include a ballerina, a jack-in-the-box, and tin soldiers.

★★Disney's Pop Century Resort. $$. The newest hotel project at Walt Disney World, this massive resort will have 5,760 rooms spread across twenty buildings; the first phase of 2,880 rooms is scheduled to open in early 2002, with completion expected by 2003.

The hotel sends guests on a trip through American popular culture, highlighting the toys, fads, technological breakthroughs, dance crazes, and catch phrases that defined each decade of the twentieth century. Each pair of buildings will be themed to a different decade.

The first phase of the resort salutes the "Classic Years" of the 1950s and 1960s. The second half of the resort covers the "Legendary Years" from 1900 to the 1940s.

Larger-than-life pop icons, like the Big Wheel, Play-Doh, Rubik's Cube, Duncan Yo-Yo, bowling pins, a laptop computer, cellular phones, and more, tower near the lodge buildings and form shapes for giant feature pool areas.

The pools at the Classic Years are shaped like a bowling pin, a flower, and a computer, while the Legendary Years' pools resemble a crossword puzzle, a soda bottle, and a highway sign.

Priced in the same budget range as the All-Star resorts, Pop Century is located in the northeast quadrant of Osceola Parkway and Victory Way, between Disney's Wide World of Sports and Disney's Caribbean Beach Resort.

★★★★Disney's BoardWalk Inn. $$$$. ☎ (407) 939-5100.

★★★★Disney's BoardWalk Villas. $$$$. ☎ (407) 939-6200. 2101 Epcot Resorts Boulevard, Lake Buena Vista. Way back before there was such a thing as a Disney theme park (yes, kids, there was such a time) our forebears ventured to the beach to grand "boardwalk" resorts, including famed Coney Island in New York, and others along the Jersey Shore. It's a place of striped awnings and balconies like those of oceanfront inns of the 1930s.

Flash forward to **Disney's BoardWalk** resort, which re-creates some of the old-time fun with 378 hotel rooms and 532 Vacation Club time-share units in a forty-five-acre area along Crescent Lake near Epcot, across the water from Disney's Yacht and Beach Club Resorts with views of Crescent Lake or gardens. Guests can walk around the lake on the boardwalk to Epcot, take a boat to Epcot or the Disney–MGM Studios, or take a bus to the Magic Kingdom and other destinations within Walt Disney World.

This is one of the loveliest spots at Walt Disney World, with hardly a mouse in sight. Take the time to explore some of the eateries and stores around the lake; there is a fascinating collection of old photos and pageant tickets from beach towns like Atlantic City. In the lobby of the hotel treasures include metal Nanny Chairs from a nineteenth century European carousel, hand-painted and gold-leafed. Nearby is a photo and beautifully detailed wooden model of Flip Flap, a 1910 coaster at Coney Island; the ride went into a complete inverted loop, not much different from today's metal coasters.

The original concept for this resort seemed to imply that Disney would add a rock-'em, roll-'em wooden coaster; as built, the coaster is a water slide that enters into the Luna Park swimming pool, including a two-hundred-foot roller-coaster water slide and water-spouting elephants.

Outside the **BoardWalk Inn**, one of the vacation resorts, is a fully operational miniature carousel dating from the 1920s from famed carousel-maker Marcus Illions.

Among the guest rooms are fourteen two-story **Garden Suites**, luxury accommodations made to look like New England homes that have white picket fences and gardens. The foremost place to stay is the two-thousand-square-foot **Steeplechase Suite** at the **Innkeeper's Club**.

The **Little Toots** child care facility is open from 4 P.M. to midnight for youngsters ages four to twelve, at a rate of $4 per hour.

The **ESPN Club** sports bar is an athletic supporter's heaven, with more television monitors and big screens than your average appliance store; they display a wide range of sporting events. The menu offers a selection of bar food and drink, including Bloody Mary Chili. Specialties include Tailgate BBQ Pork, Mighty Duck "Chick Trick," penne pasta, and the Slider Burger.

At the **Big River Grille & Brewing Works** ($), the brewmaster crafts five specialty beers, served along with pub pies, sausages, and gourmet burgers, and more substantial entrees, including yellowfin tuna marinated in teriyaki sauce, breast of chicken with shiitake mushrooms in Rocket Red Ale sauce, and "tilted" veal loaf, from 10 A.M. to 2 A.M. Flagship beers brewed on the premises are the aggressive Rocket Red Ale, Title Pale Ale, and Wowzer's Wheat, the lightest in body and flavor, featuring orange peel added during the brewing.

Atlantic Dance is a Disney-funky pop music lounge. The libations of choice include some two dozen signature martinis; you can also indulge in a hand-rolled cigar. Admission is about $3 during the week and $5 on weekends; you must be twenty-one or older to enter. Open 8 P.M. to 2 A.M. nightly.

Also at the resort is **Spoodles** ($$), featuring Mediterranean cuisine from France, Spain, Italy, Greece, and North Africa for breakfast, lunch, and dinner, from 7 A.M. to 10 P.M. A breakfast buffet offers traditional and unusual baked and stir-fried offerings. Lunch and dinner menus feature bite-sized tapas. Entrees include pasta with chicken, spinach, and roasted peppers; mushroom risotto; tuna with Moroccan spices and sun-dried tomato couscous; or a grilled rib-eye with garlic mashed potatoes, fennel, and tomatoes.

The **Flying Fish Cafe** ($$$) offers seafood and steaks each evening from 5 to 10 P.M. and later on weekends. Subtle decorations include a floor-to-ceiling backlit glass Ferris wheel, a roller coaster studded with light bulbs, and a high-energy color pattern of rich reds and blues. Guests can dine at the chef's counter by the show kitchen to watch the chefs in action.

Specialties include a *fritto misto* of rock shrimp, squid, and the catch of the day served with lemon pepper aioli and braised cranberry beans; oak-wood-grilled center-cut pork chop; spicy barbecue glazed salmon fillet with corn pudding and sugar snap peas; and potato-wrapped striped bass with leek fondue and cabernet sauvignon reduction.

Admission and parking is free for the boardwalk, shops, and restaurants; valet parking is also available.

House calls. House Med can send a medical technician to your hotel room between 8 A.M. and 11 P.M.; the technician can consult with a physician to obtain certain prescription medicines if necessary. Call ☎ (407) 648-9234 for assistance.

You can also find many walk-in medical clinics listed in the Orlando or Kissimmee phone book.

★★★Disney's Coronado Springs Resort. $$$. 1000 West Buena Vista Drive, Lake Buena Vista. ☎ (407) 939-1000. A moderately priced convention hotel, an attractive 1,967-room spread that pays homage to Francisco de Coronado's explorations from Mexico to the American Southwest.

It is also the only place in the world where Mexico and Santa Fe face Polynesia across a lake.

Located on 136 acres on the west side of World Drive, near Blizzard Beach and the Disney–MGM Studios Theme Park, the resort's haciendas lie in the shade of palm trees, nearby to a white sand beach on fifteen-acre Lago Dorado and four themed pools, including one large water hole with a slide. The resort appears as a series of three– and four-story *palacios* tinted in shades of desert sand, sunset pink, and tropical green. There are also two-story cabanas on the northern shore of the lake.

At the edge of the lagoon the five-story Mayan pyramid is the splashy centerpiece of a family fun pool, complete with twisting waterslide.

Guests stay in one of three major areas: the **Casitas**, representing urban centers such as Santa Fe; the **Ranchos**, villas landscaped with sagebrush and cactus; and the **Cabanas**, inspired by beachside resorts along the Gulf Coast.

The lobby and reception area is built around **La Fuente de las Palomas**, a fountain that bubbles up from a Spanish urn under a domed ceiling painted with images of white clouds and doves against a perfect blue sky.

The resort features a ninety-five-thousand-square-foot convention center and the largest hotel ballroom in the Southeast. Oh yes, there are also colorful plazas, palm trees, and a rocky shoreline along a lake; a fifty-foot-tall Mayan pyramid lords over the pool and water play area.

The **Maya Grill** ($$$), along the lake, is open for breakfast 7 to 11:30 A.M. and for dinner from 5 to 10 P.M. The restaurant is operated by one of the premier restaurateur families of Mexico and features a wood-fired grill where cooks braise meats and fish over an open fire. The relatively small restaurant is a hidden gem at Walt Disney World.

The **Pepper Market Food Court** ($) features Southwest, Mexican, and American dishes for all meals. You'll pick up your food from various serving stations and have your dinner card punched; a cashier translates the punch into a bill when you are ready to leave.

Francisco's ($) is a bright outdoor cafe-style eatery featuring lighter fare.

Recreational facilities include a sand volleyball court at the "Dig Site" pool area. Bicycles and watercraft are available for rent at La Marina.

Disney's Animal Kingdom Area

★★★Disney's Animal Kingdom Lodge. $$$. ☎ (407) 934-7639. Inspired by the splendor of a South African game reserve, the 1,307-room five-story deluxe resort features hand-carved furnishings and views of a thirty-three-acre tropical savannah stocked with free-roaming animals.

The lodge, located near Disney's Animal Kingdom but not directly on the theme park property, is based on a traditional semicircular *kraal* or corral, a design used in African villages to keep homes and livestock safe from harm.

The six-story resort features towering thatched roofs complemented by rich woods and golden tones. The grand lobby includes a large, mud fireplace, natural lighting, and giant dormer windows that provide spectacular views of sunrises and sunsets over the savannah.

At night twinkling lights resemble fireflies and soft-glowing campfires. Just outside the lobby, an elevated *kopje*, or rock outcropping, puts guests within fifteen feet of the animals, and gives an extraordinary, near-panoramic view of the animal reserve.

Many of the resort's guestrooms feature balconies overlooking savannahs that are home to more than two hundred mammals and birds including giraffe, zebra, Thomson's gazelle, ostrich, and sacred ibis.

Restaurants include **Jiko—The Cooking Place**, a casual restaurant with an African taste, and **Boma—Flavors of Africa**, a family-style budget restaurant.

Disney Village Resort Area

★★Disney's Port Orleans Resort. $$$. 2201 Orleans Drive, Lake Buena Vista. ☎ (407) 934-5000. A re-creation of the French Quarter of New Orleans, packed with G-rated Disney detail. The resort's swimming pool is located at **Doubloon Lagoon** and includes a sea-serpent water slide: down the tongue and into the water.

Restaurants at **Port Orleans Square** include some unusual offerings. At the **Sassagoula Floatworks & Food Factory** ($), decorated with Mardi Gras props, check out the **King Creole Broiler**, with creole specialties; **Basin Street Burgers and Chicken**; **Preservation Pizza Company**; and **Jacques Beignet's Bakery**, featuring New Orleans *beignets* (fried dough fritters).

Bonfamille's Cafe ($$) offers steaks, seafood, and other dishes with a creole flair served in an attractive courtyard setting, with dinner entrees priced from about $5 to $20 and served from 5 to 10 P.M.; entrees include jambalaya, blackened sea scallops, chicken and sausage creole, and steak dishes. Breakfast is also served from 7 to 11:30 A.M., and more adventuresome diners can order eggs with andouille sausage, crawfish in creole sauce, beignets, and turkey breast with hollandaise sauce; if you insist you can also order pancakes.

The resort includes 1,008 rooms in seven three-story buildings, a marina, and a pool. Transportation to the parks is by water taxi or bus.

★★Disney's Dixie Landings Resort. $$$. 1251 Dixie Drive, Lake Buena Vista. ☎ (407) 934-6000. A bit of the old South, this is another of Disney's moderately priced resorts. The huge 2,048-room resort, divided into "parishes," includes a marina and five pools; the buildings are styled after plantation mansions and low bayou homes. The Mansion rooms are a bit more formal, evoking memories of grand staircases and columns; the bayou rooms in tin-roofed structures look as if they would fit in well with the swamp.

There's a stocked fishing hole and a country-style water slide at **Old Man Island** at the center of the resort. Boats and bicycles are available for rent at **Dixie Levee**.

Colonel's Cotton Mill ($) food court includes the **Acadian Pizza 'n Pasta**, **Bleu Bayou Burgers and Chicken**, **Cajun Broiler**, **Riverside Market and Deli**, and the **Southern Trace Bakery**.

Boatwright's Dining Hall ($$) offers a Cajun and American menu in a reproduction of a shipbuilding shed overlooking the Sassagoula River. Specialties include gumbo, grilled catfish Bayou Teche, roasted chicken, and prime rib, with dinner entrees from about $5 to $20, served from 5 to 10 P.M.; breakfast is also served from 7 to 11:30 A.M.

Transportation to the parks is by water taxi and bus.

★★Disney's Village Resort. $$$$. Magnolia Way, Lake Buena Vista. ☎ (407) 827-1100. A collection of light and open townhouses, "treehouses," and multilevel villas in the woods near the Disney–MGM Studios Theme Park and Epcot Center.

For some families, renting one of these villa rooms may be less expensive or more convenient than taking two small hotel rooms. Most of the smaller one-bedroom Club Suites include refrigerators, and one- and two-bedroom Vacation Villas include fully equipped kitchens.

Nearby are the **Lake Buena Vista Golf Course**, five lighted pools, tennis courts, and a marina. The resort includes 585 units and a health club. Villas range from one- and two-bedroom villas to the fancier **Fairway and Treehouse Villas**. You can also rent one of four Grand Vista Suites, fully furnished homes originally intended as model homes for a residential or time-sharing resort.

Some of the best bass fishing in Walt Disney World is in the canals right outside the door of many of the villas. The resort is across the lagoon from **Pleasure Island** and next to the **Disney Village Marketplace** shops and restaurants. Groceries for the villas are available at the **Gourmet Pantry** within the resort, or you can take a short drive outside the park to the **Crossroads of Lake Buena Vista** shopping center (outside the park, it is nevertheless on Disney property . . . don't want to let any of those dollars leak out of the company's hands, do we?).

The restaurant at the resort is the **Lake Buena Vista Club** ($), a family eatery in the clubhouse on Club Lake Drive. Open all day; specialties include Key West Caesar Salad, burgers, and chicken.

Transportation to the parks is by bus.

★★Disney's Old Key West Resort. $$$$. 1510 North Cove Road, Lake Buena Vista. ☎ (407) 827-7700. Deluxe studios and one- to three-bedroom vacation homes with whirlpool tubs. Shared facilities include a video library, four pools, tennis courts, and a marina.

Olivia's Cafe ($$) is open all day with outdoor and indoor seating for Key West specialties that include conch egg rolls, conch chowder, Mangrove Snapper wrapped in a banana leaf and steamed with herb butter, Florida Paella, and Mojo Chicken drizzled with fresh lime vinaigrette. A character breakfast with Winnie the Pooh and Tigger too is offered Sunday and Wednesday.

★★★Disney's Vacation Club Resort. $$$$. 1510 North Cove Road, Lake Buena Vista. ☎ (407) 827-7700. Located on the **Lake Buena Vista Golf Course**, units range from studios that sleep four to one-, two-, and three-bedroom units and Grand Villas with beds for as many as twelve.

I could write a book about real estate. Until I do here's my best advice about buying a time-share at Walt Disney World or anywhere else: don't do it on an impulse. Talk to your accountant or a financial adviser or someone else who is not in the business of selling you something other than advice.

You don't have to buy a time-share to stay at the resort; unsold rooms, or rooms turned back to Disney for resale by owners, are available for rent.

The restaurant at the club is **Olivia's**, which specializes in Key West dishes from conch fritters to Key lime pie, with entrees priced from about $5 to $20.

★★★The Villas at The Disney Institute. $$$$. 1901 Buena Vista Drive, Lake Buena Vista. ☎ (407) 827-1100. In the woods near Disney's adult-learning complex, each home away from home can accommodate from four to eight people. At the **Seasons Dining Room**, the change of the calendar brings new choices on the menu, featuring dishes from California to the Mediterranean and beyond. The Villas are also within walking distance of restaurants at Pleasure Island and the Disney Village Marketplace.

Disney Hotel Plaza

Best Western Lake Buena Vista Resort Hotel	$89	to	$199
Hotel Royal Plaza	$99	to	$199
Courtyard by Marriott	$129	to	$229
Grosvenor Resort	$105	to	$180
Wyndham Palace Resort & Spa	$149	to	$389
Doubletree Guest Suites Resort	$152	to	$299
The Hilton Resort	$170	to	$335

Seven hotels built and operated by major (non-Disney) hotel companies are clustered near the Disney Village Marketplace and Pleasure Island. Guests can drive or use Disney buses to get to the park. These are high-quality hotels without the fanciful touch of Disney-owned properties.

★★Wyndham Palace Resort & Spa. $$$. ☎ (407) 827-2727 or ☎ (800) 327-2990. 🖳 www.wyndham.com. Formerly the Buena Vista Palace, a twenty-seven-story lakeside tower with views of much of Walt Disney World and nine restaurants and a **Recreation Island** with three pools. The resort includes more than 1,014 rooms and suites, a health club, tennis courts, and pools. Restaurants include the top-of-the-tower haute cuisine **Arthur's 27** and **The Top of the Palace Lounge**. There's also the less-formal **Outback** restaurant with seafood and steaks. Summer Kids' Klub is a program for children ages four to twelve.

★★Courtyard by Marriott Lake Buena Vista at Walt Disney World. $$$. ☎ (407) 828-8888 or ☎ (800) 223-9930. 🖳 www.courtyard.com. A family-oriented hotel with a fourteen-story central atrium and 323 rooms. This was originally the Howard Johnson Resort Hotel, until it was converted lock, stock, and towels to a Marriott.

★★Doubletree Guest Suites Resort. $$$. ☎ (407) 934-1000 or ☎ (800) 222-8733. 🖳 www.doubletreehotels.com. Each one- or two-bedroom suite includes a microwave, refrigerator, and small wet bar, and the 229-room hotel offers a pool and tennis courts. The showplace eatery is the **Streamers Restaurant**. This hotel had previously been the Guest Quarters Suite Resort.

★★★Grosvenor Resort. $$$. ☎ (407) 828-4444 or ☎ (800) 624-4109. 🖳 www.grosvenorresort.com. A lakeside tower with 625 rooms that includes a large recreation facility featuring tennis and handball courts, a children's playground, and heated swimming pools. **Baskerville's**, a British-theme restaurant, is modeled after Sherlock Holmes's 221B Baker Street home in London; next door is **Moriarty's**, a pub named after the great detective's archenemy.

★★★The Hilton at Walt Disney World Village. $$$. ☎ (407) 827-4000 or ☎ (800) 782-4414. 🖳 www.hilton.com. A large resort and conference center directly across from the Disney Village Marketplace. The hotel recently underwent a top-to-bottom renovation with a Main Street Disney theme. It includes nine restaurants and lounges, among them **Covington Mill** and a **Benihana** Japanese steak house. Also featured is an outdoor spa. The **Vacation Station Kid's Hotel** caters to kids ages four to twelve; guests at the hotel can park their kids for two hours for as little as $2.25, with additional charges for more hours.

★★Hotel Royal Plaza. $$$. ☎ (407) 828-2828 or ☎ (800) 248-7890. 🖳 www.royalplaza.com. This 396-room hotel includes two restaurants and lounges with nightly entertainment, a pool, and tennis courts.

★★Best Western Lake Buena Vista Resort Hotel. $$$. ☎ (407) 828-2424 or ☎ (800) 348-3765. 🖳 www.bestwestern.com. A lakeside hotel with a Caribbean flavor and a rooftop nightclub known as **Toppers** that offers a spectacular view of Walt Disney World. The **Traders** restaurant offers breakfast and dinner, and the **Parakeet Cafe** has pizza and snacks.

Why Stay at a Hotel Within Walt Disney World?

The hotels within Walt Disney World are among the most attractive, most imaginative places to stay at any major tourist area we know of. They offer all sorts of extras not available outside the park, and quite a few conveniences.

However, all of this comes at a price. The lowest rates at Walt Disney-owned or operated hotels, or those operated by major chains on the park property, generally start at around $77 per night in low-season, which is the middle to high end of most standard off-site hotels.

It is up to you to decide what value to place on the extras that come with your higher room rates; you should also consider the possibility of obtaining similar special treatment outside the park. (I heard of one family that booked perfectly nice rooms a few miles outside of the park and used just some of the money they saved to engage limousine service to and from the park.)

Insider advantages to guests who stay at Walt Disney World Resorts include: free parking within Walt Disney World for the length of the stay; complimentary use of the Walt Disney World transportation system, including monorail, bus, ferryboat, and launch transportation to the parks, avoiding crowded parking lots; advance reservations for dining, Disney Dinner Shows, and Disney Character Breakfasts. Guests can make reservations as soon as they receive confirmation of hotel reservations.

Preferred access to tee times on all five championship golf courses. Also available are horseback riding, swimming, tennis, health clubs, and other facilities. (Golf, horses, tennis, and other activities, though, are not free.)

Hotels Outside the Park

I-192/Irlo Bronson Memorial Highway/Vine Street Kissimmee

Katella Avenue, which fronts the main entrance to Disneyland in California, turned out to be one of Walt Disney's worst nightmares. When Disneyland was first built it was surrounded by lush green orange groves. But with the success of the park the environs became an unending stretch of unattractive strip motels, gift shops, and fast-food restaurants.

When Disney began secretly buying up tens of thousands of acres of swamp and cypress groves in Central Florida in the 1960s, it was with the intention of shielding his new park deep within a green barrier. There was to be no Katella Avenue at Walt Disney World.

And in the end, Disney was successful. The Magic Kingdom, Epcot Center, Disney–MGM Studios Theme Park, Disney's Animal Kingdom, and all of the other attractions within the park seem to exist in a world unto themselves. There are tens of thousands of hotel rooms within the park as well as places to eat for all guests and day visitors, but the sheer size of the park swallows them up and hides them from sight of each other.

But, of course, the Walt Disney Company cannot own every square mile of Florida, even though it probably would if it could. There are two principal places where Disney meets the real world: at Apopka-Vineland Road (S.R. 535) and at I-192. And then there is the rest of the Orlando-Kissimmee area.

For many decades, way before the arrival of the Hollywood mice, Kissimmee was among Florida's premier cattle raising areas, best known for its Brahma cattle.

Most of the hotels and attractions on I-192 can be found between I-4 and I-441 (Main Street/South Orange Blossom Trail) in Kissimmee. The section where I-4 meets I-192 actually lies within the southern end of the huge Walt Disney World property.

West of I-4, toward I-27, is the less popular side of I-192, although a number of new hotels have been built in the area. Room rates at low-season range from as low as $29 at I-27 to about $75 per night closer to the park; high-season rates are about double. Hotels in this area often include "Main Gate" or "West Gate" in their name.

The busier side of I-192 runs about ten miles from I-4 east to Main Street in Kissimmee. The area closest to I-4 is often called "Main Gate East." Near I-4 you will find attractions including Arabian Nights, Old Town, and Water Mania. Between the intersection of S.R. 535 and Kissimmee are Medieval Times and Fun 'n Wheels. A few miles past South Orange Blossom Trail and just short of the intersection with the Florida Turnpike is Osceola County Stadium, the spring training home of the Houston Astros.

I-192 is a many-named splendor. I-192 bears several different names in its traverse from I-27 west of the park to and through downtown Kissimmee. For much of its length near the park, it is known as Irlo Bronson Memorial Highway. (Bronson was a prominent local politician and developer.) Near Kissimmee, it is called Vine Street; past Kissimmee toward St. Cloud, it is named Thirteenth Street. Some segments are also known as Space Coast Highway. You can call it 192 anywhere and people will know what you mean.

The far distant reaches of I-192 and the backroads outside the obvious tourist areas are the homes of the lowest rung on the ladder—I have seen rates as low as $19.99 for the night. Be sure to read the fine print; some prices are for single guests only, with an additional $5 or $10 for a second person. Several hotels advertise a low price and then add a "service charge" to the nightly bill.

Lake Buena Vista, Apopka-Vineland Road, Crossroads, World Center

The "back door" to Walt Disney World can be found off S.R. 535: Apopka-Vineland Road. Here Hotel Plaza Boulevard leads into the Disney Hotel Plaza area, Disney Village, and Pleasure Island. Farther along the road are the gates to the Magic Kingdom, Epcot, Disney–MGM Studios, and the other attractions within the park.

Some of the property in this area is actually owned and controlled by the Walt Disney Company, although it is not technically within the park.

Many of the area hotels offer free transportation to Walt Disney World, and some may be on the route for transportation companies that pick up passengers at Orlando International Airport; inquire when you call for information.

★★Courtyard by Marriott Lake Buena Vista at Vista Centre. $$–$$$. 8501 Palm Parkway. ☎ (407) 239-6900 or ☎ (800) 635-8684. 🖳 www.

courtyard.com. A family-oriented resort with 308 rooms; suites include a refrigerator and microwave. The **Courtyard Cafe** offers a breakfast buffet and dinner from a menu. Formerly the Howard Johnson Park Square Inn.

★★**Embassy Suites Resort Lake Buena Vista. $$$–$$$$.** 8100 Lake Avenue. ☎ (407) 239-1144 or ☎ (800) 257-8483. 🖳 www.embassysuites.com. An all-suite hotel in Lake Buena Vista, with bedroom, living room, dining, and kitchen areas, refrigerator, and microwave.

★★**Holiday Inn Sunspree—Lake Buena Vista. $$–$$$.** 13351 S.R. 535. ☎ (407) 239-4500 or ☎ (800) 366-6299. 🖳 www.holiday-inn.com. A family resort just outside the Disney Village Marketplace area on S.R. 535. All 507 rooms include a refrigerator and microwave; some offer KidSuites, a mini-room for the youngsters within the parents' suite. There are also free activities for children ages three to twelve from 8 A.M. to midnight. Restaurants include **Maxine's**, with breakfast and dinner buffets. **Max's Funtime Parlor** has breakfast and dinner buffets with Character Shows, featuring the Kidsuite Gang: Max, Maxine, Paully Wog, Grahammie Bear, Mollee Mouse, and Mattie Mole.

★★**Hyatt Regency Grand Cypress. $$$$.** Near the Disney Village Hotel Plaza. ☎ (407) 239-1234 or ☎ (800) 233-1234. **Villas of Grand Cypress.** $$$$. ☎ (407) 239-4700 or ☎ (800) 835-7377. 🖳 www.hyatt.com. A 750-room tower plus 146 villas in and around forty-five holes of golf, twelve tennis courts, and a huge pool with waterfalls and a forty-five-foot water slide.

★★★**Marriott's Orlando World Center. $$–$$$$.** S.R. 536 and I-4. ☎ (407) 239-4200 or ☎ (800) 228-9290. 🖳 www.marriott.com. The complex sprawls across two hundred landscaped acres and includes 1,501 rooms and suites, an 18-hole golf course, several large pools, and tennis courts.

There are five restaurants, including **Mikado's**, a Japanese steak house. There's also a children's "lounge" for ages four to twelve, open from 8 A.M. to 11 P.M. The **Orlando World Center** is often used for large conventions, offering Disney and other entertainment for spouses and children while business goes on within its meeting rooms.

★★★★**Opryland Hotel Florida. $$$–$$$$.** In February of 2002 a bit of upscale country is due to move into the Disney neighborhood, about five minutes away from Walt Disney World at the intersection of International Drive and Osceola Parkway. The 1,400-room hotel and convention center, is modeled after classic old Floridian architecture, with salutes to Saint Augustine, Key West, and Everglades architecture. The design includes four acres of gardens under glass. Atop the grand atrium is a giant sun icon.

One of two swimming pools is themed like a bit of South Beach in Miami Beach; a second pool includes waterslides and a giant spouting octopus.

Theaters at the resort will present a regular schedule of major stars of various musical styles.

For information, consult 🖳 www.oprylandhotels.com/florida.

★★**Radisson Inn Lake Buena Vista. $$–$$$.** 8686 Palm Parkway. ☎ (407) 239-8400 or ☎ (800) 333-3333. 🖳 www.radisson.com. Offering two hundred rooms and a pool with water slide.

International Drive (SeaWorld to Universal Studios Orlando)

The next major stop on our tour is the international Drive area, a five-mile uninterrupted stretch of every national hotel and restaurant chain you've ever heard of, and some you probably haven't. This road serves no purpose other than for the tourist; it's a convenient midway location for the visitor looking to explore in all directions. Room rates run from about $50 to $100 in low-season at motels; a few fancy hotels have rooms at about double those prices.

One end of International Drive begins south of the Beeline Expressway at the entrance to SeaWorld. From there it wanders more or less northerly to pass by the Orange County Convention and Civic Center, the Mercado shopping area, across Sand Lake Road (S.R. 482), in front of Wet 'n Wild and then heads east across Kirkman Road near the main entrance to Universal Studios Escape.

International Drive is, then, just minutes from SeaWorld, Universal Studios, Wet 'n Wild, and half a dozen other smaller attractions. There are restaurants of all descriptions on the road, as well. The road is about a fifteen-minute drive south to Walt Disney World or north to Orlando.

North of the Beeline, International Drive branches into exotically named circles: Hawaiian Court, Samoan Court, Austrian Court, and Jamaican Court.

North of Sand Lake Road, you will be across the road from Wet 'n Wild. Just before Kirkman Road, look for American Way on the left side.

Nearby to Universal Studios are Kirkman Road, Turkey Lake Road, and Universal Boulevard (renamed from Republic Drive in 1998).

Along the way I have skipped over the hotel that may be the queen of International Drive, the elegant and somewhat unusual **Peabody Orlando**. Rooms range in price from about $300 to $390, and suites climb to $1,450. Facilities include an Olympic-sized swimming pool, a health club, and extensive meeting and convention facilities. (There are special rates for seniors and special promotions through the year.)

Restaurants include the gourmet eatery **Dux**, a Northern Italian trattoria known as **Capriccio**, and the **B-Line Diner**, which is reminiscent of a 1954 burger-and-milk-shake diner.

But I have skipped over the most unusual feature of the Peabody; while Disney has a mouse, SeaWorld has a whale, and Universal Studios has a shark, the Peabody has a squad of trained ducks. Every day at 11 A.M. five somewhat trained mallards march down a red carpet to the lobby fountain, accompanied by the official duck master, to the tune of John Philip Sousa's "King Cotton" march. At 5 P.M. the procession goes the other way and the ducks return to their **Royal Duck Palace**. The show is free and open to visitors as well as guests.

The hotel's shuttle to the theme parks, by the way, is known as the Double Ducker.

Orlando International Airport Area

The airport is located about thirty minutes away from Walt Disney World. If your plane arrives late or if you are preparing for an early-morning departure, you might want to consider staying near the airport. Room rates for "name" hotels are higher than those in the tourist areas of Kissimmee; expect to pay $60 to $125 per night in low-season and from $70 to $150 per night in high-season.

The closest hotel to your airline's arrival gate doesn't even require you to leave the airport. The Hyatt Regency Airport hotel is within the main airport building; you might want to consider one night's stay there if your plane arrives very late or leaves very early. Rates at the Hyatt range from about $119 to $220, depending on the season.

Other hotels close to the airport can be found along Semoran Boulevard (S.R. 436), which leads into Frontage Road and McCoy Road, two service roads that run parallel to the Beeline Expressway (Route 528). Also in the neighborhood are T. G. Lee Boulevard and Augusta National Drive.

Moving west from the airport you are heading for the South Orange Blossom Trail area.

South Orange Blossom Trail/Sand Lake Road/ Florida Mall Area

Near the intersection where the Beeline Expressway comes to the combined Route 17–92 and 441—which is better known as the South Orange Blossom Trail—you will find a collection of more than a dozen brand-name motels.

The farther north you travel, toward Orlando, the more likely you are to find lower-priced locally owned motels. (You'll also find some adult bookstores and strip joints.)

Rumor has it that there once was grass in the neighborhood. This is strictly a place to sleep, with the exception of the intersection of South Orange Blossom Trail with Sand Lake Road (S.R. 482). Here you will find the **Florida Mall**, with shopping, movie theaters, and chain restaurants.

Sand Lake connects to the east with McCoy Road and runs directly into the airport.

Nightly rates in this area range from about $40 to $100 in off-season and $50 to $150 per night in high-season.

A Guide to Area Motels (Outside the Walt Disney World Resort)

$	Economy: $25 to $45 low-season; $45 to $65 high-season
$$	Budget: $45 to $75 low-season; $65 to $90 high-season
$$$	Moderate: $75 to $125 low-season; $100 to $200 high-season
$$$$	Deluxe: $125 to $200 low-season; $200 to $400 high-season
★★	Better
★★★	Superior
★★★★	*Econoguide* Best

(Bronson = Irlo Bronson Highway, also known as U.S. Highway 192)

Kissimmee (1 to 10 Miles from Disney)

Adventure Motel. $. 4501 West Bronson. ☎ (407) 396-0808.

Ambassador Motel. $. 4107 West Vine Street. ☎ (407) 847-7171.

★★★**Best Western–Eastgate. $–$$.** 5565 West Bronson. ☎ (800) 223-5361 or ☎ (407) 396-0707. 🖳 www.bestwestern.com.

★★★**Best Western–Maingate. $$–$$$.** 8600 West Bronson. ☎ (800) 327-9151 or ☎ (407) 396-0100. 🖳 www.bestwestern.com.

★★★**Best Western Suites. $$$.** 4786 West Bronson. ☎ (800) 468-3027 or ☎ (407) 396-2056. 🖳 www.bestwestern.com.

Budget Inn East. $. 307 East Vine Street. ☎ (407) 847-8010.

Budget Inn–West. $$. 4686 West Bronson. ☎ (407) 396-2322.

Casa Rosa Inn. $. 4600 West Highway 192. ☎ (800) 432-0665 or ☎ (407) 396-2020.

Central Motel. $. 4698 West Bronson. ☎ (407) 396-2333.

Chateau Motel. $. 3518 West Vine Street. ☎ (407) 847-3477.

★★★**Clarion Hotel Maingate. $$–$$$.** 7675 West Bronson. ☎ (800) 568-3352 or ☎ (407) 396-4000. 🖳 www.choicehotels.com.

Comfort Inn–Maingate West. $. 9330 West Bronson. ☎ (800) 440-4473 or ☎ (941) 424-8420. 🖳 www.choicehotels.com.

Comfort Inn–Maingate. $$. 7571 West Bronson. ☎ (800) 223-1628 or ☎ (407) 396-7500. 🖳 www.choicehotels.com.

Condo Lodge. $$. 3187 West Vine Street. ☎ (800) 866-2660 or ☎ (407) 931-2383.

Continental Motel. $. 4650 West Bronson. ☎ (800) 432-1030 or ☎ (407) 396-1030.

Crown Motel. $. 3834 West Highway 192. ☎ (407) 933-4666.

Days Inn East of Magic Kingdom. $$. 5840 West Bronson. ☎ (800) 327-9126 or ☎ (407) 396-7969. 🖳 www.daysinn.com.

Days Inn Eastgate. $–$$. 5245 West Bronson. ☎ (800) 423-3864 or ☎ (407) 396-7700. 🖳 www.daysinn.com.

Days Inn Kissimmee East. $$. 2095 East Bronson. ☎ (800) 352-2192 or ☎ (407) 846-7136. 🖳 www.daysinn.com.

Days Inn Maingate West of Walt Disney World. $$–$$$. 7980 West Bronson. ☎ (800) 327-9173 or ☎ (407) 396-1000. 🖳 www.daysinn.com.

Days Inn–South Kissimmee. $$. 4104 West Vine Street. ☎ (800) 647-0010 or ☎ (407) 846-4714. 🖳 www.daysinn.com.

Days Suites East of Magic Kingdom. $$. 5820 West Bronson. ☎ (800) 327-9126 or ☎ (407) 396-7900. 🖳 www.daysinn.com.

★★★**Diplomat Resort at Maingate. $$–$$$.** 7491 West Bronson. ☎ (800) 669-6753 or ☎ (407) 396-6000. 🖳 www.maingateresort.com.

★★★**Doubletree Guest Suites Resort Orlando Maingate. $$$.** 4787 West Bronson. ☎ (407) 397-0555. 🖳 www.doubletreehotels.com.

★★★**Doubletree Resort & Conference Center. $$$.** 3011 Maingate Lane. ☎ (800) 239-6478 or ☎ (407) 396-1400. 🖳 www.doubletreehotels.com.

Econo Lodge. $. 4669 West Bronson. ☎ (800) 523-8729 or ☎ (407) 396-1890. 🖳 www.choicehotels.com.

Econo Lodge Hawaiian Resort. $$. 7514 West Bronson. ☎ (800) 365-6935 or ☎ (407) 396-2000. 🖳 www.choicehotels.com.

Enterprise Motel. $. 4121 West Vine Street. ☎ (800) 833-2655 or ☎ (407) 933-1383.

Flamingo Inn. $. 801 East Vine Street. ☎ (800) 780-7617 or ☎ (407) 846-1935.

Four Points Sheraton. $$$. 4018 West Vine Street. ☎ (407) 870-2000. 💻 www.fourpoints.com. Suites.

★★★**Four Points Sheraton Lakeside. $$–$$$.** 7769 West Bronson. ☎ (800) 848-0801 or ☎ (407) 396-2222. 💻 www.fourpoints.com.

Four Winds Motel. $. 4596 West Bronson. ☎ (800) 826-5830 or ☎ (407) 396-4011.

Golden Link Motel. $. 4914 West Bronson. ☎ (800) 654-3957 or ☎ (407) 396-0555. On Lake Cecile.

★★★**Hampton Inn–Maingate. $$.** 3104 Parkway Boulevard. ☎ (800) 426-7866 or ☎ (407) 396-8484. 💻 www.hampton-inn.com.

★★★**HoJo Inn–Maingate East. $$.** 6051 West Bronson. ☎ (800) 288-4678 or ☎ (407) 396-1748. 💻 www.hojo.com. $$

★★★**Holiday Inn Express Kissimmee East. $$.** 2145 East Bronson. ☎ (407) 846-4646. 💻 www.holiday-inn.com.

★★★**Holiday Inn Hotel & Suites Maingate East. $$–$$$.** 5678 West Bronson. ☎ (800) 366-5437 or ☎ (407) 396-4488. 💻 www.holiday-inn.com.

Holiday Inn Kissimmee Downtown. $–$$. 2009 West Vine Street. ☎ (800) 624-5905 or ☎ (407) 846-2713. 💻 www.holiday-inn.com.

Holiday Inn Maingate West. $$. 7601 Black Lake Road. ☎ (800) 365-6935 or ☎ (407) 396-1100. 💻 www.holiday-inn.com.

★★★**Holiday Inn Nikki Bird Resort. $$–$$$.** 7300 West Bronson. ☎ (407) 396-7300. 💻 www.holiday-inn.com. Resort.

★★★**Homewood Suites Hotel Orlando. $$$–$$$$.** 8745 International Drive. ☎ (888) 697-8745. 💻 www.homewoodsuitesorlando.com.

Howard Johnson. $. 4643 West Bronson. ☎ (407) 396-1340 or ☎ (888) 786-1405. 💻 www.hojo.com.

Howard Johnson Maingate Central. $. 4985 West Bronson. ☎ (888) 753-4343 or ☎ (407) 396-4343. 💻 www.hojo.com.

Howard Johnson Hotel Maingate West. $–$$. 8660 West Bronson. ☎ (800) 638-7829 or ☎ (407) 396-4500. 💻 www.hojo.com.

Howard Johnson Inn Maingate East. $–$$$. 6051 West Bronson. ☎ (800) 288-4678 or ☎ (407) 396-1748. 💻 www.hojo.com.

Howard Johnson Inn & Suites Lakefront Park. $–$$. 4836 West Bronson. ☎ (800) 952-5464 or ☎ (407) 396-4762. 💻 www.hojo.com.

Howard Johnson Kissimmee Hotel. $. 2323 East Bronson. ☎ (800) 521-4656 or ☎ (407) 846-4900. 💻 www.hojo.com.

★★★**Hyatt Orlando. $$–$$$.** 6375 West Bronson. ☎ (800) 233-1234 or ☎ (407) 396-1234. 💻 www.hyatt.com. Resort.

Key Motel. $. 4810 West Bronson. ☎ (407) 396-6200. Lakefront.

Knight's Inn–Maingate. $–$$. 7475 West Bronson. ☎ (407) 396-4200. 💻 www.knightsinn.com.

Knight's Inn–Maingate East. $$. 2880 Poinciana Boulevard. ☎ (800) 843-5644 or ☎ (407) 396-8186. 🖳 www.knightsinn.com.

Lambert Inn. $. 410 West Vine Street. ☎ (407) 846-2015.

Larson's Inn Family Suite. $$. 6075 West Bronson. ☎ (800) 327-9074 or ☎ (407) 396-6100.

Magic Castle. $. 4559 West Bronson. ☎ (800) 446-5669 or ☎ (407) 396-1212.

Magic Castle Maingate. $–$$. 5055 West Bronson. ☎ (800) 446-5669 or ☎ (407) 396-2212.

Magic Tree Resort. $–$$. 2795 North Old Lake Wilson Road. ☎ (407) 396-2300. Suites.

Maple Leaf Motel. $. 4647 West Bronson. ☎ (407) 787-3800.

Masters Inns. $. 2945 Entry Point Boulevard. ☎ (800) 633-3434 or ☎ (407) 396-7743. 🖳 www.mastersinn.com.

Masters Inn. $. 5367 West Bronson. ☎ (800) 633-3434 or ☎ (407) 396-4020. 🖳 www.mastersinn.com.

The real Old Town. Orlando was established as a campground for soldiers during the Seminole Indian War of 1835 to 1842, and it then continued as a trading post. The war resulted in removal of most Native Americans in Florida to reservations in Oklahoma.

The Orlando Metropolitan Area was the sixteenth-fastest growing area in the country, according to the 2000 Census. Its population grew 34 percent between 1990 and 2000, to 1,644,561.

Motel 6–Maingate West. $. 7455 West Bronson. ☎ (407) 396-6422. 🖳 www.motel6.com.

Motel 6–Orlando East. $. 5731 West Bronson. ☎ (407) 396-6333. 🖳 www.motel6.com.

Palm Motel. $–$$. 4519 West Bronson. ☎ (407) 396-0744.

Park Inn International Kissimmee. $$. 4960 West Bronson. ☎ (800) 327-0072 or ☎ (407) 396-1376.

Parkway Motel. $. 4529 West Bronson. ☎ (407) 396-2042.

Quality Inn. $–$$. 2050 East Bronson. (877) 586-8080 or ☎ (407) 846-4545. 🖳 www.choicehotels.com.

Quality Inn–Lake Cecile. $$. 4944 West Bronson. ☎ (800) 864-4855 or ☎ (407) 396-4455. 🖳 www.choicehotels.com. Lakeside.

Quality Inn Maingate. $–$$. 4156 Vine Street. ☎ (800) 228-5151 or ☎ (407) 870-7374. 🖳 www.choicehotels.com.

Quality Suites Maingate East. $$–$$$$. 5876 West Bronson. ☎ (800) 848-4148 or ☎ (407) 396-8040. 🖳 www.choicehotels.com.

Quality Inn Maingate West. $–$$$. 7785 West Bronson. ☎ (800) 634-5525 or ☎ (407) 396-1828. 🖳 www.choicehotels.com.

★★**Radisson Resort Parkway. $$–$$$$.** 2900 Parkway Boulevard. ☎ (800) 634-4774 or ☎ (407) 396-7000. 🖳 www.radisson.com.

Ramada Fountain Park Resort Hotel. $$. 5150 West Bronson. ☎ (800) 327-9179 or ☎ (407) 396-1111. 🖳 www.ramada.com. Lakeside.

★★★**Ramada Plaza Hotel Gateway. $$–$$$.** 7470 West Bronson. ☎ (800) 327-9170 or ☎ (407) 396-4400. 🖳 www.ramada.com.

Ramada Resort Maingate. $$–$$$. 2950 Reedy Creek Boulevard. ☎ (800) 365-6935 or ☎ (407) 396-4466. 🖳 www.ramada.com.

Record Motel. $. 4651 West Bronson. ☎ (800) 874-4555 or ☎ (407) 396-8400.

Red Carpet Inn East. $. 4700 West Bronson. ☎ (800) 462-6063 or ☎ (407) 396-1133.

Red Roof Inn #204. $–$$$. 4970 Kyngs Heath Road. ☎ (800) 843-7663 or ☎ (407) 396-0065. 🖳 www.redroof.com.

Resort Suites. $–$$$. 4694 West Bronson. ☎ (800) 432-0695 or ☎ (407) 396-1780.

Riviera Motel. $. 2248 East Bronson. ☎ (800) 226-8010 or ☎ (407) 847-9494.

Sevilla Inn. $. 4640 West Bronson. ☎ (800) 367-1363 or ☎ (407) 396-4135.

Shoney's Inn Orlando/Kissimmee Maingate. $–$$. 4156 Vine Street. ☎ (800) 222-2222 or ☎ (407) 870-7374. 🖳 www.shoneysinn.com.

Sleep Inn Maingate. $–$$. 8536 West Bronson. ☎ (800) 225-0086 or ☎ (407) 396-1600. 🖳 www.choicehotels.com.

Stadium Inn & Suites. $–$$. 2039 East Bronson. ☎ (800) 785-7567 or ☎ (407) 846-7814.

Sun Motel. $. 5020 West Bronson. ☎ (407) 396-2673.

Super 8 Motel East Lakeside. $–$$. 4880 West Bronson. ☎ (800) 325-4872 or ☎ (407) 396-1144. 🖳 www.super8.com.

Super 8 Motel Maingate. $–$$. 5875 West Bronson. ☎ (407) 396-8883. 🖳 www.super8.com.

Thriftlodge East Gate. $–$$. 4624 West Bronson. ☎ (800) 648-4148 or ☎ (407) 396-2151. 🖳 www.travelodge.com.

Thrifty Inn. $. 1620 West Vine Street. ☎ (407) 847-7224.

Traveler's Inn on Lake Cecile. $–$$. 4900 West Bronson. ☎ (800) 932-4321 or ☎ (407) 396-1668.

★★★**Travelodge Hotel Maingate East. $$–$$$.** 5711 West Bronson. ☎ (800) 327-1128 or ☎ (407) 396-4222. 🖳 www.travelodge.com.

Travelodge Suites–East Gate Orange. $–$$$. 5399 West Bronson. ☎ (407) 396-7666. 🖳 www.travelodge.com.

★★★**Westgate Towers. $$–$$$$.** 7600 West Bronson. ☎ (888) 808-7410 or ☎ (407) 396-2500.

Downtown Kissimmee (10 to 15 Miles from Disney)

Best Western–Kissimmee. $. 2261 East Bronson. ☎ (800) 547-3278 or ☎ (407) 846-2221. 🖳 www.bestwestern.com.

★★**Caribbean Villas. $$.** 2003 Trinidad Court. ☎ (800) 327-4730 or ☎ (407) 846-4405.

Days Inn Downtown. $$. 4104 West Bronson. ☎ (800) 647-0010 or ☎ (407) 846-4714. 🖳 www.daysinn.com.

Super 8. $$. 1815 West Vine Street. ☎ (800) 325-4348 or ☎ (407) 847-6121. 🖳 www.super8.com.

Lake Buena Vista (1 to 10 Miles from Disney)

Comfort Inn. $–$$. 8442 Palm Parkway. ☎ (800) 999-7300. 🖳 www.choicehotels.com.

★★**Courtyard by Marriott-Vista Center. $$.** 8501 Palm Parkway. ☎ (800) 635-8684 or ☎ (407) 239-6900. 🖳 www.courtyard.com.

Days Inn Lake Buena Vista. $$. 12799 Apopka-Vineland Road. ☎ (800) 224-5058 or ☎ (407) 239-4441. 🖳 www.daysinn.com.

Doubletree Club Hotel. $$. 12490 Apopka-Vineland Road. ☎ (800) 521-3297 or ☎ (407) 239-4646. 🖳 www.doubletreehotels.com.

★★**Embassy Suites Resort Lake Buena Vista. $$$–$$$$.** 8100 Lake Avenue. ☎ (407) 239-1144. 🖳 www.embassy-suites.com. Suites.

★★★**Holiday Inn Sunspree Resort Lake Buena Vista. $$–$$$.** 13351 S.R. 535. ☎ (800) 366-6299 or ☎ (407) 239-4500. 🖳 www.holiday-inn.com.

★★★**Hyatt Regency Grand Cypress. $$$$.** One Grand Cypress Boulevard. ☎ (800) 233-1234 or ☎ (407) 239-1234. 🖳 www.hyatt.com.

★★★★**Orlando World Center Marriott. $$$$.** One World Center Drive. ☎ (800) 621-0638 or ☎ (407) 239-4200. 🖳 www.marriott.com.

★★**Radisson Inn Lake Buena Vista. $$$.** 8686 Palm Parkway. ☎ (407) 239-8400. 🖳 www.radisson.com.

★★**Residence Inn by Marriott Lake Buena Vista. $$$.** 8800 Meadow Creek Drive. ☎ (800) 331-3131 or ☎ (407) 239-7700. 🖳 www.residenceinn.com.

RIU Orlando. $$–$$$. 8688 Palm Parkway. ☎ (800) 996-3426 or ☎ (407) 239-8500.

Sheraton Safari. $$. 12205 Apopka-Vineland Road. ☎ (800) 423-3297 or ☎ (407) 239-0444. 🖳 www.sheraton.com.

★★**The Villas of Grand Cypress. $$$$.** One North Jacaranda. ☎ (800) 835-7377 or ☎ (407) 239-4700.

International Drive and Convention Center Area (10 Miles from Disney, 1 to 5 Miles from SeaWorld and Universal Studios)

(Note: Republic Drive from the Convention Center to Universal Studios Escape is now called Universal Boulevard.)

Among better hotels is the **Renaissance Orlando Resort at SeaWorld.** Located directly across from SeaWorld Orlando with a view into the park, it is centrally located between Walt Disney World and Universal Orlando. Best of all, it's a luxurious world away from the theme parks; the resort's 778 rooms are among the largest standard rooms in central Florida. Interior rooms look into one of the largest resort atrium lobbies in the world, a ten-story space with a skylight up top and an indoor waterfall, koi pool, and aviary down below. The five restaurants in the hotel include Atlantis, the hotel's signature seafood eatery, and the elegant Haifeng, serving gourmet Asian specialties.

Rack rates for the Renaissance Orlando range from about $229 to $299, although special offers are available. The Discovery Cove Adventure Package that includes two nights at the hotel, admission to Discovery Cove (one with a dolphin swim and one general admission), a weeklong two-person pass to SeaWorld Orlando, and other features at a discount.

The ★★★★**Renaissance Orlando Resort at SeaWorld** is located at 6677 Sea Harbor Drive, Orlando. **$$$$.** For reservations, call ☎ (407) 351-5555 or consult 🖳 www.renaissancehotels.com.

★★★**Arnold Palmer's Bay Hill Club. $$$–$$$$.** 9000 Bay Hill Boulevard, Orlando. ☎ (800) 422-9445 or ☎ (407) 876-2429. 🖳 www.bayhill.com/bayclub.html.

Best Inn and Suites. $. 5858 International Drive. ☎ (800) 527-8483 or ☎ (407) 351-4410.

★★★**Best Western Plaza International. $$–$$$.** 8738 International Drive, Orlando. ☎ (800) 654-7160 or ☎ (407) 345-8195. 🖳 www.bestwestern.com.

Buena Vista Suites. $$$. 14450 International Drive. ☎ (800) 537-7737 or ☎ (407) 239-8588. 🖳 www.buenavistasuites.com.

★★★**Caribe Royale Resort Suites. $$$.** 14300 International Drive, Lake Buena Vista. ☎ (800) 823-8300 or ☎ (407) 238-8000. 🖳 www.caribe royale.com.

Clarion Hotel Universal. $$. 7299 Universal Boulevard, Orlando. ☎ (800) 445-7299 or ☎ (407) 351-5009. 🖳 www.choicehotels.com.

★★★**Clarion Plaza Hotel Orlando. $$–$$$.** 9700 International Drive, Orlando. ☎ (800) 627-8258 or ☎ (407) 996-9700. 🖳 www.choicehotels.com.

★★**Comfort Suites Orlando. $$.** 9350 Turkey Lake Road. ☎ (800) 277-8483 or ☎ (407) 351-5050. 🖳 www.choicehotels.com.

Country Hearth Inn. $$. 9861 International Drive. ☎ (800) 447-1890 or ☎ (407) 352-0008. 🖳 www.countryhearth.com.

★★**Courtyard by Marriott International Drive. $$.** 8600 Austrian Court, Orlando. ☎ (800) 321-2211 or ☎ (407) 351-2244. 🖳 www.courtyard.com.

Cypress Pointe Resort. $$$. 8651 Treasure Cay Lane, Lake Buena Vista. ☎ (800) 824-5790 or ☎ (407) 238-2300.

Days Inn Convention Center/SeaWorld. $$. 9990 International Drive, Orlando. ☎ (800) 224-5055 or ☎ (407) 352-8700. 🖳 www.daysinn.com.

Days Inn East of Universal Studios. $$. 5827 Caravan Court. ☎ (800) 327-2111 or ☎ (407) 351-3800. 🖳 www.daysinn.com.

Days Inn International Drive. $$. 7200 International Drive. ☎ (800) 224-5057 or ☎ (407) 351-1200. 🖳 www.daysinn.com.

Days Inn Lakeside. $$. 7335 Sand Lake Road. ☎ (800) 777-3297 or ☎ (407) 351-1900. 🖳 www.daysinn.com. Lakeside.

★★★**Delta Orlando Resort. $$$.** 5715 Major Boulevard. ☎ (800) 634-4763 or ☎ (407) 351-3340. 🖳 www.deltaorlandoresort.com.

★★**The Doubletree Castle Hotel. $$$.** 8629 International Drive, Orlando. ☎ (800) 952-2785 or ☎ (407) 345-1511. 🖳 www.doubletreehotels.com.

★★**Embassy Suites on the Jamaican Court. $$$.** 8250 Jamaican Court. ☎ (800) 327-9797 or ☎ (407) 345-8250. 💻 www.embassy-suites.com.

★★**Embassy Suites Orlando South. $$$.** 8978 International Drive. ☎ (800) 433-7275 or ☎ (407) 352-1400. 💻 www.embassy-suites.com.

★★**Enclave Suites at Orlando. $$$.** 6165 Carrier Drive. ☎ (800) 457-0077 or ☎ (407) 351-1155.

★★**Fairfield Inn International Drive by Marriott. $$.** 8342 Jamaican Court. ☎ (800) 228-2800 or ☎ (407) 363-1944. 💻 www.marriott.com.

★★**Hampton Inn. $$.** 6101 Sandlake Road. ☎ (800) 763-1100 or ☎ (407) 363-7886. 💻 www.hampton-inn.com.

★★**Hampton Inn at Universal Studios. $$.** 5621 Windhover Drive. ☎ (800) 231-8395 or ☎ (407) 351-6716. 💻 www.hampton-inn.com.

★★**Hampton Inn South of Universal Studios. $$.** 7110 South Kirkman Road. ☎ (800) 763-1100 or ☎ (407) 345-1112. 💻 www.hampton-inn.com.

★★**Hawthorn Suites Hotel. $$–$$$.** 6435 Westwood Boulevard. ☎ (800) 527-1133 or ☎ (407) 351-6600.

Holiday Inn Express International Drive. $$. 6323 International Drive. ☎ (800) 365-6935 or ☎ (407) 351-4430. 💻 www.holiday-inn.com.

Howard Johnson Hawaiian Court. $$. 9956 Hawaiian Court. ☎ (800) 826-4847 or ☎ (407) 351-5100. 💻 www.hojo.com.

Holiday Inn Hotel and Suites. $$. 5905 Kirkman Road. ☎ (800) 327-1364 or ☎ (407) 351-3333. 💻 www.holiday-inn.com.

Holiday Inn International Drive Resort. $$. 6515 International Drive. ☎ (800) 465-4329 or ☎ (407) 351-3500. 💻 www.holiday-inn.com.

Howard Johnson Lodge International Drive North. $$. 6603 International Drive. ☎ (800) 722-2900 or ☎ (407) 351-2900. 💻 www.hojo.com.

Howard Johnson Plaza. $$. 7050 Kirkman Road. ☎ (800) 327-3808 or ☎ (407) 351-2000. 💻 www.hojo.com.

★★**La Quinta at International Drive. $$.** 8300 Jamaican Court. ☎ (800) 531-5900 or ☎ (407) 351-1660.

Las Palmas Hotel. $$. 6233 International Drive. ☎ (800) 327-2114 or ☎ (407) 351-3900.

Masters Inn. $–$$. 8222 Jamaican Court. ☎ (800) 633-3434 or ☎ (407) 345-1172. 💻 www.mastersinn.com.

MIC Lakefront Inn. $$. 6500 International Drive. ☎ (407) 345-5340. Lakeside.

★★★**Rosen Centre. $$$$.** 9840 International Drive. ☎ (800) 800-9840 or ☎ (407) 996-9840. 💻 www.rosencentre.com.

★★**Parc Corniche Condominium Suite Hotel. $$$.** 6300 Parc Corniche Drive. ☎ (800) 446-2721 or ☎ (407) 239-7100. 💻 www.parccorniche.com.

★★★★**The Peabody Orlando Hotel. $$$$.** 9801 International Drive. ☎ (800) 732-2639 or ☎ (407) 352-4000. 💻 www.peabodyorlando.com.

Quality Inn International. $–$$. 7600 International Drive. ☎ (800) 825-7600 or ☎ (407) 996-1600. 💻 www.choicehotels.com.

Quality Inn Plaza. $$. 9000 International Drive. ☎ (800) 999-8585 or ☎ (407) 345-8585. 🖳 www.choicehotels.com.

★★**Quality Suites International Drive Area. $$.** 7400 Canada Avenue. ☎ (800) 228-2027 or ☎ (407) 363-0332. 🖳 www.choicehotels.com.

★★**Radisson Barcelo Hotel. $$.** 8444 International Drive. ☎ (800) 330-3333 or ☎ (407) 345-0505. 🖳 www.radisson.com.

★★**Radisson Hotel Universal/Orlando. $$.** 5780 Major Boulevard. ☎ (800) 843-8693 or ☎ (407) 351-1000. 🖳 www.radisson.com.

Ramada Limited. $–$$. 5625 Major Boulevard. ☎ (800) 200-8117 or ☎ (407) 354-3996. 🖳 www.ramada.com.

Ramada Resort & Conference Center. $$. 7400 International Drive. ☎ (800) 327-1363 or ☎ (407) 996-7400. 🖳 www.ramada.com.

Ramada Suites by SeaWorld. $$$. 6800 Villa de Costa Drive. ☎ (800) 663-1405 or ☎ (407) 239-0707. 🖳 www.ramada.com.

Red Roof Inn #200. $$. 9922 Hawaiian Court. ☎ (800) 843-7663 or ☎ (407) 352-1507. 🖳 www.redroof.com.

★★★**Renaissance Orlando Resort. $$$$.** 6677 Sea Harbor Drive. ☎ (800) 327-6677 or ☎ (407) 351-5555. 🖳 www.renaissancehotels.com.

★★**Residence Inn by Marriott—Orlando International Drive. $$$.** 7975 Canada Avenue. ☎ (800) 331-3131 or ☎ (407) 345-0117. 🖳 www.residenceinn.com.

Rodeway Inn. $–$$. 6327 International Drive. ☎ (800) 999-6327 or ☎ (407) 996-4444. 🖳 www.choicehotels.com.

Sheraton Suite City Hotel. $$. 5905 International Drive. ☎ (800) 327-1366 or ☎ (407) 351-2100. 🖳 www.sheraton.com.

★★**Sheraton World Resort. $$$.** 10100 International Drive. ☎ (800) 327-0363 or ☎ (407) 352-1100. 🖳 www.sheraton.com.

★★**Summerfield Suites Hotel. $$$.** 8480 International Drive. ☎ (800) 833-4353 or ☎ (407) 352-2400. 🖳 www.wyndham.com/AboutWyndham/summerfield.cfm.

★★**Summerfield Suites Hotel. $$$.** 8751 Suiteside Drive. ☎ (800) 833-4353 or ☎ (407) 238-0777. 🖳 www.wyndham.com/AboutWyndham/summerfield.cfm.

Super 8 Motel. $. 5900 American Way, Orlando. ☎ (407) 352-8383. 🖳 www.super8.com.

★★**Wellesley Inn Orlando. $$.** 5635 Windhover Drive. ☎ (800) 444-8888 or ☎ (407) 345-0026.

Westgate Lakes Resort. $$$. 10000 Turkey Lake Road. ☎ (800) 846-4253 or ☎ (407) 345-0000.

★★**Wynfield Inn Westwood. $$.** 6263 Westwood Boulevard. ☎ (800) 346-1551 or ☎ (407) 345-8000.

★★**Wyndham Orlando Marriott. $$$.** 8001 International Drive. ☎ (800) 996-3426 or ☎ (407) 351-2420.

Orlando International Airport and Southeast Orlando (10 to 20 Miles from Disney)

Baymont Inn and Suites. $$. 2051 Consulate Drive, Orlando. ☎ (800) 428-3438 or ☎ (407) 240-0500.

Best Inn. $. 7101 South Orange Blossom Trail. ☎ (800) 237-8466 or ☎ (407) 851-4300.

★★**Best Western Florida Mall. $$.** 8421 South Orange Blossom Trail, Orlando. ☎ (800) 327-9742 or ☎ (407) 855-6060. 💻 www.bestwestern.com.

Days Inn. $$. 3300 South Orange Blossom Trail, Orlando. ☎ (407) 422-4521.

Days Inn/Lodge–Florida Mall. $. 1851 West LandStreet Road. ☎ (800) 331-3954 or ☎ (407) 859-7700. 💻 www.daysinn.com.

★★**Doubletree Guest Suites Orlando International Airport. $$.** 7550 Augusta National Drive. ☎ (407) 240-5555. 💻 www.doubletreehotels.com.

Four Points Sheraton. $$. 3835 McCoy Road. ☎ (800) 325-3535 or ☎ (407) 859-2711. 💻 www.fourpoints.com.

★★**Guesthouse International Hotel Orlando. $$.** 7900 South Orange Blossom Trail. ☎ (407) 859-7900.

Hampton Inn–Airport. $$. 5767 T. G. Lee Boulevard. ☎ (407) 888-2995.

Holiday Inn Orlando International Airport. $$. 5750 T. G. Lee Boulevard. ☎ (407) 851-6400. 💻 www.holiday-inn.com.

Howard Johnson Hotel. $. 8700 South Orange Blossom Trail. ☎ (800) 654-2000 or ☎ (407) 851-2330. 💻 www.hojo.com.

★★**Hyatt Regency Orlando International Airport. $$$.** Main Terminal. ☎ (800) 233-1234 or ☎ (407) 825-1234. 💻 www.hyatt.com.

★★**Orlando Airport Marriott. $$$.** 7499 Augusta National Drive. ☎ (800) 766-6752 or ☎ (407) 851-9000. 💻 www.marriott.com.

Quality Inn & Suites. $$. 4855 South Orange Blossom Trail. ☎ (800) 444-3001 or ☎ (407) 851-3000. 💻 www.choicehotels.com.

Radisson Hotel Orlando Airport. $$–$$$. 5555 Hazeltine National Drive. ☎ (800) 333-3333 or ☎ (407) 856-0100. 💻 www.radisson.com.

Renaissance Hotel Orlando. $$$. 5445 Forbes Place. ☎ (800) 762-6222 or ☎ (407) 240-1000. 💻 www.renaissancehotels.com.

Rodeway Inn–Florida Mall. $–$$. 8601 South Orange Blossom Trail. ☎ (407) 859-4100. 💻 www.choicehotels.com.

★★**Sheraton Plaza Hotel at the Florida Mall. $$$.** 1500 Sand Lake Road. ☎ (800) 231-7883 or ☎ (407) 859-1500. 💻 www.sheraton.com.

West Orlando, Downtown Orlando, East Orlando (10 to 20 Miles from Disney)

Best Western Orlando West. $$. 2014 West Colonial Drive. ☎ (800) 645-6386 or ☎ (407) 841-8600. 💻 www.bestwestern.com.

Four Points Sheraton. $$. 151 East Washington Street. ☎ (800) 325-3535 or ☎ (407) 841-3220. 💻 www.fourpoints.com.

Holiday Inn at the Orlando Arena. $$. 304 West Colonial Drive. ☎ (800) 523-3405 or ☎ (407) 843-8700. 💻 www.holiday-inn.com.

Holiday Inn Express. $. 3330 West Colonial Drive. ☎ (407) 299-6710. 💻 www.holiday-inn.com.

Omni Marriott Downtown. $$–$$$. 400 West Livingston Street. ☎ (800) 421-8001 or ☎ (407) 843-6664. 💻 www.marriott.com.

Ramada Orlando Central. $$. 3200 West Colonial Drive. ☎ (800) 828-5270 or ☎ (407) 295-5270. 💻 www.ramada.com.

Altamonte Springs, Winter Park (25 to 30 Miles from Disney)

Days Inn Altamonte/Orlando North. $. 235 South Wymore Road. ☎ (800) 224-5059 or ☎ (407) 862-2800. 💻 www.daysinn.com.

Days Inn Orlando/Winter Park. $$. 901 North Orlando Avenue. ☎ (800) 611-6575 or ☎ (407) 644-8000. 💻 www.daysinn.com.

Holiday Inn Orlando-Altamonte Springs. $$. 230 West Highway 436. ☎ (800) 226-4544 or ☎ (407) 862-4455. 💻 www.holiday-inn.com.

Holiday Inn Orlando North at Winter Park. $$. 626 Lee Road. ☎ (407) 645-5600. 💻 www.holiday-inn.com.

Langford Resort Hotel. $$. 300 East New England Avenue, Winter Park. ☎ (407) 644-3400.

Sheraton Orlando North Hotel. $$$. 600 North Lake Destiny Drive. ☎ (800) 628-6660 or ☎ (407) 660-9000. 💻 www.sheraton.com.

Travelodge. $. 450 Douglas Avenue, Altamonte Springs. ☎ (800) 327-2221 or ☎ (407) 862-7111. 💻 www.travelodge.com.

Davenport (10 Miles from Disney)

Comfort Inn–Maingate South. $$. 5510 U.S. Highway 27 North ☎ (800) 255-4386 or ☎ (941) 424-2811. 💻 www.choicehotels.com.

Days Inn South of Disney. $$. I-4 and U.S. 27. ☎ (800) 424-4999. 💻 www.daysinn.com.

Holiday Inn Express. $$. I-4 and U.S. 27, Baseball City. ☎ (800) 225-3351 or ☎ (941) 424-2120. 💻 www.holiday-inn.com.

Campgrounds and RV Parks

Disney's Fort Wilderness Resort. $$–$$$$. Lake Buena Vista. ☎ (407) 934-7639. Within Walt Disney World in 740 acres of woods. Campsites and cabins.

Fort Summit Camping Resort. $. I-4 and U.S. 27, Baseball City. ☎ (800) 424-1880 or ☎ (941) 424-1880. Three hundred sites.

Kissimmee/Orlando KOA. $. 4771 West Bronson, Kissimmee. ☎ (800) 331-1453 or ☎ (407) 396-2400. $

Sherwood Forest Mobile Home Estate & RV Resort. $. 530 West Bronson. ☎ (407) 396-0999.

Eating for Less

As a tourist magnet, the Orlando area offers just about every type of restaurant from fancy to ordinary, from American to European to Asian. (One of the most eclectic gatherings of foreign restaurants can be found within the World

***Econoguide* to Best Food at Walt Disney World**

Best Food with a View: California Grill Disney's Contemporary Resort.

Best Steak Dinner: Yachtsman Steakhouse at Disney's Yacht Club Resort, or Concourse Steakhouse at Disney's Contemporary Resort. Second place: Le Cellier at Canada pavilion, Epcot.

Best Seafood: Fulton's Crab House at Downtown Disney. Close seconds: California Grill at Disney's Contemporary Resort and Flying Fish Café at Disney's BoardWalk.

Best Theme Eatery: Rainforest Café at Disney's Animal Kingdom. Close second: House of Blues at Downtown Disney.

Best Sushi: California Grill at Disney's Contemporary Resort. Close seconds: Kimono's at Walt Disney World Swan, and Matsu No Ma Lounge in Japan at the Epcot World Showcase.

Best Vegetarian Fare: Spoodles at Disney's BoardWalk resort. Second place: California Grill at Disney's Contemporary Resort.

Best Milkshakes: Mom's specials at the 50's Prime Time Cafe at Disney-MGM Studios, or Beaches and Cream Soda Shop at Disney's Beach Club Resort.

Best High Tea: Rose & Crown Pub & Dining Room at United Kingdom in Epcot World Showcase, and Garden View Lounge at Disney's Grand Floridian Resort & Spa.

Best Wine Cellar: Victoria & Albert's at Disney's Grand Floridian Resort & Spa. Close seconds: California Grill at Disney's Contemporary Resort, Spoodles at Disney's BoardWalk resort, and Artist Point at Disney's Wilderness Lodge.

Best Beer Selection: Big River Grille and Brewing Works at Disney's BoardWalk resort. Close second: ESPN Club at Disney's BoardWalk.

Most Exclusive Table: The Chef's Table in the kitchen at Victoria & Albert's at Disney's Grand Floridian, booked six months in advance.

***Econoguide* to Best Food at Universal Orlando**

Emeril's Restaurant Orlando. CityWalk. Bam! Quirky New Orleans and American fare.

Latin Quarter. CityWalk. Spicy food and hot dancers.

Pat O'Brien's. CityWalk. Cajun fare and exotic drinks.

Bob Marley–A Tribute to Freedom. CityWalk. A tribute to Jamaican country cooking and great music.

Mythos. Universal Studios Islands of Adventure. A mystic eatery.

Showcase pavilions of Epcot Center.) But the emphasis seems to be on "family" restaurants. If there is a single major franchise fast-food restaurant in America that is not represented in the Orlando area, I don't know about it.

The biggest collections of fast-food restaurants can be found on I-192 (Irlo Bronson) and International Drive. If you're really into deep-fried grease, you can probably find seven different McDonald's or Burger Kings or Pizza Huts, one for every night of a week's stay.

Somewhat unique to the South are the all-you-can-eat buffets, which usually offer breakfasts in the range of $2 to $5, lunches from $4 to $8, and dinners from $6 to $12. Chains include Ponderosa Steak House, Sizzler, Shoney's, and Gilligan's. Be aware that quality can vary from one buffet to the next; a great buffet deal is to be found at Sweet Tomatoes on International Drive near Universal Orlando.

By the way, don't hesitate to ask to inspect the buffet before buying your way into the buffet line.

Chapter 4
Walt Disney World: You've Got to Have a Ticket

As if you don't already face enough tough decisions—dates, airlines, hotels, and more—there is also the matter of those little pieces of cardboard called "admission tickets." Actually, they are not all that little: a family of four including two children under ten years of age visiting Walt Disney World for five days could easily spend (are you ready for this?) $825 for a Park Hopper ticket, or $941 if you want to visit the water parks, too. If the kids are over the age of ten, they (or rather, you) pay full fare; a five-day pass will set you back $911 to $1,037.

Add in a day or two at Universal Studios Orlando and a day at SeaWorld, and the cost of tickets alone is more than $1,200.

But like everything else in this *Econoguide*, there are various ways to analyze the available options. The very best thing you can do is to sit down with a piece of paper and make a plan before you leave for Florida. Don't wait until you are standing at the ticket counter with a hundred people eyeing your back, your children tugging at your sleeves, and tears in your eyes to decide on your ticket strategy.

Instead, fit your plans to one of the available ticket packages. And don't overlook the money-saving strategies we discuss here—or the collection of discount coupons for Universal Orlando, SeaWorld, and other attractions and services you'll find in the back of this book.

First the Bad News

Remember what I said about Walt Disney World being a giant vacuum aimed at your wallet? Well, the great sucking sound begins at the ticket counter.

If one of the Disney ticket plans matches your schedule exactly, you're in luck and you'll save some money. But if the plans are not exactly what you need you *could* end up wasting money instead of saving.

All ticket prices and limitations listed here were in effect in mid-2001 and are subject to change. In recent years, Disney has adjusted prices in early spring; the "adjustments" have almost always been upward.

Walt Disney World Tickets

Prices were in effect in the summer of 2001, and do not include 6 percent Florida sales tax. All prices are subject to change without notice; in recent years, Disney has raised prices each spring. You may also find other ticket plans over the course of the year.

Tickets can be purchased at Walt Disney World, through some travel agents, online at 🖳 www.disneyworld.com, and by calling ☎ (407) 560-7277.

		Adult (Ages 10 and older)	Child (3–9)
1-Park/1-day Ticket		$48.00	$38.00

Magic Kingdom, Epcot, Disney's Animal Kingdom, or Disney–MGM Studios. Good in one park only. You will be allowed to exit and return to the park on the same day; be sure to have your hand stamped.

		Adult	Child
Park-Hopper Ticket	4-day	$192.00	$152.00
	5-day	$217.00	$172.00

Admission to Magic Kingdom, Epcot, Disney–MGM Studios, and Disney's Animal Kingdom on any four or five days, any combination of parks on a day.

		Adult	Child
Park-Hopper Plus Ticket	5-day	$247.00	$197.00
	6-day	$277.00	$222.00
	7-day	$307.00	$247.00

Admission to Magic Kingdom, Epcot, Disney–MGM Studios, Disney's Animal Kingdom, on any five, six, or seven days, any combination of parks on a day. Plus two visits from among Blizzard Beach, Typhoon Lagoon, River Country, Downtown Disney Pleasure Island, or Disney's Wide World of Sports.

Parking $6.00

	Adult	Child
DisneyQuest	$29.00	$23.00
Cirque du Soleil La Nouba	$67.00	$39.00
River Country	$15.95	$12.50
Blizzard Beach	$29.00	$24.00
Typhoon Lagoon	$29.00	$24.00
Pleasure Island (18 and older)	$19.81	N/A
Disney's Wide World of Sports	$9.25	$7.25

Walt Disney World Annual Passes

	Adult	Child
Annual Pass	$349.00	$297.00

Admission to Disney–MGM Studios, Epcot, Magic Kingdom, and Disney's Animal Kingdom for one year from date of voucher redemption.

	Adult	Child
Premium Annual Pass	$469.00	$399.00

Admission to Magic Kingdom, Epcot, Disney–MGM Studios and Disney's Animal Kingdom, plus Blizzard Beach, Typhoon Lagoon, River Country, and Downtown Disney Pleasure Island, DisneyQuest, and Disney's Wide World of Sports for one year from date of voucher redemption.

Pleasure Island Annual Pass

	Adult	Child
18 and older	$54.95	N/A

Ultimate Park Hopper Ticket

Offered only to guests at Walt Disney World resorts; the ticket includes *unlimited* admission to the Magic Kingdom, Disney's Animal Kingdom, Disney–MGM Studios, Epcot, Blizzard Beach, Typhoon Lagoon, River Country, Pleasure Island, and Disney's Wide World of Sports. Tickets are good from the moment of check-in until the end of the day of departure.

Prices are only slightly lower than an equivalent Park Hopper Plus Ticket sold at the gate, but the tickets are available in a wider range of day options.

As in the past, tickets have no expiration date; if you have leftover days on a pass, you can take it with you and use it the next time you visit the park. And because park ticket prices seem to be on an inexorable march upward, you may earn a reasonable return on your investment when you return in later seasons.

In recent years Disney has made it difficult to use one nifty money-saving trick. The tickets have always been "nontransferable," but Disney had no way to enforce that rule. It used to be that you could give your unused tickets to a friend or other family member, or sell your unused passes to one of the many "gray market" ticket booths in the vicinity of the park. The gray marketeers would buy and sell extra tickets at a discount.

Disney has tried various methods to make it hard to transfer ownership of a ticket. Methods have included printing a picture of the owner on the ticket and even a high-tech device that measured the dimensions of your hand and compared it with a record on file.

Home delivery. You can purchase tickets over the internet at www.disney.com.

You can also purchase over the telephone with a credit card by calling ☎ (407) 824-4321.

To purchase with a check call the same phone number to confirm current prices and obtain a mailing address.

Be sure to leave enough time before your trip for tickets to be mailed to you.

You can also purchase tickets at Disney Stores in many malls around the country.

The current system is a credit card–like medium with information stored in a magnetic stripe on the back. When you use the ticket the data is updated by Disney's computer; it is very difficult or impossible for an individual to know the remaining value on a ticket.

Under that system there is no reason not to consider trading passes with a trusted friend or relative.

I'm a lot less enthusiastic about buying tickets from gray marketeers outside the park. If it were my money I would stay away from any of the credit-card media and would only consider buying a standard cardboard ticket and only after I examined the ticket very carefully for signs of alteration or fraud. And then I would pay for the tickets with a credit card so that I could challenge payment if necessary.

An *Econoguide* to Disney Tickets

Which type of ticket or pass should you buy? There is no one answer because no two families follow the same schedule on a trip to Central Florida.

If your plans call for a full week's stay and you plan to visit every corner of the park—from the Magic Kingdom to Epcot to Disney–MGM Studios to Pleasure Island at night, and Blizzard Beach, Typhoon Lagoon, and River Country on hot afternoons—then the Park Hopper PLUS ticket makes the most sense. You can visit multiple parks on the same day with a multi-day ticket; with the five-day ticket you can also make two visits to the water parks, Pleasure Island, or Disney's Wide World of Sports.

If you are in town for a weekend and plan only a two-day visit, you'll probably want to buy just single admission tickets.

Now, here's a more complex decision: suppose you plan to visit Disney theme parks for four days and also want to go to Blizzard Beach, Typhoon Lagoon, Pleasure Island, or River Country (or all of them) during your stay. It *may* make more sense to buy a five-day ticket. Add up the value of admission to the secondary parks you will visit and subtract them from the cost of the ticket. Then you'll have to decide what to do with the unused ticket.

What do you do if your child graduates to adult ticket status while you still have days left on your non-expiring multi-day ticket? Go to Guest Services where you can apply the value of the ticket against a new adult ticket. Or, tell your eleven-year-old to look like a nine-year-old at the ticket turnstile.

And then, here's another interesting plan. I call it the "Annual Pass Eleven-Month Year." Suppose you know that a yearly visit to Walt Disney World is in the cards for the next several years. Here's a way to save hundreds of dollars over a one-year period: purchase an Annual Pass and then schedule two trips within 365 days. For example, visit Orlando in March of one year and February of the next.

How much money could you save with an eleven-month year? Let's say you visit Walt Disney World for six days at the theme and water parks, buying a Park Hopper Plus ticket for six days. At 2001 prices this visit would cost $1,058 with tax for a family of two adults and two children. Come back again in 2002, and you'll pay at least $1,058 more for another set of passes: total ticket cost is about $2,116 for the two visits.

Now consider Premium Annual Passes, good for one year from first use. Passes for two adults and two children at 2001 rates would cost $1,840.

Your potential savings under this example: $276, which will buy more than a few meals.

But you'll have to be pretty certain about your upcoming vacation schedule: your savings would turn into a significant loss if you don't return to Walt Disney World within a year.

Buying Discount Tickets

Yes, you can get Disney tickets for less. But it takes a bit of doing. There are two routes to discounts: an unofficial, unauthorized path and an official path.

First the official ways:

1. Book an all-inclusive hotel and park admission package from the Walt Disney Company. Packages include rooms and tickets; some other deals add in use of recreational facilities, and breakfast, lunch, and dinner every day at the hotel or within the parks.

Be sure to figure the true value of the package. Ask for the regular room rate, and then add in the value—to you—of recreation and meals to determine if there is a real discount.

If the package includes airfare, compare its value against the best ticket prices you could obtain on your own.

2. Book a hotel and admission package from one of the hotels outside the park. Again, find out the regular hotel charge to determine if your admission tickets are being offered at a discount.

3. Use an admission ticket discount such as the Disney Club, described later in this chapter.

4. Be on the lookout for occasional promotions by the Walt Disney Company through some of the official tourist agencies in the Orlando area.

One good place to check is the Orlando/Orange County Convention & Visitors Bureau, which is located at 8445 International Drive. Write to the bureau at P.O. Box 690355, Orlando, FL 32869.

Disney regularly offers special deals to Florida residents, sometimes extending the discounts to neighboring states. Some of the programs allow buyers to bring guests. Do you have any friends or relatives down south?

5. Buy tickets through AAA or other travel associations or through credit card issuers that may offer slightly discounted tickets.

A mark, a yen, a buck, or a pound. Ticket booths at Walt Disney World accept American Express, MasterCard, Visa, traveler's checks, personal checks with ID, cash, pennies, children . . . just kidding about the kids.

Lines at ticket booths are usually within reasonable limits within half an hour before and after opening time; lines will build at mid-morning to as much as fifteen minutes. You can save time by purchasing tickets at all Disney-owned or -operated hotels and many large area resorts.

Unofficially Yours

Now, a few unofficial ways.

1. Buy your tickets from a tourist office. They may have discount tickets directly from Walt Disney World, or they may have some tickets that have come through the gray market, such as extra supplies from hotel packages.

2. Buy your tickets from a side-of-the-road ticket broker in one of the tourist areas. You'll likely be offered passes at 10 percent to 20 percent off the list price. Their sources include hotel packages as well as any tickets they may have bought from visitors. Be sure to examine the tickets carefully to make sure they are valid. The safest type of ticket to buy here is an ordinary one-park, one-day cardboard ticket. I'd advise against buying multi-day credit card tickets from an unofficial source.

The safest way to pay for anything is with a credit card, which allows you to enlist the aid of the credit card issuer in any dispute.

The Disney Club

One way for serious Disney fans to save a bit of money is to join the Disney Club (successor to the Magic Kingdom Club).

Members of the club receive about a 5 percent discount on multi-day admission tickets to Disneyland and Walt Disney World.

There are also discounts to Walt Disney World attractions including Disney Quest, Pleasure Island, River Country, Typhoon Lagoon, and Blizzard Beach. Based on availability and time of year, discounts at various Disneyland and Walt Disney World hotels range from 10 to 20 percent.

Other benefits include a discount at Planet Hollywood and Rainforest Cafe restaurants in Orlando, and at the House of Blues at Downtown Disney in Anaheim. You'll also receive a subscription to *Disney Magazine* and some of the benefits of the national Entertainment Club, offering discounts at hotels across North America. The card is also worth a 10 percent cut on prices at many shops at Walt Disney World as well as at Disney Stores nationwide.

An annual membership costs $39.95, with renewals of $29.95; one membership can be shared among family members. If your average savings is 10 percent the card would seem to make sense if you spend $400 or more on covered expenses per year.

Note that you may end up spending more money on a Disney hotel room than you would outside one of the parks. And discounted rooms are limited in supply.

To join the Disney Club, call ☎ (800) 654-6347 or consult 💻 www.disneyclub.com.

As with any "deal," be sure to compare prices you could obtain by yourself. For example, the airfare discount generally applies to full ticket price, and excursion fares may be cheaper; the hotel discounts may still be more costly than a direct booking at a lower-priced hotel, even another Disney property.

Tickets for Other Attractions

The other attractions in the Orlando area are much more willing to strike a deal. You can usually purchase discounted tickets for Universal Orlando, SeaWorld, many dinner theaters, and other entertainment from brokers in hotels and on tourist strips. Shop around before you buy, and examine the tickets carefully.

And be sure to check out the many discount coupons for attractions that you will find in the back of this book.

Free Tickets!

Two Disney Tickets for $5! Free Universal Studios Passes!

Impossible? Not at all.

Completely free? Well. . . .

You can't help but notice the come-ons as you travel in the prime tourist areas of Irlo Bronson Highway (Highway 192) in Kissimmee and International Drive in Orlando. And in many hotels, you'll be assaulted in the lobby.

We've already discussed the discount ticket deals, available from brokers who have tickets available for a few dollars off the list price for dinner theaters and some of the theme parks other than at Walt Disney World. (You can also use the discount coupons in the back of this book for Universal Studios, SeaWorld, Busch Gardens, Splendid China, Cypress Gardens, and a host of other attractions.) No, here we are talking about those seemingly impossible offers of free or near-free tickets.

The pitch works something like this: "All you've got to do is go to this wonderful resort, eat a free breakfast, and listen to our two-hour presentation about our time-sharing/interval ownership/vacation club. Even if you don't buy, we'll give you two free tickets to Walt Disney World. There's no pressure."

It's all true, except for the "no pressure" part.

You'll start by filling out a simple form. There are usually a few qualifying questions to see if you have sufficient income to make a timesharing purchase—the threshold is usually pretty low, around $30,000 per year in annual income. And you'll likely be asked to make a "deposit" of about $20 to hold your place at the presentation. The deposit will be returned along with your "free" tickets. (There are two reasons for the deposit: the deposit is the commission earned by the ticket broker for delivering you to the sales group, as well as an inducement to make sure you show up for your appointment.)

I've sat through a few of the presentations and have earned my free tickets and the return of my deposit, just as promised. I've also had to fight off some pretty insistent sales pitches. Sometimes the two or nearly three hours of my time have been worth the value of a pair of tickets; sometimes I've felt like it would be worth paying $100 to the salespeople to let me escape before my promised time was up.

The typical sales pitch tries to compare the amount of money you have spent on your hotel room to the annual cost of a mortgage for a timeshare. You will likely be offered a specific week, or group of weeks, at a one-time "purchase" price. But there are also additional charges for maintenance, owner's groups, and other expenses.

Mickey'll take Manhattan. The Magic Kingdom opened on October 1, 1971. Walt Disney World includes 28,000 acres or some 43 square miles of land, making it about the size of San Francisco or twice the size of Manhattan.

The Magic Kingdom takes up about 107 acres; its parking lot is even bigger, at 125 acres. (By way of comparison, Disneyland occupies just 80 acres in California.)

Here are a few more measurements of the elements of Walt Disney World: Epcot, 300 acres including a 40-acre lake; Disney–MGM Studios Theme Park, 154 acres; Fort Wilderness, 600 acres, and Dixie Landings/Port Orleans, 325 acres.

And the Disney's Animal Kingdom sprawls over some 500 acres, which is nice if you're a rhino.

Should you consider buying a timeshare? Most hard-nosed financial experts consider them to be less-than-wonderful investments. They talk about the fact that you may be locked into a location or time period that may not always work with your changing lifestyle. They worry about unexpected expenses—if the elevator fails or the swimming pool leaks or other major expenses occur, the bill will come to the homeowners. And finally, there is not a very good history of increasing monetary value for timeshare purchases.

One way to check on the value of timeshares is to go to the resale market. There are several agencies in and around Orlando that specialize in unloading timeshares from private parties. If there is a big disparity between buying from the developer and buying from a reseller, or if the reseller has an unexpectedly large inventory of shares for sale, you should be very suspicious.

In any case make sure you consult your accountant or attorney before signing anything.

Chapter 5
Walt Disney World (and Universal Orlando) with Children

Children and Walt Disney World? Could there possibly be a better fit? Well, yes and no: for many kids a visit to Walt Disney World or Universal Orlando is the biggest thing that has ever happened to them—and although it almost always will be a most wonderful vacation, there are also special concerns for youngsters and their parents.

Here are ten suggestions to make a trip with young children go well:

1. Involve the children in the planning. Obtain maps and brochures and study them at the dinner table; read sections of this book together. Work together on a schedule for the places you want to visit on each day.

2. Draw up the "rules" for the visit and make sure each child understands them and agrees with them. The basic rule in our family was that our young children always had to be within an arm's length of mom or dad.

3. Study and understand the height and age minimums for some of the more active rides at the parks. Don't build up expectations of your forty-one-inch-tall child for an attraction that requires riders to be forty-two inches in height. (Did we hear someone say something about lift pads in shoes? Just remember that the rules are there to protect children from injury.)

4. Come to a family agreement on financial matters. Few parents can afford to buy everything a child demands; even if you could, you probably wouldn't want to. Consider giving your children a special allowance they can spend at the park; encourage them to wait a day or two into the trip so they don't hit bottom before they find the souvenir they really want to take home.

5. Choose a place to meet if you become separated. Landmarks include Cinderella's Castle or the carrousel in the Magic Kingdom; Spaceship Earth in Epcot; a particular spot near the Tree of Life at Disney's Animal Kingdom; the Chinese Theater in Disney–MGM Studios; the Back to the Future steam locomotive or the Gak fountain at Universal Studios Florida; or One Fish, Two Fish, Red Fish, Blue Fish in Seuss Landing at Universal Studios Islands of Adventure. Beyond that instruct your children to find a uniformed park attendant if they are lost, and plan on checking with attendants yourself if you misplace a child.

Attach a name tag to youngsters (available at Guest Services if you don't have your own) or put a paper in your child's pocket with your name and hotel on it. Some parents even give their kids walkie-talkie radios or cell phones.

6. For much of the year, the sun in Central Florida is quite strong. Keep your kids (and yourself) under hats, and be sure to use a sunscreen, especially at midday. You may want to bring bottles of water for the entire family—it's a lot cheaper than soda at the snack bars, and better for you, too.

7. You are not supposed to bring food into the park. Then again, we've never seen a paying guest searched for hidden sandwiches. You may choose to leave lunch in your car and come out for a break—this is easy at Epcot, Disney–MGM Studios, or Animal Kingdom because of the proximity of the parking lot to the park. There are lockers outside the gates at the other parks.

8. A good strategy with youngsters, especially if you are staying inside the park or nearby, is to arrive early and then leave at lunchtime for a quick nap or a swim; return at dusk to enjoy the evening at the park. You'll miss the hottest and most crowded part of the day and probably enjoy yourself much more. Be sure to have your hands stamped when you leave the park and hold onto your tickets (including your parking pass) if you intend to return.

9. Although you can bring your own stroller, it is also easy to rent one for the day at the parks. Park the stroller near the exit to the attraction so it is waiting when you come out. Don't leave any valuables with the stroller. If you move from one Disney park to another during a single day, show your receipt at the new park to obtain a stroller when you arrive.

10. There are changing tables in most restrooms and private places for nursing mothers. You can also purchase diapers and formula; ask at Guest Services.

Dad, I Promise . . .

One of the best things about going to Walt Disney World or Universal Studios with kids is that a resourceful parent should be able to milk a few weeks of "If you don't behave right now, I'm not taking you to Florida" threats.

My resourceful son Willie came up with his own contract. Call it:

The Ten Theme Park Commandments

I. Thou shalt not leave thy parents' sight.
II. Thou shalt not go on twister rides after a meal.
III. Thou shalt not complain about the lines.
IV. Thou shalt not fight with thy sister or brother.
V. Thou shalt not ask to buy something at the shops that costs more than the admission ticket.
VI. Thou shalt enjoy any of the boring things that Mom and Dad want to see.
VII. Thou shalt stand still so Dad can take at least one picture.
VIII. Thou shalt not pester the characters to talk.
IX. Thou shalt not sing "It's a Small World After All" more than sixteen times in a row.
X. Thou shalt go on at least one educational ride, even if it has a long line.

A Kid's-Eye View of the Best of Walt Disney World and Universal Orlando

What are the best attractions for youngsters (three to ten years old)? Well, you know your particular child's interests and fears better than anyone else, but here are some favorites and a few warnings. (Key appears on next page.)

Magic Kingdom

Dumbo, The Flying Elephant ❷
Cinderella's Golden Carrousel
It's a Small World
Jungle Cruise
Pirates of the Caribbean ❶
Peter Pan's Flight
Mad Tea Party ❷
The Magic Carpets of Aladdin ❷
The Many Adventures of Winnie the Pooh
Mickey's Toontown Fair
The Barnstormer
Ariel's Grotto
Country Bear Jamboree
Tom Sawyer's Island
Tomorrowland Speedway ❸
Enchanted Tiki Room
Splash Mountain ❸

Epcot

Imagination!
Honey, I Shrunk the Audience
Food Rocks (The Land) ❶
Universe of Energy ❶
Wonders of Life ❹
The Living Seas
River of Time (Mexico)
GM Test Track ❶

Disney's Animal Kingdom

Kilimanjaro Safaris
Kali River Rapids ❹
Festival of the Lion King
Tarzan Rocks! ❶
It's Tough to Be a Bug!
Triceratop Spin ❷
Primeval Whirl ❷
Dinosaurs ❹
Affection Section
Pangani Forest Exploration Trail

Disney–MGM Studios

Fantasmic! ❶
Jim Henson's Muppet*Vision 3D ❶
The Great Movie Ride ❶
Honey, I Shrunk the Kids Movie Set Adventure
Doug Live!
Voyage of the Little Mermaid ❶
Beauty and the Beast—Live on Stage
Sounds Dangerous ❶

Universal Studios Florida

Woody Woodpecker's KidZone
Fievel's Playground
E.T. Adventure
Twister ❶
Back to the Future ❹
Wild, Wild, Wild West Stunt Show ❶
Animal Actors Stage
Funtastic World of Hanna-Barbera ❷
Earthquake—The Big One ❶/❸
Jaws ❶/❹
Men in Black ❹

Universal's Islands of Adventure

The Cat in the Hat
If I Ran the Zoo
Dudley Do-Right's Ripsaw Falls ❷
The Eighth Voyage of Sinbad ❶
Pteranadon Flyers ❷
One Fish, Two Fish, Red Fish, Blue Fish
Caro-Seuss-el
Storm Force Accelatron ❷
Me Ship *The Olive*
Jurassic Park River Adventure ❶/❷
Camp Jurassic

Notes:

❶ Loud noises and special effects (pirates, skeletons, beasts) may startle unprepared children.

❷ Can make some children dizzy.

❸ Adult must accompany small children.

❹ **Disney–MGM Studios:** Star Wars may be a bit rough for youngsters. **Epcot:** Body Wars, Cranium Command, and GM Test Track may be too intense for very young. Parental guidance advised for *The Making of Me* film at the Wonders of Life. **Universal Studios Florida:** Back to the Future and Men in Black may be too intense for some children; use your judgment based on your knowledge of your own child. Jaws, Twister, and Earthquake have some wild effects but most children find them fun. **Magic Kingdom:** Splash Mountain is charming, but it does include one drop over a waterfall; it's not as scary as it looks, but some children may not be ready. **Disney's Animal Kingdom:** Dinosaurs is a wild ride through animatronic dinosaurs and exploding meteors. Some youngsters may be scared, but most will beg for a second and third and fourth trip. Kali River Rapids is a relatively wild river raft ride that may frighten some youngsters.

Babysitting

Several independent companies offer babysitting at many hotels and resorts:

All About Kids. ☎ (407) 812-9300 or ☎ (800) 728-6506.

KinderCare Guest Services. ☎ (407) 827-5444.

Supersitters. ☎ (407) 382-2558 or ☎ (800) 972-9819.

Kid's Camps and Clubs

A number of Disney hotel resorts include evening clubs for youngsters between the ages of four and twelve; all visitors must be toilet trained. Rates in 2001 were $8 per hour, per child. Be sure to call ahead for reservations.

Cub's Den. Disney's Wilderness Lodge. ☎ (407) 939-3463. 5 P.M. to midnight daily. Includes dinner. Video games and Disney movies.

Harbor Club. Disney's BoardWalk. ☎ (407) 939-6301. 4:30–11:45 P.M. daily. Includes dinner (6–8 P.M.). Arcade games, movies, and arts and crafts.

Mouseketeer Clubhouse. Disney's Contemporary Resort. ☎ (407) 824-1000, Ext. 3038. 4:30 P.M.–midnight daily. Includes dinner (6–8 P.M.). Activities and Disney movies.

Mouseketeer Clubhouse. Disney's Grand Floridian Resort & Spa. ☎ (407) 824-2985. 4:30 P.M.–midnight daily. Includes dinner. Movies and games.

The Neverland Club. Disney's Polynesian Resort. ☎ (407) 939-3463. 5 P.M.–midnight daily. Includes buffet dinner (6–8 P.M.). Video games, films, and arts and crafts.

Sandcastle Club. Disney's Beach Club Resort. ☎ (407) 934-6290. 4:30 P.M.–midnight daily. Includes dinner (6–8 P.M.) Activities and Disney movies.

Part II
Walt Disney World

Chapter 6
The Keys to the Kingdom . . . and the Rest of Walt Disney World

So, you want to go to Disney World. Great! Which Walt Disney World?

- The world of Mickey and Minnie and Dumbo and one thousand live elephants, okapi, giraffes, two-toed sloths, gorillas, and black rhinos?[1]
- The only place on the planet where China touches Norway, where Santa Fe overlooks Polynesia, and where you can drive among the dinosaurs?[2]
- The home of R2D2, Humphrey Bogart, the Alien, Kermit the Frog, and an elevator guaranteed to fail hundreds of times a day?[3]
- The stately adult pleasure dome of Merriweather A. Pleasure, where you can boogey (almost) all night?[4]
- Florida's only ski resort and the summer golf course for Santa's elves?[5]
- A terrifying plunge down Humunga Kowabunga or a kid-friendly splashdown at Whoop 'n Holler Hollow?[6]
- The campfire sing-along at the trading post?[7]
- The place where you can hitch a ride in rock group Aerosmith's speedy luxury limo?[8]
- A place with five championship-level golf courses?[9]
- The home port of the largest private flotilla in the world, bigger than many navies?[10]
- A place where guests volunteer as crash test dummies?[11]
- A dinner table in a rainforest or parked at a drive-in movie?[12]
- A spectacular old-style baseball park, home to the Spring Training camp of a major-league team?[13]
- Or a world-class Indy-style auto racecourse?[14]

Oh, *that* Disney World.

---

[1]The Magic Kingdom and Disney's Animal Kingdom
[2]Epcot Center and Disney's Coronado Springs
[3]Disney–MGM Studios
[4]Pleasure Island
[5]Blizzard Beach and Winter Summerland
[6]Typhoon Lagoon and River Country
[7]Fort Wilderness
[8]Rock 'n Roller Coaster at Disney–MGM Studios
[9]The Magic Linkdom
[10]The Walt Disney World marinas
[11]GM Test Track at Epcot
[12]Rainforest Cafe or Sci-Fi Dine-in Theater
[13]Disney's Wide World of Sports
[14]Walt Disney World Speedway

Let's start with an important definition:

Walt Disney World is the entertainment complex that includes the **Magic Kingdom**, **Epcot**, **Disney's Animal Kingdom**, and **Disney–MGM Studios** as well as **Blizzard Beach**, **Typhoon Lagoon**, **River Country**, the six Disney golf courses, **Downtown Disney** (including **Pleasure Island**, **Disney Village**, and **Disney's West Side** encompassing **DisneyQuest** and **Cirque du Soleil**), **Disney's Wide World of Sports**, and hundreds of Disney-operated and Disney-licensed hotels and restaurants within the property lines of the World.

Covering forty-seven square miles, Walt Disney World is about the size of San Francisco, or twice the size of Manhattan. Of more than thirty thousand acres, only about one-fourth has been developed, with another quarter set aside as a wilderness preserve.

My goal in this, the largest section of the book, is twofold: first, to break down the huge World into smaller and more understandable pieces and, second, to put them back together in a way that shows how to get the most out of it.

There are nine chapters in this section:

- The Keys to the Kingdom . . . and the Rest of Walt Disney World
- The Magic Kingdom
- Epcot
- Disney's Animal Kingdom
- Disney–MGM Studios
- Disney Water Parks
- Downtown Disney
- Educational Opportunities at Walt Disney World
- Inside the World of Disney

Later on in the book, we'll return to Walt Disney World to discuss dinner theaters, sports, recreation, and educational opportunities.

Each of the theme park chapters begins with a list of *Econoguide* "Must-See" attractions and the exclusive "Power Trip" tour. I hope you'll take the time to read the chapters before you go and once again when you're in Florida.

A Few Ways Around the Waiting Lines

The good news about Walt Disney World is that things are getting better and better all the time. Recent years have seen the arrival of a hard-rockin' coaster at Disney–MGM Studios, amazing animal encounters at Disney's Animal Kingdom, and a wild automobile test facility at Epcot.

The not-so-good news: there are thousands of people in line ahead of you, especially during the busy summer season and holiday periods.

The Fastpass System

Disney's Fastpass offers some welcome relief to waiting lines; the advanced ride reservation system is available at many of the most popular attractions in all four theme parks.

To use the system insert your admission ticket into a card reader to receive a Fastpass with a scheduled return time. At the appointed hour you can walk right into the pre-show area without waiting in line.

Here's the fine print: you can only register for one Fastpass appointment at a time. If you have a reservation for a 2 P.M. coaster ride, you cannot use your ticket to reserve a river rapids expedition until after the appointed time.

Among attractions with Fastpass distribution:

Magic Kingdom: The Haunted Mansion, The Many Adventures of Winnie the Pooh, Jungle Cruise, Space Mountain, Buzz Lightyear's Space Ranger Spin, and Splash Mountain.

Epcot: GM Test Track, and *Honey, I Shrunk the Audience.*

Disney–MGM Studios: *Who Wants to Be a Millionaire—Play It!*, Jim Henson's Muppet*Vision 3-D, Rock 'n' Roller Coaster Starring Aerosmith, Tower of Terror II, Star Tours, *Indiana Jones Epic Stunt Spectacular*, and the *Voyage of the Little Mermaid.*

Disney's Animal Kingdom: Kilimanjaro Safaris, Dinosaur, and Kali River Rapids.

In recent years guests at Walt Disney World hotels who purchase multi-day passes were offered other ways around waiting in line. Magic Kingdom E-Ride Nights, offered on certain evenings at the Magic Kingdom, reopen several of the more popular attractions at the park "after hours," usually between 10 P.M. and 1 A.M.

Guests at Disney World hotels can also enter selected sections of the parks ninety minutes earlier than other visitors on Surprise Mornings.

Getting to the Magic Kingdom by Car

The idea behind the transportation system at Walt Disney World probably sounded good at the time: getting to the Magic Kingdom *should* be a magical experience. When you leave your car you *should* be in an entirely different world.

"We'll have visitors park way on the other side of a large lagoon and then let them take an exciting monorail ride or a soothing ferryboat to the main gate," the planners said. "By the time they're inside the park, they'll completely forget about the outside world."

So far, so good, but let's consider how it works out more thirty-five or so years after the planners made their drawings.

First you park way out in East Overshoe, practically the next county. Then you must walk to the central aisle of the parking lot and wait for a gigantic snake-like tram to take you to the Transportation and Ticket Center (TTC).

At the TTC you'll choose between a monorail around Seven Seas Lagoon or a ferryboat ride. Either way you'll be taken to the main gates.

Total time from parking the car to your first

Pets. Never leave your cat, dog, mouse, or other pet in your car; heat can build up tremendously in a parked vehicle, and animals can die. If you must bring a pet with you, bring proof of vaccination and use one of the Pet Care Kennels at the Magic Kingdom's Transportation and Ticket Center or at the entrance to Epcot, Disney's Animal Kingdom, Disney–MGM Studios, and Disney's Fort Wilderness Resort and Campground. Animal lovers there will also care for birds, ferrets, small rodents, and non-venomous snakes in carriers.

step onto Main Street is about thirty minutes at the start of the day and as much as an hour at peak periods from about 10 A.M. to noon, when there are long lines at the monorail or ferryboat.

At the end of the day you'll have to reverse the process. And you *did* remember where you parked your car, right?

For most visitors to the Magic Kingdom staying outside the park, there's no easy way around the process, except to follow one of our general rules: arrive early. If you're staying within Walt Disney World, consider taking the monorail, water taxi, or bus right from your hotel.

Back of the bus. Can you park at a Disney hotel lot and ride a monorail, boat, or bus directly to one of the parks? The answer is yes . . . and no. In theory, you must have a guest ID card to ride one of the internal modes of transport. However, I have never seen a driver ask for a card. And, Disney encourages guests at Walt Disney World to sample the restaurants and shops at its hotels.

If you absolutely inst, Disney also quietly sells a daily transportation ticket for $2.50.

Getting to Epcot, Disney–MGM, or Animal Kingdom by Car

The situation is different at Disney–MGM Studios, Epcot, and Disney's Animal Kingdom, where you can park and walk or take a single tram ride to the gates.

On busy days, or if I know that I will be ending my day at a different park than the one I started at, I leave my car where I want it to be at the end of the day and use Disney transportation to travel to my first park of the day.

If your plan for the day calls for a start at the Magic Kingdom and ends with a special dinner at Epcot, you might try this strategy: arrive early at Epcot and park there. Ride the monorail to the transfer point at the Transportation and Ticket Center and pick up the monorail to the Magic Kingdom. Then reverse that route in the afternoon and you will be able to stay as late as you want at Epcot and pick up your car there. The alternate plan works, too, on nights when the Magic Kingdom is open later than Epcot; park at the Magic Kingdom and ride the monorail to Epcot to begin your day.

Traffic reports. If you're driving, four low-power radio signals on three AM frequencies keep visitors abreast of information at the resort. Guests can tune to 1030 (driving toward the Magic Kingdom), 900 (exiting the Magic Kingdom), 810 (entering Epcot), and 900 (exiting Epcot).

Relativity. All of Disneyland in California could fit within the lagoon at Epcot, or within the boundaries of the parking lot at the Magic Kingdom.

From Within Walt Disney World

One of the advantages of a hotel within Walt Disney World is the availability of Disney's own bus, monorail, and boat fleet.

The buses go directly to the entrance of the Magic Kingdom, Disney's Animal Kingdom, Epcot, and Disney–MGM Studios. Similarly, the boat services from some Disney hotels go directly to the Magic Kingdom or to the back door

International Gateway entrance to Epcot. Visitors staying at a Disney hotel with a monorail stop have direct service only to the Magic Kingdom; you'll have to make a transfer at the Transportaion and Ticket Center to an Epcot train or a Disney–MGM Studios bus if either is your destination.

The principal transportation system at the Magic Kingdom—and one of the most famous—is the Mark IV Monorail system, which links the Magic Kingdom and the Transportation and Ticket Center, and a second route that runs from there to Epcot. A local version of the Magic Kingdom loop stops at several of the major hotels within the park.

Everything You Always Wanted to Know About the Monorail

Well, almost everything. The trains have eight 113-horsepower motors in various cars; the train can't be split up into smaller units.

The monorails run on 600-volt DC power drawn from Disney's own power plant north of the Contemporary Resort, across the road from the monorail maintenance shop.

The Disney tracks stretch nearly fourteen miles, including spur lines and maintenance areas. Just over half of that is the Epcot "beam"; the Lagoon beam to hotels and the Exterior beam to the Magic Kingdom are each about two-and-a-half miles in length.

A monorail waits for passengers at the Magic Kingdom

Photo by Corey Sandler. Used by permission from Disney Enterprises, Inc.

By the way, there is one row of seats in the front cab with the driver of the monorail. Ask one of the attendants to place you there for an interesting and different perspective; you may have to let a train pass by if there are many people waiting in line.

Five if by Monorail, Seven if by Ferry

Another component of the transportation system to the Magic Kingdom is decidedly low-tech: Disney's fleet of ferryboats that cross the lagoon from the TTC to the gates of the park. At most times there are two boats in constant operation with a third available for peak periods.

The scaled-down versions of the famous Staten Island Ferries in New York are double-ended vessels, meaning they don't need to turn around at either end of their trip. You walk on at one end and walk off at the other. By the way, the ferries are free-floating; unlike the riverboat at the Magic Kingdom, there is no rail beneath the water.

The ferries are a very pleasant way to travel, especially on a pretty evening at the end of a long day.

Although the monorail may look speedy, in truth it is only about a minute or two faster than the ferryboat in getting from the TTC to the Magic Kingdom. And the two ferryboats can carry about three times as many passengers as one monorail train. So, if the line for the monorail is lengthy, go by sea.

WALT DISNEY WORLD ROADWAYS

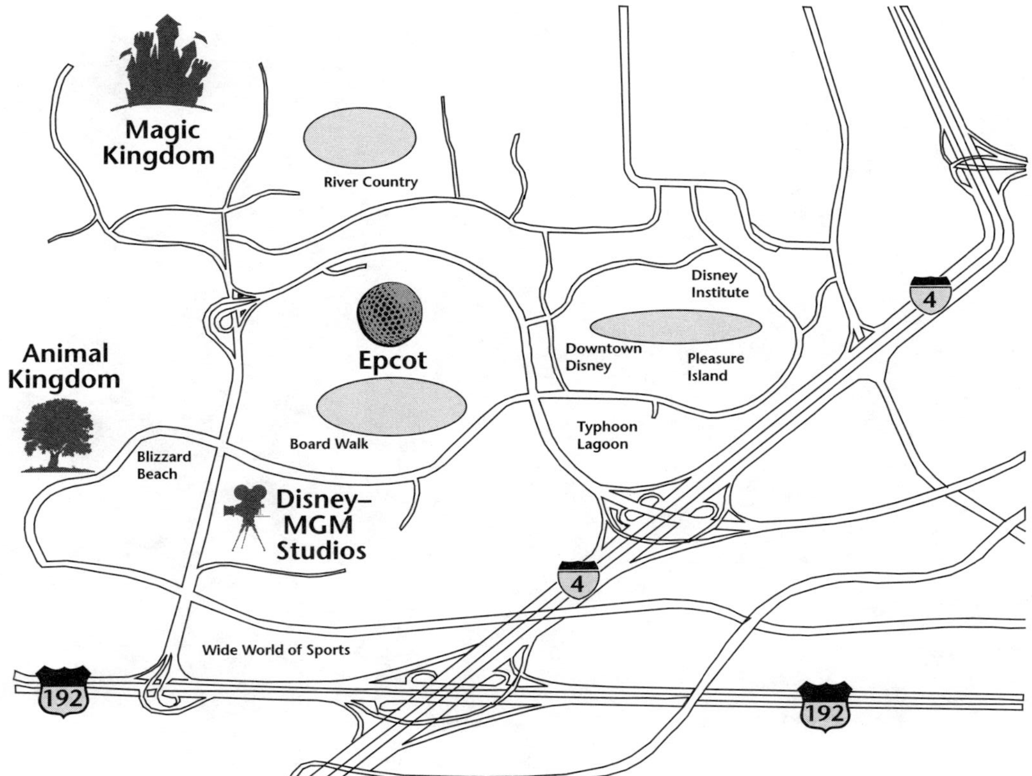

Chapter 7
The Magic Kingdom

Once upon a mouse, back in 1928, Walter Elias Disney created a short cartoon he called *Steamboat Willie*. Its star was a mouse, Willie, who soon thereafter underwent a name change and achieved stardom as Mickey Mouse.

Everything else since then has been built upon the slender shoulders of the cute little rodent, along with his gal, Minnie, and buddies Donald, Daisy, Snow White, as well as a cast of thousands of other cartoon and movie favorites.

Disney's film studio began to grow rapidly; Walt set up a little park alongside his first movie studios to entertain visitors, exhibiting his collection of scale model trains among other things. When he moved into television in the early 1950s Disney struck a deal with ABC Television to help fund the construction of the Disneyland park in California, which opened in a former orange grove in 1955. Although much has changed in the nearly fifty years since Disneyland was first planned, the basic structure of that park, and all that have followed, is the same. Walt Disney World's Magic Kingdom opened in 1971. And then here's a how-de-doo: In 1995 Disney bought the entire ABC network.

Today breathes there a man, woman, girl, boy, duck, or mouse who has not dreamed of visiting the Magic Kingdom? Walt Disney's entertainment vision—along with the incredible marketing skills of the company he left behind—has made Disney's parks and symbols probably the world's best-known popular icons. You can see Mickey Mouse T-shirts worn on the streets of Moscow, Epcot towels on the beaches of the Caribbean, Minnie dresses on the boulevards of Paris, and Roger Rabbit hats in the alleys of Tokyo.

In 1992 Disneyland Paris joined the three other parks—Disneyland, Walt Disney World, and Tokyo Disneyland—on the global map.

In Florida, by far the largest of all the Disney parks, the empire sprawls across miles of land and includes four major theme parks and dozens of other attractions. However, it is still The Magic Kingdom—home of **Main Street U.S.A.**, **Fantasyland**, **Adventureland**, **Frontierland**, and **Tomorrowland**—that visitors think of when they first set out for Orlando.

In this section you'll find the details of the Ultimate Unauthorized Tour of

MUST-SEES

WOW

Space Mountain
(Tomorrowland)

Buzz Lightyear's Space Ranger Spin
(Tomorrowland)

The Timekeeper
(Tomorrowland)

It's a Small World
(Fantasyland)

The Many Adventures of Winnie the Pooh
(Fantasyland)

Mickey's and Minnie's Country Houses
(Mickey's Toontown Fair)

The Haunted Mansion
(Liberty Square)

Pirates of the Caribbean
(Adventureland)

Jungle Cruise
(Adventureland)

Big Thunder Mountain Railroad
(Frontierland)

Splash Mountain
(Frontierland)

Tom Sawyer Island
(Frontierland)

the Magic Kingdom, area by area. I'll tell you which rides are "must-sees" and which ones are not worth crossing the road for.

Power Trip

A Fastpass Plan

For years a big crowd at the Magic Kingdom guaranteed big lines and long waits at the most popular attractions. There are few things less appealing to a four-year-old than waiting an hour for a ride on Winnie the Pooh, a teenager chilling out in a slow-moving queue for Space Mountain, or an adult stuck in the very slow lane at the corral on the dock at the Jungle Cruise.

In years past we have offered detailed battle plans to visitors to help them beat the crowds. We're happy to report that, for the most part, Disney has come to the rescue of its guests with the creation of the Fastpass, a system that lets visitors reserve a time for a popular ride. Fastpass is not perfect, but it's a whole lot better than life without it.

Here's how it works: you insert your ticket into a reader at special booths near attractions and receive a Fastpass ticket imprinted with an assigned time period. When you return, you'll enter a special gateway to the attraction with a promise or no more than a fifteen-minute wait. On all but the busiest days of the year, you're only allowed to hold one Fastpass ticket at a time; when waiting times for Fastpasses extend to two hours or more, Disney allows visitors to make reservations at two attractions.

In 2001 the Magic Kingdom offered Fastpass tickets at six attractions: The Haunted Mansion, The Many Adventures of Winnie the Pooh, Jungle Cruise, Space Mountain, Buzz Lightyear's Space Ranger Spin, and Splash Mountain. Look for the ***FAST*** icon in this book.

(Among the popular rides *not* part of the Fastpass system: Pirates of the Caribbean and the other kiddie rides in Fantasyland.)

So the Power Trip for Walt Disney World works like this:

1. Start by coming up with a list of the attractions you most want to see.
2. Divide the list into Fastpass attractions and waiting-line attractions.
3. Get to the park as early as you can.
4. Begin your day by making a beeline to the first Fastpass attraction on your list and grab a ticket.

On busy days the gates will open about thirty minutes before the park itself; you will be able to stroll to a rope barrier at the top of Main Street. On extremely busy days attractions may be open earlier than officially announced.

Head for the Fastpass machine at the attraction at the top of your list. At busy times of the year, your first Fastpass reservation will tell you to come back in an hour or two; later in the day, the gap may extend to several hours.

Now put your Fastpass in your pocket and head for the first attraction on your non-Fastpass list.

With a bit of luck, you can ping-pong back and forth between ride reservations and waiting lines.

Closing time. Closing time varies according to the season, and is sometimes adjusted from day to day based on attendance patterns; it can be as early as 6 P.M. or as late as midnight. Check at the park for details. The announced closing time is actually a relative thing, usually meaning the time when the last person is allowed to join a ride line. The parks themselves are cleared out about an hour or so after then, and the final bus or other transportation to parking lots or hotels leaves about ninety minutes after closing time.

Waiting times for the major rides are listed on a board near the **Plaza Restaurant**, just outside the entrance to Frontierland and Adventureland. Cast a quick eye on the waiting times when your first arrive to help adjust your Power Trip, and check it out any time you're in the neighborhood. Your goal: go where the crowds are *not*.

Moving beyond Fastpass, it's also important to understand the ebb and flow of traffic. We've already suggested you arrive early. You should also plan to eat lunch and dinner early, to avoid lines and to take advantage of a break in the crowds when the rest of the world is chowing down. Another reduction in crowds at attractions comes during the daily parades, shows, and fireworks.

Depending on how crowded the park is, you may want to go back for a repeat on a few of the rides in the dark. I especially like after-dark rides on Big Thunder Mountain and the Jungle Cruise. You can also catch some of the story rides at Fantasyland, and (for the hopelessly romantic or the hopelessly child-directed) It's a Small World.

In peak season and holidays you will still be able to catch the late performance of the fireworks show to end your day with a bang.

The Opening Dash

The Magic Kingdom usually opens at 9 A.M., although it may open at 8 A.M. at extremely busy times of the year. Guests at Walt Disney Resorts are allowed a head start to certain areas of the park on some days.

Lockers. Store extra clothing and other items at one of the coin-operated lockers beneath the Main Street Railroad Station and at the Transportation and Ticket Center. Your one-day rental can be transferred to Epcot or Disney–MGM Studios; consult the attendant.

Lost and found. A family of four touring Walt Disney World for four days and not losing at least one backpack, two sets of sunglasses, and three hats is unlike any we know. On the day of a loss, check at City Hall in the Magic Kingdom or Guest Services at Epcot, Animal Kingdom, or the Disney–MGM Studios. After a day, items are taken to a central office at the Transportation and Ticket Center.

The first part of the park that officially opens is Main Street; you can visit some of the shops or grab a bite to eat at the bakery or restaurants before the attractions open. Visitors are stopped at rope lines at the top of Main Street—one to the left near the Crystal Palace, one in the center heading toward Cinderella Castle, and one to the right just short of Tomorrowland.

The first rule of the Power Trip calls for you to get to the park early; the second is to get yourself a good position at one of the three gates. Bear to the left if your first goal is Splash Mountain, Big Thunder Mountain, or elsewhere in Adventureland or Frontierland. Line up at the rightmost gate if your goal is Space Mountain, Alien Encounter, Tomorrowland Indy Speedway, or another Tomorrowland ride. And head up the center to go to fulfill your need to visit Fantasyland.

Just before the gates open for the masses, you'll hear a bit of music and an announcement that quotes Walt Disney's dedication of the park; then the speaker will conclude by asking visitors to walk slowly and carefully into the park; of course, the crowds will stampede wildly instead.

Whether you walk or run, if you are anywhere near the front of the waiting line when the gates open, you should be able to get onto any ride in the park with no more than a fifteen-minute wait, which is about as good as it gets.

Or try this: enter the park before the opening, and go up to the Disney World Railroad platform; you'll find a train that will depart the moment the park officially opens. Ride to the Splash Mountain station and get off and into line; you should be able to beat most of the thundering horde racing across the park on foot.

A general rule for any part of Walt Disney World is to head immediately for the ride or rides you expect will have the longest lines and get them out of the way early. Then go on to as many other major attractions as you can before the lines become too long. Spend the afternoon visiting lesser attractions, and then go back to major draws at the end of the day as the crowds lessen and the parades and fireworks pull people out of line.

Attractions at the Magic Kingdom

Main Street, U.S.A.

Somewhere, someplace, at some time, there was an America like this. It's a place of small stores with friendly proprietors, where the streets are clean and the landscape neat, and where a paper scrap never lingers on the ground.

At the start of your visit to the Magic Kingdom you'll think of Main Street, U.S.A., as an interesting place to walk through on the way to somewhere else. But be sure to leave time to come back later to browse, shop, or eat; if you are following our advice you will have arrived early at the park with a specific destination in mind.

But when you come back marvel at the attention to detail of the storefronts and interior decorations of the shops. Most of the names on the second-story windows are those of former and present Disney employees responsible for creation or maintenance of the park.

Main Street is also the place to be if you are a parade fan; the entertainment moves toward the railroad station just inside the gates—that may be the best seat in the house to watch the parade. You can also see the parades at the circle near Cinderella Castle and on the streets of Frontierland, both of which are nearer the major attractions of the park.

The famous Disney parades change every few years, and in high-season there may be as many as three parades a day—an afternoon Disney character parade and two evening electrical events. Pick up an Entertainment Show Schedule at the entrance to the park or at City Hall.

Disney phone numbers. Walt Disney World dining reservations: ☎ (407) 939-3463
Disney resort hotel reservations: ☎ (407) 934-7639
Golf tee times: ☎ (407) 824-2270
Pleasure Island: ☎ (407) 934-7781

Meeting places. Try not to select the front of Cinderella Castle as a meeting place for groups that go their own way within the park. This location can become quite crowded during the daily parades and other events. Instead, choose the back side of the castle near the carrousel or a landmark off the parade route.

SpectroMagic

In the nostalgic world of Disney, everything old is new again, sooner of later. New in April of 2001 was a return of the venerable SpectroMagic parade, which debuted in Orlando in 1991 and ran until mid-1999 when it was replaced by the Main Street Electrical Parade, which dated back to 1977 in its original form.

Designed as a moving gallery for audiences, SpectroMagic uses state-of-the-art lighting effects to bring to life pixies and peacocks, seahorses and flying horses, flower gardens and fountains.

Highlights include:

- The Genie from Disney's *Aladdin* serves as conductor of an orchestra producing a rainbow of musical notes that flow into the air
- Practical Pig, poised before a hundred-foot-long parade segment of Disney characters, castle towers, a carousel, and a bejeweled coach, changes the colors into silvery white
- Chernabog, one of the monstrous demons from *Fantasia*, spreads his wings to a thirty-eight-foot span

- Ursula, the sea witch octopus from *The Little Mermaid*
- And, of course, Mickey Mouse in a magician's cape that transforms into a sweep of color from the base of his float to seventeen feet above his head

It takes more than 120 performers to bring the parade to life, and seventy-five tons of batteries to power more than 600,000 lights including more than 250,000 fiber optic points.

A secret spot, slightly less crowded, from which to watch parades is near the exit from Pirates of the Caribbean and the entrance to Splash Mountain near the Pecos Bill Cafe. A pathway under the railroad is the start or end of most parades.

One place worth stopping before you begin your exploration is **City Hall** in Town Square. Step up to the counter to obtain schedules of entertainment and appearances by Disney characters; maps in English, French, German, Spanish, or braille; written show descriptions for visitors with special needs; and other information.

City Hall opens when the ticket gates open (up to half an hour or so before the rope is dropped at the top of Main Street), allowing you to make a quick stop there before you join the dash to Space Mountain or Splash Mountain or Dumbo or whatever's your immediate pleasure.

Walt Disney Railroad

A pleasant way to tour the park (our favorite way to end a day), these real steam engines take passengers on a mile-and-a-half, fifteen-minute circuit of the park.

Walt Disney was a railroad nut, even running a small-scale system in his own backyard. The four engines that are part of the Magic Kingdom's rolling stock were built in the United States but spent much of their working lives in Mexico's Yucatan peninsula hauling sugar cane. The wheels, side rods, and other major parts of the engines are original, although the boilers and cabs have been rebuilt.

Originally constructed to burn coal or wood and later converted to oil, the steam engines are now powered by diesel fuel.

The *Lilly Belle*, named for Disney's wife, was built in 1928, coincidentally the same year Mickey Mouse made his screen debut. Also on the tracks is the *Roy O. Disney*, named for the boss's brother, the *Walter E. Disney*, named for the man himself, and the less-often-seen *Roger Broggie*, christened after a long-time Disney employee and friend.

The recorded spiel of the conductor has become politically correct in recent years, removing references to marauding Indians and instead extolling the friendly Native Americans waiting to greet visitors.

Cinderella Castle

The hallmark of the Magic Kingdom, Cinderella Castle matches every child's mind's-eye image of a fairytale castle. It sits at the focal center of the park marking the top of Main Street, U.S.A., and the entranceway to Fantasyland. It is especially handsome by night, lit by colored gels.

The castle is loosely based on Sleeping Beauty's castle from the fairy tale and the Disney movie that brought it to life. It is built of fiberglass and steel beams; not a single brick or stone was used in its construction.

Cinderella Castle
Photo by Corey Sandler. Used by permission from Disney Enterprises, Inc.

Way up top in one of the towers is a small apartment originally intended for Walt Disney and his family, but never used.

Cinderella Castle is 189 feet tall—nine feet higher than Spaceship Earth in Epcot.

(At Disneyland in Anaheim, California, the original bastion is Sleeping Beauty Castle. It is much smaller, its towers a mere seventy-one feet tall.)

We're told plans were drawn for a place to stay within the castle as part of the park's twenty-fifth anniversary gala; among the problems was how to deal with the fact that guests would have been inside the park after hours. One solution called for the assignment of a personal escort for all guests, which wouldn't have been too big of a deal, because room rates were expected to be several thousand dollars per night. In any case, it never happened and the rooms within remain unfinished.

You can, though, go halfway up the tower to **Cinderella's Royal Table** for a theme park theme meal. And be sure to check out the elaborate mosaics in the entranceway; they tell the familiar story of the girl with the glass slipper in Italian glass, real silver, and gold.

The Coat of Arms above the castle on the north wall (facing Fantasyland) is that of the Disney family. Outside the entrance to King Stefan's Banquet Hall are plaques for other Disney executives.

Main Street Vehicles. Old-fashioned cars, a horse-drawn trolley, and fire engines move slowly down Main Street to Cinderella Castle. (Following not far behind the horses are uniformed sanitation engineers with shovels.)

Tomorrowland

When Tomorrowland was originally conceived, it was as a showcase of the future. Ironically, the world of tomorrow at the Magic Kingdom eventually became the most dated and tired part of the park.

In 1995 Tomorrowland underwent the most complete remake of an original area at any Disney park. Today's Tomorrowland looks forward and backward at the same time: the setting is somewhat like a Buck Rogers's science fiction movie of the 1920s and 1930s.

Only in the world of Disney could a place begin way out in the future, fall way behind the times, and then be remade at a cost of millions so that it appears to be a 1930s view of the twenty-first century. The concept was first tried out at Disneyland Paris; a similar remake was undertaken at Disneyland in California.

Tomorrowland has been recast as an Interplanetary Convention Center. **Space Mountain** is now the headquarters for the Intergalactic Tracking Network. **Alien Encounter** is the setting for a trade fair for products that are a few hundred years away from your neighborhood Kmart. Gliding by overhead are the trains of the **Tomorrowland Transit Authority**, and you'll be able to visit the Metropolis Science Center for a loopy experiment in time travel, ***The Timekeeper***.

Past visitors may look up and miss something: the **Skyway** no longer crosses the park. It was retired in late 1999.

WOW Space Mountain *FAST*

Every Disney visitor with a bit of spunk—and his or her mom and dad—has to visit Tomorrowland at least once to catch a rocketship to Ryca 1.

Space Mountain is the big enchilada, the highmost high, the place where hundreds of Magic Kingdom visitors have dropped their eyeglasses, cameras, and hairpieces. It is also one of the most popular of all of the attractions at Walt Disney World (as is the similar—but not identical—ride at Disneyland; another version with an upside-down loop, named Discovery Mountain and based on Jules Verne's book, *From the Earth to the Moon*, is at Disneyland Paris).

Space Mountain is a masterpiece of Disney Imagineering, merging a relatively small and slow (top speed of about 28 miles per hour) roller coaster with an outer space theme.

The small cars zoom around indoors in near-total darkness, the only light coming from the projected images of stars and planets on the ceiling. The ride is a triumph of scene-setting, the amusement park equivalent of a big-budget movie's special effects.

The cars feel like they are moving much faster than they are because you have no point of reference in the dark. The cars do not turn upside down.

As you enter, you'll see a chart of the FX-1 Intergalactic Tracking Network, representing some of the launches and satellites of a future civilization. When you finally reach the loading area for the ride—the final queue that can give you twenty more minutes of exquisite teasing torture before you are loaded into your spaceship—check out the video monitors hung from the ceiling.

The televisions bring you reports from PNN—the Planetary News Network. You'll hear from the Hubble Traffic scanner on traffic congestion on Route 4066 in the outer galaxy. Wendy Beryllium's weather report calls for a toasty 620 degrees on Mercury and a chilly negative 360 degrees on Neptune. The extended forecast for the planet Earth calls for partly cloudy skies, rising oceans, and a giant comet smashing into the planet sometime in the next hundred million years. There's a report on the construction of the Mall of Mars. And if you hang on long enough, you will get to see an episode in the lifestyles of the rich and alien.

And be sure to catch the wild ads from Crazy Larry, the used spaceship dealer. What a deal: free floor mats with any intergalactic cruiser!

Overhead a projector paints the pictures of huge rolling asteroids; you will not be the first to observe that they look like close-ups of chocolate chip cookies. Disney has never revealed its recipe.

Finally you'll reach the busy launching pad packed with technicians and engineers loading spacecraft.

There are two tracks within the building and the ride is slightly different on each; the left side has more sharp turns, while the right side has more sharp dips. The waiting line splits into left and right queues as you enter the loading area. Each train seats six persons, one behind the other.

Professional Space Mountain riders—and there are tens of thousands of them—will argue over which seat affords the best ride. The last seat seems to benefit from a "whip" effect as the cars make sharp turns; we prefer the very front chair, where you don't have the back of someone else's head to mar the illusion of space travel and there is a terrific blast of onrushing air as you move on the track.

At busy times, you probably will not be able to cajole an attendant into allowing you to select the seat of your choice; late at night or on the occasional slow day you might be in luck.

Do keep a hand on your personal belongings; wrap camera and purse straps around your feet and make sure children are properly beneath the restraining bar. (Disney launch technicians will double-check the safety arrangements, too.)

And then it's over. The ride is about two minutes and forty seconds in length, and nowhere near as fast or as wild as a major roller coaster such as the Rock 'n' Roller Coaster at Disney–MGM Studios, or the even-bigger The Hulk or Dueling Dragons at Universal Studios Islands of Adventure in Orlando. But Space Mountain has that certain Disney touch that keeps visitors coming back again and again to wait in line for their next space voyage.

Now, speaking of lines: they can easily extend to ninety minutes or more on a busy afternoon. The general rule to avoid long lines at the Magic Kingdom especially applies here. Get to the ride when the gates first open and you may be able to stroll right on board, or come back to the ride at the end of the day. Another somewhat quiet time is during the dinner hour, from about 6 to 7 P.M.

Or take advantage of Disney's Fastpass system and reserve your space flight ahead of time.

If both tracks are operating, a crowd backed up to the front door means a wait of about an hour; sometimes, though, attendants will build up the line outside while the inside queues clear out. This is often done at the end of the day to discourage huge crowds as closing hour approaches.

Children younger than three cannot ride Space Mountain, and below the age of seven must be accompanied by an adult; all riders must be at least forty-four inches tall, and pregnant women and others with back or health problems are advised against riding.

Space Mountain, along with other major rides at Walt Disney World such as Big Thunder Mountain Railroad and Splash Mountain, offers a "switch off" arrangement if not all of the people in your party want to ride the coaster, or if you are traveling with a child too young or too small to ride. Inform the attendant at the turnstile near the launching area that you want to switch off; one parent or adult can ride Space Mountain and change places with another at the exit so everyone can take a turn.

WOW Buzz Lightyear's Space Ranger Spin *FAST*

It's *Toy Story* live, in a new ride that combines a zippy dark ride with a shooting gallery. You'll be teamed with astro-superhero Buzz Lightyear on a daring mission to rescue the universe's crystollic fusion cell supply (better known as batteries) from the clutches of the evil Emperor Zurg.

You'll be assigned to your personal two-seater XP-37 Space Cruiser, spinning through ten scenes of toys, asteroids and meteors, and strange and wondrous aliens in the Gamma Quadrant. Each car includes a joystick to spin the car and a pair of infrared laser guns to knock down all manner of threats by Zurg—basically, shoot any and all of the orange Emperor Zurg insignias scattered throughout the ride. When your laser hits a target it triggers animation, sound, and light effects, and your score—which varies according to the complexity of the shot—is tallied on an LED screen on the cruiser's dashboard.

The final scene takes you through a tunnel of energy, a fun holdover from the Take Flight attraction, which was the former occupant of the building.

At a Disney press event, I rode through the Gamma Quadrant with Buzz Aldrin, the famed NASA astronaut; does the name Buzz Lightyear ring a bell here? Aldrin scored pretty well on the ride, by the way, reaching the Planetary Explorer level, which only seemed right.

Alien Encounter: The ExtraTERRORestrial

We've come a long, long way from Mickey Mouse to an up-close-and-personal meeting with the ExtraTERRORestrial.

As you stroll through Tomorrowland, you'll see billboards from the local chamber of commerce inviting you to visit the "Tomorrowland Interplanetary Convention Center" for an exhibit by X-S Tech, a mysterious company promoting a mysterious new technology. When you enter the convention center you will see displays on some of their strange businesses, including Electro Robotics, Cryo Cybernetics, and more. There are also billboards advertising such attractions as "Lunar Disneyland—The Happiest Place off Earth" and an invitation to the "Tomorrowland Swap Meet" where the offerings include a collection of previously owned robots.

Once you're in the preshow area you will meet L. C. Clench, the otherworldly spokesman for X-S Tech . . . there's something not quite right about this guy, er . . . alien. His slogan: "If something can't be done with X-S, it shouldn't be done at all."

When you enter into the display area, you'll meet the robotic host T.O.M. 2000 (Technobotic Oratorical Mechanism, Series 2000), who is there to demonstrate the X-S Series 1000 Teleportation System. He's going to show the use of teleportation using the aid of his cute little alien friend, Skippy. Hmm . . . teleportation, as in *The Fly*? You don't suppose there's a chance of something going wrong with the device, do you?

When you are escorted into the demonstration area and locked into your seat by an overhead harness (locked into your seat!), the audience will be scanned for a suitable subject.

Of course, something goes wrong. A wild alien is loose among the audience . . . which is locked into its seats!

Much of the show consists of very loud sound effects, bright flashes, and a whole lot of screaming coming from all around you. It took us a few moments before we realized that most of the screaming was on the soundtrack.

Alien Encounter replaced the hopelessly outdated *Mission to Mars* show (so old, it was originally called *Voyage to the Moon*). There are two theaters, each seating 134 persons; visitors must be at least forty-eight inches tall.

The attraction was the subject of intensive hype before it opened; visitors were promised the chance to take part in a terrifying "sensory thriller." But when the show opened in early 1995, it lasted only a few weeks before Disney execs at the very highest level ordered it shut down and reworked to make it scarier.

Alas, I still find the encounter to be a lot more hype than horror. The show is not as technologically impressive as *Honey, I Shrunk the Audience* at Epcot nor anywhere nearly as stomach-turning as the plunging elevators at the Twilight Zone Tower of Terror II at the Disney–MGM Studios. The place is worth a visit, but I'd recommend against joining a lengthy line for the privilege.

Under foot. Among the most amazing wonders of the Magic Kingdom is one that most visitors never see. Below your feet are nine acres of underground "utilidor" corridors hiding the sewers, water pipes, air conditioning, electrical cables, communications links, and garbage collection facilities. There is also an extensive system of tunnels that allow employees to come and go within the park virtually unseen; have you ever wondered why you have never seen Mickey walking to work, or seen a Mike Fink keelboat captain strolling through Tomorrowland?

Actually, the tunnels are the first level of the Magic Kingdom. Because of the high water table of much of Florida, the tunnels were put in place first and then covered over with dirt, much of it from the excavation of the lagoon.

About that trash: as you might expect in a Magic Kingdom, Disney does not use an ordinary garbage truck. Refuse is sucked to a central collection point through a huge network of pneumatic tubes.

WOW *The Timekeeper*

Jules Verne, H. G. Wells, and a few modern-day stars lead us on a stunning multimedia exploration of time and space, presented in Circle-Vision 360. The show features wildman Robin Williams as the voice of Timekeeper.

The adventure begins with a preshow in which you are introduced to Timekeeper and his robotic assistant "9-Eyes," who has guess-how-many cameras. The amusing introduction includes a newsreel about the development and testing of 9-Eyes, including a research trip over Niagara Falls.

Listen carefully as Williams, er, the Timekeeper lets loose with a stream of quick jokes, some of the funniest in the Magic Kingdom. "No longer are we limited to traveling from place to place and losing our bags beforehand," he tells us.

Anyway, it seems that Timekeeper has perfected the long-sought-after art of time travel and is about to embark on a journey to visit some of the great visionaries of all time, including Jules Verne and H. G. Wells. Many of Frenchman Verne's predictions, including space travel, subways, and submarines have come true; Englishman Wells was a great visionary, too, but few of his dreams, including time travel and alien invasions, have (thus far) come true.

Timekeeper embarks on a grand voyage back in time to the Universal Scientific Exposition of Paris in 1900. There he meets Verne and Wells who are in the midst of an argument about their beliefs. Verne accuses Wells of being a hopeless dreamer and scoffs at his idea of time travel.

9-Eyes comes into the middle of it all when it is spotted by Verne, who grabs hold of the strange device and suddenly becomes dragged along on a fantastic voyage that includes the high-speed TGV train in modern France, downtown Parisian traffic, an undersea trip, and a stop at the madhouse of New York City ("home of ten million dreams and one parking space").

After a few more spectacular visits, including a glimpse of the higher-tech future of the year 2189 in Paris (note that the banner on the Eiffel tower celebrates the structure's three-hundredth anniversary, and watch for Jules Verne and H. G. Wells flying by in a time machine), the entourage is deposited back at the site of the science exposition of Paris.

The film may be a bit over the heads of young children—literally and figuratively, since there are no seats in the theater—but for some *The Timekeeper* is a favorite.

If you watch very carefully, it is apparent that many of the actors spoke French with English overdubbed later; the film debuted at Le Visionarium at Disneyland Paris. In the European version French superstar Gérard Depardieu made a cameo appearance as an airport baggage handler in a sequence involving the Concorde at Orly Airport near Paris.

The theater is large and at most times of the day you should be able to get in to the twenty-minute show with no more than a twenty-minute wait; if the line extends out the door you may want to come back at another time.

Tomorrowland Transit Authority

Trains of twenty-passenger cars of the Tomorrowland Transit Authority Metroliner circle slowly above Tomorrowland, offering a brief peek into Space Mountain (a good way for the faint of heart to get some idea of what the excitement is about) and an even briefer glimpse of Buzz Lightyear's Space Ranger Spin.

The former **WEDway PeopleMover**, reworked a bit as part of the remake of Tomorrowland, loads at **Rockettower Plaza**. The PeopleMover is a pet project of the Magic Kingdom, demonstrating an unusual means of propulsion—the linear induction motor. The track and the car form a motor together, as magnetic pulses pull the car down a flat coil.

There is rarely a significant line for this ten-minute ride, which we still find to be about seven minutes too long. Still, it's a seat and a bit of a view.

Astro Orbiter

A basic amusement park ride with rotating rockets and an up/down lever, but in typical Disney fashion it seems like much more.

Nowhere near as threatening (to some) as Space Mountain, it nevertheless is not for people with a fear of heights.

As part of the overall remake of Tomorrowland, the ride was rebuilt and is now one of the most recognizable features of that section of the park, with the Jules Verne theme of rotating planets and moons. It is especially impressive at night.

If you think about it Astro Orbiter is a slightly faster and somewhat higher version of Dumbo, the Flying Elephant.

Left, right, up, down. Check out the world of transportation at the right corner of the Space Mountain building near the Carousel of Progress. In one spot you can see the Disney steam train, the modern monorail, and the electric Tomorrowland Transit Authority cars. To your left is the aerial skyride and the earthbound Tomorrowland Speedway. Above it all are the Astro Orbiters. And then think of the rocket ships on rails within the mountain.

Carousel of Progress

The future ain't what it used to be. That was very evident as the Carousel of Progress grew further and further out of date in the 1980s. Its concept of the future had moved into the past.

This ride, originally presented at the 1964–65 World's Fair in New York, tells of the march of technology in American homes. It was interesting in 1964 and quaint in 1984, but hopelessly outdated in the 1990s; in 1994 a slightly updated version of the show debuted, featuring the voice of the late, lamented raconteur Jean Shepherd.

The basic Carousel is unchanged; theater seats revolve around a stationary central core populated by audio-animatronic robots. The first few scenes of the show are from the earlier version, with added narration by Shepherd and the original theme song.

Robo-stars. Disney claims that the Carousel of Progress has had more performances than any other stage show in the history of America; of course, it's not really a stage show because all of the actors have electric motors inside them.

The show starts in the early twentieth century as electricity makes its appearance in the home; the second scene takes place at the time of Lindbergh in the 1920s, and then we move on to the promising 1940s. (Many adults will be amused to see a working vibrating belt exercise machine like those that were popular into the early 1950s.)

His, hers, and its. The little signs over the restrooms in Tomorrowland depict male and female robots.

The fourth stage setting takes us a few years beyond the current day. A young boy loans his grandmother his virtual reality game, which she takes over. When grandma calls out her score of 550, the voice-actuated oven burns the turkey.

Even with the small amount of updating it is still worth noting that the Carousel is an all-white, middle-class world and not all that thrilling, and also one in which Dad is still pretty much the indisputable king of the castle. Note the eyes on the various robot dogs in each scene—the dog is the best actor in the troupe.

The best seat is down front in the center of the auditorium.

Tomorrowland Indy Speedway

Every kid we know dreams of getting behind the wheel of Mommy's or Daddy's car; most adults we know dream of taking a spin around a racecourse. Perhaps that is why this attraction, which doesn't have all that much to do with Tomorrowland that we can think of, is such a popular destination.

In 2000 the course received a bit of a facelift, adding an Indy theme including a brickyard starting line and a position pole.

There are four parallel tracks of about a half-mile each, and the little race cars have real gasoline engines that will propel them forward at up to a zippy 7 miles per hour. The steering gear works, too, allowing the driver to move the car left and right down the course, although there is a center rail that will keep the car from completely leaving the track.

Children must be at least fifty-two inches tall to ride in one of the cars alone; otherwise their feet won't reach the gas pedal. Mom or Dad, though, can sit alongside and press the pedal while junior happily steers.

Waiting lines can reach to nearly an hour on the most crowded days; visit the track early or late to make the best use of your time. A circuit takes about four minutes.

Galaxy Palace Theater at Rockettower Plaza. An outdoor theater located between the Transportarium and the Carousel of Progress, used for live shows.

Tomorrowland Arcade. The fanciful power station for the world of the future, located at the exit from Space Mountain, also contains a good-sized video arcade, minus any first-person shooting games. Disney designers again looked backward to the rounded, streamlined architecture of the Art Deco 1930s for their presentation of the future.

Fantasyland

This is the stuff of young dreams: Dumbo, Peter Pan, Alice in Wonderland, Snow White, and the toy riot of It's a Small World. Fantasyland is a bright and cheerful place, decorated in splashes of color and sprinkled with snippets of song. Over it all is Cinderella Castle (described already in the section about Main Street, U.S.A.).

Dumbo the Flying Elephant

Disney began with an ordinary amusement park ride, making it into something very special for the littlest guests.

Riders sit in fiberglass elephants, which can be moved up and down as they circle a mirrored ball and the statue of Timothy Mouse, the very clever rodent who is Dumbo's manager in the classic Disney animated movie.

Sixteen Dumbos go round a golden crown with a set of gears and pinwheels, like a kiddie drawing of a machine.

This ride has always been a huge lure for young children, with lines of up to an hour for the ninety-second ride. If your kids insist on an elephant-back ride, head for Dumbo early or late in the day.

One of the rites of passage, we suspect, is the day kids tell you they're willing to skip the lines for Dumbo and would rather make a second pass at Space Mountain.

Dumbo the Flying Elephant

Cinderella's Golden Carrousel

One of the few mostly "real" things in this world of fantasy, the carrousel dates back to 1917 and was used by generations of kids in New Jersey. Many of the horses are hand-carved originals, although the herd has been augmented with some fiberglass replicas and the overhead canopy has been Disneyfied with images from Disney films. None of the horses are identical. The musical organ, which plays selections from hit movies, is an Italian original.

The lines for the two-minute ride ebb and flow; we'd suggest you wait for the times when you can walk right on board.

WOW It's a Small World

Every little girl's wildest dream: a world of beautiful dancing dolls from all over the world. There is nothing to get your heart beating here, but even the most cynical—including little boys and adults—will probably find something to smile about in this upbeat boat ride. We especially enjoy the animatronic cancan dancers.

This eleven-minute ride was originally designed for the 1964–65 World's Fair in New York, but unlike the Carousel of Progress, the Small World ride has maintained its timeless appeal. The sound system was updated and improved in recent years.

The boats are large and the lines move pretty quickly (if two queues are being formed, the line to the left moves a bit faster), but we'd advise coming to this attraction early or late in the day. Children who like this ride will probably also enjoy the shorter Rivers of Time ride at the Mexican pavilion of Epcot.

Peter Pan's Flight

A mellow excursion into some of the scenes from Disney's version of the story of the little boy who doesn't want to grow up. Riders sit in a small pirate ship that suspends them a foot or so off the floor. Everyone's favorite scene is the overhead view of London by night, which does a pretty good job of simulating Peter's flight. Strictly for kids.

At Disneyland Paris, a jazzed-up version of this ride is one of the more popular attractions; not so at the Magic Kingdom, although lines still reach to forty-five minutes or more on busy days.

Mad Tea Party

A Disney version of a rather common amusement park ride in which circular cars move around a track and also spin around on platforms. If it sounds dizzying, that's because it is: the very young and others with sensitive stomachs might prefer the carousel across the way. However, the riders have some control over how fast the cups spin; grab hold of the wheel in the center of the cup and don't let go for the least movement.

The ride is covered over with a tent-like structure, taking the cups and most of the waiting line out of the elements. The ride has been designed like a scene from Disney's classic 1951 film *Alice in Wonderland*. Our favorite part is the drunken mouse who pops out of the teapot in the center.

The ride itself is only about ninety seconds long; the wait can be much more than that. I'd recommend hopping on board only if lines are short.

WOW The Many Adventures of Winnie the Pooh *FAST*

Oh, bother! It's a blustery day and the pages of one of our favorite books are blowing out of the building and into Fantasyland.

Welcome to a lovingly detailed step into the pages of one of the best-known children's books. Our giant honey pot vehicles carry up to six people into the pages of the book. We begin in Chapter 1, in which Pooh begins his search for honey in a very enchanted place.

"Happy Winds-day," says Gopher. "Maybe for you," replies Piglet. Pooh announces, "I'm in the mood for food," but Eeyore doubts the bear will reach the tree.

We move on to Rabbit's Garden, where Kanga holds onto Roo, flying like a kite in the wind, and into Owl's House. And then we enter the dramatic darkness of the Blustery Night, where we meet Tigger for the first time. "Come bounce with me," he invites, and so we do. Ever sat in a bouncing giant honey pot before?

One of the more dramatic scenes is Pooh's Dream, a view into his nightmare. What could he possibly fear? Why Heffalump and Woozle honey thieves, of course. Watch for the jack in the boxes.

And then Pooh wakes up in the Floody Place, and here Disney Imagineers pull out all the stops. There's water all about, and we seem to float through the room. The only one who isn't upset about the flooding is Pooh, happy to find that the rising water allows him to float to a honey bonanza high up in a tree.

All in all, this is one honey of a ride, and a great step forward in the venerable history of Disney dark rides. Pooh takes about three-and-a-half minutes, and sixteen to eighteen cars are on the track at any one time. I'd suggest coming early or late to avoid the crowds sure to come to this happy new place.

Pooh replaced an old favorite in the park, Mr. Toad's Wild Ride based on one of Disney's more obscure films, *The Adventures of Ichabod and Mr. Toad,* which was in turn loosely based on the book *The Wind in the Willows*. As good as that ride was, this one is much better.

By the way, the catchy music for the Pooh ride is by the composer of the score for *Mary Poppins* and the It's a Small World attraction.

Snow White's Scary Adventures

The word *scary* has returned to the doorway of this attraction, a tip-off to the fact that in some small ways this ride emphasizes the grimmer parts of the Brothers Grimm fairy tale, as presented in Disney's 1938 animated movie. The ride can't hold a fading candle to the spooks in the Haunted Mansion across the way in Liberty Square, but there are a few more skeletons and witches than very young children might expect.

A remake a few years ago created a kinder, gentler Snow White removing some of the darker elements of the ride, making the Florida version more like its California, Paris, and Tokyo cousins.

Parents be warned: it's still a bit scary at the start with some ghoulish ghouls and wicked witches, but it's happier at the end. The new version uses about half of the old "sets," but now Snow White herself appears for the first time in Florida. In fact, she's there in five scenes: at the wishing well in the courtyard of the castle, in the scary forest, at the dwarf's cottage, with the Prince when he kisses her to break the Witch's spell, and (of course) riding off with the Prince to live happily ever after.

The revision of the show was accompanied by a 50 percent increase in capacity for the vehicles; cars now carry six passengers instead of four.

The Legend of the Lion King

A sophisticated live actor and puppet show with special effects, music, and animation based on Disney's *Lion King* cartoon feature, presented in the

Child under tow. On a crowded day, it is possible to lose sight of your children from time to time. Discuss with them beforehand a place to meet if you get separated; you can also obtain name tags to place on your children at City Hall or the Baby Center next to the Crystal Palace. Disney employees are well trained on how to deal with a lost child; track one down for assistance.

The Baby Center is designed to assist in nursing or changing infants; most other rest rooms throughout the parks have some accommodation for these needs. The Baby Center also offers for sale emergency rations of formula, replacement pacifiers, bottles, and diapers. Strollers are available for rent beneath the railroad overpass at the park entrance.

Fantasyland Theater. The show puts the audience into the shadow of huge puppets on a 125-foot-wide stage.

The eight-minute standing preshow opens with an actor dressed as Rafiki, introducing the story of *The Lion King* and including the "Circle of Life" song from the movie.

Once you enter the theater itself, you will be asked to move all the way across the row to the far side of the auditorium. If you want to try to claim the best view in the middle, hold back until about twenty-five people have entered a row.

The characters—some of which require as many as four puppeteers beneath the stage to operate—speak and sing with the recorded voices of some of the humans who gave words to the film characters, including Jeremy Irons as Scar, James Earl Jones as Mufasa, Whoopi Goldberg as Shenzi, and Cheech Marin as Banzai.

The theater uses fantastic lighting, curtains of water, and wind machines as part of its effects. Jets of steam erupt from the floor, and lightning crashes from above. Mountains and grasslands rise from below. Some young children may find the sound a bit loud, but the familiar story of *The Lion King* will entrance all.

Lines for the twenty-eight-minute show will build during the middle of the day; come early or late or during a parade. If the waiting line extends outside from under the canopy you will not make it into the next show, which means your waiting line will be at least an hour.

Ariel's Grotto. A watery world in the shadow of Dumbo where fans of *The Little Mermaid* can meet Ariel herself. On hot days, visitors young and old may want to dance in the fountains.

Fantasyland Character Festival. Here's your chance to press the fantasy flesh of many favorite Disney characters in front of the former home of 20,000 Leagues Under the Sea. That venerable ride has been shut since 1995, with regular rumors of a new watery-themed attraction to come.

Mickey's Toontown Fair

Walt Disney World, Disneyland, and the entire Disney empire were built from the ears of the most famous rodent of all, but until 1989 Mickey didn't have a place of his own. That year, Disney honored the mouse's sixtieth (!) birthday with the first new area at Walt Disney World since its opening. Mickey's Starland became one of the most popular areas of the park for the youngest visitors.

Starland was given a major makeover, reopening as Mickey's Toontown Fair as part of the twenty-fifth anniversary celebration party throughout Walt Disney World.

There are no outer-space roller coasters or multimillion dollar water slides here; instead we have the sort of giddy happiness that has sustained the mouse's popularity for years. Disney also uses the area to present and promote some of its newer cartoon stars, including Goof Troop, Dark Wing Duck, Rescue Rangers, Tale Spin, and DuckTales. Lines to meet and greet Mickey, Minnie, and the other local stars can become quite lengthy in the middle of the day; come early or late if you can.

World's fair fare. Disney was involved in four major pavilions at the 1964–65 New York World's Fair, including Pepsi's "It's a Small World—A Salute to UNICEF" ride, General Electric's "Carousel of Progress," the Illinois pavilion's "Great Moments with Mr. Lincoln," and Ford's "Magic Skyway" ride.

The first three World's Fair exhibits were later recycled for use at Disney parks: "It's a Small World" was moved to Disneyland and became the model for very similar and popular rides at Walt Disney World, Tokyo Disneyland, and Disneyland Paris. The GE "Carousel" was moved to Walt Disney World; it was updated a bit in 1994 but remains essentially unchanged. And "Great Moments with Mr. Lincoln" was Disney's first big success with audio-animatronics and was moved to Disneyland's Main Street, where it played for many years.

WOW Mickey's Country House

If you have kids, or ever were one, then there's not a whole lot of doubt about this: you've got to visit Mickey Mouse's house. It's a walk-through tour of the Mickster's private digs. Out back, in the Judge's Tent, the man . . . er, the mouse . . . himself appears to sign autographs.

WOW Minnie's Country House

Ms. Minnie is even more sociable than her friend across the street. Minnie waits in the gazebo in her garden from time to time. You're welcome to explore the house; be sure to press the buttons on the answering machine by the telephone.

The Barnstormer at Goofy's Wiseacre Farm

A kid-sized roller coaster with kid-sized thrills. Riders sit in cars that look like old biplanes. The tracks include a wide turn that flies through a barn where kids are waiting their turn to ride. Similar to Gadget's Go-Coaster at Mickey's Toontown at Disneyland, it is about twice as long. In the distance over the top of the coaster is the real thing at Magic Kingdom: Space Mountain.

Donald's Boat. The *Miss Daisy*, which has seen better days and sprouts leaks from all over is a great place to cool off on a hot day. Disney Imagineers have created a dry lake to surround the boat—here's your chance to walk on pseudo-water. Alas, Grandma Duck's Petting Farm was removed to make room.

Toontown Hall of Fame. A shrine to the greatest Disney cartoon characters of all time, with regular appearances by local celebrities. Parents be warned: there is also a large gift shop within.

Toontown Farmer's Market. An outdoor stand where you can make your own strawberry shortcake for about $3.

Walt Disney World Railroad. The vintage railroad that circles the Magic Kingdom has a station at the back of Toontown Fair. The next stop is Main Street, and the third stop is in Frontierland.

Liberty Square

A peaceful laid-back corner of America, home of the presidents (robotically assisted), a festive riverboat (which runs on underwater tracks), and a haunted mansion (which is too creepy to pass by without a tour). The square is also home to a massive live oak tree festooned with thirteen lanterns—one for each of the thirteen original colonies—like the Liberty Trees used as political statements in pre-Revolutionary times.

WOW The Haunted Mansion *FAST*

Scare yourself silly in this masterpiece of an attraction with some of the most sophisticated special effects at Walt Disney World. During the years there have been hundreds of creepy and decrepit little improvements. If it's been a while since you last visited you should be sure to go back; be sure to bring your death certificate.

The ride is something of a rite of passage for kids, moving from Mickey and Minnie to the (humorous) dark side of Disney.

The experience begins in the graveyard waiting line; before you let the tombstones make you feel too creepy stop and read some of the inscriptions. They're a howl!

The attendants, dressed as morticians, are among the best actors in the park, almost always staying in character. They will tell you to "fill in the dead space" in the line. When the elevator at the start of the ride fills up they may announce "No more bodies." They play their roles well—we've tried our best over the course of years to make them crack a smile, without any success.

Once you are admitted to the mansion itself, you will be ushered into a strange room that has an interesting visual trick—is the ceiling going up or the floor going down? Either way, the portraits on the wall are a real scream. (Don't read this if you don't want to know. OK, you have been warned: at Walt Disney World, the ceiling moves up and the floor stays where it is; at Disneyland, the floor moves down and the walls are stationary. The stretching room was put into place in California as a way to get visitors to the loading level which is on the other side of the railroad tracks. When the Florida house was built, there was no need to go down a level, but Imagineers wanted to keep the same illusion even if it was accomplished in a different way.)

The experience is accompanied throughout by a decidedly strange soundtrack that is also among the more literate found at Walt Disney World—that is, if you are able to hear it in the rather fuzzy sound system.

Here's part of the introduction from the stretching room:

When hinges creak in doorless chambers and strange and frightening sounds echo through the halls, whenever candlelights flicker where the air is deathly still, that is the time when ghosts are present, practicing their terror with ghoulish delight.

Your cadaverous pallor betrays an aura of foreboding, almost as though you sense a disquieting metamorphosis. Is this haunted room actually stretching? Or is it your imagination? And consider this dismaying observation: this chamber has no windows, and no doors.

Which offers you this chilling challenge: to find a way out! Of course, there's always my way.

You'll arrive at a loading station for a moving set of chairs and settle in for a tour through a house that is in the control of the largest collection of spooks this side of the CIA.

Says your Ghost Host: "We find it delightfully unlivable here in this ghostly retreat. Every room has wall-to-wall creeps and hot and cold running chills."

We've ridden the ride many times and see something different each time. Among the best effects are the dancing ghouls at the dinner party, the moving door knockers, and the face within the crystal ball.

This ride is probably the single best combination of Disney design, filmmaking, and audio-animatronics anywhere at the Magic Kingdom. There are all sorts of delightful details on the ride, enough to make it worth several rides if you have the time. Here are a few you might want to look for: the needlepoint that reads "Tomb Sweet Tomb"; the legs sticking out from under the banquet table in the ghostly wedding reception; the skull-shaped notes rising out of the top of the organ at the reception.

You'll meet Madame Leota, a disembodied guide who will help you attempt to make contact with the spirits within the mansion.

Rap on a table, it's time to respond, send us a message from somewhere beyond. Goblins and ghoulies from last Halloween, awaken the spirits with your tambourine. Wizards and witches wherever you dwell, give us a hint by ringing a bell.

The best special effect of the ride is the wedding party scene, where guests move from mortal coil to diaphanous spirit and back. After the party, you'll meet the famous Grim Grinning Ghosts, captured within luminous globes. Despite surviving dozens of rides at the Magic Kingdom, Disneyland, and Disneyland Paris it took use years before we were still unable to figure out what they were saying. Here's part of their song:

When the crypt doors creak and the tombstones quake, spooks come out for a swinging wake. Happy haunts materialize and begin to vocalize; grim grinning ghosts come out to socialize.

Now don't close your eyes and don't try to hide, or a silly spook may sit by your side. Shrouded in a daft disguise, they pretend to terrorize; grim grinning ghosts come out to socialize.

As the ride comes to an end, Madam Leota will urge you to hurry back. Make final arrangements now.

In recent years, Disney has been subtly increasing the realism of the ride, perhaps in reaction to the overall explicitness of our society. The skeletons are just a bit more real, the ghosts are just a bit more ghoulish. Most noticeable is

Tomb with a view. Our favorite Haunted Mansion tombstones include: "Dear departed brother Dave. He chased a bear into a cave"; "Here rests Wathel R. Bender. He rode to glory on a fender"; and "Here lies good old Fred. A great big rock fell on his head." And there is "Rest in peace cousin Huet. We all know you didn't do it."

More favorites, from the cemetery at the exit of the ride: Bluebeard's tomb reads, "Here lyeth his loving wives. Seven winsome wives, some fat some thin. Six of them were faithful, but the seventh did him in." Other pun-full names on the wall include Paul Tergyst, Clare Voince, Metta Fisiks, and Manny Festation.

Many of the names are drawn from the Imagineers who designed the original ride.

a new ending, sending your moving chair on a detour through a graveyard full of creepy tombs and ghostly trees.

Some very young children may become a bit scared, although most kids of all ages can see the humor among the horrors. And speaking of jokes, stop to read the inscriptions on the tombs at the exit.

Lines for this show vary greatly; the best times to visit are early or late in the day. Try not to join the crowds streaming toward the mansion's door each time the Hall of Presidents lets out or the riverboat arrives. The ride lasts about nine minutes, including a two-minute preshow.

The original Haunted Mansion was at Disneyland in California. Because it was to be built near the New Orleans area of Frontierland, the idea was to make it look like an early 1800s Southern mansion; however, it actually ended up looking more like an old home in Baltimore. Walt Disney himself vetoed one design that made the house appear to be derelict (Disney's first falling-down house would come some thirty years later at Disney–MGM Studios with the construction of the Twilight Zone Tower of Terror.)

The original plans called for a walk-through tour, with visitors escorted by a butler or maid who would tell the story. The first story line was quite different, too, and not at all sugarcoated: it told of a wealthy sea merchant who built a fabulous mansion for his new bride but then killed her in a rage when she learned he was really a bloody pirate. Her ghost came back to haunt him and tormented him so much that he finally hung himself from the rafters, giving the mansion two unhappy spirits.

About all that is left of the gruesome story is a brief glimpse of a hanging body above the stretching room, the weathervane in the shape of a sailing ship on the top of the cupola of the mansion, and some nautical-theme paintings.

The Hall of Presidents

Within the ornate theater is a living history lesson featuring some of Disney's more impressive audio-animatronics. The show is derived from the Illinois pavilion at the 1964–65 New York World's Fair, designed by Disney. Fairgoers were startled when a seated Abe Lincoln wearily came to life to address the audience. In the Magic Kingdom version of the show all forty-two American presidents are represented on stage.

In late 2001 the attraction will unveil a new George W. Bush figure and give him some words to speak, recorded by the president. Bill Clinton was the first sitting president to have a speaking role in the pageant, with a speech recorded in the Oval Office. In the new version, Clinton steps back into the chorus with all of the other former presidents.

Shows start on the hour and on the half-hour. The first part of the show involves a series of detailed paintings projected on the large center screen; then the curtains pull back to reveal the assembled presidents.

The first part of the show features a narration by poet Maya Angelou, one of the few women and African Americans given individual recognition in the park. Her presentation includes a brief but frank discussion of slavery.

The flag-waving show and a spectacular film that precedes the robotics may have particular appeal to school children studying American history. Others may enjoy the technical artistry of the robots, and some may enjoy studying the details of the costumes on each of the chief executives.

The show takes about twenty-two minutes; the seven-hundred-seat auditorium quickly eats up waiting lines and the maximum wait should be no more than two shows, or about forty minutes.

By the way, the show at the American pavilion at Epcot, the American Experience, has similar themes but is much flashier, focusing on other great figures from the history of our nation.

Liberty Belle Riverboat

A new golden oldie took to the waters in 1997 with the arrival of the *Liberty Belle*, a steam-powered sternwheeler.

The riverboat replaced a pair of older Disney replicas, the *Admiral Joe Fowler* and the *Richard F. Irvine*; they were taken out of service after carrying some ninety million people during their careers.

The boat circles the half-mile Rivers of America connected to an underwater rail. This is by no means a thrill ride, but it is a very pleasant reprieve on a hot day.

The narrator is Sam Clemens, best known as the author Mark Twain. The cruise takes about twenty minutes.

Liberty Belle *Riverboat*
Photo by Corey Sandler. Used by permission from Disney Enterprises, Inc.

Mike Fink Keelboats

Small riverboats that follow the same circuit as the riverboat, a bit faster and a bit more personal with your own guide. Mike Fink was a riverboat captain of legend who had an adventure with Davy Crockett.

The small boats, the *Bertha Mae* and the *Gullywhumper*, take about ten minutes for a circuit. Because of the small capacity of the boats, we'd advise against joining a long line if there is one; we'd also suggest against duplicating a trip on the keelboats and one on the riverboat. The keelboats run only during the day and may not run during the off-season.

Adventureland

Ahoy, mateys: welcome to a most unusual corner of Central Florida, where you will find a Caribbean island, an African veldt, a South Pacific bird tree, and more. Adventureland includes some of the most dramatic landscaping touches in the Magic Kingdom and the most popular band of pirates since Penzance.

WOW Pirates of the Caribbean

Yo, ho, yo . . . one of Disney's very best. After an approach through a dank dungeon waiting area (and past a parrot wearing an eye patch!), you'll settle into a broad-beamed boat for a cruise into the middle of a pirate raid on a Caribbean island town.

You'll love the moonlit battle scene as your boat passes beneath the guns of two warring ships; cannonballs will land all around you in the cool water. Pay attention, too, to the jail scene where a group of pirates tries to entice a mangy dog to bring them the key. The ride includes a wondrous collection of audio-animatronic humans and animals, including robotic chickens and pigs.

Some young children may be scared by the simulated cannon fire and the skulls and bones that are fairly liberally strewn about in some of the caves of Pirates of the Caribbean. And some adults may find bones of their own to pick—things such as the depiction of women as objects for sale at auction. However, the ride might offer an opportunity to discuss such unhappy elements of history with youngsters.

The ride begins with a little bit of a watery drop; your boat is dropping below the Disney World Railroad tracks overhead to the ride area, which (like Splash Mountain and Space Mountain) actually lies mostly outside the boundaries of the park.

In any case Pirates of the Caribbean is a masterpiece of Disney artistry. You don't want to miss this one!

And not content to leave a good thing alone, Disney has introduced a much improved audio system to the ride. I was thrilled to finally be able to understand the background warning at the entrance to the lagoon: "Dead men tell no lies." And a bit further into the ride you'll also be able to hear some of the boasts and taunts of the pirates as they go about their good-natured dastardly deeds.

And finally, listen for the parrot in the treasure trove at the end of the ride: he's singing, "Yo ho, yo ho, a pirate's life for me."

Lines can become quite long at midday; head for this popular trip when the park first opens or in late afternoon. As you enter the queue, keep to your left to save a few minutes in line. The waiting area is mostly under cover, which makes it a good place to be in the rain or on a very hot day. The ride itself takes about seven minutes.

Swiss Family Treehouse

This is one of those "no accounting for taste" attractions—you'll either love it or hate it, probably depending upon how deeply the story of the *Swiss Family Robinson* is engraved upon your memory. Actually, this attraction is a remembrance of the 1960 Disney movie version of the classic novel *Swiss Family Robinson*, written by Johann David Wyss and completed by his son Johann Rudolf Wyss in 1813.

The treehouse winds up and across a simulated of a banyan tree (constructed of sculpted concrete and steel). There are a lot of stairs to climb and a few ropewalk bridges; on a busy day your view may be mostly the backside of the tourist in front of you. It takes five to ten minutes to walk up, through, and down the tree; incredibly, there can sometimes be lengthy lines for the privilege; if there's a line and you're determined to climb this tree come back late in the day.

The "tree" received a remake at the end of 1997, with new and improved details added to this old house.

The Magic Carpets of Aladdin

Kids can pilot their own flying carpet at a new carnival ride that debuted in 2001. Sixteen four-passenger vehicles circle a giant animated Genie's lamp, across from the Swiss Family Treehouse. Riders can control their own carpet, moving up or down or pitching forward or backward. All the while, animatronic camels "spit" at the riders going by. Music from Disney's 1992 animated feature *Aladdin* plays throughout the ride.

Alongside the ride, the **Agrabah Bazaar** features a Disney version of a Middle Eastern open-air marketplace, selling vases, brass, spices, clothing, and souvenirs.

WOW Jungle Cruise *FAST*

Another Disney classic, this is an escorted boat tour through a simulated wild kingdom that somehow stretches from the African veldt to the Amazon rain forest to the Nile valley and the jungles of Southeast Asia.

You'll see some of Disney's most famous special effects, like the automated hippos who lurk just below the water's top and the cavorting elephants who will spray water from their trunks. The shores are lined with robotic zebras, lions, and giraffes. The best part of the ride is the hokey but still entertaining patter of the tour guides in pith helmets. ("Be sure to tell all your friends about Jungle Cruise," our guide told us. "It cuts down the lines." As we were readying to board our boats, we were advised to guard against confusion in loading. "Note that there is one dock to the left, and one to the right: it's a paradox."

Ouch. As we passed into a section of Egypt's famous river, we were told, "If you don't believe me, you're in da Nile."

And another guide told us, "Don't worry about looking stupid—I'm doing that for you." But my favorite bad joke involved horticultural commentary: "I'd like to point out my favorite plants in the jungle. I like that one, and that one, and that one."

Amateur gardeners may be thrilled by the amazing collection of plants, flowers, and trees—most of them real—that Disney groundskeepers manage to keep alive. One of the tricks is a network of gas heaters that warms the occasionally chilly air of Florida in the winter.

The ride is about ten minutes; the line to get on board, alas, can sometimes wind around and around the corral for more than an hour. Go early or late on busy days. It is actually most dramatic by night, and especially silly.

Sources say that Jungle Cruise is due for an update and expansion.

Enchanted Tiki Room—Under New Management

The Tropical Serenade is among the strangest of all of the attractions at the Magic Kingdom, and you're not likely to enjoy it unless you are in exactly the right frame of mind. In 1998 the birds debuted a new version of the venerable, corny show.

The Tiki Room is the home of the **Enchanted Tiki Birds**, a collection of more than two hundred wisecracking, wing-flapping, automated winged creatures, along with a collection of singing flowers, totem poles, and statues.

Hollywood featherweights Iago, from Disney's animated feature *Aladdin*, and Zazu, from *The Lion King*, have become the new landlords of the popular Adventureland attraction that opened with the park October 1, 1971.

The interior of the theater is as tacky as ever, and the exceedingly annoying theme song "In the Tiki, Tiki, Tiki, Tiki, Tiki Room" is preserved for the ages.

The original group of animatronic characters continue to star in the show including José, Michael, Fritz, and Pierre. Walt Disney imagineers had three of the four original actors re-record audio segments for the new show.

But the story line is a bit more interesting, made all the better because of a greatly improved audio system. Now you can hear all of the corny jokes, including Iago's taunting insult to the Polynesian gods. They warn: "When you mess with Polynesia, the Tiki gods will squeeze ya."

The Enchanted Tiki Room—Under New Management blends the original cast into a new version of the corny, strange show. One song guests will likely recognize is a stirring rendition of "Friend Like Me," sung by Iago.

Midway through the song, Iago, voiced by the professional annoyance Gilbert Gottfried (who provided the voice of Iago for *Aladdin*), interrupts: "Stop the music!"

Iago announces the Tiki Room will house a brand-new show. Zazu warns Iago that any changes ill anger the tiki gods. No problem, says Iago.

Among the musical highlights is a rendition of "In the Still of the Night," when all of the Tiki icons around the room come to life, complete with a disco mirror ball.

And so, when the new show begins Uh Oa, the tiki goddess of disaster, rises up from the center of the room in a horrible blast of green vapor. She raises her staff and sends a bolt hurling towards Iago. When it connects Iago disappears in a cloud of smoke.

After the tiki gods perform a hip-hop rap number, Iago reappears wrapped in bandages and on crutches declaring the tiki gods the greatest act he has ever heard. He joins Zazu and the rest of the animatronic cast for a musical grand finale.

The waiting area for the show includes a stop in front of a waterfall that features volcano flames.

The show also features a funny preshow starring a couple of wise-cracking bird-agents, William and Morris, voiced by comedians Don Rickles and Phil Hartman. The birds are late for the show. "Maybe they hit traffic," says Morris. "Don't say that!" says William.

The Tiki birds were among Disney's first attempts at audio-animatronics, representing the state of the art as it existed around 1963 when a very similar show was introduced at Disneyland.

We know some young children who have been absolutely enchanted by the birds; the very young and the very cynical may want to pass. In any case the show is blissfully short, and it's nice and cool inside on a hot Florida day.

Shrunken Ned's Junior Jungle Boats. This set of coin-operated remote-control boats stands near the Jungle Cruise. If you say the name quickly, you'll get the minor joke.

Frontierland

Almost anything goes in this wild western corner of the Magic Kingdom, home of Davy Crockett, Tom Sawyer, a bunch of vacationing bears, a runaway mining train, and the park's newest, wettest, and wildest big splash.

WOW Big Thunder Mountain Railroad

One of the best rides at the park, it is at the same time much more than and much less than it appears.

Big Thunder is a Disneyfied roller coaster, one of only three "thrill" rides in the Magic Kingdom (along with Space Mountain and Splash Mountain). As roller coasters go, it is fairly tame, with about a half-mile of track and a three-and-a-half-minute ride with a few short drops and some interesting twists and turns. But in the Disney tradition it is the setting and the attention to detail that make this one of the most popular places to be.

You will ride in a runaway mining train up through a quaking tunnel, across a flooding village, and back down around and through a 197-foot-high artificial mountain, bedecked with real mining antiques from former mines out West. As you enter the waiting line, you'll see part of a "stamping mill" made by the Joshua Hendy Works in San Francisco, possibly made for one of the mines of the Comstock in Nevada. Stamping mills were used to crush large pieces of rock into smaller pieces to allow the removal of ore.

One-upsmanship. Big Thunder Mountain Railroad at Disneyland Paris has a much sharper drop than its older American cousin.

Look, too, at the audio-animatronic animals and birds, and watch for the old coot of a miner in a bathtub as you zoom by. The telegraph office lists the manager's name as Morris Code; get it?

Construction of the ride, completed in 1981, cost $17 million, which equals the entire price tag for Disneyland when it opened in 1955.

Picking the right time to visit the railroad can make a real difference at this very popular attraction; waits of more than an hour are common at midday in peak season. The shortest lines are early in the day or just before dinnertime. Coaster fans say the best ride (meaning the wildest) can be had with a seat in the last row of seats; we also like the very front of any coaster ride because it gives you a view of the perils ahead, over the top of the engine in front.

The line outside, near the rafts to Tom Sawyer Island, is only a small portion of the queue. There is a large upper corral and a winding path down through the mining station to the railroad. The ride takes on a very different feeling at night, and true fans should experience it then as well as during the day.

Children younger than seven must be accompanied by an adult; no one under forty-two inches is allowed to ride. Warn young children about the loud noises they will hear as their railway car is pulled up the first lift on the ride.

Big Thunder Mountain Railroad at night is like another ride altogether. Like Space Mountain, the fun is increased because the darkness hides the track ahead of you.

WOW Splash Mountain FAST

Disney's "highest, scariest, wildest, and wettest" attraction is a wild ride to contemplate; you may have a long time to contemplate it as you wait your turn on a busy day.

Splash Mountain includes three lifts and four drops, with the biggest plunging about fifty feet at a forty-five-degree angle and a top speed of about 40 miles per hour—Disney claims it's the steepest flume ride in the world. The big drop, visible to the crowds along the Rivers of America in Frontierland, will make it appear as if the log car has fallen into a pond.

Some of the best special effects take place within the mountain, with a story based on Disney's classic *Song of the South* cartoon, made in 1946. The ride follows Brer Rabbit as he tries to outwit Brer Fox and Brer Bear on a wild journey to the Laughin' Place.

The entrance to Splash Mountain is beneath the reconstructed Frontierland railroad station. (As you approach on the train, you will be able to see a small portion of Splash Mountain—it's the *Zip-a-dee Lady* paddlewheeler that is at the end of the ride, *after* the big drop.)

Disney has hidden the waiting lines within an open inner courtyard not visible from the entrance, and then a long and winding queue within the building itself; be sure to ask the cast member at the measuring pole (forty-four inches minimum for youngsters) about the length of the line. We'd suggest you come back another time—very early or late—if the line is too long. As usual at many of the attractions, you often will save a few minutes by choosing the left-side line over the right. The capacity for the ride is about 2,400 passengers per hour, with fifty log boats in use at a time.

Once you enter the Splash Mountain building, there are a few interesting exhibits including a series of Brer Fox story needlepoints ("Some critters ain't never gonna learn" and "You can't run away from trouble. Ain't no place that far" among them). Check out the animated shadows on the wall in some of the dark areas.

The interior waiting line for Splash Mountain is not the place for claustrophobics. It is dark in places and tight—closer than the waiting queue for Pirates of the Caribbean.

You'll start by loading into your "log"; you may find the seats slightly wet. The logs will climb up into the mountain—you'll see the bottom of the big drop, and first-time riders will certainly be expecting a sudden sharp drop over the precipice they've seen from the ground. And, just to build up the tension a bit, there are several small teasing drops.

But instead of the great fall, your log will move gently through a beautiful, tuneful, and peaceful water world filled with some sixty-eight animatronic characters and lots of delightful details. At the end of the first room there's a drop—but again it's not the big one.

Midway through the ride you'll pass through an opening to the outside and you'll be treated to one of the better views of the park—Thunder Mountain to your left, Cinderella Castle straight ahead, and Space Mountain and the distant Contemporary Resort behind it. (This peek is reminiscent of another Disney classic—the Matterhorn at Disneyland in California.) You'll also likely see a crowd of people staring up at you from below—actually, they're looking beyond you to the big drop over your shoulder.

All of a sudden you're back in the mountain and it's dark. Is this the big drop? Actually, no; you enter into another large room, this time one

Inside Splash Mountain. Disney engineers carefully control the amount of water in the flumes. Too much water will cause too much turbulence and splashing; too little can cause a loaded boat to bottom out. On the big drop, about one-quarter of the water is diverted around the boat to control the speed of the drop.

In any case, there's an emergency braking system at the bottom of the big drop; the brake is turned on if an infrared beam determines that two boats are too close together for safety. Pressurized air inflates a set of air bags that lift the underside of the moving boat and push it against rubber strips in a safety channel on the side of the boat, bringing it to a halt.

By the way, the big splash at the bottom of the drop is not caused by the boat—it's an artificial splash produced by water cannons.

Department of Redundancy Department. If you look carefully, you can spot a fire sprinkler system in the ceiling of the water tunnels within Splash Mountain.

How wet do you like it? Splash Mountain is a watery place, and the log cars make a huge wave as they land at the bottom of the big drop, but the fact is that you won't get very wet on the ride. The two wettest places seem to be the very first row of seats and the last—the wave flies over the car. The front row has the best view of the drop; the last row has the most suspense.

No charge. Splash Mountain, because it is one of the high places in the park and because of the watery path, is occasionally forced to close when a lightning storm is in the area.

illuminated with black light. Check out the bees circling around the bee hive. There's lots of water now, with splashing fountains and little squirts of water overhead. And there are now some signs of warning: "Enter at your own risk," "Danger," "Go Back, Beware, Watch Out."

But instead of going down, you'll go up one more sharp climb. Why do you suppose there are a pair of vultures hanging over the top of the hill? Listen to what they say: "Everybody's got a laughing place, maybe this is yours."

This is it, folks. The big one, the spectacular waterfall you've seen from the walkway below. You're over . . . and down in about four seconds.

There is one final surprise at the very end, yet another sparkling interior room, home to a "Welcome Home Brer Rabbit" party.

Splash Mountain is actually one of the longer rides at the Magic Kingdom at nearly eleven minutes, and despite the brevity of the final drop it does give you a lot more for your waiting time than Thunder Mountain or Space Mountain.

If you can convince the kids (or the adults) to look past the short drop, they are sure to love the rest of the ride which is pure Disney. And try the ride again in the the night; the view of the park from near the top is worth the wait.

There are Splash Mountains at Disneyland and at Tokyo Disneyland; in California guests sit one behind another while the Japanese and Florida versions load side by side.

Tom Sawyer Island

Another essential, at least for the youngsters, is the raft ride over to this little island in the middle of the Rivers of America. Based upon Mark Twain's classic book, you'll find dark caves, waterwheels, a barrel bridge, and a rope bridge to bounce on; at the far end of the island is a little bridge to Fort Sam Clemens, where kids can scramble around the parapets and fire air guns at passing sidewheelers.

The little snack bar at the fort sells, along with beverages, a most unusual fast food: whole sour pickles. There's also an interesting little gazebo out on the water known as Aunt Polly's Landing, selling picnic-basket fare: things such as peanut butter and jelly sandwiches, cold fried chicken and apple pie. Nearby is a half-whitewashed fence with notable graffiti, including a scrawl that declares: Tom♥Becky.

Parents will appreciate the space to let their children burn off a bit of energy after standing in lines all day; be advised, though, that it is fairly easy to misplace a youngster in one of the simulated caves or on a trail. Discuss with your children a meeting place in case you become separated.

Lines for the raft rarely require more than ten minutes waiting. The island closes at dusk.

Country Bear Jamboree

A doggedly cute show starring some twenty robotic bears of various sizes, shapes, and personalities, full of corny jokes and strained puns. Where else could you possibly expect to see a trio of bears named Bubbles, Bunny, and Beulah singing a bowdlerized Beach Boys hit, "Wish They All Could Be California Bears"? (The soundtrack is changed annually for a Christmas hoedown.)

We find this fifteen-minute attraction just barely (sorry) easier to take than the Enchanted Tiki Birds; youngsters and fans of Disney audio-animatronics will probably want to argue strongly in its favor. And despite our opinion, the Jamboree is a very popular shown. The best time to visit is early, late, or during one of the parades. The best seats are at the very front or back of the hall.

Diamond Horseshoe Saloon Revue

Disney's just slightly-risqué version of a Western dance hall revue is a lot of fun for young and old. Expect some funny crude humor, mostly made at the expense of the visitors. This is a good place to take a break for lunch; come early or late to avoid crowds.

The audience is greeted by one of the show's two hosts: Wildcat Kate or Dr. Bill Ya Later. Guests may see one or three different acts, depending on when they arrive. Some will be treated to a traveling troubadour of the Old West, a singer accompanying himself on banjo or guitar, who strolls through the saloon, talks to audience members and leads sing-alongs. Another regular show features a Wild West magician performing tricks and sleight-of-hand.

Rounding out the repertoire is the saloon's featured singer and her two dancing girls, "Miss Lucille Lamour and Her Lovely Ladies." They perform a variety of dances, including the can-can, clog stomp, and other saloon numbers. And heavens-to-Mickey: one of them may even end up perched in the lap of some lucky guy in the audience.

Check the daily schedule for the shows, which last about forty-five minutes. Show up about half an hour early to grab one of the limited seats. You can order sandwiches and salads priced at about $6 and ice cream at the "bar."

Frontierland Shootin' Arcade. A durn-fancy shooting gallery, sort of a live video game and not like any other shooting gallery you have seen at a county fair. Players aim huge buffalo rifles at a Disney replica of an 1850s frontier town. The rifles fire infrared beams at targets on tombstones, clouds, banks, jails, and other objects; direct hits make the targets spin, explode, or otherwise surprise. Some of the signs on the objects tell a story: "Old Tom Hubbard died with a frown, but a grave can't keep a good man down." If you hit the skeleton of a steer, his horns will spin around.

To use the rifles you must pay an additional charge for a specific number of "bullets."

Eating Your Way Through the Magic Kingdom

There are three types of restaurants at the Magic Kingdom: overpriced and bad, overpriced and barely acceptable, and overpriced and almost good. Well, OK, there are a few meals that are overpriced and good.

In any case we'd recommend that you not consider meals to be an important part of your experience at the Magic Kingdom; save your time and money for one of the somewhat better Epcot Center or Disney–MGM Studios restaurants or for an evening outside of the Disney borders.

You do, though, have to eat. Disney has a rule against bringing your own sandwiches or other food into the park. In dozens of visits to Walt Disney World, though, we have never seen an attendant search a backpack or shoulder bag for peanut butter and jelly on white bread, and you certainly can pack a baby's formula and a few candy bars for the kids.

If you don't pack your own food it is possible to pick and choose among the offerings at the park. Disney does offer a few nonstandard and more healthful dishes, like pasta salads, turkey burgers, and smoked turkey legs at some of its stands. Nevertheless, each year guests at Walt Disney World eat more than seven million hamburgers, five million hot dogs, five million pounds of french fries, and 265,000 pounds of popcorn, as well as drink forty-six million Cokes.

We include general price ranges in our listings and mention specific prices for some items. Pricing on food and menus is subject to change. All food establishments within Disney World offer soft drinks at prices of almost $3. (Did I hear someone say, "Why, I'll just throw a few cans of soda in a backpack."? Thought so. If you're discreet, you can find a way to carry your own.)

Main Street, U.S.A.

Main Street Wagons. Located throughout the Main Street area. Espresso, cappuccino, soft drinks. Hot dogs and baked goods. Fresh fruit and vegetables and fruit drinks priced from about $1 to $3. A few umbrella-shaded tables are available on East Center Street beside the Main Street Market house.

Main Street Bake Shop. On Main Street near the Plaza Ice Cream Parlor. Unusual baked goods and beverages, $2 to $4. Cookies about $1. Watch cookies being made from scratch through the large window fronting on Main Street. There is a small seating area inside the pleasant, floral decorated shop, but most customers take their goodies to go, either to sit at one of the nearby umbrella tables or to carry with them as they move deeper into the park.

The bake shop is very crowded at opening time as guests grab breakfast sweets and coffee. A separate cookies and pastries line is available to the right of the entrance if that is all you want.

Plaza Ice Cream Parlor. On Main Street, near the Bake Shop. A pleasant, old-fashioned ice cream shop; it gets very crowded at times. Most items about $3.

Casey's Corner. At the top end of Main Street. Hot dogs, soft drinks, and coffee. Serving

Key

= Fast food

= Pub

= Full-service restaurant

staff in vintage baseball outfits offer hot dogs (about $2.50 and $3.95) with a toppings bar, plus other snacks.

The Crystal Palace. At the top of Main Street, toward Adventureland. Breakfast, lunch, and dinner buffets. Breakfast $13.95 for adults and $7.95 for children ages 3–11. Lunch for $14.95 (adults) and $7.95 (children). Dinner $19.95 (adults) and $9.95 (children). Breakfast offerings include scrambled eggs and omelets, French toast, and breakfast lasagna. At lunch, there is an assortment of salads, soup, pastas, and deli sandwiches. For dinner you can choose from carved meats, pastas, and chicken, beef, and fish dishes. A children's buffet is also offered.

The building is a replica of the Crystal Palace, built for the International Exhibition in New York in 1851. The atmosphere is bright and airy with floral designs in a Victorian gazebo setting and a Dixieland jazz group often entertains diners.

Tony's Town Square Restaurant. Just inside the entrance to the right. Italian food, steaks, seafood, hamburgers, and salads, $15 to $21; appetizers, $3 to $8. Breakfast, lunch, and dinner from 8:30 A.M.; closing time depends on park hours. Reservations recommended; check in at the restaurant lobby.

The restaurant is modeled after the cafe in Disney's classic *Lady and the Tramp* movie. Seating for about two hundred.

Entrees include steak fiorentino, a T-bone steak rubbed with garlic and peppercorns; chicken florentine, grilled breast served with spinach cream sauce and polenta; and veal marsala with wild mushrooms and marsala wine. Breakfast specialties include Italian frittatas, *Lady and the Tramp* waffles, and traditional favorites.

The Plaza Restaurant. At the top of Main Street toward Tomorrowland. Gourmet hamburgers, soups, sandwiches, and salads. Lunch and dinner. Open from 11 A.M. Entrees, $7 to $9.

This pleasant nineteenth-century–style dining room offers table service inside and bright yellow-and-white umbrella tables outside. Specialties include reubens and other sandwiches, basic burgers and grilled mushroom-and-onion burgers with provolone cheese, and supercalifragilisticexpialidocious sundaes.

Adventureland

Sunshine Tree Terrace. At the north end of Adventureland, behind the Enchanted Tiki Birds' Tropical Serenade, this is worth a quick stop for a drink or light snack. Offerings include citrus drinks, frozen yogurt, shakes, and desserts, $2 to $3.

Aloha Isle. Pineapple and fruit drinks, about $2. Try fresh pineapple spears for about $1 or raspberry/vanilla swirl.

El Pirata y el Perico Restaurante. Mexican fast food for lunch and dinner. Specialties include tacos and nachos.

Frontierland

Pecos Bill Cafe. Just past the Country Bear Vacation Hoedown. Burgers, chicken barbecue, salads, and hot dogs, $5 to $7. Western saloon atmosphere in the side-by-side restaurants that share a common menu. Look carefully at the animals mounted on the wall; they're talking and singing robots.

The chicken and bean salad or a barbecue chicken sandwich is a good alternative, but if hamburger fits your fancy, try the Pecos Bill Trail Bacon Cheeseburger Basket. A fixings bar offers your basic toppings.

Turkey Leg Wagon. One of the strangest sights you are likely to see in Frontierland are visitors walking along the pathway absently chewing on what looks like the leg of a large dog. Actually, they're smoked turkey legs sold at a stand directly across from the Country Bear Vacation Hoedown for about $4. Just follow the smell to the end of the line. As you carry along one of these interesting treats, watch out for seagulls; they'll sometimes fly right at the turkey leg trying to take a bite out of it!

Diamond Horseshoe Saloon Revue. Sandwiches, ice cream, and snacks with a free Old West vaudeville show. Check daily schedule.

Liberty Square

Columbia Harbour House. On Liberty Square across from Ichabod's Landing. Battered shrimp and chicken, cold sandwiches, pasta salads, salads. Lunch and dinner, $3 to $7. Children's menu includes a chicken sandwich or hot dog for about $4.

Seafood dining in seafaring atmosphere. The dark, cool decor provides a comfortable respite from the sun. Larger tables seat six to eight. A few, small, semiprivate dining rooms accommodate groups.

For an unusual snack or meal try the clam chowder served inside a round loaf of dark bread. When the chowder is gone, you can eat the bowl. A fruit plate is about $5.25. Sandwiches include smoked ham and cheese, tuna salad, and smoked turkey. Apple cobbler or chocolate and banana cream pies for dessert are about $3. A children's "Little Mariner's Meal" includes entree, cookies, and small beverage for about $2.49.

Liberty Square Wagon. On the walkway between Columbia Harbour House and the Hall of Presidents. Baked potatoes with toppings and beverages, $2 to $3. There's also a fresh fruit and pickle stand nearby.

In an area where sandwiches and fast foods average about $5, the potato wagon is a popular alternative for a filling, low-cost lunch or snack. Fresh-baked white and sweet potatoes with a variety of toppings, about $2.50.

Fruit and Vegetable Wagon. On the square behind the Columbia Harbour House and the Liberty Square Wagon. Various fruits and vegetables from a "farmer's market" wagon.

Attractively presented offerings including apples, peaches, grapes, star fruit, and even pickles, squash, and potatoes.

Liberty Tree Tavern. Next to Diamond Horseshoe Revue and open for lunch (11:30 A.M. to 4 P.M.) and dinner (from 4:30 P.M.). Sandwiches, beef, chicken, seafood, salads, $7 to $16. Reservations recommended; request a seating time at the door.

Sit-down dining in a colonial atmosphere with a lot of interesting details, including maple bench seats, fireplaces, and simulated peg flooring. A variety of sandwiches is available from about $7 to $10. Seafood and other entrees from about $10 to $14. Luncheon specialties include New England Pot Roast, Pilgrim's Feast turkey dinner, and Cape Cod pasta with shrimp and vegetables.

At dinner time the Liberty Tree features a Disney characters family-style dinner for about $20 for adults and $10 for children age nine and younger. The meal includes salad, roast turkey, glazed ham, and marinated flank steak.

Fantasyland

Pinocchio Village Haus. Next to It's a Small World. Turkey hamburgers, turkey hot dogs, chicken, salads, pasta. Lunch and dinner.

A large dining hall in a Disneyfied Tudor style. You'll find several small rooms, including a favored location overlooking the It's a Small World ride. Meals from about $5 to $6 with french fries or grapes and a regular beverage include choice of cheeseburgers (beef or turkey), a quarter pound turkey hot dog, or a grilled bratwurst.

The eatery includes a relish bar with pickles, tomatoes, onions, mushrooms, sauerkraut, barbecue sauce, cheese sauce, and more.

Also available is a smoked turkey sub with provolone cheese, lettuce, and tomatoes for about $4.50.

As at many Disney fast food restaurants, the service lines move slowly at peak time. Come early or late to avoid wasting time.

Cinderella's Royal Table. Upstairs in Cinderella Castle. Character breakfasts, lunches, and dinners.

If you enter the castle from the Fantasyland side, the restaurant is on the outside left. Lines for lunch begin early because seating is limited. Among the more expensive restaurants in the Magic Kingdom, Cinderella's Royal Table has a special draw for some children, especially little girls who dream of meeting Cinderella herself. Reservations are accepted at the door on the day you wish to dine; guests at Disney hotels can make telephone reservations up to two days ahead of time.

You enter the restaurant through a "great hall" entrance on the ground floor. This interesting room is complete with torch lanterns and swords on the wall. The slate floor and high, exposed-beam ceiling enhance the "castle" feeling of the restaurant. You'll move upstairs via an interesting, winding stairway or in an elevator.

Tomorrowland

Cosmic Ray's Starlight Cafe. Cosmic Ray's (get it?) is the largest fast food eatery in the Magic Kingdom, the former Tomorrowland Terrace. Decorated in brushed aluminum, purples, and blacks, there's a little stage at the back of the room for shows. Offerings include hamburgers, vegetarian burgers, chicken, soups, and salads at several food court–like stands within. Specialties include the Chick Encounter family meal for three to four, featuring a whole rotisserie chicken, and the Coop Canaveral chicken drummettes.

Plaza Pavilion. In the walkway between Main Street and Tomorrowland. Pizza, sandwiches, salads, $3 to $5. Covered outdoor dining in a pleasant setting for about 650 people. There are three dining areas, including one that overlooks a portion of the central lagoon and Cinderella Castle. The area offers cool shade and ample seating away from the main service area and transient crowds.

Try the Italian hoagie at about $4.25 or the chicken parmesan sandwich for a dollar more. Deep dish pizza is available by the slice for about $3.25 to $4.75. Fix up your ice cream with the brownie sundae for about $2.75 or an ice cream float for about $2.30.

Auntie Gravity's Galactic Goodies. Across the broad plaza from Space Mountain at the base of the Astro Orbiter tower. Juice, snacks, frozen yogurt, $2 to $3.

MAGIC KINGDOM

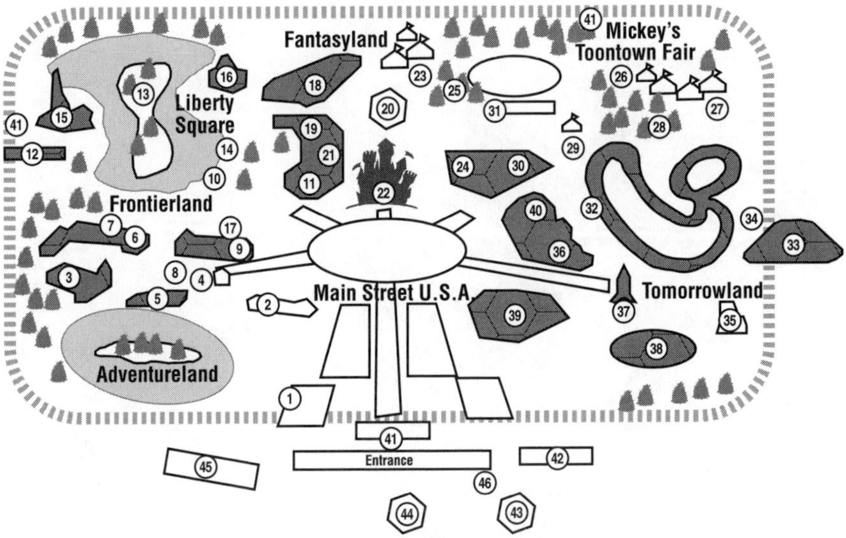

① City Hall
② First Aid
③ Pirates of the Caribbean
④ Swiss Family Treehouse
⑤ Jungle Cruise
⑥ Enchanted Tiki Room
⑦ Country Bear Jamboree
⑧ The Magic Carpets of Aladdin
⑨ Diamond Horseshoe Saloon Revue
⑩ *Liberty Belle* Riverboat
⑪ The Hall of Presidents
⑫ Splash Mountain
⑬ Tom Sawyer Island
⑭ Mike Fink Keelboats
⑮ Big Thunder Mountain Railroad
⑯ The Haunted Mansion
⑰ Frontierland Shootin' Arcade
⑱ It's a Small World
⑲ Peter Pan's Flight
⑳ Cinderella's Golden Carrousel
㉑ *The Legend of the Lion King*
㉒ Cinderella Castle
㉓ Dumbo the Flying Elephant
㉔ Snow White's Scary Adventures
㉕ Ariel's Grotto
㉖ Toontown Hall of Fame
㉗ Mickey's and Minnie's Country Houses
㉘ The Barnstormer at Goofy's Wiseacre Farm
㉙ Mad Tea Party
㉚ The Many Adventures of Winnie the Pooh
㉛ Fantasyland Character Festival
㉜ Tomorrowland Indy Speedway
㉝ Space Mountain
㉞ Tomorrowland Transit Authority
㉟ Tomorrowland Stage
㊱ Alien Encounter: The ExtraTERRORestrial
㊲ Astro Orbiter
㊳ Carousel of Progress
㊴ *The Timekeeper*
㊵ Buzz Lightyear's Space Ranger Spin
㊶ Walt Disney World Railroad Station
㊷ Magic Kingdom Bus Transportation
㊸ Ferryboat to Parking
㊹ Boats to Discovery Island and Fort Wilderness
㊺ Monorail Station
㊻ Stroller Rental

Chapter 8
Epcot

Epcot is Disney's permanent world's fair, a place where the nations and the global multinational corporations of the world meet their tourists and customers. Oh, and it's a heck of a lot of fun, too.

Spaceship Earth, the park icon, received a makeover for the twenty-first century with the addition of shimmering script letters as much as thirty-six feet tall, spelling out "Epcot." The golf ball was first altered as part of Disney's millennium celebration with the addition of a twenty-five-story-high Sorcerer Mickey's arm and hand holding a gigantic magical wand.

This is no small sign. All told, Mickey's gloved hand, the wand, and the word "Epcot" weigh some 100,000 pounds.

After entertaining millions of Epcot guests, the *Tapestry of Nations* spectacle and the sky-filling fireworks-and-laser dazzler, *IllumiNations: Reflections of Earth,* have been extended indefinitely with twice-daily parades.

Lead by the "Sage of Time," 120 huge figures in the "Tapestry of Nations" appear from hiding places around the lake. They are controlled from twenty feet below by puppeteers who look like marionettes to the figures. The puppets and costumes were created by the costume designer of the Broadway production of the *Lion King*. To the accompaniment of music, the puppets join sixteen percussion units, designed to resemble colossal timepieces.

IllumiNations: Reflections of Earth is a dazzling finale on and above World Showcase Lagoon; the night is filled with the fiery glow of torches, lasers, high-energy music, and booming fireworks. The sky transforms into a kaleidoscope of colorful pyrotechnic bursts. Comets streak across the sky as video images are displayed on the giant Earth Globe, the floating centerpiece. Then, the sphere blossoms like a flower, revealing a brilliant ball of fire. The music builds, lasers shoot skyward, fireworks light the night, and flames leap across the surface of the lagoon.

The Millennium Village, a pavilion created especially for the millennium celebration, closed on January 1, 2001. The space was converted to a convention and meeting facility.

Disney gives Epcot a hand

Epcot's biggest draw is the GM Test Track. That is, at least until sometime in 2003 when **Mission: SPACE** arrives. That much-awaited attraction, which replaces Horizons, promises to take visitors into a simulation of space flight, using the highest of ride technology.

The Epcot Story

Walt Disney's concept called for a modern city built from scratch to include factories, homes, offices, and farms as a showcase for new ideas and technologies from industry and education. Disney gave his dream the name Experimental Prototype Community of Tomorrow, which is the almost-forgotten name behind the Epcot acronym.

Disney lived long enough to set the broad outlines for Epcot, but the park as built was quite different from the prototype community he first planned. Roughly half the park is given over to imaginative pavilions that explore the frontiers of science: communication, energy, human life, transportation, technology, creativity, agriculture, and the seas. And then spread around the World Showcase Lagoon are exhibits, films, and a handful of rides that share some of the cultures of the globe: from Canada, France, Morocco, Japan, Italy, America, Germany, China, Norway, Mexico, and the United Kingdom.

Epcot, at 260 acres, is more than twice the size of the Magic Kingdom. The World Showcase Lagoon is about forty acres in size; the promenade that circles it and leads to the pavilions of nations is 1.2 miles in length. Construction costs were about $1.3 billion in 1982; at the time it was one of the largest private construction jobs ever undertaken.

Although for most visitors it is the Magic Kingdom of Mickey and Minnie that brings them to Walt Disney World, many adults and quite a few children will tell you that the memory they bring home comes from Epcot: the wild ride at GM Test Track, the dinosaurs at the Universe of Energy, the troll at Norway, or the film view of the Great Wall at China.

MUST-SEES

WOW

Future World

Spaceship Earth

Innoventions

Universe of Energy

Body Wars
(Wonders of Life)

Cranium Command
(Wonders of Life)

GM Test Track

Honey, I Shrunk the Audience
(Imagination!)

Living with the Land
(The Land)

Circle of Life
(The Land)

World Showcase

El Rio del Tiempo
(Mexico)

Maelstrom
(Norway)

Wonders of China
(China)

The American Adventure
(United States)

Epcot's Special Events Calendar

Epcot includes an interesting range of special events. In recent years these events have included Holidays Around the World at Christmastime, featuring a candlelight processional, the Christmas Story presented at the America Gardens Stage, and a "living" Christmas tree. The events were free to all ticket holders, but Epcot also made available a specially priced ticket that offered entrance to the park, reserved seating at the processional, free preferred parking, and special discounts on Epcot merchandise.

Another favorite is Disney's **Candlelight Processional**, a retelling of the Christmas story. It is presented at least twice nightly at the America Gardens Theatre in World Showcase from just after Thanksgiving through December 30.

Each program features a guest celebrity narrating the traditional story of Christmas, interwoven with music of the season by 450 choral voices, a fifty-piece orchestra, and a handbell choir. A limited number of seats are available to guests at Epcot, with lines forming several hours before show time. Disney also sells Candlelight Processional packages that include dining at select Epcot restaurants and preferred seating at one of the shows. In recent years the packages began at about $40 for adults, not including admission to the park; a special package with an after–4 P.M. admission to Epcot sold for about $60.

The Lights of Winter is a sparkling canopy of thirty thousand synchronized lights above the bridge from Future World to World Showcase, plus nightly tree-lighting ceremonies with carolers, fanfare trumpeters, and holiday storytellers. And in recent years there has also been ***Holiday IllumiNations***, a seasonal version of the nightly laser, light, and fireworks show.

And gardeners and nature lovers can soak up the grandeur of the gardens, topiaries, and flowers from late April through the end of May at the Epcot International Flower & Garden Festival. For information about this and other festivals at Epcot, call ☎ (407) 824-4321.

Many of the international pavilions have special celebrations on their national holidays. Chinese New Year is celebrated in February at China; Moroccan Throne Day is observed on March 3; and Italy holds a Carnivale Celebration at the opening of Lent.

Epcot operates on a split schedule, with Future World open for much of the season from 9 A.M. to 9 P.M., and the World Showcase at the back of the park open from 11 A.M. to 9 P.M. One more thing: on most days the gates actually open at 8:30 A.M., with Spaceship Earth and some of the restaurants ready for early arrivals; when the park starts to get very busy with the opening of the GM Test Track, I'd recommend an early spot in line.

And remember that operating hours are subject to change; call the park or check at the front desk of one of the hotels within the park for current information.

Epcot is unique among the four parks at Walt Disney World in that it has two entrances—the

Springtime treat. If you arrive at Epcot in March, April, or May, pay attention to the trees just at the base of the golf ball. The striking ornamental trees with blue trumpet-shaped flowers are jacaranda, native to northwestern Argentina.

main gate, which leads directly to the Spaceship Earth, and a second, less-used International Gateway at the World Showcase, between the United Kingdom and France pavilions. Trams or ferries run between the International Gateway and the BoardWalk, Swan, Dolphin, Beach Club, and Yacht Club resorts.

Here's an insider tip for a classy way to spend the day at Epcot: take the launch from World Gateway to the BoardWalk Resort for lunch or dinner to escape the madding crowds.

Power Trip

This plan is based on the split schedule that opens Future World two hours before the World Showcase, and taking advantage of the Fastpass system.

The key to getting the most out of a visit to Epcot, as with every other attraction, is once again to adopt a contrarian view of the park. Most visitors saunter into the park in mid-morning and join the crowds at the pavilions of Future World before beginning a slow—and crowded—circle of the World Showcase section in a clockwise direction. Another important bit of information is the fact that **Spaceship Earth** and the surrounding Innoventions usually open a bit before the rest of Epcot.

At Epcot the GM Test Track and *Honey, I Shrunk the Audience* have Fastpass booths.

Before you go to the park, make up a list of your personal must-sees. Get to the park early. If you're up for a thrill ride this is the time to make tracks to the **GM Test Track**. Bear to the left from the entrance and follow the signs. If the lines are short go ahead and take a spin; otherwise grab a Fastpass reservation and come back at the appointed hour.

While you're in the neighborhood, retrace your steps a bit to the **Universe of Energy** pavilion and see the show there. Then sprint across Future World to the Imagination! pavilion for the ***Honey, I Shrunk the Audience*** show. Grab a seat or a Fastpass reservation.

By this time, it should be near 11 A.M. and time to jump out ahead of the crowds. Move into the World Showcase.

The biggest crowds at the **World Showcase** can usually be found at the **Norway**, **Mexico**, and **American** pavilions. If you are at the head of the throng, go immediately to Mexico and then next door to Norway and then continue in a clockwise circle around the lagoon. If you find yourself behind the madding crowd, you might want to travel in the opposite direction, going counterclockwise and starting at Canada.

After you leave the World Showcase, tour the remaining pavilions of **Future World**, this time moving in a clockwise direction—starting at the **Imagination!** pavilion, and heading toward the front of the park and Spaceship Earth.

Double back at the golf ball and visit **Innoventions** and **Wonders of Life** to complete your tour.

With luck, you will complete the tour of Epcot at nightfall and can enjoy a leisurely dinner before coming out to the lagoon for a view of the spectacular ***IllumiNations*** show.

Here's a by-the-numbers Power Trip, pavilion-by-pavilion. 1: **GM Test Track**; 2: **Universe of Energy**; 3: ***Honey, I Shrunk the Audience***; 4: **Mexico**; 5: **Norway**; 6: **China**; 7: **Germany**; 8: **Italy**; 9: **The American Adventure**; 10: **Japan**; 11: **Morocco**; 12: **France**; 13: **United Kingdom**; 14: **Canada**; 15: **Imagination!**; 16: **The Land**; 17: **The Living Seas**; 18: **Spaceship Earth**; 19: **Innoventions**, and 20: **Wonders of Life**.

Attractions at Future World

WOW Spaceship Earth

The huge geodesic sphere that is the symbol of Epcot—referred to by most visitors as the "golf ball"—is 180 feet (eighteen stories) high and 165 feet in diameter with 2.2 million cubic feet of space within. The outside of the sphere is made up of some eleven thousand triangular tiles, made of a composite of ethylene plastic bonded between two aluminum panels. It weighs almost sixteen million pounds, including 1,750 tons of steel.

As impressive as the shell is, the real excitement of Spaceship Earth can be found on the ride within, which is sponsored by communications giant AT&T. (Each of the major exhibits at Epcot's Future World is sponsored by a major American corporation, but the commercialism is relatively low-key.)

The original exhibit was designed by a collaboration that included science fiction author Ray Bradbury, the Smithsonian Institution, and newsman Walter Cronkite. The ride was updated in 1995 with some new areas, a new narration by actor Jeremy Irons, and a new musical score. (The cloying "Tomorrow's Child" song is gone.) There's nothing here that will set your heart to pounding, but the lighting, video, and computerized special effects are among the best at Walt Disney World.

You'll board "time machine" chairs for a trip into the sphere that will take you back through history from the age of the Cro-Magnon man some thirty thousand years ago to the present, along the way passing through the great ancient civilizations of Egypt, Phoenicia, and Rome. The narration may be a bit beyond the comprehension of young children, but they'll still enjoy and learn from the sights.

You'll note some of the important developments of our time, including the creation of an alphabet and written language, the first books, the development of the printing press, and on to modern communications. You'll also see great cultural figures from Michelangelo at work in the Sistine Chapel to Howdy Doody and Ed Sullivan. At the very top of the ball is the most spectacular sight of all, a huge sky of stars and planets.

Not all of the special effects of this ride are visual ones; Disney engineers even created smell

Tubular, dude.
The Spaceship Earth sphere is built from four structural parts. The outer shell is strictly for decorative purposes and is connected to an inner waterproof sphere by hundreds of small support columns. A column that runs up the center of the ball supports the internal ride, which circles around the column like a spiral staircase. And finally, a platform at the bottom of the sphere supports the inner structure and the ride itself.

cannons that fill the air with appropriate odors, including the ashes of burning Rome.

The page from the Bible that Johannes Gutenberg is examining is an exact replica of a page from one of his early Bibles. In an ancient Egypt setting the hieroglyphics on the wall are reproductions of actual graphics; the words being dictated by the Pharaoh were taken from an actual letter sent by a pharaoh to one of his agents.

Hard ride. As befits the unusual building, the time machines in this ride take an unusual route. You'll slowly spiral up, up, and up around the sides of the ball until you reach the starfield at top; then your chair will turn around for a steep, backward descent to the base. Some riders might find the trip down a bit uncomfortable.

And then we move into the near future where we see a young boy communicating in his room over the information superhighway. At the very top of the golf ball we move into a startlingly beautiful planetarium-like dome with Spaceship Earth and the stars all around it. Our chairs move into a view of a futuristic classroom embarking on a virtual field trip.

The dazzling finale puts the audience in the heart of interactive global networks that tie the peoples of the earth together. Fantastic special effects, animatronic robots, and laser beams that surround and encase the visitors on a simulated trip into a microchip.

At the exit is the **Global Neighborhood** for hands-on demonstrations of new technologies in voice recognition, video telephony, and the information superhighway.

Because of its position at the front of the park, lines for this ride are usually longest at the start of the day, although early arrivals can still expect to be able to walk right on. If the line builds up, though, we'd suggest coming back in the afternoon or on your way out of the park at the end of the day.

WOW Innoventions

Innoventions is the most commercial part of Walt Disney World, which is saying quite a bit. This is the World's Fair core of Epcot.

What Disney has done is truly an amazing thing: they have found a way to charge visitors nearly $50 each to enter a somewhat ordinary convention hall–like building and look at exhibits of commercial products.

The light fantastic. Disney designers snuck a little extra bit of magic into the construction of the Innoventions building. Fiber optics embedded in the tiles of the walkways outside are computer controlled to dance along with the nightly *IllumiNations* show on the lagoon.

Even more amazing is the fact that Disney is able to charge major corporations millions of dollars for the right to build their own exhibits.

Although products are not sold in exhibit areas, representatives are on hand to explain and demonstrate. Guests can use computer terminals to request information by mail.

Most of the exhibits are changed every few years. Youngsters and fans of electronic gadgets will likely want to bear to the right of Spaceship Earth to **Innoventions West**, home of exhibits

Epcot ecology. As a planned community, Epcot includes many interesting experiments in ecology.

The huge Disney development uses a tremendous amount of water, which is a particular problem in the wet Florida environment. Some of the effluent of the wastewater treatment plant is sprayed on the 145-acre Walt Disney World Tree Farm to make use of nutrients in the water. Another project involves the growth of water hyacinths in a pond fed by the wastewater plant; the plants help purify the water by absorbing nutrients and filtering solids through their roots. Grown plants are harvested and composted for use as fertilizer.

by companies that in recent years included IBM, Sega of America, Xerox, and Monsanto. On the left side of Spaceship Earth in **Innoventions East** are exhibits aimed mostly at adults, including displays in recent years from General Motors, Motorola, Panja, Disney, and others.

Fast food eateries within the Innoventions area include the **Electric Umbrella Restaurant**, **Fountain View Espresso & Bakery**, and **Pasta Piazza Ristorante**.

Parental guidance: Innoventions is a tremendous lure for the video kid generation. I don't know about you, but I'm not very happy about the thought of spending thousands of dollars and traveling thousands of miles to Orlando to see my children head off to play video games for hours at a time. Other parents might be willing to trust their kids to stay in one place for a few hours while they head off to a leisurely dinner.

In either case be sure to have a plan to keep track of your children as they roam the sprawling Innoventions buildings.

Innoventions West

In recent years, exhibitors at Innoventions West have included:

Beautiful Science. An exploration of the life sciences at work on world food and health problems, as presented by Monsanto.

The Knowledge Vortex. Ways to capture, organize, and share information, from Xerox.

Medicine's New Vision. Advanced radiological technologies.

Networked Living. IBM's PlanetRider demonstrates the World Wide Web.

Ultimate Home Theater Experience. High-definition television sets, high-tech lighting, advanced surround sound, and more, from Luton.

Video Games of Tomorrow. Demonstrations of games from Sega.

Innoventions East

In recent years, exhibitors at Innovations East have included:

Communications Dream Forum. Starnac the robot offered a glimpse into the future, as seen by Motorola.

Future Cars. General Motors showed off prototype vehicles, including cars powered by fuel cells and batteries.

The House of Innoventions. A tour of a smart home of the future, including a refrigerator connected to the Internet, as presented by Panja.

WOW Universe of Energy

Forward to the past, and back to the future: one of the favorite pavilions at Epcot has been given a fresh jolt of . . . energy.

The pavilion is based around an entertaining film known as *Ellen's Energy Crisis*, starring comedian Ellen DeGeneres and featuring some exciting special effects. In the movie, Ellen dreams she is a contestant on the "Jeopardy!" television game show. She's up against the reigning champion Dr. Judy Peterson, played by Jamie Lee Curtis. The third contestant: Albert Einstein.

And the categories? They're all about energy, a subject that is clearly not Ellen's specialty.

Ellen has a secret weapon, though: her neighbor Bill Nye the Science Guy. She summons him for some hints, and he responds by taking Ellen—and all of the guests seated in the pavilion's famous moving grandstands—on a tour that travels back in time to the birth of the planet, and then on to a world tour of today's energy need and research.

The show begins with a standing-room-only preshow where we are introduced to Ellen, her cats, her neighbor Bill, and her nemesis, the brainy Dr. Peterson—Ellen insists her nickname was "Stupid Judy." Also making cameo appearances are game-show host Alex Trebek, Willard Scott with the 1 million B.C. weather, and Len Berman with the back, back, back sports report.

From the preshow guests move into the old moving theater cars for an expedition 220 million years back to the Big Bang and from there to the dawn of the dinosaurs, with Ellen wisecracking all the way along.

(There are six sections; the seats all the way forward to the left lead the parade, while the back right section moves out last. We prefer to be in front.)

The show is a major draw at Epcot and contributes to a lopsided draw to the west side of the park along with the new GM Test Track. Head there early, or come back late in the day to avoid lines that may stretch for eons.

Wonders of Life

A world of its own. Under one geodesic domed roof you will find two of Epcot's best attractions, plus a healthful Fitness Fairground for children of all ages and entertaining and informative films and presentations on subjects from exercise to reproduction.

You could easily spend a few hours here; it's an excellent place to escape bad weather.

WOW **Body Wars.** Strap on your seat belts and prepare for blast-off on a journey to inner space. Body Wars is a fantastic simulator ride that takes you on a repair expedition inside a human body—a training mission to remove a splinter from *within*.

(Check out the pilot's cockpit for the Body Wars vehicle; we especially like the pink baby shoes hanging over the windshield.)

Super helix. The huge sculpture at the entrance to the Wonders of Life pavilion is a seventy-five-foot-tall representation of a DNA molecule, the basic building block of life. A human built to the same scale would be several million miles tall.

Secret Mickey. There is a hidden image of Mickey Mouse in the mural above the waiting area for Body Wars.

How'd they do that? The geodesic dome for the Wonders of Life pavilion is 250 feet in diameter and 60 feet tall at the center; to construct it, engineers built a temporary tower crane in the center. Rings of triangles were then hoisted by cables attached to the tower and anchored to columns around the circumference. When the dome was up, the crane was dismantled and removed.

As usual in a sci-fi story like this, something goes wrong within the body and the medical craft begins to lose all power from its fuel cell. So our pilot decides he must go to the brain and cross the blood-brain barrier and park next to a synapse in hopes that it will fire and recharge the cell. Our cabin bounces and twists through the veins and arteries of the human body, ending up with an electrical bang.

Amazingly for a vehicle that doesn't really go anywhere, this ride carries as many health warnings as a roller coaster. Pregnant women and visitors with back or heart ailments are advised not to come aboard, and an adult must accompany any child younger than seven; those younger than three years of age cannot ride. If you're the type who gets queasy on an elevator—and you know who you are—you might want to pass this one by.

Any serious movie fan will recognize the Body Wars story as a spin-off of the classic science fiction flick, *Fantastic Voyage*, which featured Raquel Welch in a body suit.

Cranium Command. A wild and offbeat show, unlike almost anything else at Walt Disney World, this is a combination audio-animatronics and film journey into one of the most unstable places on earth. Your screaming leader, General Knowledge, will inform you that you have been assigned to pilot the most erratic craft in the fleet—the mind of a twelve-year-old boy.

This is a presentation that has something for everyone, from corny jokes and a food fight for the kids to smart one-liners and comic performances from well-known comedians, that include George Wendt (Norm from "Cheers") as superintendent of the stomach, Bobcat Goldthwait as a hysterical adrenaline gland, and Charles Grodin as the smug, all-knowing Right Brain. All this is to teach about the benefits of stress management!

It's a very clever show and rarely more than a fifteen- to thirty-minute wait; don't miss it.

Fitness Fairgrounds. The various exhibits in the center of the dome can occupy visitors for hours and are a great place to get out of the sun or rain. Our only warning about this place is that it is quite easy to misplace young children in the busy aisles.

- **Goofy About Health.** You wouldn't ordinarily include our old friend Goofy on a list of contenders for the Olympic team, but this very entertaining film presentation teaches about the value of exercise and health habits as it entertains.
- **AnaComical Players.** A lively and pun-filled tour of the human body,

presented by a clever improvisational theater group. Are you really ready for "Flossed in Space"?

• ***The Making of Me.*** OK, parents: here's an opportunity to teach your children some of the facts of life in an entertaining fourteen-minute film starring comedian Martin Short. He begins with a visit to the birth of his Mom and Dad and follows them right through his own conception (lovemaking is described as a private moment between lovers, with just enough detail to guarantee your kids will come up with their own questions). There is spectacular footage of the beginnings of life and childbirth. Lines for this show, presented in a tiny theater, can begin to stretch to as much as an hour at the most crowded parts of the day; go early or late. Highly recommended.

• **Coach's Corner.** Step up to the batting tee, the tennis net, or the fairway for a quick sports lesson. Your swing will be videotaped and you'll receive a quick taped comment from one of sport's greatest players. It's all in good fun, although some adults seem to take their moment of stardom *very* seriously.

• **Wondercycles.** A high-tech set of exercise bicycles that present videodisc images keyed to your pedaling speed. You can "visit" Disneyland, scoot in and among the floats in the Rose Bowl Parade in California, or enjoy a hilarious low-level pedal through Big Town, U.S.A., in which your cycle passes humans, dogs, cars, and furniture at rug-rat level.

• **Sensory Funhouse.** A set of interesting demonstrations of human senses, including sight, sound, and touch. You'll discover some unusual demonstrations, such as an area where you stick your hands through a black curtain so you can't see what you are touching; like the old story of the blind men and the elephant, it's amusing to hear the descriptions visitors make of items that include a pair of ski goggles, a chess piece, a gyroscope, a toy train, and a toy dinosaur.

• **Met Lifestyle Revue.** A computer will ask you all sorts of personal questions and then offer a personalized set of lifestyle suggestions.

The best way to tour Wonders of Life is to keep an eye on waiting lines for Body Wars and Cranium Command and dive in when they seem reasonable. There is plenty to occupy visitors between trips to those attractions.

Mission: SPACE *(Coming in 2003)*

The next major attraction at Epcot promises to boldly go where no thrill ride has gone before: deep space.

According to Disney, the state-of-the-art attraction will launch guests into a simulated space adventure, from pulse-racing lift-off to weightlessness in outer space. Mission: SPACE is expected to blast off sometime in 2003. It will bear the corporate sponsorship of Compaq Computer Company.

Walt Disney Imagineering says it will use new technologies, making it the first ride system ever created to take guests straight up in simulated flight. Set decades into the future, guests will be transported in time and place to an international space training center were they will encounter challenges similar to those faced by real astronauts. The ride is expected to last about five minutes.

Six-time NASA shuttle astronaut Story Musgrove is one of the consultants on the project. NASA has no formal relationship with Disney for the attraction but has agreed to allow depiction of its training methods. One possibility: guests may be able to communicate with astronauts on the real international space station.

The pavilion occupies the former site of the **Horizons** attraction, one of the sentimental favorites of Epcot.

Horizons was an extension of the theme from the Magic Kingdom's Carousel of Progress, presenting a vision of the future that included the Omega Centauri space colony, the Sea Castle underwater city, and the robotic farm station Mesa Verde.

WOW GM Test Track *FAST*

Fasten your seat belts for the longest, fastest, and most technologically complex ride at Walt Disney World, a wild salute to GM's proving grounds for automobiles. You'll climb hills, careen through hairpin turns, jounce down bumpy roadways, zip along straightaways, and enter into a fifty-degree banked turn at 65 miles per hour, zooming across the front of the pavilion. Trust me, it feels like twice that speed.

The Test Track climbs, spirals, and snakes through the 150,000-square-foot pavilion; the former home of the World of Motion was completely gutted and rebuilt for this new attraction at Epcot. About half of the 5,246-foot-long track loops outside the pavilion where maximum speeds are obtained; a full ride takes about five-and-a-half minutes. (By comparison, Space Mountain lasts about three minutes, reaching a top speed of just 32 miles per hour, half that of the test vehicles here.)

This is sure to be the number one draw at Epcot for some time to come; if you have any doubt consider the fact that the ride is set up with the largest waiting area in Walt Disney World. If the outside queue is filled, the last person in line can expect as much as a ninety-minute wait. Once you set foot inside the building, the wait should be about forty-five minutes.

(One way to get around the waiting lines is to volunteer for the "singles" crew. You'll be ushered right to the training theater, to wait in a much shorter line for the odd open space in the cars. Even better: make a ride reservation using Disney's Fastpass system.)

On the plus side the inside queue is actually one of the more interesting places I know of to stand around and wait. You'll pass through a simulation of a GM test facility with all sorts of torture devices for vehicles—from door slammers and seat belt twisters to crash test dummies in all sorts of extreme distress. The much-abused star here is Chester, who allows himself to be repeatedly thumped in the chest by a swinging weight. By the way, real crash test dummies cost as much as $100,000 each, wired with as many as 120 data channels for instruments.

You'll also learn about emissions, braking, and safety engineering at GM.

At the end of the waiting area, the line is split into groups of twenty-four and ushered into small theaters for a briefing by the test track coordinator.

A vehicle rounds the curve at the GM Test Track

You'll learn about acceleration, braking, and rollover tests . . . oops, no rollovers today. Note the pictures on the walls of actual GM test tracks around the world.

Your guide will select a menu of tests for you and your vehicle:

Hill Climb Test. An accelerating climb up a three-story, eighteen-degree hill, demonstrating the measurement of the generation of heat and stress on engines and transmissions.

Road-Surface Test. Your vehicle will clamber across stretches of rough German and Belgian blocks in a trial for the suspension system.

Brake Test. The car makes a high-speed run at a set of traffic cones, with and without computer-controlled ABS braking. Without ABS, of course, the cones become orange road kill. Monitors give you an instant replay.

Environmental Chamber. The vehicles move into a 120-degree heat lamp oven and then an indoor 20-degree arctic in a test of the effects of temperature and corrosion on the body and system; from there the car (and passengers) endure a corrosive mist sprayed by industrial robots.

Ride and Handling Test. A pass through a hairpin and loops set the stage for high-speed trials to come.

Barrier Test. Off to the left side of the car you can watch another test vehicle—with test dummies instead of vacationers—crash into a barrier. And then your vehicle will accelerate rapidly and slam at full speed into a solid wall. NOT! But it will come very, very close.

High-Speed Test. On the other side of the wall is the outdoor high-speed test track, a wild ride into the backyard of the pavilion and then a great swoop around the front on a fifty-degree bank where the vehicle reaches its top speed of just under 65 miles per hour. Passengers experience about two Gs of force on the banked turns.

The ride draws its inspiration from GM's famed Milford proving ground northwest of Detroit; the facility dates back to 1924 and includes 132 miles of test roads of nearly every construction. The vehicles are not derived from an actual GM car but instead are adaptations of a HYGE sled. HYGE, which stands for "hydraulic-controlled gas-energized," is a test sled that allows engineers to simplify and standardize the proving grounds process.

Guests enter into a six-passenger Test Track vehicle; vehicles pull up four at a time. When they leave, cars are spaced about ten seconds apart; the ride should be able to accommodate about 1,800 persons per hour.

There are three seats in front and three in back, and each passenger has a shoulder harness and seat belt. (There is no steering wheel, accelerator, or brake pedal—the vehicle is entirely under the control of the computer.) A video screen in front of each row of seats helps explain the testing process.

Passengers will feel the wind; I'd recommend angling for a front seat—there's a bit more protection from the wind and the view of the track is clearer. The ride will likely continue to operate in light rain but shut down in heavier conditions. Trust me, you wouldn't enjoy the ride in a Florida thunderboomer.

The ride is fun anytime of the day, but I particularly recommend the experience by night when darkness accentuates the outdoor experience.

The gas caps on the body of the car are strictly for show. The vehicles use electric motors in the rear that draw 480 volts of power through a slot in the bottom of the track, like a super-sized slot-car racer. The motors generate about 250 horsepower and can accelerate from 0 to 65 miles per hour in about 8.8 seconds; the electric motors are also part of the braking system.

A trio of computers manages acceleration, deceleration, and braking; together the onboard computers perform more calculations per second than the brains of the Space Shuttle. A central computer in the ride's control room manages distance between the cars on the track.

The vehicles are constructed entirely out of composite material, with no steel between the front and rear wheels. Cars run about 145 miles per day on a "Tailhook" track surface, based on the coating material used on aircraft carriers. The abuse is tough on the tires, which must be replaced several times a year. During the course of a year, each vehicle will travel the equivalent of twenty-one round-trips from Orlando to Detroit.

A two-year delay in opening the ride was directly related to the complexity of the technology. It is by far the most intricate ride at Walt Disney World.

At Test Track Disney had to invent everything, he said; there were no off-the-shelf mechanisms to be customized. (By comparison the Rock 'n Roller Coaster at Disney–MGM Studios uses a track and car system already proven at other parks, albeit within a building fitted out with Disney theming.)

The show is not over when you exit your vehicle; you'll walk into an impressive simulation of a robotic assembly line with a stamping mill shaking the floor and parts of vehicles moving by overhead.

In the Driving Technologies Lab you'll have a chance to sit at one of ten high-tech driving simulators to test out new automotive technologies, including night vision sensors. Your chair will rumble and bounce in sequence with your driving, and you'll feel the thud of any collisions. (Two of the ten stations are set up with hand controls for drivers who have disabilities.)

Finally, there is a display of some of the latest production cars from General Motors, backed by a flashy set of video walls. Here's where the ride turns from thrills to marketing, although for many visitors there's a lot to be said for a car showroom without a car salesperson in sight.

Imagination!

Every once in a long, long while Disney suffers from a lack of imagination. That was the case with the ExtraTERRORestrial Alien Encounter at the Magic Kingdom, and that seems to be the case with the much-awaited remake of the dark ride at Imagination!

Journey into Your Imagination. In its previous incarnation, this attraction included some of the most unusual special effects at Epcot and was a clear favorite among youngsters. The ride introduced us to Dreamfinder and his pet purple dragon Figment (as in "of imagination") on an expedition to collect colors, sounds, shapes, and stories with which to create new ideas.

The new show dispenses with most of the "cuteness," instead creating a story based on the Imagination Institute that is featured in the fun-filled *Honey, I*

The monorail passes in front of Journey into Your Imagination

Photo by Corey Sandler. Used by permission from Disney Enterprises, Inc.

Shrunk the Audience show. Dreamfinder is gone, and Figment has a tiny supporting role to actor Eric Idle.

The resulting dark ride, though, is as flat as Spaceship Earth is round. It seems little more than a very weak carnival funhouse show, with upside-down rooms, a dark room filled with the sound of an approaching train, and lots of mirrors. Not very imaginative, in other words.

Disney insiders say that the ride is not a hit with management, either, and may be reworked once more.

The best part of the building is the redone Kodak exhibit at the end of the ride where visitors can play with all sorts of high-tech video and audio devices.

WOW ***Honey, I Shrunk the Audience*** FAST

A spectacular 3-D thriller that takes off where the two shape-altering Disney films (*Honey, I Shrunk the Kids* and *Honey, I Blew Up the Baby*) left off. In this case, it's the audience that shrinks instead of the kids. This is a theatrical performance that is simply not to be missed.

It begins outside the theater with a preshow sponsored by Kodak and based on their "true colors" advertising theme, an attractive and somewhat inspiring collection of photographs on the general idea of imagination and an extension of the imagination exhibit upstairs.

Then we find ourselves as honored guests at the presentation of the "Inventor of the Year" award to Wayne Szalinski, played by actor Rick Moranis. Other members of the film cast also appear in the feature, and are joined by funnyman Eric Idle of Monty Python's Flying Circus.

And finally we are invited within to see a demonstration of some of Wayne's greatest new inventions, including the Dimensional Duplicator and the No Mess Holographic Pet System.

You'll go through the doors on the left side of the preshow auditorium into the theater. You'll be asked to move all the way across a row to fill up all the seats; if you want to try to grab one of the best seats hold back a bit until about twenty-five people have entered a row and then enter.

As far as what happens next, we don't want to spoil the fun or play a cat-and-mouse game with you; oops, disregard that last hint.

The wild conclusion of the show comes when one of the machines goes berserk and ends up shrinking the entire audience down to toy size. "Stay in your seats and we will blow you up as soon as possible," says Wayne.

The auditorium conspires with the 3-D images to complete the illusion with moving seats, spectacular lighting, special film effects, and unusual effects that will tickle your fancy and sprinkle you with laughter.

The large theater seats 575 guests and will eat up a full waiting line inside the building; if the line stretches out onto the plaza you can expect at least a forty-five-minute wait. Lines will ebb and flow at the theater, reached from an entrance inside the doors of the Journey into Imagination to the left of the loading area for the theme ride. Go early or late to avoid lengthy waits.

The Land

Everyone has to eat, and The Land is a tasty collection of informative exhibits about food and our environment. The building, in part a giant greenhouse, also includes a popular food court restaurant. The sprawling pavilion is as large as all of Tomorrowland in the Magic Kingdom.

Wide world of food. The Land is one of the largest attractions at Walt Disney World. It covers some six acres and is as big as the entire Tomorrowland area in the Magic Kingdom. Stop and take a look at the huge mosaic at the entrance: some three thousand square feet in size, it is made of 150,000 separate pieces in 131 colors of marble, granite, slate, smalto (colored glass or enamel), Venetian glass, mirror, ceramic, pebbles, and gold.

WOW **Living with the Land.** A boat ride through the past and future of agriculture. Disney Imagineers created a storm scene as an introduction to a tour that passes through a rain forest, desert, and plain—traditional sources of food—and then into some amazing experiments with hydroponic farms, cultivated shrimp and fish, and a desert made to bloom with crops with the assistance of high-tech irrigation.

The opening storm scene now includes some very nice special effects with lightning and a rain forest, and a cast of animatronic creatures. Another significant change is that the opening segment of the ride is introduced by a woman, one of the few female voices in the park; once the boats enter into the farming areas the guide at the front of your boat will take over.

Among the advanced techniques you will see are "intercropping" of different plants to make the best use of soil and nutrients (coconut, cacao, and sweet potatoes in one example); growing plants vertically in hydroponic (soil-less) containers, which makes them easier to feed and inspect for pests; and an experiment in growing plants in simulated lunar soil, based on analysis of the real thing brought back from the moon by American astronauts.

On a recent visit the garden included bananas, papayas, ferns, rice, peanuts, bok choy, sugarcane, casaba, sweet potatoes, and some incredible varieties of squash. The simulated tropical and desert farms of The Land create vegetables for some of the restaurants in the pavilion.

One section of the farm includes a computer-controlled watering system that delivers individual amounts of moisture to plants as needed.

A fish farming "aquacell" grows crops of fish selected for their ability to thrive in a crowded environment. Fish under development on various trips have included sunshine bass, tilapia, catfish, pacu, sturgeon, and the strange-looking paddlefish, which is cultivated for its caviar. Some fish and vegetables you see here are served at some of the restaurants.

Among the most educational of all the exhibits at Epcot, Living with the Land is also a good place for a quick break. Preschoolers may be bored, but anyone else is sure to find something to learn. Lines build by midday to as much as an hour in length; come early or late.

Behind the Seeds Guided Greenhouse Tour. Serious gardeners and eaters will want to sign up to take this one-hour walking tour of The Land's greenhouses and labs, concentrating on soil-free gardening, fish farming, plant biotechnology, and pest management. Sign up for the tour at the desk near the Green Thumb Emporium on the lower level. There are only a limited number of places on the tours, which are offered from 10 A.M. to 4:30 P.M. Tickets are $6 for adults and $4 for children ages three to nine.

Food Rocks. This revue gives new meaning to the term *vegetable*. Only Disney would dare give us edible versions of our favorite rock 'n' roll stars. The Peach Boys (Beach Boys) sing about "good, good, good, good nutrition"; Pita Gabriel (Peter Gabriel) wants to be your High Fiber; Chubby Cheddar (Chubby Checker) tells you "Come on baby, let's exercise"; Neil Moussaka (Neil Sedaka) sings "Don't take my squash away from me; don't you leave me without broccoli. Eat your spinach. Yes, it's true, cause vegetables are good for you."

Cher-acudda (Cher) begs you to "Just keep him lean"; and The Wrapper (Tone Loc) discusses nutrient information labels. But wait, there's also Refrigerator Police (Sting) watching every little knish you eat, and The Get-the-Point Sisters (The Pointer Sisters). Who is real and who is artificial? Neil Sedaka, Cher, Little Richard, and Chubby Checker actually performed their own songs for the "Food Rocks" show. The other stars had singing stand-ins.

The Food Rocks Theater has a capacity of 250 for the thirteen-minute show and there should rarely be more than a fifteen-minute wait. The show replaced the overly cute Kitchen Kabaret show.

Before you enter the theater, by the way, take a moment to read some of the interesting food facts in the waiting area. There I learned why cashews are never sold in the shell: they are related to poison ivy and their shells contain an irritating oil. I also found out that many famous French sauces, including Mornay and Hollandaise, were not named for the chefs that created them but instead for the noblemen who featured them at their tables.

WOW ***Circle of Life.*** The animated stars of *The Lion King* reappear as the "actors" in an environmental spectacular.

Simba the lion, Timon the meerkat, and Pumbaa the warthog appear in colorful 70-mm glory, along with actors in a fable that begins when King Simba finds that Timon and Pumbaa are planning a new subdivision in the jungle, the "Hakuna Matata Lakeside Village."

Simba warns his friends about the mistakes made by a creature who has from time to time forgotten how everything is connected in the Circle of Life. Those creatures, of course, are humans.

You'll learn about some of modern science's efforts to deal with thoughtful use of land in urban and rural settings around the world. The film includes scenes of polluted wildlife and an oil spill, an ironic antidote to the Exxon Pavilion across the way. There is some very spectacular photography that builds off the *Lion King* film. For example, the famous thundering herds of animals of the cartoon move into a film of the real thing.

The auditorium for the *Circle of Life* is a bit strange for Disney World; once you leave the waiting area you'll go down a series of narrow stairways into the seating area. It may be a difficult climb for some. Those who climb all the way down will have to put up with a sometimes overly loud soundtrack.

The Living Seas

An ambitious but ultimately unsatisfying bust. There are one or two interesting exhibits here, but if you or your children are truly interested in learning about the watery two-thirds of our planet, you would be much better off making a visit to SeaWorld or a big-city aquarium.

But as long as you are here, check out the exhibits and interactive areas, including some of the antique diving equipment in the entrance and waiting area. When you enter the auditorium for a short film, lag back a bit and get a seat along the left side so that you will be first in line to enter the "hydrolators." The film—a superb explanation of the birth of the oceans and the origin of life from within them—is about twelve minutes. The ride that follows is about three minutes; allow about forty-five minutes for the full exhibit.

The movie does make one interesting point: humans have spent less time at the deepest points in the ocean than on the surface of the moon.

Caribbean Coral Reef Ride. The idea was great: take visitors on a tour within a huge saltwater aquarium filled with strange and wonderful marine life that include sharks, stingrays, parrot fish, and more. But the trip takes just three minutes and the setup to the ride—the trip deep down below the sea in elevator-like "hydrolators"—is hokey and there's no chance to stop and study. Check out the "Department of Pelagic Safety" certificate in the hydrolator.

Don't read this. We don't want to spoil the illusion here. So, if you don't want to know an inside tip about the hydrolators, stop reading this sidebar right here. OK? You've been warned. The hydrolators don't really dive down beneath the sea; the floor moves a few inches to simulate movement and bubbles move up the sides of elevator. Then you walk out the door on the other side of the wall. It's the same principle used in the Haunted Mansion and in more dramatic fashion in other simulator rides.

Sea Base Alpha. A set of exhibits about sea life and underwater technologies. Spend a bit of time studying the wave tank to understand the physics of breakers at the beach. Youngsters will enjoy climbing into the diving suits, and adults can grab a good picture when they poke their heads into the breathing bubbles.

Dolphins at the exhibit are participants in a project that uses a large keyboard to communicate with humans; scientists believe the dolphins are responding to instructions given them by humans, and are able to communicate with their handlers using the same device.

Epcot DiveQuest. Leave it to the folks at Disney to invent the ultimate dive site: guaranteed calm seas, no current, incredible visibility, vivid coral formations, more than sixty-five kinds of marine life, and an audience on the other side of a window.

After suiting up in waist-deep water, groups of eight divers are guided by a Living Seas specialist for a twenty-minute dive, followed by a twenty-minute free-dive period. The entire three-hour program includes a presentation on marine life research and conservation and a backstage overview of The Living Seas.

Divers must show proof of scuba certification (no junior certification) and sign a legal waiver. All gear is provided, with lockers for changing and showering. In 2001 Epcot DiveQuest cost $140, and Epcot admission is not required. Dives are scheduled daily at 4:30 P.M. and 5:30 P.M. For reservations call ☎ (407) 939-8687.

Eating Your Way Through Epcot's Future World

Innoventions

Electric Umbrella. A large fast-food eatery inside Innoventions East, offering burgers, chicken, and salads. An outdoor terrace is a good bet in temperate weather. The restaurant features an unusual electronic scoreboard for menus (easy to adjust offerings and prices). Items include a chicken sandwich with fajita seasoning for $6.59, hot dogs for $4.34, cheeseburgers for $4.34, and a meatless burger with fries for $5.24.

Fountain View Espresso and Bakery. Baked goods. Espresso, cappuccino, latté, cafe mocha, and other hot drinks priced about $2.50. Also offered are coffees with Amaretto, Bailey's Irish Cream, Frangelico, or Sambucca for about $4.29, plus beer and wine. This is a good place—if you can get one of the relatively few seats—to sit and watch the fountain show. You can't see the fireworks from here, though.

Ice Station Cool. An unusual bit of marketing, this little igloo celebrates the global culture of Coca-Cola culture. A soda fountain offers free samples of soft drinks from around the world. On one visit the samples included Smart Watermelon from China, Kinley Lemon from Israel, Lilt Pineapple from the United Kingdom, Vegitabeta from Japan, and Krest Ginger Ale from Mozambique. You can also purchase Coke T-shirts in languages that include Japanese, Arabic, Russian, and Korean.

Key

= Fast food

= Pub

= Full-service restaurant

Pasta Piazza Ristorante. Pizza, pasta, and more.

Wonders of Life

Pure and Simple. Within Wonders of Life, across from the AnaComical Players' stage. Waffles and fruit, salads, sandwiches, frozen yogurt, and sundaes. "Guilt-free goodies," $1.50 to $5.

Well-named for its small offerings of frozen yogurt, shakes, muffins, and other healthful fare, presented in an attractive cafe-like setting. Seating is at colorful blue metal tables and chairs, like something out of "The Jetsons."

Special offerings priced from about $3 to $5 include a beta carotene salad (assorted veggies with a cantaloupe–balsamic vinaigrette dressing), venison chili soup, and a submarine with turkey pastrami, turkey ham, turkey breast, turkey salami, low-fat mozzarella, lettuce, and tomato on a multigrain roll. Sweets include nonfat yogurt sundaes, fruit cups, and fruit juice "smoothies."

The Land

Sunshine Season Food Fair. An attractive food court downstairs in The Land pavilion. One of the best things about eating at The Sunshine Season Food Fair in The Land is that everyone in your party can eat something different, shopping at the various stands and meeting at a table in the court. Just don't promise your kids a hot dog, a greasy burger, or fries when you arrive to eat; you'll have to get those elsewhere.

Stands include the **Barbecue Store**, offering beef and chicken sandwiches (about $5) or chicken and ribs (about $7); the **Picnic Fare** selling cheese, fruit, and sausages; the **Bakery**, a fine place for bagels, rolls, muffins, cakes, and cookies; the **Potato Store**, selling baked potatoes with stuffing that includes cheese, bacon, and beef ($2 to $3.25); and the **Cheese Shoppe**, offering quiche, pasta, vegetable lasagna, and . . . cheese. Dessert counters include the **Beverage House** ($1.25 to $2.50) and the **Ice Cream Stand** ($1.50 to $2.75). Also, select a double chocolate brownie, giant cookie, or apple pie. There is also a selection of beers, wine, piña coladas, and margaritas.

All stands share the same kitchen and there is some duplication; the same excellent brownie, for example, is available at several counters.

The Garden Grill. Upstairs in The Land pavilion. One of the most attractive and interesting full-service restaurants in Future World. The entire

Early value meals. Epcot sometimes offers discount early-bird meals at many of its restaurants for diners who arrive between 4:30 and 6 P.M. Check at Earth Station when you arrive at Epcot to see if this unadvertised special deal is in effect when you visit.

Fast food? The speed of rotation of the Garden Grill is adjusted to about one revolution per meal. The lunchtime speed is slightly quicker (about 448 feet per hour); dinnertime slows the turntable down to about 422 feet per hour. Either way, you're not likely to suffer from jet lag.

room revolves around a portion of the boat tour down below. It is now given over to character dining "experiences" starring Mickey, Minnie, and Chip 'n Dale.

Breakfast includes scrambled eggs, grilled smokehouse ham steak, grits, and biscuits. Lunch and dinner specialties include rotisserie-cooked chicken, hickory-smoked steak, and various fresh vegetables, including some from the gardens at the pavilion. Breakfast is priced about $14.95 for adults and $8.25 for children ages three to eleven; lunch costs about $16.95 for adults and $9.95 for children ages three to eleven; and dinner is priced at $17.50 for adults and $9.95 for children.

Parties holding reservations can bypass lines and enter directly into The Land pavilion within fifteen minutes of their reservation time.

Outside the entrance is a display of some of the fresh herbs and vegetables grown in the pavilion's greenhouses and served in the restaurant. You will see basil, chives, rosemary, parsley, thyme, and some beautiful peppers, beans, squashes, cucumbers, and eggplants.

The Living Seas

Coral Reef Restaurant. In the lower level of The Living Seas exhibit, to the right of the main entrance. Fish, shellfish, beef, chicken, and salads. Lunch, $6 to $15; dinner, $19 and up. Beer, mixed drinks, and a full wine list. Reservations are suggested; make them at the Earth Station. Open for lunch from 11:30 A.M. to 2:45 P.M., and for dinner from 4:30 P.M. to the closing hour for the park.

This place gives a new meaning to the idea of a seafood restaurant. You see food, the food sees you. We kept seeing diners nervously eyeing the passing sharks in the coral reef behind the huge windows alongside the tables; we suspect they worried *they* were going to be the seafood.

The best seats in the tank, er . . . restaurant, are eight tables along the glass wall. Other tables are as much as twenty feet from the fish. However, the restaurant is arranged in three terraces that give all guests a relatively good view of the aquarium wall.

Anyhow, there is a fine selection of fish and shellfish; there are also some beef and chicken selections. Specialties include grilled fillet of tuna wrapped in plantains, the Coral Reef Clambake with half a lobster and shrimp, maple-glazed salmon, and steak and chicken offerings.

Attractions at World Showcase

The rest of the World's Fair at Epcot is the World Showcase, a collection of entertainment-education-tourism-trade exhibits from an unusual mix of countries. With the possible exception of the United Nations, nowhere else will you find Germany between Italy and China, or Mexico beside Norway.

And though other parts of the vast Disney empire may be individually more impressive, there are few vistas more spectacular than the viewing area at the six o'clock position on World Showcase Lagoon. Displayed in a circle before you are the pavilions of the select nations of the world; all around is lush vegetation (sometimes adapted to the vagaries of Central Florida weather) including tens of thousands of rose bushes and trees, Callery pears, Washingtonia fan palms, and camphor trees.

Most of the young staffers come from the country of the pavilion they work at, participating in the World Showcase Fellowship Program. During a one-year stay, the young people take part in a work-study curriculum.

As at any World's Fair, it is important to draw an important distinction here: going to the Mexico pavilion is not the same as experiencing the ancient reality of Mexico. Seeing the spectacular movie at the Chinese exhibit does not mean you have been to Mongolia or Beijing. And taking the water ride at Norway does not qualify you to say that you have explored the Norwegian fjords.

Instead, the pavilions—some better than others—do an excellent job of whetting the appetite for travel and educating us all on how different and alike we are. If you can get your kids excited about a visit to England or Canada or Italy, then a trip to Orlando may pay dividends all around; or, maybe it's your kids that have always wanted to go to Japan and they needed to convince you.

One welcome addition in the World Showcase is the **Kids Zone** outside many pavilions where young visitors can engage in arts and crafts and educational activities related to each international destination; check the schedule when you arrive.

Mexico

The pavilion is set within a striking pre-Colombian–style pyramid, festooned with giant serpent heads and sculptures of Toltec warriors and patterned after the Aztec Temple of Quetzalcoatl at Teotihuacán. Quetzalcoatl, the god of life, is represented by large serpent heads that can be seen along the entranceway.

The landscaping around the Cantina de San Angel depicts the arid desert regions of Mexico; the moist tropics of the Yucatan jungle are echoed with the lush greenery around the Mayan temple.

Inside is a magical wonderland of a happy Mexican village. You'll enter into the colorful **Plaza de Los Amigos**, filled with carts selling handcrafted sombreros of varying sizes, toys, sandals, and other objects—sold at prices that are relative bargains within Walt Disney World. On a terrace near the "river," a mariachi band lets loose with its almost impossibly happy sound.

And down by the water, there's a charming Mexican cantina. The food is good, not great, but in the **San Angel Inn and Restaurant** is one of the most spectacular settings for dinner within the park, a magical indoor setting. Take a few moments on your way into or out of the pavilion to look at the small but spectacular collection of ancient Mexican art.

El Rio del Tiempo. A charming, happy journey to Mexico—sort of a south-of-the-border version of the Magic Kingdom's It's a Small World. This six-minute boat ride, though, is sure to appeal to children of all ages. There's a touch of Mexico's majestic past as a regional power, a greeting from a Mayan high priest, a humorous acknowledgment of the country's present day as a tourist mecca (enjoy the salespeople who scuttle from screen to screen to try to sell their wares), and a dazzling indoor fireworks salute as dozens of animated dolls dance around you. The indoor fireworks of El Rio del Tiempo ("The River of Time") are produced with cool fiber optics.

The Mexican pavilion can become quite crowded at midday; I'd suggest a visit before 11 A.M. or after dinner.

Norway

The Land of the Midnight Sun has constructed one of the more interesting exhibits at Epcot. You'll enter on cobblestone streets of a simulated ancient village; take special note of the wood-stave church modeled after one built in 1250 A.D. There's also an interesting—and very expensive—set of stores offering clothing, crafts, and toys. Children will love the Legos table in the gift shop; Legos are made by a company in neighboring Denmark.

The wooden building outside the main pavilion is a *stavkirke* or Stave Church, styled after the Gol Church of Hallingdal, which dates to about 1250; within is a display of Norse artifacts.

The pavilion incorporates four distinct Norwegian architectural styles. The Puffin's Roost and Kringla Bakeri are built in Setesdal style with grass roofs and thick log walls. The Fjoring shop uses the gables of Bergen style. The castle represents the Oslo-style fourteenth-century Akershus, which still stands guard in the harbor of Oslo. And the stucco and stone Informasjon building is built in Alesund style.

Maelstrom. A dramatic and fun look at Norway from Viking times through modern day on a storm-tossed oil platform in the North Sea. You'll board Viking longboats modeled after those used by Erik the Red one thousand years ago and set sail into a world of fjords, forests, and the occasional troll. Some very young visitors may be momentarily scared by the "monsters"; all riders are likely to be thrilled by the indoor lightning storm in the North Sea.

You'll know you are in trouble near the end of the short four-minute ride when one of the trolls gets angry: "I cast a spell: back, back, over the falls." Sure enough, your boat will appear to travel over a cliff to land in the World Showcase Lagoon of Epcot, before reversing direction for a gentle plunge down a waterfall.

There's a movie at the end of the ride that I find much less thrilling than the ride; if you move quickly you can walk right through the theater and out the door before the lights go down.

The Maelstrom ride can become quite crowded at midday; visit early or late.

Shops feature trolls, beautiful (but pricey) knit sweaters from Scandinavia, trolls, leather items, trolls, candy, and trolls.

China

One of the most successful of all of the Epcot pavilions at transporting the visitor to a foreign land. The building is a small-scale but beautifully replicated version of Beijing's Temple of Heaven. On busy days look for dragon dancers and acrobats performing outside near the replica of the *Zhao Yang Men* ("Gate of the Golden Sun").

The Hall of Prayer for Good Harvests is a half-scale reproduction of the actual hall within the Temple of Heaven near Beijing. There are twelve outer columns supporting the roof, representing both the months of the year and the twelve-year cycle of the Chinese calendar. Near the center of the room are four columns representing the four seasons; the columns support a square beam, which stands for the Earth, and the assemblage is topped off by a round beam, representing heaven.

WOW ***Wonders of China: Land of Beauty, Land of Time.*** Simply breathtaking and not to be missed. A Circle-Vision 360 tour of China guaranteed to open your eyes to the beauty and vastness of this still scarcely known nation. We've all seen pictures of the Great Wall, although never so spectacularly as presented here. And recently, we've been granted views of the fabulous Forbidden City of Beijing. But consider the thrill of being able to look back over your shoulder at the gate through which you came. But then, there is more: the incredible Shilin Stone Forest, the Gobi Desert, the Grand Canal, tropical palms, and snow-capped mountains.

A Disney film crew had to carry the six-hundred-pound camera 4,500 steps up the steep slopes of Huangshan Mountain in Annui Province for what ended up as just a few seconds on the screen.

By the way, if you are thrilled by the images of China presented in the film, you may want to make a visit to the Splendid China theme park in Kissimmee; read about it in Chapter 23.

Lines for the nineteen-minute film build during the day, but rarely add up to more than about half an hour; come early or late to avoid them altogether. The only drawback to this presentation is the fact that the theater has no seats. There are rails to lean upon—sitting on them is frowned upon—and small children and short adults may have a hard time seeing the screen without a lift. To make things worse, no strollers are allowed.

Land of Many Faces. An impressive exhibit that introduces many of China's ethnic minorities.

Yong Feng Shangdian Department Store. A shopping mall of merchandise from China, including silk clothing, embroidered items, and crafts. The huge collection includes some of the more interesting foreign items at Epcot, including silk robes, wooden toys, jewelry, and prints.

You can also have your name written in Chinese characters on a scroll, T-shirt, or sweatshirt at a booth outside.

How high's the water? You may not even notice as you cross it, but there is a small drawbridge between the Chinese pavilion and Germany near the Village Traders shop. Each day at about 5 P.M. the bridge lifts and some of the floating props for the parade are taken through onto the lake for the nightly show.

Dragonslayer. The statue in the center of the square is of Saint George and the dragon he slayed on a pilgrimage to the Middle East. Saint George is the patron saint of soldiers, and statues in his honor are common in Bavaria.

Germany

Wunderbar! A visit to a make-believe German village complete with a beer garden, teddy bear toy shop, wine cellar, and a pastry shop of your dreams. The high wall at the back of the showcase is based on the Eltz Castle on the Mosel River, and Stahleck Castle on the Rhine.

Biergarten. Almost as loud and fun as a hall at the Oktoberfest in Munich—especially as the night goes on. The lively restaurant offers an all-you-can-eat banquet of red cabbage, sauerbraten, sausage, rotisserie chicken, and smoked pork loin. Desserts include apple strudel.

Der Bücherwurm. Here's a bookworm's delight, filled with books from and about Germany. The facade of the building is modeled after the Kaufhaus, a sixteeenth-century merchants' hall in the Black Forest town of Freiburg.

Der Teddybär. You've been warned: this is a children-parent-grandparent trap full of fabulous toys, dolls, and various stuffed animals.

Die Weihnachts Ecke. Every day is Christmas in this shop full of ornaments, decorations, and gifts.

Glas und Porzellan. An outlet of Goebel, the glass and porcelain maker best known as the maker of Hummel figurines.

Süssigkeiten. We're uncertain whether to recommend you visit this shop on an empty or a full stomach. Let's put it this way: a full stomach will save you a lot of money. The cookies, candies, and pretzels are unlike anything you will find this side of Germany, and are worth a trip from anywhere.

Volkskunst. A crafts market of clothing, carved dolls, cuckoo clocks, and more.

Weinkeller. The shop stocks several hundred varieties of German wines, as well as a selection of beer mugs, wine glasses, and other drinking items. Germans are serious about their beer; if you have any doubts, check out the mugs for sale at the Weinkeller. One of them is big enough to hold a couple of gallons of brew.

Italy

Like China, the Italian pavilion is one of the more successful efforts in terms of giving the visitor a feeling of walking the streets of a foreign land. Take the time to study the various architectural styles. Out front is a 105-foot-tall "campanile," or bell tower, a version of one of the landmarks of Saint Mark's Square in Venice, and the replica of the square itself is beautifully constructed; all that is missing are the pigeons, which explains why this version of Saint Mark's is so Disney-clean.

The detailed replica of the angel on top of the campanile in the re-created Venice is covered with real gold leaf. The marble stones for the buildings, though, have no marble in them: they are actually fiberglass that has been painted and treated.

At the top of one of the columns at the entrance to Saint Mark's Square is a likeness of Saint Theodore, an important military leader in early Venetian history. Topping the other column is the winged Lion of Saint Mark's, the mythical guardian of the city of Venice. The stairway and portico alongside the Doge's Palace are drawn from Berona, while the town hall is reminiscent of the style of northern Italy.

Landscaping around the garden area includes bougainvillea, citrus plants including orange and lemon trees, and colorful blue, white, and pink hanging baskets. Down at the edge of the World Showcase Lagoon is a gondola mooring. And around the square is a collection of delicious and attractive stores. Outside the square look for the lively and irreverent performances of *Il Commedia di Bologna*.

Delizie Italiane. An open-air market with sweet delicacies of all description.

La Cucina Italiana. Gourmet foods and wines, as well as fine cooking accessories.

Il Bel Cristallo. Fine crystalware, including colorful Venetian glass and porcelain figurines.

United States

WOW **The American Adventure.** In our early visits to Epcot the United States pavilion was one we passed by as the day got long. It's located at the very "back" of the park, and besides, we're Americans, so why should we be interested in something known as "The American Adventure"?

Boy, were we ever wrong! The exhibit here is the ultimate in Disney animatronics, a rip-roaring, flag-waving show on a larger scale than almost anything else at Walt Disney World or anywhere else. The unlikely costars of the production are author Mark Twain and statesman and inventor Ben Franklin. Never mind that Twain wasn't born until forty-five years after Franklin died; such things don't matter when figures from history are brought back as robots.

The walls of the main hall are adorned with an interesting group of quotes from an unusual collection of Americans, including:

Wendell Willkie: "Our way of living together in America is a strong but delicate fabric. It is made up of many threads. It has been woven over many centuries by the patience and sacrifice of countless liberty-loving men and women."

Walt Disney: "Our greatest natural resource is the minds of our children."

Charles Lindbergh: "I don't believe in taking foolish chances, but nothing can be accomplished without taking any chance at all."

Ayn Rand: "Throughout the centuries there were men who took first steps down new roads armed with nothing but their own vision."

Herman Melville: "Our blood is as the flood of the Amazon, made up of a

Grumpy and Dopey were absent that day. In the auditorium of The American Adventure, the twelve statues flanking the stage are said to represent the Spirits of America. On the right, from the back of the hall to the front, are Adventure, Self-Reliance, Knowledge, Pioneering, Heritage, and Freedom. On the left, from back to front, are Discovery, Compassion, Independence, Tomorrow, Innovation, and Individualism. The forty-four flags in the Hall of Flags represent the banners that have flown over the colonial, revolutionary, and independent United States.

No mistake. The clock on the facade of the United States building uses a IIII instead of IV for the four o'clock hour; this is an accurate reproduction of Georgian architecture of the time.

thousand noble currents all pouring into one . . . we are not a nation so much as a world."

The twenty-nine-minute show starts with the Pilgrims landing at Plymouth Rock, moves on to the Boston Tea Party and General George Washington's winter at Valley Forge. There's an eclectic collection of well-known and lesser-known figures of American history and culture.

To Disney's credit, the pantheon of heroes here includes women, Native Americans, and African-Americans. We meet characters such as Susan B. Anthony, Alexander Graham Bell, Frederick Douglass, Chief Joseph, and Martin Luther King Jr., Charles Lindbergh, and Teddy Roosevelt,

On the cultural side are representations of Muhammad Ali, Lucille Ball, Marilyn Monroe, John Wayne, and Walt Disney himself. And don't overlook the imposing Georgian building itself and the paintings and statues in the hallways.

Among special effects used in The American Adventure is multi-plane cinematography, developed by Disney technicians to add the illusion of depth to animated films, including *Snow White and the Seven Dwarfs* and *Pinocchio*.

The buildings at the pavilion reflect American architecture from the late 1790s through 1830, including English Georgian, during the reign of King George III. Other examples are drawn from Williamsburg, Independence Hall, the Old State House in Boston, and Thomas Jefferson's Monticello home.

By the way, the 110,000 "bricks" on the exterior of the main building are made from fiberglass formed and colored to appear the correct age. The landscaping is in the style of an historic formal garden in Philadelphia.

Lines at The American Adventure can build at midday but, except on the busiest days, are rarely larger than the seats in the large auditorium. The best seats are in the first few rows nearest the stage.

Japan

A typically understated but elegant Japanese setting, featuring a reproduction of an eighth-century pagoda from the Horyuji Temple, the oldest completely preserved temple complex in Japan. Each of the five levels of the Goju-no-to (five-story pagoda) symbolize one of the five basic elements: earth, water, fire, wind, and sky. Amateur gardeners will marvel at the detail in the rock gardens and ponds. Fish fanciers should check out the koi in the ponds. Rocks symbolize the long life of the earth; the water symbolizes the sea, a source of life.

Most of the plants and trees of the Japanese garden are native to the southern United States but were selected because they were similar in appearance to those in Japan.

The red Gate of Honor (Torii) at the entrance to the Japanese pavilion is a sign of good luck. The gates were originally intended as perches for roosters to welcome the daily arrival of the sun goddess. The one at the pavilion is modeled after one in Hiroshima Bay.

Bijutsu-Kan Gallery. A small museum of Japanese arts, culture, and craft. The exhibition is changed from time to time.

Mitsukoshi Department Store. The farthest west branch of a large Japanese department store, offering a selection of clothing, dolls, toys, and trinkets. The food section includes some unusual items such as fried sweet potatoes, shrimp flavored chips, and tomato crackers. Gardeners may want to bring home a grow-it-yourself bonsai kit.

Morocco

Step through the Bab Boujoulad gate to a beautifully detailed replica of the Koutoubia Minaret in Marrakesh. It's a world of fezzes, saris, and belly dancers.

Bab Boujoulad is the main gate to the ancient city of Fez, known as the Medina. It was founded in the year 786 by the Idrissids. In the Medina section of the pavilion is a reproduction of the Chella Minaret in the capital city of Rabat. There is also a reproduction of the Nejjarine Fountain in Fez.

Check out the very full Senegal date palm to the right of the pavilion. The intricate tilework of the Morocco pavilion is among the most authentic recreations of a foreign nation at Epcot; note that none of the tiles are perfect, because Muslims believe that only Allah is without flaw.

The folklore, dances, and music of Morocco presented in the square outside the pavilion. Belly dancing and music from the regions of Tangiers, Fez, Casablanca, the Andaluz, and Marrakesh are presented at the Restaurant Marrakesh.

Gallery of Arts and History. A museum of arts, crafts, and culture, with a changing display. Nearby is a branch of the **Moroccan National Tourist Office** with information for visitors who would like to make a journey to the real thing.

Within the courtyard is a collection of fascinating shops, including **Casablanca Carpets** for handmade Berber and Rabat rugs; **Tangier Traders** for leather goods, woven belts, and fezzes; **Medina Arts** for crafts; and **Jewels of the Sahara**, selling silver, gold, beads, and precious and semiprecious jewel items. There's a sign at the shops inviting shoppers to "make an offer" for items they want to purchase; start with a large discount from the list price and be happy with a small break.

France

Vive la France! France lives in a small-scale reproduction of a section of the streets of Paris, complete with an elegant theater, shops, and a bakery and

Ooh, la la. The costumes of the pretty jeune filles at France's pavilion are modeled after dresses worn in Edouard Manet's famous nightclub painting, Le Bar aux Folies-Bergère.

Eiffel tiny. The one-tenth-scale replica of the Eiffel Tower was constructed using Gustave Eiffel's original blueprints.

sweet shop of your dreams. There's even a one-tenth scale Eiffel Tower atop the pavilion. It's for appearance only, though—there is no top-level observation tower as there is in the real thing.

Take a few moments to look at the architectural styles, which include mansard roofs and ironwork harking from France's *Belle Epoque* ("Beautiful Age") in the late nineteenth century. The park on the right side of the pavilion is stocked with Lombardy poplars, looking somewhat like the famous setting of Seurat's painting, *Sunday Afternoon on the Island of La Grande Jatte*.

Impressions de France. Within the Palais du Cinéma is a lovely eighteen-minute film that hits all of the highlights of France—from Paris to Versailles to Mont Saint Michel to Cannes, and lots of lesser-known but equally beautiful settings, accompanied by lovely and familiar music, including "Gaité Parisienne" by Jacques Offenbach, "Trois Gymnopédies" by Eric Satie, "Carnival of the Animals" by Camille Saint-Saëns, "Claire de Lune" by Claude Debussy, "Daphnis et Chloé" by Maurice Ravel, and other familiar French works. The large screens extend two-hundred degrees around the theater, which has the added advantage of seats for all viewers.

Lines build at midday; visit early or late on crowded days. Stop and take a look at the postshow area, which is modeled after Les Halles, the former commercial marketplace of Paris.

Plume et Palette. One of the most high-tone of all shops in Epcot, with its entranceway modeled after one of the more famous decorative entranceways to the Paris Metro subway. The interior of the store and the showcases compete with the lovely gifts and artworks for sale here.

La Signature. Get a whiff of the perfumes and a peek at the clothing.

For the gourmand, there is **La Maison du Vin,** which, as its name suggests, is a Gallic House of Wines. And send your sweet tooth to **Galerie des Halles,** a bakery and candy store in a building that is modeled after the famous Parisian market.

United Kingdom

Merry Olde England (and the rest of the United Kingdom) is represented at Epcot by a selection of attractive shops and a first-class pub that sports a nice selection of British beers; it may be one of the few places in Florida where you can get a decent kidney pie.

Look for typical attention to detail in the construction of the buildings in the interesting streets of the United Kingdom. Never mind that the thatched roofs are made from plastic fibers (for fire protection) or the smoke stains applied by artists with paint brushes; you probably didn't notice that until I pointed it out. The streetscape includes a thatched-roof cottage from the 1500s, a formal square with a Hyde Park–like bandstand, a London city square, and an exterior facade of the style of Hampton Court.

If you fancy you have a Green Thumb, or wish you did, be sure to check out the perfectly tended little English garden next to the Magic of Wales shop. The gardens include all sorts of roses from many parts of the former British Empire.

By the way, the secret garden also is an excellent place to watch the *IllumiNations* show on the lagoon.

The Toy Soldier. Playthings for men and boys, women and girls of all ages. The shop's exterior is modeled after an ancient Scottish manor.

Lords and Ladies. More toys, of a slightly nobler fashion: chess sets, dartboards, beer mugs, stamps, coins, and more, inside a hall where the Knights of the Round Table would have felt at home.

Pringle of Scotland. Lay down your chips for beautiful knit sweaters and other articles of clothing.

The Queen's Table. Her highness may be the only one among us with the available cash to do some serious shopping here, but it's fun to poke (carefully) among the fabulous Royal Doulton china, figurines, and Toby mugs. The crests for four of the realm's most famous schools (Oxford, Cambridge, Eton, and Edinburgh) are displayed in the upstairs windows of the shop.

The Magic of Wales. A gift shop of small items and souvenirs from Wales; prices are the most reasonable among emporia here.

The Tea Caddy. Here you'll find considerably more kinds of leaves in bags and cans than you're likely to find at the corner grocery.

Canada

The vast range of experiences of Canada is reflected in the landmarks of the pavilion. At front is a native totem pole; out back is a scaled-down Canadian Rocky Mountain; and between is a scaled-down reproduction of the stone Château Laurier in Ottawa. The gardens of the Canada pavilion are based on the famed Butchart Gardens of Victoria, British Columbia, in western Canada.

O Canada! Another breathtaking Circle-Vision 360 movie that brings you up close and personal to bobcats, wolves, bears, and other creatures of the wild, to human glories such as the Cathédral de Notre Dame, to the ski slopes of the Rockies, and onto the ice of a hockey game in a scene so real you'll wish you had a goalie's mask on. Did we mention getting caught in the middle of the rodeo ring in the Calgary Stampede or the breathtaking camera ride down the toboggan slide at Québec City?

The waiting area for the film is a cave-like mountain lodge from the Canadian Rockies. Be advised that you'll have to stand to watch this extraordinary eighteen-minute movie.

Northwest Mercantile. A modern-day version of a frontier trading post. You'll trade dollars (credit cards accepted, too) for sheepskins, lumberjack shirts, maple syrup, and Indian artifacts and crafts.

La Boutique des Provinces. Products from Canada's French-speaking regions, including Québec and parts of Ontario and the Atlantic provinces.

Eating Your Way Through Epcot's World Showcase

Mexico

Cantina de San Angel. Tacos, salads, and burritos, \$3.50 to \$6. This outdoor cantina is located opposite the Aztec pyramid, beside the lagoon. Get a quick Mexican fix at this attractive outdoor cafe: tortillas, tostadas, and sweet churros (fried dough dipped in powdered sugar and cinnamon).

Small, round, wooden tables seat four under colorful umbrellas during the day and under high, soft-light lanterns at night. Meals are accompanied by Mexican music in a setting that includes native flowers on a tiled patio inside a stucco wall. The platos Mexicanos include corn or flour tortillas filled with chicken or beef, priced from about \$4 to \$6. Side dishes include refried beans or chips and salsa. Desserts, priced from about \$2 to \$3, include flan or churros.

The outdoor Cantina de San Angel, outside the Mexico pavilion along the lagoon, is an interesting place to view the nightly *IllumiNations* show over a cold beer or soft drink. Tables fill up early.

San Angel Inn. Lunch from \$5 to \$15. Dinner from \$15. Children's menu. Reservations are suggested and necessary in busy season.

This restaurant is inside a simulated Aztec pyramid in the center of the Mexican exhibit, our favorite location for a restaurant at Epcot. Diners sit on a terrace overlooking the passing boats on the River of Time (*El Rio del Tiempo*), under a make-believe starlit sky. It feels about as real as any Mexican place north of the border; in fact, the eatery is run by the same company that operates the well-known restaurant of the same name in Mexico City.

Live percussion and a mariachi band add to the atmosphere. Look beyond the River of Time to view pyramids, a volcano, and a campfire.

The menu offers above-average Mexican fare. Specialties include *carne asada Tampiquena, huachinango a la Veracruzana*, tacos, burritos, and enchiladas.

On visits we have made, lunchtime offerings have included the interesting and traditional *mole poblano* (chicken and spices with a chocolate-based sauce) and a combination platter (beef taco, enchilada, quesadilla, and avocado dip). At dinner we have been offered baked California lobster (\$26) and *camarones enchiladas* (shrimp sautéed with pepper).

Dos Equis and Tecate beers, margaritas, and wine are also available.

Lunch or dinner children's offerings include soft tortilla with chicken or beef, fried chicken, or grilled beef taco. Traditional Mexican desserts include flan or *capirotada* (bread pudding). Libations include Mexican coffee with Kahlua, tequila, and cream.

Key

= Fast Food

= Pub

= Full-service restaurant

Norway

Kringla Bakeri og Kafé. Open-faced sandwiches and pastries, \$3 to \$4.

This interesting kafé is located on the left side of the Norwegian pavillion, behind the replica of the church.

What else would you expect to be offered at a Kringla Bakeri than fresh *kringles*? All right, then: a kringle is a candied pretzel. Also available are *vaflers*, which are waffles covered with powdered sugar and jam and other sweets. Sample the wonderful white rice cream pudding or chocolate ball, like a three-inch truffle.

Open-faced sandwiches ($3 to $5) are very well presented for a medium-to-small serving. Offerings include tongue, beef, smoked salmon, mackerel, and ham. And of course, there's a herring platter.

Early bird meals. Oslo, the capital and major port of Norway, lies at the head of the Oslo Fjord. The earliest settlement was on the Akershus Peninsula, where a royal fortress was built about 1300. The building still stands, used for state banquets.

Chairs and tables are available outside, between Norway's Ancient Church and the shops at the pavilion.

Restaurant Akershus. Buffet with hot and cold meat, cheese, pasta, and dessert. Lunch, $11.25 for adults and $4.25 for children; dinner $17.25 for adults and $7.50 for children. Reservations are available and necessary on busy days. Open from 11:30 A.M. to 3:30 P.M. for lunch, and 4:30 to 8:30 P.M. for dinner.

This restaurant is located inside a replica of the famous castle of Akershus in the Oslo harbor on the right side of the Epcot Norway exhibit.

Visitors are offered a version of a Royal Norwegian Buffet *koldbord*, or "cold table," with more than forty items. You'll find more types of herring than you ever imagined possible, along with hot and cold smoked salmon, turkey, or mackerel. You can also find meatballs, scrambled eggs, lamb with cabbage, mashed rutabaga, hot smoked pork with honey mustard sauce, and more. Be sure to take advantage of the offer by the waiters and waitresses for guided tours of the *koldbord*. Desserts, wine, beer, and soft drinks are a la carte; free refills are offered on soft drinks.

Akershus is an interesting excursion for the adventurous, although most children we know will find the offerings a bit strange and unappealing. Even some adults will consider the buffet to be an unending selection of appetizers without the main course. In recent years the offerings have been broadened to include more pedestrian fare: peel-and-eat shrimp, meatballs with gravy, and macaroni and cheese.

The white stone walls and tile floors offer a pleasant, cool atmosphere for lunch or dinner. The rustic elegance of high ceilings and wooden beams are enhanced by the appetizing (to some) odor of cabbage and vinegar.

China

Lotus Blossom Cafe. Stir-fry, eggrolls, sweet-and-sour chicken, soup, and more, $2 to $6. Lunch, dinner.

This is a quality fast-food restaurant located near the entrance to the China pavilion beside the Nine Dragons Restaurant. It offers covered outdoor dining in a cafe or patio setting. The dining area is tastefully decorated; the food is better than most fast-food operations.

Goes great with chili dogs. For an unusual treat, try the red bean ice cream offered as a dessert at the Nine Dragons restaurant in China.

For the most variety for your money try one of the combination platters. For a lighter meal, sample a bowl of soup for about $3. Chinese beer, tea, and soft drinks are available.

Nine Dragons Restaurant. Varied traditional Chinese cuisine in Mandarin, Cantonese, Kiangche, and Szechuan styles, plus appetizers. Luncheon entrees range from $5 to $15; dinner entrees start at $15. Reservations are required at busy times. Open daily from 11 A.M. through the closing time for the park.

In a setting like an Oriental palace, this quiet restaurant is located near the entrance of the China exhibit, on the left side as you enter. Look up as you walk into the waiting area to see an interesting golden dragon hanging from the ceiling. An ancient robe hangs on the back wall of the waiting area.

As fancy as it is, the selection of food is no better than many average Chinese restaurants, and not as impressive as gourmet Asian eateries. Specialties include *kang bo* chicken and red bean ice cream. Chinese beer as well as specialty drinks and Chinese cordials also are available.

Outpost

Village Traders. Located in a dead area (space for a new pavilion?) between Germany and China. A group of huts there offers vegetarian delights, including a "vegetable box" for $1.40 (you might call it a salad); the box with dips costs $2. A selection of fresh fruit is also available.

Germany

Biergarten. Traditional German fare including potatoes, pork, and bratwurst, served for lunch and dinner in all-you-can-eat banquet-style dining. The luncheon buffet, offered from 11:30 A.M. to 3 P.M. was priced at about $9.95 for adults, and $4.75 for children eleven and younger; offerings include sausages, rotisserie chicken, salads, red cabbage, and potatoes. At dinner the menu expands to include sauerbraten and smoked pork; prices increase to $15.75 for adults and $6.99 for children eleven and younger.

Located at the rear of the German exhibit off the Sommerfest courtyard, the Biergarten offers a loud and raucous atmosphere that gets louder as the evening wears on. Inside you'll feel like you are in a German beer hall at night.

One million bottles of beer on the wall. . . . The famous Oktoberfest is celebrated in Munich, Germany, every October. Germany has the highest per capita beer consumption in the world, about forty gallons per person per year.

You'll dine at long tables, served by waiters and waitresses in alpine dress. The setting includes some small-town shops and a stage for the nightly musical shows.

Wash it all down with a huge thirty-three-ounce stein of beer (up to $7.50) or German wine and sit back and enjoy the floor show of oompah music and other lively tunes. All in all, a lot of noisy fun.

Sommerfest. Bratwurst und strudel und Black Forest cake und beer for about $2 to $4. Lunch, dinner, snacks. Sommerfest offers German fast-food treats served at an attractive outdoor cafe located at the right rear of the German exhibit outside the Biergarten. You won't have any trouble finding this interesting and different establishment; follow the sharp odor of wurst and sauerkraut. Select a German beer to accompany one of the sandwich offerings.

Italy

L'Originale Alfredo di Roma Ristorante. Veal, chicken, pasta, and seafood entrees plus appetizers and dessert in an Italian atmosphere; there are strolling musicians at dinner. Lunch menu items range from about $5 to $20; dinner entrees start at $15.

A children's lunch and dinner menu is offered. Reservations are required; stop by the Earth Station on the day you wish to dine.

You'll enter across a stone-paved square, beside the huge Neptune fountain and walled patio. The pink stucco exterior, stone benches, columns, and lanterns provides an appropriate atmosphere.

Originally elsewhere. L'Originale Alfredo di Roma Ristorante is not the original Alfredo's; the real thing is in Rome and is credited with the creation of the creamy pasta fettuccine Alfredo.

A semiformal decor with interesting wallpaper and upholstered seating welcomes you to the cool interior and pleasantly lively atmosphere. Check out the numerous photographs on the wall of the waiting area; you'll see many familiar personalities being served pasta.

The menu features freshly made pasta (including spaghetti, rigatoni, ziti, lasagna, and more) with various delectable sauces. Specialties include Cornish chicken legs in focaccia bread and oregano crust, *Ossobuco di Vitello*, and grilled salmon with Italian ratatouille in basil sauce. House wines available by the glass or by the liter.

United States

Liberty Inn. Burgers, sandwiches, chili, and salads, $2 to $6. Lunch and dinner. Child's menu, $3.50 to $4. Indoor and outdoor seating with traditional stateside fare. There's nothing here to startle a youngster or, for that matter, to educate the palate of an adult, but the food is acceptable and typical of what many American families eat most of the time.

The outdoor patio is a very pleasant, tree-shaded place offering umbrella tables and a bit of natural shade and colorful landscaping. The inside dining room is very spacious and has large window walls to maintain a bright, light atmosphere, even late in the day.

The menu changes little between lunch and dinner. Offerings include a chicken breast sandwich served with french fries for about $5 for lunch or dinner. At dinner, you can also choose a roasted half chicken with french fries and cole slaw for about $6. The evening offerings also include jambalaya, a southern stew that includes pork, shrimp, crawfish, chicken, sausage, vegetables, and rice. For the children there is fried chicken and hot dogs.

Japan

Yakitori House. Japanese fast food including beef, chicken, seafood, and salads, for about $3 to $8. Lunch, dinner.

Yakitori is located in the rear left portion of the Japanese exhibit, behind the fountain, within the Japanese gardens in a replica of a teahouse in the five-hundred-year-old Katsura Imperial Summer Palace in Kyoto. Dine indoors or outside; the rock-walled patio with fragrant landscaping is a pleasant getaway for lunch or dinner. By night, the patio is lit by lanterns.

The restaurant offers Japanese fast food, serving yakitori (skewered chicken basted with soy sauce and sesame), teriyaki chicken and beef, and guydon (a beef stew served over rice). The Shogun Combo offers a good selection, including beef teriyaki, seafood salad, and soups.

Japanese Shaved Ice. In hot weather, the snack bar on World Showcase Lagoon just to the left of the Japanese pavilion sells kaki-jori, which is your basic snow cone done Japanese style with tasty fruit syrups. Flavors include cherry, strawberry, honeydew melon, tangerine, or mixed for $1.50.

Matsu No Ma Lounge. Exotic drinks, sushi, and more, ranging from about $2 to $8. The lounge is located upstairs at the right side of the pavilion. Here you can sample sake (warm rice wine), Japanese beer, or exotic mixed drinks. Nonalcoholic drinks include *Ichigo* (strawberries, pineapple juice, lemon), and *Mikan* (Mandarin orange and pineapple juice with lemon).

Appetizers include tempura, Kabuki beef or chicken, sashimi, and assorted Nigiri sushi.

Teppanyaki Dining Room. Japanese beef, chicken, and seafood dishes prepared at your table. Lunch entrees from about $10 to $20; dinner entrees from about $15 to $30. Children's menu available. Reservations are usually necessary; make them at the Earth Station on the day you want to eat.

Find this interesting restaurant on the second floor of the building on the right of the Japanese exhibit, above the Mitsukoshi Department Store.

An entertaining and tasty break from the hubbub of Epcot. Groups of diners are assembled around a hot table, facing a chef equipped with a set of sharp knives; he carries salt and pepper shakers in holsters. Depending on the luck of the draw, your chef may be a multilingual comic, playing games with the chicken, shrimp, and beef as he slices and stir-fries the food. Teppanyaki fare is fresh and simple, featuring vegetables and meat over rice.

The dining experience is definitely not for someone who wants a leisurely and private time. But children—and adults who enjoy a floor show with their meal—are certain to have fun. Dinner entrees are the same as at lunch, but the prices are higher and the portions slightly larger.

Other specialties include exotic alcoholic and nonalcoholic drinks. One summer favorite is the Sakura, built from strawberries, light rum, white curaçao, and lemon juice.

Sipping rice. Sake, pronounced sah'-key, is a colorless, sweet alcohol, sometimes called rice wine. It is made from rice fermented with yeast. It is traditionally served warm.

Note that there are several teppanyaki-style Japanese restaurants nearby Walt Disney World; most offer better prices and smaller crowds.

Tempura Kiku. Batter-fried meat and vegetables, sushi, sashimi, shrimp, scallops, lobster, and fried beef and chicken strips. Lunch entrees from about $10 to $12; dinner entrees from about $15 to $23. Open from 11 A.M. to 3 P.M. for lunch, and from 5 P.M. to park closing for dinner.

Tempura Kiku is located upstairs at the right side of the Japanese pavilion, next to the Matsu No Ma Lounge. Exotic drinks from the lounge are available at the restaurant. Reservations are not accepted; there are only twenty-five seats.

Minimalist meals. The Japanese style of raw or lightly cooked foods in small, elegantly prepared portions is said to come from that nation's history of being overpopulated and short of both food and fuel.

Morocco

Restaurant Marrakesh. Traditional Moroccan food. Lunch entrees range from about $10 to $15. Dinner entrees range from about $17 to $20. Children's lunch and dinner selections. Reservations necessary in busy season; stop by the Earth Station or sign in at the podium at the front of the Morocco exhibit. Best deal: lower-priced lunches.

One of our favorite spots at Epcot, this place does a good job of making you feel as if you have traveled to an exotic place. When you arrive, wind your way through the Fez gate to the back of the Medina to find the Marrakesh amid the narrow streets and quaint shops.

Waiters in ankle-length *djellaba* robes, strolling musicians, and belly dancers provide an interesting and entertaining backdrop for a delightful meal. Even if you have to wait in the lobby briefly for your table, you'll be entertained by the music, native costumes, and decor. The dining area's raised dining rooms overlook the stage.

Among the traditional delicacies offered for lunch are *meshoui* (lamb roast in natural juices with rice, almonds, raisins, and saffron) and *couscous* (rolled semolina) steamed with garden vegetables, chicken, or lamb. Consider trying one of the sampler plates with small portions of various offerings for yourself or to share with someone.

The dinner menu is similar, but offering more variety and larger portions. Try the Tangier sampler for a selection of items, including specialties marinated in spices such as ginger, cumin, garlic with olives, paprika, and pickled lemon.

It's all topped off with some delicious honey-sweetened pastries or crepes.

Tangierine Cafe. A recent addition to the pavilion offers lentil salad, hummus, and slow-roasted lamb.

Veiled threat. Belly dancing first came to America in 1893 at the Chicago World's Fair when a Syrian dancer who called herself "Little Egypt" scandalized viewers with what later came to be known as the "hootchy-kootchy." Belly dancing is believed to have originated in Persia (now Iran) and is still popular throughout the Middle East.

Moorish Cafe and Pastry Shop. Baklava and other delectables for about $1.50 each. Moroccan Flag Beer for about $3.

France

Boulangerie Pâtisserie. French pastries and fresh croissants, priced from about $2 to $4. Breakfast, snacks.

This quaint bakery shop is across the narrow French street from the Bistro de Paris. It's a wonderful place to grab breakfast or a sweet snack any time of the day. The bakery is managed by the Chefs de France, which is as tasty a recommendation as can be found at Epcot.

Any of the tarts, apple turnovers, quiche Lorraine, and chocolate treats are good. Dark, flavorful coffee makes a good accompaniment for the sweet treats.

Bistro de Paris. Traditional French cuisine in a light, quiet setting. Dinner and lunch (in peak season only). Dinner entrees start at about $15 and rise from there. Children's menu.

A window seat upstairs at the Bistro may be the best place in the park to view the nightly *IllumiNations* show.

Reservations are available and necessary on busy days.

Upstairs over the Chefs de France, this bistro is entered through a rear door at the back of the building. A bistro is an intimate little cafe or pub, and that's what the designers of the Bistro de Paris had in mind in this lighter and (usually) quieter version of Chefs de France. The same master chefs designed the menu, which includes a variety of appetizers, soups, entrees, and desserts.

Specialties include grilled beef tenderloin with mushrooms, glazed onions, and green peppercorn sauce; grilled swordfish with a tomato-béarnaise sauce; and sautéed veal tenderloin with apple and Calvados sauce.

Appetizers and entrees vary by season and are occasionally changed. In recent years offerings have included appetizers such as salad of duck liver pâté at $14, *gratin d'escargots de Bourgogne* (casserole of snails in herbal butter) at $7.50, cream of lobster soup at $4.50, or a mixed green salad with true Roquefort dressing and walnuts at $7.50.

Entrees have included a sautéed breast of duck with cherries and red wine sauce for $20; a rack of lamb with vegetables for two is $48.

At least ten dessert items are available. On some visits I have been offered fruit and sherbet with raspberry sauce, and vanilla creme in a puff pastry shell topped with caramel sauce.

Au Petit Café. French cafe fare from soup to quiche, $4 to $14.50. Children's offerings, about $4. Lunch, dinner, snacks.

This Parisian-style sidewalk cafe is located to the left of Chefs de France. You'll find it through the smell of fresh flowers coming from the many hanging baskets that adorn the posts that support the awning over the patio.

The World Showcase is not quite the Champs-Elysées, but the little sidewalk cafe with its formal black-jacketed waiters gives a nice taste of the time-honored people-watching stations on the streets of Paris.

The menu includes traditional onion soup with cheese, *coq au vin*, and sautéed strip steak with Bordelaise sauce. Moderately priced offerings include such familiar items as quiche Lorraine and salads. Luncheon entrees range from $5 to $15; dinner plates begin at $15.

Fruit sorbets, ice cream, pastry shells filled with light cream and chocolate sauce, and ice cream soufflé with Grand Marnier sauce round out the menu.

No reservations are accepted, and the waiting lines can become quite long on busy days.

Chefs de France. Traditional French cuisine. Lunch, $8 to $15. Dinner from $15. Children's lunch and dinner menu. Reservations are suggested.

C'est merveilleux! Right here in Epcot, just across the way from umpteen hot dog and pizza stands, is a restaurant nearly as fine as any in France.

The chefs of France who are behind the restaurant are Paul Bocuse and Roger Vergé, operators of two of the country's finest restaurants, and Gaston LeNôtre, considered a national treasure for his pastries and desserts. The eatery is located on the ground floor of the large building at the left of the entrance to the France exhibit, to the right of the Au Petit Café outdoor dining area.

Enter this intriguing restaurant under the red awning off the stone-paved street of the France exhibit. The building is of classic French architecture with stone walls and a metal roof. Inside is an elegant French dining room complete with fresh tablecloths, paintings, and chandeliers; table service in elegant continental style with a bustling, active atmosphere. Pleasant and helpful personnel speak French (English, if you insist) and are ready and willing to help you make selections.

Lunch and dinner meals include ten or more salads and appetizers and about as many entrees. All of this comes at only a slightly high price, compared to other Epcot table-service restaurants.

Menu items change from season to season. On recent visits we have seen fresh fillet of snapper and spinach baked in puff pastry, sautéed scallops and crab dumplings with lobster cream sauce, and sautéed tenderloin of beef with raisins and brandy sauce.

As you might expect, desserts are worth drooling over, with plenty more than a dozen selections. We have dreamed about *crème caramel* (baked French custard with caramel sauce).

United Kingdom

Rose & Crown Pub and Dining Room. English pub fare in a pleasant atmosphere. Lunch entrees from $5 to $15, and dinner from $15. Children's menu. Lunch, dinner, snacks. Traditional afternoon tea at 4 P.M. Reservations for the dining room are recommended and necessary on busy days; no reservations are accepted for the pub.

Located across the street from the main portion of the United Kingdom exhibit, the Rose & Crown is an interesting British dining experience. Very ordinary pub food in England seems very exotic in Orlando. On previous visits, we have been offered steak-and-kidney pie, lamb and barley soup, chicken and leeks, and fish and chips. The dinner menu expanded to include Cornish game hen, herb-roasted lamb, and Argyle prime rib with Yorkshire pudding. A selection of sweets, such as traditional sherry trifle, was also available.

There is a decent selection of beers, stouts, and ales, including Bass from England, Tennent's from Scotland, and Guinness Stout and Harp ale from Ireland. They're sold by the pint and "yard" for those with powerful thirsts.

The decor is appropriately rough and dark, with elements of both city and country drinking establishments in the United Kingdom. Frosted and etched glass adds an elegant interest to this beautiful setting.

The pub, which can become quite crowded, offers appetizer-sized portions of the dinner menu along with beers and mixed drinks.

Harry Ramsden's. Classic fish and chips.

Canada

Le Cellier Steakhouse. Steaks, pasta, and seafood in a quiet corner of the park. Lunch, served from noon to 4 P.M., has entrees priced from about $8 to $10; dinner is served from 4 to 9 P.M. with entrees from about $10 to $15.

EPCOT

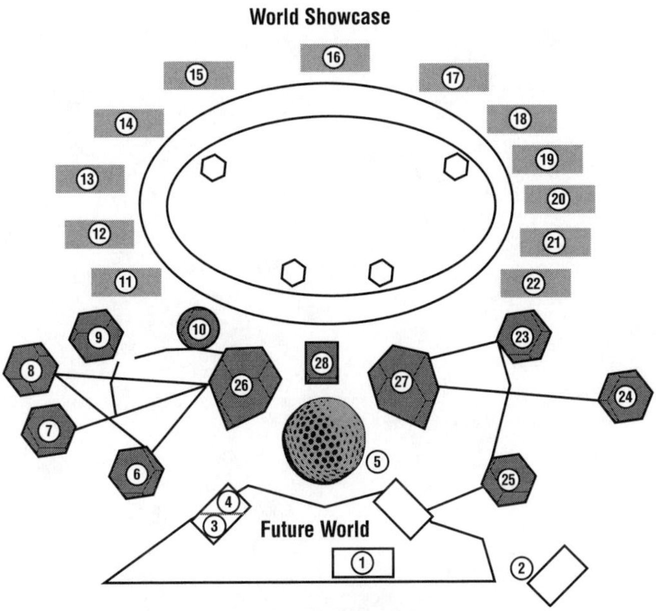

Epcot Center

1. Monorail station
2. Bus terminal
3. Banking
4. Strollers
5. Spaceship Earth
6. Universe of Energy
7. Wonders of Life
8. Mission: SPACE *(Coming in 2003)*
9. GM Test Track
10. Special events
11. Mexico
12. Norway
13. China
14. Germany
15. Italy
16. United States
17. Japan
18. Morocco
19. France
20. International Gateway
    ferry terminal to Epcot resorts
21. United Kingdom
22. Canada
23. Imagination!
24. The Land
25. The Living Seas
26. Innoventions East
27. Innoventions West
28. Fountain of Nations

Chapter 9
Disney's Animal Kingdom

Disney's Animal Kingdom is a perfectly logical progression. After all, the entire worldwide Disney empire began with a mouse.

Now there is a cast of more than a thousand animals at work at a wondrous kingdom that celebrates the creatures real, extinct, and imaginary with rides and attractions, shows, dramatic landscapes, and close encounters with all sorts of exotic creatures.

Mickey is still around, too.

From the moment you enter the park through a lush oasis, you are immersed in a meticulously re-created world: Africa and Asia brought to the swamps and meadows of Florida. Gardeners planted more than four million trees, plants, shrubs, ground covers, vines, epiphytes, and grasses from every continent but Antarctica.

The employees of the park include more than one thousand birds and mammals, plus iguanas, chameleons, and other reptiles. On the human side, Disney recruiters traveled to Uganda, Zimbabwe, Ghana, Botswana, Cameroon, and South Africa to hire nearly one hundred college students, many seeking careers in the hospitality industry. You'll find Africans working at many of the gift shops and attractions in the park.

Disney's Animal Kingdom is five hundred acres of sweeping vistas, including the wide-open plains of Africa populated by great herds of animals. By comparison, the Magic Kingdom is just 107 acres and Epcot just 260 acres.

The park is located in the southwest corner of Walt Disney World at the end of the Osceola County Parkway near All-Star Resorts. Although you wouldn't know it from the outside, it lies just north of U.S. 192.

Among the highlights:

- A safari across Africa, bringing us up close to real lions, elephants, zebras, giraffes, and dozens of other familiar and rare animals. There's a touch of an environmental message, too, with a harrowing chase after a group of elephant poachers.
- A stroll through Asia, where tigers rule the ruins of a Maharajah's palace

MUST-SEES

WOW

The Tree of Life
(Safari Village)

It's Tough to Be a Bug!
(Safari Village)

Kilimanjaro Safaris
(Africa)

Pangani Forest Exploration Trail
(Africa)

Conservation Station
(Conservation Station)

Kali River Rapids
(Asia)

Maharajah Jungle Trek
(Asia)

Dinosaur
(Countdown to extinction at DinoLand U.S.A.)

Tarzan Rocks!
(DinoLand U.S.A.)

Festival of the Lion King
(Camp Minnie-Mickey)

- A voyage millions of years back in time to rescue a dinosaur moments before a fiery meteor slams into the earth, dooming the entire species
- A 3-D glimpse of the world from a bug's-eye view
- A striking sculpture known as the "Tree of Life," which sets the theme for the park with images of animals large and small
- A lively stage show that combines a bit of Broadway, a circus big top, and a Disney parade
- And you'll find Disney's favorite creatures: Mickey Mouse and Minnie Mouse among them, strolling the park and making regular appearances in a beautiful garden

The Park Is Born

Disney's Animal Kingdom officially opened on Earth Day, April 22, 1998.

"Just as this theme park has its roots in our films, it also represents a major departure," said Roy W. Disney, Walt's nephew and vice chairman of the company.

"Once a movie is completed, it's done forever. On the other hand, Disney's Animal Kingdom—like the animal world itself—will evolve and grow. It's truly a living thing."

Speaking at the dedication of Conservation Station in the park, Disney lauded a group of "eco-heroes," including gorilla researcher Dr. Jane Goodall.

"Walt Disney advocated 'stealth education,'" he continued. "Remember the song: 'A Spoonful of Sugar Helps the Medicine Go Down.'"

Walt Disney Company chairman Michael Eisner read from the dedication plaque for Disney's Animal Kingdom at the ceremonies for the formal grand opening of the park:

"Welcome to a kingdom of animals . . . real, ancient, and imagined: a kingdom ruled by lions, dinosaurs, and dragons; a kingdom of balance, harmony, and survival; a kingdom we enter to share in the wonder, gaze at the beauty, thrill at the drama . . . and learn."

The Asia section opened in 1999, adding a

thrilling trek through the habitats of some extraordinary animals, including tigers, tapirs, and komodo dragons, and a wet river rafting adventure that has an ecological message.

One apparent problem at Disney's Animal Kingdom has been the relative paucity of activities for young children. The next new thing at the park will improve a bit on the range of offerings. **Chester & Hester's Dino-Rama** is a small midway of dinosaur-themed games and two rides—the **Triceratop Spin** and the **Primeval Whirl**.

About the Park

Disney's Animal Kingdom is a more leisurely experience than the Magic Kingdom, Epcot, or Disney–MGM Studios. The beauty is in the details, and you'll miss a lot if you rush from attraction to attraction.

There are seven main areas, each at the end of a spoke radiating out from the Tree of Life at the center of the park:

The Oasis. The entrance plaza leads into this very green and lush tropical garden. Most visitors will zoom right through; make a point to explore the Oasis later in the day or on your way out.

Safari Village. The island at the center of the park is home to the Tree of Life and *It's Tough to Be a Bug!*

Africa. You'll enter through the East African port of Harambe to some of the most spectacular parts of the park: the Kilimanjaro Safari, the Pangani Forest Exploration Trail, and the Wildlife Express train to Conservation Station.

Conservation Station. An inside peek at the care and preservation of wildlife, and some hands-on participation at the Affection Section.

Asia. One of the most beautifully realized areas of the park, home to the very wet Kali River Rapids and the Maharajah Jungle Trek, a stroll through the jungles of Asia.

Dinoland, U.S.A. About as close as you could hope to get to the world of the dinosaurs. Explore the Cretaceous Trail and the Boneyard; then load onto a Time Rover for a wild, high-tech trip back in time to the days when the dinosaur was king.

Camp Minnie-Mickey. An old-fashioned summer camp populated by Mickey and his pals, the Lion King and his troupe, and for those who prefer the real thing, some fascinating smaller animals.

The layout of the park is somewhat confusing because you cannot see landmarks; the Tree of Life is only visible when you are in the center of the park and cannot be seen from outlying lands. Study the map and pay attention to the signs.

There's no Main Street or obvious gathering place, although the thriving port city of Harambe is likely to be a favored hangout for many visitors. Be sure to bring a hat and suntan lotion; parts of the park are about as hot and exposed as, let's say, Africa.

The park is generally open from early in the morning until dusk; Disney has installed lighting on the savanna and may operate the park into the night on some of the busiest days of the year.

There remains quite a bit of undeveloped space available for expansion at the park. Disneyphiles note that the early renderings for the park included an area named Beastly Kingdom, the home of mythical creatures such as unicorns and dragons. And they point to the logo for Animal Kingdom, which includes a winged dragon in the middle of a march of real creatures. We can hope.

Power Trip #1

Breakfast with the Animals

There are two good reasons to get to the park early and head for Harambe: First of all, the **Kilimanjaro Safari** is one of the biggest draws of the park, and lines build by mid-morning. Secondly, many of the animals on the African savanna are morning creatures. (Lions, for example, sleep as much as eighteen hours a day and are particularly fond of siestas in the heat of the afternoon.)

Dedicated animal lovers and photographers will want to arrive at the park as early as possible and head for Harambe. If you're lucky you may be able to make two safari trips before most visitors park their cars.

Of course you could also use the Fastpass system to grab a reservation for a safari expedition; in fact, you might want to ride once in the morning and again later in the day to see a variety of animals.

If it's a warm morning head for Asia and the **Kali River Rapids** for a wet tour through a tropical rainforest; if there's a chill in the air you might want to wait for later in the day, although lines will build in the afternoon. Kali River Rapids also offers Fastpass reservations.

Walk through the thrilling **Maharajah Jungle Trek** while you're there. Move on to DinoLand, U.S.A., for **Dinosaur** and Camp Minnie-Mickey for the ***Festival of the Lion King*** show. Leave ***It's Tough to Be a Bug!*** in the Tree of Life and the front of the park for last.

The live shows at the park fill quickly; one great strategy is to pick up a Fastpass for an attraction like the Kilimanjaro Safari or Dinosaur and put it in your pocket while you head for a show. When the entertainment is over, you should be able to amble into an attraction without waiting in line.

Power Trip #2

A Contrarian's Tour

OK, so we know that most visitors are likely to head first for the Kilimanjaro Safari, but you have other goals in mind. Take advantage of the major flow to the left side of the park in the morning by going the other direction instead.

Head first for DinoLand, U.S.A., for **Dinosaur** and then Camp Minnie-Mickey for the ***Festival of the Lion King*** show.

Move counterclockwise against the flow toward Africa and the **Kilimanjaro Safari**. Catch lunch early and then head out into the savanna during the noon-time lull in search of snoozing cats and frolicking elephants. The cooling **Kali River Rapids** are definitely worth a visit; lines will build on warm afternoons.

The Oasis

You'll enter the park though the cool green of this lush garden. Colorful and unusual animals inhabit a miniature landscape of streams, grottoes, waterfalls, and glades. It's a place of cool mists, fragrant flowers, and the sights and sounds of playful animals.

Most visitors are going to sprint through the Oasis to get into the park itself . . . and that's not a bad idea on a busy day. But do take the time to revisit the area, or at least make a more leisurely stroll when you leave at the end of the day. This is Disney's horticultural and animal imagineering at its best, a lovingly created small world after all.

There are lovely and exotic plantings at almost every turn, and caves, waterfalls, and grottoes that offer welcome respite from the Florida sun.

And tucked away are hidden animal delights, including tropical birds and small animals such as anteaters, tufted deer, muntjac, two-toed sloths, otters, macaws, and scarlet ibis. My favorites include the tree kangaroos.

At the far end of the Oasis, a stone bridge crosses the Discovery River to bring visitors to Safari Village.

The gardens are colored by hundreds of flowering trees from nearly every tropical and subtropical region on earth, including jacarandas, tabebuias, calliandras, cassias, michellias, bauhinias, and tipuana. Disney landscapers promise plants and trees will be in bloom no matter what time of year you tour the park.

The Animal Kingdom's population of plants is at least five times as large as the lush world of Epcot. All told, Animal Kingdom has more landscaping than the three other Walt Disney World parks combined.

On the African savanna the challenge includes keeping the huge area looking like a piece of Africa while dealing with the fact that many of the animals will insist on eating the landscaping. Elephants, for example, can completely devour large stands of their favorite grass. Handlers place precut leafy branches and 1,300 pounds of fresh grasses in various spots each day to attempt to lure some of the larger eaters away from the live vegetation.

Absolutely no insecticides or other chemicals that might endanger the animals are used in the park, according to Disney.

Another challenge comes from Florida's occasional winter freezes. Water sprays help prevent frost, and heaters are used in some areas such as The Oasis where the plants are lush and tropical.

Disney's plant kingdom. The plant collection at Disney's Animal Kingdom includes 600 species of trees, 350 species of grasses, and 1,800 species of shrubs, vines, ferns, mosses, epiphytes, and perennials. All told, more than 100,000 trees and more than 4 million individual grasses and shrubs were planted or grown from seed.

Secrets of the kingdom. Architectural scale is suppressed to allow trees to overshadow buildings; overall building height is limited to thirty feet, while the major trees of the park were at or above forty feet at opening.

Safari Village

The crossroads of adventure at Disney's Animal Kingdom, this island of tropical greenery and equatorial architecture is the hub through which you'll pass to reach other lands. Safari Village is circled by Discovery River.

There are some 1,500 hand-painted wooden folk art carvings scattered about, a fusion of pre-Columbian, Peruvian, African, and Polynesian forms. They were crafted on the island of Bali by native craft workers.

WOW The Tree of Life

Towering 145 feet above Safari Village is the Tree of Life, 170 feet wide at its base and surrounded by shimmering pools and meadows filled with birds and small mammals noted for their playful behavior. The trunk of the tree is carved as an intricate swirling pattern of animal forms that symbolize the richness and diversity of animal life on earth.

More than a dozen artists and Imagineers worked for seventeen months to create the 325 animal carvings from majestic lions to playful dolphins, from humble armadillos to camels, baboons, and elephants; they had between six and ten hours to finish each sculpture before the plaster hardened.

Hungarian sculptor Zsolt Hormay assembled a team of artists from around the world. Native Americans carved the bear, bald eagle, bobcat, and mountain lion. Hormay himself sculpted the baboon, koala, and scorpion.

The images were carved in a thin layer of cement attached to steel rods bent into the rough forms of the animals; some of the animals highest up in the tree are made of foam to reduce weight.

The tree itself has some eight thousand branches adorned with more than 103,000 artificial leaves that blow in the wind; the entire structure—built upon a framework designed with the assistance of an oil rig builder—sways a bit in the wind.

At its base are small pools and meadows that are home to animals that include otters, flamingos, capybaras, ducks, storks, cranes, cockatoos, lemurs, tamarins, tortoises, and red kangaroos.

WOW Tree of Life Theater: *It's Tough to Be a Bug!*

Like Spaceship Earth at Epcot, the central symbol of Disney's Animal Kingdom also houses an exciting attraction. Guests step inside the Tree of Life to experience a 3-D adventure about creatures of a much smaller scale than most of the others in the park: insects.

Based on *A Bug's Life*, the animated film from Disney and Pixar (creator of *Toy Story*), the humorous film and special-effects theater provide a bug's-eye view of the world.

The queue for the 430-seat theater wends its way around the base of the Tree of Life before eventually ducking into a cool, dark room; listen carefully for the rustle, buzzes, and chirps of the stars of the show. While waiting read some of the amusing movie posters promoting the greatest hits of insect cinema, facetious titles include: *Web Side Story*, *Beauty and the Bee*, *My Fair Lady Bug*, *Antie*, *A Cockroach Line*, and my favorite, *Little House of Hoppers*.

When the doors open, pick out a place to sit on a log and admire the tangled-root and vine architecture all around. The orchestra of creatures tunes up below while a buzzing can be heard from the wasp nest projection booth.

Try to sit in the middle of the theater—midway in from both sides and halfway back from the screen—for the best 3-D effects.

The show is ready to begin. The announcer has a request: Please refrain from buzzing, chirping, stinging . . . or pollinating.

With a pair of 3-D "bug glasses" in place you're right in the midst of things as Flick, the ant master of ceremonies, welcomes visitors as honorary bugs and introduces us to some of the cast of millions.

"Take it from an ant. It's tough to be a bug," says the emcee. "That's why we've developed some amazing survival techniques."

Assisted by a pair of acorn weevils with a slingshot, Chili the Tarantula shows off his ability to throw poison quills. And yes, they're zooming out toward the audience.

Next an acid-spraying soldier termite, "the Termite-ator," defends his mound by spraying intruders—that's us—in the seats below. The stinkbug soloist, Claire DeRoom, astonishes us with a malodorous performance.

But the big artillery arrives with a villainous grasshopper, a bug on a mission to wipe out the audience of intruders. "You guys only see us as monsters!" he says. "Maybe it's time you 'honorary bugs' got a taste of your own medicine!" Suddenly we're under assault by a giant flyswatter, a blinding fog of "Bug Doom" spray, and a nasty hornet squadron.

I won't spoil the ending, but it does have a certain biting edge.

The butterfly curtain closes, and the announcer reminds the audience to remain seated while all the lice, bedbugs, maggots, and cockroaches exit first.

Africa

The adventure into and across the wilds of Africa begins in Harambe, a well-aged, modern-day town on the edge of a wildlife reserve. Harambe (pronounced Ha'-rahm-bay) is based on the Arab-influenced Swahili culture and architecture of coastal Kenya, with white coral walls, thatched roofs, and a *hakuna matata* attitude toward life.

Disney Imagineers lavished a tremendous amount of detail on Harambe; be sure to read some of the signs and notes on the wall. The hand-plastered walls often expose their coral rock substructures. I was at first surprised to find that Disney had allowed the place to look so dusty on Grand Opening Day, until I realized that the piles of wind-blown dirt inside the hallways of some of the buildings were actually created by designers and cemented into place.

At the end of Harambe's main street an ancient gnarled baobab tree, a symbol of the African savanna, beckons visitors toward the Kilimanjaro Safari.

Check out the Ziwani Traders shop at Mombasa Marketplace to explore an interesting selection of hand-carved masks, sculptures, clothing, and other items from Kenya and other African nations. The decorative gourds on display are used by Masai tribes to hold milk until it is sour enough to meet their taste preferences.

WOW Kilimanjaro Safaris *FAST*

The adventure begins in Harambe beneath a forty-foot-tall baobab tree, where the queue winds its way through a warehouse stocked with safari gear. The waiting area is huge . . . and well-hidden from view; be sure to check the posted wait time at the outside of the safari shed before staking your claim in line.

Disney has added a few touches that make the wait a bit less painful. Near the start of the covered portion of the line you'll circle around the base of *Mzee Mbuyu baobab* (Swahili for "Old Man Baobab"), one of the signature trees of the Harambe reserve. A bit later on, the queue passes through a few live animal habitats, including that of a group of crowned cranes.

Environmental messages play from video monitors overhead. The safari will help you learn about the importance of protecting animal life; the game warden quotes a Swahili saying: "What you see with your eyes you value with your heart."

Eventually you will be bouncing across the rugged terrain in an open-sided, thirty-two-passenger motor lorry; you can call it a safari truck. In the driver's seat is an experienced guide who will help identify the animals and keep in radio contact with a bush pilot flying ahead in a spotter plane.

The trucks follow a twisting trail through a lush green forest, across small river crossings, and into the Serengeti grasslands rich with antelope, giraffes, zebras, baboons, rhinos, elephants, crocodiles, lions, hippos, and many more animals.

Crossing the Bongo Pool, where many animals come to drink, be on the lookout for black rhinos, among the most fascinating animals in Africa. They may be along the shores, wallowing in the water, or lurking just below its surface. If you're lucky you may spot a glimpse of a rare okapi, a large mammal related to the giraffe but lacking the long neck.

Rounding the bend, you'll come to a woodland of date and fan palms, the home of a colony of shiny black and white colobus monkeys.

A set of cascading waterfalls forms a pool that is home to African crocodiles, which can grow to as much as twenty feet in length, much larger than American alligators. A very rickety bridge crosses directly over their heads; do you think it's strong enough to support the weight of your safari lorry?

Safely across, the safari emerges from heavy vegetation for a spectacular view of the vast savanna, where you'll see spotted giraffes, black and white striped zebras, sable antelope, Thomson's gazelles, and speedy ostriches that are capable of outrunning the truck.

The landscape of the savanna includes strange vegetation such as maringa trees—known as sausage trees—with foot-long seed pods used by natives to make a lemonade-like drink. Termite mounds stand up to twenty feet tall.

Out on the grasslands baboon families sightsee from rocks and trees as the trucks pass by. Around another bend, a herd of elephants moves among the trees. The truck fords a small stream and moves into elephant company.

If you're lucky you may catch a glimpse of one or more lions; they are hard to spot, especially in midday when they're likely to be snoozing.

Kilimanjaro Safaris

A home for the animals. Most of the animals in Africa spend their days working the crowds on the Kilimanjaro Safaris and from along the Pangani Forest Exploration Trail, and then retire for the night to their hotel suites.

Most of the animals at the park were born in captivity at zoos and other preserves.

Among the tasks undertaken by Disney animal managers was to give them more room to roam than most have ever known, while conditioning them to come to shelters each night for their own security and for daily care.

Each area has its own sound signal used to summon animals to their "backstage" homes. The Thomson's gazelles have learned to come back to their shelter each night when they hear a "goose call." Giraffes respond to a coach's whistle, and zebras listen for a cowbell.

When the animals were first introduced to the African savanna and forest there were temporary fences erected to help them learn where they were expected to roam.

Subtle barriers including water, gratings, and hidden wires help reinforce the training.

The driver communicates by radio with the spotter plane in search of "Big Red" and her elephant newborn "Little Red," a favorite pair of pachyderms who weere given their names because they seem to enjoy rolling in the rust-red dust.

Keep your eyes open (and cameras ready) for a glimpse of white rhinos in nearby pools; you may spot kudu, scimitar-horned oryx, Zimbabwean Klipspringer, long-horned eland, and cheetahs out in the grasslands.

The beauty of the scene is soon disturbed by a message from one of the game wardens: it seems ivory poachers have wounded Big Red, and Little Red is missing. The bush pilot asks us to help out by forcing the poachers eastward along the gorge toward the waiting wardens.

We hear the sound of the poachers' jeep ahead of us and even the sound of bullets; off to our left we pass their hurriedly abandoned camp, fires still smoldering.

And then comes the good news from the spotter plane: the poachers have been caught. As we come around a bend we find a ranger training a rifle on a pair of poachers cornered inside their crashed vehicle. Beside it in the back of a small flat-bed truck is a baby elephant still covered with rust-red dust; Little Red is safe and will be taken back to his mother.

Detouring around several waterfalls and across a one-hundred-foot pool, we rejoin the main road and enter the most lush vegetation in all of the safari, a place of giant bamboo, palm, and other big-leaf trees; we are near the heart of gorilla country and the start of the Pangani Forest Exploration Trail.

About the Safari

The trucks sit high off the road and offer good views. There is a canvas awning that provides a bit of shade from the sun, but in heavy rain you can expect to get wet. Serious photographers will want to try to get one of the outside seats. No guarantee, but I found more action on the driver's side of the vehicle.

The safaris run all day until dusk, and you are likely to see different animals each time you go for a trip. Most of the creatures are more active in the morning, often seeking cool shade for long siestas in the heat of the afternoon.

The Kilimanjaro Safaris are one of the major draws of Disney's Animal Kingdom, and they're likely to have long lines at certain times of the day. On busy days, lines can reach to as much as two hours in mid-morning and mid-afternoon, dropping to a reasonable fifteen minutes at lunch. It is almost always worthwhile to use the Fastpass system here.

My suggestion is to arrive early and ride the safari before the crowds form and while the animals are most active, and then come back again in mid-afternoon for another safari. And don't stay away just because it may be raining a bit; some of the animals are much more active when it is cool or wet.

The animals all perform their roles well, but the unsung stars include Disney's landscaping crew. The trick was to find a way to simulate the wilds of Africa in an environment that includes moving safari trucks and free-ranging animals.

Disney's planners laid out the plant bed lines using spray paint from a motorcycle moving at the same speed as the trucks because guests would experience the landscape at that speed.

Snorkel-derms. Unless you've been to the continent of Africa, you might not know that elephants can swim. Most animal parks don't have pools big enough or deep enough. In Disney's African savanna, though, there are three pools twelve feet deep and sixty feet long where elephants can swim and even "snorkel," breathing from underwater through their trunks.

A woman's place. African lions live in large prides of one or two males with females and cubs. Female lions do the hunting, but males eat first.

The park's chief landscape designer took some horticultural tips from a wise old elephant while he was scouting Africa for savanna landscape materials; the animal grabbed some favorite snacking grass with its trunk and passed it over to the designer. The seeds from that eualopsis grass were eventually planted at Animal Kingdom.

The rutted safari road is also part of the landscape design. The Imagineering team matched concrete with the surrounding soil, then rolled tires through it and tossed stones, dirt, and twigs into it to create a bumpy, remote African road in the wilds of Walt Disney World.

This is central Florida, of course, and not central Africa and so some creative compromises were necessary. The seven distinctive baobab trees were re-created in concrete, and the towering acacias are actually thirty-foot-tall southern live oaks given a carefully maintained crew cut.

WOW Pangani Forest Exploration Trail

The end of the safari ride is also the beginning of the Pangani Forest Exploration Trail, where you can take a walk through the domain of two troops of lowland gorillas, observe hippos from an underwater viewing area, and get close to exotic birds in an aviary.

Have thatch, will travel. Disney designers went back to Africa to obtain tribal craftsmen and traditional thatching grass to create the pole-supported thatched roofs of Harambe and the research outposts along Pangani Forest Exploration Trail.

During construction, Disney imported thirteen Zulu craftsmen from Kwazulu-Natal in South Africa and fifteen trailer loads of thatch.

Trading their tribal garb for American blue jeans—and putting hard hats over familiar straw caps and bandannas—the builders did object to air conditioning in their hotel rooms. They were eventually moved to houses where they could open the windows and let in the mid-summer warmth of Florida.

The roofs were constructed with wild Berg thatch, which resists insects and decay and provides excellent insulation and waterproofing.

The battens, which secure the thatch to hardwood rafters, are made of eucalyptus pods stripped bare, coated with mud, and kiln-dried to produce a mottled dark brown finish.

The roofs are expected to withstand the effects of Florida's sun and rain for up to sixty years.

Highlights include close-ups of African mammals including hippos (with an over- and underwater viewport); you'll also be able to see families of lowland gorillas through windows in the gorilla observatory and from a swaying rope bridge that crosses through a small valley. And you can spy herds of antelope from a thatch-roof observation station.

Many of the animals are too small or too shy to be seen from passing safari trucks. Instead they are presented up close along the trail. One display shows cutaways into the burrows of naked mole rats—some of the most unusual creatures in the park. The creatures are actually not rats at all, but rather relatives of the common mole; they organize themselves like bees or ants, with a queen who is the center of society.

Giant African bullfrogs hop around a lily-pad pool outside a wildlife research center that features interactive displays and maps. Research areas include telescopes, video displays, and animal- and bird-spotting guides.

At the exit from the research office you'll enter a canopy of trees filled with as many as thirty-five species of exotic tropical birds nesting among the palms and bushes. In pools below are many rare fish, including the colorful cichlid that is found only in Lake Tanganyika.

Moving across the aviary you'll find another open air shelter that has a dam on the far wall with a large panel of inch-thick glass holding back the mill pond. The water is home to a trio of giant hippopotamuses and a pair of coal-black African cormorants; and the glass offers an above- and underwater view.

A bit further along is a platform overlooking the savanna with a view of giraffes, tiny dik-diks, and other rare members of the antelope family grazing in knee-high grass.

The trail leads through a leafy canyon to the gorilla research camp. Experts answer questions and assist with research materials. Just beyond a large plate glass window a family of gorillas—two females and a silverback adult male—make their home. Disney hopes for the patter of little gorilla feet in the years to come.

Beyond the research camp the path crosses a small canyon over a swaying suspension bridge to present another view of the gorilla family. On the other side of the bridge is another group of young male gorillas, part of a study of bachelor groups within the Gorilla Species Survival Plan (SSP), a program of the American Zoo and Aquarium Association.

The end of the trail leads to Harambe station where you can catch the Wildlife Express train to Conservation Station.

Tree farm. A Brazilian flowering tree named Markhamia normally grows as straight as a telephone pole in the rainforest. Grown from seed at the Animal Kingdom, the tree started out in a straight line until it reached a shade canopy above. Then it "turned on its blinker and made a sharp left-hand turn," said Paul Comstock, the park's chief landscape designer. The plant grew toward the light, then made another sharp turn toward the sky, ultimately resembling a giant stairstep.

Another of the trees in the "valley" of Pangani Forest is one with an exceptionally long Latin name: *Schizolobium parahybum excelsum,* better known as the flowering Bacurubu tree from Panama.

Wildlife Express to Conservation Station

The Wildlife Express departs from the East African Depot near Harambe. The colonial-style, narrow-gauge steam trains of the Eastern Star Railway offer a glimpse at some of the nighttime homes for the animals as well as some of the park's veterinary facilities.

"Karibuni Harambe!" announces the train conductor. "Welcome to Harambe." There's to be no drinking, no smoking, and "absolutely no cooking on board."

And while we're at it: *"Kuwa macho wajangili!"* ("Keep a lookout for poachers!")

The puffing steam engines and open-air carriages hark back to British railroads in the mountains and jungles of far-off colonies. For nearly a century, engines like these were shipped to South Africa, Rhodesia, and India to carry European explorers and the native populations to mines, agricultural areas, and animal lands.

The passenger carriages are partially enclosed by waist-high, wood-louvered shutters; carpetbags, boxes, crates, and wicker luggage are stacked high on the roof. The classic depot is patterned after the stucco structures with open-air waiting areas built by the British in East Africa during the early 1900s.

The narrow-gauge (3.3-foot rail width) track was used in many areas where that design was easier to use along canyon walls and around horseshoe bends.

Three engines and two sets of cars were built in 1997 by the model-railroad firm of Severn Lamb in Alchester, England, a few miles from William Shakespeare's cottage in Stratford-upon-Avon. The company makes trains for parks located around the world, including one in use at Disneyland Paris.

Each five-car train seats 250 passengers on side-facing benches for the 1.2-mile circle tour that runs down a shallow valley between Africa and Asia. The tour offers a behind-the-scenes look at the modern animal care facilities, includ-

Train buff alert. The model for the engines at Disney's Animal Kingdom was discovered in the archives of the Indian Peninsula Railroad; they feature an unusual Aspinwall side-tank 2-4-2 design first built in 1898 at Horwich Locomotive Works in England. The stubby locomotives combine engines and tender in one car. Unlike the American-style engines at the Magic Kingdom with their bells and low-moaning whistles, the Wildlife Express' whistles sound like the scream of a wounded piccolo.

Although a handful of the nineteenth-century trains may still be operating in some isolated corners of the world, the Wildlife Express is believed to be the only train of its type now carrying passengers.

ing night shelters for lions, elephants, warthogs, and antelope herds.

On the return from Conservation Station the train offers some peeks into the Asian area of Disney's Animal Kingdom.

WOW Conservation Station

Conservation Station offers a backstage look at the veterinary headquarters and center for conservation programs at Disney's Animal Kingdom.

Located in the north side of the park near the edge of Africa, Conservation Station is reached by a short journey aboard the Wildlife Express train. From the depot it's a short walk through a jungle to a building dominated by a giant montage of animal faces, including those of the gorilla, wolf, elephant, lion, panda, turtle, baboon, and others.

Just inside the building, in the Hall of Animals, another mural presents hundreds of other animals looking directly at their visitors. "The animals are looking at you and to you—the human species," says curator Jackie Ogden. "Man represents both the greatest danger to the animals and their environment and the greatest hope."

Here guests can meet animal experts and learn about the behind-the-scenes operations of the park and how they can help the animals they have met. Around the room are high-tech interactive computer displays and video observatories with a view into the park's veterinary operating room. Veterinarians may describe surgeries or procedures as they perform them; an attendant can relay questions and answers. The operating room includes blood analyzers, anesthetic equipment, and EKG machines; it even has a laparoscope connected to an overhead television monitor so guests can see into the bodies of patients in certain surgeries.

Animal-care experts are on hand to explain goings-on and to answer questions about many of the creatures. There are also regularly scheduled presentations allowing you to get up close and personal to live animals, including aardvarks, chinchillas, a miniature donkey, a golden eagle, goats, guinea pigs, rock hyrax, a great horned owl, porcupines, and rabbits.

To the right is Rafiki's Planet Watch, a giant screen that projects a world map spotlighting eleven areas of the world where animals are most threatened by destruction of habitats and the encroachment of human civilization.

Nearby is Animal Cam, four sets of computer touch-screens that allow visitors to control cameras trained on some of the animal habitats. A video and computer system allows visitors to hear messages from well-known wildlife conservationists and to find out about ecological programs in their own backyards.

Research activities directed from the facilities include radio transmitters that allow scientists to track the movement of herds, and endocrine studies that let scientists check on the health of animals without disturbing them.

Next comes a series of rooms with large picture windows that allow visitors to peek in on baby mammal nurseries, brooder rooms for birds, reptiles, and amphibians, and veterinary laboratories and operating rooms.

Near the center of Conservation Station is the EcoWeb computer, where guests can learn about conservation efforts around the world and in their hometowns.

I don't usually make recommendations about visiting bathrooms, but you might want to take a side trip into the public facilities here; while you are tending to your business you can learn things such as the fact that an elephant pees as much as twenty gallons per day.

Chow time. Food service for the one thousand animal employees of Disney's Animal Kingdom is one of the more complex and demanding assignments in the park. Do *you* want to tell a 425-pound gorilla or a three-ton rhino that supper is late?

A full-grown elephant chomps down something like 125 pounds of hay and pelleted chow each day. Anteaters don't eat just ants—they prefer a mix of ants and grubs.

Giraffes have their own smorgasbord hidden high up in the re-created baobab trees: hidden sixteen-foot-wide turntables deliver bamboo, willow, and acacia shoots throughout the day.

The park includes an eight-acre "browse farm" to feed the animals with a stand of acacia, hibiscus, mulberries, and shrubs to replace natural forage for giraffes, gorillas, baboons, elephants, and antelope.

Affection Section

This is your basic petting zoo, done very nicely in Disney style. Here you'll find pygmy goats, Nigerian dwarf goats, a miniature donkey, guinea pigs, and Tunis sheep, plus live demonstrations featuring unusual and exotic animals such as llamas, porcupines, aardvarks, and lesser anteaters.

The animals have hideaways where they can escape over-handling from visitors.

There's a fanciful hand washer built into the snout of an elephant sculpture at the entrance.

Asia

As you cross the Asia Bridge, you enter into the mythical Kingdom of Anandapur ("place of delight"), filled with the crumbling ruins of an ancient village, its temples, and even a maharajah's palace.

In many small ways Anandapur is the most realistic and engaging area of the Animal Kingdom. We enter into a collage of Asian themes, including Nepalese, Indian, Thai, and Indonesian architecture, ruins, and animal carvings. A stand of trees grows from the ruins of a tiger shrine, and two massive monument towers—one Thai and one Nepalese—provide an idyllic setting for two rival families of gibbons who create a hooting racket all day.

The pathway from Harambe to Asia offers one of the best views of the Tree of Life. Overall, this is a place to go slow and enjoy the scenery and the animals and the sense of place. Asia opened in the spring of 1999, almost a year after the rest of the park; plans call for continued expansion over the years, along the shores of Discovery River.

Humankind and animals have lived in relative harmony for centuries here in the rainforest. But today the lush Asian lands are in danger: fires are burning, trees are falling, and animals are losing their habitat. An environmental message about logging and development underlies much of this area.

WOW Kali River Rapids FAST

Aboard twelve-passenger rubber rafts, adventurers zoom down the raging whitewater Chakranadi River through rapids and waterfalls and through dense jungles and into a modern-day parable about the effects of thoughtless development. *Chakranadi* is a Thai word meaning "river that runs in a circle."

Traveling into a huge bamboo tunnel, rafters are surrounded by a jasmine-tinged mist as they are lifted forty feet to the river's headwaters. The tour begins with a close call with a geyser from the river bottom; if you're lucky you'll watch the people sitting opposite you take a surprise shower.

At the top of a climb a giant carved tiger face peers from behind a waterfall. Gliding on through a rainforest and temple ruins, the raft emerges from a thicket of bamboo, and the smell of jasmine is lost to the acrid smell of smoke from burning trees. The raft twists and spins through the river, swollen by uncontrolled runoff from rain, the unpleasant result of environmentally careless logging.

Disaster narrowly avoided, more thrills await on a white-knuckle race through turbulent waters, some of the more energetic I've seen on a river raft ride. The large rafts move comfortably; take advantage of the dry storage section in the center of the boat for backpacks.

Depending on luck (and how heavily weighted down your raft is) you will end up somewhere between damp and drenched.

The setup to the ride has some lovely attention to details. The queue winds its way through a wooden temple; beyond the rails you can spot stone gods in the jungle. The counter at the entrance to the rapids holds a sign saying the owner is away, "gone to temple." The shelves are stocked with native guidebooks, and Kodak film in Indian-language packaging.

Speaking of queues: You can expect the water ride to be very popular on hot Florida afternoons. I'd suggest heading there early or late on crowded days.

WOW Maharajah Jungle Trek

At the end of the river ride lies a trail through an Asian wonder world, through temple ruins partially reclaimed by the jungle.

Komodo monitor dragons, which grow up to twelve feet long, perch on rocks near a stream bed. Across a wooden foot bridge are Malayan tapirs, families of bats, rare Asian birds, and other exotic creatures.

Tapirs are strange creatures that look like a long-nosed pig dressed in a tony gray Cardigan sweater.

A distant relative of the rhinoceros and horse, tapirs are most active in the early morning and late afternoon.

The ruins of a maharajah's palace are home to a group of Bengal tigers. Beyond them lie a herd of blackbuck antelope and Elds Deer. The animals are visible from the top of a parapet, through a bamboo stand, and from a bridge amid the recreated ruins near an old herb garden. On one of the visits I made, I watched as one of the tigers spent much of the warm morning swimming back and forth in a moat.

Maharajah Jungle Trek

© Disney Enterprises, Inc.

Gibbons let loose hoots as they swing from a Thai temple to a Nepalese monument tower.

Near the end of the trek is a walk-through aviary, home to species of ground-, mud-, and tree-dwelling birds.

There's also a bat room, with visitors standing on the free side of an open wood grate with slats too wide for the creatures to pass through. (There's also a go-round for those too squeamish to face the bats up close and personal.)

Flights of Wonder

Birds swoop low over the audience gathered at Caravan Stage, a 1,250-seat amphitheater overlooking the Discovery River just across the bridge to Asia.

Flights of Wonder demonstrates the skills of some of the world's most interesting birds, including falcons, macaws, vultures, hawks, and owls in a twenty-five-minute show that is presented several times daily.

Here you'll meet Luke, the youngster whose discovery of a treasure map takes him back to the land of his ancestors, an Anandapur village in southern Asia. There's a cast of dozens of rare birds from at least twenty species.

And then there is the phoenix, the wise old bird of mythology who emerges from an explosion of fire and smoke to befriend Luke and, with the assistance of several trainers, reveals the wonders of birds.

The show is set in a crumbling fortified town in Asia, a centuries-old way station on the fringe of the desert. The buildings are pockmarked to provide homes for some of the avian actors as they wait for their cues to perform. Others even fly from the top branches of the 145-foot-tall Tree of Life just on the other side of the Discovery River.

A Harris hawk or a Barbary falcon swoops down and swipes Luke's hat. Toco toucans catch grapes at ten paces. A black-legged seriema, a large crane-like bird, body-slams a real-looking serpent. Tumbler pigeons do midair backward somersaults.

Other stars include a green-winged macaw, king vulture, Eurasia eagle owl, and moulacan cockatoo. At some shows, an augur buzzard flies out and lends a hand by scratching the head of the phoenix.

Although the show is carefully rehearsed, the birds are taught to show off their natural talent rather than perform tricks. Trainers demonstrate how birds respond to special audio or visual clues.

Casting will vary from show to show. At one performance, a troop of Indian runner ducks will dash across the stage on cue; another time the role might be taken by Abyssinian ground hornbills in flight.

DinoLand, U.S.A.

A celebration of America's fascination with all things dinosaur, this section of the Animal Kingdom looks like a quirky roadside attraction of the 1950s, complete with an old Airstream trailer, a Quonset hut, pink (plastic) flamingos, and other bits of dino-Americana. You will enter into the area beneath the skeleton of a fifty-foot-tall brachiosaurus.

Dinoland, U.S.A., features the Boneyard playground, a rambling open-air dig site filled with fossils; kids can slide, bounce, and slither through the bones of *Tyrannosaurus rex*, triceratops, and other long-gone giants.

New in 2001 is **Chester & Hester's Dino-Rama!**, rides and games aimed at the youngest visitors.

WOW Dinosaur *FAST*

Dinosaur is housed within what we're told is the "once-secret research project of the Dino Institute, built as a discovery center and ongoing research lab dedicated to uncovering the mysteries of the past." (Does this sound like Jurassic Park? More than a little, actually.)

The attraction, which opened as Countdown to Extinction, was renamed in 2000 to support Disney's film of the same name.

Enter into the institute's rotunda, filled with murals, dioramas, and fossils telling the scientific theory of how the dinosaurs became extinct. A video starring Disney's favorite techno-geek Bill Nye explains that scientists now believe that an asteroid—six miles across and traveling 60,000 miles per hour—slammed into the earth in a fiery crash sixty-five million years ago at the end of the Cretaceous Era. The resulting "nuclear winter" blocked the sun and dropped temperatures for several years, devastating plant life. Much of the planet's animal life, deprived of food, followed into extinction.

Cast of dino characters. Here is the dinosaur crew, in their order of appearance in Dinosaur: Styracosaurus, Alioramus, Parasaurolophus, Raptor, Carnotaurus, Saltasaurus, Cearadactylus, Compsognather, and Iguanadon.

According to Disney Imagineers, the show was cast as if it were a movie, with a hero and a villain. The hero is the iguanadon, a plant-eating dinosaur large enough to make an impression anywhere he goes, but gentle-looking with a wise, beaked face.

Planners wanted to surprise visitors with a villain few had ever encountered in films, museums, or books: the carnotaurus. The name means "meat bull" and the creature matches its fearsome name with the blunt face of a bulldog, a gaping mouthful of savage teeth, and two huge horns. The creature in the show was based on a nearly complete skeleton of a carnotaurus that was uncovered recently in Argentina. The audio-animatronic version, though, is larger and even more fearsome than the real thing—that's show biz.

As many as eighty guests at a time are ushered into a briefing room for a video conference with the director of the institute, Dr. Helen Marsh. "I hope you enjoyed the quaint exhibits in the old wing," she says. "Today that bare bones approach is history. The Dino institute has created the Time Rover—an amazing vehicle that can literally transport you to the age of the dinosaurs."

The idea is to take guests back to the start of the Cretaceous Era for a thrilling but safe romp amongst the dinosaurs. And, we're promised, we'll be whisked back to the present day well before that asteroid crashes into the planet. As Dr. Marsh assures us, "The future is truly in the past."

Of course, nothing could possibly go wrong, right? Well, wait until you meet paleontologist Grant Seeker (nudge, nudge: Get the egghead joke?). It seems Seeker has a plan of his own: he wants to use the Time Rover to retrieve a living, breathing iguanadon. And to do so, he needs to send us very close to the end of the Cretaceous period. You know, when the asteroid is due.

Dr. Marsh is in charge, of course, and Seeker promises her the Time Rovers are properly programmed. But why is he winking at you?

Finally, we descend into the loading area for the twelve-passenger Time Rovers, three rows of four seats. Buckle yourself into a seat and put your cameras and personal belongings into the pocket in front of you; you're going to need your hands to hold on tight.

And then we're off, into a cloud of fog and a blizzard of flashing lights . . . we're going back, back, back in time.

Suddenly we emerge into a sunless prehistoric forest, a place of strange insects and birds, and the honking and shrieking of giant beasts. As our Time Rover climbs a small hill, the headlights reveal a styracosaurus. Nearby, an alioramus indelicately dines on a giant lizard.

As we move through the fantastic landscape, we can hear the voice of Grant Seeker as he helps us search for the iguanadon of his dreams. He doesn't seem all that concerned about the sudden hail of meteorites that is falling from the sky, smashing into the vehicle and making it swerve off the road . . . and directly into the path of a fearsome carnotaurus.

But wait! The big meteor is on its way. Will Grant Seeker manage to pull you back sixty-five million years to the Dino Institute before it hits the earth, or before you become a dino dinner?

You will, of course, survive to spend another day at Disney. As you stumble out of the institute and back to the present day at the park, be sure to check out the security camera images near the exit; is that an iguanadon wandering the halls?

Everyone is going to enjoy the show, although some riders may find that the loud jumble of noises and flashes make the story a bit difficult to follow; others may find the ride itself a bit jarring.

The CTX Rovers are versions of the vehicles used at Disneyland's Indiana Jones Adventure, Temple of the Forbidden Eye ride. The Rovers use a Disney technology known as Enhanced Motion Vehicle, which controls the movement of the transport forward and backward, up and down, and side to side, as well as the sounds and some of the special effects of the ride. Each vehicle can stop, back up, slow down, or go faster based on computer decisions.

Guests must be at least forty-six inches tall to ride, and pregnant women and visitors who have medical conditions are advised against travel.

Chester & Hester's Dino-Rama! The dinosaurs are in charge in this family ride area. New in 2001 and 2002 are a pair of carnival rides and half a dozen midway games. Chester and Hester's Dinosaur Treasures is a re-creation of a quirky roadside stand of the (believe it or not) pre-Disney era in America, selling all manner of dinosaur souvenirs. The fun fair includes carnival games like Ringosaurus where guests toss beanbags into dinosaur jaws.

Triceratop Spin. A hub-and-spoke spinning ride; sixteen four-person vehicles move up, down, and around in a ride that transforms into a giant spinning toy top. The top rises to reveal—what else?—a dinosaur.

Primeval Whirl. In the spring of 2002 Disney will unveil a small family coaster ride with thirteen rider-controlled spinning cars. Chester and Hester's homemade "time machine" is a wacky run that sends riders through curves, short drops, and the jaws of a dinosaur.

The Boneyard

Not since the days of the dinosaurs has there been a playground like this: bones, fossils, and reconstructed dinosaur skeletons are everywhere. Children of all ages can dig in the sand to uncover the pieces of the past (returning them later for other explorers to find). There's also a set of walkways, rope bridges, and slides that lead in every which way.

Cretaceous Trail

A walk through the past, where guests can wander through a garden of cycads, palms, ferns, and other surprising survivors from the age of the dinosaur, including soft-shelled turtles and Chinese crocodiles.

The cycad collection of more than three thousand ancient fern-like plants is the third-largest in North America. It includes direct descendants of four botanical epochs of plant evolution dating back hundreds of millions of years, such as ferns, mosses, conifers, broadleaf plants, and the first flowering plants.

Dinoland, U.S.A., features twenty species of magnolia, a flowering plant that dates back to the Cretaceous period.

WOW *Tarzan Rocks!*

A high-energy stage and rock show, based on Disney's *Tarzan* film.

Think of this lively show as a Disney rock opera, with a theme song of "Two Worlds, One Family." The story begins as jungle creatures drop for the forest canopy overhead; then the curtain parts to reveal a modern-day rock band.

The music and effects are very loud and flashy. Among the stars are the acrobats on ropes, and the roller-skating monkeys who perform airborne tricks on a track that extends into the lower orchestra.

The show debuted in mid-1999, marking the first major change among attractions at Disney's Animal Kingdom. *Tarzan Rocks* replaced *Journey into Jungle Book,* a musical show based on Disney's classic animated film, which in turn was loosely based on Rudyard Kipling's writings.

The 1,500-seat covered outdoor amphitheater is a nicely shaded setting.

Fossil Preparation Lab

At DinoLand, U.S.A., in 1999 and 2000, staffers from Chicago's Field Museum performed some of the studies of "Sue," the largest, most complete skeleton of a *Tyrannosaurus rex* ever found.

Sue is now on display in Chicago. A life-sized replica of the fifty-foot-long dinosaur was due to be created and displayed at Disney's Animal Kingdom.

The T-rex, 85 percent complete and including 350 bones, was uncovered in South Dakota in 1990 by fossil hunter Susan Hendrickson; it's her name the dino bears. Only twenty-two other T-rex remains have ever been found.

The skeleton was purchased in 1997 at auction by the Field Museum with support from Walt Disney World and other companies.

Camp Minnie-Mickey

Since the Disney empire did start with a mouse (and then his girlfriend, and then various dogs, ducks, and other creatures), it was obvious from the start that some of the most famous animals of our time would have an area of their own. (And yes, Goofy is a dog.)

Just across the Discovery River southwest of Safari Village, Camp Minnie-Mickey is a child's paradise of woodland trails and "meet-and-greet" pavilions, set in a Northeastern forest of cedar and birch trees. Benches and other furniture were handcrafted by artisans from the Adirondacks. Each trail leading to a character meeting spot is themed to set up an exciting character encounter.

As guests cross a wood-hewn bridge from Discovery Island to Camp Minnie-Mickey, they stroll alongside a babbling brook to find life-like images of Mickey,

Goofy and Donald Duck at their favorite fishing hole. You'll also find Winnie the Pooh and Tigger camped out in a grove of maples and oaks.

WOW *Festival of the Lion King*

Here's Disney's stagecraft at its best, a rollicking combination of Broadway, an indoor parade, and a circus. Oh yes, there are also stilt walkers, fire twirlers, singers, dancers, acrobats, and floats.

The theater is a one-thousand-seat hexagonal timber structure. Guests are assigned to one of four triangular rooting sections: elephant, giraffe, warthog, and lion.

Giant stages move in from four directions to bring us up close to Simba and other animal heroes of *The Lion King*, along with singers, dancers, and acrobatic performers costumed in African tribal garb or dressed to depict exotic African animals. The show opens with a rousing rendition of "I Just Can't Wait to Be King."

A twelve-foot-tall figure of Simba rises from Pride Rock. To the left is Elephant Waterfall, where a playful pachyderm spouts water from his trunk. Across the way is a pair of swaying giraffe heads. And nearby is a jungle mesa topped by Pumba and Timon.

The unbilled stars of the show, though, are a troupe of acrobats who perform a comic—but impressive—routine on a trampoline and trapeze at center stage. A pair of adagio dancers performs to "Can You Feel the Love Tonight?" and the girl returns later in a flying harness to soar above the crowd. Kids from the audience are brought forth for a production of "Wimboweh."

The twenty-eight-minute show is performed eight times daily. Lines can build at midday; one strategy to avoid crowds is to visit the show early, or aim for a show that takes place near starting time for one of the two daily March of the Animals parades.

Pocahontas and Her Forest Friends

Pocahontas takes to a rustic stage to help us discover the secret to saving America's forests and the creatures that live there.

With the help of Grandmother Willow—a spirit in a tree trunk—as well as a live armadillo, red-tailed hawk, skunk, boa constrictor, and several rabbits, Pocahontas and the audience learn that only humans can save the animals and the forest from civilization.

The twelve-minute show is presented through the day in a 350-seat outdoor theater. Trees offer shade to part of the seats.

Animal Kingdom's Top Ten

They're all stars, but here are ten of the most unusual and interesting creatures in the park:

• **Gerenuk.** An antelope with a pencil-thin neck, oversized ears, and delicate features, it stands on its spindly hind legs to feed on vegetation. Look for these other-worldly creatures on the savanna from Kilimanjaro Safaris or from the savanna overlook at Pangani Forest Exploration Trail.

• **Naked Mole Rat.** A homely, cold-blooded creature from Kenya and Ethiopia that lives in an underground colony centered around a queen, the only female in the colony capable of reproduction. Pink and virtually hairless, these members of the mole family seem to "moonwalk" along tunnels. A glass wall exposes the colony along the Pangani Forest Exploration Trail.

• **Marabou Stork.** It's been called the "world's ugliest bird" and it's not hard to understand why: it sports a pick-ax bill, two unsightly pouches, and a naked cranium that has scab-like spots. Standing as much as five feet tall, they were slaughtered in large numbers at the turn of the century for hat makers who sought the downy feathers under their tails. One of the largest groups in North America can be seen on the savanna.

• **Okapi.** One of the largest mammals discovered in the twentieth century, okapi are found only in the Ituri Forest of the Republic of Congo. Resembling a cross between a giraffe and zebra, it is a shy, solitary, and short-necked member of the giraffe family. They can be seen near the start of the Kilimanjaro Safaris tour and from the Pangani Forest pathway.

• **Sable Antelope.** Large and aggressive antelope from southern Africa with scimitar-shaped horns that allow them to stand up to large predators, including lions. When at rest, they lie in a circular star pattern with their heads facing out and their young in the middle to protect them from predators. A herd of sable can be seen from the Kilimanjaro Safari.

• **Carmine Bee-Eater.** One of the most beautiful African birds, about a foot long with an iridescent turquoise head and a flaming carmine red body. It performs amazing acrobatics in pursuit of bees, one of its favorite foods. One of the largest flocks in North America can be seen in the aviary on Pangani Forest Exploration Trail.

• **Red Kangaroo.** This marsupial's unusual reproductive system allows her to have one offspring at foot while another nurses and grows in her pouch and a third is in the embryonic stage; she can produce two kinds of milk at the same time for these different-aged joeys. Boomers (males) are reddish in color, while females are bluish gray. They can leap distances of up to forty feet, reaching speeds of 30 miles per hour. A group can be seen in the Tree of Life area.

• **Ring-Tailed Lemur.** About the size of a large house cat, gray with a long black-and-white striped tail, they spend their leisure time sunbathing. One of the few primates that gives birth to multiple young, its horrific screaming is mostly bluster. A colony can be seen in the Tree of Life area.

• **White Rhinoceros.** Not really white—you go and tell him—but actually brownish-gray, its name comes from a mistranslation of the Afrikaans word for "wide," which describes the animal's upper lip. This creature, as much as three tons in weight, has been poached for years for its horn, which is used for ceremonial dagger handles in northern Africa and in Chinese folk medicine. Though they don't swim, they like to take dips to cool off. They can be seen from the Kilimanjaro Safari.

• **Black Rhinoceros.** More rare than white rhinos, these animals from eastern and southern Africa are also more aggressive. They use their hooked lip to grab the shrubs they eat. Fewer that five thousand are left in the wild; like the white rhino, they have been poached for their horns. They can be seen on the savanna from the Kilimanjaro Safari.

According to Disney most of the animals on display were born in zoological parks; others were rescued from endangered habitats or are orphans that have been saved by wildlife officials.

Eating Your Way Through Disney's Animal Kingdom

There are several interesting fast-food restaurants in the park as well as one sit-down restaurant, the Rainforest Cafe, near the entrance. You'll also find snacks that include dinosaur legs (well, OK, they're large turkey legs) in DinoLand, U.S.A., fresh-baked cookies in an Adirondack cabin at Camp Minnie-Mickey, and ice cream bars that have the imprint of Simba's paw from stands throughout the park.

The park can be quite hot in the Florida sunshine; be sure to drink lots of water to avoid dehydration. Bottled water is available from vendors and there are free fountains in many locations.

And, unlike the Magic Kingdom, Disney's Animal Kingdom fully embraces alcohol. You can purchase beer in many of the restaurants, and there's even a house brand of wine at a bar in Harambe.

Rainforest Cafe

Somewhat hidden behind a sixty-five-foot waterfall to the left of the entrance is a branch of the quirky Rainforest Cafe chain, the second outlet at Walt Disney World (the other is at Disney Village). There are entrances from inside and outside the park. (You'll need to have your hand stamped and hold on to your ticket to reenter the park; visitors coming just for the restaurant will have to pay for parking in the Animal Kingdom lot.)

The Rainforest Cafe is the only full-service restaurant at the park, and waits for seats in the 575-seat dining room can be as long as several hours. Advance reservations are not accepted, but arriving guests will be given a "passport" with an expected departure time for a dining "safari." Not coincidentally, a large gift shop lies between the check-in desk and the dining room, and your presence—and money—will be welcomed there while you wait. If your safari time is several hours in the offing, you could go back into the park.

There are other sights to see while you wait, though, including real parrots on perches below giant toadstools, giant cylindrical aquariums, and a bubbling water wall at the base of the juice bar. And you've got to love the stools at the bar—I wonder where the front halves of those animals went?

Key

= Fast Food

= Pub

= Full-service restaurant

Safari Village

Pizzafari. Open-hearth oven pizzas, offered with unusual toppings. One of the more Disney-esque places in the park, the inside of the restaurant is nevertheless worth a peek; the walls are covered with animal murals and the ceiling is lined with colorful animal figurines. Small pies sell for about $6. Also available is a mesquite-grilled chicken Caesar salad.

Flame Tree Barbecue. Specializing in wood-roasted meats with tomato-based or mustard sauces. Open for lunch and dinner, there is indoor seating as well as an outdoor dining pavilion along the river. The menu includes smoked beef brisket, pork shoulder, and turkey for about $7, and barbecued rib platters for $8.50.

DinoLand, U.S.A.

Restaurantosaurus. A basic fast-foodery with a slightly altered McDonald's menu, minus the golden arches. You'll find Chicken McNuggets, Happy Meals, french fries, plus hot dogs, sandwiches, and salads. Complete meals are priced at about $6.

A daily character breakfast starring Mickey Mouse, Donald Duck, Goofy, and Pluto is also presented here.

Africa

Tusker House Restaurant. Chicken cooked on the rotisserie, roasted, grilled, or fried, plus prime rib, lasagna, and roasted vegetable sandwiches with tabbouleh. The restaurant sprawls out onto a weather-beaten outdoor patio. Open for breakfast, lunch, and dinner. Prices range from about $7.25 to $9.

Kusafiri Coffee Shop & Bakery. An attractive eatery featuring warm cinnamon rolls, coffee, espresso, cappuccino, and other delicacies. Kusafiri is designed like an east African bazaar, with Arabic archways and ceilings draped in exotic fabrics.

DISNEY'S ANIMAL KINGDOM

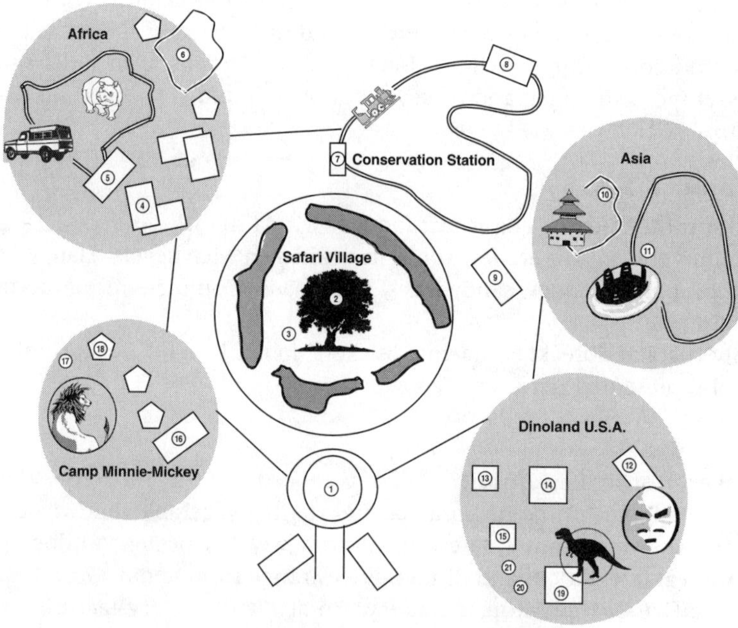

1. Oasis
2. The Tree of Life
3. *It's Tough to Be a Bug!*
4. Harambe
5. Kilimanjaro Safaris
6. Pangani Forest Exploration Trail
7. Wildlife Express
8. Conservation Station
9. Flights of Wonder
10. Maharajah Jungle Trek
11. Kali River Rapids
12. *Tarzan Rocks!*
13. The Boneyard
14. Fossil Preparation Lab
15. Cretaceous Trail
16. *Pocahantas and Her Forest Friends*
17. *Festival of the Lion King*
18. Character Greeting Area
19. Dinosaur
20. Triceratop Spin
21. Primeval Whirl

Chapter 10
Disney–MGM Studios

Let's go to the movies: The Disney–MGM Studios celebrates the magic of film-making and television.

In recent years the park has begun to emerge from the shadows of the other, splashier parks at Walt Disney World. The first step was the installation of the **Twilight Zone Tower of Terror II**, a wild journey that expands on a story from the revered television show. Then came the astounding ***Fantasmic!*** nighttime show and the **Rock 'n' Roller Coaster** starring Aerosmith.

And the park will be one of the centerpieces of the celebration of the one-hundredth anniversary of the birth of Walt Disney, in a year-long observance that begins October 1, 2001.

A 122-foot-tall Sorcerer Mickey hat will crown the studios as its new icon, representing the magic of show business and Disney wizardry. The 156-ton icon, at the end of Hollywood Boulevard directly in front of the Chinese Theater, salutes Mickey's famous role in the animated classic *Fantasia*.

The hat, by the way, is a size 605⅞. It would fit a 350-foot-tall mouse.

New in 2001 was ***Who Wants to Be a Millionaire—Play It!***, a live version of the television hit. Other recent arrivals for the young set include ***Doug Live!*** and ***Bear in the Big Blue House***. Children of all ages will enjoy the audio thrills of ***Sounds Dangerous***. And just to make things interesting, the Tower of Terror was reprogrammed to make it even more terrifying.

The idea behind Disney–MGM Studios is to allow guests to step into some of the greatest—or at least the most popular—movies and television hits of the twentieth century. Not surprisingly, many of them are Disney hits, including *Beauty and the Beast, The Little Mermaid, Mulan, Toy Story, The Hunchback of Notre Dame*, and *Honey, I Shrunk the Kids*.

The overall theme of Disney–MGM Studios seems to be "Nothing is what it appears to be." This will be apparent from the moment you spot the park's distinctive Earffel Tower (a set of mouse ears atop a 130-foot-tall water tower) to when you first see the movie-realistic New York street scenes or see some of the inside magic of the studio production tours.

MUST-SEES

WOW

Who Wants to Be a Millionaire—Play It!
(Mickey meets Regis)

Fantasmic!
(the best nighttime spectacular at Walt Disney World)

Rock 'n' Roller Coaster
(an outrageous coaster for thrill-seekers of all ages)

Twilight Zone Tower of Terror II
(more white-knuckle drops than ever)

The Great Movie Ride

Doug Live!
(adults not wanted)

Sounds Dangerous
(eyes wide shut)

Indiana Jones Epic Stunt Spectacular

Star Tours

Voyage of the Little Mermaid
(adults excused)

Jim Henson's Muppet*Vision 3D

Disney–MGM Studios Backlot Tour

You'll also be able to see the Twilight Zone Tower of Terror II, a creepy derelict hotel. It's fun to think of the Tower as a counterpoint to the squeaky-clean real hotels spread throughout Walt Disney World.

The *Fantasmic!* show is not to be missed. It is quite simply one of the best outdoor entertainments at any theme park anywhere.

Find the time to stroll **Hollywood Boulevard** near the entranceway—I'd suggest coming back to this area at midday when the lines at attractions are at their longest.

The boulevard is a continuous street theater. Pretty girls may be approached by "producers" handing out their business cards. Actresses on the prowl for producers will give men the eye; vain stars will expect you to swoon at their feet. Actors perform skits and gags from old silent films. The street actors stay in character all of the time they are "on"; for fun try asking one of them for directions or some personal questions about their careers.

In recent years Disney beefed up its shopping district on **Sunset Boulevard** to include a Planet Hollywood shop, joining the larger store at the chain's restaurant at the **Disney Village Marketplace**.

The Sunset Boulevard area now includes the four biggest draws at MGM: *Fantasmic!*, Rock 'n' Roller Coaster, the Twilight Zone Tower of Terror II, and the *Beauty and the Beast—Live On Stage* show.

If you arrive late or are visiting on a busy day, start your day with a glance at the **Studios Tip Board** at the top end of Hollywood Boulevard. A chalkboard here will tell you how long the waits are for many of the attractions at the park; the hosts are kept up to date by walkie-talkie reports from head counters. You may need to alter your Power Trip based on unusual conditions.

One more note: the layout of the park make it one of the hottest places in the Walt Disney World Resort. Be sure to wear a hat and use sunscreen lotion any time of the year.

How does Disney–MGM Studios compare to the other movie-themed park in Orlando, Universal Studios Florida? In my opinion, anything within Walt Disney World offers a more polished and better planned experience than almost any other theme park. That said, Universal Studios Florida is larger and has several rides and attractions that are unlike anything else at Walt Disney World, including the Twister, Men in Black, Terminator 2, Earthquake, and King Kong attractions. (The other theme park across town, Universal's Islands of Adventure, includes the Jurassic Park River Adventure, plus phantasmagoric rides loosely based on cartoon characters as well as some of the hairiest roller coasters for older kids of all ages.)

If you have the time I suggest you visit both Disney–MGM and Universal's two parks; if you are on a very tight schedule and must choose among them, I'd suggest Disney–MGM if you are with young children, Universal's Islands of Adventure for teens, and Universal Studios Florida for older parties.

Christmastime at MGM Studios

While we're on the subject of wild fantasies, MGM is also home each Christmastime to the Spectacle of Lights show on its Residential Street and Washington Square back lot.

The display began as a private show that lit up the house of businessman Jennings Osborne; he—or at least his show—was eventually run out of Little Rock, Arkansas, because of electrical excess.

The street is open for strolling each evening from just after Thanksgiving through early January. The back lot tram tour is ended early each day to allow pedestrians to walk around.

The rest of the park is hardly neglected. Live plantings of poinsettias line the paths, a giant set of mouse ears adorns the landmark Earful Tower near the road entrance to the park, and a spectacular Christmas tree occupies the plaza outside The Great Movie Ride.

Power Trip #1

For Adults and Adventurous Kids

Arrive early. This tour allows for a quick fast-food lunch and a more leisurely dinner. Stop by the **Production Information Window** just inside the gates on the right side to see if there are any tickets for tapings of television shows.

Before you start your day, draw up your list of personal must-sees. Order them into attractions that offer Fastpass reservations and those that do not. At Disney–MGM Studios, you can obtain Fastpass reservations at *Who Wants to Be a Millionaire—Play It!*, Jim Henson's Muppet*Vision 3D, Rock 'n' Roller Coaster, Tower of Terror II, Star Tours, *Indiana Jones Epic Stunt Spectacular*, and *Voyage of the Little Mermaid*.

If you're looking for thrills in the morning, I would go the length of Hollywood Boulevard and turn right and head down Sunset Boulevard toward the **Twilight Zone Tower of Terror II**. Make a quick stop at the Fastpass dispenser for the **Rock 'n' Roller Coaster** and then head for the still-short line at the Tower of Terror. If the lines are short and you are so inclined—if you can pardon that pun—check into the hotel again before the lines reach intolerable lengths later in the day.

Now head to the Rock 'n' Roller Coaster in Studio 15 to the left of the Tower of Terror II. Once your stomach is back in its customary position, zoom out of Sunset Boulevard and back to Hollywood Boulevard; make a left at the first corner along Echo Lake. Note the Hollywood & Vine and '50s Prime Time Cafe as possible dinner stops; you may want to make a reservation as you go by.

Your next goal is to pick up a Fastpass for ***Who Wants to Be a Millionaire—Play It!*** If you can get in right away, go for the big bucks; if not, plan to come back in the afternoon with your pass in hand.

Head for **Star Tours.** (Pass by the *Indiana Jones Epic Stunt Spectacular*—it'll wait for later.) After you're back from the moons of Endor, make a sharp left turn and visit **Jim Henson's Muppet*Vision 3D**, a treat for all ages. While you're in the area, check out **Mama Melrose's Ristorante Italiano**, another interesting food stop, or the **Sci-Fi Dine-In Theater Restaurant**, a must-see eatery; make reservations early for these dining options.

The next stop is **The Great Movie Ride** at the top of Hollywood Boulevard. (Along the way, you have passed by *Doug Live!* and *Sounds Dangerous*.)

Continue moving in a counterclockwise direction through the archway to the studio section of the park.

It should be time for lunch now; the **Soundstage Restaurant** is in the studio area and is as good a fast-food stop as any other.

Go next to **The Magic of Disney Animation** tour; don't let youngsters talk you out of this visit—they'll enjoy the movie in the preshow and you'll want to see the artists at work. Nearby is ***Bear in the Big Blue House***, a small live production based on the children's television show of the same name.

At this point, you will have visited all of the attractions that have the longest lines. Backtrack or continue in a counterclockwise direction to see shows such as the ***Indiana Jones Epic Stunt Spectacular*** (consult the daily schedule for show times), ***Doug Live!*** (for younger visitors) and the clever ***Sounds Dangerous*** for movie and Drew Carey fans.

Remember that crowds at many rides and restaurants will be shorter during the afternoon parade; check the schedule on the day you arrive.

And finally, you'll want to end your day at one of the nighttime showings of ***Fantasmic!*** On a busy day you may need to secure a seat as much as an hour before show time.

Power Trip #2

For Young Children and Adults Who Are with Them

This tour skips three rides that may be too wild for youngsters: Twilight Zone Tower of Terror II, the Rock 'n' Roller Coaster, and Star Tours.

Arrive early. Make restaurant reservations for lunch or dinner. Then head up

Hollywood Boulevard and go straight to **The Great Movie Ride**. When you're through, enter into the studio section of the park and join the line for the ***Voyage of the Little Mermaid*** stage show.

Head over to ***Bear in the Big Blue House*** near the soundstages for the short stage show. The next stop is the **Disney–MGM Studios Backlot Tour**.

Now cross over the top of the park to visit the ***Honey, I Shrunk the Kids*** **Movie Set Adventure** and one of the outdoor stage shows such as the ***Hunchback of Notre Dame***.

It's time to go inside to take a load off your feet and your mind with some inspired silliness at **Jim Henson's Muppet*Vision 3D**, a treat for all ages.

Go next to **The Magic of Disney Animation** tour.

Depending on the ages of your children, you may want to visit the ***Indiana Jones Epic Stunt Spectacular*** (consult the daily schedule for show times, and be aware that there are some loud noises and flashes in the show), ***Doug Live!***, and ***Sounds Dangerous***.

And then end the night at ***Fantasmic!***, a treat for all ages. Get there an hour early if the park is crowded.

Attractions at Disney–MGM Studios

WOW *Who Wants to Be a Millionaire—Play It!* FAST

In April 2001, Regis Philbin himself arrived at Disney–MGM Studios accompanied by Mickey Mouse and armored trucks loaded with collectible prizes.

Philbin handed the "keys to the hot seat" to six theme park hosts charged with re-creating the drama delivered in the hit game show, "Who Wants to Be a Millionaire?"

Guests experience "Millionaire" in exacting detail, seated in a replica of the high-tech set, complete with the dramatically lit hot seat. The one difference: guests play for points, not dollars, winning unique prizes along the way. Prizes range from collectible pins and hats to a grand prize of a trip to New York City to view a taping of the ABC-TV game show.

The live show runs continuously throughout the day in a six-hundred-seat studio located in Soundstages 2 and 3 at the Disney–MGM Studios.

Like the television show, the fastest finger determines the first contestant to sit in the coveted hot seat. All audience members play along, using individual keypads at their seats as their scores are tallied throughout the session. They also get involved when players use the "ask the audience" lifeline. Other guests could be called upon for help with the "phone a complete stranger" lifeline.

The "phone a stranger" phones are spread around the theme park. One is in a corridor near the soundstages on the Backstage Tour. A second is near the Fastpass machines for the show. And a third phone, just in case no one answers anywhere else, is in an office in the *Millionaire* production facilities.

At least for the moment, the *Millionaire* show will sharply reduce the use of the studios at the park for film production; Disney has had only limited success in luring film companies to the lot in recent years.

Production at the stages has included the HBO series "From the Earth to the Moon." Films shot at the studios include: *Marvin's Room, Passenger 57, Oscar, Quick Change, Ernest Saves Christmas*, and *Splash Too*. TV shows taped at the studios include: "Sheena," "Full House," "Wheel of Fortune," "ESPN College Football Awards," "World Championship Wrestling," "Talk Soup," "Step by Step," "Barbara Walters Special," and "Live! With Regis & Kathie Lee."

WOW *Fantasmic!*

The fabulous *Fantasmic!* nighttime music, light, water, and animation show, which has been thrilling visitors to Disneyland in California for years, made its way east to the Disney–MGM Studio and became an immediate hit.

The show is presented twice nightly at a 6,500-seat amphitheater behind the Twilight Zone Tower of Terror II off Sunset Boulevard; the stadium half-circles a 1.9-million gallon lagoon. There's also room for another three thousand standing guests, making it the largest amphitheater at Walt Disney World.

Under the baton of Mickey Mouse himself, the spectacular attraction features fifty performers and combines lasers, dazzling special effects, animation, and dancing waters synchronized to the melodies of beloved Disney classics. Three water mist screens are used to project Disney animation.

The twenty-five-minute show takes guests inside the dreams of Mickey Mouse—a world where his magic creates dancing waters, shooting comets, animated fountains, swirling stars, balls of fire, and other amazing wonders. When Disney villains intrude on Mickey's fantasy and turn his dreams into nightmares, he uses the power of good to triumph over the evildoers.

The show opens subtly, with a faint musical note in a darkened theater. As the music swells, a brilliant light bursts in the night sky, illuminating the entire island and casting a spotlight on Mickey Mouse. Mickey's imagination gives him the power to make the waters dance as he conducts the musical score.

Next an animated comet soars across the sky, sprinkling stars against a giant water-screen backdrop. Under Mickey's direction, the stars dance in unison to the "Sorceror's Apprentice"; as the stars burst forth in color they transform into blooming floral images.

To the sounds of African drums and the chatter of wild animals, costumed animal characters emerge from behind the water screens to perform a version of "I Just Can't Wait to Be King" from *The Lion King*.

A cascade of bubbles fills the water screens for a medley of hits, including "Under the Sea." Old friend Jiminy Cricket rises up the screen, trapped within a bubble; Jiminy escapes only to find Monstro the whale in pursuit.

Love is in the air as we are visited by famous couples Pocahontas and John Smith, Cinderella and Prince Charming, Belle and Beast, Aladdin and Jasmine, Ariel and Eric, and Snow White and her Prince.

The merriment fades rapidly with rumbling thunder and crashing waves. The Evil Queen from *Snow White* brews a magical spell with the aid of lightning, flares, and smoke effects. Her plan to defeat Mickey brings together classic Disney villains Ursula, Cruella, Scar, Jafar, Maleficent, Hades, and others to harness the positive energy of Mickey and turn it to evil. Mickey is terrified when Maleficent unexpectedly transforms into a forty-foot-tall dragon whose breath ignites the waterway into a sea of flames that overtakes the island.

But once again it's Mickey to the rescue as the mouse rises high above the water, summoning forth a giant water curtain to surround the island. The fountains begin to dance again, smothering the fierce flames while Mickey defeats the dragon. When MM triumphs, Tinkerbell heralds the arrival of the good guys, and the *Steamboat Willie* River Boat full of all-time favorites comes steaming around the bend.

Fantasmic! is a major draw at the theme park every night, which means two things: Get to the amphitheater early to claim a seat (the gates open ninety minutes before show time), and if you're not going to the show, take advantage of the fact that thousands of people will be out of circulation and not on line at major attractions such as The Twilight Zone Tower of Terror II.

There are no bad seats, although the best view is about ten rows up from the water in the center of the amphitheater, roughly rows I through L. If it's a cool night and the wind is blowing from the stage, I'd recommend sitting a bit further back—the wind can carry some cold mist into the seats.

There's also no cover in the theater—the show will go on in light rain but is likely to be canceled in heavier weather.

WOW **Rock 'n' Roller Coaster** FAST

The Mouse meets hard-rockers Aerosmith for some bodacious partying at Walt Disney World's first serious roller coaster.

The coaster is hidden within a building styled to look like the other working soundstages at Disney–MGM Studios. Stage 15, we find, is the headquarters of G-Force Records. We enter beneath a forty-foot-long Fender guitar into the record company's lobby, beautifully decorated with details that include carved guitar-head columns.

Here's the buzz: the mega-rock group Aerosmith is in the house, recording a new song. Even better, this must be the VIP Tour, for we are ushered through the Artist's Entrance to the recording studio. Music blasts through the closed doors of Studios A and B, and then the door opens to Studio C. Alas, the recording session is over, but wait: there's the band listening to playback in the control room beyond. And they're happy to see us, too; what's a rock band without a following of frenetic fans?

But then a producer rushes in to tell the boys they're already late for a major concert across town. Time to go . . . but not without the fans. It's time to order up the largest, fastest limousine in town.

We step out of the studio and into a wonderfully seedy Hollywood alley, the back door to the Lock 'n Roll parking garage and the Down Under Club. The concert is about to begin and there is no time to waste; we're ushered into our stretch limo, a twenty-four-passenger pink Caddy that shines with chrome. (There are six coaches, each with two rows of two seats.)

Before you've got the time to ask yourself, "How'd a nice person like me end up in a place like this?" your vehicle is launched into a traffic tunnel and the chase is on. And I do mean "launched." The coaster accelerates from 0 to 57 miles per hour in 2.8 seconds. The takeoff is unusual because it is flat rather than up a hill; once the cars reach maximum speed they will climb up to the top of the building under their own momentum.

From there it's a wild trip through Beverly Hills, downtown Los Angeles, over the traffic jam intersection of I-10 and the 101, and through one of the "O"s of the HOLLYWOOD sign. The large signs and thirty sets are illuminated with black light.

All of this is accompanied, of course, by a rock 'n roll soundtrack performed by Aerosmith and blasted through 108 speakers in each train. (There are five different songs, so serious fans will have to ride at least that many times to hear all of the music.)

I visited the coaster during the final days of testing and was treated to an unusual view of the interior of the building with the lights on. The most amazing sight was the first climbing hill at the end of the launch tube—it heads almost straight up the rear wall; it's probably just as well that you won't have to see that stretch of track.

At the top of the hill the coaster almost immediately goes into a double inversion. There's a third inversion a bit further along in the ride.

Disney points out that the coaster was not adapted to fit within an already-built structure. Instead, the tracks were designed and installed at the park and a building was put up around them. This is one reason, Imagineers say, the ride is as smooth as it is.

Riders must be at least forty-eight inches tall to ride. The coaster is located off Sunset Boulevard to the left of the Twilight Zone Tower of Terror II.

WOW **Twilight Zone Tower of Terror II** *FAST*

Behold the mysterious Hollywood Tower Hotel, a relic of Tinseltown's golden age moved to Disney–MGM Studios, complete with a set of high-speed elevators guaranteed to fail on a regular basis.

The Tower of Terror was an instant hit when it opened several years ago; in 1999 Imagineers put into effect the third major reworking of the popular ride, ratcheting up the terror factor and adding a "II" to the title.

The ride begins with a launch skyward. There's a brief moment of panic when the cables of the elevator seem to snap in a shower of electrical sparks. The vehicle then plunges thirteen stories, falling faster than the force of gravity. Then it lurches back upward, only to fall again and again.

I counted seven plunges of various lengths and intensities, including a final drop that delivered a few moments of palpable weightlessness. I might have missed a few drops; it's not easy taking notes in a falling elevator.

Computer technology permitted ride engineers to make changes to the ride with adjustments to the software. According to Disney, engineers tested thirty-three versions to come up with the most exciting variation. The amount of time in the elevator shaft is about the same as it was before the changes.

You'll approach the hotel across its beautifully landscaped grounds; if the waiting line extends outside the building, you are in for a lengthy wait.

Even before you enter the lobby of the abandoned hotel, there are signs of danger high up on the side of the 199-foot-tall building—the tallest structure anywhere at Walt Disney World—you'll see a sparking electrical wires in a sign hanging above a gaping hole in the tower walls.

The Twilight Zone Tower of Terror II
© Disney Enterprises, Inc.

Legend says a full guest wing was once attached to that damaged wall.

What happened to the wing? And more important, what happened to the people who were in the tower when it disappeared?

Well, you'll be given a not-at-all-subtle hint of what lies ahead when you spot an out-of-control elevator cage plunging down the shaft, visible through open doors high on the outer wall.

Once inside, you'll be in the lobby, with the concierge's table and the front desk. Check out the rich details. For example, on the left side you'll see a dusty unfinished mah-jongg game and a pile of 1930s newspapers. Many of the furnishings of the lobby came from old hotels in Hollywood and Los Angeles, including the famed Jonathan Club, an L.A. landmark built in the 1920s.

Eventually you'll make it to the bellhop's podium where you will be sent to one of the four libraries. (Warning: if you're prone to claustrophobia, you may feel uncomfortable in the library; then again, if the library scares you, then the elevator will definitely terrify you.)

The introduction begins in the darkened hotel library as a flash of lightning energizes a television in the corner. Our host, Rod Serling (long dead, but that doesn't matter in the Twilight Zone), tells the story of the dark and stormy night—Halloween of 1939, to be exact—when the guests disappeared from their elevator and stepped into a nightmare.

"This elevator travels directly to . . . The Twilight Zone."

We learn that when the lightning bolt struck, all the main elevators of the building were lost; only the creaky old service elevator still functions.

And then the library doors open to reveal the entrance to the hotel's basement, a creepy world of boilers, generators, and electrical boxes. It even smells like a basement.

There's another waiting line down in the basement; the line splits into left and right queues that head to one or the other of the two elevator shafts in the building. The rides are the same, although the shaft to the right offers a brief view of the park from the top, while the left shaft overlooks the Disney road system.

The cars seat twenty-two passengers with three rows. If you want to sit in the front row of the car, you'll need to camp out on one of the spaces marked 1 or 2 in front of the elevator; to snag the center seat on the top row—a seat with an unobstructed view and a seat belt instead of safety bar to hold you in place, you'll want to ask for Seat 4 in Row 5. The elevator operator at the door may be willing to cooperate with you in making your choice.

The doors of the elevator will open on the first floor where you will see a happy family and bellhop suddenly struck by lightning; the view changes to a star field. Your car will move forward into the lights and the shaft.

When you arrive at the "fifth dimension" you will look out at what seems to be an elevator shaft. Wait a minute! Are you going up or sideways? And who are those people who seem to have hitched a ride in your elevator? They seem like ghostly doubles of you and those around you.

Finally, you are in the vertical elevator shaft in the most severely damaged part of the hotel; your cab rises up higher and higher. At each floor, you can catch glimpses of the happy theme park outside. At the very top, you will reach the damaged elevator motors; they are sparking and flashing ominously.

The door opens for a view of the park; guests watching from outside will be able to see the elevator cab hanging in space for a few seconds.

The elevator cab is actually driven downward by high-power motors so that it travels faster than it would in free-fall. The rest of the way down, the cab travels in what the engineers call "controlled deceleration." That means putting on the brakes. And, by the way, the drop is advertised as a thirteen-story drop but the top floor is the twelfth. Ah, but you got on the elevator in the basement.

How good is the ride? Well, it definitely is worth a WOW in this *Econoguide*. But it is a very short experience once you are in the elevator, about two minutes with just ten seconds or so of drop. Personally, I love the ride, but I work real hard to avoid waiting in line for two hours for ten seconds of thrill.

On busy days be sure to get to the park early and ride the Tower of Terror immediately, especially in the summer and in holiday periods.

On one of my visits in March, the official opening hour for Disney–MGM Studios was 9 A.M. but the gates opened at 8:30 A.M. and people poured into the park. We were on the ride by about 8:40, off by about 8:45, and back on ten minutes later. By 11 A.M., the wait was up to nearly an hour. But during the midday parade the lines fell away and the wait was a reasonable ten minutes.

WOW The Great Movie Ride

A celebration of some of the most famous movies of our time within a reproduction of the famous Mann's Chinese Theater in Hollywood.

The interior of the Chinese Theater is a bittersweet reminder of how full of marvel were the grand theaters of the early years of movies and how ordinary are our local quintupleplex mall theaters. In the lobby you'll find what may be the world's most expensive slippers: Dorothy's ruby shoes from the 1939 MGM classic *The Wizard of Oz*. You'll also find a carrousel horse from the 1964 *Mary Poppins* movie, and a portion of the set from the 1979 *Alien* film.

Your first stop is a waiting area in a theater that is continuously showing original trailers from some of the most beloved movies of all time, including *Singin' in the Rain*; *Fantasia*; *Footlight Parade* with Jimmy Cagney, Joan Blondell, and Ruby Keeler; and a stark preview of *Alien*. You'll go within all of those movies and more in the ride to come.

Your moving auditorium will be presided over by a host or hostess who will narrate the tour. After a few introductory scenes, through, your leader will be hijacked by a 1920s gangster or a Wild West desperado (depending on which set of seats you are in). Don't worry, though: the good guys always seem to prevail later on in the ride.

In addition to old Chicago and the West, the moving chairs visit "By a Waterfall" (with more than sixty animatronic dancers) from Busby Berkeley's *Footlight Parade*.

From there the chairs move into the *Nostromo* spaceship, home of the Alien himself; an extended *Raiders of the Lost Ark* set including wriggling robotic snakes; the jungle world of *Tarzan*; Mickey Mouse's *Fantasia*; and finally a drive down the Yellow Brick Road of *The Wizard of Oz*.

The last stop on the ride is a high-tech theater that surrounds you with the sound and images of a short film that strings together some of the best-known scenes of all time. Some visitors come back to see how many stars and films they can recognize as they fly by.

The lines for this attraction build at midday. If the lines extend outside the building, I'd suggest you come back at another time; there is still a lengthy queue within the theater. The ride itself takes about twenty minutes once you're seated.

The ride is worth a visit, although it could use a freshening; it has remained essentially frozen in time since Disney–MGM Studios was opened. Insiders say that a reworking of the attraction, perhaps using some advanced virtual reality technologies, may happen in years to come.

The sidewalk outside the ride includes hand- and footprints from celebrities minor and major.

Look closely to find Pee-Wee Herman, dated 1984, before he became a persona non grata at Disney. Leonard Nimoy's handprint gives the V-shaped Vulcan "Live long and prosper" salute.

Going my way?
The Great Movie Ride brings to Disney–MGM the same "moving theater" cars first introduced at the Energy pavilion at Epcot.

Fly it again, Sam.
According to the Hollywood myth-makers, the Lockheed Electra 12A on display in the *Casablanca* set was used in the real movie, a happy accident.

The heart of darkness.
The spaceship that is invaded by the murderous alien of *Alien*—the most chilling scene of the Great Movie Ride—was named "Nostromo." That name comes from a 1904 book by the Polish/English novelist Joseph Conrad, who spent much of his early life as a seaman on a succession of freighters.

WOW *Doug Live!*

The Beets are coming to town, but Doug is worried that his beloved Patti may go to the concert with Roger. Will love conquer all? Will Quailman and Quaildog triumph over the evil Dr. Rubbersuit? Do you have any idea what I'm talking about here?

If you do know, then you are either a preteen or you hang around one. This musical stage show, based on the ABC Television show "Doug," follows twelve-year-old Doug Funnie, his dog Porkchop, best friend Skeeter, secret crush Patti, and class bully Roger through the ups and downs of preteen life.

It's a lively and fun show for kids, with a talented group of young singers and actors, along with an onstage rock group drafted from audience members. The characters move in and out of doors in the screen.

The message of the show: Be yourself. "That's a cool theme," says Doug. "Why do you think they call this a theme park?" answers Patti.

Outside the building, you'll find the **Academy of Television Arts and Sciences Hall of Fame Plaza** honoring television legends. The Academy was founded in 1946, the same year network television was born; the real Hall of Fame is located at the Academy's headquarters in Hollywood. Among those honored in Orlando are Red Skelton, Bill Cosby, Mary Tyler Moore, Sid Caesar, Rod Serling, James Garner, Andy Griffith, Milton Berle, Danny Thomas, Barbara Walters, Carol Burnett, and, of course, Walt Disney.

WOW ABC Sound Studio: *Sounds Dangerous*

How better to demonstrate the power of audio in storytelling than to take a whole audience of visitors and lock them up in the dark . . . with a high-tech stereo and 3-D sound system, that is.

That's the idea behind *Sounds Dangerous*, starring comedian Drew Carey as a bumbling police detective.

Everything starts out like your basic television sitcom, with Drew in search of a smuggling ring. He's equipped with a hidden video camera and he's in broadcast communication with headquarters. Ah, but something goes wrong and the video camera shuts off . . . and we're all left in the dark. *Very* dark, actually; there's barely a peep of light in the auditorium.

Ah, but we can still hear Drew in our headphones and we learn the entire story from his description and some truly amazing sound effects. Have you ever experienced a haircut and shave in the dark? There's a trip to the circus—watch out for those elephants. And then there is that jar full of killer bees; you don't suppose the glass will break, do you? Can you imagine the sound?

Justice triumphs, and the smuggling ring is unmasked. It's all a clever lesson in how important a role sound plays in movies and television.

Outside the theater is an interactive playroom where you can experiment with some of the arts of movie sound, including a Foley stage for sound effects and computer stations where you can put your own voice or noises you select into a classic Disney cartoon.

WOW *Indiana Jones Epic Stunt Spectacular* FAST

A cast of stunt performers, helped by a dozen or so volunteers from the audience, help Indy save Marion, the heroine of the film *Raiders of the Lost Ark*, from machine-gun-toting German soldiers, an airplane crash, and various other assaults.

The stunt show starts with a real bang as a double for Indiana Jones rocks and rolls across the huge stage. It's a thirty-two-minute world of Nazis, Arab swordsmen, fiery explosions, and bad jokes.

The set received a complete makeover in 2000, with new lighting, sound, and special effects. Many of the enhancements reflect technical advances that weren't available when the show first opened in 1989.

Inspired by the blockbuster film *Raiders of the Lost Ark*, the show re-creates scenes with seventeen stunt performers. The professionals are joined by about a dozen "extras" drawn from the audience. Wearing costumes appropriate for the Middle-Eastern setting, they act as bystanders while Indiana saves Marion from the machine-gun fire of German soldiers and an out-of-control truck that explodes on impact.

The two-thousand-seat covered outdoor theater—a good place to get out of the sun—fills up by show time, even earlier on busier days. The best seats are in the center of the theater; they are filled first and it is from this section that the "casting director" usually selects "extras" to participate. All must be over the age of eighteen; there's a ringer among them.

WOW Star Tours FAST

"Whenever your plans call for intergalactic travel," say the travel posters, "please consider flying Star Tours to the vacation moon of Endor." And watch this space: Disney insiders say a new Star Tours show, perhaps involving some new high-tech projection systems, is in the offing.

Disney builds the atmosphere and excitement beautifully from the moment you walk beneath the huge space machine outside; it continues as you walk through the indoor waiting area that simulates a gritty space garage. The clumsy mechanics are our favorite flaky robots, R2-D2 and C-3PO.

Most of the queue for Star Tours is inside the building; if the line reaches outside the building onto the plaza, you've facing a forty-five-minute wait; if the line extends outside and into the covered space "forest," you might want to plan your expedition to Endor for later in the day. Better yet: grab a Fastpass.

When your time comes you will enter a forty-passenger simulator cabin and meet your pilot, Captain Rex. The doors will close and your seat belts tightly cinched before he informs you that this is his first trip. Too late—you're off. You'll make an uneasy takeoff and then blast (acciden-

Another big adventure. The original voice of the robot pilot at Star Tours was none other than the exceedingly strange Paul Reubens, also known as Pee-Wee Herman. After Pee-Wee was, err, exposed as someone a bit out of the Disney mold, a new (less interesting) voice was dubbed in to replace his.

tally) into and through a frozen meteor, stumble into an active intergalactic battle zone, and finally make a wild landing at your goal, the vacation moon of Endor.

This is quite a wild ride, at about the same level of twisting, turning, and dipping as the Body Wars show at Wonders of Life in Epcot Center. It's a short ride, but a bit rough for the very young; pregnant women and those with health problems are advised to sit this one out.

After the ride note the travel posters for other Star Tour destinations, including lovely Hoth and Tatoine.

Disney insiders say a new film is in the works for the attraction.

WOW *Voyage of the Little Mermaid* FAST

This is presented throughout the day at a theater that includes all sorts of bits and pieces of Disney magic, including snippets from the movie, more than one hundred puppets, lasers, holographic projections, live performers, and audio-animatronic robots. The fifteen-minute show can draw huge lines on a crowded afternoon; it is presented twenty-two times a day. If this film is a favorite of your youngsters, you would do best to head there early. Very young kids may become a bit startled by some of the special effects used in the show; prepare them ahead of time.

At the start of the show the curtain becomes running water, and laser beams overhead create the feeling we are descending beneath the waves. An opening sequence of black-light puppetry is especially enchanting.

Bear in the Big Blue House

A fifteen-minute live stage show featuring some of the characters from the Disney Channel show for youngsters. There are no seats in the theater; you'll camp out on a carpeted floor.

Beauty and the Beast—Live on Stage

Off-off-Broadway, this twenty-minute live-action show at the outdoor Theater of the Stars uses elaborate props, extravagant costumes, colorful production numbers and dramatic special effects to tell the fairy-tale love story of Belle and the Beast.

Many elements from the film are also used in the stage show, including the recorded vocal talents of stage and screen stars such as Robby Benson (Beast), Angela Lansbury (Mrs. Potts, the teapot), Jerry Orbach (Lumiere, the candelabra), David Ogden Stiers (Cogsworth, the clock) and young Bradley Pierce (Chip, the cup).

As the show opens audiences are welcomed by "Be Our Guest," performed by a collection of dancing chefs, bubbling bottles, and a lovely sherbet parfait that becomes a beautiful show girl.

"The Mob Song" takes place in a dark forest pierced with streaks of lightning, wolves' eyes, and huge bats. Here Gaston leads the villagers on a rampage to "kill the beast." Belle proves that love conquers all as the Beast miraculously transforms—on stage—into a handsome prince!

In the final scene Belle and her prince dance to "Beauty and the Beast," as recorded by Angela Lansbury, while surrounded by dazzling special effects, white doves, and serenading beaus and maidens.

Check the daily entertainment schedule for times.

Hunchback of Notre Dame

A thirty-two-minute stage spectacular based on Disney's cartoon of the same name, presented just off the streets of New York at the Backlot Theater near the Muppet*Vision show.

The costumes, music, and staging are a cut above most other shows at Walt Disney World. Pick your favorite dancers: Quasimodo, stone gargoyles, and lovely peasant girls. The confetti gun special effects are a hoot at the Festival of Fools.

Honey, I Shrunk the Kids Movie Set Adventure

A most inventive playground based on the hit movie about a mad inventor whose shrinking ray accidentally reduces his children and a few friends. Play areas include giant cereal loops, ants, spiders, a huge roll of film, and a leaky garden hose. The ground is carpeted in a spongy rubber.

It's a great place for youngsters to burn off some energy; be advised, though, that it is quite easy to misplace a child in the playground. The best strategy is to station an adult by the single exit from the playground, rather than chasing through the various adventures.

WOW Jim Henson's Muppet*Vision 3D *FAST*

We have to admit that we passed by this attraction the first few times we took our kids to the studios—Bert and Ernie and Kermit the Frog seemed a bit too silly, even for an eight-year-old. Were we ever wrong!

The fun begins once you enter the theater, which also happens to be Muppet World Headquarters. Pause just inside the entrance to read the office directory on the wall. Listings include the Institute of Heckling and Browbeating—Statler and Waldorf, Curmudgeons-in-Chief; the Sartorial Accumulation Division, run by Miss Piggy, of course; and the Academy of Amphibian Science, under the tutelage of Kermit the Frog. The security desk at the door advises that the guard will be back in five minutes, but the key is under the mat.

The preshow area for Muppet*Vision includes a wonderfully goofy collection of packing cases with equipment for the Muppet Labs (Tongue Inflators, Gorilla Detectors, and Anvil Repair Kits) and road-show suitcases for the Muppet band, Dr. Teeth and the Electric Mayhem, including paisley bell bottoms, Nehru jackets, Beatles boots, and love beads. There's a big pink trunk that bears the label, "Miss Piggy Satin Evening Gowns"; below that is "More Satin Evening Gowns," and finally, "The Rest of the Satin Evening Gowns." Another favorite: a cargo net filled with orange and green cubes and labeled "A-Net-Full-of-Jell-O" in a tribute to original Mouseketeer Annette Funicello.

But the real fun is within the beautiful 584-seat theater, which is decidedly more opulent than your neighborhood quintupleplex. There's a robotic all-penguin orchestra in the pit (they took the job just for the halibut) and a private box at the front for Waldorf and Statler. The film includes some marvelous 3-D special effects, as well as flashing lights, a bubble maker, smell-o-vision, and a surprise from the skies, as well as a live actor and a cannon.

Don't pass this extraordinary multimedia show by. If you don't have a kid with you, you can pretend you're with the ones in front of you in line. And when you leave, be sure to check out the statue outside: It's Miss Piggy as the Statue of Liberty.

The same show now plays at Disney's California Adventure in Anaheim.

WOW Disney–MGM Studios Backlot Tour

Disney–MGM Studios is a working movie lot, and the backlot shuttle tour is a great way to see some of the real—and not-so-real elements of moviemaking. Films and TV shows under production vary, but have included in recent seasons "Star Search," "Mickey Mouse Club," professional wrestling shows, and bits and pieces of major films, including *Honey, I Blew Up the Baby* and the HBO Films series "From the Earth to the Moon."

The tour begins with a visit to the Water Effects Tank. This pool, home of the *Miss Fortune* tugboat and other miniature or partial boat sets, demonstrates how technicians use fans, explosions, and a four-hundred-gallon splash tank to re-create a raging storm and a battle at sea. Two volunteers from the audience will get to play captains courageous.

From there it's on to a walk through a portion of the prop warehouse. Signs indicate some of the more recognizable objects; pay attention to the tags on some of the items on the shelves for clues to the more obscure.

The large trams run continuously, and lines are generally short in the morning and late in the day. Remember this: the left side of the cars (the first person into each row) is the wet side, no matter what the guide says at first. (Not very wet, by the way—more of a splash than a soaking.)

As you pull out of the tram station, you will first pass by the **Car Pool**, which includes some of the vehicles used in your favorite movies.

The trams next pass through the **Costuming** shops. Artisans at the **Scenic Shop** can build just about anything and everything for the movies; you'll also glimpse the huge stock of lighting fixtures for filmmaking. The interior of a 747 plane was used for scenes in *Passenger 57*; it is part of an actual jetliner retired from Delta Airlines.

The back lot of the studios has a **Residential Street** that holds some vaguely familiar sights—you may recognize homes used in "Golden Girls," "Empty Nest," and many other movie and televi-

Two pants, one jacket. Tailors at the costume shop make as many as 12,000 costumes a year. Disney claims the world's largest working wardrobe, with more than 2.5 million items available. Among articles on display is a hot red dress from *Pretty Woman* and Michael Jackson's "Captain EO" suit.

Fishy statue. Note the statue between the Studio Catering Co. and the Special Effects Tour. It's the actual mermaid fountain from the 1984 film *Splash*.

sion settings. These are empty shells used for exterior shots; interior filming is done within soundstages in California or elsewhere.

At the end of the street you'll make a right turn past the **Boneyard**, home of some of the larger props from former movie productions. Look for the trolley from Toontown in *Who Framed Roger Rabbit* and the UFO from *Flight of the Navigator,* among other props. Parked on a corner is a Gulfstream airplane owned by Walt Disney and used in 1964 during the scouting for land for Walt Disney World in Florida.

And finally it is on to a demonstration of large-scale special effects in the area known as **Catastrophe Canyon**, which simulates a working oil field in a narrow desert canyon. We won't spoil the fun except to point out that the "set" features a series of tanks storing seventy thousand gallons of water, hydraulic shaker tables, flames, explosions, and . . . your tram.

The tour includes a stop at the AFI Showcase, honoring American film heritage. Presented by the American Film Institute (AFI), the Showcase includes rare movie artifacts and memorabilia, a video wall, and exhibits on the careers of AFI's twenty-five Life Achievement Award recipients.

Among the many pieces of movie history that have been shown are Rosebud, the sled from *Citizen Kane*; Humphrey Bogart's suit from *The Maltese Falcon;* the cheesy little miniature saucer used in the 1955 sci-fi classic *The Day the Earth Stood Still*; and sketches from *Toy Story*.

The Showcase also has displays on film preservation and the various disciplines of filmmaking taught at the AFI Conservatory, including editing, directing, producing, cinematography, screenwriting, and production design.

Funds raised from sale of items at the Showcase goes to AFI's preservation efforts, such as the restoration and distribution of the recently discovered 1912 film *Richard III*, the oldest surviving American feature film, found in the basement of a Portland, Oregon, home where it had lain untouched for some thirty years.

Lines build by midday; come early or late in the day to avoid a long wait.

Fill 'er up. The oil field at Catastrophe Canyon bears the markings of Mohave Oil, a fictitious company that is also represented at the old-timey Oscar's Super Service Station on Hollywood Boulevard.

Movie souvenirs. If you are a movie fan, Sid Cahuenga's One-of-a-Kind shop near the entrance gate at Crossroads of the World offers large color posters for many classic movies from Disney, MGM, and other studios (we found *Bambi, Sleeping Beauty,* and *Pinocchio* for about $15 each). Also available are small lobby cards for about $3 and even original press kits for major motion pictures.

Sounds like . . . The Foley Stage is named after the acknowledged creator of the Hollywood sound-effects stage, Jack Foley.

The same sort of devices were used in adding sounds to live radio dramas of the 1930s and 1940s.

The work of the audio engineer is known as "sweetening" and includes the use of sound filters, the addition of echo, and the inclusion of sound effects.

Eating Your Way Through Disney–MGM Studios

Disney–MGM Studios includes some of the more interesting eateries at Walt Disney World. Be sure to check when you arrive for Early Value Meals offered at some of the restaurants, and for special meal deals for youngsters.

ABC Commissary. A large fast-food cafeteria offering basic fare that includes burgers, large hot dogs, chicken breast sandwiches, and stir-fry chicken, prices range from about $4 to $5. Children are offered hot dogs, chicken strips, and more for about $4.

Backlot Express. In the Studio Shops between Star Tours and the Indiana Jones Epic Stunt Spectacular. An interesting setting for a burger and hot dog fast-foodery, set among the props of the Studio Shops. Offerings include charbroiled chicken with flour tortillas, burgers, hot dogs, chili, and chef's salad, prices range from $4 to $7. The condiment bar includes a healthy (and otherwise) selection of about two dozen toppings.

Dinosaur Gertie's Ice Cream of Extinction. Across from the Indiana Jones Epic Stunt Spectacular. Cold treats from within the belly of a dino, or so it appears. Some of the same items can be purchased from wagons around the park. The eatery's name is a tribute to Gertie the Dinosaur, one of the first animated cartoon stars; Gertie was a big hit in 1914 in vaudeville shows.

'50s Prime Time Cafe. Along Echo Lake, near the Indiana Jones Epic Stunt Spectacular. Step right into a kitchen of the 1950s; Mom will greet you at the door, and your waitress will stand by to make sure you clear your plate. Luncheon appetizer offerings include Mom's Chili over angel hair pasta for about $4, Dad's Bachelor Chili for about $2.50, and fried zucchini for about $3. Entrees include Magnificent Meatloaf, Chicken Pot Pie, Granny's Pot Roast, and the All-American Burger, for about $8 to $15.

Dinner offerings include Auntie's Roasted Lamb and a charbroiled T-bone steak, prices range from about $13 to $23. Book reservations early.

Hollywood & Vine. At Hollywood and Vine, on the main gate side of Echo Lake. Breakfast and lunch buffets with Minnie Mouse and friends.

The Hollywood Brown Derby. At the end of Hollywood Boulevard, near the entrance to the studios; this is one of the nicer restaurants within any of the Disney theme parks. The Brown Derby was the "in" restaurant and night spot of Hollywood in the 1930s. Owner Bob Cobb reportedly told his friends that food was all that mattered—in fact, he said, his menu would be so good that people would eat out of a hat. So he built his restaurant in the shape of a derby.

This replica of the Hollywood landmark features an Art Deco interior and drawings of movie stars on the walls. Lunch includes the famous Cobb salad introduced at the original Brown Derby, as well as corned beef and cabbage, and pasta with seafood; prices range from about $9 to $18. Dinner entrees include peppercorn-crusted tuna with balsamic syrup, sautéed grouper, rack of lamb, and tomato-garlic penne, prices range from about $15 to $24.

Mama Melrose's Ristorante Italiano. In the streets of New York near the Muppet*Vision theater and Star Tours attractions. A very attractive eatery, filled with the enticing smells from the wood-fired pizza oven.

"Tutta La Pasta Che Puoi Mangiare" (all the pasta you care to eat) costs about $10.50; grilled tenderloin of beef is priced at about $14. Other offerings include fresh fish, vegetable lasagna, and chicken marsala. Your basic (small) pizza sells for about $9.50 and is available in basic, Italian combo, four-cheese, chicken, and pesto varieties, among others. There are also vegetarian, ham, Mexican, and other varieties. The child's menu includes spaghetti, pizza, hot dogs, and chicken strips, for about $4 to $6. There are 292 seats available, but things can become quite hectic between 1 and 3 P.M. Reservations are accepted.

Key

= Fast food

= Pub

= Full-service restaurant

Min and Bill's Dockside Diner. On Echo Lake near SuperStar Television. Belly up to the hatchway in the SS *Down the Hatch*, moored at a dock on the studio pond. Snack offerings include nachos with cheese, fruit cup, Danish, soft yogurt, and ice cream sodas, prices range from about $2 to $3.

Sci-Fi Dine-In Theater Restaurant. Behind Monster Sound and across from Star Tours. Ya gotta see this place—it's a must-see eatery, among the most unusual settings of any restaurant anywhere. Each group of diners is shown to their table—inside a little convertible—by a parking attendant. Each four-seat car with a 1955 license plate faces a large drive-in movie screen showing coming attractions for weird and wonderful science fiction movies of the 1950s and 1960s. Reservations are essential.

On one visit, the films included *Cat Women of the Moon, Devil Girl from Mars* (a creature without mercy), *The Horror of Party Beach* (teenagers, beach, rock 'n' roll, bikers, and atomic monsters) and Peter Graves in *It*, and the original trailers for *Attack of the 50 Ft. Woman*. (The girl in one of the horror films says to the guy she is with, "I expected to be frightened on my wedding night, but not like this.")

The reel of trailers also includes a few newsreels; it runs about forty-five minutes before repeating itself, which is enough time to order, eat, and leave.

All in all, the Sci-Fi Restaurant is a hoot. The food is appropriate for a drive-in theater—very ordinary, but that's not really the reason you came.

Samples from the menu include Journey to the Center of the Pasta, Attack of the Killer Club Sandwich, Return of the Killer Club Sandwich, Revenge of the Killer Club Sandwich, and Beach Party Panic (fillet of fish, of course), prices range from about $8 to $12.

At dinner look for some of the same dishes, plus Red Planet (linguine and tomato sauce) and Saucer Sightings (a rib-eye steak), with entrees priced from about $10 to $17.

Starring Rolls Bakery. Almost hidden to the right of the Brown Derby, offerings include bagels, small loaves of bread, croissants, pastries, donuts, muffins, and cheesecake, priced from about $2 to $4.

Studio Catering Company. Off the streets of New York, next to the *Honey, I Shrunk the Kids* playground. It's an outdoor fast-food restaurant under a corrugated tin roof. Just outside is an ice cream and sundae bar.

Sunset Market Ranch. As you rush to or from the Twilight Zone Tower of Terror II, don't overlook the attractive outdoor eatery on Sunset Boulevard. Included in this area is **Rosie's Red Hot Dogs, Catalina Eddie's** frozen yogurt stand, and **Echo Park** and **Anaheim Produce** fruit and vegetable stands. The market is a tribute to the famed Los Angeles Farmer's Market.

Toy Story Pizza Planet. A pizza parlor near Star Tour, with a collection of the latest in video games—or is it the other way around?

DISNEY–MGM STUDIOS

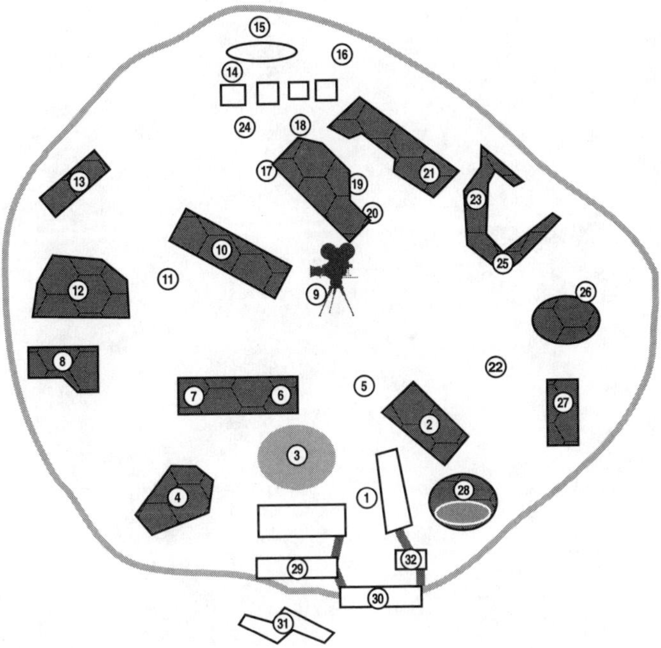

1. Hollywood Boulevard
2. *Beauty and the Beast—Live on Stage*
3. Echo Lake
4. *Indiana Jones Epic Stunt Spectacular*
5. Plaza
6. *Doug Live!*
7. ABC Sound Studio: *Sounds Dangerous*
8. Star Tours
9. The Great Movie Ride
10. Honey, I Shrunk the Kids Movie Set Adventure
11. New York Street
12. Jim Henson's Muppet*Vision 3D
13. *Hunchback of Notre Dame*
14. The Backlot
15. Catastrophe Canyon
16. Residential Street
17. Inside the Magic
18. Soundstage I
19. *Who Wants to Be a Millionaire—Play It!*
20. *Bear in the Big Blue House*
21. Production Center
22. Sunset Boulevard
23. *Voyage of the Little Mermaid*
24. Disney–MGM Studios Backlot Tour
25. The Magic of Disney Animation
26. Rock 'n' Roller Coaster
27. Twilight Zone Tower of Terror II
28. *Fantasmic!*
29. First Aid
30. Entrance Plaza
31. Guest Relations
32. Lockers/Strollers

Chapter 11
Disney Water Parks

On hot New York City summer days when I was a kid, we sometimes managed to unscrew the covers from fire hydrants and turned them on: instant water park!

Over the course of years, water parks have grown much more ambitious. All over America you'll find one-hundred-foot towers of fiberglass and steel, lubricated with rushing water. Beneath them you will find swimming pools that have massive wave machines.

But once again, leave it to Disney to take what has become the ordinary water park and make it extraordinary. It's all in the setting.

Each of Disney's watering holes—**Blizzard Beach**, **Typhoon Lagoon**, and **River Country**—are state-of-the-watery-art. They are a great way to cool off and have a ton of fun on a hot summer or summer-like day—a season that in Florida can extend from March and sometimes February through December.

If you've got an all-parks admission ticket, it's not a bad idea to plan on splitting your day into thirds: start at one of the theme parks in the morning, break away to a water park in the heat and crowds of the afternoon, and then return to one of the theme parks in the evening for more rides and the nightly fireworks or parade.

The water parks have fast food eateries. You can also bring your own lunch in a cooler; no bottles or alcohol are allowed.

If you're on an a la carte plan, jump at the chance to unwind at a water park on the hottest day of your trip. And don't overlook Wet 'n Wild, nearby to its owner, Universal Studios Florida.

Blizzard Beach

You are, of course, perfectly willing to suspend disbelief—that's why you're at Walt Disney World in the first place. So you'll have no problem getting this concept: after a freak storm dumped a ton of snow on Orlando, Blizzard Beach was quickly constructed as Florida's first ski resort. Unfortunately, temperatures quickly returned to normal.

Electricity overhead. Thunderstorms can come up quickly and powerfully in Florida, especially in the late afternoons of hot days. Lifeguards will clear the pools and slides of Typhoon Lagoon or Blizzard Beach if a storm is near, and they may even close the park if necessary.

Whoa! It's you against gravity as you plunge down the flumes at River Country, Typhoon Lagoon, and Blizzard Beach.

You can somewhat control your speed, though, by the way you lie down.

Fastest: Lie on your back with your hands over your head. Arch your back so that only your shoulders and heels touch the track.

Fast: Lie on your back with your hands crossed on your chest and your ankles crossed.

Slow: Sit up.

Slowest: Walk back down the stairs.

And so what we've got here is a ski resort for swimmers. Blizzard Beach is built around ninety-foot **Mount Gushmore**, served by a chairlift to the top of the ski jump.

This is no bunny hill; nearly every one of the seventeen slides are a few notches above the level of Typhoon Lagoon over on the other side of Walt Disney World. It also has the only ski lift I know of where there's a beach umbrella over the chairs.

Downhill Double Dipper. The world's first side-by-side racing slide.

Summit Plummet. This is the big one, the ski jump starting 120 feet up. (It actually begins at a platform thirty feet above the top of Mount Gushmore!) As far as we know it is the highest free-fall water slide in the world. From below, it looks as if skiers . . . er, sliders . . . are heading off a ski jump at the top of the mountain.

Sliders may reach a top speed of 60 miles per hour down the five-hundred-foot-slide at an angle of sixty degrees; the slide passes through a ski chalet on the way down. For those in training for the water slide Olympics, there's a timing clock at the bottom to report your results.

If you make it to the top of Mount Gushmore but lack the courage to take the dive, you can take a slightly easier way to the bottom: **Slush Gusher**, a double-humped slide about half the length of the plummet but still a spectacular plunge delivering speeds of as much as 50 miles per hour.

Another way off the top is **Runoff Rapids**, an inner-tube ride that suddenly drops into a dark section within a pipe.

"Snowmaking" jets spray water over the course as you bounce your way to the bottom on **Snow Stormers**, a twisting and turning inner-tube slide that looks like a slalom ski course.

Ski Patrol Training Center. Activities for the hotshots include the T-bar at the Ski Patrol Training Center, where you can hang on to an overhead trolley for a trip over—or into—a pool. You'll also find the **Thin Ice Training Course**, which presents a pathway across treacherous icebergs in the pool. And the **Krinkle Tin Slide** is an enclosed pipe that deposits sliders into a deep pool.

Teamboat Springs. A record-setting five-person, 1,500-foot raft ride down through waterfalls.

Toboggan Racer. An eight-lane competitive waterslide; unlike the other slides, this one puts riders head-first on a mat. Nearby is another mat slide,

Snow Stormers; this trio of flumes races down the mountain on a switchback course through slalom gates.

Melt Away Bay. A 1.2-acre wave pool at the base of Mount Gushmore.

Cross Country Creek circles the park, pushing visitors on inner tubes on a half-mile circuit; the creek passes through an ice cave where the "icicles" melt onto the paddlers below.

For youngsters there's **Tike's Peak**, which has miniature versions of Mount Gushmore's slides and a snow castle fountain.

The forty-two-acre park is located north of Disney's All-Star Sports Resort, across World Drive from Disney–MGM Studios.

Blizzard Beach is a hot draw and may attract crowds beyond your tolerance during busy times of the year; a contrarian approach calls for taking advantage of Typhoon Lagoon instead. Disney planners will close admission to the park once the lot is full; only guests at Disney resorts arriving by bus will be admitted; come early during peak times. Note that during the off-season in the early months of the year, Blizzard Beach is closed on Sundays.

Typhoon Lagoon

According to Disney legend, this was once a beautiful tropical resort until a rogue typhoon roared through. What was left standing was knocked down by an earthquake. Oh, and then there was a volcanic eruption. (Sounds like a lovely place to vacation.) But the villagers refused to give up, and they rebuilt their paradise in and among the ruins.

The fabulous water slides are built into realistic miniature mountains; the huge wave pool has a sandy beach; and the river rafting ride passes through jungle canopies, a rain forest, and caves. There is hardly any sign of the artificial nature of the park—the water that cascades down the mountain emerges from rivers and creeks without a pipe in sight.

Mount Mayday is one of the tallest peaks in Florida, even if it is a Disney-created simulation. It rises some ninety feet into the air and is topped by the wreckage of the shrimp boat, *Miss Tilly*. The smokestack on the boat erupts in a plume of water every once in a while, adding to the cascades all around.

The namesake central pool is **Typhoon Lagoon**, which is almost three acres in size. Every ninety seconds you can catch some of the world's largest man-made waves, walls of water as high as six feet tall. You'll hear a thunder-like rumble as the wave is generated and a scream from the bathers as the water is released. Two sheltered pools, **Whitecap Cover** and **Blustery Bay**, serve the less adventurous, with shallows for young children.

Up before down. As enjoyable as Typhoon Lagoon is, be aware that there is quite a bit of climbing involved in using the slides. There is a bit less climbing if you use the ski lift at Blizzard Beach, but you can expect long lines at busy times there.

Hang on to your bathing suit as you drop 51 feet at speeds of up to 30 miles per hour, down the 214-foot-long **Humunga Kowabunga** water slide. Do we actually pay good money and wait in line for the privilege of falling this far, this fast? The moment of truth will come when you reach the

Slip, sliding away. According to local myth, more than a few women have lost their bikini tops on the old Kowabunga. Always trying to please, Disney has built a little viewing stand at the bottom.

I spent part of an afternoon there—strictly for research purposes—but the only lost articles I observed were sunglasses.

By the way, I'd strongly recommend wearing an eyeglass strap or carrying your glasses in your folded hands when you ride one of the slides. You should also use plenty of sunscreen.

top; try not to stop and consider the folly of it all. There's nothing to do but to lie on your back, cross your ankles, and fold your arms over your chest. Once you've survived, come back another time and try the slide with your eyes open.

And just to make things more interesting, Disney later added a third Kowabunga slide and put all three within dark tunnels.

Or try the nearby **Storm Slides**. The three body slides, **Rudder Buster**, **Jib Jammer**, and **Stern Burner**, crash through caves, geysers, and waterfalls. Each of the slides is somewhat different—on a busy day you'll have to take the slide assigned by the lifeguard at the top of the stairs. If you have a choice, our favorite is the center slide, which passes through an unexpected dark tunnel midway down the hill. The top speed on the slides is about 20 miles per hour, which seems mighty fast.

Mayday Falls and **Keelhaul Falls** let you loose on a large inner tube through waterfalls, fountains, caves, and more. Mayday is the taller and longer of the slides, about 460 feet in length. Keelhaul is shorter, about four hundred feet, but features include sharper twists and turns.

Entire families can go for a relatively tame white-water adventure at **Gangplank Falls**. Your circular boat will work its way down the mountain in and among waterfalls and obstacles. Don't say the wrong thing to the person who loads your raft at the top of the slide—with the flick of a wrist, he or she can send your raft under the waterfall at the loading zone. The rafts can hold up to five or six persons, and you may end up with strangers if lines are long.

For the youngest swimmers **Ketchakiddie Creek** features water slides, boats, squirting animals, and other toys for children only.

And finally, you can take a tour on the lazily flowing **Castaway Creek** that circles the park for almost half a mile; it takes about thirty minutes to circle completely around. If the traffic gets too thick or if the float is too lazy, you can get out and walk in the three-foot-deep creek or even leave and cross the park to your starting place.

Perhaps the most unusual attraction at the park is the **Shark Reef**, where guests get to strap on a snorkel and float through an artificial coral reef in and among small nurse and bonnethead sharks, and thousands of other colorful little fishies. We're assured that these are peaceful creatures. In fact, naturalists worry more about visitors damaging the fish with their suntan lotions and other pollutants; you'll be asked to take a shower first. It's an absolutely captivating experience and highly recommended.

Lockers and sometimes-crowded changing rooms and showers are available along the right side of the lagoon as you face Mount Mayday. You can also rent towels. During the summer the park is open into the evening; in spring and fall it often closes as early as 5 P.M. Typhoon Lagoon typically closes for maintenance in January or February.

We have found that dragging a towel and shirt around the park is more of a nuisance than it is worth—you can't bring the towel up the waiting line for slides, and the exits are usually not in the same place as the entrances. If it's warm enough to go swimming, you might want to do without a towel.

Although you are allowed to wear water shoes and glasses, you should take care to hold on to both in the water and on slides.

Snack bars in the park include **Lowtide Lou's**, **Leaning Palms**, **Typhoon Tilly's**, and **Let's Go Slurpin'**. Prices range from $3 to $5 for fried chicken, burgers, and fried fish dishes; you can also get soft drinks, beer, and ice cream.

There's also a gift shop, **Singapore Sal's Saleable Salvage**, where you can buy bathing suits, T-shirts, and souvenirs. They also have suntan lotion; you can save a few dollars or more by shopping at a drugstore outside the park.

Note that during the off-season in the early months of the year, Typhoon Lagoon is closed on Saturdays.

Surfing Lessons

Here's your chance to hang ten: every Tuesday the surf boys and surf gals at Typhoon Lagoon offer surfing lessons and a private chance to catch ten waves. Surf's up for two-and-a-half hours before the park opens or after it closes.

By the way, the waves in Typhoon Lagoon's surf pool can get as high as eight feet, which is better than you'll find at many surfing beaches.

Tickets for the surfing classes are $125 per person. Call ☎ (407) 939-7529 for reservations.

River Country

River Country is Disney's version of Huck Finn's swimmin' hole. Get there by driving to the Fort Wilderness parking lot and taking the Disney bus from there to the park. Or you can hop a short boat ride from the Magic Kingdom across Bay Lake.

The walk from the bus stop to River Country takes you past the **Fort Wilderness Petting Zoo**, a small, pleasant shaded area that has goats, sheep, horses, and other animals. Admission to the zoo is free; there is a small fee for the pony ride, with an adult leading the very docile steed around the track.

At the heart of River Country is **Bay Cove**, featuring rope swings, a ship's boom, and other interesting ways to fly out over and into the water below.

Bay Cove is actually a part of Bay Lake, which is itself connected to Seven Seas Lagoon at the Magic Kingdom. Across the cove from the beach are the **Whoop 'n Holler Hollow** corkscrew flume rides. Also emptying into the cove are the inner

Night slide. Consider ducking out of the Magic Kingdom or Epcot some hot summer afternoon for a cooling dip as the sun goes down. River Country is open until 8 P.M. during summertime, and ticket booths have in past years offered lower-cost tickets after 3 P.M.

tube rafts that have come down **White Water Rapids**, which despite its name is actually a rather slow, 330-foot-long meander.

Be aware there is a health warning about swimming in Bay Lake—and most every other pond or lake in the state of Florida. Swimmers are advised not to swim underwater near the bottom of the pond because of the presence of certain bacteria and algae that thrive in the warm waters.

The **Upstream Plunge Pool** is a large heated swimming pool that includes **Slippery Slide Falls**, a pair of water chutes that come to an end about seven feet above the water; you're on your own for the rest of the way down.

River Country is a pleasant break from crowds at higher-energy water parks Typhoon Lagoon and Blizzard Beach; parents can watch children from the comfort of the sandy beach. From the beach you can look across Bay Lake to the monorail, the ferryboats, and a distant peek at Space Mountain.

In the summer, though, the park can become quite crowded, and the gates are sometimes shut before noon; they'll reopen in late afternoon, and the park stays open late in season.

You don't need to pay a parking charge for River Country; head for the Magic Kingdom, and move all the way to the rightmost toll booth. Tell the attendant you are going to River Country and bear right after the toll plaza.

Discovery Island, RIP

Disney's eleven-acre zoological park, stocked with a small but interesting collection of wild animals, closed in the spring of 1999, a victim of the success of Disney's Animal Kingdom.

The island was reached by ferryboat from a dock near River Country, and joint tickets with the two smaller attractions were offered.

Disney is mum on plans for the small island, which lies in an attractive location. One rumored use is as a super-luxury honeymoon island, another as the site of a high-tech scavenger hunt.

Chapter 12

Downtown Disney: Disney West Side, Pleasure Island, Marketplace, Cirque du Soleil

A city of entertainment the size of Walt Disney World deserves its own downtown, a place to unwind at the end of a long day of business, do some shopping, and catch a meal at a place that doesn't use paper napkins and plastic forks. Of course, the business of Walt Disney World is Disney entertainment, and so Disney has created its own very quirky metropolis of restaurants, nightclubs, shops, and theaters.

Set in a crescent curve along one shore of Buena Vista Lagoon, Downtown Disney is made up of:

- **Downtown Disney West Side.** The hottest area of downtown, home to a collection of "celebrity" restaurants, the indoor virtual theme park Disney Quest, and one of the world capitals of weird, Cirque du Soleil.
- **Downtown Disney Pleasure Island.** The original downtown district for adults, it includes a collection of unusual clubs and restaurants.
- **Downtown Disney Marketplace.** Originally known as the Disney Village Marketplace, here you'll find all things Disney as well as a mega-LEGO store and an outpost of the Rainforest Cafe.

Parking is free at Downtown Disney, but sometimes you may feel as if you have parked in East Overshoe, Iowa; there are more than seven thousand spaces in several lots. Valet parking is available for $5 after 5:30 P.M.

If you are staying somewhere at Walt Disney World, consider using bus transportation from your hotel to Downtown Disney.

Downtown Disney West Side

WOW DisneyQuest

Disney's most far-out park exists within the purple walls of DisneyQuest, a place that stands at the cutting edge of virtual entertainment.

How different is this theme-park-in-a-box? Check out its icon: "Hurricane

MUST-SEES

WOW

DisneyQuest
(an indoor high-tech theme park)

Cirque du Soleil: *La Nouba*
(weird and wonderful)

House of Blues
(Disney West Side)

Wolfgang Puck Cafe
(Disney West Side)

Bongos Cuban Cafe
(Disney West Side)

Planet Hollywood
(Disney West Side)

BET SoundStage Club
(Pleasure Island)

The Adventurers Club
(Pleasure Island)

The Comedy Warehouse
(Pleasure Island)

Rainforest Cafe
(Downtown Disney Marketplace)

Mickey," a swirling version of Walt Disney's classic cartoon mouse.

The 100,000-square-foot building was a five-story flagship for Disney's hopes for a chain of similar attractions in dozens of domestic and international locations. Alas, in 2001, Disney closed its second DisneyQuest, in Chicago.

In 2001 general admission was $29, and tickets for children (3–9) were $23. The pass provides all-day use of the facility, including all the video games and pinball you can play. Everyone must have a ticket to enter, and guests twelve and younger must be accompanied by an adult.

Unlimited use of DisneyQuest is now included on the Ultimate Park Hopper ticket for Walt Disney World Resort Guests. Other guests might want to consider purchasing a DisneyQuest annual pass for $79 for adults and $63 for children.

Disney estimates people will make visits of two to three hours. The attraction is usually open from 10:30 A.M. until midnight; there is a capacity limit, and long lines can be expected from time to time, especially on rainy days.

Call ahead for more information and special hours during holiday periods.

You enter DisneyQuest through the "Cybrolator." Your bumbling guide is Aladdin's madcap Genie of the Lamp. When the doors open, you find yourself standing at the Ventureport, a crossroads of adventure leading to four entertainment environments.

Though you will probably be anxious to begin your quest, take a moment to soak in one of the most amazing interiors at Walt Disney World. The crossroads puts you in the middle of a gigantic armillary sphere, an ancient astronomical instrument composed of rings representing the positions of important circles of the celestial sphere. It's a stunning piece of work easily missed.

Many of the DisneyQuest attractions are designed to be changed or updated regularly. Disney say its plans to change 20 percent to 30 percent each year, keeping the place fresh for returning visitors.

New in 2001 was Pirates of the Caribbean: Battle for Buccaneer Gold, a high-tech challenge inspired by one of the most popular attractions at the Magic Kingdom. A crew of four boards a ship-themed motion platform, then works together as captain and cannoneers on an action-packed, five-minute journey. The 3-D adventure culminates in a final showdown with Jolly Roger and his ghost ship.

At **Radio Disney SongMaker**, you can enter a private sound booth to produce your own greatest hit, combining lyrics and music styles to create a one-of-a-kind song. SongMaker offers a choice a few dozen musical styles, including hip-hop, swing, country, dance, and even opera or yodeling. Song titles range from the serious ("I Love You Mom") to the downright silly ("My Dog Gets More Dates Than I Do") and serve as the inspiration for the lyric lines guests string together to form the song. More than a thousand vocal performances by professional studio singers and top musicians are available. You can download the song to a CD (for an extra charge) to show your family and friends your debut as a musical producer.

The **Explore Zone** gateway is through the tiger's head from Aladdin's Cave of Wonders. The entrance is through a 150-foot-long slide that drops two stories (there are stairs, too, for those who prefer to stay on their own feet).

On one of my visits one of the stars here was the **Virtual Jungle Cruise** where visitors were able to navigate a primeval world, where dangers include hungry dinosaurs and a cataclysmic comet. Guests strap their feet into toeholds on a real raft and paddle your way in a virtual reality re-creation of the wildest whitewater expedition ever.

You can drive a miniature camera-equipped, radio-controlled car on a hunt for the **Treasures of the Incas** beneath the glass floor at your feet.

You can fly through the streets of Agrabah on a hunt to release the Genie in **Aladdin's Magic Carpet Ride**, an entertainment that was previewed in a prototype version at Epcot several years ago. Sitting on motorcycle-like simulators and wearing virtual-reality headgear, players become Abu the monkey on a tour on Aladdin's flying carpet in search of the Genie of the Lamp. Participants compete against the clock and each other.

And you'll be able to join Herc and his friends in a battle against Hades in **Hercules in the Underworld**. At **Score Zone**, you can go sword-to-sword with supervillains as you fly through a 3-D comic book world in **Ride the Comix!** As many as six visitors at a time put on head-mounted virtual-reality helmets and brandish laser swords against Disney villains.

Rescue earth colonists under attack in **Invasion! An Alien Encounter** while piloting a planetary walker. This is an extension of the Alien Encounter attraction at the Magic Kingdom. You travel in X-S 5000 Rescue Units, developed to defend human colonists from a succession of nasties. Among the creatures are Alien Warbeasts and riders, slow but numerous Alien Grunts, and bloodthirsty Alien Heavy Weapons Commanders.

And you can become the joystick on a human-sized motion base—a Hover-Disc Motion Base—and hip-check your friends in **Mighty Ducks Pinball Slam**. A hydraulic system lifts the discs slightly off the floor, and players maneuver their ball on the screen by moving their bodies. It's fun to play and to watch.

The **Create Zone** is an Imagineering studio where you can design the roller coaster of your dreams . . . and then buckle up and ride your creation on **Cyber-Space Mountain**, a 360-degree pitch-and-roll simulator. You'll begin at a computer console where you can select ride elements—lifts, drops, rolls, loops, and just about any diabolical twist of fate you'd like to try with some ten thousand feet of virtual track to play with. Ride elements include figure-eights, spirals, barrel rolls, loops, banked S-curves, camelbacks, and straightaways. And then you're off on a ninety-second ride inside a simulator that can roll like a barrel, climb, and drop—in some ways it is more radical than the real thing.

You can learn some of the secrets of Disney animation at the **Animation Academy**, an eighteen-seat video training classroom.

The entry to the **Replay Zone** is through a retro art collection from the moon-crazy '50s; on the other side are three levels of classic rides and games with a futuristic twist. Climb into a bubble-top bumper car and shoot it out with oversized playground balls in **Buzz Lightyear's AstroBlaster**. There are two passengers in each car—one driver and one gunner. If you hit a target on another vehicle, they'll spin out.

And there's a section of carnival games with rewards, including **Dumbo's Water Race** and **Mickey's Lunar Rally**. There's even a **Game Graveyard** where the golden oldies of video gaming live on.

DisneyQuest includes a pair of unusual fast food eateries as well: **FoodQuest**, offering salads, sandwiches, pizza, and fun food, and **Wonderland Cafe**, with indulgent desserts, including offerings from **The Cheesecake Factory**.

For information, call ☎ (407) 828-4600 or consult 💻 www.disneyquest.com.

WOW Cirque du Soleil: *La Nouba*

Wonderfully weirder than most anything else at Walt Disney World, Cirque du Soleil's *La Nouba* brings together an international cast of sixty performers twice daily, five days a week, in a seventy-thousand-square-foot, 1,671-seat theater that resembles a concrete circus tent with a 160-foot-tall mast.

The Montreal-based circus has no elephants and dancing tigers, and its aerialists and clowns march to a decidedly different beat from what you'll find under any other big top.

Created in 1984 by one-time street performer Guy Laliberté, Cirque du Soleil is a striking mix of the circus arts and street entertainment. The circus has permanent show facilities in Las Vegas at the Treasure Island and Bellagio casinos. Other shows tour in Europe, Asia, and North America.

The name of the show comes from an Algerian French phrase, *faire la Nouba*, which roughly translates as "party hearty." The strangeness begins with a nightmare opening scene with a startling moment when a bicyclist pedals by upside-down, suspended from a wire. And the weirdness goes on from there, including the introduction of a raft of creatures who rise up from beneath the floor.

Cirque du Soleil's La Nouba *at Downtown Disney West Side*

Photo courtesy of Cirque du Soleil

There's a bit of a story involving *La femme de ménage* ("The Cleaning Lady") who seems to discover this strange world going on behind the scenes, and there's a wonderfully bizarre strong man who prances about making comically menacing poses.

On my visit four tiny Chinese girls, ages eleven to fourteen, stole the show with a display of incredible acrobatics using the diabolo, a Chinese yoyo.

Another star turn is performed by Vasily Dementchoukov with his chair act, which somehow defies the laws of physics and gravity. At one point he balances precariously on a stack of eight chairs atop a table twenty-five feet in the air, all the while spinning a birthday cake lit with candles. You'll have to see it not to believe it.

A group of bicyclists in modern dress climb and descend stairs, performing some heart-stopping maneuvers at the edges of the stage and open pits. One of the bikers hops his bike over the body of a draftee from the audience.

But my favorite act came near the end when a whole troupe of acrobats perform on the power track and trampoline that rise from beneath the stage. They become human spider-men, launching themselves and climbing the walls of a building that rises from the stage.

And then somewhere in the amorphous story, the cleaning lady kisses a frog and finds her prince.

All in all, this is a spectacular way to spend ninety minutes. Not cheap, though: in mid-2001, tickets for La Nouba were priced at $67 plus tax ($39 plus tax for children). The show schedule varies from season to season. In the busy summertime, advance purchase is essential.

Sight lines in the U-shaped theater are very good; the best seats are in the center about midway up from the stage. Tickets in the 100 series are on the lower level and those in the 200 series are in the balcony.

No photography or videotaping is permitted. The music and sound effects are rather loud, which may be a problem for some guests and children. The show is under contract to Walt Disney World through the year 2010; the show may change slightly over that time as some of the acts rotate in and out.

AMC Pleasure Island 24

☎ (407) 827-1300. 🖳 www.amctheatres.com. Already the most successful multiscreen theater complex in Florida when it had a mere ten screens; the place expanded to two dozen screens a few years ago, making it the largest cineplex in the state.

Sixteen of the theaters feature "stadium seating"—two with balconies and three-story-tall screens. Call for show times.

Virgin Records Megastore

A state-of-the-art music, video, and book mecca; the circular, three-level store features three hundred CD listening stations and an elevated exterior stage for live performances.

Downtown Shops

Also on the West Side is a collection of eclectic shops, including:

- **Guitar Gallery**. Selling one-of-a-kind and celebrity model acoustic and electric guitars.
- **Magnetron Magnetz**. All things magnetic, and not just refrigerator stick-ups, although you can buy those, too. Every few minutes, the store's "magnetic generator" comes to life, energizing the whole place and all that is within it in wondrous ways.
- **Celebrity Eyeworks Studio**. Somewhere out there, someone is looking to buy a replica of eyewear worn by movie stars; this is the place.
- **Sosa Family Cigars**. Stogies from a renowned Cuban family in a store modeled after the living room of founding father Don Juan Sosa Acosta.
- **Hoypoloi**. An unusual gallery of art glass, ceramics, sculpture, and other decorative items.
- **Starabilia**. Nostalgic and collectible old stuff, run by the founder of a similar store at the Forum Shops at Caesars Palace in Las Vegas.
- **Forty Thirst Street**. A high-tone coffee and juice bar with a computer-operated lighting system and fiber optic menus.

Disney West Side Restaurants

House of Blues. ☎ (407) 934-2583. The sign out front of the huge five-hundred-seat restaurant and two-thousand-seat music hall, television production, and radio broadcasting facility reads: "In Blues We Trust."

The place is modeled after an old-time Mississippi juke joint, with rusted metal and fall-down wood trim. It gets even funkier inside, with a collection of folk art paintings and sculptures.

Live blues, R&B, jazz, and country music are presented nightly, plus a rollicking Sunday Gospel Brunch. The restaurant features eclectic cuisine with a delta heritage. Signature dishes, priced from about $9 to $22, include jambalaya, the Elwood (chicken breast Cajun style), the Jake Burger, and étoufée.

There is, of course, a gift shop that sells souvenirs and, more importantly, books about blues and folk art and well-known and obscure blues recordings.

There's even a blues time for youngsters ages four to fifteen. Gumbo Yo Yo, a live, interactive stage show, is presented Saturday mornings, focused on teaching the House of Blues mission of "Unity in Diversity" through comedy, music and storytelling.

Tickets are available at the door, or by calling ahead; parents and children of other ages are free. A portion of ticket sales proceeds go to the International House of Blues Foundation to support various educational outreach programs.

Wolfgang Puck Cafe. The famed chef's first Florida restaurant features his innovative California cuisine in a casual setting adorned with colorful mosaic tiles.

Specialties include wood-fired pizzas with toppings such as spicy chicken and smoked salmon.

There are 550 seats inside in three dining rooms, plus a walk-up Wolfgang Puck Express restaurant. Inside is a sushi and raw bar, a casual dining restaurant downstairs with some seats allowing a view of the kitchen, and a more upscale, reservations-only restaurant upstairs with a view of Buena Vista Lagoon.

Wolfgang devotes his creative energies to the food, while his wife and partner Barbara Lazaroff designs the eating places—the bill was said to reach $8 million for decorating. Be sure to check out the bar counter, which includes a spread of $30,000 worth of semiprecious stones, and the tile work out front.

Bongos Cuban Cafe. A Cuban cafe/nightclub, created by Latin superstar Gloria Estefan and her husband, Emilio, brings the sizzle of Miami's South Beach to Disney.

A giant concrete pineapple outside and elaborate mosaic murals inside speak of the hot, hot, hot heyday of Cuba in the 1940s and early 1950s; there's even a Ricky Riccardo look-alike working as a greeter.

The 471-seat restaurant includes a menu created by Quintin and Carmen Lario, founders with the Estefans of Larios on the Beach, a very popular eatery on Miami's South Beach.

Key

= Fast food

= Pub

= Full-service restaurant

The Cuban style of cooking, comidas criolla or Creole, combines tropical and European elements. Staples include white sweet potatoes, squash, corn, rice, beans, and simmered sauces known as "soffritos."

WOW **Planet Hollywood.** This three-story four-hundred-seat restaurant, on its own plot of land between West Side and Pleasure Island, is one of the busiest eateries on the planet. The club, which has several major film stars among its owners, including Sylvester Stallone, Arnold Schwarzenegger, Bruce Willis, and Demi Moore, is a cinema equivalent to the Hard Rock Cafe chain. (Not at all coincidentally, there is a Hard Rock restaurant at Universal Studios Florida across town.)

The restaurant is decorated with movie and TV scripts, artifacts, and costumes; the sounds of music and film clips echo throughout. Surprisingly, the food is above average, including huge Caesar salads, Cajun chicken breast, hot wings, burgers, and pizza. Entrees start at about $10. Open daily from 11 A.M. to 2 A.M.

Pleasure Island

Merriweather Adam Pleasure, also known as MAD Pleasure or the Grand Funmeister, disappeared in 1941 on a circumnavigation expedition of the Antarctic. By 1955 his beloved home island was in disrepair; the coup de grace was administered by a rogue hurricane.

The six-acre island languished in ruins until it was rediscovered by Disney archaeologists, who painstakingly rebuilt the town.

If you believe that story perhaps you'd like to join the Pleasure Island Histerical Society, whose plaques dot the landmarks of Pleasure Island, which is located next to Disney Village. Even if you don't, a visit to Pleasure Island is a worthy nighttime entertainment.

It's New Year's Eve every night of the year at the nightly **New Year's Eve Street Party**. The celebration begins at 11:45 P.M. and includes music, dancers, confetti, and fireworks.

There's also a Mardi Gras celebration in late February, including a week's worth of partying, live music, and Cajun and Creole specialties. Twice nightly a Mardi Gras procession led by the Krewe of Caesar parades through Pleasure Island. And then there's the Cinco de Mayo celebration of Mexico's Independence Day, held, naturally, on May 5 and featuring festive music, decorations, and authentic cuisine.

There is no cover charge or age restriction to visit Pleasure Island during the day, or at anytime to enter the restaurants. The shops open at 10 A.M. The ticket gates go up at 7 P.M., charging $19.81; after 7 P.M., visitors younger than the age of eighteen must be accompanied by a parent.

Pleasure Island is included in Park-Hopper tickets at Walt Disney World, and annual passes are available at roughly the price of three one-day admissions.

WOW BET SoundStage Club

This upscale waterfront club features jazz, rhythm and blues, soul, and hip-hop in live performances, as well as programming from BET SoundStage Network.

BET operates Black Entertainment Television, a cable programming service. (The club replaced the Neon Armadillo Music Saloon.)

Mannequins Dance Palace

A contemporary club that has a rotating dance floor and a high-tech (recorded) sound, light, and dance show starring the Pleasure Island Explosion Dancers, on stage several times each night. There are also a bunch of strange mannequins scattered about, bubble machines, and more. You must be twenty-one to enter.

Pleasure Island Jazz Company

A club celebrating America's native music with live performances in an old warehouse; all around is amusement park and carnival equipment.

Rock 'n' Roll Beach Club

Live bands perform the classics of rock; a DJ spins stacks of vinyl—well, stacks of CDs anyway—during breaks. Be sure to check out the second floor where you'll find a selection of pool and air hockey tables and video and pinball machines; check out the shark hanging from the ceiling with a bikini top in its teeth. Menu items include pizza by the slice.

8TRAX

If you can remember what an 8-track tape player was, you'll understand the basic concept of this celebration of the '70s (starring The Doors, Iron Butterfly, Janis Joplin, bell-bottoms, bean bag chairs, and lava lamps). The dance floor includes your basic disco mirror ball and a fog machine.

Half the pleasure. You can enter Pleasure Island during the day without buying a ticket; this will allow you to visit the shops and restaurants for free. Guests who are within the gates at 7 P.M. can stay at Pleasure Island and see all the outdoor shows without buying a ticket, although a Pleasure Island ticket is required to enter any of the clubs. The clubs generally open at 8 or 8:30 P.M.

Designated drinkers. Note that the drinking age in Florida is twenty-one, and visitors to Pleasure Island who are not obviously over that age will be required to show proof of their birthdate; once "carded," you'll receive a wristband you can wear for the rest of the evening. There is, however, no requirement that you buy any drinks in any of the clubs—just say "no" and you'll be left alone to watch the shows.

WOW The Adventurers Club

Kungaloosh! Welcome to the decidedly unusual private club of Mr. Pleasure and his friends. Don't worry, though, you'll be welcomed as a guest . . . and offered a free membership and a secret password. We're sworn to secrecy ourselves . . . but it begins with a K. Five strange rooms filled with strange actors and you, their guests. Stick around and see what happens.

The Adventurers Club is one of the most entertaining "performance spaces" you'll find at Walt Disney World. According to the cover story, this is the place where Mr. Pleasure stored the strange items he brought back from his journeys; it's enough fun just to cruise among them. You'll likely meet the curator, the maid, and other oddball friends of Pleasure who will share their stories, and you'll be invited to enter into the library for an oddball show, including the Balderdash Cup Competition, the Curator's New Discovery, the Second Annual Radiothon Talent Show, the Maid's Sing-a-long, and the Bon Voyage Party.

Get in early and grab a seat in the main parlor on the lower level. There's no pressure to buy drinks; you can just sit and watch the strange goings-on.

WOW The Comedy Warehouse

This place is a hoot, offering an evening of improvisational humor, with somewhere between a PG and R rating—by Disney standards it can get downright risqué. (I'll leave it to the comics to express themselves, but on one of my visits the skit—directed by instructions called out by the audience—progressed to a love scene on the beach in which Ariel the mermaid lost her strategically placed seashells and was revealed to be a man.) There were even a few gentle jibes at Disney, including a fake movie poster on the wall advertising a film dubbed as *Dumbo, First Blood*.

There are several shows each night; the club is small and seats are often filled well before show time. If you want to sit through two sessions, you'll have to exit and get back in line for a later show. From time to time television crews tape comedy specials here. When a "name" comedian is appearing there may be an extra charge for admission.

When you are offered a seat in the amphitheater-like club, think twice about whether you really want to sit by a telephone. You don't suppose it may ring during the show, do you?

As at all of the clubs here, you will be approached by a waiter or waitress but you do not have to purchase anything if you don't want to. Drink prices include small beers for about $3, up to a sixty-ounce pitcher for about $9. Special drinks include Laughter Punch, made with Midori, rum, and pineapple juice. Sodas, popcorn, pretzels, and banana splits are also available.

Pleasure Island Restaurants

The major restaurants on Pleasure Island are located outside the turnstiles between Pleasure Island and Disney Village and can be visited without purchasing a ticket.

Fulton's Crab House. By the shores of Disney's inland sea is a seafood restaurant on a re-created paddlewheeler. The crab house promises to change its menu daily to reflect the latest and greatest seafood available in season. (They'll even post the air freight bills on the wall!) Entrees, from about $15 to $35, include Nantucket Bay Scallops, Mustard Crusted Trout, and Fulton's Cioppino. Appetizers begin with a well-stocked oyster bar, and also include such delicacies as alderwood smoked salmon with potato crostini lemon chive cream. Open for a popular character breakfast with seatings at 8 and 10 A.M., lunch daily from 11:30 A.M. to 4 P.M., and dinner 5 P.M. to midnight. Dinner entrees about $20.

Portobello Yacht Club. ☎ (407) 934-8888. A first-class northern Italian eatery, with offerings ranging from thin-crust pizza cooked in a wood-fired oven ($7 to $8) to steak, chicken, and fish dishes. Lunch salads, priced from about $5 to $8 may include *insalata Caesar di pollo* ("Caesar salad with chicken"). A sample of entrees, priced from about $13 to $25, includes Spiedini di Gamberi, charcoal-grilled garlic shrimp on a rosemary skewer; center-cut pork chop with herb crust; veal rib eye breaded and sautéed with a balsamic vinaigrette topping; and Spaghettini all Portobello, a house specialty including Alaskan crab, scallops, clams, shrimp, and mussels with tomatoes, garlic, olive oil, wine, and herbs.

A child's menu is also available. Open daily 11:30 A.M. to midnight; call for reservations.

The club is outside the gates of Pleasure Island; Pleasure Island visitors can come and go if they hold on to their ticket for the evening.

We're impressed. On one of our visits to Pleasure Island, a sign at the entrance to the parking lot read, "Impress your date. Use our valet parking services." Actually, though, you might consider it worth the fee to use the valet in bad weather because the outlying parking spaces can seem like they are in the next state.

Wildhorse Saloon. Live country music, dance, and entertainment venue, plus American barbecue restaurant. This location is the first outpost of the world-famous Wildhorse Saloon in Nashville.

There is, of course, a gift shop, selling a mix of traditional and contemporary Western-inspired casual apparel for men, women, and children; plus jewelry, accessories, and souvenir merchandise.

Downtown Disney Marketplace

When the going gets tough, the tough go shopping, and the Marketplace is one of Disney's most interesting collections of shops, including a large Lego outlet and the mother of all Disney Stores. There's also another outlet of the unusual Rainforest Cafe chain.

You can drive to the Village and park in the huge parking lot (it adjoins and mixes with the spaces for Pleasure Island), or you can take a water taxi from the Port Orleans Resort, Dixie Landings Resort, or the Disney Vacation Club. The stores are open from 9:30 A.M. to 10 P.M.

During the Christmas holiday period there's ice skating on a small rink at Downtown Disney Marketplace, the only outdoor rink in Florida. Skate rentals are available.

Of course, there are lots of shops selling T-shirts, sweatshirts, and hats with pictures of Mickey or Minnie, but perhaps the single largest collection is at the warehouse-sized **World of Disney**, with twelve rooms of toys and souvenirs, clothing (including Disney lingerie!), and more.

Another favorite is the **Lego Imagination Center**, a retail shrine to the little plastic bricks. It features an outdoor play area and huge Lego models, including a sea serpent rising out of Buena Vista Lagoon and a UFO model complete with an alien family. The store features every Lego product available in the United States, including blocks, games, puzzles, bedsheets, and clothing.

It's Christmas all the time at **Disney's Days of Christmas**, where you can purchase American and European ornaments and Disney holiday merchandise. At **Toys Fantastic**, you'll find guess-what from guess-who, plus a selection of Barbie toys. **Eurospain** sells an interesting collection of hand-crafted Spanish crafts. **Harrington Bay Clothiers** and **Resortwear Unlimited** offer sportswear for men and women, respectively.

You'll be able to indulge that chocolate addiction with a visit to **Ghirardelli's Ice Cream Soda Fountain and Chocolate Shop.** You'll find chocolate in all forms, as well as sundaes, shakes, malts, and more. The shop is designed like a turn-of-the-century San Francisco shop.

Downtown Disney Marketplace Restaurants

WOW **Rainforest Cafe**. Wild and wacky, with trees, birds, crocodiles, and rainfall . . . real and animatronic.

This is not your basic roadside cafe, unless your neighborhood eatery sports an animatronic gator at the door, an active (simulated) volcano, and a menu that emphasizes non-endangered fish, beef from countries that pledge not to deforest their lands for grazing, and some imaginative vegetarian offerings as well. Every once in a while the room lights go dim, and a (dry) thunderstorm breaks out inside the restaurant.

Be sure to check out the wishing pond to the right of the entrance. The spectacular parrots on perches are real; the huge alligator below is not.

Lines for the 550-seat restaurant can become oppressive at prime lunch and dinner hours; your best bet is to come earlier or later than the crowds. Of course, you can also while away the time in the impressive gift shop.

Specialties include the Amazon Natural herbal burger constructed of nuts, grains, and beans; Rumble in the Jungle—roasted turkey tossed with Caesar salad and stuffed into a pita bread; Jamaica Me Crazy!—grilled pork chops dusted with Jamaican and Cajun seasonings; and Rasta Pasta with bow-tie pasta, grilled chicken, walnut pesto, broccoli, red peppers, spinach, and fresh herbs in a garlic cream sauce.

Open for lunch and dinner from 10:30 A.M. to 11 P.M. Another Rainforest Cafe is located at the entrance plaza to Disney's Animal Kingdom.

Cap'n Jack's Oyster Bar. Lunch, dinner. A little bit of Cape Cod in a pretty setting on a shack built into the village lake. Lobster tails, crab claws, clams, chowder, frozen margaritas. $5 to $15. Child's menu features pasta, $4. Open from 11:30 A.M. to 10 P.M.

Wolfgang Puck Express. Lunch and dinner service for California-style pizzas.

Ronald's Fun House. A one-of-a-kind outpost of the fast food chain featuring fanciful rooms and decor based on Ronald McDonald and some of his McDonaldland friends. Among the settings: Ronald's Dining Room, with a formal twenty-foot serpentine dining area; Birdie's Music Room, featuring a giant french fry organ; and Grimace's Game Room, with video monitors. Oh, and they sell burgers and fries, too.

Chapter 13
Educational Opportunities at Walt Disney World

Feeling bad about taking your kids out of school for a vacation at Walt Disney World? How about giving them a little homework, Mickey-style?

Feeling too old to justify leaving your job at the law firm to spend a week with Mickey and Minnie? How about mixing in a bit of adult education? (While you're there, you can still sneak in a flight with Dumbo the Flying Elephant.)

Disney offers a range of educational seminars for youngsters and adults. You might want to discuss some of the options with your children's teachers.

Should You Take Your Kids Out of School?

In the best of all worlds, probably not. There are enough interruptions in the normal school year as it is. However, if work and school vacation times do not coincide, or if you are taking our advice seriously and trying to avoid crowds, there are ways to work with your schools.

Meet with your children's teachers to determine if there are particular times when an absence of a few days (wrapped around or including a weekend or minor holiday) will not make a big impact on schoolwork. Consult your school calendar in search of local holidays or "workshop" half-days.

See if you can coordinate special assignments for your children. If there is an upcoming unit on Mexico, for example, perhaps they could be assigned to produce a report with research performed at Epcot Center's Mexican pavilion.

Behind the Scenes Tours

Walt Disney World conducts tours of its parks and facilities as part of educational programs for visiting school and corporate groups. You may be able to participate as an individual or family if space is available. For information, call ☎ (407) 939-8687.

Gardens of the World. A three-hour study of selected gardens in Epcot's World Showcase, conducted by a Disney horticulturist. The education includes tips to bring home to your own garden. Tickets in 2001 were $49 per person; theme park admission is required.

Inside Animation. Follow in the mouseprints of Walt Disney on a two-and-a-half-hour exploration of the history of animation and the beginnings of the Disney Studio. Guests create their own cel paintings. Tickets in 2001 were $49; theme park admission not required.

Hidden Treasures of World Showcase. Three-hour walking tours of Epcot's World Showcase to point out the subtle details of the architecture. Tickets in 2001 were $49 per person; theme park admission is required.

Hidden Treasures of World Showcase Plus. Five-hour walking tours of Epcot's World Showcase, plus a backstage look at the Epcot wardrobe department, and a lunch at the German pavilion. Tickets in 2001 were $85 per person; theme park admission is not required.

Disney by Design. After an overview of architectural design and terminology, guests take a three-hour tour of Disney's "Entertainment Architecture" at resorts, offices, and other unique structures. Tickets in 2001 were priced at $99 per person; theme park admission is not required.

Backstage Magic. The ultimate in insider peeks, a seven-hour expedition that includes the "Utilidor" tunnel system beneath the Magic Kingdom, backstage technology at Epcot, and behind-the-scenes looks at selected attractions. Includes lunch. Tickets in 2001 were $199 per person; theme park admission is not required.

Disney Youth Education Series

For information on courses aimed at visiting school groups, call ☎ (877) 939-6884. Programs in recent years have included:

Animal Encounters. Hands-on learning adventures in the wilderness areas of the Walt Disney World Resort.

Arts & Literature. Explorations of storytelling, animation, and theater

Humanities & Life Management. Real world applications of leadership, business, and cultural studies.

Natural Science & Conservation. Studies of animal care and management issues faced by scientists at the Walt Disney World Resort and around the world.

Physical Science & Mathematics. Explorations of the science and math behind some of the all-time favorite Disney attractions.

The Disney Institute

In 2000 Disney pulled the plug on its ambitious Disney Institute. The facility was intended as an adult education center, an idea that never seemed to catch fire within Walt Disney World.

The Institute began ambitiously, offering eighty courses with twenty-seven studios, a broadcast-quality performance center, cinema, garden, an outdoor amphitheater, and closed-circuit television and radio stations.

The institute continues to offer courses to groups and conventions by advance reservation. The attractive and private Disney Institute villas are available for rent through the Disney reservations department.

Chapter 14
Inside the World of Disney

Disney Cruise Line

Ahoy, Mickey! *Disney Magic* and *Disney Wonder* are just like any other cruise ship . . . except for those six letters on the bow and all that they mean for guests.

The *Disney Wonder* makes three- and four-day cruises to the Bahamas, featuring a visit to Nassau and Castaway Cay, Disney's private Bahamian island.

Disney Magic sails alternating week-long cruises to the eastern and western Caribbean, including a stop at Castaway Cay.

Both vessels depart from Port Canaveral on Florida's east coast, about an hour away from Orlando.

Disney has built its ships with adults as well as kids in mind. Youngsters have their own deck: Disney's Oceaneer Adventure is open late into the night. Features include Disney's Oceaneer Club, a play area for younger kids, and Disney's Oceaneer Lab that offers electronic games played on giant video walls and interactive computer activities. And teens have their own private hangout, Common Grounds.

Adults can join in the activities on the sports deck or catch the latest scores at the ESPN Skybox up top. They can dance the night away at Beat Street, an adult nightclub district with dance, jazz, and improv comedy clubs.

Guests rotate to one of three themed restaurants each evening. French continental cuisine is offered at Lumières on the *Disney Magic* and Triton's on the *Disney Wonder*. The flavors and spirit of the Bahamas is featured at Parrot Cay. And then there is Animator's Palette, where the room magically transforms from a black-and-white artist's sketch to full-color animation over the course of dinner. There's also Palo, an adults-only restaurant, and a kids-only pizza parlor.

After dinner, families can enjoy one of three Broadway-style shows at the Walt Disney Theatre, or catch a movie at the Buena Vista Theatre. And there's Studio Sea, a nightclub for the entire family.

The Disney Cruise Line fleet

At Castaway Cay, a one-thousand-acre Bahamian island with miles of white sand beach, activities include snorkeling, sailing, kayaking, paddle boats, and inflatables. The crew will offer an island barbecue.

The ships, built in Trieste, Italy, feature a "classic exterior design reminiscent of the majestic transatlantic ocean liners of the past." And they have in many ways delivered on the promise, with some of the most elegant shipboard spaces I have seen, and a vessel with stunning lines that will please even the most finicky cruise connoisseur. I don't recall the *Queen Mary* offering Disney character breakfasts and shows, though.

For full details on the Disney cruise line, you can consult another title in this book series, *Econoguide Cruises.*

Disneyland Paris

The French have an apt phrase: *Le plus ça change, le plus c'est la même chose.* It means: "The more that changes, the more things are the same."

The French hate American culture, right? Tell that to *La Belle au Bois Dormant* (Sleeping Beauty), *Blanche-Neige et les Sept Nains* (Snow White and the Seven Dwarfs), and, of course, to Mickey Mouse (no translation needed).

Most of all, tell that to the millions of visitors who head twenty miles east of the City of Lights to Marne la Vallée, home of the City of Mickey.

Disneyland Paris opened in 1992. Although many cultural highbrows sniffed haughtily, and bean counters objected to some of the financial underpinnings of the hotels and real estate operations surrounding the attraction, the Magic Kingdom park quickly began drawing tourists.

In 2002 Disney Studios, a second theme park, will open at Disneyland Paris.

Should you go all the way from North America to visit Disneyland Paris? Well, on the one hand, this is one of the most advanced theme parks in the world, decades younger than the Magic Kingdom in Orlando, and the even-older Disneyland in Anaheim. But, it is also very similar, albeit with a French accent.

For us the beauty of Disneyland Paris is this: it's a wonderful way to convince the kids to come to France to visit to the Cathedral of Notre Dame, the Louvre, the Champs Elysée, Versailles, the Pompidou . . . and Mickey and Minnie.

On several of my trips I chose to make Disneyland Paris my base, venturing west to Paris and Versailles five days in a week, and spending two days in the park. Hotels at the park, although not cheap, are still less expensive than many hotels in downtown Paris. The RER train service to London is easily accessible, or you can rent a car and use the highways.

Mouse mouths. Walt Disney himself performed the voices of Mickey and Minnie in the earliest cartoons, including *Steamboat Willie,* which was the first Mickey Mouse cartoon with sound—but not the first movie starring the rascally rodent. That honor went to *Plane Crazy.* The current voice of the Mickster is Wayne Allwine.

Although Disneyland Paris is very much an outpost of American culture, as defined by Walt Disney and as refined during a half-century by the moviemaking and theme park empire he created, there is nevertheless a definite French and European gloss to the park. But worry not: though the rides and attrac-

Main Street U.S.A., in Disneyland Paris

Courtesy Disneyland Paris. © Disney

tions are narrated in French, you'll find English and other translations readily available. Nearly every park employee speaks multiple languages, and English is very common.

The Magic Kingdom is laid out very much like its cousins in California and Florida. One exception: the American Tomorrowland is called Discoveryland in France.

Among the highlights of the park:

Phantom Manor. It's got 999 ghoulish French ghosts . . . and this is the highest-tech version of this Disney classic (known as the Haunted Mansion in Florida and California).

The story, if you need one, involves a bride who was jilted at the altar. Forever in her wedding dress, she haunts the house and all who visit.

Pirates of the Caribbean. Yo, ho, yo . . . this is one of Disney's very best. A slightly Frenchified version of the classic watery adventure, it's a cruise into the middle of a pirate raid on a Caribbean island town.

Among the highlights are a moonlit battle scene as your boat passes beneath the guns of two warring ships; cannonballs land all around in the cool water. Pay attention, too, to the jail scene where a group of pirates tries to entice a mangy dog to bring them the key. The ride includes a wondrous collection of animatronic humans and animals, including robotic chickens and pigs.

***Indiana Jones et le Temple du Peril* (Indiana Jones and the Temple of Doom).** A truly wild roller coaster that careens through the long-buried ruins of the Temple of Peril, right-side up, upside down, and straight at the waters below. In 2000 Disney turned up the thrills a few notches by reworking the track, mounting the cars backward, and sending guests on a ride that lets them concentrate on where they've been instead of where they're heading. The mine cars back their way through a spiraling inverted 360-degree loop.

***Le Château de la Belle au Bois Dormant* (Sleeping Beauty's Castle).** The centerpiece of the park is this very European castle. Located upstairs is *La Galerie de la Belle au Bois Dormant* (Sleeping Beauty's Gallery), which displays the story of Sleeping Beauty through hand-painted storybooks, stained glass windows, and finely woven tapestries. Beneath the castle is *La Tanière du Dragon* (The Dragon's Lair) where a huge animatronic dragon sleeps restlessly

Dumbo the Flying Elephant. A worldwide favorite for youngsters, who wait in line (along with their cranky parents) for the chance to ride on Dumbo in a circular pathway above Fantasyland.

"It's a Small World." Every little girl's wildest dream: a world of beautiful dancing dolls from all over the world. There is nothing to get your heart beating here, but even the most cynical—including little boys and adults—will probably find something to smile about in this upbeat boat ride.

Star Tours. The Starspeeder 3000 departs regularly on a short and eventful voyage to outer space in this simulator ride based on the *Star Wars* films of George Lucas.

Le Visionarium. A Cinematronic 360-degree theater presenting a beautifully produced film about French science fiction author Jules Verne, in a spectacular time-travel adventure that soars through Europe. A version of that film was imported to Walt Disney World in Orlando as *The Timekeeper.*

Space Mountain: *De la Terre à la Lune* ("From the Earth to the Moon"). A triumph of imagineering, a roller-coaster trip to the moon. This version of the classic ride goes way beyond the originals at Disneyland and Walt Disney World, beginning with the takeoff: every thirty-six seconds the Cannon *Columbiad* launches a twenty-four-passenger rocket train through its barrel.

Space travelers shoot to the top in a heart-stopping 1.8 seconds, floating through a moment of zero-gravity at the top before descending in the dark through the trip from the earth to the moon with upside-down spirals, and twists and turns.

For information, consult www.disneylandparis.com.

Suspended animation. A recurring rumor about dear old Walt Disney is that he chose to be cryogenically frozen when he died of lung cancer in 1966, in hopes of a defrost in another day and age. Actually, according to the company, he went to the other extreme and was cremated before burial at the famous Forest Lawn Memorial Park in California.

Tokyo Disneyland

Hai, Mickey-san. If ever proof was required of the global impact of American popular culture, it came with the opening of Tokyo Disneyland in 1983. The park, six miles outside of Tokyo, is owned by a Japanese company under license to Disney. It includes familiar Disney attractions as well as new shows such as Pinocchio's Daring Journey, The Eternal Seas, and Meet the World.

Instead of Main Street, U.S.A., you'll find World Bazaar as the gateway to Adventureland, Fantasyland, Tomorrowland, and Westernland. Adventureland attractions include the Jungle Cruise, Enchanted Tiki Room, and Pirates of the Caribbean. In Westernland you'll find the Mark Twain Riverboat, Tom Sawyer Island, The Golden Horseshoe Revue, and Country Bear Jamboree. At Toontown the cartoon characters are in charge.

Fantasyland includes the Pinocchio ride, plus It's a Small World, Haunted Mansion, Snow White's Adventure, and the Mickey Mouse Revue. There are also venerable favorites Dumbo the Flying Elephant, and Cinderella's Golden Carrousel.

Tomorrowland includes yet another Space Mountain, as well as Meet the World, an attraction based on Japanese history and the country's influence on the rest of the world.

A new park, Tokyo Disney Sea, was due to open on September 4, 2001, overlooking Tokyo Bay, adjacent to Tokyo Disneyland. Surrounded by water (and aided by construction tricks that seem to extend the horizon of a small moat), the park is centered around a globe-shaped fountain known as the AquaSphere, alive with the flow of water. Representing our Earth, the "water planet," the AquaSphere is intended to amaze viewers with cascades of water that flow down and around the globe, mysteriously clinging to its surface.

In a scheme that sounds somewhat like Universal's Islands of Adventure in Orlando, plans for the new Tokyo park call for seven distinct "ports of call."

Guests will experience the old-world charm of the romantic southern European seaport of Mediterranean Harbor; discover portals to fantastic adventures deep within a smoldering volcano known as Mysterious Island; find the whimsical "under the sea" world of Ariel and all her friends from the classic Disney animated film *The Little Mermaid* in Mermaid Lagoon; encounter Aladdin and his playful Genie pal when they explore the exotic enchantment of "1001 Arabian Nights" along the shores of Arabian Coast; confront ancient perils and hidden mysteries in the jungles of Lost River Delta; travel across the horizons of time to Port Discovery, a futuristic marina that celebrates the thrills, adventure, and excitement of new frontiers in the sea and sky; and take a step back in time to American Waterfront, which nostalgically showcases the harbors of New York and Cape Cod at the beginning of the twentieth century.

In Mysterious Island guests will venture to the ocean floor to explore the lost city of Atlantis in *20,000 Leagues Under the Sea*, and take a thrilling journey far below an active volcano in Journey to the Center of the Earth.

In Arabian Coast, guests will board boats in "Sindbad's Seven Voyages " and set out with the famous sailor on a storybook journey through his treacherous travels. Well-worn transports in the Indiana Jones Adventure—Temple of the Crystal Skull will take visitors to the jungles of Lost River Delta where they will join intrepid Indiana Jones on a perilous journey through the secret corridors of a foreboding Central American pyramid. Guests will also experience all the thrills of soaring high above the clouds and diving into the eye of a storm when they board StormRider in Port Discovery.

Located on the park's main waterfront in Mediterranean Harbor, the Tokyo DisneySea Hotel MiraCosta will offer breathtaking views of the park and Tokyo Bay. The MiraCosta will allow guests to stay overnight in the park.

The park will be connected to Tokyo Disneyland by monorail.

For information, consult 🖳 www.tokyodisneyland.co.jp/index_e.html.

Part III
Universal Orlando

Chapter 15
A Burgeoning Universe

Orlando is no longer just a small world after all. The kingdom of the mouse now has some serious—and fun—competition across town at the growing Universal Studios empire.

Universal Orlando now offers two theme parks, a water park, a sprawling nighttime dining and entertainment complex, and a pair of impressive hotel resorts. The bottom line: a claim on at least two days of an Orlando visit with more to come.

- **Universal Studios Florida** celebrates the worlds of moviemaking and television.
- **Universal Studios Islands of Adventure** is one of the most advanced theme and thrill parks in the world, with a collection of high-tech simulators, roller coasters, and strangeness unmatched at Walt Disney World.
- **Universal Studios CityWalk** by night is a lively rock, blues, and culinary magnet.

The first three of five large resort hotels is open: the elegant 750-room Portofino Bay Hotel, the 650-room Hard Rock Hotel, and the 1,000-room Royal Pacific Hotel. Two additional hotels planned for years to come will bring the total number of rooms on the park property to about five thousand.

Universal Studios also owns the Wet 'n Wild water park nearby on International Drive. And if that's not enough, Universal Studios is noodling around with plans for two thousand more acres of land on the other side of I-4 that may one day hold a few more theme parks, another group of resort hotels, and other attractions.

The Universal Story

It was almost ninety years ago that movie legend Carl Laemmle began to allow visitors—at twenty-five cents a head—to come to his studios to watch silent movies being made. The tours at Universal Film Manufacturing Company in Hollywood were stopped when sound was added to film; in 1964 the renamed Universal Studios reopened its doors to visitors.

Universal Orlando Tickets

Prices were in effect for the summer of 2001 and are subject to change. One-day tickets are valid at either Universal Studios Florida or Universal Studios Islands of Adventure. Multi-day tickets allow moving back and forth between the parks on any day the tickets are in use. Prices do not include tax. Universal Orlando offers a variety of discounts such as AAA, AARP, HIA, and the Orlando MagiCard, and offers a discount for online purchases at www.universalstudios.com.

One-Day (Admission to Universal Studios or Islands of Adventure on a single day)

Adult	$48.00
Child (3–9)	$39.00

Two-Day (Admission to Universal Studios and Islands of Adventure for two days; unused days do not expire. Includes park-to-park entrance on same day and Universal Express privileges. Also includes a CityWalk Party Pass to selected venues.)

Adult	$89.95
Child (3–9)	$76.95

Three-Day (Admission to Universal Studios and Islands of Adventure for three days; unused days do not expire. Includes park-to-park entrance on same day and Universal Express privileges. Also includes a CityWalk Party Pass to selected venues.)

Adult	$104.95
Child (3–9)	$91.95

2-Park Annual Pass (Entrance to both parks. Includes free parking, admission to special events, 10 percent savings on additional single-day passes for up to six guests, 10 percent savings on purchases at stores)

All passes	$164.95

2-Park Seasonal Annual Pass (Not valid summer, Christmas, Easter periods)

Adult	$119.95
Child (3–9)	$104.95

Universal Studios Florida Celebrity Annual Pass (Valid at USF only)

Adult	$89.95
Child (3–9)	$74.95

Orlando FlexTickets

Prices were in effect in the summer of 2001 and are subject to change. Prices do not include tax. Visit any of the parks within the same day. Parking fee required only once each day at first park visited.

4-Park Orlando FlexTicket: $159.95 (adult); $127.95 (ages 3–9) Unlimited admission to Universal Studios Florida, Universal Studios Islands of Adventure, SeaWorld Orlando, Wet 'n Wild Orlando. Valid fourteen consecutive days.

5-Park Orlando FlexTicket: $196.95 (adult); $157.95 (ages 3–9) Unlimited admission to Universal Studios Florida, Universal Studios Islands of Adventure, SeaWorld Orlando, Wet 'n Wild Orlando, Busch Gardens Tampa. Valid fourteen consecutive days.

Parking: $7
Valet parking: $14

For information, call ☎ (407) 363-8000, or consult www.uescape.com or www.universalstudios.com

Universal Studios Islands of Adventure by night

Universal's Hollywood lot became the third most popular tourist attraction in the nation; visitors board trams that take them in and around the historic back lot and soundstages of Universal City and along the way into some very special attractions based on some of the movie company's greatest hits.

In 1990 Universal moved east to Florida with the opening of Universal Studios in Orlando. Here are a few things to understand about the sprawling resort, now home to two theme parks:

• Universal Studios Florida is more than twenty years newer than most of Walt Disney World, and Universal Studios Islands of Adventure is as state of the art as theme parks come. Both parks include some of the most spectacular and state-of-the-art rides and attractions in the world, well beyond Pirates of the Caribbean.

• The facility is a working studio, producing movies, television shows, music videos, and commercials.

• Universal Studios CityWalk offers some very sophisticated places to eat and to party, and best of all it sits at the entrance to both theme parks. You can break away from the rides for lunch or dinner, or end your day there. This is a worthy competitor to Downtown Disney at Walt Disney World.

The best times to come to Universal Orlando are the same as for other area attractions. Arrive between September and November, between Thanksgiving and Christmas, or in mid-January, and you may be able to walk around like you own the place. Show up during Christmas break, Easter vacation, or midsummer, and you'll meet what seems like the entire population of Manhattan or Boston or Cleveland in front of you in line.

Universal Orlando is open 365 days a year. Hours of operation of the parks

Universal Studios Islands of Adventure from above

are adjusted based on projections for attendance and are subject to change. Check before you make plans for late evenings.

Some of the shows are opened on a staggered basis. When you first walk in the door at a quiet time of year, you may find that some of the shows don't offer performances before 11 A.M. or noon; head for the rides first.

Travel to the park: Universal Orlando is located near the intersection of Interstate 4 and the Florida Turnpike in Orlando. The main entrance is about one-half mile north of I-4 at exit 30B–Kirkman Road (Highway 435). Another entrance is located on Turkey Lake Road.

From Orlando International Airport: Take 528 West (the Bee-Line Expressway) toward Tampa and Walt Disney World. Watch for signs to Interstate 4 East (to Orlando); take the Universal Studios exit 30B.

From Walt Disney World: Take I-4 East (to Orlando) to the Universal Studios exit 30B.

Or, take Universal Boulevard (formerly Republic Drive) into the park.

Universal Orlando is a unit of Universal Studios, a part of CANAL+, the TV and film division of Vivendi Universal, a global media and communications company.

Universal Express

Few things are less exciting to theme park visitors than to find ninety-minute waiting lines at attractions. Lines will never completely go away, but in 2000 Universal Studios joined Walt Disney World in offering guests a way to make an appointment for a bug hunt with the Men in Black or to zoom with mythical monsters at Dueling Dragons.

The program is called **Universal Express**, and on all but the most impossibly crowded days guests should be able to stroll onto their favorite rides and attractions after no more than a fifteen-minute wait.

Resort guests staying at on-site Universal hotels have all-day priority access to virtually all rides and attractions simply by showing their hotel room keys. That program is available for guests staying at the Portofino Bay Hotel, the Hard Rock Hotel, and the Royal Pacific Resort after it opens in 2002.

Multi-Day ticket holders (two-day or three-day tickets) can choose times and receive express passes to as many as three rides or attractions by presenting their ticket at any Universal Express distribution center located in either park. Guests can choose one of two possible windows of time in which they can return to the rides or attractions they have selected. They can get another Express Pass after visiting all three attractions or after all the chosen windows of time have passed.

Single-Day ticket holders can choose one of two possible windows of times for a single ride or attraction, and receive an Express Pass for that ride or attraction. They can get another Express Pass after visiting the attraction, after the chosen window of time has passed, or after two hours have passed.

Express Passes cannot be used at Pteranodon Flyers, for front-row seating on the Incredible Hulk Coaster and Dueling Dragons coaster at Islands of Adventure, or at Fievel's Playland Slide or Woody Woodpecker's Nuthouse Coaster at Universal Studios.

Very Very Important Persons

Universal Studios offers two types of VIP tours for people who hate to wait in line; like, who doesn't?

The basic **VIP tour** is a five-hour guided walking tour of either one of the Universal parks with as many as fifteen guests. Departing daily at 10 A.M. and noon, visitors are given priority entrance to at least eight attractions.

At Universal Studios Florida the tour usually includes JAWS, Kongfrontation, Twister, Back to the Future: The Ride, E.T. Adventure, and Men in Black Alien Attack.

At Universal's Islands of Adventure, the tour usually visits Incredible Hulk Coaster, Dudley Do-Right's Ripsaw Falls, Jurassic Park River Adventure, The Amazing Adventures of Spider-Man, The Cat in the Hat, Dueling Dragons, The Eighth Voyage of Sindbad, and Dr. Doom's Fearfall. In 2001, tickets for the VIP tour, including admission, were $120.

If you want to be alone, you can purchase an **Exclusive VIP Tour** for as many as fifteen guests of your choice. The tour, of as much as eight hours, departs at a time of your choice, and visits any attractions at one park. In 2001, tickets for the Exclusive VIP tour were $1,700 for the group.

If you are really pressed for time, you can pay for the **Universal Orlando 1-Day/2-Park Exclu-**

Upgrading your ticket. If you decide you want to come back for a second day at Universal Studios, visit Guest Relations to upgrade your ticket to a two-day pass. You must do this on the day of purchase of the original ticket. During the off-season, Universal sometimes offers a "second day free" promotion. And if you are a regular visitor to Orlando, you might want to consider buying an annual pass, available for year-round or seasonal periods.

sive VIP Tour. For a mere $2,800 per group of as many as fifteen, a guide will offer priority entrance to as many attractions as possible in both parks in an eight-hour day.

The **Universal Orlando Ultimate Escape Tour** the VIP treatment to two days at both parks, for $3,000 per group of as many as fifteen.

The tours do not include lunch. As expensive as the tours are, they might begin to make sense if you are forced to visit the park on a day when all of the major rides have ninety-minute waits. About a dozen tour guides are available.

One downside is that you'll miss some of the clever entertainments presented in the waiting lines; then again, you'll miss the waiting lines.

For information and reservations for a VIP tour, call Universal Studios Vacations at ☎ (800) 711-0080.

A Place to Spend the Night

Part of the master plan for Universal Orlando is to capture as many visitors as possible to spend their entire vacation time on Universal property.

The **Portofino Bay Hotel at Universal Orlando** is an especially attractive resort, set alongside a lagoon, re-creating a bit of the charm and romantic harbor setting of the Mediterranean seaside village of Portofino in Italy.

The hotel, managed by Loews, includes eight restaurants and lounges, two swimming pools, a pair of bocce ball courts, and a large convention and meeting space.

The **Hard Rock Hotel** showcases the architectural styles of a California mission. Public areas are decorated with pieces from Hard Rock's extensive collection of rock 'n' roll memorabilia.

In 2002 the **Royal Pacific Resort at Universal Orlando** will open, adding one thousand luxury guest rooms and suites. Its architecture is influenced by the tropically lush region of the Asia Pacific.

All of the hotels are connected to each other and to Universal Studios, Universal Studios Islands of Adventure, and Universal Studios CityWalk by a walkways and scenic waterways plied by water taxis.

Guests are also offered priority reservations at restaurants in the hotels and the parks.

UNIVERSAL ORLANDO

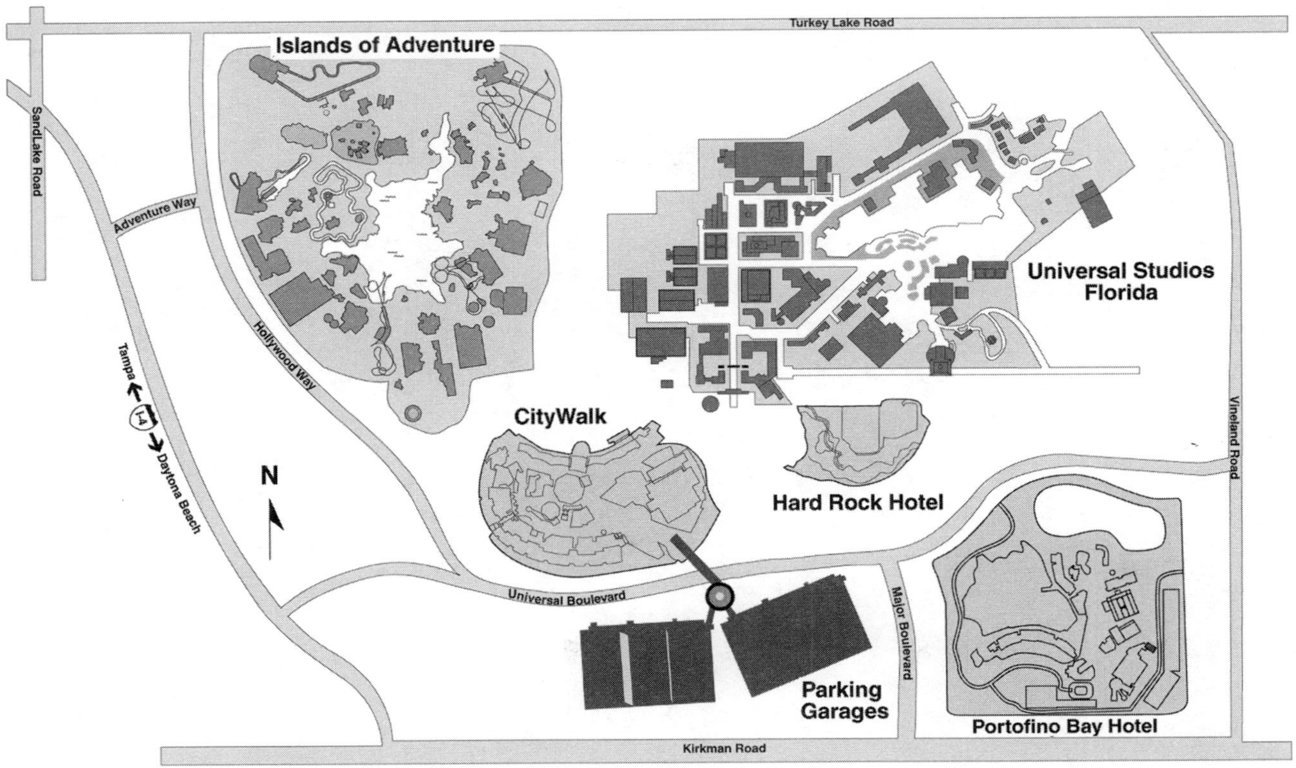

Chapter 16
Universal Studios Florida

Ride the movies. Then surf the TV shows. And while you're at it, immerse yourself in one of the most thematically consistent theme parks in the world.

Universal Studios Florida is a place where fans of Hollywood's greatest hits can extend the experience of the big screen into thrilling and clever state-of-the-art rides and shows.

This is the home of, among others, Jaws, King Kong, the Terminator, E.T., and Beetlejuice. For kids of all ages, here you'll meet the universe of Hanna-Barbera, Woody Woodpecker, Barney, Feivel, and Curious George. Fans of the classics can pay tribute to Alfred Hitchcock, Lucille Ball, Hollywood makeup magicians, stuntmen and -women, and even animal star actors.

And then there is the supremely weird world of Men in Black, the Ultimate Bug Hunt. The huge techno-thriller ride merges a high-tech ride mechanism with some of the liveliest animatronics in Orlando.

Another recent addition is Woody Woodpecker Kidzone, which includes *Animal Planet Live!*, E.T. Adventure, *A Day in the Park with Barney*. Feivel's Playland, Woody Woodpecker's Nuthouse Coaster, and the wet and wild Curious George Goes to Town.

Power Trip #1

An Express Tour

You can still choose to stand on line at Universal Studios if you insist, but there's a much smarter way to travel now. The Universal Express system allows visitors to make reservations for most of the major attractions.

Guests at hotels on the property are offered unlimited express privileges; purchasers of two- or three-day multi-park passes can hold as many as three reservations at a time, and one-day ticket holders can reserve one attraction at a time.

The best strategy here is to obtain a reservation for your number one goal, and then head for the shortest line at the next place on your list.

Power Trip #2

First Things First

If you don't have a Universal Express reservation, lines at some of the more popular attractions can build to as much as ninety minutes on busy days; the Power Trip puts you on a fast track for the major magnets in the morning, with a more leisurely pace for the rest of the day.

Men in Black is the current top draw at the park; head there first or last to avoid the crowds.

After the intergalactic bugs, the spectacular **Terminator 2 3-D** show, the **Twister** attraction, the **Jaws** ride, and the older but wilder **Back to the Future** simulator are the most popular. Therefore the smartest plan is to head for one of them as soon as you arrive at the park—and the earlier the better. Make your first right turn on Rodeo Drive and go directly to Terminator 2 3-D; if you're in the first crush of visitors you should be able to meet your robotic fate within half an hour. When the show lets out, continue up Hollywood Boulevard to Sunset Boulevard and head directly for Back to the Future. Lines should still be at manageable levels in the morning. When you're back to the present, continue around the lagoon to Jaws.

Warning: in our judgment, many young visitors and some older ones may find these rides to be too wild; if you're not up to the journey go instead to the **E.T. Adventure** as your first stop.

When you are through with your early targets you can check out the lines at rides you missed, or make plans to come back late in the day.

Continue around the lagoon in a counterclockwise direction to come to **Earthquake—The Big One** and ride the subway to San Francisco. Exit that ride and continue to **Kongfrontation**.

Now head to the front of the park and **The Funtastic World of Hanna-Barbera**, where you will probably find a growing line. It's worth the wait for youngsters; adults may choose to pass it by, especially if they've been to The Future already.

Youngsters will certainly want to visit **Nickelodeon Studios**. Adults will appreciate **Alfred Hitchcock: The Art of Making Movies**.

You have now seen the major attractions of the park. Check the daily schedule for show times and then make a second tour to visit ***The Gory, Gruesome & Grotesque Horror Make-Up Show***, the E.T. Adventure if you missed it the first time around and if the lines are at a reasonable length, ***Animal Planet Live!***, and the ***Wild, Wild, Wild West Stunt Show***.

Power Trip #3

Counter-Revolutionary

Here's an alternate plan for use on the very busiest days. It works especially well when you have a full day and the park is open late.

Start your day by going clockwise, moving against the crowds sprinting for Men in Black: Alien Attack, Twister, Terminator 2 3-D, Jaws, or Back to the Future. Instead, your first goal is one of the big draws near the entrance.

Go to **Kongfrontation**, then **Earthquake**, and then, depending on the lines, **The Funtastic World of Hanna-Barbera** and **Alfred Hitchcock**. By this time, the park should be pretty crowded; have an early lunch. For the rest of the afternoon, visit the less-crowded live shows including **Nickelodeon Studios**, ***Animal Planet Live!***, ***The Gory, Gruesome & Grotesque Horror Make-Up Show,*** and the ***Wild, Wild, Wild West Stunt Show***.

Have an early dinner. As other visitors rest from waiting in lines all day, use the evening to see the most popular attractions: **Men in Black**, **Twister**, **Terminator 2 3-D**, **Jaws**, **Back to the Future**, and **E.T. Adventure**, plus any other live shows you missed in the morning.

Attractions at Universal Studios Florida

Expo Center

WOW Men in Black: Alien Attack

You are aware, of course, that the twin observation towers of the New York World's Fair of 1964–65 and the Saint Louis Arch aren't really mere American architectural landmarks. They are, of course, actually landing beacons for alien spacecraft.

If you didn't know that then maybe you also wouldn't realize that the entrance to a pavilion called "The Universe and You" isn't really an ordinary theme park attraction, either. You see, what we've got here is the cleverly hidden global headquarters of the Men in Black (MIB) organization.

And you, you're about to become the newest recruit in the MIB army.

You'll enter an elevator in what just might seem like an ordinary office building, and then come out into the fantastic coffee break

MUST-SEES

WOW

Men in Black: Alien Attack

Back to the Future . . . The Ride

E.T. Adventure

Animal Planet Live!

Woody Woodpecker's Nuthouse Coaster
(A little coaster for little coasters)

Curious George Goes to Town
(Don't get into trouble, kids)

Earthquake—The Big One

Jaws

Twister

Kongfrontation

Hitchcock's 3-D Theatre

The Funtastic World of Hanna-Barbera
(Children of all ages)

Nickelodeon Studios
(Kids and their escorts)

Terminator 2 3-D

room where you can chat with some of the friendly (but very sassy) alien workforce; from there it's on to the immigration center.

The ride begins with a training lecture by MIB director Zed (voiced by actor Rip Torn, who held the role in the movie) warning new trainees that aliens are living among us. Our job is to round them up and keep track of them. In fact, a shuttle is ready to take off immediately to deport some rather nasty alien criminals to Planet LV-428. After a lecture on the finer points of alien spotting and the proper use of alien zappers, visitors are turned loose on their very own training mission.

Ah, but something goes wrong: the space shuttle bound for Planet LV-428 has crashed, and armed aliens are running around New York City, something that—despite appearances to the contrary—is not an ordinary occurrence in the Big Apple.

"Everybody hit the streets. This is not a drill."

Your six-passenger training vehicle (with two rows of three seats) heads out into the streets, and suddenly the bugs are everywhere: in the windows, hanging from the lamp posts, and peeking out of mailboxes. There are two similar but not identical tracks, with a pair of vehicles competing against each other and the aliens.

It's zap or be zapped in a wild, cosmic turkey shoot—if the alien wins a duel, your vehicle will spin out of control.

"Alien life forms detected! Look out, the other car is full of bugs!"

The end of the adventure lies within the slimy belly of the largest animatronic creature ever built, a warehouse-sized thirty-foot-tall alien bug with eight-foot teeth and twenty-foot claws.

You'll receive an individual score, a group score, and the score of the vehicle you competed against. There are about thirty different endings for your experience, and fellow recruit Will Smith will give you an appropriate send-off.

Men in Black is a ride-through interactive video game experience, a wackily weird entertainment that combines a bit of the streetscape of Kongfrontation, the state-of-the-art ride mechanism of The Amazing Adventures of Spider-Man, some of the dizzy fun of The Cat in the Hat, and an improvement over the intergalactic target-shooting at the Magic Kingdom's Buzz Lightyear's Space Ranger Spin.

The ride, located between Back to the Future and the *Wild, Wild, Wild West Stunt Show*, is reputed to be the largest dark ride ever built, with more than an acre and a half under roof. The building is the largest at the park.

WOW **Back to the Future . . . The Ride**

Dive into the world of the record-breaking movie trilogy, *Back to the Future* in Universal's incredible simulator adventure. This is about as wild a ride as anything you'll find in Florida, with the possible exception of the real Space Shuttle. There is absolutely nothing like it at Walt Disney World.

It seems that weird Doc Brown is back home and conducting new time travel experiments. He has created another vehicle—an eight-passenger Time Vehicle that is faster and more energy efficient than anything before . . . or since. That's the good news. The bad news is that Biff Tannen has broken into the Institute of Future Technology and threatens to end the universe as we know it! It's up to you to jump into your own modified DeLorean and chase down Biff.

Surrounded by images and sound and buffeted by the motion of your flight simulator, you will soar into Hill Valley in the year 2015, blast back to the Ice Age for a chilling high-speed encounter with canyons of sheer ice, explode into the Volcanic Era for a once-in-a-lifetime encounter with a *Tyrannosaurus rex* and then through a volcano and over the edge of a molten lava fall.

This is a state-of-the-art attraction that combines an amazing 70-mm film with a set of simulator ride vehicles (bearing Florida license plates "OUTTATIME"). The eighty-foot-diameter domed Omnimax screens occupy all of your peripheral vision, making the screen seem to vanish and take you into the scene.

The Institute of Future Technology in the waiting area features actual props from the *Back to the Future* movie series, including a set of hoverboards (futuristic skateboards without wheels) and the all-important flux capacitors for time travel.

Check out the bulletin board in the waiting area where you will see the names of some of the visiting scientists who have offices in the building. They include guys by the names of Thomas Edison, Albert Einstein, and Francis Bacon.

There are actually two identical rides in the building, each with its own set of twelve eight-seater DeLoreans and movie dome. Each area has cars on three levels with three cars at the top, five in the middle, and four at the bottom.

Universal insiders say the very best experience can be had by sitting in the front row of the center car on the second tier; dispatchers call it Car 6. This particular vehicle is in the absolute center of the movie dome and you cannot easily see any other cars that might distract from the illusion.

At about the midway point of the waiting line visitors are divided among three ramps, one to each level. If you can manage to go through portal number two to the middle level, you will have

Coming attraction. If you have really sharp eyes and a good sense of balance, keep an eye out during your wild Back to the Future ride for the movie poster on the wall in Hill Valley; it advertises *Jaws 19.*

You're being watched. I took a backstage tour of Back to the Future, visiting the computer rooms and the security "tower" where operators monitor all twelve cars in each theater using see-in-the-dark video cameras.

Operators are able to turn off individual cars if anything goes wrong or a rider becomes ill or faints.

From 2001 to the future. The director of the Back to the Future ride-film was renowned movie special effects designer Douglas Trumbull, who created special effects for hits including *2001: A Space Odyssey* and *Close Encounters of the Third Kind.*

The four-minute 70-mm movie portion of the ride took two years to make and cost as much as a feature film. Elaborate hand-painted miniatures were created for the filming.

Don't say you weren't warned. Back to the Future is described as a "dynamically aggressive ride." Visitors suffering from maladies including dizziness, seizures, back or neck problems, claustrophobia, motion sickness, and heart disorders, as well as pregnant women, are advised to sit this one out. The ride also won't work for persons of a certain size or shape who cannot fit into the seats and safety harness. We suspect you know who you are.

a one-in-five chance of grabbing a choice seat in magic Car 6.

If you are concerned about getting motion sickness, you may want to try to get onto the lower level of the ride. (Speaking for myself, I prefer a Dramamine in the morning and Car 6.)

When you enter into the holding room for the simulator, try to maneuver near the door to get a seat in the front of the car. (Some visitors find the small waiting room a bit confining; you can ask the attendant to leave the door open if you feel it necessary. Trust me: a much more intense experience is coming.)

As you wait to board the simulator, pay attention to the little movie about time travel safety; we enjoyed watching crash dummies "Fender" and "Bender" at work. When you feel the floor rumble beneath your feet, you'll know the car is returning to its base.

The preshow and the movie in the ride itself were made specially for the simulator. Doc Brown (Christopher Lloyd) and Biff Tannen (Thomas Wilson) took part in the movie, but Marty McFly (Michael J. Fox) is nowhere to be seen.

The glass case in the preflight waiting room includes some juicy little details for fans of the film. In the famous Car 6, you'll find a notepad discussing the results of various flights in which Doc Brown reports he discussed the theory of electricity with Benjamin Franklin and philosophy with Mark Twain. On one of the flights, Brown reports he attended a presidential inauguration, noting that "she is quite a woman."

The DeLorean vehicles rise about eight feet out of their garages at the start of the movie. Once in the air, four actuators drive the car—three for vertical and one for fore-and-aft movement. Although it may feel as if your car is soaring and dropping hundreds of feet, the entire range of movement for the vehicle is about two feet.

To give the feeling of traveling through space, the cars are surrounded with a fog made from liquid nitrogen.

This is a great place to use a Universal Express pass. Without a reservation on a busy day, lines easily reach to ninety minutes or more. Remember that the crowd you see out on the plaza is only about half the backup—there are internal walkways and hallways as well.

Each ride takes nearly five minutes, with about ninety-six persons entering each of the two simulator theaters at a time. By the end of a quiet day, there may be no line at all. But it still takes five minutes or so to walk into the gate, up the stairs, into a waiting room for one of the simulators, and into your seat.

Before or after you join the line, check out the large prop to the left of the building. The Jules Verne Train was used in the closing scene of *Back to the Future III*, when Doc Brown returns from 1885 in this steam engine adapted to become a time machine.

Woody Woodpecker's Kidzone

E.T. Adventure

One of the best-loved movies of all times is given life in this imaginative ride, which begins where the film *E.T.* left off. You will share a bicycle with our favorite extraterrestrial in a voyage across the moon to save E.T.'s home, a planet dying for lack of his healing touch.

As marvelous as the ride itself is, don't overlook the incredible fantasy world of the waiting area. It will start when you register at the door and are cast as an actor in the coming adventure; be sure to hold on to the special card you are given until it is collected as you climb onto your bicycle.

Meeting spot. If you're planning to do a baby swap, ask for advice from one of the attendants on the proper place to wait. And if you need to meet someone after the ride, pick a specific spot such as the Jules Verne Train, because there are two exits from the building.

Triple A. Most of the gift shops and several of the sit-down restaurants within Universal Studios will give a 10 percent discount to AAA members; bring your card.

The entrance line wends its way through a mysterious redwood forest populated with all sorts of human and otherworldly creatures. All around you government agents search for E.T.

Finally, you are at your bicycle. As with most of the other rides at Universal, the E.T. ride has been subtly improved over the years. The beginning is now much scarier as your bicycle is pursued by police cars with searchlights. Nicer effects include a gorgeous star field using fiber optics; throughout the rest of the ride the colors have been brightened. New fog and smoke effects were also added. It's the same wonderful ride it used to be, only better.

You'll seem to climb higher and higher, until the city beneath you looks like a toy set. Director Steven Spielberg created a phantasmagoric cast of new characters for the adventure, including Botanicus, Tickli Moot Moot, Orbidon, Magdol, Big Zoms, Tympani Tremblies, Water Imps, Horn-Flowers, Gurgles, Squirtals, and Churtles. Will you arrive home at the Green Planet in time?

Well, yes: and the celebration begins as E.T.'s friend the Tickli Moot Moot laughs again, Orbidon sparkles, and Magdol sings. Baby E.T.s will dance and play all around you, and E.T. will thank you . . . personally.

The huge miniature city beneath your bicycle includes 3,340 tiny buildings, 250 ultra-compact cars, and one thousand street lights. The stars twinkle from some 4,400 points of light.

The music for the ride was written by Academy Award–winning composer John Williams, also responsible for the movie score.

WOW *Animal Planet Live!*

Animal stars, including many refugees from animal shelters, take center stage at *Animal Planet Live!* The show brings Animal Planet television network's favorite shows together with the behind-the-scenes movie magic.

Animal Planet Live! features video clips from such popular Animal Planet television shows as "Emergency Vets," "The Planet's Funniest Animals," "The Jeff Corwin Experience," "Wild on the Set," and the network's lively animal sports programs.

Many of the animal stars featured in *Animal Planet Live!* have extensive credits in film and television production. In 2001 the stars of the show included:

- Meesha, the talented gray Himalayan, who costarred with Robert De Niro and Ben Stiller, as Jinx, the toilet-using cat, in *Meet the Parents*
- Sniffles, a rescued raccoon, who shared the spotlight with Jim Carrey in *Ace Ventura: Pet Detective*
- Spooner, a four-year-old Australian Shepherd, who was discovered at an animal shelter before landing his break-out role in the Baha Men's video "Who Let the Dogs Out?"

The open-air stadium, the former home of the Animal Actors Stage, will accommodate 1,500 people for its twenty-five-minute show; it is a good place to take an afternoon break when lines at attractions are longest and the sun is at its hottest.

Woody Woodpecker's Nuthouse Coaster

WOW Woody Woodpecker's Nuthouse Coaster

Equal rights for kids: why should adults have all the thrills? In 1999 the Woodster arrived with his own kid-sized roller coaster, installing a brilliant red eight-hundred-foot-long track through a cartoon factory, and there's lots of small surprises for young riders. This ride is not The Hulk or Dueling Dragons—the monster rides next door at Universal Studios Islands of Adventure—but then kids aren't allowed on those coasters anyway. Think of Nuthouse Coaster as a thrill ride with training wheels.

The coaster's highest point reaches a top speed of 22 miles per hour, reaching a maximum height of twenty-eight feet; the sixteen-car train takes ninety seconds from start to finish.

Riders must be at least three years old and able to sit up; kids under forty-eight inches must be accompanied by an adult.

WOW Curious George Goes to Town

Everyone's favorite mischievous monkey now has a home at Universal Studios Florida. (For the record, he pushed aside the creepy Psycho House movie false front that had stood on a hill nearby. We suppose that's a good thing.)

It's a wet and wonderful world. It seems that George has let loose a bit of havoc by freeing the animals from their cages, leaving the doors open for kids to climb through. Following George's footsteps into the town's plaza there's a dream of a playground, centered around a room packed with 12,500 foam balls to throw, shoot, and dump on each other. Outside a pair of balconies face each other across the plaza with water cannons. Up above two five-hundred-gallon buckets fill up every few minutes and then dump their load on watchers below. Restrooms are nearby for changing clothes.

Fievel's Playland

Now here's *serious* entertainment for the very youngest visitors to Universal Studios, and a good place to burn off some energy.

The playground, based loosely on the *An American Tail* animated movies, is located between the E.T. Adventure and *Animal Planet Live!* The surroundings are padded with a soft absorbent surface to protect kids who might fall. It includes a carnival air pillow for jumping and a thirty-foot climbing net.

The kids-only water slide has a measuring post at about forty inches that says: "If you ain't this tall, bring an adult." Another sign warns that the slide will give you wet breeches, and this is quite true. The slide itself, on a small raft, is short and not nearly as wild as bigger rides at water parks. The line for the slide can become quite long, and parents who do not accompany their kids will probably want to park themselves at the bottom of the slide to retrieve them.

It might be possible to let your kids run loose at the playground while an adult waits in line at E.T.; I'd suggest you keep them out of line for the water slide, though, since it would be impossible to retrieve them quickly if they were way up in the queue.

A Day in the Park with Barney

This interactive musical show and hands-on educational playground stars the ubiquitous purple dinosaur, his best friend Baby Bop, and her big brother BJ. Actors at the 350-seat theater-in-the-round teach lessons about life through song, dance, and play.

Special effects take guests through the seasons of the year with wind, falling leaves, light rain, and even snow; clouds and stars appear magically on a projection screen. Songs include some of Barney's favorites, such as "Mr. Knickerbocker," "If You're Happy and You Know It," and his chart-topping hit, "I Love You." Adults are excused unless accompanied by an insistent youngster.

Visitors enter the attraction through a landscaped park to a central courtyard where a statue of the dino-star is surrounded by playful streams of water. Gently winding paths meander through the park, inviting guests to try out the interactive Humming Stone, a kaleidoscope, or the sand sculpture wheel.

The centerpiece is the Barney Theater, of course. In the preshow area, visitors are met by a new character, Mr. Peekaboo, a bumbling but good-hearted fellow who introduces himself to the crowd with a lighthearted but forgetful song. When children remind him of who they came to see, he urges them to use their imaginations . . . encouraged by a colorful waterfall wall that beckons them into the theater.

After the show children of all ages are invited into Barney's backyard, which features interactive delights that include a water-harp that plays music as visitors run their fingers through its streams of water, and a wood-pipe xylophone. Brightly colored rocks emit musical tones when stepped on, and rainbow lights sparkle everywhere.

San Francisco/Amity

WOW Earthquake—The Big One

Why in the world would any sane human being want to travel all the way to Orlando, fork over a not-small number of hard-earned bucks, and then wait in a long line for the privilege of walking right into a devastating earthquake?

Well, it has to be because this ride is devastatingly fun. This spectacular attraction is based on the motion picture *Earthquake*, which was the first movie in history to win an Academy Award for special effects.

Six visitors—usually three women, a man, and two kids—are picked as extras and "grips" for a demonstration of movie special effects. The kids get to fulfill an ultimate fantasy: dropping (foam) boulders on a bunch of adults; the male extra is in for a surprise dive.

Before the action you'll see a short film about some of the special effects used in the original

Backstage at the earthquake. We took an exclusive tour into the control room and observed the computer controls for the sophisticated ride. You can see the room along the right side of the train in the catastrophe station; it's the operator who runs out with a megaphone at the end of each adventure.

movie. Most interesting is probably the miniature city constructed for one of the most spectacular scenes in the movie. It took six months to build, at a cost of about $2.5 million, and about six minutes to destroy; the actual sequence in the movie takes even less time than that.

I'd suggest you move all the way across the rows in the demonstration area so you can move quickly to the train for your choice of seats. When the demonstration is over, you will enter into a re-creation of a subway station in Oakland and board a subway train heading to Embarcadero Station in San Francisco.

The front of the two-hundred-seat train is to your left; the best car for the ride is the second car from the front. The first row of each car has a somewhat blocked view; try to grab a seat in the middle. The right side of the train (the far side of the row as you get in) has the best view of the flood; the left side of the train (where the last person in the row gets on board) is closest to the explosions and the train crash.

The train pulls out of the station and under the bay to Embarcadero Station. Suddenly, something goes very wrong. The train begins to shake violently, lights flicker, and the ceiling starts to collapse. The street above your head caves in, and a huge propane tanker truck crashes through the ceiling and toward you. But that's only the beginning: another train bears down on you at high speed aiming for a head-on crash. Finally, a huge tidal wave races your way.

Cut!

Amity Games. Down by the waterfront, there's a movie set version of a boardwalk, complete with games of chance that include **Short Shot** basketball, **Milk Can Menagerie**, **Shark-Banger** (a version of the familiar whack-a-mole game), **Wave Roll**, **Goblet Lob**, **Quarter Pitch**, **Hoop Toss**, and **Dolphin Dash**.

WOW Jaws

Just when you thought it was safe to go back to Florida, Universal Studios went and opened Jaws, a spectacular ride based on the movie classic that

Heavy effects. The special effects of Earthquake—The Big One are among the most spectacular ever created for an amusement park. To begin with, the rocking and rolling of the simulated earthquake would actually register a whopping 8.3 on the Richter scale. The mega-tremor releases sixty-five thousand gallons of (recycled) water every six minutes. The falling roadway slab weighs forty-five thousand pounds.

By the way, the tracks themselves remain stable; all of the rocking and rolling is done by lifters within the train itself.

Out of business. On the streets of San Francisco, note the impressive facade of Ferries & Cliff, one of the biggest department stores in the city at the turn of the century. It collapsed in the great earthquake of 1906 and was never rebuilt, except at Universal Studios.

And then check out the photos along the walls of the preshow area. Universal researchers uncovered a treasure trove of photos from the family of a survivor of the 1906 San Francisco earthquake.

Land line. How long is that line for Jaws? Here is a formula to estimate the wait: there are eight boats, each capable of holding forty-eight visitors, and the ride takes six minutes. Allowing two minutes to load and unload, that means each boat will carry about 336 passengers an hour. The eight boats, then, will move about 2,688 victims per hour across Amity Harbor.

By the way, the Jaws boat ride may be shut down if an electrical storm is in the area.

Vital stats. The Jaws ride employs space-age underwater technology never before used in an amusement attraction.

The seven-acre lagoon holds five million gallons of water and there are eight boats. Much of the New England memorabilia scattered about was found in Gloucester, Massachusetts, and surrounding fishing towns.

The thirty-two-foot shark is made of steel and fiberglass, with a latex skin; its teeth are made of urethane.

When it attacks, it moves through the water at realistic shark speeds of twenty feet per second, with thrusts equal to the power of a 727 jet engine.

kept millions out of the ocean twenty-five years ago . . . and still keeps many out of the surf.

It's always the Fourth of July when you visit the picturesque seaside resort of Amity. You can walk the boardwalk and try your hand at carnival games or grab a sticky snack. And, of course, you are certainly going to want to hop on board the Amity Harbor tour boat for a peaceful cruise.

The five-minute jaunt starts out well enough. The vicious shark that had previously terrorized Amity hangs lifeless from a hook in the village. What could possibly go wrong?

Well, OK, we imagine you have guessed what lies ahead. Your boat will motor gently around the corner, past a pretty little lighthouse to find a wrecked tour boat just like the one you're in. A few moments later, the harbor explodes with terror as an awesome thirty-two-foot-long, three-ton killer great white shark arrives to invite all of you to lunch. *His* lunch, that is.

It starts with a quick glimpse of a dorsal fin that zips past and then under your boat. Then he comes back!

Your boat captain will attempt to save the day, firing rifle grenades in a desperate attempt to stop the attacker. Somehow he will steer the boat into the safety of a deserted boathouse. Hah! Suddenly there's a crash on the side of the boathouse and the wall all but comes down with the force of Jaws breaking through.

Now it's a race for life as the boat is chased by the frenzied creature. The captain wildly fires his gun, hitting a chemical tank along shore and the lagoon fills with burning fuel as he attempts to break for safety on a barge that carries the main power supply cable to Amity Island.

Once again the shark attacks, but this time he grabs hold of the main power cable: instant fish fry! At last you're safe . . . right?

Some young visitors may find the explosions and the hot steam that envelops you at the end of the ride frightening; the fright level of the Jaws ride has ratcheted up a bit in recent years.

The left side of the boat is definitely the place to be for the more adventurous traveler; that's the side closest to the explosions, fire, Jaws, and . . . water. The fifth row of the boat lines up directly with the shark in some of the most spectacular scenes. By the way, when the ride first opened, Universal set decorators included a pair of mouse ears in the shark's mouth, but the top brass decided it was too scary for youngsters . . . and Disney.

Wild, Wild, Wild West Stunt Show

Guns blaze, cowboys brawl, and dynamite creates an instant urban renewal district in Universal's re-creation of a nineteenth-century western town. Hollywood stunt players demonstrate how they simulate the dangerous action.

The show, held in a two-thousand-seat arena, is short, intense, and suitable for kids of all ages, although some of the explosions and gunfire are a bit loud. There's a little story about a rough and tough "Ma" and her gang of boys; the guys in the white hats win, but not before there's a terrific battle down in the corral, up on the roofs, and even out on the ropes that hold the sign ("Square Dance and Hanging, Saturday Night") across Main Street.

There is a block of seats near the well at the left front of the stage that is marked "splash zone." Sit there if you are overdue for a shower. The water doesn't come from the "well" on the stage, though; that's a stunt pit, about six feet deep and padded on the bottom with a trampoline.

New York

WOW Twister

Here's your chance to step into the room with a murderous tornado.

That's the story line of the spectacular attraction, based on the wildly successful movie of the same name and basically the same story.

Guests entering into the waiting line find themselves in an outdoor field littered with re-creations of some of the film's props and artifacts. The setting is Wakita, Oklahoma, population 585. You'll see old farm equipment, an Esmoo Dairy truck with its signature cow symbol, and a collection of storm-tracking vehicles. Monitors overhead show footage of actual tornadoes.

Eventually you'll make your way into the preshow area where actor Bill Paxton deadpans his way through an introduction to the art and special effects used in the film. The 300-mile-an-hour twister in the film, Paxton says, is classified as an "F5, a once-in-a-lifetime monster tornado." Some call a twister of that magnitude the "finger of God," he tells us.

Actress Helen Hunt livens up the place later with more details about filming in and around the real town of Wakita, in "tornado alley." Some of the scenes in the film, we learn, were enhanced with the winds produced by a commercial jet engine. The room is decorated with actual props from the film.

We enter into what is left of Aunt Meg's home, destroyed by a twister in the film, and from there into one last area where we look out on the Galaxy Drive-In, a scene from the movie. The marquee at the theater promises "A Night of Horror."

Drink in the details. You'll hear the sound of crickets. Look for the shadow of a worker inside Erik's Garage. If you watch very carefully, you'll see a snippet of the famous shower scene from *Psycho* on the screen.

But it's showers of another sort that grab our attention. Rain begins to pelt the drive-in; we're somewhat protected by the tin roof over the shelter where we stand.

The storm begins to intensify. A window in the projection booth shatters. A storm-chaser truck, with the film's "Dorothy" experiment on its flatbed, blows in from the left and knocks over a fire hydrant. A bolt of lightning splits a tree, and the wind and rain is suddenly very intense. The flimsy tin roof over our heads doesn't provide much shelter any more.

Finally, the event that has drawn us volunteers: a five-story tornado grows before our eyes. We feel the wind, see the finger of God, and hear its freight train rumble.

Was that an Esmoo cow flying over our heads?

And then a truck slides across the parking lot to strike the gas pumps outside of Erik's Garage. A line of flame moves toward the leaking gas.

Boom! And it's over . . . and we lucky survivors get to walk out into the gift shop, a place where you can buy souvenirs that declare to the world that you have been to a place where cows fly.

Twister replaced the *Ghostbusters* attraction that had a long run there; the building was almost completely rebuilt within its exterior shell. Twister was originally scheduled to open in 1998 but was delayed out of respect for several Florida communities ravaged by real tornadoes in February of that year.

A trip through the Twister attraction will take about twenty minutes, plus the length of the waiting line. The tornado scene itself takes only about two-and-a-half minutes. If the outdoor queue is full when you arrive expect about an hour's wait; if the line extends out the door and onto the street you'd probably be better off coming back later.

Kongfrontation

The big banana himself is in town, and you are a helpless captive in New York's Roosevelt Island tram. In fact, you're so close you can smell the bananas on his breath.

The four-and-a-half-minute adventure begins as you walk through a beautifully constructed replica of a Manhattan subway station, complete with advertising posters appropriately redecorated with graffiti. Up above are television sets, and as you move through the building watch for news bulletins about the escapades of the famous ape.

The Big Apple has been turned into a frightening war zone, with wrecked cars, burst water mains, and massive fires. As your sixty-seat tram makes a turn, you arrive at the Queensboro Bridge to find the big guy hanging from the supports. Uprooting telephone poles as if they were toothpicks, he reaches for your tram . . . until a helicopter makes a brave attempt to distract him.

Phew! You're safe. But are you, really?

The Kongfrontation set is based on Manhattan's lower west side in 1976, the setting for the remake of *King Kong* which starred Jessica Lange and Jeff Bridges. Pay attention to the little details as you travel on the tram—peek into some of the windows of the tenements and see school-kid drawings, posters, and boxes of food.

New Yorkers will note that the moviemaking magic ignores a few key Big Apple facts. For example, you'll enter into the ride through a replica of Penn Station, which is on the west side of Manhattan; to find the loading platform for the Roosevelt Island Tram, which is on the east side.

Expensive stains. The New York streets are made of concrete; a mold was applied to make the roads appear to be constructed of cobblestones. All of the cracks in the road, bubble gum on the sidewalks, and rust stains on the stone (Styrofoam, actually) walls were applied by artists.

Before the park opened, Universal hired a graffiti artist from New York to decorate the walls of the tram waiting area. Since then, amateurs have added to the work.

King Kong wears a seven-thousand-pound fur coat. Four stories tall and weighing six tons, he has an arm span of 54 feet. The rescue helicopters are molded from real National Guard OH6 choppers.

Beetlejuice's Graveyard Revue

This is the ultimate in graveyard rock, a tuneful singing and dancing show presented in a shaded outdoor amphitheater and starring everybody's favorite creep, Beetlejuice, and a monstrous cast of characters that includes Wolfman, Dracula, Frankenstein, the Phantom of the Opera, and the Bride of Frankenstein. The background music is tape recorded, but the singing and dancing is live and very entertaining, although the very young and older adults may find it a bit loud.

Pay attention to some of the inside jokes: Beetlejuice takes a gander at the creepy old horror set and comments, "Hey, it looks like Tim Burton's summer home." He introduces Frankenstein as "a man of many parts—all of them used." And the Bride: "this month's cover girl from *Popular Mechanics*."

We especially enjoyed the stage performance of the "Banana Song" from the movie, as Beetlejuice dances with a pair of shrunken head dummies.

The Beetlejuice Revue is even better at night; the crowd is usually a bit more rowdy and the lighting effects look especially impressive against the dark sky. Check the schedule for the hours of performance.

Beetlejuice is a character on loan from Warner Brothers, while the rest of the awful actors are from Universal classics.

Arcades

As if you needed any more excitement, there is a state-of-the-art video arcade in the New York section that offers a good selection of current games.

Production Central

WOW Hitchcock's 3-D Theatre

At a theme park that celebrates the art of moviemaking, this show is the most serious exploration of the role of the director and a very entertaining stop for film fans.

Alfred Hitchcock made more than fifty films in his career, along the way creating some of the most famous scenes in the history of motion pictures. From the terrifying shower scene of *Psycho* to the dizzying heights of *Vertigo* to the relentless aerial attack of *The Birds*, you will learn the techniques behind Hitchcock's brilliance. The Hitchcock show, especially the assemblage of great clips shown in the theater, demonstrates moviemaking at its highest art form.

Hitchcock made ten feature films for Universal, beginning in 1934 with *The Man Who Knew Too Much* and ending with *Family Plot* in 1976. Universal was also the company behind his television series.

Enter the 258-seat **Tribute Theater** for a giant screen film journey through many of Hitchcock's works, including a portion of the rarely seen 3-D version of *Dial M for Murder*. (The movie was shot in 3-D, but while it was still in production the public's fascination with 3-D was deemed to have passed and the movie was released in a standard version.) You're also in for a surprise conclusion, courtesy of some of the flying fiends of *The Birds*.

Then it's on to an interactive area where you can explore more of Hitchcock's technique. Actor James Stewart will be your guide in an exploration of the visual shocks of *Vertigo*. John Forsythe will assist you in the reenactment of the murder on a carousel in *Strangers on a Train*. Norman Lloyd, who played the villain in *Saboteur* and later produced Hitchcock's television shows, will lead you up the gigantic torch of the Statue of Liberty, the climactic scene in that film.

In 1999 a portion of the show that included a comic re-enactment of the famous shower scene from *Psycho* was replaced by walk-through exhibits about Hitchcock's films.

Be sure to climb the stairs for a fascinating recreation of the famous apartment building scene

Rapid cutting. The shower scene in Alfred Hitchcock's *Psycho* is made up of seventy-eight different shots, edited in rapid sequence to simulate the violence of the attack. However, the knife is never shown piercing the skin. Hitchcock shot the film in black and white to lessen the gore. The "blood" is actually chocolate syrup; stage blood photographs as grey in a black and white print.

Check it out. In the Bates Motel replica at the end of the tour, notice that the key to Room 1 is missing. Even more interesting is what you'll uncover if you move the painting to the left of the check-in desk!

The shop also offers some of the more unusual souvenirs of the park: Bates Motel towels.

Doubles. One of Hitchcock's signatures was that he always had a minor walk-on in his movies. In Anthony Perkins's film introduction to the *Psycho* set, pay attention when the technicians remove the set and lighting equipment; there is a Hitchcock look-alike walking off in the distance.

in *Rear Window*. You'll be able to peer through binoculars at a wall of windows, each showing a different scene—in one of them, a murder takes place.

Back downstairs, Shirley MacLaine narrates a presentation about Hitchcock's famous cameos—his brief appearances in each of his films. Note the life-size mannequin of the director in the room; the master was only about 5′3″ tall.

You can also enter into the gift shop and the interactive area without waiting in line for the show itself.

WOW The Funtastic World of Hanna-Barbera

Yabba-dabba-doo. Children won't need to be persuaded, but adults: don't pass this one by. This show combines a wide-screen cartoon with state-of-the-art simulators—it's a wild ride for children of all ages. Think of it as a Junior Back to the Future.

Each group of eight seats in the ninety-six-seat auditorium is actually a flight simulator without the cabin, offering a glimpse at the technology—that is if you can take your eyes off the screen during the show. Remember the view when you ride the much wilder Back to the Future attraction, which uses similar but more aggressive technology.

The adventure begins with a three-minute preshow that introduces us to Bill Hanna and Joe Barbera, the rarely seen artists who launched some of our best-loved *non*-Disney characters, including Yogi Bear, the Flintstones, the Jetsons, Scooby Doo, and more. Their work garnered eight Emmys and seven Oscars. Hanna died in 2001.

Hanna and Barbera introduce us to the story of the adventure that lies ahead, as if such things really matter. We learn that Bill and Joe want to make Elroy Jetson their cartoon star of the future. But that's not all right with that diabolical dog Dastardly, who kidnaps Elroy. It's up to you, Yogi, and Boo Boo to rescue him.

While you are in the preshow area, if you listen carefully, you can hear from the other side of the door the screams of the people who are already riding. When it is your turn the doors will open and you will be ushered into the auditorium full of simulator cars.

Yogi will lead the entire audience—seated in its simulators—to a spaceship for a blastoff into the stratosphere and then back down into Bedrock for a prehistoric tussle featuring Fred, Wilma, Barney, Pebbles, Bam-Bam, and the entire Flintstones family. And so we are on to Scooby Doo's weird world and the fantastic future of the Jetsons.

The four-minute trip is every bit as silly as it sounds, but it's an exhilarating ride all the while.

Medical news. If you are prone to dizziness or upset stomach on wild rides like Back to the Future or The Funtastic World of Hanna-Barbera, you might want to take one or two Dramamine motion sickness tablets at the start of the day (before you take any rides). They work like a charm. Check with your family doctor first, especially if you are taking any other medications or if you have any allergies or unusual conditions. And be aware that the pills may make you a bit sleepy; you may want to assign a designated driver for the end of the day.

Back door. You don't have to wait in the sometimes-lengthy lines to the ride to get to the nifty play area of Funtastic Adventures. Enter through the Hanna-Barbera Store. This is a good place to let kids burn off some energy or get out of the rain.

Studio lingo. As you stroll the back lot, look for the three types of movie sets. A "facade" is a false front that has nothing behind it. A "shell" has a front, back, and side, but no useable interior space. A "practical set" is a shell that can be used for movies or other purposes.

Lean back for the best ride. The auditorium includes a row of seats down front that don't move; the elderly, the very young, pregnant women, and those with back problems are advised to sit there. By the way, if you get queasy here, you will get sick at Back to the Future.

The fun and learning doesn't stop after Elroy is rescued, either. An interactive play area allows you to play with sound effects, color your own cartoon cel with an electronic paint box and even see yourself as a cartoon character, shrunk in size to play in Pebbles's dollhouse.

The Boneyard

The storage place for some of the largest props from movies old and new. In recent years we have seen props from The *Flintstones*, *Casper*, and *Flipper*; the houseboat from *Cape Fear*; the Love Rock from *Problem Child 2*; fake topiary from *Edward Scissorhands*; and creepy things from *The Mummy* and *The Mummy Returns*.

Films shot here have included *Psycho IV: The Beginning*; Sylvester Stallone's *Oscar*, and *Problem Child 2*. Television projects include dozens of commercials and numerous Nickelodeon series.

WOW Nickelodeon Studios

If you have children they'll already know the way to The Network for Kids once they spot the seventeen-foot-tall Green Slime Geyser out front; it's the planet's only known source of the stuff.

This is a real working television studio, producing nearly three hundred episodes per year of Nickelodeon favorites.

Nickelodeon, which began in 1979, is owned by MTV Networks, which is itself owned by Viacom International.

Check out some of the funny signs overhead as you wait in line for a Nickelodeon tour or a television taping. One particularly interesting sign offers translations of common proverbs from English to foreign tongues. For example, in English you might say, "Don't waste your breath"; in France you would say (in French), "Save your saliva." An American might observe that something minor is "nothing to lose sleep over"; in Hawaii you could say, "It's a heap of relish made of octopus liver." And finally, "All that glitters is not gold" is translated in Haiti as "not all hair is real."

Admission to the Nickelodeon studio tour is free to Universal Studios visitors. You'll be invited to tour the production facilities and the two large sound stages for the cable television network.

From glassed-in catwalks above the stages, you can watch episodes in rehearsal or tapings, as well as look in on control rooms, makeup rooms, and the "kitchen" where slime and gak are made.

At the end of each studio tour, kids and their families enter the **Game Lab**, where the youngsters can try out some of the stunts used on the shows; the kids, by the way, get the best seats while their parents are sent to the bleachers. And, of course, at least one kid will get slimed!

If you or your kids are hoping to be in the audience for the taping of one of the game shows, stop by early in the day and see if they are handing out tickets alongside the door to Stage 18. You can also call the Nickelodeon operator at ☎ (407) 363-8586 and ask to be connected to the "hot line" number. Most taping is done on weekdays. The odds are not great: there are only a few hundred seats for each taping and they are usually snapped up by the first few hundred youngsters through the gates.

Your child's chances of appearing as a contestant on a Nickelodeon show are also pretty slim; most kids come from the Orlando area because they must be available on short notice to meet the schedules of the producers.

Inside slime. Try as we could, we were unable to obtain the secret recipe for gak and slime. We can tell you, though, that slime is the stuff that is poured over people while gak is dumped. And slime sorta tastes like applesauce while gak is a bit like butterscotch pudding gone wrong.

In addition to thousands of kids, movie director Steven Spielberg has also enjoyed a good sliming.

Production schedule. To find out what is in production at the studios, call the Guest Services office at ☎ (407) 354-6356.

Hollywood

WOW Terminator 2 3-D

He's back . . . and with a vengeance. This is a tour de force of film, live action, and computerized special effects that puts the audience in the middle of an epic battle between and among the fearsome "cinebotic" robots, stunt performers, and the reunited stars of *Terminator 2*: Arnold Schwarzenegger, Linda Hamilton, Robert Patrick, and Eddie Furlong, along with director James Cameron and special effects wizards from the series. In this newest Terminator adventure—which begins in the present day and jumps to the Los Angeles of 2029 covered in the film—Cyberdyne Systems, the dreaded creators of Skynet and its fearsome Terminator cyborgs, has moved its corporate headquarters to Universal Studios Florida's Hollywood Boulevard.

Guests twist and turn in their seats as menacing Cyberdyne Systems "T-70" cinebotic warriors train their sights on random targets throughout the theater, firing across the theater. The audience will leap back in three-dimensional shock when the T-1000 Terminator "cop" from the *Terminator 2* movie morphs to life before their very eyes, then cheer with relief as Schwarzenegger's T-800 cyborg literally charges off the screen to save the day astride a 1,500-pound

Harley Davidson "hog" that actually lands on the stage and then dives back into the screen and into the scene.

And not to spoil the fun, but you'll want to hold on to your seats for the jaw-dropping finale. You'll understand what we mean when your feet are back on solid ground.

The show begins with a "super" entertaining preshow sales pitch by a Cyberdyne associate. "Imagine a world where butterflies run on batteries," she asks, expecting you to do so with happy anticipation, "where human error is a thing of the past. Our goal is complete control of global communication."

Just after the associate unveils Skynet, a computer-controlled defense system, something goes wrong with the promotional video: it seems that hackers have broken into the system to warn us against Cyberdyne.

Terminator creator James Cameron, who directed this third installment of the saga, regards Terminator 2 3-D as a true sequel to his earlier blockbusters. "It's definitely the next film," he said. "The only difference is this film is only twelve minutes long and you can't see it in just any theater."

Because the audience is in the present day, the story uses T-70 cinebots, a design of robots not seen in the movies, which take place several decades in the future. The six T-70s each stand eight feet tall; they rise from their hiding places along the walls of the theater with the aid of a hydraulic system.

This is the first time interlocking three-dimensional images are projected onto multiple screens, surrounding guests in 180 degrees of action. For its climactic third act, the film opens up from one fifty-foot center screen to simultaneous projection on three screens, arranged at sixty-degree angles for a sense of enveloping the audience. Spanning 165-feet, Terminator 2 3-D enjoys the distinction of being the world's largest 3-D installation and the first to use the triple screen setup and six 70-mm Iwerks projectors.

According to its producers, the twelve-minute-long film is, frame for frame, the most expensive film every produced.

Live-action portions of the film took place in a two-week shoot at Kaiser Eagle Mountain, an abandoned steel mine in Desert Center, California, rebuilt in spectacular fashion to resemble Los Angeles after a nuclear war. More than a hundred cars, trucks, and buses were hauled in from wrecking yards and strewn about the one-million-square-foot location set. The background consisted not of mockups but of actual buildings that were blown up during filming, lending a scale authenticity that surpassed many big-budget Hollywood action flicks.

Additional scenes were shot on a Los Angeles soundstage, where an elaborate twenty-four-foot "miniature" of Skynet, the pyramid-shaped headquarters of Cyberdyne Systems, was constructed. Through the magic of cinema trickery it will appear to be eight hundred feet tall on screen.

The show has a seating capacity of 700, and can accommodate about 2,400 guests per hour. Much of the waiting area for the show is within the Cyberdyne building; if lines extend out onto the street you may want to come back later in the day. The best seats for the 3-D effects are from the middle to the back of the theater; the best seats to see the live action, including the arrival of the Harley on stage and the frozen breakup finale, is third or fourth row, center.

Lucy: A Tribute

On the left side of Rodeo Drive, keep your ears open for the world's largest indoor collection of Lucy screams. If you are a fan of Lucille Ball and everyone around her, you'll be enthralled with this collection of photos, scripts, and memorabilia and a continuous showing of episodes from her television show. Among my personal favorites is Lucy as part a barbershop quartet.

There is a diorama showing how the original television show was filmed in front of a live audience. The show was photographed (on 35-mm black-and-white film) on one large set; episodes were edited and combined.

We don't know very many other places in the world where you can see a collection of Desi Arnaz's conga drums or view some of the original scripts from "I Love Lucy." There's a Lucy trivia quiz, including questions like, "What was the biggest laugh in Lucy history?" Here's a hint: the answer involves Lucy, Ricky, a bunch of raw eggs, and a wild and romantic dance.

Desi Arnaz was born as Desiderio Alberto Arnazey Acha III in Santiago, Cuba, in 1917. The son of a Cuban senator, he lived in great luxury until the revolution of 1933 when they fled the country. Arnaz worked at various jobs, including cleaning birdcages.

Eventually he got a job in a band and soon became one of the leading band leaders in New York. Signed to the lead in the New York musical *Too Many Girls*, he played a Latin football player. When he went to Hollywood to play his role in the movie version of the show, he met the studio ingénue Lucille Ball, and in late 1940 they began a bicoastal marriage.

After World War II, looking for a way to work together in Los Angeles, Lucy and Desi hired the writers of Lucy's radio show "My Favorite Husband" and produced a pilot for "I Love Lucy." Their new company, Desilu Productions, became the largest television and film production company in Hollywood. Arnaz died in 1986; Lucy passed on in 1989.

Lucy, I'm home! The original TV show was unusual in that the creators worked with three or four permanent sets that stood side-by-side in the studio, avoiding the flimsy looking sets typical of television shows at the time. The permanent setting also allowed for more advanced lighting, allowing cameras to move quickly from one area to another. All of the sets were painted in carefully chosen shades of gray to control the contrast of the finished black-and-white film.

The Gory, Gruesome & Grotesque Horror Make-Up Show

It's nearly all in the name; they left out "gross."

Most everyone loves a good monster or horror movie. Here's your chance to learn some of the secrets behind the special effects. For example, where else would you find the recipe for gore: shrimp sauce, oatmeal, and red dye.

Among the devices demonstrated in the twenty-five-minute show is the teleportation scene from *The Fly*, somewhat humorously reenacted on stage.

A film clip explains how Meryl Streep is turned around in her body in *Death*

Becomes Her, a special effect that involved blue-screen technology. Streep was videotaped walking backward wearing a blue bag over her head, and then her face was electronically superimposed onto the bag for the effect.

Some children may find the GG&G show to be much too gory, gruesome, and grotesque: parents be warned.

One extra from the audience—usually a woman—gets her arm sliced open and suffers other simulated indignities. There are 355 seats in the theater, and visitors are often turned away at midday; go early or late on busy days.

AT&T at the Movies

An interactive electronic playground that may interest some visitors; it does have buttons for kids to push, and it is a good place to duck in out of the rain or the sun and enjoy a few Epcot-like science and computer games.

At the **Movie Make-Up** screen, you can pose in front of a TV camera and then apply different ears or mustaches or beards or other facial adornments. Nearby is what may be the world's largest working telephone, a booth where the entire family can enter to place a speakerphone call (on your dime, not theirs).

And there is the **Dawn of Sound** where you can listen to some of the most famous early sound clips of all time, including Al Jolson, news clips from Prohibition, the early talkies, and of all things, a bit of *Steamboat Willie*—the first Mickey Mouse cartoon with sound.

Special Events

Most any day in the summer and during holiday periods the rest of the year you can expect a high school or college marching band to high-step around the park at mid-morning. And Universal Studios also regularly throws itself a party for special events; call ☎ (407) 363-8000 for calendar updates.

New Year's Eve Celebration. A blazing fireworks show and other seasonal entertainment welcome the new year.

Spring Break and Daytona Speed Week. The park offers special discounts to college students during spring break.

Mardi Gras at Universal Studios Florida. Presented each year from mid-February through the end of March or early April, and featuring fifteen or so full-sized floats from the streets of New Orleans, more than two hundred costumed street performers, including stilt walkers, fire eaters, unicyclists, and ten marching bands. In addition, more than 150 elaborately costumed characters will ride on the floats; many of them are guests selected from the audience. The parade takes place nightly at closing time; admission is included in the day's ticket. In addition, major musical groups will perform on stage each Saturday during the Mardi Gras celebration, and the park's restaurants will add New Orleans favorites, including crawfish, jambalaya, and étouffée. You can also buy a potent Hurricane, a rum-based drink concocted by Pat O'Brien's, a restaurant that now has its own location at Universal CityWalk.

Fourth of July. A special fireworks show, with music from movie favorites.

Halloween Horror Nights. Hundreds of monsters, maniacs, and mutants crawl out from the back lot from mid-October through Halloween. This is an amazing effort, not for the squeamish or very young. Scattered about the park are a half-dozen dark mazes populated by all manner of creepy creatures and scarified with the aid of sound effects, fog machines, and laser projectors. One of the highlights is a Halloween walking tour *through* the set of King Kong, a place only viewed from the safety of a cable car the rest of the year.

The park attracts huge crowds for the Halloween Horror Nights; a separate admission ticket is required.

Eating Your Way Through Universal Studios

There are some interesting choices for food at Universal Studios, including a variety of foreign and ethnic foods. There are many more choices, too, with the opening of Universal CityWalk. You can leave Universal Studios Florida (get your hand stamped for re-entry) and go out to lunch or dinner at CityWalk, choosing from a nice variety of unusual to haute cuisine.

Near Nickelodeon Studios, there's a new exit from the park that leads to Hard Rock Cafe and NBA City, as well as offering a shortcut that connects to Universal Studios Islands of Adventure and Universal CityWalk.

The Front Lot

Beverly Hills Boulangerie. A selection of gourmet sandwiches and pastries.

Just inside the entrance gates, at the corner of Plaza of the Stars and Rodeo Drive, the Boulangerie offers a selection of sandwiches, coffee, and drinks.

Sweets include cherry turnovers, cheese Danishes, overstuffed muffins, macadamia and chocolate chip cookies, croissants, hazelnut éclairs, and slices of key lime pie, for about $2 to $3.

Key

= Fast food

= Pub

= Full-service restaurant

The Fudge Shoppe. Just like the sign says—no more, no less—The Fudge Shoppe is located beside the Studio Store across from the main entrance. This is a good stop to get something special for the road or for a quick sweet treat on your way into the park.

Expo Center

International Food Bazaar. Gyros, brats, burgers, pizza, and more, $2 to $8. In the rear of Expo Center, next to Back to the Future, this food court offers American, Chinese, German, Italian, and Greek fast food. The advantage of this eatery is evident to families: everyone in the party should be able to indulge their own tastes in one place.

Hollywood

Cafe La Bamba. This attractive eatery lost its Mexican flavor in favor of more ordinary fare such as barbecued baby back ribs, rotisserie chickens, and barbecued pork, for about $7 to $10.

The cafe is decorated within like an old villa, with fancy pillars and art; albeit with a cafeteria line within. During Universal's celebration of Mardi Gras, the restaurant takes on a New Orleans menu.

A quiet bar near the entrance offers a variety of alcoholic beverages and soft drinks.

Mel's Drive-In. Burgers, hot dogs, salads, chips, and drinks in a 1950s diner, modeled after the eatery from *American Graffiti*.

You can't miss Mel's. Just look for the garish pink and blue building with its large neon sign on the corner of Eighth and Hollywood Boulevard. Unless you are a child of the '50s, you may not immediately appreciate the true beauty of the pink and white 1956 Ford Crown Victoria parked next to an absolutely cherry 1957 black Chevrolet out front.

Inside, a sock-hop theme prevails, with period music and booths that have individual juke box selectors. Check out the old 45-rpm records pasted to the wall and the pedal pushers worn by the attendants.

Notice I didn't say "waitresses." Forget the personal, at-table service you knew in the '50s, because you have to stand in line to retrieve your fast food here. You'll also have a lot of company in line at this popular place.

Schwab's Pharmacy. A classic old-time drugstore fountain just waiting to be discovered.

Hard to miss, on Hollywood Boulevard next to the Brown Derby Hat Shop. Look for the giant blue neon sign, and walk into the bright white drugstore fountain area.

This is a typical 1950s drugstore with a few booths and seating around a curved counter. Soda jerks in blue jeans, white shirts, and classic paper hats take your order and prepare the treats while you watch. The walls are decorated with vintage photos from the original Schwab's in Hollywood and some of its famous patrons.

If you remember the '50s with its custom, handmade ice-cream treats (or even if you don't), you'll have a hard time selecting from the familiar Schwab's offerings.

Main courses include hot dogs and turkey or chicken salad sandwiches for about $6 or $7. Ice cream cones and milkshakes sell for about $2.50 to$3.50.

Schwab's is also a good place to pick up an emergency supply of aspirin, Tylenol, Rolaids, or cough drops—some of which you may need after the treats you go through. They also sell Dramamine, useful to some for thrill ride relief.

San Francisco/Amity

Boardwalk Snacks. Hot dogs, chips, fruit, and drinks. On hot days this is the place to go for an emergency Slush Puppy.

For a quick, takeout snack or light meal on the go, stroll into the Boardwalk on the small wharf on Amity Avenue. The shop offers a nautical theme, with outdoor dining at picnic tables that offer a view of the lagoon.

Boardwalk fare includes hot dogs and chili dogs, and corn dogs for about $4 to $6; turkey drumsticks go for about $4.75. You can also buy cotton candy and frozen yogurt.

Chez Alcatraz. Quick seafood treats and drinks. Located over the water on the first wharf in San Francisco/Amity, this walk-up stand gives you a chance to sample shrimp cocktails, clam chowder, soft drinks, or beer and wine while you watch the activities in the lagoon.

An interesting crab salad "Conewich" gives you a one-handed shot at seafood salad on the go, or you can try a crab cocktail. Entrees range in price from about $3 to $6.

Lombard's Landing. Steak, pasta, and seafood served in an elegant 1800s warehouse, this is, by most visitors' accounts, the most attractive restaurant in the park with a nice view of the lagoon. Lunch entrees range from about $8 to $15 for adults and $3.50 to $5 for children. Dinner entrees start at about $15 and reach to about $25 for adults and $5 to $8 for children.

Fish choices include swordfish, grouper, tuna, mahi mahi, salmon, and lobster, priced at market rates from about $15 to $25. You can begin your meal with New England Clam Chowder, or lobster bisque. Other entrees include pan-seared bison rib eye for $24, and buffalo burgers for $10.

If you time your visit perfectly, you will have a front-row view of the stunt show in the lagoon; the best seats would be out on the balcony overlooking the water.

Located on the wharf next to the Pastry Company, Lombard's entrance is marked by a bright blue awning. Inside, the warehouse has been upgraded with jade green, simulated marble tables, fish fountains, and aquariums. Notice the exposed iron work and wooden beams with bright copper bases.

The large "port hole" aquarium in the center of the rear dining room is not to be missed. And while you select your food, you can read the newspaper story of the great San Francisco Earthquake of 1906.

Entrees for lunch include fish and chips, grilled chicken, crab cakes, New York strip steak, or chicken and chive fettuccine. The signature sandwiches include the Lomberger (a hamburger on a sourdough bun with Swiss, cheddar, or boursin cheese), a fried grouper on sourdough with a dill *rémoulade* sauce, and a veggie burger on a seven-grain bun.

The catch of the day can be grilled, blackened, or sautéed; fish selections include swordfish, red snapper, tuna, salmon, and lobster.

Midway Grill. Carnival fare: grilled Italian sausage with peppers and onions for about $6, Philly cheese steak for about $6.50, plus hot dogs and chicken fingers.

Pier 27. Barbecue, hot dogs, clam chowder, beer, and chips. You'd almost have to know this little eatery was here or find it by accident tucked into the back of Golden Gate Mercantile on Pier 27.

Draft and imported bottled beer complement the limited but rather nice selection of barbecue pork sandwiches, clam chowder, or hot dogs.

Richters Burger Company. Richter, as in Richter scale, and as in The

Big One (a $6 burger with fries), The San Andreas (chicken breast on bun with fries), and The Trembler (a hot dog platter with fries). Entrees range from about $5 to $8. Located directly opposite the entrance to Earthquake, the tables in the back have a view of the lagoon.

San Francisco Pastry Company. San Francisco–style pastries and sweets, croissant sandwiches, plus espresso and cappuccino and the best selection of beers at any casual restaurant in the park.

At the front of Pier 27, on the Embarcadero across from Earthquake: The Big One. The European cafe design opens off of brick-paved streets, and the patio overlooks the lagoon.

Production Central

Classic Monsters Cafe. A gustatory celebration of some of Universal's greatest monster hits. You'll order your food from a cafeteria line and take it back to one of four monstrous dining areas stocked with artifacts and memorabilia from great movies: Egypt (including items from *The Mummy*), a Gothic haunted house (*Phantom of the Opera* and *Frankenstein*), outer space (films such as *This Island Earth*, one of the worst sci-fi movies ever made, so bad it's a classic), and a sea creature lair (*Creature from the Black Lagoon*).

Items on display include original scripts, props, posters, and costumes. The background music includes great hits from monster films and even some parodies such as *The Rocky Horror Picture Show*. Video monitors show clips from Universal classics.

Appetizers include chef, Caesar, and chicken and shrimp Caesar salads priced from about $3 to $9. Pastas include four-cheese ravioli, penne pasta, linguine primavera, and wood-fired oven pizza from about $7.

New York

Finnegan's Bar and Grill. Traditional Irish fare, including stews and meat pies. About $10 to $15.

Finnegan's occupies a prominent position on Fifth Avenue across the street from Kongfrontation. In movie-set style, the corner Regal Cafe is just another entrance to Finnegan's.

This is a typical New York City community bar, complete with brick-paved sidewalk and awning-covered entrance. The neon signs in the windows add to the festive saloon atmosphere. The pressed tin ceilings are high and accented with hanging lights and slow-moving fans.

Lighter items include a Blarney baguette filled with your choice of roast beef, corned beef, ham, or turkey with wedge fries for about $9, and a Shamrock steak sandwich, also for about $9. It's Saint Patrick's Day every day here, including Irish stew with lamb, potatoes, and fresh vegetable for $7.95. And there is London Times fish and chips (fish fillets in ale batter with fries and malt vinegar), served on the front page of the *London Times* for about $10.50. And, of course, there is corned beef and cabbage (about $11) every day.

Other offerings include shepherd's pie and bangers and mash (hot dogs and mashed potatoes), each for about $10.

Louie's Italian Restaurant. Italian antipasto, pizzas, salads, and more. Located right on Universal's Fifth Avenue at Canal Street, Louie's offers a wide selection of Italian specialties from antipasto to pizza, soups to salads, plus pasta and ices. You can also buy beer.

The dining area here is very large and open with studio-type lighting. The high ceiling and large front windows give an open, bright atmosphere. Two serving lanes offer the same fare on either side, but veteran Louie's visitors say the left side usually is shorter.

The portions are large and the food fresh. Pizza is available by the slice for about $3.50 or by the pie from about $16 to $18.

UNIVERSAL STUDIOS FLORIDA

1. Production Center Information
2. Nickelodeon Studios
3. The Funtastic World of Hanna-Barbera
4. Hitchcock's 3-D Theatre
5. *Future attraction*
6. The Boneyard
7. Production Studios
8. Twister
9. Men in Black: Alien Attack
10. Kongfrontation
11. Performance stage
12. *Beetlejuice's Graveyard Revue*
13. Earthquake–The Big One
14. Jaws
15. *Wild, Wild, Wild West Stunt Show*
16. Back to the Future . . . The Ride
17. AT&T at the Movies
18. *Animal Planet Live!*
19. *A Day in the Park with Barney*
20. Fievel's Playland
21. E.T. Adventure
22. *The Gory, Gruesome & Grotesque Horror Make-Up Show*
23. Terminator 2 3-D
24. Lucy: A Tribute
25. Woody Woodpecker's Nuthouse Coaster
26. Curious George Goes to Town

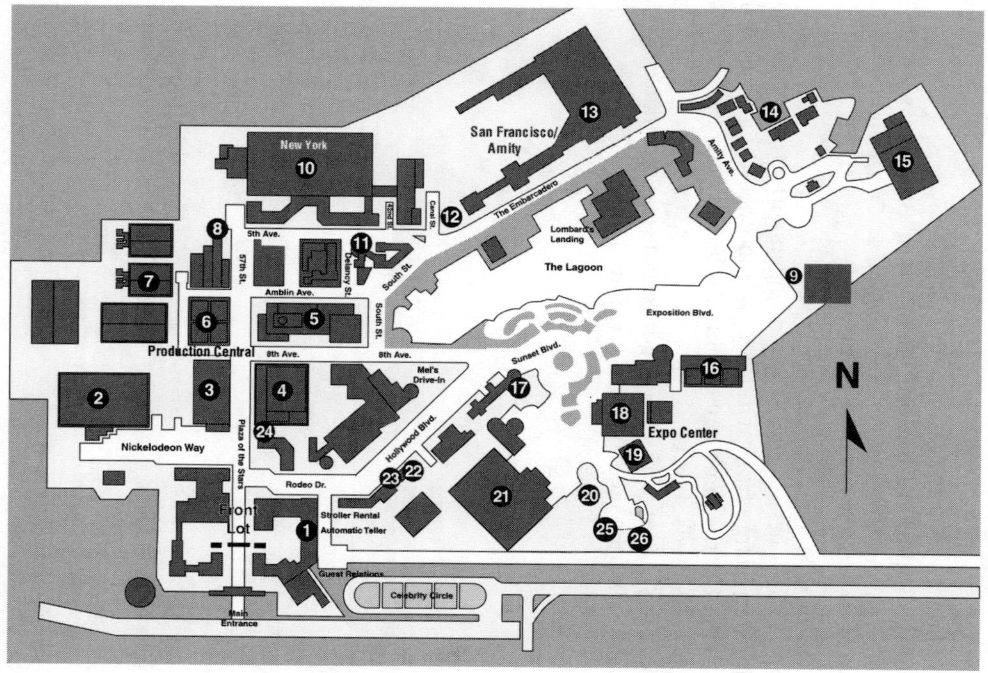

Chapter 17
Universal Studios Islands of Adventure

Universal's Islands of Adventure is the most technologically advanced, wild and woolly theme park in Orlando. It's got something for everyone, with thrill rides, spectacular simulations, entertainment, worlds of wonder for children of all ages, and delights for the eye at most every turn.

This is also Florida's most beautiful theme park by night, a world of fire and water, fog and light.

On 110 acres, roughly the same size as Walt Disney World's Magic Kingdom, you'll find the world's first duel racing roller coasters; the first combined 3-D film, live action, and moving motion base simulator; and a high-speed coaster that has a zero-G heartline inversion.

The crown jewel of Islands of Adventure is the Amazing Adventures of Spider-Man, an attraction that is unlike anything else anywhere on the theme park planet; if comparisons must be drawn, think of Back to the Future and The Terminator 2 3-D . . . on wheels.

Then there are the awesome roller coasters. The glowing-green Incredible Hulk Coaster dominates the skyline as you drive by on I-4 and overhangs Marvel Super Hero Island to your left as you enter the park; a couple of times a minute the area rumbles with the launch of a train 150 feet up the takeoff tunnel and then echoes with the screams of the riders as they immediately enter into an inverted zero-G heartline roll. But not to be overlooked is the mind-boggling spaghetti bowl of red and blue tracks in the back right corner of the park; the two Dueling Dragons coasters run side-by-side, above, below, and straight at each other.

It certainly gets hot in Florida but you'll have plenty of opportunities to take a shower with your clothes on at entertaining water rides Dudley Do-Right's Ripsaw Falls and Popeye & Bluto's Bilge-Rat Barges.

You can visit places heretofore only viewed in the mind's eye, at state-of-the-art simulations such as the Jurassic Park River Adventure, Triceratops Encounter, and Poseidon's Fury: Escape from the Lost City.

And then there is Seuss Landing, where the wonderfully weird world of Dr. Seuss comes to life for children of all ages.

MUST-SEES

WOW

The Amazing Adventures of Spider-Man

Incredible Hulk Coaster

Doctor Doom's Fearfall

Dudley Do-Right's Ripsaw Falls

Popeye & Bluto's Bilge-Rat Barges

Jurassic Park River Adventure

Pteranadon Flyers

Dueling Dragons

Poseidon's Fury: Escape from the Lost City

The Eighth Voyage of Sindbad

The Cat in the Hat

Caro-Seuss-el

One Fish, Two Fish, Red Fish, Blue Fish

At opening ceremonies in 1999, Steven Spielberg, creative consultant to Universal Studios, gave an interesting insight to the design process: "Making a theme park is like making movies and plays, and then building an entire city to contain them."

A Tour of the Islands

The adventure begins at the Port of Entry and continues through five "islands" connected by walkways, bridges, and a water taxi. Clockwise from the Port of Entry, you'll find:

- Marvel Super Hero Island
- Toon Lagoon
- Jurassic Park
- The Lost Continent
- Seuss Landing

Power Trip #1

The Express Tour

The Universal Express system allows visitors to make reservations for most major attractions. Guests at Universal's hotels are given unlimited express privileges; purchasers of two- or three-day multi-park passes can hold as many as three reservations at a time, and holders of one-day tickets can reserve one attraction at a time.

The best strategy here is to grab a reservation for your number one goal, and then head for the shortest line at the next place on your list.

Power Trip #2

Everything Is New

Face it: Islands of Adventure is going to be one bustling island for years to come. The biggest draws are the major thrill rides, **The Amazing Adventures of Spider-Man**, **Dueling Dragons**, and **The Hulk**. On a Florida sizzler (which can happen almost any time of the year, but especially from May through September), **Jurassic Park River Adventures** and **Dudley Do-Right's Ripsaw Falls**, and **Popeye & Bluto's Bilge-Rat Barges** are likely to draw long, hot lines of guests in search of a cooling drench.

And if you're intent on riding the simple but charming **Pteranadon Flyers**, don't wait too late in the day either. You'll need a kid as an escort, though.

Follow the basic *Econoguide* strategy: arrive early, head deep into the park to your number one goal, and try to stay one step ahead of the crowds who will likely work their way from front to back.

If you're heading to Jurassic Park or the Dueling Dragons, you might consider jumping on a water taxi at the landing where Port of Entry meets the lagoon; the shuttles run to a dock near the **Jurassic Park Discovery Center**. If there's a line for the boat, though, you'll probably do better by walking.

Remember that Jurassic Park, Dudley Do-Right, and Bilge-Rat Barges are not billed as water rides for nothing. (So, too for **One Fish, Two Fish, Red Fish, Blue Fish** for the kiddies.) Consider whether you want to start the day with a wet bottom, especially on a cool day.

Eat lunch and dinner early and head for major attractions while other park visitors wait in line for food.

Port of Entry

You'll present your passport (admission tickets, actually) at a dramatic plaza in the shadow of a towering lighthouse modeled after the famous Pharos light at ancient Alexandria. If you have a moment, check out the notice about currency exchange rates at the USIOA Guest Services booth. In addition to cash, credit cards, travelers checks, and currency from a number of major nations of today, you can also learn that USIOA values one Spanish doubloon as four pigs and one donkey, and one Alsation franc at one goose.

Notable shops in the Port of Entry include **Universal's Islands of Adventure Trading Company** (the major souvenir shop of the park), **Silk Road Clothiers** (travel gear, leather bags, and jewelry), **Island Market and Export** (gourmet foods from around the world), and **Ocean Trader Market** (carvings from Africa, mehndi skin colorings from India, and more exotica).

Universal Studios Islands of Adventure

Give yourself a few moments to enjoy the attention to detail around you at eye level and up above. My favorite sign in the Port of Entry: "Sooths Sayed While You Wait."

At the end of the shopping district lies the entryway to the park itself, a pass through a set of gates held back by impressively large chains.

A fleet of three eccentric water taxis, **Island Skipper Tours**, runs from the Port of Entry across the Inland Sea to a dock at the Jurassic Park Discovery Center. It's a pleasant trip, only a bit faster than walking if your timing is right, but the taxis do offer spectacular views of The Incredible Hulk Coaster and other sections of the park unavailable anywhere else.

Marvel Super Hero Island

Imagine: an entire island populated by superheroes the likes of Spider-Man, The Hulk, and the Fantastic Four.

For most of us this place is eerily familiar, a step into the fantasy comic book pages of yesterday and today. Just like in the cartoons, the storefronts are generic. You'll find a store named "Store," an arcade "Arcade," and a frozen ice stand advertised as "Frozen Ice."

You'll also find a trio of awesome thrill rides guaranteed to make you marvel.

The Amazing Adventures of Spider-Man

You've got to see this, though you still won't believe it. Quite simply, this is the state of the art in theme park rides, a 3-D video, virtual reality motion base simulator on wheels. There's nothing like it anywhere else in the universe.

There's an outdoor queue in the delivery docks of that well-known New York newspaper, the *Daily Bugle*, home of mild-mannered photographer Peter Parker. (Background information for the comically impaired: the bite of a radioactive spider changed shy high school student Peter Parker into a superhero with the speed, agility, and strength of a spider-man. He earns his keep as a cameraman, acting as a one-man vigilante army whenever he can spare the time.)

Eventually, we make our way into the lobby of the *Bugle*. Spend some time to soak in the attention to detail in the waiting area. It begins with a collection of headlines of recent events you may have missed while you were away on vacation. For example, "Terror Coast to Coast: Magnetic Mutant Seizes Missile Base." There are also some *Bugle* editorials by the unknowing Spider-Man detractor J. Jonah Jameson, who asks: "Is Spider-Man Through?"

Past the hallway we enter Peter Parker's office and darkroom. Look closely at the name on the door; it seems that the previous occupant of the small room was named "Broom Closet."

Signs on the wall give the *Bugle*'s operating procedure: "Remember! First get the pictures. Then get the stories. And after that . . . safety first."

And next we enter the newsroom. Lights flash on old-style telephones, an incongruous mix with modern computer screens. Note the color scheme: most everything in the background is in pale green, like the muted backgrounds of a comic book. The foreground is decorated in bright poster-like colors.

There is news in the air. Headlines trumpet: "Emergency Declared! Statue of Liberty Stolen!" Who could possibly have done such a dastardly deed other than Doctor Octopus, Electro, Hydro-Man, Hobgoblin, and Scream, AKA The Sinister Syndicate?

Drafted as a civilian posse, we're given the chance to join with Spider-Man to retrieve the missing national treasure. Our vehicles are "Scoops," more formally known as "Surveillance Communications Patrols."

A funny cartoon tells of the do's and don'ts about loading into the car. Watch carefully and see if you can spot the funny jab at the GM Test Track at Disney's Epcot; it comes during the cartoon's recommendation that you be sure to use the Scoop's lap bars.

Each car holds a dozen volunteers in three rows of four. Two Scoops are loaded at the same time. The rows are numbered from the rear of each vehicle (and assigned a name for a section of the *Daily Bugle's* circulation area in New York City). Row 1 is Queens, the back row of the second vehicle in line. Row 2, Bronx, is the middle row. Row 3, Brooklyn, is the front row. In the first vehicle in line, Row 4, Coney Island, is the back of the bus. Row 5, Staten Island, is in the middle. Row 6, Manhattan, is the front row.

All of the seats in the Scoop vehicle give a good view of the action, The front row offers the most dramatic views—without someone else's head between you and the action. But the middle and last rows offer the most motion.

And then we're off on a twenty-block tour of New York City, a huge acre-and-a-half set where we are thrust into the middle of a battle between good and evil.

Seen through our 3-D glasses, Spider-Man greets us and then things go seriously wrong. Flaming pumpkins and spewing water pipes hurled by the forces of evil seem to fly toward riders and smash into our vehicle.

It all comes to a chilling conclusion when Doc Ock takes aim at us with his Doomsday Anti-Gravity Gun. One blast sends us four hundred feet in the air and then into a four-hundred-foot freefall. If you're wondering whether you should take out new flight insurance, remember that it's all simulated—a technology known as "sensory drop." That doesn't mean it doesn't feel very real.

According to Universal Studios the challenge in creating Spider-Man was to get guests directly involved in the action as they view 3-D films and move at high speed past props and special effects. The technology employs a "moving point of convergence" and uses twenty-five large-format movie projectors and dozens of smaller projectors.

I went for a behind-the-scenes peek at the control room for the high-tech ride. There I saw with my own eyes what my mind had refused to believe. The actual rise and fall of the vehicles—including the "four-hundred-foot drop" that is at the heart of the ride—is only about three or four feet.

Knowing the secret, I went back and rode the Scoop once more—and I still felt the bottom of my stomach rising to meet my throat as we "fell" forty stories.

WOW Incredible Hulk Coaster

It seems that Dr. Bruce Banner is playing around with the rules of physics once again, conducting special gamma-ray accelerator tests.

We lucky visitors are offered the chance to participate in the experiment. How can we say no?

In a ride of about two minutes and fifteen seconds, the thirty-two passengers, seated four-abreast, experience seven rollovers and plunge into a pair of deep subterranean tunnels.

Not that you're going to be able to read this book—or remember much of what I wrote here—while you're riding on The Hulk, here's a summary of your ride. Your trip begins when your car is catapulted in three seconds up a 150-foot launch tunnel with the same force as a U.S. Air Force F-16 fighter attack jet on takeoff. Exiting from the tube at 40 miles per hour, there's an immediate twist onto your back in a weightless heartline roll more than 110 feet above the ground. The cars then dive at 60 miles per hour in a steep plunge toward the water, and then straight back up 109 feet.

Still with me? OK, now we go into a sharp twist into an upside-down roll to the right, then a tight turn and upside-down roll to the left . . . followed by yet another plunge to the water. Back up we go, into a narrow oblong loop, upside-down at the top, of course.

We complete the front side of the ride with a drop to—and below—the surface of the lagoon and beneath a bridge full of gawkers crossing from the Port of Entry to Marvel Super-Hero Island. Coming up from the tunnel, we make a slow, twisting climb to the left, which ends in a sideways loop. From there we're into an upside-down loop and into a semi-hidden area of the park behind the Hulk building.

The Incredible Hulk, Doctor Doom's Fearfall, and Marvel Super Hero Island

Out back where there are few witnesses, we flip over and then plunge upside-down to earth and immediately back up into one inverted loop and then another and then onto our sides in a small, tight loop that goes upside-down at the top.

If you have your eyes open, you may be able to see the end of the ride, but between here and there are a few more high-G twists and turns to burn off speed.

Whew! Now you can say you've experienced The Incredible Hulk. Was it good for you, too?

The queue for The Hulk begins outside and wends its way into the Gamma Radiation Testing Zone, your basic sci-fi cartoon laboratory with flashing lights, green overhead pipes, and video monitors that tell the story of the experiment through the words of Dr. Bruce Banner.

(In case you're not an expert on all things Marvel, scientist Bruce Banner's basic constitution was altered when he was caught in the rays of a gamma bomb explosion; he's a nice enough guy as long as you don't get him angry or agitated. When he is, he transforms into the rampaging Incredible Hulk, glowing a lovely shade of green.)

Just short of the loading area, the line splits. Keep to the left for a seat in the front car, or keep to the right to enter the faster-moving line for the rest of the train.

Short story. Alas, the smallest visitors to Universal's Islands of Adventure will be unable to ride the fastest and wildest attractions. Don't fight the rules: they are there for the child's protection. Here are the minimum heights:

Pteranadon Flyers. Thirty-six inches

The Amazing Adventures of Spider-Man. Forty inches

Jurassic Park River Adventure. Forty-two inches

Dudley Do-Right's Ripsaw Falls. Forty-four inches

Popeye & Bluto's Bilge-Rat Barges. Forty-eight inches

Doctor Doom's Fearfall. Fifty-two inches

Dueling Dragons and **The Incredible Hulk.** Fifty-four inches

Note that even if a child meets one of the lower height requirements, they must be accompanied by an adult on restricted rides if they are under 48 inches in height.

At night the metal coaster track glows an eerie green, an especially dramatic sight for guests walking across the bridge to the island; the tracks loop over and then under the walkway.

WOW Doctor Doom's Fearfall

Looming above the island are a pair of two-hundred-foot towers of steel. Victor Von Doom, absolute dictator of the otherwise insignificant nation of Latvaria has much bigger goals: total world domination. The creation is Doctor Doom's infernal device to drain fear from all visitors.

We enter through the portals of the Latvarian Embassy, guarded by a squad of Doctor Doom's army in their armored finery. Doom's enemies, of course, are the Fantastic Four, although to tell you the truth these guys did absolutely nothing to prevent the bad doctor from sending me shooting up a tower into the sky.

We lucky visitors are strapped into four-passenger seats on the outside of the tower, feet dangling free below. With a sudden burst of energy, the seats zoom 150 feet up the tower; there's a brief pause of weightlessness at the top and then a powered descent back down the track to the bottom.

This ride gives many of us about as much of the feel of weightlessness as we're going to experience until we win a ride on the Space Shuttle. As we flew up the tower the press credentials on a lanyard around my neck floated off and hung in space at the top. I had just enough time to reach out and grab it.

The chairs give you two or three bounces on the way down. And then when your feet and the rest of you are more or less back on terra firma, you'll exit the ride into a video arcade.

Storm Force Accelatron

A dizzying spin for younger visitors, the Accelatron features the powers of the X-Men superheroine, Storm, in a battle to defeat Magneto.

As guests enter into a geodesic dome topped by a twenty-foot lightning rod they learn that Storm, majestic mistress of weather, has requested the aid of her mentor, Professor Xavier and all of the visitors who stop by. Guests board the circular Power Orb, specially designed by Professor Xavier to convert human energy into electrical forces through the power of "cyclospin." Recruits can hold onto the Power Orb's rudder, spinning the Accelatron faster and faster, generating enough power to defeat Magneto.

Translation: a high-intensity carnival thrill ride.

Toon Lagoon

A place where the funnies come to life, from the snow-capped peaks of Ripsaw Falls to Popeye's ship, the Olive to Wimpy's burger stand.

Comic Strip Lane salutes cartoon heroes old and new. In addition to Cathy and Shoe and the Marvel superheroes, you'll also find cutouts of classic toon characters such as Pogo, Snuffy Smith, Little Orphan Annie, Betty Boop, Beetle Bailey, Hagar the Horrible, Krazy Kat, Betty Boop, and Dennis the Menace.

Hanging from the storefronts and trees are cartoon blurbs. A few samples: "Don't have the mushroom pizza before you ride Ripsaw Falls." My favorite, hung outside of Blondie's: "I have a feeling people can read my thoughts."

Also outside of Blondie's is a fun photo opportunity. Pose a family member or friend pulling on Marmaduke's leash; turn your camera sideways and you can expect a picture right out of the comic books.

WOW Dudley Do-Right's Ripsaw Falls

Dudley Do-Right must save Nell from evil Snidely Whiplash in this wild flume ride. It's a familiar setting for Dudley, the dim-bulb Canadian Mountie who was part of the beloved "Rocky and Bullwinkle Show."

It's our assignment to help Dudley on a wild and wet rescue attempt through a lagoon and log flume that ends with a drop through the roof of a ramshackle dynamite shack ("Danger Zone. Highly Kamboomable.") and a dive fifteen feet below the surface of the water.

You'll work your way up through queues that wind outside the building and then within. There is, of course, water, water, everywhere. The plunging logs splash onto the queue below, and water cannons fire spurts here and there.

When you finally enter the building you'll learn the story of Ripsaw Falls, told with tongue decidedly planted in cheek. Movie posters advertise such slightly-skewed hits as *Saw Wars, Paws,* and *Three Men and a Grizzly.*

You'll meet the Beaver and the Bear, performing a standup comedy routine (actually a hang-up comedy routine from their mounted position on the wall.) Listen carefully to the very bad jokes, including a few gentle jabs at the Mouse across town. I guess it is a small world after all.

My favorite sign at the loading platform: "Please remove hats and antlers."

There are three rows of seats in the log-like car. You can load as many as six per log if you're very friendly with another person in your party, one behind the other in the same seat.

The first lift takes you out on a floating pathway with a great view of Toon Lagoon and other parts of the Islands of Adventure. When we emerge from a mine section, we find our heroine Nell, fit to be tied.

Then Dudley loses his train of thought; we all regain it quickly when we seem to meet an oncoming locomotive. Get it?

After several false drops we come to the big one. In case you miss the point, a sign warns: "Scenic overlook ahead!"

The plunge down the falls is dramatic . . . and wet. The front row of the log gets soaked, the middle gets wet, and the third seat gets seriously damp. But a good time is had by all.

"And so," we are told, "our hero proves a Mountie always gets his man, but not always his girl."

WOW Popeye & Bluto's Bilge-Rat Barges

The villainous Bluto is the proprietor of this establishment, and so you can count on things going awry.

Popeye tells us that "Bluto has taken me girlfrien' Olive down the White Waters of Sweet Haven. I need shipmates to join me rescue. Don't ferget to bring yer spinach."

You might want to bring a rain parka, too.

We start out on a path for Popeye's pleasant boat ride, but we come to a detour in the waiting line erected by Bluto. Suddenly we are in the line for Bluto's boat, which seems like a much less friendly cruise line.

The long and complex queue eventually wends its way into Bluto's office. Among the awards and plaques for evil-doing is a framed greenback, labeled "First Dollar Stolen."

The twelve-passenger circular rafts move along at a zippy sixteen feet per second. There are lots of spins and tight turns but only a short drop. That doesn't mean you won't get wet, though. If the splashes from the rapids and the unexpected geysers don't get you, one of the kids up on the deck of Me Ship, *The Olive* just may have you in the sights of his water cannon.

This is, after all, just another raft ride, not all that different from another

Popeye & Bluto's Bilge-Rat Barges

Orlando attraction, Kali River Rapids at Disney's Animal Kingdom. Where the Bilge-Rat Barges shines, though, is in the theming. There are funny little surprises at every turn, including Bluto's Boatwash, and various other opportunities for some extra wet surprises.

You will get wet, especially in the seat of your pants. You're in most danger when your side of the raft is moving backwards into a wave. There is a covered storage area in the center of the raft, but you'd do better using a locker for valuables or leave them with someone on shore.

Me Ship *The Olive*

A fun spot for kids with some great slides and hidey-holes. There are also water squirters to aim at the Bilge Rat Barges passing by below. There are bells to ring and telescopes, and all sorts of toys.

Actually, this place is worth a visit by kids of all ages just for the view of the lagoon and the rest of the park from the upper level.

Jurassic Park

The dinosaurs are back, and here's your chance to meet them face to face. The robotic creatures (you didn't really expect scaly flesh and blood, did you?) take over the Jurassic Park River Adventure. Elsewhere you will meet dinos up close and personal at the Triceratops Encounter, check in on the DNA recombination process at the Jurassic Park Discovery Center, and hitch a ride on the back of a Pteranodon for a prehistoric bird's-eye view of the park.

The entry to this part of Islands of Adventure wends its way through tropical jungle that is enclosed by electric fences and alarms. Beyond the mists of the ancient forests, you can hear distant roars. (Be sure to make a return visit to this area if you're in the park at night.)

WOW Jurassic Park River Adventure

Hop aboard a small boat for a pleasant little journey back in time, the ever-flowing river. We are, of course, in the ultimate theme park, the world of the dinosaur brought back to life by scientists who have extracted dino DNA from an ancient insect trapped in amber.

The boats carry twenty-five persons, in five rows of five seats, into a beautifully landscaped, ferny re-creation of earth as it existed millions of years ago.

"The river flows through a newborn world, where giants walked the earth," says our guide. "Welcome to . . . Jurassic Park."

First stop on our voyage is Ultrasaur Lagoon, home of a species of gentle vegetarian giants who pose no threats to us. From there we float into Stegosaur Springs, where the natives seem just a bit more threatening, but we're harmless tourists, right?

And then there is Hadrosaur Cove, and here these guys are suddenly not very hospitable at all. In fact, one of them roars up out of the water so close to our boat that it diverts us into the wrong channel: we're pushed through the Jurassic Park Animal Control Gate Number 13 into the Raptor Containment Area. And that's not good at all.

Alarms and flashing lights are everywhere. We see the destroyed remains of a crashed tour boat just like ours. (Shades of the crashed tour boat at Jaws in Universal Studios Florida.)

Close by, a pair of small spitters fight over the remnants of a Jurassic Park uniform.

As we pass further along we come beneath a crane holding a crate marked "Raptor Transport Unit." Something inside is moving around and making nasty noises. Will it drop on our heads?

And then we are into the warehouse building. We are pushed way back against our seats as the boat makes a very steep climb in near darkness. At the top we seem to pause for just a moment . . . and then we plunge back to the surface of the lake, in an eighty-four-foot plunge down one of the longest, fastest, and steepest water descents anywhere.

This is, of course, at heart a water ride and you will get wet—the first row gets soaked, with a bit less water as you move toward the back of the boat. You can use one of the lockers outside the waiting queue for valuables; when the park opened they were free for one hour, with a charge of $1 for each additional thirty minutes. (When the park is very busy, the waiting time may well extend more than an hour, putting you into the red.)

The long queue splits left and right to a pair of loading stations. As long as you've got to be waiting in line, you might as well learn something about the various species of dinosaurs in the park; there's an informative video on overhead screens.

By the way, gardeners will be thrilled by the plantings around the ride and along the river pathway.

The ride is a near-duplicate of the original Jurassic Park attraction at Universal Studios Hollywood.

The Jurassic Park Discovery Center glows by night

Jurassic Park Discovery Center

An interactive educational experience where visitors can observe as a raptor is hatched from an egg, examine dinosaur skeletons, and learn how biochemists at Jurassic Park brought these prehistoric creatures back to life.

One of the stations demonstrates DNA sequencing in a process that is supposed to mix a bit of your personal characteristics with those of a compatible dinosaur. You begin by choosing between ancient creatures that were herbivores or carnivores, armored or camouflaged, large or small, and members of herding groups or solo folk. Then you lean into a "brain scanner" that takes a video image of your face, and give a simulated snippet of your DNA to a sampler that scans your hand.

The final step is an instruction to the computer to genetically recombine with your receptor dinosaur. The result: a new dinosaur with a bit of your face and personal characteristics. For some reason the dino I created was not carrying a reporter's notebook.

At another station a lab technician assists you in using a "pre-emergent nursery scanner" to examine the life growing within huge eggs. There's also a neutrino scanner that examines fossils in a wall of rock.

At Beasaurs, you can use a periscope-like device to get some idea of how the world looked through the eyes of a dinosaur—an unusual effect when you consider that for many of the beasts, their eyes were on opposite sides of their head.

The Discovery Center is an ambitious attempt at edutainment, but falls a bit flat; I expect Universal will step up the investment here in years to come.

WOW Pteranadon Flyers

Here's a chance to get a prehistoric bird's-eye view of the island, soaring in a chair beneath the ten-foot wings of one of these flying dinosaurs. This very simple ride is a charming diversion, and it immediately proved much too popular for its own good.

Universal planners thought of the ride as a diversion for the kids, and it surely is attractive to youngsters. But its simple charm and the view of the park it offers made it appealing to adults as well. The result: there can be lengthy lines for the very short ride. There are only three of the two-seater birds on the track at any one time. Lines can stretch to an hour or more, and, alas, the ride is way too short to justify that. The rule: adults need to be accompanied by a child.

The two-seat metal birds are pulled by a chain lift about forty feet into the air and then descend under the quiet power of gravity along a winding track that circles above Camp Jurassic. The chairs move along at a brisk but unthreatening speed, swinging out from side to side a bit as they move around turns.

Some youngsters may be uncomfortable riding alone, but they must be willing and able to occupy their own seat. There is both a lap bar and a seat belt to hold riders in place, and there are no loops and dives on the track.

Triceratops Encounter

A dino-petting zoo: for the first time ever, humans can pet a "living" dinosaur. At the feed and control stations, trainers teach guests about the biology of the twenty-four-foot-long, ten-foot-tall Triceratops.

Here's your chance to get up close and personal with a real, live triceratops. You'll meet Chris, making a visit to the veterinarian for a case of the sniffles. Well, OK, she's not real, but she moves around, interacts with her concerned doc, and sniffles and sneezes. (You have been warned.)

Guests are escorted through in groups of about thirty, stepping onto a scale near the entrance for a group weigh-in. Our small contingent totaled about 6,315 pounds, or about the weight of a small triceratops we were told.

The walk-through to the encounter begins at the Jurassic Park Game Warden Station. There you'll be able to look at—and touch—all sorts of buttons and switches on the control system for the park. Yes, you really can play with the switch that turns on or off the electric-fence systems and the surveillance cameras and all of the other safety systems that are there to protect us from the beasts outside the compound. I'm sorry to have to tell you this, though: the switches aren't really connected to anything. And, the dinosaurs aren't real. You knew that already, right?

The next stop is a lab area (including lockers of Dilphosaurus Acid Protection Suits). You'll find huge bales of "Dino Chow" as well as samples of stomach contents and dino dung. And then we're in the examining room with Chris. Attendants there will check her temperature, listen to her vital signs, and collect a sinus sample and a urine sample, which is something you don't see every day. There are a few other bathroom jokes here, as well, which you can experience for yourself without my help.

Chris, powered with high-tech hydraulics and robotics, moves and responds to trainers and visitors. And a lucky visitor will get to pet the gentle giant.

Camp Jurassic

A children's play area sitting in the shadow of Jurassic Park River Adventure, the camp includes a fantastic collection of climbing nets and slides. Some of the areas are nicely shaded.

The nets look a lot flimsier than they are. There are steel cables hidden within the webbing of many of the supports.

Best of all for parents: there is only one exit from Camp Jurassic, so you can let the kids run free and park yourself at the gate to catch them if they start to wander off toward the dinosaurs and other lures.

At the base of the climbing area is the Amber Mine itself, stocked with glowing gems (some including insects trapped in the amber, which according to the story of Jurassic Park, was the source of the dinosaur DNA for the resurrection of the beasts).

Outside the mine be sure to step on the large dino footprints on the walkway. (If you don't step on them on purpose, you're almost certain to do so by accident.) Each print triggers a mighty or mini-roar from the maker of the mark, along with an accompanying rumble in the ground below your feet.

The Lost Continent

A crumbling statue of Poseidon, the Greek god of the sea, presides over a land long ago lost in the mists of time. Exotic traders peer from behind mountains of rich fabrics and precious metals, inviting guests to join them in the search for even greater treasures.

WOW Dueling Dragons

"A stroll through this forest can be a dangerous proposition," says Merlin. "Living within it are two fierce dragons. One breathes fire; the other breathes ice. In order to escape, you must prove your bravery by mounting the back of one of the creatures and riding it to freedom."

That's the good news; the bad news is that we're talking about a roller coaster here—one of the most terrifying yet conceived.

Dueling Dragons features two intertwined tracks that whiz guests over, under, and around each other through the trees of a medieval forest and then out over Dragon Lake.

From the top of the 125-foot common lift, the Fire Dragon drops to the left and the Ice Dragon heads off to the right, with each track following its own layout. But they don't stay apart forever—three times the coasters zoom straight at each other, turning away or diving above or below each other at the last moment. At times the two tracks and their passengers—their feet dangling below (or above) them, are separated by a mere twelve inches.

The seats in the dragons are four-abreast with eight rows, for a total of thirty-two volunteers; the cars are suspended from the overhead track except when they are upside down and the track is under your head. The tracks invert five

Dueling Dragons

times during the ride of about two minutes and twenty-five seconds. As each train is loaded, a computer calculates its weight and decides which of the two coasters should leave first and at what speed, so that the near-collisions occur right on schedule.

And here's something you don't see in a press release every day: Universal says the queue for the Dueling Dragons, at 3,180 feet, is the longest and most elaborate waiting line in the world. Trust me, it just goes on and on and on.

The good news is that because there are two separate coasters, the line moves twice as fast, gobbling up about 3,264 riders per hour. The bad news is that nevertheless, this is one very long line; If you arrive at the coaster and find the line reaching to the outside of the queue, you're in for a wait that might reach two hours.

Just when you think you're heading for the loading station, the queue takes off in another direction into a whole new yard full of lines. Finally you enter into the building in a medieval churchlike setting, a place of shattered glass and crumbled stones that once was a castle so fair, where Merlin will tell you the story of the dueling dragons.

Slow down a bit to read the inscription in the open book in the next room. It's Merlin's entreaty to the gods to release us all from the thrall of the dragons. "Serpent of fire, obey my command. Abandon your hold upon this land." And, "Dragon ice, abominable scourge, from this blighted land diverge."

The next waiting area (yes, there's still more) is a creepy cavern, marked with the scrawls of ancient graffiti artists. "Don't be a bonehead," it says, just above a collection of skulls. And then there is "Enter in peace, exit in pieces."

And then finally, it is time to "Choose thy fate." The waiting line diverges into the final queues. Head left to Fire, right to Ice.

The two loading stations are next to each other. There is one final queue for those visitors who insist on sitting in the front of the car. The cars leave the station about the same time, climbing the hill in tandem and taking off on their near-collision course together.

The Fire track is a few seconds faster to the finish. Coaster experts say that the Ice side offers better twists and turns; sit toward the front for the best views of the next close encounter. Fire is a bit faster and wilder; ride at the back for the best whips.

Trust me: anything that is not locked up will fall out. Use the lockers outside the queue to store your possessions.

WOW *Poseidon's Fury: Escape from the Lost City*

The "Keeper" seems to be extremely pleased with the unexpected arrival of guests to his cavern. After all, it's been hundreds—perhaps thousands—of years since his city disappeared into the sea.

This walk-through show puts visitors in the middle of a battle between the watery powers of Poseidon and the fiery authority of his archenemy Zeus.

You'll enter through the moldy, crumbling ruins of an ancient city. Once you're inside, the hallway is very dark, damp, and cool, barely lit by flickering lamps. When your eyes finally adjust to the light, check out the interesting details on the walls and ceilings, including the shell sconces on the walls.

About 150 to 200 persons at a time are allowed into the first theater; you'll stand around the walls surrounding a circular platform in the center. A trap door drops from the ceiling, and we meet the "Keeper of Tales," who will be our guide. "Call me Keeper," he says.

What we've got here, unsurprisingly, is a battle between the good and beneficent god Zeus and the evil Poseidon and his followers in the breakaway province of Atlantis. The battle went on for a thousand years or so, until Zeus triumphed and Atlantis and Poseidon were banished beneath the seas.

And so we move on to the next room, a creepy stone temple ruled by The Oracle, the Gatekeeper to Atlantis. But where has she gone? "Never trust a voice without a head," the Keeper advises. Ah, but there she is, speaking from a perch above a giant door; it is, we learn, the portal to Atlantis.

The Oracle introduces us to a set of secret symbols we need to unlock the portal. And darned if the portal doesn't start moving around like a giant puzzle. It's like a giant bank vault door; when the pieces finally align, a vortex to Atlantis is revealed. As befits a visit beneath the sea, this is one wet and wild vortex. A tube of water flows up and around us as we move into the world of Atlantis. This is definitely a frizz-the-hair, fog the glasses kind of place, but you won't get wet.

And then we are welcomed to the spectacular Temple of Poseidon, with a view through windows into the undersea world. "It's beautiful," says the Keeper, "but I do not judge a shark by his smile." Right he is, for soon thereafter Poseidon himself and his army of followers fill a dramatic water screen across the room. (The images are dramatic, an even better, indoor version of Disney's *Fantasmic.)*

"Welcome to your new home," Poseidon tells us, but his welcome sounds like more of a threat. Who among us can stand up to a fearsome visage such as Poseidon? Not you or me, but what has come over old man Keeper? Suddenly, the Keeper reveals his true identity; let's just say we find out that he holds a much loftier position than a mere teller of tales.

The ensuing battle between the gods fills the room with fire and water and fog . . . and with victory, a sudden return to the other side of the vortex.

WOW *The Eighth Voyage of Sindbad*

Apparently, seven voyages were not enough for this great hero of the past, and so he sets out once again on a great search for riches.

Here's the story line in three sentences: "Sindbad: We're as rich as kings," says Kebab. "Yes, but only if we can make it back alive," replies Sindbad. And, look: "the princess is imprisoned in a circle of fire!"

So, you see, the goal is to escape the clutches of evil, with the riches . . . and the princess . . . intact.

Sindbad and his friend Kebab ("Shush, Kebab," says Sindbad at one point in the story) are entreated by the captive princess to snatch away the enchanted jewel, "The Sultan's Heart." But when they do so, the lovely princess transforms into the evil sorceress Miseria who proceeds to torment Sindbad, Kebab, and the real princess. ("That's so typical," says Kebab. "Give your girlfriend a big rock and she changes on you.")

The show involves explosions, fireworks, and other pyrotechnics. And, there are also a few wet surprises. One splash zone is in the middle section of the center of the theater near the mast; another is down low on the right side.

When Miseria and her henchmen battle against Sindbad and his buddy, you'll see just them throwing axes, hammers, knives . . . and a kitchen sink.

The finale features Miseria's flaming plunge from the upper level of the set into the pond below. (Watch carefully and see if you can spot the stuntman in a flame-resistant suit substituting for Miseria at the last moment.)

There are 1,700 seats in the canopied theater, which should allow for enough space for last-minute arrivals except on the busiest of days.

While you're in the area, be sure to pause to contemplate the statue outside of the entrance to the theater. There's a hidden camera and speakers within, along with an array of water hoses. The controller talks with the guests . . . with his or her hands on the spray buttons. It's fun to watch or participate.

Flying Unicorn

At the end of a meandering path under the trees between Jurassic Park and the Lost Continent are traces of long-lost mythical creatures, fairies, and gnomes.

According to legend, an ancient wizard gathered scraps of knights' armor, wood from magic castles, and iron from witches' cauldrons to build a cart resembling the noble steed he rode as a young man. As he was constructing the vehicle he came across a miraculous find: a unicorn's horn which he placed on the head of the cart; when he did so, it came alive, soaring over the treetops.

Translation: a relatively tame roller coaster for younger visitors.

Mystics of the Seven Veils

One of the stranger offerings at a theme park, a team of rent-a-psychics operate under a tent near Sindbad's show. You can buy readers from five minutes to half an hour, for about $10 to $50. Or you can send the money to me and I'll send you the tea leaves from my last cup of Lipton's.

Seuss Landing

Ten whimsical acres where Dr. Seuss's famous characters come to life. This is the most fun part of the park, a draw for kids of all ages.

There's hardly a straight line to be found on the island, and Universal's horticulturists have even managed to find and grow some strangely misshapen trees to match the strange foliage of the books of Dr. Seuss. (Some of the palms were transplanted from southern Florida where they had been bent by the fury of Hurricane Andrew.)

Near the entrance to the land near the Port of Entry is a dedication to Theodore Geisel, better known under his pen name. "We dedicate this land to Dr. Seuss. May his genius forever be on the loose."

At the other end of the land, beneath an arch at the entrance to The Lost Continent is a Seussian quote: "Think left and think right. Think low and think high. Oh, the things you can think up, if only you try!"

The Cat in the Hat

A ride through the pages of Dr. Seuss's best-known book, and one of the best dark rides anywhere. (This ride is the most Disney-like attraction at Universal's Islands of Adventure, the highest possible compliment for a ride aimed at youngsters.)

Up to 1,800 guests per hour travel on six-passenger couches through eighteen scenes from the book. At the heart of the ride is a twenty-four-foot revolving, mind-bending tunnel. The couches twist and turn and spin on their bases.

The adventure features more than thirty robotic characters, including the Cat himself and the mischievous Thing 1 and Thing 2. Those Things tear the house apart in wonderful ways, then race to make everything right once Mom comes back home.

"Should we tell her about it?" we're asked. "Well, what would you do if mother asked you?" We're not sure.

Caro-Seuss-el

Claimed to be the most elaborate and interactive carousels ever built—who are we to argue with Dog-a-lopes and Cowfish?

Seven different Seuss characters, a total of fifty-four mounts, circle around; the creatures will respond to their riders in wonderfully weird ways.

Characters include Cowfish from *McElligot's Pool*; Elephant-birds from *Horton Hatches the Egg*; AquaMop Tops and Twin Camels from *One Fish, Two Fish, Red Fish, Blue Fish*; Dog-a-lopes and Mulligatawnies from *If I Ran the Zoo*; and Birthday Katroo from *Happy Birthday to You*.

One Fish, Two Fish, Red Fish, Blue Fish

WOW One Fish, Two Fish, Red Fish, Blue Fish

Young visitors (and lucky adults in their company) steer one of twelve two-passenger Seussian fish up and down fifteen feet in the air as they travel through water spouts and streams. Topping off the ride is an eighteen-foot-tall sculpture of the "Star Belly Fish" of the story.

You know which fish you are. If the song says that one fish should go down and red fish should head for the sky, pay attention unless you'd like a free bath from the water cannon on the next turn.

If I Ran the Zoo

An interactive playground that tells the story of Gerald McGrew and his quest to create a totally different zoo of strange and unusual animals. The three areas include Hedges, Water, and the New Zoo.

At McElligot's Pool you can drop a coin in the creature's mouth if you'd like to see what happens. Let me give you a hint: the humor here is not dry. (By the way, Universal promises to give all of the coins to charity.)

Sylvester McMonkey McBean and His Very Unusual Driving Machines *(Coming Attraction)*

Based on Dr. Seuss's *Sneeches* tale that teaches children about discrimination, this indoor-outdoor elevated attraction has been on hold since the opening of the park in 1999.

According to the original plans, guests will be able to choose between the Star Belly side or the Plain Belly side, each offering a different ride experience on a track elevated fifteen feet in the air. The vehicles travel slowly on a track above Seuss Landing and through six show scenes, including the Circus McGurkus Cafe Stoopendous where the cars pass nearby a gigantic hanging mobile of Seuss characters.

Eating Your Way Through Universal's Islands of Adventure

By theme park standards, Universal has done a great job of creating interesting food fare at Islands of Adventure, from green eggs and ham to Dagwood sandwiches, from burgers to exotic Asian noodle dishes. Fast-food meals will likely cost about $10 with a drink; the upscale Mythos and the quirky Confisco Grille offer restaurant service for about $12 to $20 for entrees alone.

Port of Entry

Confisco Grille. Run by a band of thieves (No, I wouldn't call Universal Studios such an unpleasant thing. These thieves are the wait staff within this unusual—and inventive—restaurant on the right side of the Port of Entry as you near the lagoon. The manager may warn you, though, that if you find something missing from your table to let him know; he'll see about getting it back for you.)

The unusual lobby features some odd mechanisms and stairways to nowhere. Inside there's Kraft paper on the tabletops and the smell of a wood fire in the air.

On recent visits, specialties priced from about $10 to $20 included Thai chicken salad, a portabella mushroom burger, Shrimp Alla Confisco, and a grilled sirloin steak. Side orders include Confisco fries for about $4, served in a cone with dipping sauces such as Buffalo-style (hot sauce and blue cheese) and Southern-style (peach chipotle barbecue sauce.)

Key

= Fast food

= Pub

= Full-service restaurant

Croissant Moon Bakery. A pleasant bakery with only a handful of inside tables. Specialties include soups and salads for about $3 each, and unusual sandwiches priced at about $7 include peppered roast beef and smoked Gouda cheese, and smoked turkey and brie. And there is a sumptuous spread of cakes, cheesecakes, and cookies, priced about $2 to $3.

Marvel Super Hero Island

Cafe 4. A salute to the Fantastic Four (scientist Reed Richards, his wife Sue, her kid brother John Storm, and Ben Grimm), near the entrance to Spider-Man.

Offerings include pizza by the slice (about $3.50) or the pie (up to $17.45) with choices including cheese, pepperoni, and barbecued chicken with boursin cheese. Other choices, priced from about $5 to $8, include an Italian hoagie, sausage sub, minestrone soup, and Caesar salad.

Captain America Diner. Good old American fare, including chicken sandwiches, burgers, and Freedom Fighter French Fries, with diner-style entrees from about $5 to $7.

Toon Lagoon

Blondie's: Home of the Dagwood. We're talking real sandwiches here, huge stacks of stuff between slices of bread. Of course, the featured sandwich includes the Dagwood (ham, salami, turkey, bologna, Swiss and American cheeses). The Dagwood and other handfuls are priced at about $7. You'll also find vegetable soup and salads.

Comic Strip Cafe. Offering just what you'd expect comic book heroes to order. You'll find counters serving fish and chips, Chinese, Mexican, and pizza and pasta offerings.

Wimpy's. You already know what kind of food this guy likes. Just head for the counter marked "bovine perfection." Wimpy promises, by the way, that he "personally supervises the culinary construction of each hamburger."

Alas, the burgers cost more than a nickel, and you'll have to pay for them today, or on Tuesday (if your visit is on a Tuesday). A basic burger with fries is about $5. If you insist, you can also order a chicken sandwich or chili dog for about $7. And attention Popeye, there's even a spinach salad for $3.

Cathy's Ice Cream. The weight-conscious comic-strip heroine's favorite food is offered to all.

Jurassic Park

Thunder Falls Terrace. A glass wall lets diners watch hapless guests plunge down the final drop at the Jurassic Park River Adventure.

The interior is Jurassic Park primitive, with huge wooden beams. It's an attractive setting with good food, albeit a bit on the pricey side for a cafeteria.

Some of the more unusual theme park appetizers (Stegosaurus Starters, actually) include peel and eat shrimp for about $7, and roasted corn and conch chowder for $3. Entrees, priced from about $7 to $12, include rotisserie chicken salad, barbecued chicken wings, and char-grilled baby back ribs.

Pizza Predattoria. Small personal pies, including pepperoni and barbecued chicken with pineapple, are priced about $7. Other entrees include meatball sandwiches, and a Caesar salad in a pizza crust. There's also a combination platter of pizza, salad, and soda for about $9.95.

The Burger Digs. A basic fast-food joint, offering burgers, cheeseburgers, and grilled chicken for about $6 to $9.

The Watering Hole. You've got to like a bar in Jurassic Park that advertises itself as the "home of the original lounge lizard."

The walk-up outdoor stand offers coffee and a full range of drinks, including rum runners, pina coladas, and margaritas, priced at about $3 plain, or $5 with a shot of alcohol. There's also a nice selection of imported and microbrews.

The Lost Continent

Mythos Restaurant. The showpiece of the Islands of Adventure, Mythos lies on the shore of the Inland Sea within a volcanic rock formation.

Stop and take a look at the intricate details on the Mythos building, with carvings and hidden figures, in some ways a rocky version of the striking Tree of Life at Disney's Animal Kingdom. The interior is like a limestone cavern.

Appetizers, priced from about $5 to $10, include tempura shrimp with wasabi and soy, grilled asparagus with citrus butter. Salads include poached artichoke.

Entrees from about $10 to $20 include linguini with Thai spices, including mint and cilantro, grilled yellowfin tuna Nicoise with kalamata vinaigrette, and grilled chicken sandwich with Vidalia onions, fontina cheese and green olive mayonnaise.

Enchanted Oak Restaurant (and Alchemy Bar). Designed to commemorate the oak tree trunk into which legend says Merlin was frozen by the Lady of the Lake. The eatery on The Lost Continent features oak-fired barbecue dishes and Dragon Scale Ale. The great sorcerer himself may make guest appearances if you're lucky. Entrees from about $7 to $15 include chicken and ribs, barbecued spare ribs, and hickory smoked chicken.

Seuss Landing

Green Eggs and Ham Cafe. What else do you expect on the menu than this famed dish from Dr. Seuss? There's more, of course, but don't you want to try something green?

Green Eggs and Ham Cafe

In case you were wondering, the eggs are colored with parsley puree. Entrees at the outdoor are priced about $6, including green eggs and hamwich, hamburgers, and cheeseburgers.

Circus McGurkus Cafe Stoopendous. A fun place to eat with animated mobiles of Seuss circus creatures overhead.

Above the seats is a section of track from the delayed Sylvester McMonkey McBean and His Very Unusual Driving Machines ride; test vehicles pass by from time to time.

Booths are named after Seuss characters, including "Rolf from the Ocean of Olf" and "The Drum-Tummied Snumm."

Entrees include basic kid stuff like deep-fried chicken, lasagna, pepperoni pizza, meatballs and spaghetti, and the like. Entrees are about $7. There's also the old standby of alphabet soup for a relative bargain of about $3.

Moose Juice Goose Juice. A drink stand offering moose juice (also known as Turbo Tangerine) or goose juice (sour green apple). Both are available fresh or frozen for $2 to $3. If you can't decide between them, order a mix of both.

A Musical Escape

Among the delights of the park is a suite of original music composed and performed as a background theme. A different soundtrack is heard in each of the five islands, as well as in the Port of Entry. Musicians from around the world came together in the resonant chambers of a desanctified monastery and professional studios in Seattle to make a recording that was one of the most ambitious musical events ever.

Port of Entry features music performed by a Javanese gamalan, a traditional orchestra, which traces its roots back to 230 A.D.; it consists mainly of percussive instruments, including gongs, drums, bells, and wooden-keyed xylophones, as well as violins, flutes, and zithers. The music changes as the visitor walks through an exotic bazaar, culminating in a grand, lush signature theme as guests pass under a grand arch and, like explorers discovering a new world, view the one-hundred-acre vista of the Islands of Adventure for the first time.

A Celtic band recorded additional music for the Port of Entry and for The Lost Continent. The band included some of the most ancient instruments in Western culture including the bagpipe, double oboe, flute, and harp. Also featured in the recording are a pennywhistle, a handheld Celtic drum known as a "bohdran," a concertina, and an Irish alto flute.

Also contributing to music for The Lost Continent was a Greco-Etruscan band, featuring instruments from the Middle East, India, and Greece. Among instruments were a Greek lyre named a "kithara," a wind instrument played with a double reed known as a "shawm," a stringed instrument from Western Asia named a "cembalo" with strings struck by a pair of small hammers, a stringed instrument from India named a "vina," a sitar and its larger cousin the "surbahar," a long-necked Indian lute known as a "tambura," a pakawaj talking drum, and a bowed stringed instrument carved from a single block of wood called a "sarangi."

At Seuss Landing, musicians bring the fantastic sounds of cartoons to life. The result was a score that involved some newly created but wacky instruments, including a harp that used rubber bands instead of strings. For Toon Lagoon, where two-dimensional cartoons populate the landscape, they worked with familiar melodies such as "The Sailor's Hornpipe" (better known to us as Popeye's theme), and music from the beloved cartoons of Jay Ward, creator of Rocky and Bullwinkle.

UNIVERSAL STUDIOS ISLANDS OF ADVENTURE

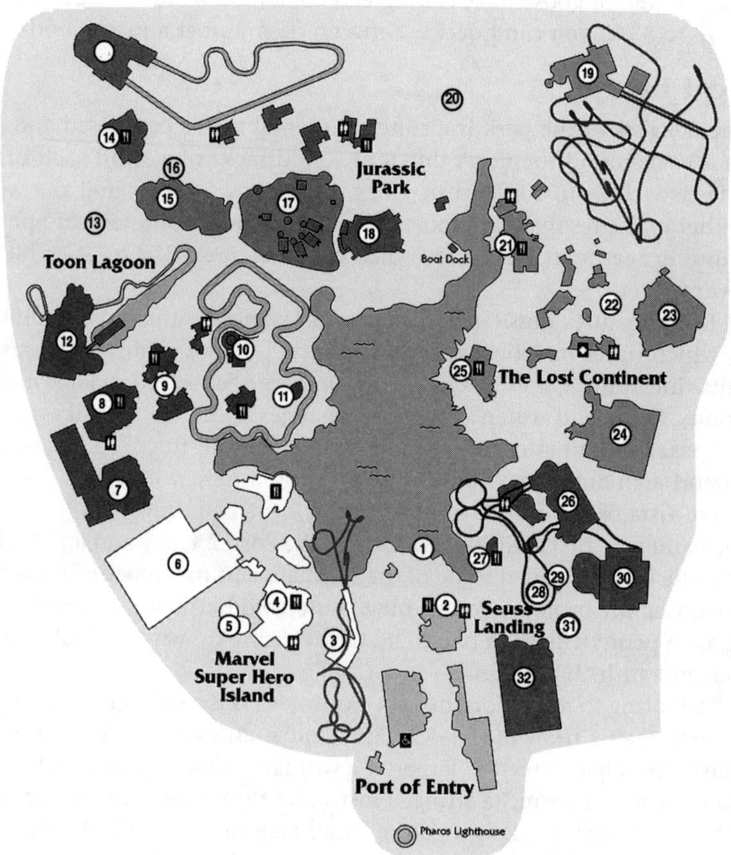

1. Island Skipper Tours
2. Confisco Grille
3. Incredible Hulk Coaster
4. Cafe 4
5. Doctor Doom's Fearfall
6. The Amazing Adventures of Spider-Man
7. Special Events
8. Comic Strip Cafe
9. Comic Strip Lane
10. Popeye & Bluto's Bilge-Rat Barges
11. Me Ship *The Olive*
12. Dudley Do-Right's Ripsaw Falls
13. Storm Force Accelatron
14. Jurassic Park River Adventure
15. Thunder Falls Terrace/Camp Jurassic
16. Pteranadon Flyers
17. Triceratops Encounter
18. Jurassic Park Discovery Center
19. Dueling Dragons
20. Flying Unicorn
21. Enchanted Oak Restaurant (and Alchemy Bar)
22. Mystics of the Seven Veils
23. *The Eighth Voyage of Sindbad*
24. *Poseidon's Fury: Escape from the Lost City*
25. Mythos Restaurant
26. Future attraction: Sylvester McMonkey McBean and His Very Unusual Driving Machines
27. Green Eggs and Ham Cafe
28. Caro-Seuss-el
29. Moose Juice Goose Juice
30. Circus McGurkus Cafe Stoopendous
31. One Fish, Two Fish, Red Fish, Blue Fish
32. The Cat in the Hat

Chapter 18
Universal CityWalk Orlando

In Orlando, even adults deserve a place all their own. (Kids can come along, too, most of the time.)

Universal CityWalk, a thirty-acre day-and-night entertainment center, serves as the front door to Universal Studios Florida and Universal Studios Islands of Adventure. Visitors are deposited there when they exit one of the two gigantic parking garages.

The two-tiered promenade wraps around a four-acre lagoon.

Admission to CityWalk is free, and visitors can come and go between Universal Studios Florida and Universal's Islands of Adventure; your options for lunch or dinner are greatly improved by the addition. Some of the venues have a cover charge of about $3 to $5 in the evening when there is entertainment, and may have a higher entrance fee for some special events.

You will, though, have to park you car in Universal's lot and pay a $7 fee for the privilege, something that is not popular with some visitors.

In 2001 Universal offered two nighttime deals: a CityWalk Party Pass for $8.43 for all clubs, except for special events, or $12.67 for club access plus a ticket to a movie at the Universal Cineplex. Both prices include tax.

On the moving sidewalk from the parking structure into CityWalk, to your right is the Hard Rock Hotel. A bit farther in the distance to your right is the elegant Portofino Hotel.

At the end of the walkway you will find yourself in CityWalk. Head right to Universal Studios Florida and left to Universal's Islands of Adventure.

The first CityWalk was opened at Universal Studios Hollywood, and was an immediate success. At Walt Disney World, Pleasure Island and Downtown Disney West Side were clearly influenced by that success in California.

For many visitors the best thing about CityWalk is its proximity to the two theme parks at Universal Orlando. For the first time in Orlando, it is possible to exit a theme park and walk to a sophisticated dining and adult entertainment district for lunch or dinner and then return to the park.

A CityWalk Walkabout

Bob Marley—A Tribute to Freedom. At Bob Marley's the room is hot, the music is hot, the dancing is hot, and some of the food is hot: the jerk chicken with black bean sauce will clear out your sinuses nicely.

The restaurant is a one-of-a-kind celebration of music and culture based around the music and philosophy of Jamaican reggae legend and cultural icon Bob Marley. The restaurant and club is patterned after Marley's actual home and garden in Kingston, Jamaica; in a touch of realism it is not air conditioned. It includes an inner courtyard that is open to the sky and there's a stage for performances. The menu features light Jamaican fare, including meat patties, roti, Red Stripe beer, and grapefruit-flavored Ting soda.

Open for dinner weekdays from 5 P.M. to 1:30 A.M., and lunch and dinner on Saturdays and Sundays from 11 A.M. to 1:30 A.M. Cover charge $4.25 after 7 P.M.

CityJazz. CityJazz is very elegant, a wood-trimmed cathedral to jazz that is endowed with impeccable acoustics. The Down Beat Jazz Hall of Fame honors the musicians hallowed in the pages of *Down Beat Magazine* since 1952. And the stars of today are featured at a live performance stage.

Nearby is an outdoor stage facing Central Plaza for small performances. A much larger stage offers seats facing the water; it is used for major concerts.

Open for downing from 8:30 P.M. to 1 A.M. The Down Beat Jazz Hall of Fame Museum is open from 3 to 6 P.M. Cover charge $5.25 after 8:30 P.M., with higher charges for special performances.

Emeril's Orlando. Bam! From the bayous of Louisiana, a sophisticated and "kicky" culinary hotspot that features chef Emeril Lagasse's Creole-based cuisine. The focal point is a bustling open kitchen where diners can watch their meals prepared. A squad of waiters descends on tables to deliver meals to every diner at the same moment—they call it "gang service."

Located in a separate building near the waterfront, this is a very upscale eatery—not a cheap date. A meal for two with wine can easily hit $200. And speaking of wine, the house collection holds something like twelve thousand bottles. Lagasse himself makes occasional appearances.

When the restaurant opened, appetizers included Maine lobster cheesecake, Louisiana oyster stew, and lump crabmeat and Florida hearts of palm strudel, priced from about $8 to $12. Entrees, priced from about $18 to $32, included Portobello mushroom confit, Andouille-crusted Texas redfish, grilled veal chop, and pan-seared filet of beef with parsley crust. Wood-fired pizzas included wild and exotic mushroom truffle pizza, sweet barbecue salmon pizza, and Southwestern-style seafood pizza with cilantro black bean sauce.

There's also a six-course "degustation" or sampler, served to the entire table.

Open for lunch from 11:30 A.M. to 2 P.M. and dinner daily from 5:30 P.M. to 10 P.M., and until 11 P.M. on Friday and Saturday.

The Groove. The Groove is a high-tech, high-end dance club, with all of the requisite toys: fog machines, strobes, spotlights, and video screens. Oh, and the music was so loud that I could barely take notes. The walls are decorated with all things dance, from funk to disco to the Folies Bergere and even a bit of exotic dancing. One of the prized posters advertises an appearance by Josephine Baker at the Folies Bergere in Paris.

The Blue Room is like a set from the "Jetsons," serving martini drinks such as the Hippie Chick and the Mood Ring. The Green Room is a spooky place lit by electric candles, featuring scotch and aperitifs such as Nectar of the Gods. The Red Room (reminiscent of an old, old bordello, or so I am told), offers fruit drinks including the Scarlet Letter and the Red Velvet. The club includes live performances by Universal/MCA acts.

Open nightly from 9 P.M. to 2 A.M. Guests must be twenty-one or older to enter. Cover charge is $5.25.

Hard Rock Cafe Orlando. The world's largest Hard Rock Cafe includes a 650-seat restaurant. There is, of course, a gift shop. The spectacular eatery replaces the earlier version at Universal Studios Florida. (The old building near the Universal Studios Florida closed, but may be recast for another use.)

Hard Rock Cafe features classic American cuisine in a high-energy atmosphere, surrounded by rare and unique pieces of memorabilia from the past five decades of rock and roll. Signature dishes include Pig Sandwich, grilled fajitas, veggie burgers, and the Outrageous Hot Fudge Brownie.

Open from 11 A.M. to 2 A.M.

Hard Rock Live. The first live-concert venue in the chain is modestly fashioned after the Roman Forum in a modern "retro" style. Capable of seating as many as 2,500 people, Hard Rock Live hosts concerts by cutting-edge and rock-classic artists.

More than 140,000 square feet in size, complete with imposing columns, majestic archways, and a grand entrance, the hall includes the latest in sound and light technology. The arena includes opulent luxury boxes, as well as general seating.

Hard Rock Live at Universal CityWalk

The Hard Rock Live House Band, which includes members who have backed up some of rock's greatest names, performs from Monday through Thursday. Cover charge is $9.

Ticket prices for headliner acts vary by performer.

Jimmy Buffett's Margaritaville Cafe. Perched like a parrot on the edge of the CityWalk lagoon, this quirky restaurant celebrates the island music and lifestyle of cult hero musician Buffett. There are, of course, margaritas on tap . . . in fact they may flow out of a bubbling volcano. The cafe is appropriately located overlooking the water near the bridge to Islands of Adventure.

Food is "high-end" bar food, including seafood, "cheeseburgers in paradise" and other fare related to Buffet's songs. The Volcano Bar erupts with margaritas, and there are also themed areas, including the Shark Bar and the 12-Volt Bar. If you don't catch the references just ask the nearest Parrothead: they just might sing you the appropriate line from the master.

Open for lunch and dinner from 11 A.M. to 2 A.M. Cover charge $3.25 after 10 P.M.

Latin Quarter. Hot, hot, hot: a salsa beat and a delicious spread of Hispanic food from twenty-one nations from Mexico to South America. Add in a dance floor and the infectious music, and you'll see why this place is one of the liveliest places in CityWalk. A dance troupe, including some outrageous costumes, performs salsa, merengue, tango, and other hot, hot, hot routines.

The extensive menu includes appetizers priced from about $5 to $8, including *ceviche de corvina y camarones* (Corvina fish and shrimp marinated in a spicy lemon and lime juice with jalapenos, tomato, and cilantro), *nachos casi machos* (plantain chip nachos with Monterrey Jack cheese and jalapenos), and *tamal en majo de maiz con mujo* (cornmeal stuffed with seasoned pork wrapped in a corn husk and served on a black bean puree.)

Entrees, priced from about $14 to $20, include *churrasco* (grilled skirt steak with chimichurri sauce over garbanzo beans sautéed with ham and chorizo sausage), *costillas de Cornero al morno* (spiced rack of lamb), and *atun a la cana de Azucar* (sugar cane tuna loin on a bed of roasted garlic boniato).

Open from 11 A.M. to 1:30 A.M. for lunch and dinner. Cover charge $3.25 after 10 P.M.

Motown Cafe. The Motown Cafe is a temple to the icons of R&B and soul. The centerpiece is a revolving triple-threat statue of the Supremes in full spangle regalia. Around the room are other statues and pieces of memorabilia from other superstars such as the Temptations, the Four Tops, and the Jackson Five. There's also the Motown Moments, two house bands that perform hits by the Temptations and Supremes.

The menu features "slow cooked" homestyle Detroit dishes, such as Smokey's Ribs and french-fried sweet potatoes. There is, of course, a gift shop.

Open for dinner from 5 P.M. to midnight during the week, and until 2 A.M. on Friday and Saturday. Cover charge $3.25.

NASCAR Cafe. This is fast food of a different sort, with diners immersed within rows of gleaming Winston Cup Cars, a surround-sound video wall, electronic and multimedia games, and various memorabilia and artifacts from the world of NASCAR racing. The atmosphere continues on to the menu and the pit-crew wait staff.

Car parts are everywhere, of course. An entire race car hangs over the bar on the ground floor, surprisingly close to the ground floor video arcade where you'll find driving games, including a Virtual Reality Race Simulator, priced at about $5 per ride.

The menu includes basic American food, some of the items named in honor of racing heroes. Offerings are priced from about $8 to $10 for burgers (including a Daytona chili burger and a vegetarian Gardenburger) and from about $11 to $20 for entrees such as the Bill France pork chop, the DW Dude Filet (Darrell Waltrip's steak of choice), the Crew Chief Roasted Chicken, and a Chicken Pastry Pot Pie.

Appetizers, priced from about $6, include Talladega Tenders, Winston Cup Wings, Supercharged Chili, and popcorn shrimp.

Open daily from 10 A.M. to 10 P.M. No cover charge.

NBA City. A high-energy cafe, next door to the Hard Rock Cafe near the entrance to Universal Studios Islands of Adventure. This is the first in what is intended to be a new chain of theme restaurants, a partnership between the National Basketball Association and Hard Rock Cafe.

Outside is the tallest basketball player in Orlando since Shaquille O'Neal left town, a gigantic hoopster in bronze. Down below are handprints from NBA stars including Hakeem Olajuwon, Charles Barkley, and WNBA star Sheryl Swoopes. You won't be the first to place your small mitt in theirs.

The restaurant includes the CityWalk Cage, a dining area featuring contemporary American cuisine with entrees such as steak, chops, and pizza priced from about $9 to $20, the NBA City Playground with games and attractions, and the NBA City Club where guests can watch live and classic games.

Open from 11 A.M. to 2 A.M. No cover charge.

Pastamoré. A lively outdoor street cafe, with a few indoor seats. Specialties include panini, a spiced and decorated bread, priced about $10. Offerings include panini al verdura with beefsteak tomatoes, grilled eggplant, fresh basil, olive oil, and balsamic vinegar; panini capicola with Italian meats and Fontina cheese; and panini di polle é pesto, with grilled marinated chicken, Fontina cheese, and pesto mayonnaise.

You'll also find antipasto and salad selections, along with a selection of Italian and domestic beers and wines. Desserts include ultra-rich Italian gelato ice cream; flavors include cappuccino, pistachio, and chocolate with hazelnuts.

The cafe is open from 8 A.M. to midnight, and the small restaurant operates from 5 P.M. to midnight.

Pat O'Brien's. A replica of the famous watering hole in New Orleans with a Main Bar and a Dueling Pianos bar. Famed for its old-world character and flaming fountain patio, Pat O'Brien's is also the birthplace of the world-famous Hurricane drink. The restaurant's wine collection features more than four thousand bottles with many of them on display around the dining room; an extensive cigar humidor is located within the "chimney" of the eatery.

Founded in 1933 as Club Tipperary, one of the leading speakeasies of New

Orleans, Pat O'Brien's moved to its current location in 1942. The CityWalk outpost is a close replica of the original, built of weathered red brick, wrought iron, and dark wood fixtures. Overhead in the entranceway are seven muskets representing the seven countries that once occupied New Orleans.

Pat O'Brien's does a great job of transporting the feel of New Orleans to Orlando. Upstairs over the open courtyard are a few handsome smaller rooms. Among them is the Briars Suite, named in honor of Napoleon Bonaparte's favorite retreat on the Isle of Saint Helena, where Napoleon came to visit and all but refused to leave.

I sampled a fiery jambalaya, a lot different from the weak imitations you may find at your neighborhood diner.

Open for lunch and dinner from 11 A.M. to 1 A.M. Cover charge $3.25 to enter the Dueling Pianos bar, which is open from 6 P.M. to 2 A.M. and restricted to guests twenty-one and older.

Universal Cineplex. A twenty-screen, 5,200-seat Cineplex Odeon theater complex that employs state-of-the art projection and sound systems. The seating is laid out in a "stadium" design, assuring unobstructed views. One of the theaters, especially large and lavish, is used for movie premieres.

CityWalk Shops

All Star Collectibles. Autographed, labeled, licensed, or otherwise touched by someone or something associated with just about every sport.

Captain Crackers. Your basic Florida T-shirt and knickknack shop, gone wild in a jungle theme.

Cigarz at CityWalk. Cigars, of course, and fine tobacco, as well as cordials, single malt Scotch, and coffees.

Dapy. Wind-up, flashing, beeping, and clicking toys and gifts. Dapy, which originated in Paris, is related to Spencer Gifts and Universal itself.

Elegant Illusions. Lower-priced, high-quality copies of expensive jewelry.

Endangered Species. A clothing and gift shop that has an environmentally aware message.

Fossil. An upscale version of the trendy watch, sunglass, and accessory marketplace.

Glow! An eclectic, electric, and glimmering collection of clothing, accessories, and gifts.

Quiet Flight. Beachwear and ware.

Silver. Retro jewelry in a re-creation of an old cruise ship.

Tabasco Country Store. Hot sauce, hot clothing, and hot toys.

The Universal Studios Store. Did you expect a Disney store?

Part IV
SeaWorld Orlando

Chapter 19
SeaWorld Orlando, Discovery Cove by SeaWorld

Four-fifths of the earth's surface is water, and almost five million visitors a year swim upstream to visit SeaWorld Orlando, the world's most popular marine life park.

SeaWorld's appeal has always been its focus on nature and its amazing collection of marine creatures, but in recent years it has had to deal with two powerful competitors: the animal attraction of Disney's Animal Kingdom, and the human appeal of thrill rides at Universal Orlando and Walt Disney World.

In the new millennium SeaWorld has begun to expand its base with attractions that celebrate thrills as well as animals.

The king of the wild animals at the park is **Kraken**, the longest, tallest, steepest, and most stomach-churning roller coaster in Florida. Kraken flies alongside another thrill ride, **Journey to Atlantis**, an unusual mix between a coaster and a water ride.

Across the road is a new and most unusual theme park: **Discovery Cove.** Think of it as a marine attraction where the animals outnumber the human visitors and where the food and service is more like a first-class resort than a fast-food drive-through. Visitors pay handsomely for the luxury.

Located ten minutes south of downtown Orlando and fifteen minutes from Orlando International Airport at the intersection of I-4 and the Beeline Expressway, SeaWorld is open every day from 9 A.M. to 7 P.M., with additional hours during the summer and holidays. Call ☎ (800) 327-2424 or ☎ (407) 351-3600 for more information, or consult 💻 www.seaworld.com.

Discovery Cove is adjacent to SeaWorld. For information and reservations, call ☎ (877) 434-7268 or consult 💻 www.discoverycove.com.

SeaWorld Orlando

SeaWorld has a pleasantly different feel from many other attractions in Central Florida, including Walt Disney World and Universal Orlando. The emphasis is on all things natural: marine animals, birds, and lots of greenery. Most of the

MUST-SEES

WOW

Kraken
(among the extremest of coasters on land or sea)

Journey to Atlantis
(wet and slightly wild)

Wild Arctic

Key West at SeaWorld

Shamu's Happy Harbor
(adults excused)

Manatees: The Last Generation?

Shamu Adventure

Clyde and Seamore Take Pirate Island

The Intensity Water Ski Show

Terrors of the Deep

scheduled show take place in outdoor theaters that seat as many as five thousand visitors. With rare exception on the busiest of days, you won't see waiting lines; you simply walk into the theater about fifteen or twenty minutes before the event and pick a seat. If the theater is full, you'll be invited to return for a later scheduled show.

Average attendance at SeaWorld is about fifteen thousand per day, with summer and holiday peaks of almost twice that level.

SeaWorld estimates it should take about eight hours to tour the entire park. I recommend that you see the shows first and then spend the remaining time visiting areas not regulated by the clock. If you really want to see it all, plan on arriving at opening time (usually 9 A.M.) and staying through dusk.

Try to arrive for any presentation at least fifteen minutes ahead of show time. This gives you the best chance at the seat you want and allows you to view the preshow activities offered at some of the theaters. Most shows are just short of thirty minutes long. Presentations usually start right on time, but you should be able to slip in a couple of minutes late without disturbing the show.

Saturday and Sunday are generally the busiest days of the week at the park, with Monday through Thursday the quietest.

As you enter the park, stop to consider the introductory plaque near the entrance that quotes the African Environmentalist Baba Dioum: "For in the end, we will conserve only what we love, we will love only what we understand, and we will understand only what we are taught."

Power Trip #1

Thrills and Chills

If you want to make the most of a thrill-filled day at SeaWorld head for the coasters early in the day.

Here's one scenario: when the gates open, start your day with an eye-opener on the **Kraken** roller coaster. When you're back to earth, head next door to **Journey to Atlantis**, another top draw for thrill seekers; if the morning is chilly, though, you might want to wait until later in the day before enjoying Atlantis's somewhat wet thrill.

Then make a beeline to **Wild Arctic** for a simulated but still-chilly helicopter adventure.

Now, pick up the schedule of shows and work your way through the park for the rest of the day. Sometime in late afternoon, the lines at the coasters and the simulator will probably be short enough for a return visit.

End your day at the ***Shamu Rocks America*** finale at Shamu Stadium.

Power Trip #2

Seeing the Shows

Many visitors to SeaWorld come for the traditional animal shows and to stroll through the attractive grounds; they get sufficient thrills from their up-close visit with Shamu.

Begin your tour by studying the park map and show schedule you'll receive at the entrance gate. Take note that some of SeaWorld's shows and events are presented only a few times each day. Decide which of these you most want to see, and then work the schedule.

The schedule is designed to allow you to walk from show to show easily. Your best bet is to see the scheduled shows in the order they occur from your arrival time; after you've done that, spend the rest of your day viewing exhibits and visiting any rides that appeal to you, like **Kraken, Journey to Atlantis**, and **Wild Arctic**. This may sound inefficient, but the SeaWorld property isn't all that large; you can crisscross a few times if you need to.

Attractions at SeaWorld

WOW Kraken

Rising up out of the sea, or at least up out of SeaWorld, is a monster of a roller coaster, Kraken.

With the sudden explosion of roller coasters in Orlando, including the fabulous Dueling Dragons and the Hulk at Universal Studios Islands of Adventure, and the raucous Rock 'n' Roller Coaster at Disney–MGM Studios, SeaWorld waited an extra season to introduce the highest, fastest, and longest coaster in town, located alongside the Journey to Atlantis ride.

Kraken is a floorless and topless coaster. Before you get too excited, let me explain what that means; we're not talking about the dress code. Coaster seats are mounted on a pedestal a few feet above the wheels and track. There is no "car," no roof or sides, and riders' feet will dangle off the bottom of their chairs.

Think of being strapped into your favorite chair and taking off up a 149-foot-high hill and then careening off into space at speeds of up to 65 miles per hour. Oh yes, and your chair turns upside down seven times, with elements

SeaWorld Tickets
Prices, which do not include 6 percent tax, were in effect mid-2001 and are subject to change.

One-Day SeaWorld Ticket

Adult	$47.95
Child (3–9)	$38.95

4-Park Orlando FlexTicket

Adult	$159.95
Child (3–9)	$127.95

Unlimited admission to Universal Studios Florida, Universal Studios Islands of Adventure, SeaWorld Orlando, Wet 'n Wild. Valid seven days.

5-Park Orlando FlexTicket

Adult	$196.95
Child (3–9)	$157.95

Unlimited admission to Universal Studios Florida, Universal Studios Islands of Adventure, SeaWorld Orlando, Wet 'n Wild, Busch Gardens Tampa. Valid ten days.

SeaWorld Florida/Busch Gardens Tampa Bay Value Ticket (One day at each park)

Adult	$78.95
Child	$63.95

Silver Passport SeaWorld Annual Pass

Adult	$79.95
Child	$64.95

SeaWorld, Busch Gardens Tampa Annual Pass

Adult	$124.95
Child	$109.95

SeaWorld, Busch Gardens Tampa, Adventure Island Annual Pass

Adult	$154.95
Child	$139.95

Parking $6.00
Open daily from 9 A.M. to 6 P.M., with extended hours in the summer and holiday periods. For general information, call ☎ (407) 351-3600 or ☎ (800) 327-2424 or consult 💻 www.seaworld.com.

including a cobra roll, a zero gravity roll, several vertical loops, and some flat spins. The first drop is an impressive 144 feet, heading into a 101-foot diving loop. All this with a view of nothing but sky or ground.

Greek and Norse myths say Kraken was a massive underwater beast held a prisoner by Poseidon. At SeaWorld, the sea serpent has been set free . . . and boy, is he ever angry. The waiting line features some displays of baby eels—Kraken's offspring, we are told.

A good portion of the 4,177-foot-long track runs over water. The track plunges underground three times; one stretch dives below the lagoon.

Riders stay pretty dry, but onlookers are rewarded with a major splash as the coaster goes by.

The track runs fairly close to the ground for most of its path, rising and falling like the undulating back of a serpent. One very nice touch: at the top of the lift hill there's a false drop just for effect and then an extended flat stretch where you can contemplate the plunge that's ahead.

The ride takes about three minutes and thirty-nine seconds. There are usually three trains on the track (eight cars of four passengers each), accommodating about 1,500 to ride per hour.

The Swiss-designed ride is unique in Orlando, although it is similar to a ride named the Medusa at Six Flags Great Adventure in New Jersey.

WOW Journey to Atlantis

This unusual attraction is part water ride, part roller coaster, totally wild. SeaWorld's first thrill ride delivers two of the steepest, wettest, fastest drops anywhere.

Here's the concept: Journey to Atlantis

plunges riders into the middle of a fierce battle between good and evil for the lost city of Atlantis.

According to historical lore, the city of Atlantis sank beneath the waves eons ago. Now it has risen again in the Greek fishing village of Thera. The Atlantis set spans an area larger than six football fields and towers taller than a ten-story building.

You'll enter into an eight-passenger fishing boat, two per row. The front and back seats offer the best ride; you may get slightly less wet in the middle row.

The boats enter into an underwater setting with coral, an area filled with what SeaWorld calls "aqualusions." The attractive siren Allura, representing evil, and Hermes, as the force of good, play happily together for a few moments before the siren morphs into a wicked creature.

(Hermes, the golden seahorse that transforms into a glittering guide, looks like a horse but he is actually a fish. Hermes's live counterparts, yellow Indo-Pacific and lined Caribbean seahorses, reside in aquariums in the gift shop.)

Riders are pulled into Atlantis and the dark and mysterious depths of the siren's lair. (The piercing scream of the angry siren is actually made up of a combination of eight animal voices, including a lion, bear, and rattlesnake.)

Suddenly the boats nose-dive sixty feet at a sixty-degree angle, reaching a speed of up to fifty miles per hour through a tidal wave of water.

You'll fall through a dark vortex with fog and light. A second drop of just nine feet may get you wetter than the big fall. Allura calls: "Leaving so soon? I think not!" and then each fishing boats is drawn back up into the building, this time connected to the rails of a roller coaster.

The coaster drop is also about sixty feet, with sharp S-curves and other elements . . . and there's one more big splash at the base of the coaster's drop.

The last, most spectacular drop is unlike any other. Cars nose-dive at highway speeds into a series of careening, S-curves before emerging into the daylight.

The attraction adds some spectacular "aqualusion" effects to give us a view of an ancient city beneath the water. Statues seem to come to life, then magically transform into rivers of shimmering water. Entire

Journey to Atlantis
Photo courtesy SeaWorld

Realistic fantasy. The structure that houses Journey to Atlantis is modeled after a Greek palace, Knossos. Hieroglyphics on the walls of the attraction are duplicates of ones taken from murals and pictorial works in historical Etruscan books. In filming for the attraction, Santa Barbara, California, stood in for Greece.

sets appear and then disappear, metamorphosing into Olympian vistas. Advanced technology uses hologram and LCD images. Nearly twenty-four thousand fiber-optic lights illuminate the travels of Hermes, the attraction's hero who guides guests beyond the dark depths of the siren's dangers to relative safety.

The attraction is located at the back of the park near Kraken and between the Manatees display and Penguin Encounter; guests driving on International Drive can see the superstructure along the right side of the road.

The ride is usually much more crowded on hot summer days, when the idea of a cool bath and high speed is relatively attractive. Avoid Atlantis just after one of the major shows lets out.

The entire trip takes about seven-and-a-half minutes. You do not want to bring any cameras or other items not meant to get wet. There are unlocked storage cubbies for riders at the loading area; rental lockers with keys are also available before you get in line.

Note there is a forty-two-inch height minimum.

Just to add insult to injury, there is a bank of coin-operated water hoses at the bottom of the first sixty-foot water drop for use against riders.

Be sure to check out the **Jewels of the Sea Aquarium Gallery** inside the gift shop at the base of the building that supports the ride; it includes eight aquariums, including an unusual glass tank set into the floor. Beneath your feet are stingrays and various fish; over your head are bonnethead sharks.

Wild Arctic

The Wild Arctic coexists in balmy central Florida, a combination of a state-of-the-art simulator ride and an impressive re-creation of some of the wonders of the frozen north.

The adventure begins with a thrilling "flight" over the frozen north in the jet helicopter *White Thunder* to the remote Base Station Wild Arctic, surrounded by the beauty of the arctic and kicking up snow at takeoff in a race to outrun an approaching storm.

As the chopper flies out of the hangar, the arctic landscape unfolds. The journey is relaxing—at first—as the sweeping vista is filled with frozen mountains, glacier peaks, and clouds. The craft's diving and banking levels out over the sea, and passengers are treated to a spectacular view of narwhals, walruses, and other marine life.

Unsettled briefly by buffeting winds and blinding fog banks, the jet helicopter swoops toward the pack ice for a closer view of polar bears. The radio crackles a warning: the blizzard is bearing down.

Following the frigid Franklin Strait, the helicopter skims low over the arctic sea. At Larsen Sound a huge glacier fills the horizon. Gently touching down on the ancient frozen floe, visitors absorb the beauty . . . until a deep rumbling starts, and the copter starts to tumble into a deep crevasse. The copter smacks into the sea just as the rotors reach full thrust. We make a spectacular escape through the close walls of an ice cavern and eventually to the base station.

There are three helicopter simulators in the Wild Arctic building, each seating fifty-nine people. The attraction accommodates up to 1,800 guests per hour when all three simulators are in operation. Handicapped access is provided. High-definition video laser-disc projectors provide the visual stimulation, backed up by 1,200-watt, six-channel laser-disc sound systems.

Each cabin moves six ways—yaw, pitch, roll, heave, surge, and sway. Sometimes the cabin moves as much as nine feet, and in some directions it moves at speeds up to twenty-four inches per second.

Stepping from the simulator, guests enter a chilly passageway into a frozen wonderland of Base Station Wild Arctic with ice walls, where they will come close to some of the real animals that live at the North Pole.

Forget you're in Florida and buy into the story: The base station was built by modern scientists around the decrepit hull of a 150-year-old British exploration ship frozen in the ice for all these years, a unique vantage point for viewing arctic sea life, including polar bears, beluga whales, and walruses. The viewing position allows views of the animals above and below the water as they forage for food, dive, swim, and interact with Base Station workers.

High-tech equipment sits in and around the ship's remains, with measuring devices next to old anchors and video receivers perched on old shipping crates. The base station makes extensive use of computers and touch-screen monitors to allow guests to communicate with reports from field researchers, and guests can use computers to communicate with research base "scientists." You'll be able to gauge your ability to hold your breath against polar bears (two minutes), beluga whales (twenty minutes), walruses (twenty-five minutes), and the local champion, harbor seals (twenty-seven minutes).

The arctic is a place of mystery to most people, assumed to be a frozen desert. Instead, it is a vast, ever-changing ocean, teeming with life and closely linked to the rest of the planet.

Among the stars of Wild Arctic are Klondike and Snow, a pair of polar bears. Abandoned by their mother at birth, the bears were hand-raised by experts at the Denver Zoo. Weighing about 1.3 pounds at birth, by adulthood the male, Klondike, may weigh about 1,800 pounds and the female, Snow, about 900 pounds. Lack of space at the zoo demanded the bears be relocated, and in late 1995 the pair were brought to Orlando.

They live in a special enclosure that includes a chilly pool stocked with fish (the cubs had never seen live food and had to learn how to fish for themselves). The bears' hunting instincts are further satisfied with morsels hidden in nooks and crevices of the habitat.

Polar bears are among the most beautiful and dangerous of animals, and are found only in the arctic. The animals are born white; coats turn yellow in the summer sun, and turn white again after a spring molt. The hair itself is hollow to trap warm air, oil coats their fur, and a thick layer of fat provides insulation from the cold. When awake, polar bears spend much of their time stalking or feeding on seals, walruses, and sometimes even beluga whales.

Beluga whales, sometimes known as "sea canaries," are born gray and turn white as they age, making a natural camouflage from predators as they move among the icebergs and ice floes. They weigh from 1,500 to 3,300 pounds and measure from ten to fifteen feet. Like other toothed whales, belugas "echolocate," sending out sonar-like sounds to find breathing holes in the ice and to locate prey such as squid, octopi, shrimp, and a wide variety of other bottom-dwelling fish.

Walruses have one pair of flippers in front and a second in back. A thick layer of fat, or blubber, helps regulate heat loss.

Children may explore polar bear dens (without the bears), or pop their heads through openings in a simulated ice floe, just as they saw the harbor seals doing before them.

The pool contains 900,000 gallons of manufactured seawater, maintained at a cool fifty degrees in a two-story habitat above and below the surface.

WOW Key West at SeaWorld

A showcase for the island beauty and funky tropical charm of the southernmost city in the United States, with a mix of New England and Bahamian architecture, framed by stands of palm trees, hibiscus, and bougainvillea. Visitors stroll along river rock and pathways and boardwalks; restaurants feature Caribbean cuisine. Street performers and vendors and perhaps a tightrope walker brighten the landscape.

The five-acre site is on the park's east side, alongside Manatees: The Last Generation? Naturalistic animal habitats allow up-close encounters and interaction with bottlenose dolphins, sleek stingrays, and one of the world's few saltwater-adapted reptiles, the sea turtle.

The largest section at Key West is **Dolphin Cove**, home to more than two dozen inquisitive bottlenose dolphins, the species most often seen in the coastal waters of the Gulf of Mexico and off Key West.

Dolphin Cove, SeaWorld

A wave maker moves chilled seawater through the deep 600,000-gallon pool, creating tides that ebb and flow. There is also an area where guests can touch and feed the animals. And an underwater window allows glimpses of the dolphins below the surface.

> **Life of a dolphin.** Bottlenose dolphins inhabit temperate and tropical waters throughout the world, and are the most common dolphin species along the United States, from Cape Cod to the Gulf of Mexico. They live in groups known as "pods" or "herds," varying in size from two to fifteen animals; the members of the pod rank themselves and establish dominance by smacking their tails against the water, butting heads, and other actions.

At **Turtle Point**, you can come up close to threatened and endangered species of sea turtles, including the green, loggerhead, and hawksbill. The hunting of sea turtles was a major industry in Key West until federal laws protecting the animals were enacted in the 1970s.

Stingray Lagoon, a longtime local favorite at SeaWorld, features a wide variety of graceful rays, including cownose, Southern, roughtailed, Atlantic, and yellow stingrays, as well as guitar fish. Visitors are encouraged to touch and feed the two hundred or so rays.

These fascinating creatures swim close to the edge of the pool where you can easily rub their rubbery skin and feel their fins; their poison sacs have been removed, and these stingrays are used to humans. A new nursery cove exhibits newborn rays.

Nearby is **Sunset Square**, with Key West–theme shops, restaurants, and entertainment.

WOW Shamu's Happy Harbor

If you asked active, adventurous kids to come up with the design for the ultimate outdoor playground, they might come up with something just like this. Shamu's Happy Harbor is, quite simply, one of the most spectacular playgrounds we have ever seen. In the learned opinions of the kids we asked, it stands head and monkey bars over Fievel's Playground at Universal Studios; *Honey, I Shrunk the Kids* Movie Set Adventure at Disney–MGM Studios; and Tom Sawyer Island at the Magic Kingdom. We cannot imagine higher praise.

And higher is the word that comes to mind first. The central feature of the three-acre playground is a pair of gigantic nets that each extend about forty feet in the air. The netting—actually double netting to prevent accidents—winds back and forth and makes turns like flights of stairs. Way up at the top is a tire swing, safely allowing youngsters to fly out as if into space.

The base of the net lets out into a long slide. Down below is **Pete's Water Maze**, a pirate ship with water cannon, a large sand play area, and other activities. On very hot days you might want to dress your children in bathing suits and let them cool off on the small wet slides there.

Parents can park at the bottom of the net and keep an eye on their kids as they climb; a snack bar serves the area. Most of the area is under a roof, blocking the sun and some rain.

If all of this is too rambunctious for your young ones, they can explore **Boogie Bump Bay**, a special area for small ones that includes bubble bikes, a mini-ball crawl, an air bounce, a fence maze, and many other activities appropriate to their size.

WOW Manatees: The Last Generation?

SeaWorld is doing its part to answer the question it poses with a "no."

This fascinating attraction winds through a river-like setting, filled with the gentle manatee giants, as well as turtles, fish (including tarpon, gar, and snook), and birds. A seamless, 126-foot-long acrylic panel permits underwater views. Nearby is a nursing pool built for manatee mothers and their babies.

The area includes the **Manatee Theater**, which presents a special film using Bi-Vision technology with stunning underwater footage to make it seem as if you are completely surrounded by manatees.

The manatee is an air-breathing marine mammal; when it submerges, special muscles pinch the nostrils tightly closed to keep the water out. If you look carefully you will also see sparse hair on the manatee's skin. Manatee calves nurse from their mothers.

In the wild an adult manatee dines exclusively on plants; each day a full-grown specimen may eat as much as one hundred pounds of sea grass, water hyacinths, and other types of plants. At the park, the favorite food for the manatees is romaine lettuce, one of SeaWorld's bigger expenses. If you're in the viewing area at one of several feeding times, watch as the manatees use their flippers almost as hands to grab the lettuce.

All of the manatees on display have been rescued from their only natural enemy—man. Most have been injured by propellers on boats, fishing nets, or plastic items thrown in the water by boaters. Adult manatees are released back into the wild once they are able to survive there. Orphans will probably spend the rest of their lives in the park.

Also on exhibit are some of the vehicles and equipment used by **SeaWorld's Beached Animal Rescue Station**. Since 1973 the park's marine animal experts have rescued more than a hundred manatees found seriously injured, ill, or orphaned in the wild. The crews are also called upon to help at dolphin and pygmy sperm whale strandings.

One of the slogans in the manatee area is "Extinction is forever. Endangered means we still have time."

The fish that you see in the manatee ponds that look at first glance like an alligator are something known as alligator gar (lepisosteus spatula). From the side, they look ordinary but from the top and bottom they certainly could fool all but the bravest.

Pacific Point Preserve

This re-created coastal setting for California sea lions and harbor and fur seals is a great way to get up-close and personal with some of SeaWorld's most amusing aquatic creatures.

Able to swim at birth, a harbor seal pup stays close to its mother for short nursing periods. The female's fat-rich milk helps the pup to more than double its weight by the time it is four to eight weeks old. Then the pup is weaned, goes its own way, and fends for itself.

You'll be able to purchase a package of smelt to feed the seals. Washing stations are nearby to help remove the smell of smelt from your hands.

Seals and sea lions are not morning creatures; they are most active in the midday sun.

Anheuser-Busch Hospitality Center

SeaWorld is owned by Anheuser-Busch, which also owns Florida attractions Busch Gardens Tampa Bay and Adventure Island and other parks around the United States. The Hospitality House offers a bit of the corporate message along with free samples of the company's beers.

Set amid tropical lagoons and lush foliage, the center displays antique brewery equipment, including a turn-of-the-century Studebaker wagon used for hauling more than six tons of Budweiser beer behind a team of Clydesdale horses. New in 2001 was the **Clydesdale Hitch Barn**, an area where guests can watch stable hands suit up the majestic horses in their harnesses and formal attire before their twice-daily parades through the park.

Adults can sample Anheuser-Busch products, including Michelob and Budweiser beers. A separate counter offers soft drinks and snacks at the going SeaWorld prices.

An outside terrace offers a quiet, shady spot for sampling and resting and also provides a good view of the associated gardens and waterfalls, and the Clydesdale paddocks close by.

Ten or more of the giant Clydesdale workhorses are on display at any given time, either in the outside paddock or in indoor stalls near the Hospitality Center. These huge horses, the symbol of Anheuser-Busch, are sometimes dressed in elaborate harnesses and hitched to their famous wagon to march in procession through the park.

The driver of an eight-horse hitch pulling a beer wagon like the ones at SeaWorld must wrestle more than forty pounds of reins to control the horses. A Clydesdale horseshoe measures twenty inches end-to-end and weighs about five pounds.

Shows at SeaWorld

WOW Shamu Adventure

A lone kayaker paddles into a fog-shrouded Alaskan bay. Through the magic of video, projected on the huge ShamuVision screen, animal expert Jack Hanna takes us to Alaska, Norway, and the Crozet Islands of the antarctic.

An unusual feature of the show comes when a bald eagle in free flight soars from the rafters to pick up a lure on the water. (The eagle is actually an African Fisher Eagle, which looks like its American cousin but is not an endangered species.)

The 5,200-seat Shamu Stadium, a short walk down the hill from the Bayside Ski Stadium on the same side of the lagoon, was built around a five-million-gallon saltwater pool that is home to the Shamu family of killer whales.

The stars of the show are the black-and-white members of the Shamu family. The largest weighs some five tons—ten thousand pounds. The young star is two-year-old Tuar, a male killer whale. Mimicry and observational learning are lifelong activities for whales, and Tuar is learning not only from his mom, Kalina, but from the entire Shamu family. His participation in *Shamu Adventure* is steadily increasing. Currently, he is still most frequently paired with mom in the show, but he is gaining independence slowly but surely.

Tuar was born June 22, 1999, in SeaWorld's Shamu Stadium facility. His mother was the first whale to be born and thrive in the care of man, a major milestone in 1985. In eighteen months, Tuar grew tremendously; in mid-2001 he was approximately twelve feet long and weighed a whopping 1,400 pounds; his diet consisted of more than fifty pounds of fish each day.

The majestic, mysterious killer whale mostly lives in a world unto itself, traveling in pods from frigid waters off the coast of Iceland to warmer climates near the tip of South Africa. On islands off the coast of Argentina, researchers have observed them hunting in great packs, and have called them the "wolves of the sea."

Whales are aquatic mammals and not fish, though they are good swimmers. Killer whales can remain submerged up to twelve minutes before surfacing.

But killer whales have also shown an unusual capacity for sharing special relationships with humans.

In the show, many of the whale's actions are prompted by trainers' hand signals. For example, when the trainer holds up an open hand toward the audience, the whales face the audience and open their mouths. Also listen carefully for the faint sound of high-pitched training whistles during the show.

The best seats in the stadium—if you don't mind getting wet—are in the first six rows. Here you will be able to see under the water through the glass wall of the tank, as well as the show up above. If you prefer to stay dry, sit toward the front of the second bank of seats, in the middle of the stadium. You'll have a good view of the video screen and of the platform where the whales frequently beach themselves during the show.

Don't say we didn't warn you: The lower fifteen rows are marked as the "splash zone." That may at first seem like a bit of overkill—it does not seem possible that a whale can send water up that high over the glass. And in fact, for the first three-quarters of the show only those brave souls in the very closest seats are likely to be splashed by one of the animals as it passes by.

But don't congratulate yourself too soon. The conclusion of the show is one wet finale. Wet as in water that washes over the top of the glass in a spectacular wave and soaks the people in those front fifteen rows. Water. Wave. Soaks. Fifty-five-degree saltwater. Actually, it's two waves. Get the picture?

One problem with the stadium shows at SeaWorld is that when one of the presentations lets out, a large number of people are deposited onto walkways leading toward the restaurants. If you are planning to eat after a show, head directly to a restaurant or consider sending someone ahead to place an order.

Shamu: Close Up! SeaWorld's 1.7-million gallon killer whale research facility allows visitors to get closer than ever to Shamu and his friends. It also allows scientists opportunities to study the development of killer whales. The habitat is located alongside the Shamu stadium and includes shallows that will encourage the whales to engage in some of their favorite activities: back scratching and tummy rubbing. Special devices include a huge scale, capable of measuring weights up to forty thousand pounds.

Dolphin Stadium. At the ***Key West Dolphin Fest***, the stars swim, flip, and splash in a variety of stunts with their trainers and with a young volunteer and his or her family from the audience.

On the trainer's command, the dolphins "dance" in time to Key West–style music or stand up in the water to take a "bow" after they have done well. Among our favorite feats are Dolphin Powerboating, when two dolphins push a trainer around the tank by placing their noses on the bottom of his or her feet, and Dolphin "Roman Ride," when the trainer, riding with one foot on each dolphin, holds a loose harness around each animal and goes for a ride.

In addition to dolphins this show features a pair of pseudorca crassidens, or false killer whales. Their beautiful, solid black color and smooth features make them unusual performers. These fast swimmers and fun performers are up to twenty-five feet long.

Perhaps the most spectacular trick in the show is the "Bouncing Trainer," when a pseudorca surfaces with a trainer balanced on its nose, pushing the trainer about twenty feet into the air.

Before and after the show you can walk up to the glass on the tank, nose to nose with the dolphins, but visitors are asked not to touch or slap the side.

The first four rows, especially toward the center of the arena, are the wet seats. The views from anywhere are good, but the best seats are mid-stadium within the first ten rows. The stairs to the seats in the stadium are quite steep and might pose a difficulty for some people; the easiest seats are at the bottom, where you may get a bit wet, or at the top where you are the farthest away.

WOW *Clyde and Seamore Take Pirate Island*

It's a dramatic tale of treasure, treachery, and the quest for fish, beginning somewhere in the Caribbean as a pirate ship sails by an island inhabited by two marooned buccaneers. But when an otter purloins the treasure map and seeks the assistance of the stranded pirates, who will end up with the gold?

Some of the funniest bits at SeaWorld are to be found here, at the three-thousand-seat Sea Lion and Otter Stadium. The humans in this show are more than actors: they are skilled animal handlers who are chosen for both their animal knowledge. The stars are the sea lions, a tiny otter, and the only trained walrus we've ever seen.

Depending on the time of day and season, much of the stadium may be facing the sun; come early to find a shaded area. The first four rows are marked as "splash zones"; we're talking about little spurts, nothing like the tsunamis at Shamu Stadium. Early arrivals also get to watch the talented mime make fun of late arrivals, one of the most popular mini-shows at SeaWorld.

Pelican Exhibit

On the left side of the walkway toward the Atlantis Stadium is a small but spectacular collection of pelicans. Among the birds you will see there are American white pelicans, denizens of marshy lakes and the Pacific and Texas coasts; they winter chiefly in coastal lagoons from Florida and southern California south to Panama. Unlike Florida brown pelicans, white pelicans do not dive for their food. Instead they fish in groups, capturing their prey cooperatively by forming a crescent and beating their wings and driving the fish into shallow water where they use their large pouched bills to catch and then swallow their meal.

WOW *The Intensity Water Ski Show*

The lagoon show includes SeaWorld's talented water stunt actors, wakeboarders, and skiers, mixing theatrical acts with gymnastics and athletic competition.

A twenty-person team tests its mettle in contests that include speeding through a buoy course at 40 miles per hour, freestyle wakeboarding, and an "air chair" competition. Barefoot skiers rip past the grandstands, and long-distance jumpers soar 120 feet in the air from a ramp in the water. The high-flying Ty Cobb Daredevils perform incredible stunts and gymnastics on twin forty-foot tumble tracks.

Seats for the show are in the 3,800-seat **Bayside Ski Stadium** on SeaWorld's seventeen-acre lagoon.

After you've seen this show once, consider coming back for the next showing, but this time view it from the gift shop in the middle of the walkway over the lagoon. Here you can see some of the backstage preparations for some of the special events.

Nautilus Theatre

SeaWorld's 2,400-seat theater is used for special presentations. Special effects include aerial stunts, a dramatic water curtain, fog, lasers, and special lighting. Check the schedule when you arrive at the park.

SeaWorld Theater: *Pets Ahoy!*

An all-star cast features pigs, cats, dogs, birds, the occasional rat, and a few not-so-well-trained humans in a skit with a vague sea adventure theme.

One aspiring young actor or actress even gets into the act, costarring with a sloppy-kissing Great Dane. Finally, guests receive training tips for their own pets. And before you make excuses for the limited repertoire of your own pets at home, consider that nearly all performers come from animal shelters.

Continuous Viewing Exhibits

A number of SeaWorld exhibits are open all day without scheduled events. You can enter them for a quick walk-through or a leisurely study. The premier facilities of this type at SeaWorld include Key West at SeaWorld, Terrors of the Deep, Penguin Encounter, and Tropical Reef. You'll see a number of other interesting places as you walk through SeaWorld, including a tropical rain forest and Pacific Point Preserve.

WOW Terrors of the Deep

A unique collection of dangerous sea creatures. You will find yourself immersed in the secret hiding places of menacing eels, venomous fish, hungry barracuda, and . . . sharks. The creatures in this exhibit all can be potentially dangerous, it is true, but the message of this exhibit is clear: "Respect them, don't kill them." For example, sharks have a bad reputation for attacking humans, but there are few documented instances of wanton attack. As with most injurious encounters between humans and sea creatures, these attacks usually are the result of mistaken identity: the human was mistaken for food.

A short video at the entrance offers some excellent background; don't rush through. The shark movie and aquarium portion of the show are timed to give you about twenty-five minutes to view the tunnel area and the other displays. If you rush through these sections you'll have to stand in line waiting your turn for the shark theater.

The show takes about forty minutes, including the film and walk-through.

The first aquarium displays more than five hundred eels in a ten-foot-deep tank. Grouper, snapper, lookdowns, and jacks—predatory fish that are native to the same ecosystems inhabited by eels—are housed nearby.

A high-tech system simulates the currents and wave action of the reef, and a single light source is placed to simulate the sun.

The best part of this exhibit is the acrylic tunnel that runs through the bottom of the aquarium; you can walk through the tank to view the "terrors." Among the creatures you'll see are moray eels (some more than six feet long), spotted morays, and purple-mouthed eels.

After the first tunnel, you'll come to a display of venomous lionfish and scorpionfish. The graceful lionfish will captivate you with their movement and the colors of the fins that hide their dangerous spines. Scorpionfish show how they camouflage themselves in the sand and wait for an unsuspecting meal to swim overhead.

A separate tank showcases clown fishes, with beautiful but highly poisonous spines. Also on display are nasty surgeon fish. When they are agitated, they will sweep their tails and threaten antagonists with their spines; a swipe from one of the razor-sharp extensions can seriously slash another fish or injure a fisherman attempting to remove them from nets or hooks.

Bad PR. Sharks have gotten a great deal of bad PR. Two times more people die of bee stings each year than succumb to shark attacks.

Hungry sharks? Sharks eat only about once a week. Check with the park for the current feeding schedule; if you can make it, you will understand what the term *feeding frenzy* really means. This is not an experience for the squeamish.

Shark tunnels. The clear viewing tunnels can support the weight of 372 elephants, which is more than strong enough to keep you and the 450 tons of water above you apart.

One of the scenes from the film *Jaws 3-D* was shot inside the shark tunnel.

SeaWorld's education department occasionally schedules sleepovers within the tunnels for school groups.

There's also a collection of barracuda, creatures that ordinarily feast on fish, squid, and shrimp, attacking with a single swift strike at speeds of as much as twenty-eight miles per hour. Viewed from the side the barracuda is hard to miss, but from the front the slender fish is nearly invisible. Barracuda attacks on humans are rare and accidental. Murky water makes it hard to see and barracuda are apt to confuse shiny objects such as jewelry for fish; swimmers in tropical waters are advised not to be between the fish and the sunny surface of the water.

The final stop on the journey comes when you descend fifteen feet below the surface to the territory of the shark through a six-inch-thick clear acrylic tube. You'll travel through the 125-foot-long shark-filled habitat on a PeopleMover, as dozens of nurse, brown, bull, and sand tiger sharks swim overhead and in front. Among the shark skeletons on display is a set of jaw bones from a seventeen-foot male great white caught in western Australia.

If you are claustrophobic and choose to avoid the tunnel, simply exit to your left through the unmarked door beside the tunnel entrance. You can wait for the rest of your party at the end of the line.

Penguin Encounter

Hot house. When it's snowing in the penguin exhibit, these fascinating animals are swimming in fifty-five-degree water. That's cold to us, but compared to the thirty-two-degree refrigerated air of their enclosure, it is relatively warm.

Penguin and eggs. If you see groups of penguins huddled along the back wall of the exhibit, chances are they are hatching eggs. SeaWorld has a very successful penguin breeding program.

The largest, most technically advanced exhibit of its kind, it is the home to hundreds of penguins (from the antarctic) and alcids (from the arctic). The science center goes beyond entertainment to educate guests about the need to protect and preserve polar life.

In a setting so realistic that you can expect to see snowflakes inside, this exhibit moves you past living arctic and antarctic displays on a 120-foot PeopleMover. Glass windows give an unobstructed and unobtrusive view above and below the water where stately king penguins, gentle gentoos, and bounding rockhoppers live

At the alcid exhibit you'll come face-to-snout with more than a hundred puffins, buffleheads, smews, and murres from the arctic. While these are not related to penguins, they are considered their ecological counterparts.

SeaWorld animal experts match temperature and daylight as closely as possible to the animals' native territory so their seasons change as they would if they were living in the wild. After the ride past the live exhibits, you enter a hall with many fascinating, lighted displays. Press on the kid-sized handprints within each display to hear a recorded message.

The largest penguins at SeaWorld Orlando are king penguins from the antarctic; at SeaWorld of California they have a colony of emperor penguins, which are the largest in the world.

And be sure to stop at the SeaWorld Learning Center just past the moving walkway. A globe depicts antarctic explorers. You will see Scott's expedition of 1910 to 1913, and his somewhat friendly adversary Amundsen's from 1910 to 1912. Further back is Drake's route around South America from 1578 to 1579, and Cooke's expedition from 1712 to 1715, which was the first known circumnavigation of the antarctic—marked on the map as "Terra Incognita."

Tropical Reef and Caribbean Tide Pool

More than one thousand tropical fish live in the 160,000-gallon exhibit, the largest South Pacific coral reef display in the United States. The Caribbean Tide Pool gives you close-up views of tropical fish and invertebrates such as starfish, sea urchins, crabs, and anemones. Smaller aquariums exhibit clown fish, sea horses, and octopi.

Sky Tower

This four-hundred-foot needle tower can be seen from miles around SeaWorld, marking the park location and helping you find your way in. Once inside the park, you can ride a sit-down, circular elevator to the top for a panoramic view of SeaWorld and much of Central Florida.

Admission is not included in the daily park pass; in 2001 tickets were $3. The elevator may not operate during heavy winds or other bad weather.

Take your SeaWorld map on this five-and-a-half-minute ride; it will help you orient yourself to the layout of the park as well as other attractions in the area such as Walt Disney World, which you can see from your rotating, four-hundred-foot perch.

Eating Your Way Through SeaWorld

In general SeaWorld food offerings are a bit simpler than you will find at Epcot or Universal. Menus are more limited, but the food generally is of high quality, and the portions are large.

By the way, watch out for marauding seagulls, too. They are quite capable of swooping down and grabbing some of your food if you are eating at one of the outdoor restaurants.

Aloha Polynesian Luau Dinner and Show. Polynesian luau and show: adult, $35.95; child (8–12), $25.95; child (3–7), $15.95. Seating begins at 6:35 P.M. and is limited. Reservations required. Call ☎ (800) 227-8048 or ☎ (407) 351-3600, or stop by the information desk at the main SeaWorld entrance. The meal varies but usually consists of salads, seafood such as mahi-mahi with piña

Key

= Fast food

= Pub

= Full-service

colada sauce, pork loin, sweet and sour chicken, rice, vegetables, and dessert. One cocktail or beer is included in the price of the meal.

Bimini Bay Cafe. Seafood sandwiches ($7 to $8) and platters ($10 to $15). A recommended appetizer: the Key West Conch Chowder. Child's sandwich, $4. The glassed-enclosed dining room overlooks Atlantis Lagoon.

Chicken 'n Biscuit. Fried or baked chicken . . . and biscuits, $4 to $6. Child's menu.

Dockside Smokehouse. Chicken and ribs. Entrees, $5 to $7. Hickory-smoked chicken or ribs, coleslaw, and roll. Picnic tables with umbrellas are available dockside overlooking the Atlantis Lagoon, with a back-door view of the ski show from the lagoon-side seats.

Mama Stella's Italian Kitchen. Near the Penguin area, this pleasant restaurant with indoor seating offers spaghetti for about $5 and pizza for about $4. You can also purchase a garden salad and garlic bread.

Mango Joe's Cafe. Chicken or beef fajitas, fried fish, and club sandwiches, priced from about $6 to $12. Children's meals include chicken or steak fingers served with french fries for about $4. The chicken fajitas at Mango Joe's are quite good. About those "fingers": they are grilled pieces of meat, not fried; we'd vote them among the best snacks at the park.

Spinnaker's Cafe. Hamburgers and sandwiches, $5 to $6. Interesting salads and desserts, $2. An outdoor cafe. The real forte at Spinnaker, however, are desserts. Select from Black Forest cake, Key lime pie, cheesecake, strawberries and cream, and other delectables for about $2 each.

Special Tours and Programs

As befits a place of discovery, SeaWorld offers a range of interesting special tours and educational programs. Most require advance reservations and may be difficult to join in the busiest summer and holiday periods.

Adventure Express Tour. A guided tour with front-of-line access to rides, reserved seating at shows, and special animal feeding opportunities. In 2001 the five-and-a-half-hour tour cost $55 per adult and $50 per child (3–9); a separate park admission ticket is required. Make arrangements at the Guided Tour Counter inside the park's entrance.

Trainer for a Day. From training techniques to food preparation, participants learn firsthand how SeaWorld animal trainers care for and train the animals. The eight-hour program is limited to only three people per day. Participants must be in good physical condition and at least 13 years old. In 2001 the cost was $349 and included a special souvenir T-shirt, a waterproof disposable camera, and lunch. For reservations, call ☎ (407) 370-1382.

To the Rescue! An hour-long behind-the-scenes visit to the park's animal rescue and rehabilitation program for manatees, sea turtles, aquatic birds, and seals. In 2001 tickets were $7.95 for adults, $6.95 for children (3–9).

Predators Tour. Explore the myths behind shark attacks and uncover the mysteries of shark behavior with park experts. Then visit backstage at Shamu Stadium to learn about the awesome power of killer whales. In 2001 tickets were $7.95 for adults, $6.95 for children (3–9).

Polar Expedition Tour. An hour-long tour from the North Pole to the South Pole, including a face-to-face encounter with a Magellanic penguin, a visit behind the scenes at SeaWorld's Penguin Research Facility, and a view of the backstage support areas for Wild Arctic. In 2001 tickets were $7.95 for adults, $6.95 for children (3–9).

Camp SeaWorld and SeaWorld/Busch Gardens Tampa Bay Adventure Camps. SeaWorld's education department offers more than two hundred summer camp classes, including sleepover programs inside the shark tunnels and adventures for kids as well as the whole family. For information call ☎ (407) 363-2380 or ☎ (866) 468-6226.

Discovery Cove

Theme parks are crowded, impersonal, and expensive. Not so at **Discovery Cove**, which opened in 2000 across the road from SeaWorld Orlando.

At Discovery Cove you're greeted by a concierge, escorted to your personal chaise in the shade of a thatched roof, offered a reservation for your lunch or dinner, and, most importantly, given an appointment to swim with the dolphins and get up close and personal with a pool full of bat rays, and ten thousand tropical fish.

The experience is uncrowded, personal, relaxing . . . and *very* expensive. Admission to the park is limited to about one thousand visitors per day by reservation, with an entrance fee in 2001 of $199 per person.

How can they justify that price? Consider that the ticket includes admission,

Discovery Cove by SeaWorld

Discovery Cove Tickets

Prices, which do not include 6 percent tax, were in effect mid-2001 and are subject to change.

Discovery Cove tickets include a full day's use of the park; a supervised swim with the dolphins; use of a mask, snorkel, swim vest, towels, and lockers; plus lunch or dinner. Tickets also include a seven-day pass to SeaWorld Orlando, valid in the week before or after your visit to Discovery Cove.

Visitors younger than six are not permitted in the dolphin pool.

All-Inclusive General Admission	$199.00
Non-Dolphin Swim for Adult or Child (3–5)	
June 1–August 31	$109.00
All other times	$89.00
Trainer for a Day	$369.00

as well as a full meal, towels, umbrellas, lockers, snorkels, vests, lounges, and hammocks. Then add in a scheduled swim with the dolphins (which used to sell for $159 at SeaWorld all by itself) and a one-week pass to SeaWorld across the street (worth about $80), and you may be able to find a way to justify buying a set of admission tickets to Discovery Cove.

That said, it's still $796 plus tax for a family of four, a world record for theme park prices. It makes sense if you want to take a swim with the dolphins, and if you make use of the SeaWorld pass for at least a second day of your stay.

The heart of the thirty-acre park is **Dolphin Lagoon**, home to about thirty of the friendly marine mammals. Guests receive an appointment for the lagoon; children below the age of six are not permitted.

Groups of three guests receive personal instruction from a trainer in shallow water and then enter the lagoon to swim and play with the dolphins.

At **Coral Reef** swimmers and snorkelers can play hide-and-seek with rainbows of ten thousand tropical fish in a million-gallon pool. Brightly colored angelfish and delicate butterfly fish compete for attention with silvery jacks, black-and-white spadefish, and more than seventy-five other species. Swimmers also come within inches of barracuda and sharks—safely isolated from the pool behind clear panels in the water. At another point the hull of a shipwreck has acrylic panels that hold off barracudas on the other side.

Ray Lagoon is a quiet protected area where guests can snorkel, wade, and play with hundreds of southern and cownose stingrays, gentle animals that can grow up to four feet in diameter.

The quarter-mile-long **Tropical River** meanders its way throughout most of Discovery Cove, passing by beaches, walkways, and rocky lagoons. There is a dense tropical forest, an Amazon-like river, a tropical fishing village, and an underwater cave. The river ranges in depth from about three to eight feet; all visitors must wear one of the park's swim vests, which provides just enough buoyancy to let you float along.

Swimmers pass under a waterfall on the Tropical River to enter an immense aviary, home to some three hundred colorful birds from around the world. Many are trained to eat from the hands of guests.

The aviary holds softbills such as starlings and thrushes, roseate spoonbills, multicolored Turacos, nectar-eating lorries, and tawney frogmouths.

The saltwater in the reef and dolphin pool are maintained at seventy-eight degrees; the freshwater river is a constant eighty-five degrees. The park makes its own saltwater; it is not chlorinated, but instead treated with ozone and other chemicals not threatening to wildlife.

Visitors check in for the day at a reception area like a grand hotel. A concierge schedules time with the dolphins and hands out a pass with a charge account for any purchases made at the park.

The buildings at the park are designed with a tropical theme, many with real thatched roofs. All visitors are given a pass for a meal, which will feature stir-fries and grilled fish.

If you insist on spending more money you can also purchase snacks or a second meal, beer or wine, photos, gifts, and souvenirs.

Discovery Cove also offers a **Trainer for a Day** program. For a fee of $369 per person a small group of guests can spend the day working with the trainers and animals at the park.

Snorkeling in the coral reef at Discovery Cove
Photo courtesy SeaWorld

SEAWORLD

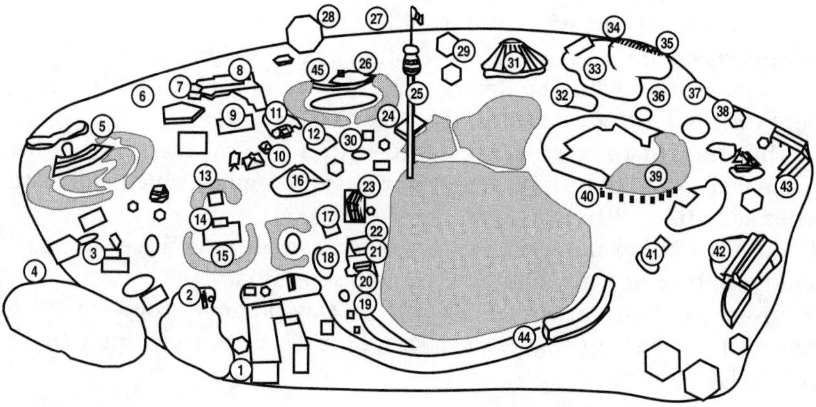

1. Ticket Plaza
2. Treasure Isle-Ice Cream
3. Key West at SeaWorld
4. Stingray Lagoon
5. Manatees: The Last Generation?
6. Special Exhibits
7. Friends of the Wild
8. Penguin Encounter
9. Mama Stella's Italian Kitchen
10. Dockside Smokehouse
11. Florida Citrus Growers' Plaza
12. Chicken 'n Biscuit
13. Tide Pool and Caribbean Tide Pool
14. Tropical Reef
15. Flamingo Exhibit
16. SeaWorld Theater: *Pets Ahoy!*
17. Tropical Rain Forest
18. Dolphin Interactive Program
19. Pelican Exhibit
20. Spoonbill Exhibit
21. Aloha Polynesian Luau Dinner and Show
22. Bimini Bay Cafe
23. *South Seas Revue*
24. Spinnaker's Cafe
25. Sky Tower
26. Pacific Point Preserve
27. Kraken
28. Journey to Atlantis
29. Terrors of the Deep
30. Special events
31. Nautilus Theatre
32. Flamingo Lagoon
33. Clydesdale Hamlet
34. The Deli
35. Anheuser-Busch Hospitality Center
36. Midway Games Area
37. Play Area
38. Radio Control Boats & Trucks
39. Shamu Stadium: Shamu Adventure
40. Shamu: Close Up!
41. Mango Joe's Cafe
42. Wild Arctic
43. Shamu's Happy Harbor
44. Bayside Ski Stadium: *The Intensity Water Ski Show*
45. Sea Lion and Otter Stadium: *Clyde and Seamore Take Pirate Island*

Part V
Dinner Shows and Character Meals

Chapter 20
Dinner Shows and Character Meals

If you're on vacation, why should the entertainment stop when you sit down to eat? That's the thinking behind one of the fastest-growing industries in Orlando and the surrounding area—the dinner show. You can eat a Chinese meal while being entertained by Asian acrobats; you can pull apart a chicken with your bare hands while knights on horseback joust for your entertainment.

There are more than a dozen major dinner shows inside and outside Walt Disney World. Nearly every one of them has something to offer.

Prices for adults generally range from about $25 to $45 and usually include all courses and drinks; be aware that almost every show offers discounts from the listed price (you'll find some coupons in this book). You may be able to buy cut-rate tickets to dinner shows from ticket booths in hotels or on tourist roads; shop around a bit for the best deal.

One word of warning: most of the shows try to pad their nightly take with all sorts of gimmicks. They'll try to sell you photos taken in the lobby, photos taken at your table, souvenir booklets, flags, and other items. If you're not in the market for extra trinkets just say no.

Call for hours of performance for any show; in the busiest seasons some theaters will have two shows in a night.

Two long-time favorites closed in the summer of 2000: Wild Bill's Dinner Show and King Henry's Feast.

Within Walt Disney World

The dinner shows at Walt Disney World resorts generally require advance reservations and purchase of tickets. Call ☎ (407) 934-7639 for reservations; most times of the year you'll need to do this weeks or even months before arrival. Guests at hotels within the park get a head start for reservations, too. Prices and times are subject to change.

Hoop-Dee-Doo Musical Revue. Pioneer Hall in Disney's Fort Wilderness Resort. ☎ (407) 939-3463, or ☎ (407) 824-2803 on the day of the show. Reservations are necessary most days; a walk-up waiting list is also begun at Pioneer Hall about forty-five minutes before show time.

A Western singing and dancing show, featuring all-you-can-eat chicken, ribs, corn, and strawberry shortcake. This is a hugely popular, raucous, thigh-slappin', hee-haw of a show; if that's the sort of entertainment you like, this is a fine example. Entertainment includes piano and banjo music, terrible jokes and gags, and an audience-participation washboard finale. In between is a bit of improvisational humor as cast members make up songs about some of the guests in the audience.

The large hall has two levels; the best seats are at the front of the balcony or a few rows back from the stage on the main level. Seats are assigned at the time of the reservation.

Veterans observe that although this is an all-you-can-eat adventure, the courses (including fried chicken, BBQ ribs, and strawberry shortcake) come and go pretty quickly and there is a show to watch, too. Disney also trimmed a half-hour off the starting time of the late show by shortening the overall performance and turn-around times a bit. Seatings at 5, 7:15, and 9:30 P.M. Adult, about $46; child (3–11), $24.

If you're not already at Fort Wilderness as a guest and plan to use Disney transportation, you'll need to leave about an hour before your show time to make connections to the resort and walk to the Pioneer Hall, which is located near the beach on Bay Lake. There is also a parking lot at Fort Wilderness.

Hayrides at Pioneer Hall. Horse-drawn tours of the Fort Wilderness area are offered each evening at 7 or 9:30 P.M. Sign up at the booth outside Pioneer Hall. Adult $6, child $4.

Polynesian Luau. Disney's Polynesian Resort. ☎ (407) 939-3463 An all-you-can-eat feast that features barbecue pork ribs, roasted chicken, mahi-mahi, fruit, and drinks, including frozen piña coladas, accompanied by singers, hula dancers, fire acts, and other entertainment.

Highlights of the Polynesian Luau include a Samoan Slap Dance and Hula.

There's a partial roof over the dining room, with the stage open to the sky; mosquito repellent is worth adding to your preshow preparations in bug season. The show is much more dramatic when it is dark; the early show in summer is presented while it is still light. (By the way, it is possible to see portions of the show from the courtyard of the Polynesian Resort without paying for a seat and meal.)

Guests at park resorts can reserve seats when they reserve their rooms; others can make reservations within thirty days of the day of the show.

Seatings are at 5:15 and 8 P.M. Adult, $46; child (3–11), $24.

Nearby Walt Disney World

Arabian Nights Dinner Attraction. 6225 West Irlo Bronson Highway (U.S. 192), east of the intersection with I-4 in Kissimmee. ☎ (407) 239-9223 or ☎ (800) 553-6116. 🖳 www.arabian-nights.com.

Beautiful horses, handsome caballeros, pretty young women, and a theatrical presentation in one of Orlando's largest and oldest dinner theaters. This is first and foremost a horse show: more than fifty of them, including Arabians, Lippizans, Andalusians, Belgians, and Percherons, perform in the 1,200-seat Palace of Horses. Favorite stunts include "Airs Above the Ground" maneuvers, horse-drawn "water skiing," a chariot race, and a most unusual square dance on horseback.

The arena itself was renovated in 1999 to bring the audience a bit closer to the show and create more of a palace-like atmosphere. And a spectacular new special effect brings "snow" to Central Florida every night.

The dinner features prime rib and salad; vegetarian lasagna is also available. The meal is accompanied by beer, wine, and soft drinks. The serving staff is extremely solicitous, and the audience is much less rowdy than at some of the other dinner shows in town.

Arabian Nights is also one of the only family-owned attractions in the area; it is the creation of Mark and Galen Miller, who previously owned an Arabian show farm near Gainesville, Florida. Shows are presented Sunday to Tuesday at 7:30 P.M., and Thursday to Saturday at 8:30 P.M. Adult, $36.95; child (3–11), $23.95.

Capone's Dinner & Show. 4740 West Irlo Bronson Highway (U.S. 192). ☎ (407) 397-2378. 🖳 www.alcapones.com.

A musical comedy review with guns and an unlimited Italian buffet that offers items such as lasagna, baked ziti, sausage and peppers, baked chicken, pasta salad, plus beer, wine, sangria, and rum runners. Set in 1931 gangland Chicago. Adult, $39.95; senior, $19.98; child (12 and younger), $24.

Medieval Times Dinner & Tournament. 4510 West Irlo Bronson Highway (U.S. 192), near Route 441 in Kissimmee. ☎ (407) 396-1518 or ☎ (800) 229-8300. 🖳 www.medievaltimes.com.

Come to dinner as the guests of the royal family in the eleventh century. The feast includes spectacular pageantry, dramatic horsemanship, swordplay, falconry, sorcery, and a jousting contest. The meal—which is served without silverware—includes a hearty vegetable soup, roasted chicken, spare ribs, potato, and dessert, plus beer, sangria, and soft drinks.

Medieval Times is one of the old-timers among dinner theaters, dating back more than twenty years in Florida, nearly forty years in Spain, and about one thousand years in history. Twenty-five years ago, Jose De Montaner converted his farm in Majorca, Spain, into a barbecue dinner show and then a medieval-theme show for tourists. There are now Medieval Times dinner attractions in California (near Disneyland), New Jersey, Illinois, Texas, South Carolina, and Toronto, Canada.

The entertainment takes place in the 1,100-seat Great Ceremonial Hall; seats are not reserved—arrive early for the best seats (down low at midcourt). The show begins with some impressive demonstration of horse training and riding skills, including the Carousel, a display of intricate horse maneuvers.

The tournament begins with knights on horseback with lances galloping at full speed toward three-inch hoops suspended from posts; the next challenge is a javelin toss on horseback. The final confrontation pits knights against each other in jousting tournaments and hand-to-hand fighting.

Alongside the theater is the **Medieval Life** exhibit, an extraordinary collection of strange artifacts brought over from Europe.

Adult, $42 plus tax; child (12 and younger), $26. Tickets include admission to Medieval Life.

Medieval Life. 4510 West Irlo Bronson Highway, off Route 441 in Kissimmee. ☎ (407) 396-1518 or ☎ (800) 229-8300. 🖳 www.medievaltimes.com.

A little piece of ancient Spain, Medieval Life includes a truly amazing collection of tools, personal items, and some of the darker elements of the Medieval times, including dungeons and torture chambers. This place is for real—an exhibit unlike most anything else in Central Florida or elsewhere in the United States.

Your visit will start at the architect's house, the home of one of the most respected members of the community; the craftsmen exhibits include authentically dressed tradesmen and artisans including potters, blacksmiths, millers, carpenters, and glassblowers.

Then—parents of young children be warned—it's into the dungeon where you'll see replicas and real instruments of torture that include the garrote, iron torture masks known as "branks," and the interrogation chair, a large wooden chair covered with sharp iron spikes used to "convince" a person charged with a crime to offer a confession. And be prepared to explain—or steer your kids around—a few real chastity belts.

MurderWatch Mystery Dinner Theatre. Grosvenor Resort at Walt Disney World Village. ☎ (800) 624-4109 or ☎ (407) 827-6534. 🖳 www.murderwatch.com/murderwatch.html.

A lively evening of food, song, and murder presented in the attractive restaurant, with above-average dinner buffet fare. Baskerville's has a replica of Sherlock Holmes's 221B Baker Street office on display.

We enjoyed a campy, funny show involving an engagement party for the daughter of a mafia don; before we could begin the salad course, an FBI agent (who also played the piano) checked out our table for bombs, listening devices, and leftovers. Other characters, including detective Shirley Holmes, worked the tables during the show. Before the night was over, the dopey chanteuse was murdered, the marriage was off, and a good time was had by all.

Tickets, including dinner, are $34.95. Children (3–9) can attend for $10.95. Presented Saturday evening with one or two shows per night.

International Drive/Universal Studios Area

Aloha Polynesian Luau at SeaWorld. 7007 SeaWorld Drive. ☎ (407) 363-2559 or ☎ (800) 327-2424. 🖳 www.seaworld.com/programs/swfluau.html.

Eat, drink, and be entertained by the Hawaiian Rhythms troupe. (Located at the perimeter of SeaWorld, you do not need a ticket to the park.) Adult, $35.95; juniors (8–12), $25.95; child (3 to 7), $15.95. Served from 6:30 to 8:45 P.M. nightly.

Mark Two Dinner Theater. 3376 Edgewater Drive. ☎ (407) 843-6275, ☎ (800) 726-6275. 🖳 www.themarktwo.com.

Live Broadway shows, preceded by a buffet dinner featuring prime rib. Open Wednesday through Sunday; some matinee performances. Tickets are priced from about $35 to $43. Tables surround the stage on three sides.

Pirate's Dinner Adventure. 6400 Carrier Drive. ☎ (407) 248-0590, ☎ (800) 866-2469. 🖳 www.orlandopirates.com.

Ahoy, mateys. Just off International Drive near Wet 'n Wild and Universal Studios Escape, the impressive set includes a full-scale pirate ship afloat in a 300,000-gallon indoor lagoon. Pirates swing from ropes over your head, and battles rage all around. Presented nightly. After the show, guests can attend the Pirate's Buccaneer Bash to mingle with cast members and attempt to learn the latest dance steps. Adult, $41.95 plus tax; child (3–11), $25.50.

Sleuths Mystery Dinner Show. 7508 Republic Drive, off international Drive behind Wet 'n Wild. ☎ (407) 363-1985 or ☎ (800) 393-1985. 🖳 www.sleuths.com.

Step into the scene of the crime. Mix with the characters, search for clues, and help track down the culprit. Among recent titles in the troupe's repertoire is "Island for Sale." You'll also eat dinner along the way. One, two, or three shows per night. Adult, $39.95 plus tax; child (3–11), $23.95.

Disney Character Meals

For reservations at character meals at Walt Disney World properties call ☎ (407) 939-7741 or ☎ (407) 939-3463.

Artist Point Character Breakfast. Disney's Wilderness Lodge. Starring Tigger, Winnie the Pooh, and Eeyore. Breakfast 7:30 to 11:30 A.M. Adult, $14.95; child (3–11), $8.95.

Baskerville's Character Breakfast Buffet. Grosvenor Resort. Call ☎ (407) 828-4444 for reservations and current information. Breakfast offered 8:30 A.M. to 10:30 A.M. on Tuesday, Thursday, and Saturday; $9.95 for adult and $5.95 for child.

Chef Mickey's Buffet. Contemporary Resort. Starring Mickey and Minnie Mouse, Goofy, Chip 'n' Dale, and Pluto. Breakfast from 7 A.M. to 11 A.M. Adult, $15.95; child (3–11), $8.95. Dinner from 5 to 9:30 P.M. Adult, $21.95; child (3–11), $9.95.

Cinderella's Royal Table/Once Upon a Time Breakfast. King Stefan's Banquet Hall in Cinderella Castle. Cinderella, Captain Hook, and friends. Daily from 8 to 10 A.M. Magic Kingdom ticket required. Resort guests can use early-morning entry for breakfast from 7:30 A.M. on Monday, Thursday, and Saturday. Reservations required. Adult, $14.95; child (3–11), $7.95. A separate admission ticket to the Magic Kingdom is required.

Crystal Palace in the Magic Kingdom. Winnie the Pooh and friends for breakfast on Main Street from 8 to 10:30 A.M. Adult, $14.95; child (3–11), $7.95. Lunch from 11:30 A.M. to 3 P.M. Adult, $15.95; child, $8.25. Dinner 3:30 P.M. to closing. Adult, $19.95; child, $9.95. Magic Kingdom admission ticket required.

Donald's Breakfastosaurus. Restaurantosaurus at Disney's Animal Kingdom. Donald Duck, of course. Park opening until 10:30 A.M. Adult, $13.95; child, $7.95. Separate Animal Kingdom admission ticket required.

Garden Grill Character Experience. Minnie, Mickey, and Chip 'n Dale. Breakfast, lunch, and dinner at The Land pavilion of Epcot Center. Family-style breakfast from 8:40 to 11:10 A.M. Adult, $14.95; child, $8.25. Lunch from 11:30 A.M. to 4:20 P.M. Adult, $16.95; child, $9.95. Dinner 4:40 to 8:10 P.M. Adult, $17.50; child, $9.95. Epcot admission ticket required.

Garden Grove Character Breakfast. Walt Disney World Swan. Goofy and Pluto. Saturday 8 to 11 A.M. Family-style meal adult, $12.95; child (3–11), $7.50. Menu items also offered.

Gulliver's Grill Character Dinner. Walt Disney World Swan. 6 to 10 P.M. Rafiki and Timon Monday and Friday. Winnie the Pooh and Tigger Thursday. Disney characters Sunday and Wednesday. Order from menu.

Goofy's Beach Club Breakfast. Cape May Cafe at Disney's Beach Club. Admiral Goofy and friends. 7:30 A.M. to 11 A.M. daily. Adult $15.95; child (3–11), $8.95.

Harry's Safari Bar & Grill Character Brunch. Walt Disney World Dolphin. 8:30 A.M. to noon daily. Adult, $15.50; child (4–12), $9.25.

Liberty Tree Tavern Character Dinner. Dinner from 4 P.M. to park closing with Mickey and Goofy. Lunch includes Colonial Chicken, pasta, turkey burgers, pot roast. Dinner includes chicken and flank steak entrees. Adult, $19.95; child (3–11), $9.95 plus theme park admission.

Minnie's Menehune Character Breakfast. 'Ohana at Disney's Polynesian Resort. Mickey, Goofy, and Chip 'n Dale. 7:30 A.M. to 11 A.M. daily. Adult, $15.95; child (3–11), $8.95.

1900 Park Fare Character Buffet. Disney's Grand Floridian Beach Resort. Breakfast with Mary Poppins, Alice in Wonderland, the Mad Hatter, and friends from 7:30 to 11:30 A.M. daily. Adult, $16.95; child, $9.95. Dinner features Disney villains, with a cast of characters including Cruella De Vil, the Snow Queen, Captain Hook, and Prince John. Served from 5:15 to 9 P.M. Adult, $21.95; child (3–11), $12.95.

Olivia's Cafe Breakfast. Disney Old Key West Resort. Winnie the Pooh and Tigger. Sunday, Monday, and Wednesday from 7:30 to 10:15 A.M. Adult, $14.95; child, $8.95.

Sunday Disney Character Breakfast. Wyndham Palace Resort, Hotel Plaza. Sunday from 8 to 10:30 A.M. Order from menu or buffet. Adult, $14.95; child, $9.95.

Part VI
Sports and Recreation Within Walt Disney World

Chapter 21
Disney's Wide World of Sports, Golf, Auto Racing, Marinas, Fishing, Tennis, and Health Clubs

Depending upon your point of view, Walt Disney World is either four theme parks surrounded by ninety-nine holes of golf, or a country club so huge it holds within it four theme parks.

Or the place is so big that it can park a baseball stadium, professional tennis complex, and track fieldhouse in one corner and an Indy-class auto racetrack in another without running out of popcorn and liniment.

If there were no Magic Kingdom, Epcot, Disney–MGM Studios, or Animal Kingdom, the Walt Disney World resort would deserve recognition just for its sports complexes.

Disney's Wide World of Sports

Lace up your sneakers, Mickey: Disney's Wide World of Sports offers world-class athletic facilities for man, woman, and mouse.

It's a field of dreams for more than thirty sports. The two hundred acres of facilities includes a handsome baseball stadium, a softball quadraplex, a field-house that has six professional-quality basketball courts, eleven clay tennis courts, four soccer fields, and much more.

The site, which draws its name from the famous ABC sports television show—now part of the Disney corporate family—has become the Spring Training home of the Atlanta Braves, the training site for the Harlem Globetrotters, and the headquarters of the Amateur Athletic Union (AAU). The AAU plans as many as a hundred annual championship events at Walt Disney World.

In 2001, visitors could purchase a day pass to the facilities for $9.25 for adults and $7.25 for children (ages 3–9) and observe training and many amateur tournament activities anywhere on the property. Parking is free. Some special events, such as Spring Training baseball games and Globetrotter performances, have an additional charge.

Tickets for all events are available through Ticketmaster outlets or by visiting the box office at the entrance to the complex. For updated schedules call the Disney's Wide World of Sports Information Line at ☎ (407) 363-6600 or consult 🖳 disney.go.com/DisneyWorld/wideworldofsports.

Major League Soccer schedules its spring training at the Disney facility, in mid-February. The Harlem Globetrotters also hold an annual holiday series at the complex.

The sports complex is within Walt Disney World, near I-192; it can also be reached on an internal bus via a transfer at the Blizzard Beach station.

Baseball Stadium. A field with major-league dimensions and 7,500 permanent seats. The Atlanta Braves work out and play their home Spring Training games in February and March of each year.

The handsome stadium is reminiscent of sturdy 1950s-style architecture; it includes a number of nice touches such as extra-wide seats and a pair of concession stands that face the field so fans won't miss a pitch if they're off on an emergency safari for hot dogs. Serious baseball fans and just about anyone else will appreciate how close you can get to the game. Seats are mostly exposed to the rain or sun, except for rows P through U of the lower deck.

The Spring Training home season includes about sixteen games from late February through the end of March; there are also intrasquad games and practice sessions. For information, call ☎ (407) 939-1500. Tickets range from about $9 to $18 and are available at the stadium or through Ticketmaster at ☎ (407) 839-3900.

When the Atlanta Braves complete Spring Training, the complex is taken over by Orlando Rays, the Class AA Southern League affiliate of the Tampa Bay Devil Rays. The Rays have a seventy-game home schedule that runs from early April to early September. Tickets range from $5 to $8 and can be purchased through Ticketmaster at ☎ (407) 839-3900 or at 🖳 www.ticketmaster.com.

The **Doyle Baseball School** conducts a school for young players several time a year; the school is run by former major leaguers Brian, Blake, and Denny Doyle. For information, call ☎ (407) 363-6600 or consult 🖳 www.doylebase ball.com.

Fieldhouse. Six hardwood basketball courts with main-floor seating for five thousand spectators. The Harlem Globetrotters train here and play a series of holiday-season games each December. The fieldhouse is also expected to be used for gymnastics and special events.

Softball/Baseball Quadraplex. Four softball diamonds with bleachers, three Major League–sized fields with five hundred seats each, and two youth baseball fields.

Track and Field Complex. A four-hundred-meter polyurethane track, long jump and triple jump runway, and other facilities.

Tennis Complex. Eleven clay courts, nine of them lighted. One thousand permanent seats at center-court stadium, with additional temporary seating available. The U.S. Tennis Association (USTA) Men's Clay Court Championship has been held at the facility.

Beach Volleyball. Five sand courts.

Velodrome. The cycling facility from the 1996 Centennial Olympics in Atlanta was moved to Orlando for training and events.

All of the facilities are open to organized tournaments only.

Official All-Star Cafe. Just outside the main entrance to the baseball stadium, a spectacular outpost of the themed dining restaurant also features stages for special events and sports radio and television shows. Nearby is a huge **Foot Locker Super Store**, stocked with the latest in athletic gear.

Walt Disney World Golf Courses

Disney is one version of golfing heaven. Ever on the search for a cute phrase, Disney has taken to calling it "The Magic Linkdom." It's a way for Mom and Dad and even junior to come to Walt Disney World without having to spend all their time in the company of a bunch of cartoon mice.

There are five championship-level 18-hole golf courses within the World, plus the 9-hole Oak Trail practice course. Two of the courses are good enough to be stops on the PGA Tour.

Instruction is available through the **Walt Disney World Golf Studio** at the

More, you say? In addition to the Walt Disney World courses, there are dozens of municipal, public, and semiprivate golf courses in and around the Disney area in Orange County. Here is a selection.

Crystal Brook Golf Course. Kissimmee. ☎ (407) 847-8721.
Cypress Creek Country Club. Orlando. Semiprivate 18 holes. ☎ (407) 351-2187.
Dubsdread Golf Course. Orlando. Municipal 18 holes. ☎ (407) 246-2551.
Eaglewood. Orlando. Public 18 holes. ☎ (407) 351-5121.
Eastwood Golf & Country Club. Orlando. Semiprivate 18 holes. ☎ (407) 281-4653.
Falcon's Fire Golf Course. Kissimmee. Public 18 holes. ☎ (407) 239-5445.
Grand Cypress Resort. Orlando. Resort 45 holes. ☎ (407) 239-4700.
Hunter's Creek Golf Club. Orlando. Public 18 holes. ☎ (407) 240-4653.
International Golf Club. Orlando. Resort 18 holes. ☎ (407) 239-6909.
Kissimmee Golf Club. Kissimmee. Public 18 holes. ☎ (407) 847-2816.
Lake Orlando Golf Club. Orlando. Public. ☎ (407) 298-1230.
Marriott's Orlando World Center. Orlando. Resort 18 holes. ☎ (407) 239-4200.
Meadow Woods Golf Club. Orlando. Semiprivate 18 holes. ☎ (407) 850-5600.
MetroWest Country Club. Orlando. Semiprivate 18 holes. ☎ (407) 299-1099.
Orange Lake Country Club. Kissimmee. Semiprivate. ☎ (407) 239-1050.
Osceola Golf Club. Kissimmee. Public 18 holes. ☎ (407) 348-4915.
The Pines. Orlando. Public 18 holes. ☎ (407) 647-4067.
Ventura Country Club. Orlando. Semiprivate 18 holes. ☎ (407) 277-2640.
Wedgefield Golf & Country Club. Orlando. Semiprivate 18 holes. ☎ (407) 568-2116.
Winter Park Municipal. Winter Park. Municipal 9 holes. ☎ (407) 623-3339.
Winter Pines Golf Club. Winter Park. Public 18 holes. ☎ (407) 671-3172.
Zellwood Station Country Club. Zellwood. Semiprivate 18 holes. ☎ (407) 886-3303.

Magnolia driving range. The fee is $50 for a half-hour lesson for adults, or $30 for juniors (17 and younger). Call ☎ (407) 824-2270 for reservations.

Junior golfers can participate in a five-day-long summer golf camp.

The Walt Disney World Golf Classic, a stop on the PGA Tour, has been held in late October in recent years. Tickets are available through Golf Sales.

Golf Fees

Prices were in effect in mid-2001 and are subject to change. Carts included. Rates do not include tax.

Resort guests can reserve tee times as much as ninety days in advance; day guests can reserve up to thirty days in advance. All reservations must be guaranteed with a credit card. For reservations, call ☎ (407) 939-4653. You may also be able to reserve a starting time on the same day you want to play by calling the Pro Shop at each course directly. Complimentary taxi service is provided to guests at Walt Disney World resort hotels coming to play at one of the courses; contact the valet desk or bell services for assistance.

Replay rates are 50 percent of full rate on the same day, on a space-available basis, and may not be reserved in advance.

Times for **Twilight** rates vary during the year; price allows play for as many holes as possible before nightfall. In recent years the courses offered a **Summer Price Slice Special** from mid-May to late September, with reduced prices of $45 to $60 at any of the five championship courses after 10 A.M. There are also reduced-price tee times after 3 P.M. and 5 P.M. daily.

Eagle Pines, Osprey Ridge	**Day Visitor**	**Resort Guest**	**Twilight Rate**
May to late September			
Eagle Pines	$105	$100	$60
Osprey Ridge	$115	$110	$70
September to late April rates are slightly higher			
Lake Buena Vista, Magnolia, Palm			
May to late September	$95	$90	$55
Early September to late April rates are slightly higher			
***Oak Trail* (9-hole walking course)**			
Adult	$35		
Junior (17 and younger)	$20		

Reduced rates for midday tee-offs, as low as $10 for 5 P.M. start. Pull carts are available for $5.

Rentals	
Graphite clubs	$45
Steel clubs	$40
Oak Trail clubs	$15
Range balls	$6
Shoes	$7

Magnolia. At the Shades of Green (formerly the Disney Inn). Named for the more than 1,500 magnolias on the course, this course plays to 6,642 yards from the middle tees and is the setting for the final round of the Walt Disney World Golf Classic. There's water on ten of the eighteen holes. In 1993 the Magnolia received a complete facelift by course architect Joe Lee. The **Garden Gallery** offers breakfast, lunch, and dinner. The **Disney Golf Studio** offers lessons and videotape analysis. Pro Shop: ☎ (407) 824-2288.

Course information: Par 72. Yardage: 5,232–7,190. Course/Slope Ratings: 69.4–74.9/123–136.

Palm. Considered the second most difficult course at Walt Disney World, it is included among *Golf Digest*'s Top 25 resort courses. It plays to a relatively short 6,461 yards from the middle tees, but water and sand seem to be almost everywhere. The 18th hole has been rated as the fourth toughest on the PGA Tour. Also located at Shades of Green, it shares the Garden Gallery and Pro Shop with the Magnolia course.

Course information: Par 72. Yardage: 5,311–6,957. Course/Slope Ratings: 69.5–73.9/124–138.

Lake Buena Vista. A wide open and heavily wooded course that reaches to 6,655 yards, extending from the Disney Village Clubhouse. Located at Disney's Village Resort near the Hotel Plaza. The **Lake Buena Vista Restaurant** in the clubhouse serves breakfast, lunch, and dinner. The **Lake Buena Vista Golf Studio** offers lessons and analysis. Pro Shop: ☎ (407) 824-3741.

Course information: Par 72. Yardage: 5,194–6,819. Course/Slope Ratings: 68.1–72.7/120–128.

Osprey Ridge. By most accounts the most difficult course at Walt Disney World, it was designed by acclaimed golf course architect Tom Fazio. The course includes a circulating 18-hole routing with holes that play in every direction.

The course extends a total of 6,705 yards from the middle tees, including some remote tropical settings. Some of the tees, greens, and viewing areas are as much as twenty-five feet above grade; much of the earth was moved from the excavation at nearby Eagle Pines.

The namesake "ridge" plays an important role in the course: you'll climb the ridge for the tee for Hole 3, the green for Hole 12 is built into its side, and the green for Hole 16 is atop it. Located at the Bonnet Creek Golf Club, it includes the **Sand Trap Bar & Grill**, a lunch spot with a view of the greens. The **Bonnet Creek Golf Studio** offers lessons and analysis. Pro Shop: ☎ (407) 824-2675.

Course information: Par 72. Yardage: 5,402–7,101. Course/Slope Ratings: 68.9–73.9/121–135.

Eagle Pines. Eight of designer Pete Dye's courses are included in *Golf* magazine's Top 50.

Courses, rated. According to the pros at the courses, here are the difficulty levels from most difficult to easiest:

1. Osprey Ridge
2. Palm
3. Magnolia
4. Eagle Pines
5. Lake Buena Vista

No word on mouse ears. Disney enforces a dress code requiring golf attire that bans T-shirts and short shorts.

Unlike the high mounds and ridges of Osprey Ridge, this newer course offers a low profile, although many balls will end up in the surrounding pines. Eagle Pines plays 6,224 yards from the middle tees and is considered a bit more forgiving than the other courses. Dye included a lip on the edge of fairways along water hazards to reduce the number of wet balls. The course shares the Bonnet Creek Golf Studio, pro shop, and Sand Trap restaurant with Osprey Ridge.

Course information: Par 72. Yardage: 4,838–6,772. Course/Slope Ratings: 66.3–72.3/111–131.

Oak Trail Executive Course. At the Shades of Green. A 9-hole, 2,913 yard, par-36 course with small rolling greens and elevated tees. It's no push-over, though, with some of the most difficult greens at Walt Disney World. No golf carts are allowed.

Course information: Par 36. Yardage: 2,552–2,913.

Miniature Golf

Winter Summerland Miniature Golf. In true Disney fashion, this pair of miniature golf courses is unlike any you will find in your neighborhood shopping mall. It seems late one Christmas Eve, Santa was flying back to the North Pole and glanced down to see an unbelievable sight: snow in Florida at Blizzard Beach. It was, Santa decided, the perfect place for a vacation getaway for his hard-working elves, a Winter Summerland.

The only thing the area lacked was a golf course; the elves took care of that, dividing the area into two camps, one that enjoyed the warm Florida sun and another that preferred the snow and cold of the North Pole. And so they built two courses: a "sand" course and a "snow" course.

On the summer course Santa slumbers beneath a large mound of sand, and inner tubes litter the "beach." Parked nearby is a small aluminum "Elfstream" camper. The winter course includes Squirty the Snowman who stands in the way and sprays golfers with water if they get too close.

Whichever course you choose, you'll end up in an old log campground lodge for the final hole; you'll need to putt your ball between two model trains that circle below a decorated Christmas tree. When you put the ball in the cup, you'll travel through cyberspace for a special greeting direct from Santa.

The course is located off the parking lot of Blizzard Beach, to the right of the ticket plaza.

Both courses are open from 10 A.M. to 11 P.M. daily; greens fees for either course are adults $9.25, children $7.50. A second round of golf is offered for a 50 percent reduction. For information, call ☎ (407) 560-3000.

Fantasia Gardens Miniature Golf. The original small golf course at Walt Disney World offers two 18-hole courses near the Swan, Dolphin, and BoardWalk resorts. Hippos dance, fountains leap, and broomsticks march at the course, with a theme taken from Disney's classic animated film *Fantasia*.

The course includes hazards based on the film. At "Toccata & Fugue" good shots are rewarded with musical tones. "The Nutcracker Suite" features quirky obstacles including dancing mushrooms. "The Pastoral Symphony" presents a forty-foot-tall Mount Olympus with waterfalls. At "The Dance of the Hours" good timing and accuracy are needed to pass *Fantasia*'s famous alligator and a hippo pas de deux. Then there is "The Sorcerer's Apprentice," starring Mickey Mouse, his troop of out-of-control broomsticks and dazzling water effects.

Alongside is **Fantasia Fairways**, a par-3 or -4 putting course with exaggerated contours, water hazards, and sand traps, with holes ranging from forty to seventy-five feet.

Both courses are open from 10 A.M. to 11 P.M. daily; greens fees for either course are adult $9.25, child $7.50. For information, call ☎ (407) 560-8760.

The Walt Disney World Speedway

The Walt Disney World Speedway, a $6 million 1.1-mile course to the left of the access road to the parking lot for the Magic Kingdom, hosted the first Disney World Indy 200 in 1996, drawing tens of thousands of fans and creating a major slow-speed traffic jam.

The speedway, with fifty-one thousand seats, is expected to be a regular stop each January in the new Indy Racing League (IRL) and the Chevy Trucks Challenge, the opening race of the NASCAR Craftsman Truck Series calendar.

The **Richard Petty Driving Experience** moves motor sports fans out of the grandstands and into the driver's or passenger's seat of an authentic stock car capable of speeds of up to 145 miles per hour. Program offerings include the eight-lap **Rookie Experience**, the sixteen-lap **Cup Experience**, and the **Experience of a Lifetime**, a series of three ten-lap sprints.

For those who'd rather leave the driving to a pro, Richard Petty Driving Experience also offers the **Ride-Along Experience**, including three laps as a passenger in a stock car with a professional driver, traveling at a top speed of 145 miles per hour.

Instructors put participants through the paces in all sessions, beginning with classroom instruction on safety and fundamentals. It continues with on-track technique for handling, passing, and drafting with the stock cars.

Sessions at Walt Disney World Speedway are planned for February through September, with limited additional opportunities in October, November, and December.

Programs are run with a lead car ahead of the students. The instructor is in the lead car with two students following single file about six to eight car lengths apart. The lead instructor car is in radio contact with a flagger, pit road instructor, and coordinator.

Driving experiences are available for those at least eighteen years of age with a valid driver's license and the ability to drive a vehicle equipped with a standard transmission.

Fans at least sixteen years of age can participate in the Ride-Along Experience. Riders under eighteen years of age must be accompanied by their parent or legal guardian.

For information on the program, call ☎ (407) 939-0130 or ☎ (800) 237-3889.

On the Water

Walt Disney World Marinas

Walt Disney World offers the country's largest fleet of pleasure boats, more than many navies of the world. There are three major areas: the Seven Seas Lagoon, which sits between the Magic Kingdom and the Ticket and Transportation Center and is surrounded by the monorail; Bay Lake, the largest body of water, which includes Discovery Island; and the Buena Vista Lagoon, a thirty-five-acre body of water that fronts on Pleasure Island and Disney Village.

Marinas are located at the **Contemporary Resort**, **Fort Wilderness**, **Polynesian Resort**, **Grand Floridian**, **Caribbean Beach**, **Yacht Club**, and **Beach Club**. You'll also find a rental counter at **Disney Village**, where a variety of boats are available for rental to day visitors as well as guests at Disney resorts. In the summer waiting lines for boats can become lengthy at midday.

Guests at some of the Disney resorts can purchase a pass that includes unlimited use of boats during their stay; if you're planning to make use of Disney's navy more than twice during a week-long stay, the pass will save you money.

Parasailing. The sky is the limit for parasailing adventures high above Bay Lake. Single and tandem fliers get a bird's-eye view of the Magic Kingdom at altitudes nearing six hundred feet for seven to ten minutes. Instead of the usual water approach, the special boats permit take-off and landing from the back of the craft. For reservations, ☎ (407) 939-0754.

People-Power. One-person pedal boats, rented for about $8 an hour, are available at most marinas. Canoes for canal paddling can be rented at the Fort Wilderness Bike Barn ☎ (407) 824-2742 for about $4 per hour, or $10 for the day.

Slow Boats. Pontoon Flote Boats putter about, very slowly, from Disney Village and other resort marinas. Rentals cost $30 per half hour. You may also be offered Water Mice boats, which replaced the Canopy Boats, these rent for about $20 per half hour.

Sailboats. Wind-powered vessels, from little two-seater Sunfish and speedy Hobie Cat catamarans to heavier six-seater Capris are available at Contemporary, Polynesian, Grand Floridian, Fort Wilderness, Yacht Club, and Beach Club marinas. Prices range from about $10 to $15 per hour.

Boating away. The Kissimmee Waterway, a fifty-mile-long series of lakes, connects Lake Tohopekaliga with Lake Okeechobee and, through that body of water, with both the Atlantic Ocean and the Gulf of Mexico. There are boat ramps at Granada (2605 Ridgeway Drive) and Partin Triangle Park on Lake Tohopekaliga, and at Sexton on Fish Lake (2590 Irlo Bronson Memorial Hwy. [I-192]), all in Kissimmee.

Hunting and fishing licenses. Fishing (fresh and saltwater) and hunting licenses for persons sixteen and older may be obtained from the Osceola County Tax Collector's office. More information is available from the Florida Game and Fresh Water Commission at ☎ (407) 846-5300 or the Florida Marine Patrol (saltwater fishing) at ☎ (800) 342-5367.

Water Skiing. Sammy Duvall's Water Sports Centre at the marina at the Contemporary Resort offers a variety of water sports including water skiing, kneeboarding, and wakeboarding on Bay Lake near the Magic Kingdom with guidance from a professional instructor. The rate in 2001 was $125 per hour for up to five guests. For information, call ☎ (407) 939-0754.

Water Mice. Small and low-powered, they're still zippy enough to be a lot of fun. They rent by the half hour for about $20; children younger than twelve are not allowed to drive. Available at Contemporary, Polynesian, Grand Floridian, Fort Wilderness, and Disney Village.

General information on many water activities is available by calling ☎ (407) 824-2222. You can also call the Fort Wilderness Marina at ☎ (407) 824-2757.

Guided Pontoon Cruises

Nightly guided pontoon cruises, timed to coincide with nighttime shows at Epcot and on Bay Lake are offered at several resorts.

Each night a pontoon boat, with a capacity of up to fifteen persons, departs any of the lakeside resorts for a circle of Bay Lake; the charge (with a driver) is $120 for a party of up to ten persons. A moonlight pontoon cruise on Bay Lake, including champagne and snacks, costs $175 for up to seven persons, and $230 for up to twelve guests.

Each evening a pontoon boat departs Disney's Yacht Club at 8:40 P.M. for a visit to Crescent Lake and the World Showcase with a great view of the nightly IllumiNations show at Epcot. The cost is $160. A similar cruise, at the same price, leaves the Boardwalk resort. For information, call ☎ (407) 939-7529.

Fishing Within Walt Disney World

Though not quite a Florida wilderness experience, there's still some pretty good fishing to be had on Bay Lake, Lake Buena Vista, Crescent Lagoon, and other waterways within Walt Disney World.

Trophy-sized largemouth bass in the fourteen-pound range lurk in lakes and canals almost within casting distance of Cinderella Castle.

During construction of the Magic Kingdom in the late 1960s, more than seventy thousand bass fingerlings were released into Bay Lake and Seven Seas Lagoon. Organized fishing tours didn't start until 1977, leaving the bass to grow and breed undisturbed for years.

Water, water everywhere. Not to drink, but to swim in, boat and water-ski on, and parasail over. In addition to the offerings within Walt Disney World, there are numerous places for aquatic recreation in the Orlando area.

Turkey Lake Park offers sand beaches, swimming pool, and nature trails. For general information, call ☎ (407) 299-5594.

You can rent a houseboat for cruising on the Saint John's River through **Hontoon Landing Marina** at ☎ (800) 248-2474.

Experienced divers can explore the Atlantic or Gulf Coasts or inland springs with equipment from **The Dive Station.** Call them at ☎ (407)) 843-3483.

The result is some spectacular fishing that has even caught the attention of professional bass fishermen. Three professional bass fishing events—FINS, Bass & Race, and Bass & Golf—have been held on Bay Lake and Seven Seas Lagoon and televised on ESPN. The heaviest largemouth bass caught and recorded at the Vacation Kingdom was fourteen pounds, six ounces.

Two-hour guided tours are offered daily on an advance-reservation basis, using pontoon boats. Boats are fully stocked with rods, reels, cold drinks, and a camera to prove you're not telling "fish stories."

Tours start at Disney's Polynesian, Contemporary, Grand Floridian, Wilderness Lodge, and Fort Wilderness resort docks on Bay Lake and Seven Seas Lagoon; at Disney's Yacht Club and Beach Club resorts and Disney's BoardWalk on Crescent Lake; and at Downtown Disney Marketplace and Disney's Port Orleans Resort.

A party of up to five people can participate in the catch-and-release tour. No fishing license is required. In 2001 a tour cost $160 for the whole party.

Disney also offers a two-hour guided experience designed just for children ages five to twelve. Cost is $30 per child.

For information and reservations for a fishing tour as much as two weeks in advance, call ☎ (407) 939-7529 and choose option 4.

Guests at Fort Wilderness or Disney Village can fish from the shore or on any of the canals. Equipment is available for rent at the Bike Barn (rods and reels) or at the Fort Wilderness trading posts (cane poles and lures).

Finally, there is the **Fishin' Hole on Ol' Man Island** at Disney's Dixie Landings Resort hotel. The hole is stocked with bass, blue gill, and even catfish; they'll provide bamboo poles and bait. After all that, though, you'll have to return the fish to the pond after you catch them; this fishin' hole is just for sport. The cost is about $4 per hour, with a family rate of about $13.25 for up to six people. For information, call ☎ (407) 934-5409.

Pool and Beach Swimming

Guests at Disney resorts are surrounded by water, with swimming encouraged almost everywhere. There are more than five miles of white sand beach along the shores of **Bay Lake** and **Seven Seas Lagoon**. Both bodies were engineered by Disney; sand was mined from beneath the lake muck during construction.

Beaches can be found at Contemporary, Grand Floridian, Caribbean Beach, Fort Wilderness, Polynesian, Yacht Club, and Beach Club resorts. At certain times of the year, swimming may be restricted because of environmental or health concerns because of algae and natural bacteria growth; check with the resort for information.

All of the hotels within Walt Disney World offer swimming pools, some more exotic than others. For example, water slides can be found at the Polynesian and Caribbean Beach Resorts. Use of these pools is restricted to guests at Disney resorts.

Day guests looking for cooling water are encouraged to visit River Country, Typhoon Lagoon, or Blizzard Beach.

Snorkeling

Swim with the fishes: leopard and nurse sharks, rays, rainbows of tropical fish, and an upside down sunken ship—without venturing into the ocean. **Shark Reef** at Disney's Typhoon Lagoon water park offers guests the opportunity to explore in snorkel gear, free with admission to Typhoon Lagoon.

For an extra charge, guests can arrange for a supplied-air (scuba assisted) snorkeling program. For information, call ☎ (407) 824-4321.

Surfing

Never mind that Walt Disney World is fifty miles inland; you can still learn to hang ten. **Craig Carroll's Cocoa Beach Surf School** conducts classes at Typhoon Lagoon's 2.75-million-gallon wave pool Tuesday mornings from 6:30 to 9 A.M. before the park opens to the public.

The pool produces waves from three to six feet high every ninety seconds—and no sharks are allowed. Classes are available to any strong swimmer older than age eight; boards are provided.

According to Carroll, 70 percent of participants have never surfed, and 90 percent "hang ten" by the end of the class.

The two-and-a-half-hour lesson, priced at $125 is conducted in the wave pool at the water park; surfboards are included. For information call ☎ (407) 939-7529.

Out and About

Tennis Courts Within the Park

For information on tennis clinics and instruction, call Disney's recreation information at ☎ (407) 939-7529. Instruction, including **Peter Burwash International** courses, are presented at the Grand Floridian, Disney's Contemporary Resort, and the Disney Institute.

Disney's Contemporary Resort. ☎ (407) 824-3578. **The Racquet Club** has six lighted clay courts, open to all resort guests from 7 A.M. to 6 P.M. Rates are $15 per court per hour, or $50 per family for the duration of the stay. Racquets and ball machines are available for rent.

Disney's Grand Floridian Beach Resort. ☎ (407) 824-3000. Two groomed clay courts are available to resort guests by reservation from 8 A.M. to 9 P.M. Rates are $15 per court per hour, $50 to play against the Pro, and $30 (for a half-hour private) to $60 (for a one-hour private) lesson. Racquets and ball machines are available for rent.

Disney's Yacht Club & Beach Club Resort. ☎ (407) 934-7000. Two hard courts available to all resort guests from 7 A.M. to 10 P.M. for no charge; no reservations are taken.

Disney's Fort Wilderness Homes/Campgrounds. ☎ (407) 824-2742. Two hard courts are available to resort and day guests from 8 A.M. to 5 P.M. for no charge; no reservations are taken. Racquets available for rent.

Horseback Riding

Trail rides depart from the Trail Blaze Corral at Fort Wilderness campground several times a day. Riders must be at least nine years old; the horses are very gentle, and experience is not required for the forty-five-minute guided tour. Only one rider per horse is permitted, and there is a weight limitation of 250 pounds. The rides cost about $23. Call ☎ (407) 824-2832 between 8 A.M. and 3:30 P.M. for information and reservations.

Hayrides

A hay wagon leaves Pioneer Hall at Fort Wilderness every night at 7 and 9 P.M. for a forty-five-minute tour. Tickets are sold by the driver.

Biking Within Walt Disney World

More than eight miles of bicycle paths can be found at Fort Wilderness and at the Disney Village Resort; other places to bike include some of the spread-out resorts such as Caribbean Beach. In an unusual departure for Disney entertainment, use of the paths is free—that is, if you bring your own bike. You can pick up maps wherever bicycles are rented.

Rental bikes can be engaged at the Bike Barn at Fort Wilderness, the Villa Center at Disney Village, or the marina at Caribbean Beach. Rates are about $5 per hour or $12 per day; tandems (bicycles built for two) can be rented at the **Bike Barn**. Call ☎ (407) 939-7529 for information.

Port Orleans and Dixie Landings. A two-and-a-half-mile tour around the Carriage Path and along the riverfront. Dixie Landings: single or tandem bikes at Dixie Levee near the marina. Port Orleans: single or tandem bikes at Port Orleans Landing near the marina.

Fort Wilderness Resort and Campground. More than eight miles of roads and trails in and among forests, beaches, trails, waterways, and boardwalks. Single and tandem bikes are available at the Bike Barn.

Disney's Village Resort and Disney Vacation Club. Easy riding along the golf course, waterways, and residential streets of the resort. You'll have to share the road with cars, buses, golf carts, and joggers. At this location bicycles are available for rental only to guests at a resort within the park. **Village Resort:** single bikes at the Reception Center. **Vacation Club:** single and tandem bikes at **Hank's Rent 'n Return**.

Disney's Caribbean Beach Resort. A leisurely, flat circuit around Barefoot Bay Lake, including bridges to Parrot Cay Island and other interesting destinations. Rent single bicycles at the **Barefoot Boat Yard**.

Jogging

Lace 'em up for a run on one of Walt Disney World Resort's scenic jogging trails. A sylvan 2.2-mile trail offers guests a view of Disney's Fort Wilderness Resort and Campground. There's a 1.8-mile pathway through the landscape at Disney Institute. The 1.4-mile promenade around the lake at Disney's Caribbean Beach Resort is ideal for jogging. Small jogging trails are offered at Disney's Contemporary Resort, Disney's Polynesian Resort, and Disney's Grand Floridian Resort and Spa. You can also take a leisurely three-quarter-mile stroll on the promenade that surrounds Crescent Lake and connects the Epcot resorts.

Walt Disney World Marathon

Disney theme parks become part of the "playing field" when thousands of marathoners traverse a magical course past landmarks of the world in Epcot, down a Tinseltown boulevard at Disney–MGM Studios, and through a storybook castle at the Magic Kingdom as part of the Walt Disney World Marathon. The annual 26.2-mile run is scheduled in early January of each year; in 2002 the event is scheduled for January 6.

There's also a Family Fun Run 5K race, a half-marathon, and a two-day Health and Fitness Expo at Disney's Wide World of Sports complex.

Registration begins ten months before the race, in March of each year. Slots are limited to the first thirteen thousand athletes for the marathon and the first five thousand for the half marathon. In 2001 both races reached capacity by five months before the event. In 2002 fees are $75 for the marathon and $45 for the half-marathon. Registration can be done on-line at 💻 www.runningnetwork.com or 💻 www.disneyworldsports.com. A paper application can be requested by calling ☎ (407) 939-7810.

Disney Health Clubs

Disney's BoardWalk Inn & Villas. Muscles and Bustles Health Club. Nautilus, circuit training, steam rooms, massage. Open daily 6 A.M. to 9 P.M.

Disney's Contemporary Resort. Olympiad Fitness Center. Nautilus, circuit training, cardiovascular, sauna, massage, tanning booths. Open daily from 6:30 A.M. to 8 P.M.

Disney's Grand Floridian Beach Resort. Spa & Health Club. Whirlpools, saunas, steam rooms, couples treatment room, personal training, massage therapies, body treatments including facials, watery therapy and soaks, manicures, pedicures, and leg treatments. Open daily 6 A.M. to 9 P.M. For reservations call ☎ (407) 843-3000.

Disney's Yacht & Beach Club Resorts. Ship Shape Health Club. Nautilus, cardiovascular equipment, weight training, sauna, spa, steam room, massages. Open daily 6 A.M. to 9 P.M.

Disney's Old Key West Resort. Exercise Room. Nautilus, free weights, massages. Open 6:30 A.M. to midnight.

The Villas at the Disney Institute. Spa & Fitness Center. Cybex, cardiovascular equipment private treatment rooms, steam room, sauna, whirlpool. Open daily 6 A.M. to 8 P.M. Call ☎ (407) 827-4429 for reservations.

Chapter 22
Outside Walt Disney World: Participant and Spectator Sports

Walt Disney World is not the only game in town: there's also professional baseball, basketball, football, and, if you can believe it, ice hockey.

Major and Minor League Baseball and Spring Training

Spring Training is a dream fulfilled for the serious baseball fan and an enjoyable sojourn for the casual observer. You are so close to the superstars of baseball, the young hopefuls trying for a one-in-a-million spot on a major league roster, as well as some of the greats of yesteryear soaking up the spring sunshine as coaches. Listen to the enthusiastic chatter of the ball players—talk of "taters" (home runs) and "hacks" (swings) and "beep" (batting practice).

There are two parts to Florida's Grapefruit League: the training and the not-quite-prime-time practice games. Pitchers and catchers usually arrive in Florida in mid-February to work themselves into shape with exercise and steadily lengthening throwing sessions. Their teammates usually arrive a week or two later. In general the teams can be found at their practice fields each morning until early afternoon; check with the Spring Training sites before heading out. At most parks there is no admission charge for the workouts, and you may be able to wander in and among the superstars.

Most teams invite many of their upper-level minor league players as well as promising rookies to their camps; you'll see uniform numbers as high as 99.

Practice games begin about March 1, and most early games take place in the afternoon. Toward the end of the season, in early April, some games may be scheduled under the lights. Teams tend to play nearby neighbors to cut down on travel time; some of the games are "split squad," meaning that half of the large preseason roster may be playing elsewhere at the same time.

Ticket prices range from about $5 to 12. You can usually obtain tickets as late as the day of the game, except for the more popular matchups, such as Yankees versus Mets or Mets versus Red Sox.

If you're a golfer you might want to check out a course near one or another of the training camps; many players and coaches share that sport and can be found on the links in the afternoon.

Once the big leaguers depart, many leave behind their minor league farm teams who play a full summer season in the Florida League.

As we know, of course, Disney wants it all, and so it came as little surprise to learn that Walt Disney World has snared a major-league team of its own—at least as a Spring Training tenant. The Atlanta Braves make their Florida base at Disney's Wide World of Sports. *See Chapter 21 for more details.*

Outside the theme park, other nearby training camps are for the Houston Astros, Kansas City Royals, Florida Marlins, and Detroit Tigers.

Spring Training Camps Near Orlando

Tickets for many Spring Training events can be purchased through the Ticketmaster website, at 🖳 www.ticketmaster.com.

Atlanta Braves. The Braves train at Disney's Wide World of Sports within Walt Disney World. For information, call ☎ (407) 363-6600.

Houston Astros. Osceola County Stadium, 1000 Bill Beck Boulevard, Kissimmee. ☎ (407) 933-5400. Tickets $7 to $12. The Osceola County Stadium and Sports Complex is also the summer home of the Osceola Astros of the Florida State League at the Class A professional level; their season is in the summer. The complex includes a 5,120-seat stadium plus four other practice fields as well as clubhouse and training facilities.

Kansas City Royals. Baseball City Stadium, 300 Stadium Way, Davenport. ☎ (941) 424-2424. Tickets: $6 to $10.

Florida Marlins. Space Coast Stadium, 5800 Stadium Parkway, Melbourne. ☎ (407) 633-9200. Tickets: $5 to $15.

Detroit Tigers. Joker Marchant Stadium, Lakeland Hills Boulevard, Lakeland. ☎ (941) 688-7911. Tickets: $5 to $10.

Other Grapefruit League Teams in Florida

Baltimore Orioles. Fort Lauderdale Stadium, 5301 N.W. Twelfth Avenue, Fort Lauderdale. ☎ (954) 776-1921. Tickets: $6 to $9; box seats, are $12. Ticketmaster: ☎ (954) 523-3309.

Boston Red Sox. City of Palms Park, 2201 Edison Avenue, Fort Myers. ☎ (941) 334-4700. Tickets: $10 to $11.

Cincinnati Reds. Ed Smith Stadium, Twelfth and Tuttle, Sarasota. ☎ (941) 955-6501. Tickets: $5 to $12. Standing room tickets, $4.

Cleveland Indians. Chain O' Lakes Stadium, Winter Haven. Call ☎ (863) 293-3900 for information or ☎ (407) 839-3900 for tickets. Tickets: $5 to $21.

L.A. Dodgers. Holman Stadium, Dodgertown, 4101 Twenty-sixth Street, Vero Beach. ☎ (561) 569-6858. Tickets: $5 to $12. Standing room tickets, $5, available for sold-out games.

Minnesota Twins. Lee County Sports Complex, 14100 Six Mile Cypress Parkway, Fort Myers. ☎ (800) 338-9467 or call ☎ (612) 338-9467 in Minnesota. Tickets: $9 to $12.

Montreal Expos. Roger Dean Stadium, 4751 Main Street, Jupiter. The Expos share facilities with the Saint Louis Cardinals. ☎ (561) 775-1818. Tickets: $6 to $18.

New York Mets. Thomas J. White Stadium, 525 N.W. Peacock Boulevard, Port Saint Lucie. ☎ (561) 871-2115. Tickets: $6 to $15.

New York Yankees. Tampa's Yankee Stadium at Legends Field, 3802 Martin Luther King Boulevard, Tampa. A modern ten-thousand-seat home; tickets sell quickly. Call ☎ (800) 969-2657 for ticket information. Tickets $8 or $10.

Philadelphia Phillies. Jack Russell Memorial Stadium, 800 Phillies Way, Clearwater. ☎ (813) 442-8496. Tickets: $9 to $12.

Pittsburgh Pirates. McKechnie Field, 1750 Ninth Street, West Bradenton. ☎ (941) 748-4610. Tickets: $6 to $9.

Saint Louis Cardinals. Municipal Stadium. 715 Hank Aaron Drive, West Palm Beach. Tickets: $5 to $15.

Tampa Bay Devil Rays. Al Lang Stadium, 180 Second Avenue S.E., Saint Petersburg. ☎ (813) 825-3137. Tickets: about $8 to $12.

Texas Rangers. Charlotte County Stadium, 2300 El Jobean Road, Port Charlotte. ☎ (941) 625-9500. Tickets: $7 to $9.

Toronto Blue Jays. Dunedin Stadium at Grant Field, 311 Douglas Avenue, Dunedin. ☎ (813) 733-0429. Tickets: $8 to $10.

NBA Basketball

The **Orlando Magic** of the National Basketball Association play at the Orlando Arena from October to April of each year.

The arena, which opened in 1989, seats 15,291 for basketball and includes a spectacular video screen used for replays and special encouragements to the fans. Tickets have been easier to obtain in recent years as the team's fortunes have waned. For ticket information call ☎ (407) 916-2255. Seats may be available at the Orlando Arena, through Ticketmaster for a fee by calling ☎ (407) 839-3900, or on-line at 🖳 www.nba.com/magic.

IHL Hockey

Professional hockey in Orlando? That's the concept for the **Orlando Solar Bears,** the southernmost member of the International Hockey League. The team plays at the Orlando Arena in a season that runs from late October through early May. For information call ☎ (407) 872-7825 or consult 🖳 www.ihlsolarbears.com.

Tickets are available at the Orlando Arena box office or through Ticketmaster for a service charge by calling ☎ (407) 839-3900. And the **Solar Bears Ice Den** at the RDV Sportsplex is open to the public for ice skating. For information call ☎ (407) 916-2550.

Arena Football League

The **Orlando Predators** play a fourteen-game schedule at the Orlando Arena from mid-April through August. The league features eight-man "Ironman" football on a fifty-yard indoor field; with the exception of the quarterback and an offensive specialist, players must play both offense and defense. Tickets are priced from $7.50 to $37. ☎ (407) 648-4444. 🖳 www.orlandopredators.com.

The Citrus Bowl

The **Florida Citrus Bowl Classic** college football game is held at the seventy-thousand-seat stadium on New Year's Day, pitting the champions of the Big Ten Conference against the South Eastern Conference (SEC). For information, call ☎ (407) 849-2500 or consult 🖳 www.fcsports.com.

Greyhound Racing

Melbourne Greyhound Park. Put your money on the dogs. Evening races Wednesday, Friday, and Saturday; matinees Monday, Wednesday, Thursday, Saturday, and Sunday. The track is located in Melbourne. ☎ (407) 259-9800. 🖳 www.fldncgreyhounds.com.

Sanford-Orlando Kennel Club. Racing from November 1 through May 2, nightly at 7:30 P.M. except Sunday, and matinees Monday, Wednesday, and Saturday at 12:30 P.M. General admission, $1; clubhouse, $2. A new clubhouse opened in late 2000. The track is located at 301 Dog Track Road, Longwood. ☎ (407) 831-1600. 🖳 www.orlandogreyhoundracing.com.

Seminole Greyhound Park. Nightly in May and June at 7:30 P.M. except Sunday and Tuesday; matinees Monday, Wednesday, and Saturday at 12:30 P.M. Clubhouse $2, grandstand free. Located at 2000 Seminola Boulevard, Casselberry. ☎ (407) 699-4510.

Roller and Ice Skating

Orlando Iceplex. Spectacular lighting, sound, a DJ . . . and indoor ice skating. 7500 Canada Avenue, off International Drive near Sand Lake Drive. ☎ (407) 352-0613. 🖳 www.iceplexholding.com/Orlando.htm.

Skate Reflections. Roller skate to the latest music on seventeen thousand square feet of solid maple floor. Located at 1111 Dyer Boulevard, Kissimmee. ☎ (407) 846-8469. 🖳 users.kua.net/~sk8.

Fishing

Backcountry Charter Service. Inshore saltwater trips on the Indian River near the Kennedy Space Center and on the Saint John's River. ☎ (407) 668-5516. 🖳 www.floridabackcountry.com.

Bass Anglers Guide Service. ☎ (407) 656-1052. 🖳 www.fishing-boating.com/bassanglers.

Bass Challenger Guide Service. ☎ (407) 273-8045 or ☎ (800) 241-5314.

Cutting Loose Expeditions. Freshwater and saltwater expeditions. ☎ (407) 629-4700 or ☎ (800) 533-4746. 🖳 www.gorp.com/cutloose.htm.

Horseback Riding

Grand Cypress Equestrian Center. $45 trail rides and $100 (for experienced riders only) for trail rides, private lessons $55 half hour, $100 hour. Located at

1 North Jacaranda, off Route 535, Orlando. ☎ (407) 239-1938 or ☎ (800) 835-7377. www.grandcypress.com.

Rodeo

Kissimmee Rodeo. Every Friday from 8 to 10 P.M. Adults, $15; children, $7. Located at the Kissimmee Sports Arena, 958 South Hoagland Boulevard. ☎ (407) 933-0020. www.ksarodeo.com.

Silver Spurs Rodeo. ☎ (407) 847-5118 for tickets; ☎ (407) 847-4052 for information. Kissimmee. The largest rodeo east of the Mississippi, with bull and bronco riding, steer wrestling, and more, is held for one weekend in mid-February and early October only. The Silver Spurs began in March 1944 during World War II as a fundraising event to sell war bonds.

Bungee Jumping

The Orlando area seems to feature more bungee-jumping establishments than you could shake a tourist at; it's a very changeable industry, with cranes or towers moving from one open lot to another. If this is the sort of thing you're looking for cruise Irlo Bronson Highway or International Drive, and look up.

Boating and Cruises

Airboat Rentals U-Drive. Adults, $27 per airboat up to four adults; electric boats $22 for up to six adults. Airboats, electric boats, and canoes available for rental and use in a cypress swamp. Located at 4266 West Highway 192, Kissimmee. ☎ (407) 847-3672. www.airboatrentals.com.

Boggy Creek Airboats. Guided tours in Florida wilderness; night alligator hunts available in summer. Adult, $16.95; children (3–12), $10. Located at 3701 Big Bass Road, Kissimmee. ☎ (407) 344-9550. www.bcairboats.com.

Rivership *Romance*. Cruises on 110-foot vessel on the Saint John's River. Dinner cruises Friday and Saturday nights ($50 all tickets); no children younger than sixteen. Adult, $35; child, $25 for three-hour lunch cruise; adult $45, child $35 for four-hour lunch trip. Located at 433 North Palmetto Avenue, Sanford. ☎ (407) 321-5091. www.rivershipromance.com.

Blimps, Hot Air Balloons, and Sightseeing Flights

Kissimmee Aviation Services. Aerial tours of central Florida. All passengers $41 for one to three persons for half-hour flight; $82 for one-hour flight. Located at 3031 West Patrick Street, Kissimmee. ☎ (407) 847-9095.

Orange Blossom Balloons. One-hour sunrise champagne hot air balloon flights over central Florida and the theme parks. Adults, $165; children (10–16), $95 with adult. Departs from the Days Inn Maingate West, near Disney. ☎ (407) 239-7677. www.orangeblossomballoons.com.

Rise & Float Balloon Tours. Adults, $165; children, $85. $85 introductory offer. Located at 5767 Major Boulevard, Orlando. ☎ (407) 352-8191.

Skyscapes Balloon Tours. Sunrise champagne brunch flights. Adults, $175. www.skyscapesballoontours.com. Located at 5755 Cove Drive, Orlando. ☎ (407) 856-4606.

Part VII
Attractions and Shopping In Kissimmee and Central Florida

Chapter 23
Gatorland, Skull Kingdom, Splendid China, and Other Attractions

Orlando-Kissimmee Attractions

Gatorland

Gatorland is about as real a place and as un-Disney a theme park as you are likely to find in Central Florida, and it is one of our favorite places in the world. It is, quite simply, a shrine to the alligator, and when they say they have the world's largest collection of the fascinatingly creepy creatures, they're not exaggerating: there are thousands of them at every turn in this fifty-acre park.

Gatorland is one of the older attractions in Central Florida, dating back to 1949. During the years, the park has grown from a handful of alligators with a few huts and pens into the Alligator Capital of the World and an active breeding station. You'll stroll along a boardwalk through a cypress swamp to see gators, herons, and dozens of other wild creatures. Other creatures on display include snakes, deer, goats, talking birds, and even a Florida bear. Semi-brave visitors can even "pet" an alligator—a baby with his mouth taped shut.

The park is also a mecca for birdwatchers, with thousands of native birds nesting in the area, making use of the alligators as protectors of their nests from natural predators such as raccoons and opossums.

The **Jungle Crocs of the World** display features Nile, Cuban, American, and Australian saltwater crocodiles in a swamp-like setting. Visitors meander through the swamp on a raised walkway. Each of the species of crocodiles has a slightly different stalking behavior, according to Gatorland experts. Cuban crocs tend to attack on land, while their saltwater cousins usually hide under the surface of the water and explode out to snap at any tempting target.

A walk-in aviary that is home to a flock of Australian Lories that may come to perch on your hand.

Florida "Crackers" (the term comes from the sound made by bullwhips cracking over the heads of cattle) were the first alligator wrestlers—of necessity. They would often have to fight gators that had grabbed calves for a

A trainer gets up close and personal at Gatorland
Photo courtesy Orlando/Orange County Convention & Visitors Bureau

snack. At Gatorland you'll see an exhibition of stunt wrestling in the eight-hundred-seat **Wrestlin' Stadium**. Another highlight is the **Gator Jumparoo**, where giant alligators as big as fifteen feet and one thousand pounds jump out of the water to be hand fed.

The park includes an alligator breeding marsh, a three-story observation tower, the **Gatorland Express Railroad**, and the **Snakes of Florida** show.

Lilly's Pad is a small water park for kids.

Gatorland also offers a line of alligator boots, belts, wallets, and meat. Yes, meat: **Pearl's Smoke House** offers smoked alligator ribs, deep fried gator nuggets, and gator chowder. We tried the nuggets: they (of course) taste just like chicken.

Rumors are afoot for a major expansion of the park that could double its size, although it would retain its quirky character as the alligator kingdom.

Open daily from 9 A.M. to dusk. Visitors should allow several hours; to catch the full cycle of shows, we'd suggest arriving early or at lunchtime. Tickets in 2001 were $17.93 for adults, $8.48 for children ages three to twelve. Various combination tickets are available with other smaller attractions in the area.

Located at 14501 South Orange Blossom Trail (S.R. 441) in Orlando, about a twenty-minute drive from Walt Disney World. ☎ (407) 855-5496 or ☎ (800) 393-5297. 💻 www.gatorland.com.

Green Meadows Farm

The ultimate petting farm for children of all ages, Green Meadows Farm includes a two-hour guided tour with introductions to more than three hundred animals including pigs, cows, goats, sheep, donkeys, chickens, turkeys, ducks, and geese. Everyone gets to milk a cow, and children can go for pony rides, a tractor-pulled hayride, and a ten-minute train ride.

This is a lovely place for animal lovers of all ages to while away a warm afternoon; the farm setting could not be more different than a theme park with real oohs and aahs at every turn. On one of our visits the tour came to a complete halt in front of a pen occupied by three-day-old Vietnamese potbelly pigs. My children fell in love with some of the exotic chickens, including a variety named *mille fleurs* ("thousand flowers") because of the intricate pattern on their back.

The farm is one of six similar operations around the country, the brainchild of Bob and Coni Keyes of Waterford, Wisconsin. It started in Wisconsin when that farm began to allow visitors to come and pick vegetables and raspberries. It expanded from that to allow urban youngsters to get up-close to farm animals. There are similar farms in Illinois, California, New Jersey, and New York.

The farm is located in the town of Kissimmee. Take I-192 east toward Kissimmee; turn right at Poinciana Boulevard and go five miles to the farm. Admission: $15; children under 2, free. Open every day but Thanksgiving and Christmas from 9:30 A.M. to 4 P.M. For information, call ☎ (407) 846-0770 or consult 🖳 www.greenmeadowsfarm.com.

Guinness World Records Experience

The Guinness book has long been the official recorder of things large and small and unusual; this attraction at The Mercado allows visitors to experience some of those celebrated oddities. Highlights of the exhibit include the Shrinkenator, where guests are seemingly miniaturized and transported on a journey inside a computer; the Molecular Expander, which expands guests to normalcy; a micro-playground of computer chips and circuit boards, including some of the latest video games; an inverted pyramid that provides a visual kaleidoscope of eighty different images depicting people who have achieved some of the most extreme human accomplishments; and Guinness Town, a multimedia streetscape of record holders.

Finally, guests can "ride the records" on a motion simulator.

Ticket prices in 2001 were $12.95 for adults; $7.95 for children (5–12). The attraction is located at 8445 International Drive. For information, call ☎ (407) 345-9337 or consult 🖳 www.themercado.com.

The Holy Land Experience

A "living Biblical museum" spread over fifteen acres near Universal Studios Florida, the Holy Land Experience opened in early 2001. The place re-creates in elaborate and authentic detail the city of Jerusalem and its religious importance between the years 1450 B.C. and A.D. 66. A cast of characters re-create stories and events included in the Bible.

In 2002 the **Scriptorium: Center for Biblical Antiquities** will open; the museum, built in the fourth-century Byzantine architectural style, will house a collection of biblical artifacts, ancient cuneiform, scrolls, and manuscripts.

The attraction is located at Conroy and Vineland roads, off exit 31A of Interstate 4. Open weekdays from 9 A.M. to 6 P.M., Friday and Saturday 9 A.M. to 9 P.M., and Sunday noon to 6 P.M. Admission: adult, $17; child (4–12), $12. For information, call ☎ (866) 872-4659 or ☎ (407) 872-2272 or consult 🖳 www.theholylandexperience.com.

Orlando Science Center

Orlando's science museum is a hands-on exploration of our environment and the universe. You'll be greeted by live animals in an eight-thousand-gallon cypress swamp. You can become a Cosmic Tourist in an exploration of space, or travel through the human body as a piece of food in BodyZone.

The Darden Adventure Theater features daily performances by the Einstein Players. The Dr. Phillips CineDome and planetarium offers a selection of Imax films and special presentations.

Adult, $9.50; child ages three to eleven, $6.75. Combo ticket including exhibits plus one film or planetarium show: adult, $12.50; child ages three to eleven, $9.25. Double combo including two films: adult, $14.50; child, $11.25. Senior tickets $1 off.

Located at 777 East Princeton Street, the center is open Tuesday through Thursday from 9 A.M. to 5 P.M., Friday and Saturday from 9 A.M. to 9 P.M., and Sunday from noon to 5 P.M. Closed Monday. For information, call ☎ (407) 514-2000 or ☎ (888) 672-4386 or consult 🖳 www.osc.org.

Orlando Science Center

Photo courtesy Orlando/Orange County Convention & Visitors Bureau

Ripley's Believe It or Not!

This is one strange place—something that will be immediately obvious when you look at the building; think of it as the leaning museum of Orlando and you'll get the idea. Among the oddities you'll find here are a replica of the *Mona Lisa* made from slices of toast, a 1907 Rolls-Royce constructed from more than a million matchsticks, and extraordinary humans, including the world's tallest man and Liu Ch'ung, the man with two pupils in each eye.

The Orlando branch of the chain of museums also includes a portion of the Berlin Wall, a reproduction of Van Gogh's self-portrait created from three thousand postcards, and a Disasters Gallery.

And the Orlando Ripley's even made it into the *Wall Street Journal* in late 1995 with a "believe it or not" of its own: eight of the twenty staffers at the museum became parents in a single year, each after touching an African fertility totem in the office lobby. A ninth pregnancy was a delivery woman for an air express company.

This is a must-see for visitors who have a taste for the bizarre; it's even stranger than a theme park that celebrates a talking mouse. Allow about ninety minutes for a self-guided tour. Located at 8201 International Drive, one block south of Sand Lake Road, the attraction is open daily from 9 A.M. to midnight. Adult, $12.95; child (4–12), $8.95. For information, call ☎ (407) 363-4418 or ☎ (800) 998-4418 or consult 🖳 www.ripleys.com/orlando2.htm.

Skull Kingdom

A haunted family attraction, this shrine to scarification stands at the top of International Drive, across from Wet 'n Wild. Enter, if you dare, through the Giant Skull Entrance. The theming never lets up, from the ticket booth within a giant winged dragon to a spider-web chandelier in the entry chamber where groups of visitors are divided into small groups to walk through the sprawling building.

The concept is "fun and fright," and it is accomplished with some high-tech apparatus, including hydraulics, smoke machines, robotics, and theatrical lighting. Live actors pop out of the walls and respond to the actions of visitors—without touching them. One of the final sections of the adventure presents a fully animated alien that will knock your knees extraterrestrially.

The Skull Kingdom is open weekdays from 6 to 11 P.M. and weekends from noon to 11 P.M. In July and August the attraction is open every day from noon to 11 P.M. Admission is $11.79; the recommended minimum age is 8. For information, call ☎ (407) 354-1564 or consult 🖳 www.skullkingdom.com.

Splendid China

A journey of ten thousand miles and five thousand years within a seventy-six-acre theme park that includes miniature replicas of The Great Wall of China, The Lunan Stone Forest, and The Forbidden City. Performances and exhibits include Chinese acrobats, artists, Mongolian wrestlers, and martial artists.

The park, which opened at the end of 1993, is a near-twin to the original Splendid China, which is located in Shenzhen, China, near Hong Kong.

The "Mysterious Kingdom of the Orient" show features more than seventy acrobats; it is performed nightly at 6 P.M. Tuesday through Sunday. Admission is included with a Splendid China ticket; separate tickets can also be purchased. If you visit the park on Monday you can use your admission ticket for a show later in the week.

A new cast of acrobats is rotated in every six months.

Areas of the park include **Suzhou Gardens**, a life-sized replica of a commercial street in the "water city" of Suzhou in eastern China of seven hundred years ago; construction of the city included construction techniques utilized by the Chinese of the twelfth and thirteenth centuries.

Near the entrance are some unusual **Tihu Stones**, rocks found in Tihu lake and other lakes in eastern China. The rock is much admired by the Chinese for its *shou* (slimness), *lou* (leaking), *znou* (folding), and *tou* (transparent) characteristics. The Chinese as a people greatly value mountain and water landscapes and go to a great deal of effort to create gardens to celebrate these themes; the Tihu stone is often used to re-create mountains in miniature.

The Great Wall of China, scaled down to a half-mile in length, includes six million replica bricks that were hand-laid by Chinese artisans. The Great Wall stretches 4,200 miles from east to west—wider than the entire continental United States. Beacon towers were built at regular intervals from which sentries could send smoke and fire signals if an enemy approached.

The grand 9,999-room **Imperial Palace** is the centerpiece of Beijing's **Forbidden City**. Built in 1420, it was the seat of power. The reproduction of the Forbidden City and Imperial Palace occupies a central location at the park.

The **Potala Palace** is a copy of the Lhasa capital of the Tibet region, built in the seventh century by King Song Song Gombo for his bride. The thirteen-story palace atop a cliff has one thousand rooms.

The spectacular **Leshan Buddha Statue** in Sichuan Province is located at a point where three rivers come together, creating turbulent waves and violent eddies that have caused many shipwrecks. More than a thousand years ago, a monk tried to end the disasters by carving a huge Buddha out of the hillside where the three rivers met. The 236-foot-tall statue was eventually completed. Two people can stand side-by-side in each of his ears, and more than one hundred people can sit on each of his feet.

One of the most spectacular sights in the park is the re-creation of the **Stone Forest**. Some 300 million years ago limestone was deposited in thick layers on the ocean floor; about 30 million years ago the seabed rose above sea level to reveal the stone, and over the course of the following centuries, the wind and rain have sculpted the limestone into a strange forest of nearly sixty-six thousand acres. Some of the stone forest peaks have been given vivid names such as "A Leisurely Stroller," "A Galloping Horse in the Sky," and "A Phoenix Combing Her Wings." Even in miniature, the reproduction towers over visitors.

The wonders of Splendid China also include the **Stone Sculptures of the Dazu Grottoes**, some fifty thousand statues. Although they were completed as early as the thirteenth century, they remained hidden until 1939. Most of the statues are dedicated to Buddhism, but others represent Taoism, Confucianism, and the ordinary life of the times.

A now-gone culture somehow built the **Cliffside Tombs of Eban** in southwest China some six hundred years ago; their well-preserved wood coffins still hang on cliffs, along with paintings of horse races, martial arts, dances, and religious activities.

The **Dai Village** includes reproductions of the simple but efficient bamboo homes of the Dai people, which include a form of climate control.

When the sun shines, the thatches of the roof curl upward and allow the sunlight in and the heat to escape; when it is raining the thatches absorb moisture and expand to seal the roof.

Every April the Dai celebrate a ceremony in which each man and woman takes a bucket of water and splashes each other in a joyous celebration that is hoped to bring good luck.

Splendid China
Photo courtesy of Orlando/Orange County Convention & Visitor Bureau

The **Guanyin Statue** is also known as "1,000 Eyes and 1,000 Hands." It celebrates the Bodhisattaba Buddha, a disciple of Buddha who was supposed to have sprouted all those eyes so he could see all human anguish and all the hands so he could appease the suffering.

The **Terra Cotta Warriors & Horses** display reproduces another wonder of China: the 1974 discovery of a hidden cave that had more than eight thousand life-sized and individually carved statues of soldiers and horses. The "army" was a guard of honor for the spirit of Quin Shihuang.

Restaurants include the **Hong Kong Seafood Restaurant**, offering Cantonese, Mandarin, Mongolian, Chiu Chow, Peking, Szechuan, and Hunan cuisine. Informal dining is also available at **The Seven Flavors** cafeteria in Suzhou Gardens.

Busy times at the park include spring and fall, plus Christmas and Chinese New Year in January or February.

Splendid China is open daily from 9:30 A.M. to 7 P.M. year-round; the Hong Kong restaurant remains open until 9 P.M.

The park throws itself a big two-week-long party for Chinese New Year's, which occurs near the end of January. Included are special athletic and musical entertainments and special dishes at the Suzhou Pearl.

At night the park takes on another dimension, with small white lights outlining the roof lines of the buildings in Suzhou Gardens, just as they do the buildings of the Forbidden City of Beijing.

The park is located on Splendid China Boulevard, two miles west of Disney World on U.S. 192. Admission, including tax, in 2001 was adult, $28.88; senior, $25.99; child, $18.18. A guided tour of the park by golf cart is available for $5.35 per person. You can also purchase an evening ticket to the "Mysterious Kingdom of the Orient" show for $16 for adults, or $10.65 for children. These prices are for the meal and show only, not park admission. If you pay the full ticket price of $28.88, you will receive the meal and show. For information, call ☎ (407) 396-7111 or consult 🖳 www.floridasplendidchina.com.

***Titanic*—Ship of Dreams**

The *Titanic* lives again in this high-tech re-creation of some of the more interesting details of the great ship, at the Mercado on International Drive.

The display includes more than two hundred artifacts from private collections, many on public display for the first time. Among them are a deck chair recovered from the Atlantic following the sinking, first-class china and dinnerware, personal letters on *Titanic* stationery that survived the sinking, and a life jacket.

Actors in period costume share stories of those aboard.

Also on display is memorabilia from the movie *Titanic*, including a costume worn by Leonardo DiCaprio, plus items from older classics, including *A Night to Remember* and *The Search for Titanic*, hosted by Orson Welles.

The controversial letter of deceased *Titanic* survivor Nellie Walcroft, purchased at auction in England, is shown. The letter sheds new light on the disaster and stirs up fresh controversy. Walcroft tells of the alleged shooting of some steerage passengers who attempted to find a place on one of the doomed *Titanic*'s lifeboats.

The attraction is located at 8445 South International Drive. In 2001, tickets were adult, $16.95; child, (6–11), $11.95. For information, call ☎ (407) 345-9337 or consult 🖳 www.themercado.com.

Wet 'n Wild

It's all in the name in this large water park, owned by nearby Universal Studios Florida. According to industry sources, Orlando's Wet 'n Wild is the busiest water park in the country, drawing about 1.3 million visitors in recent years, a bit more than Walt Disney World's Blizzard Beach and Typhoon Lagoon.

Although it doesn't have the Disney "theme" magic, Wet 'n Wild does have some of the wildest—and most unusual—water rides anywhere around.

Attractions at the park include **Bomb Bay**. Volunteers climb into a snug compartment shaped like a large bomb with fins and are slowly maneuvered onto a ledge hanging out over a six-story water slide. When the spring-loaded bomb bay doors open, the rider plunges into a near-freefall at speeds close to 30 miles per hour through an angled chute.

Blue Niagra features three hundred feet of intertwined looping slides that twist from six stories above the park to a splash landing. **The Surge** dispatches a four-passenger bouncing tube down a six-hundred-foot path including high banked turns.

Der Stuka, claimed to be one of the highest, fastest water slides in the world, sends riders in a freefall down a 250-foot slide, then allows them to coast to a stop along a 115-foot long water runway. At the **Black Hole** a two-person raft is propelled by a thousand-gallon-a-minute blast of water for a thirty-second runaway journey through five hundred feet of twisting, turning darkness.

Bubba Tub sends groups of five people splashing down a triple-dip slide. **The Flyer** is a watery toboggan run with eight-foot long toboggans.

At **Hydra Fighter**, riders sit in back-to-back swings equipped with water cannons. By regulating water pressure, they'll be able to control how high and fast the swing goes. Serious players can send their gondola on swings that get them swinging ninety degrees or more from perpendicular. About once an hour the area's lifeguards take to the ride to show amateurs how it's really done.

Our favorite here is **Knee Ski**. You'll snap on a life vest and a helmet and then plant your knees in a surfboard; then hold onto the handle for dear life as you are launched out onto the lake and towed by an overhead cable around a half-mile course. We've yet to see someone make it completely around on the first try, but after a few exciting tries, most visitors master the Knee Ski. My hotshot teenage daughter couldn't get enough of this unusual ride. I was perfectly happy to make it around once before retiring to a beach umbrella.

At **Wild One** you and a friend ride on a pair of bouncy tubes pulled around the pond by a jet-ski; there's an additional charge.

There's also the **Surf Lagoon** wave pool and the **Kids' Playground**, with smaller versions of the park's most popular rides.

Located at 6200 International Drive, just off I-4, the park is open year-round, dependent on weather conditions. For most of the year, the park is open until 5 P.M.; from June until Labor Day, Wet 'n Wild is open until 9, 10, or 11 P.M.

During summer nights from mid-June to early August, the park is open from 9 A.M. to 11 P.M., with a concert stage on the deck of the Surf Lagoon Wave Pool for nightly music and entertainment.

Admission: adult, $31.75; child (3–9), $25.39. Seniors (55 and older) are admitted for half-price. Ten dollars off the price of general admission is offered after 5 P.M. on nights the park is open late. Tubes rent for $4; towels are available for $2. For information, call ☎ (800) 992-9453 or ☎ (407) 351-1800 or consult 💻 www.wetnwild.com/orlando.

Other Attractions in Orlando, Kissimmee, and Nearby

Air Orlando Helicopter Service. 8990 International Drive. ☎ (407) 352-1753. Rides over SeaWorld, Universal Studios, Walt Disney World, and Orlando range from $15 to $395 per person with a minimum of two adult fares per flight.

Congo River Golf & Exploration Company. 6312 International Drive, next to Wet 'n Wild. Orlando. ☎ (407) 352-0042. 4777 West Highway 192, three miles east of I-4. Kissimmee. ☎ (407) 396-6900. A miniature golf course and more, with exploration games, an arcade, and go-carts (International Drive) or paddle boats (Kissimmee). Golf fees for Orlando, $7.50 for 18 holes, $10.95 for 36 holes; for Kissimmee, $7.50 for 18 holes, $11.50 for 36 holes; children younger than four years old, free. Open from 10 A.M.

Flying Tigers Warbird Air Museum. At Kissimmee Airport, off I-192 on Hoagland Boulevard. ☎ (407) 933-1942. 🖳 www.warbirdmuseum.com. An impressive collection of American warplanes in working condition or in the process of restoration by mechanics and artisans. The private collection features dozens of planes including a B-17 Flying Fortress bomber, P-51 Mustang fighter, and antique biplanes. Tour guides take you through the hangars. Open daily 9 A.M. until 5 P.M. Adult, $8; senior (over 60), $7; child (6–12), $6.

Haunted House at Old Town. 5770 West Irlo Bronson Highway. ☎ (407) 397-2231. 🖳 www.old-town.com. Two floors of spooks and special effects. Adult, $7; child (10 and younger), $5. Open noon to 11 P.M. daily.

Jungleland Zoo. 4580 West Irlo Bronson Highway, Kissimmee. ☎ (407) 396-1012. Primates, cats, birds, unusual animals from around the world, and indigenous animals of Florida are among more than five hundred animals on display. Open daily 9 A.M. to 6 P.M. adult, $11.95; child (4–12), $6.95.

Kartworld Kissimmee. 4708 West Irlo Bronson Highway, Kissimmee. ☎ (407) 396-4800. 5370 International Drive, Orlando. ☎ (407) 345-9225. Indy-style and double-seater go-karts on a nearly mile-long track that goes over and under bridges. $3.50 per lap. Children must be at least eleven years old.

Katie's Wekiva River Landing. 190 Katie's Cove, Sanford. ☎ (407) 628-1482. 🖳 www.ktland.com. Downstream canoe runs, with equipment rental and shuttle service. Open 7:45 A.M. to 7 P.M. Call for rates. Runs range from six to nineteen miles.

Malibu Grand Prix. 5863 American Way, Orlando. ☎ (407) 351-4132. Grand Prix–style fun in three-quarter-scale models of racing cars. Open in season Monday through Thursday noon to 10 P.M., Friday noon to midnight, Saturday 10 A.M. to midnight, and Sunday 10 A.M. to 10 P.M. Call for hours in off-season.

Monument of States. Lakefront Park, downtown Kissimmee. Erected in 1943, the Monument of States is a fifty-foot-tall solid concrete structure. More than 1,500 stones represent every state in the nation and twenty-one foreign countries. Minerals and ores include gold and silver, plus chrome, cobalt, copper, iron, lead, platinum, and zinc. Stones include agate, alabaster, alva, coquina, coral, diamond-bearing rocks, feldspar, flint, Florida keystone, granite, limestone, marble, meteors, mica, petrified wood, petrified teeth and bones, quartz, sandstone, schist, slate, stalactites, stalagmites, and travatia.

Mystery Fun House/Starbase Omega. 5767 Major Boulevard, Orlando. Across from the main gate of Universal Studios. ☎ (407) 351-3356. A houseful of surprises, including the Forbidden Temple, an Egyptian tomb, a miniature golf course, a video arcade and the wild "Ultimate Lazer Game—Starbase

Omega." Fun House tickets are $10.85 for all. Starbase Omega tickets are $9.95, available by reservation only. Miniature golf tickets are $4.95. Open from 10 A.M. to 9 P.M. daily; later in holiday periods.

Paintball World. 3445 Vineland Road, Orlando. ☎ (407) 396-4199. 🖳 www.paintball-world.com. A paintball preserve with trenches, forts, bases, spectator areas, concessions, and a pro shop (honest!). Open every day; reservations required during the week. About $25 per person, including one hundred paintballs.

Pirate's Cove Adventure Golf. 8501 International Drive, Orlando. ☎ (407) 352-7378. 2845 Florida Plaza Boulevard, Kissimmee. ☎ (407) 396-7484. 12545 S.R. 535, Crossroads Shopping Center, Lake Buena Vista. ☎ (407) 827-1242. 🖳 piratescove.net.

A clever pirate-theme golf course. In Orlando and Lake Buena Vista there are two 18-hole challenges. Captain Kidd's course: adult, $7.99; child (12 and younger), $6.99. Blackbeard's Challenge: adult, $8.49; child, $7.49. At the Kissimmee location, adult, $5.50; child, $4.

Pirate's Island Adventure Golf. 4330 West Irlo Bronson Highway, Kissimmee. ☎ (407) 396-4660. Two 18-hole courses set in a tropical paradise. Adults, $6 and $7; children, $4.50 and $5.50.

Race Rock. 8986 International Drive, Orlando. ☎ (407) 248-9876. 🖳 www.racerock.com. A restaurant packed with racing cars and memorabilia, including stock, funny, and Indy cars, plus monster trucks, hydroplanes, and dragsters. Open Sunday to Thursday from 11 A.M. to 10:30 P.M., Friday and Saturday until 11 P.M.

Church Street Station. Orlando's original downtown entertainment district, which predated Walt Disney World's Pleasure Island and Universal Studios Citywalk by twenty years, was on life support in mid-2001, a mere shadow of its once funky glory.

In mid-2001, all that remained was the south side of the street, including the **Cheyenne Saloon and Opera House, Crackers Seafood Restaurant,** and the **Buffalo Trading Post.**

Gone were Rosie O'Grady's Good Time Emporium, Apple Annie's Courtyard, Lili Marlene's Aviator's Pub and Restaurant, Phineas Phogg's Dance Club, and other operations.

A new owner was expected to announce redevelopment plans for the property; one possibility would result in an office building on the site.

Reptile World Serpentarium. 5705 East Irlo Bronson Highway, St. Cloud. ☎ (407) 892-6905. Cobras and other poisonous snakes. Open Tuesday through Sunday, 9 A.M. to 5:30 P.M. Adults, $5.50; students, $4.50; children (3–5), $3.50.

River Adventure Golf. 4535 West Irlo Bronson Highway. ☎ (407) 396-4666. Water-themed courses. All tickets $6.50; children younger than four, free.

SAK Comedy Lab. 380 West Amelia Street in downtown Orlando. ☎ (407) 648-0001. 🖳 www.sak.com. A small, informal storefront theater that features improvisational and scripted comedy shows. The young cast works without a net, and unlike the Comedy Warehouse at Pleasure Island, there are no Disney minders anywhere on the property. Two shows on Friday at 8 and 10 P.M. and three shows on Saturday at 8 P.M., 10 P.M., and midnight. General admission is $13.

Trainland. 8990 International Drive, Orlando, behind Pointe Orlando. ☎ (407) 363-9002. Toy trains from the 1920s to the present, one of the largest indoor model train layouts in the country, and a gift shop for collectors. Admission: adults, $8.95; seniors, $7.95; and children (3–12), $5.95.

Water Mania. 6073 West Irlo Bronson Highway. ☎ (407) 396-2626 or ☎ (800) 527-3092. 💻 www.watermania-florida.com. Catch a wave at this water park right on I-192 in Kissimmee, in and among many of the off-site hotels. The slides are not as artfully decorated as those at Typhoon Lagoon or as wet and wild as at Wet 'n Wild, but they're still fun. There's the Banana Peel two-person raft plunge, the Rain Forest children's water playground, and the Anaconda family raft ride. Open from early March to late October, 10 A.M. to 5 P.M. daily. Admission: all tickets, $16.95. Parking $5.

WonderWorks. Pointe*Orlando, International Drive, Orlando. ☎ (407) 351-8800. 💻 www.wonderworksonline.com. It's hard to miss this place, even in the midst of the wall-to-wall, grab-your-eye tourist district: it's the place that looks exactly like it has fallen from the sky and landed upside down on International Drive.

WonderWorks is a place where science has gone crazy—a sort of hands-on science museum for children of all ages. Here's the cover story: since the end of World War II, the super-secret WonderWorks laboratory has been located on a remote, uncharted island off Florida—within the Bermuda Triangle—and has served as a haven for investigators of the unexplainable. But in 1997 something went awry in a top-secret experiment to harness the power of a tornado: the energy vortex lifted the research lab from its foundations and dropped it, upside-down, in Orlando.

Inside the building you'll find hands-on demonstrations of the forces of nature, including a hurricane chamber, the Earthquake Experience, and an antigravity room. In the Physical Challenge Lab you can try out the Shocker Chair, test your coordination on a virtual balance beam, play virtual basketball, and arm wrestle a computer. In the UFO Lab you can split your image and distort your body, make music with a theramin or computer drums, and morph your voice.

Guests can also attend *Shazam*, a ninety-minute magic show and pizza dinner, offered nightly except Monday at 7 P.M.

Plan to stay for at least two hours in the building; Mom and Dad may want to shop next door. Admission: Adult, $15.95; child (4–12), $11.95. Admission and dinner magic show: adult, $28.95; child, $24.95.

A World of Orchids. 2501 Old Lake Wilson Road, Kissimmee. ☎ (407) 396-1887. 💻 www.aworldoforchids.com. Botanical gardens and an arboretum containing an ever-changing display of more than two thousand varieties of orchids which bloom throughout the year. Open daily except Monday from 9:30 A.M. to 4:30 P.M. Admission free.

Other Attractions Outside Orlando

Bok Tower Gardens. Florida's historic bell tower, centerpiece of a magnificent garden, is at Florida's highest point—all of 295 feet. Bok Tower Gardens was dedicated in 1929 to the American people by Dutch immigrant Edward Bok, Pulitzer Prize–winning editor of the *Ladies' Home Journal*. Some of the fifty-seven bronze bells weigh as much as twelve tons. The 128 acres of gardens include thousands of azaleas, camellias, magnolias, and other flowering plants. The gardens are home to a colony of wood ducks and more than one hundred other species of birds. A forty-five-minute carillon recital is presented daily at 3 P.M. Located in Lake Wales, about fifty-five miles south of Orlando, off U.S. 27 to Alternate 27, the gardens are open daily 8 A.M. to 5 P.M. Adult, $6; child, (5–12), $2. For information, call ☎ (941) 676-1408 or consult 🖳 www.boktower.org.

Cypress Gardens. Florida's first theme park, established in 1936, Cypress Gardens is home of the famous water-ski team, Dixie Belles in hoop skirts, and thousands of varieties of plants, birds, and other creatures. There's also much more in this lush, green park off U.S. 27 near Winter Haven, Florida, about forty-five minutes from Orlando. The famed botanical gardens include more than eight thousand varieties of plants from ninety countries.

New in the summer of 2001 was the **Wacky Water Park**, including slides and entertainments for kids and adults. Admission to the park, near Carousel Cove, is included in general admission to Cypress Gardens

The mid-sized attractions include **Flumarama**, home to five flumes. **Coral Reef** is an open flume ride with a twelve-foot drop into a splash pool.

The enclosed **Pineapple Pipeline** lets splashers bodysurf through forty-three feet of twists and turns. The wide-open blue **Barracuda Blaster** sports a swooping big bend. The **Rio Raceway** offers side-by-side racing slides. The largest ride is the **Typhoon Twister**, which drops 25 feet across a 170-foot-long speed tube. There's also a kiddie pool with six small slides.

Cypress Gardens has added dressing rooms and lockers. The water park is open daily during the summer from 10:30 A.M. until 5 P.M.

The ***Southern Breeze***, a re-created Old South paddle wheel boat, cruises from Port Cypress on Lake Eloise. The one-hundred-foot-long ship (designed to have a draft of only twenty-eight inches for the shallow lake) is a replica of a nineteenth-century Mississippi riverboat. It can carry as many as two hundred passengers.

The ship takes passengers on half-hour excursions on the lake; tickets are $5 for adults, $4 for seniors, and $2 for children (6–17).

The *Southern Breeze* also offers two-hour dinner cruises, with prices ranging from $11 to $20, and Sunday brunch cruises from $10 to $16.

Wings of Wonder is a walk-through glass conservatory that is home to more than one thousand free-flying butterflies from more than fifty species. Two glass-enclosed chrysalis houses contain unhatched butterflies imported from farms in Ecuador and El Salvador, a practice that helps protect species that come from the rain forests. The conservatory is also home to a flock of green and neon iguanas, mandarin ducks from Asia, ringed teal ducks from South America, and South African cape teals.

Guests are encouraged to snip and sniff a wide variety of herbs, including oregano, garlic, mint, lemongrass, rue, mallow, and safflower in the **Herb and Scene Garden**. The **Vegetable and Fruit Garden** bursts year-round with crops that include colorful burgundy queen cauliflower, tango onions, red Boston lettuce, sparkler radishes, and jade pagoda cabbage.

Nonedible but spectacular is the famed **Rose Garden**, which includes Europeana red, French Lace white, Summer Fashion yellow, and Angel Face lavender roses in appropriate seasons.

Founder Dick Pope Sr. closed his first Florida real estate deal at the age of twelve. When the local market went bust in 1927, he went into the PR business, promoting some of the first outboard motors with races across the state.

In the heart of the Depression, Pope convinced federal agencies to beautify and rebuild the canals and lakes around Winter Haven. Pope dreamed of a tropical paradise in the middle of a muck-filled marsh.

The lush gardens opened in 1936. Boat rides were added two years later. The Southern Belles arrived in 1940 when park employees dressed warmly for an unseasonable cold snap. Today you'll find Southern Belles in huge hoop skirts and other heavy accoutrements sitting out in the broiling Florida sun all year round; don't worry too much about them, though: they have a parasol above and a hidden air conditioning vent in the bench below.

During the years, the park became best-known for **The Greatest American Ski Show**, a water-ski extravaganza that showcases high-powered boat races and ski-jumping feats and a team of several dozen skiers. Cypress Gardens' first water-ski show took place in 1943 when a group of local skiers gathered on Lake Eloise to entertain military troops on leave. Since then skiers have recorded more than fifty world records, including the first four-tier human pyramid.

The Cypress Gardens ski show
Photo courtesy of Cypress Gardens

In the 1950s and 1960s Elvis Presley and Esther Williams made films here.

Variété Internationale has a changing selection of performers. Other entertainment includes a magic show and an elaborate model railroad, **Cypress Junction**, which includes twenty high-speed model trains touring tiny replicas of U.S. landmarks on 1,100 feet of track.

The **Eco Tour** is an electric boat ride through the man-made canals that wind through the two-hundred-acre park; the ride is included in the general admission charge.

Island in the Sky is a 153-foot-high revolving platform that offers an aerial view of Cypress Gardens, the surrounding Chain of Lakes and countryside.

The signature show at the park is **2001 Ski Odyssey**, featuring the latest ski techniques and water skiing stunts performed by world-class athletes.

Girls of all ages and most sizes can dress up like the world-famous Southern Belles. The two-hour-long experience invites participants to stroll the park grounds for family picture-taking. The cost in 2001 was $44.95 plus tax.

And finally, at certain times of the year Cypress Gardens almost outdoes itself with special festivals:

Spring Lights, early February to early May. The park is transformed into a bouquet of spring flowers set amid the twinkling of four million lights, including the Tree of Life with lighted blossoms, bees, and butterflies. Each evening features a Starlight Spectacular laser light show.

Spring Flower Festival, mid-March to mid-May. The park is decorated with several dozen stuffed topiary figures, many in bloom.

Mum Festival, early November to late November. More than three million brilliant blooms in magnificent arches, baskets, and other arrangements, with a thirty-five-foot cascading waterfall as its centerpiece.

Poinsettia Festival, late November to mid-January. More than forty thousand poinsettia blooms shape towering holiday trees, baskets, and beds. Other highlights include a miniature European village nestled among poinsettia alps.

Garden of Lights Holiday Festival, late November to mid-January. More than four million lights transform the park into a holiday fantasyland.

In 2001 admission was $32.95 for adults and $16.95 for children (6–12). For information, call ☎ (941) 324-2111 or ☎ (800) 282-2123 or consult 💻 www.cypressgardens.com.

Fantasy of Flight. A celebration of the wonders of flight, built around the personal collection and dream of founder Kermit Weeks. The sprawling three-hundred-acre facility includes indoor and outdoor displays of antique and unusual aircraft dating back to near the dawn of flight and featuring World War I and II fighting craft. There are also several multimedia exhibitions including a chilling re-creation of a World War I battlefield and a walk-through a B-17 Flying Fortress. A state-of-the-art flight simulation known as **Fightertown** puts visitors at the controls of a World War II fighter on a Pacific mission; the eight planes are mounted on a full-motion simulator base that responds to your movements of the stick and rudder. As you fly your mission you'll be in radio contact with a controller and the other flyers in your air group.

Visitors can also venture five hundred feet above the central Florida countryside in **The Great Balloon Experience**, a fifteen-minute trip in a tethered balloon. On clear days, the view can extend as far as the Gulf of Mexico and downtown Orlando. The 115-foot-tall balloon is moored by sixteen anchor points that can secure the balloon in wind speeds up to eighty knots.

Fantasy of Flight also offers introductory flights aboard ultra-light aircraft with experienced FAA Certified Flight Instructors. During the ultra-light introductory flights, conducted Tuesday through Sunday, guests as young as six years old can actually take over the controls of the aircraft.

Weeks, born into a wealthy oil family, put together his first home-built aircraft at the age of seventeen. A few years later he was flying in aerobatic competitions. He twice won the United States National Aerobatics Championship.

Fantasy of Flight, located in Polk City, off exit 21 of I-4, about twenty miles southwest of Walt Disney World, is open daily except Thanksgiving and Christmas Day from 9 A.M. to 5 P.M. Admission: adult, $24.95; child (5–12), $13.95; and senior (60 and older), $21.95. Tickets include admission to exhibits, Fightertown Flight Simulators, and The Great Balloon Experience (weather permitting). For information, call ☎ (863) 984-3500. 🖳 www.fantasyofflight.com.

Kennedy Space Center Visitor Center. The home base of the Space Shuttle is the fifth most popular attraction in Florida, drawing nearly three million visitors each year; it's also one of the best tourist bargains anywhere.

The Space Center is about fifty-five miles from Orlando, and there's enough to occupy you for a full morning or afternoon. Here's your chance to wander through the *Explorer*, a full-scale replica of the Space Shuttle, accurate down to the switches in the cockpit. The **Gallery of Space Flight** includes a fabulous collection of spacecraft, moon rocks, and other items.

The entry to the center is themed after the International Space Station, complete with huge replicas of the station's solar panels. **Robot Scouts** is a walk-through exhibit that introduces NASA's most far-reaching space explorers, the robotic planetary probes. Highlights include the Viking Mars lander, Cassini Saturn probe, Lunar Prospector, and Hubble Space Telescope.

New in 2001 was a live stage show, *Mad Mission to Mars 2025*. The comic antics of Professor Pruvitt, and his wacky colleagues, Kelvin, WD-4D, and Dr. Gimbal, magically transform guests into "astronaut trainees" and virtually transports them to the Red Planet.

The film *Quest for Life*, presented at the **Visitor Complex**, explores the mysterious spark of life that made our planet unique in the solar system. The film blends recent findings on the planet Mars with theories from leading scientists. And it reveals how the process that lead to life on Earth may have been replicated on as many as two billion other planets that are believed to have the needed ingredients.

The **International Space Station Center** offers the opportunity to look over the shoulders of workers assembling elements of the $30 billion orbiting research facility that will be jointly operated with the Russians.

The **LC39 Observation Gantry** gives an eagle's-eye view of the space shuttle as it is prepared for flight. It stands just half a mile from one launch pad and a mile from the other and also allows a peek into the massive Vehicle Assembly Building where the pieces of each spacecraft are brought together before flight.

At the space station center visitors view a video about the program, narrated by one of the astronauts who will help assemble the craft in space. From there, guests can walk through mock-ups of the space station, including the crew quarters and labs.

Visitors can spend as much time as they want at each attraction; buses are available to transport guests from location to location on a frequent schedule.

The Kennedy Space Center tour offers views of **Space Shuttle Launch Pads A and B**, the massive **Vehicle Assembly Building**, and an authentic 365-foot-long *Saturn V* moon rocket—one of only three in existence—housed in the new *Apollo/Saturn V* center. The Firing Room Theater re-creates the atmosphere of the original firing room as it existed during the Apollo era. The Lunar Surface Theater restages the fateful moments of Apollo 11 when astronauts Neil Armstrong and Buzz Aldrin placed the first human footprints on the moon.

Also available is a tour of the **Cape Canaveral Air Force Station**, where the U.S. space program began in the 1960s. And an exhibit at the center explores the **Merritt Island National Wildlife Refuge**, which surrounds the spaceport. Visitors can explore re-creations of the continental shelf, beach, grasslands, salt marshes, and lagoons and learn about some of the species that inhabit the area, including alligators, loggerhead turtles, manatees, black mice, scrub jays, and indigo snakes.

Spectacular Imax movies are shown on the huge screen of the Imax Theater. One of the most popular is the thirty-seven-minute *The Dream Is Alive*, which shows astronauts living and working in space.

The **Astronauts Memorial** honors the fifteen American astronauts who gave their lives in the line of duty (including the crew of the *Challenger* and the *Apollo 1* spacecraft, as well as others killed in training accidents). The forty-two-foot-high Space Mirror is set by a quiet lagoon near the entrance.

The 140,000-acre space center itself is an interesting wildlife area with some fifteen endangered species making their homes there. Watch for alligators in the canals along the roadways; the cape is also home to numerous wild pigs.

NASA's schedule hopes to have one Shuttle in space, one ready to go, and two in processing at any time. With luck, you may see one of the vehicles—mated to its external tank and rockets—moving down the three-and-a-half-mile road

A massive Saturn V moon rocket
Courtesy Kennedy Space Center Visitor Center

from the Vehicle Assembly Building to the launch pad on board a transporter. The entire assemblage weighs about twelve million pounds. Shuttles typically spend several weeks on the pad as they are prepared for launch.

Most orbiters return for a landing on a special runway at the space center, making a double sonic boom as they cross over central Florida.

It is especially interesting to visit the center while a Shuttle is in orbit; the air crackles with radio traffic to and from the orbiter and special displays track the progress of the current mission.

The center tends to be less busy on weekends than weekdays and is open every day of the year except for Christmas Day, from 9 A.M. to dusk. The visitor center may be off-limits on launch days, and bus tour routes may be altered or canceled when rockets are being prepared or launched.

The center is located off S.R. 405, NASA Parkway, seven miles east of U.S. 1. From Orlando, take S.R. 528 (the Beeline) to S.R. 407, about one hour total driving. From Atlantic Coast Florida, take Exit 78 off I-95. Follow signs for Kennedy Space Center.

In 2001 a Maximum Access Pass for a tour of the space center and two Imax films sold for $24 for adults and $15 for children (3–11).

The Cape Canaveral: Then and Now Tour combines the Maximum Access Pass with a historic tour of the Mercury, Gemini, and Apollo launch pads. $44 for adults; $35 for children (3–11).

The Wildlife Tour combines the Maximum Access Pass with a guided tour of Merritt Island Wildlife Refuge (reservations are required). $44 for adults; $35 for children (3–11).

For information, call ☎ (321) 449-4444 or ☎ (800) 572-4636 in Florida, or consult 🖳 www.KennedySpaceCenter.com.

Space Shuttle Launch Viewing. From outside the Space Center, the best places to watch a launch are along U.S. Highway 1 in the city of Titusville and along Highway A1A in the towns of Cocoa Beach and Cape Canaveral on the Atlantic Ocean.

Free launch viewing passes that permit vehicles to enter the Space Center and park at a site six miles from the pad are available by sending a letter three months in advance of a launch date to NASA Visitor Services, Mail Code: PA-Pass, Kennedy Space Center, FL 32899.

The Space Shuttle departs Florida
Courtesy Kennedy Space Center Visitor Center

The visitor center at Kennedy Space Center sells about 1,500 tickets to board buses to a viewing site six miles from the launch pad. Come to the center within five days in advance of a launch to purchase tickets, priced at $15, or $22.50 with admission to one Imax film. Tickets sell out quickly for daylight launches. In addition, if there is an afternoon launch, you may be able to park at the Visitor Center and watch the blastoff from there.

Tickets are generally available six weeks before a scheduled launch.

Current information on launches is available by calling NASA at ☎ (407) 867-4636 or ☎ (321) 449-4444, or the Kennedy Space Center Visitor Center from within Florida at ☎ (800) 572-4636.

Lion Country Safari. The nation's first drive-through zoo when it opened in 1967, the park includes more than one thousand wild animals from all over the world, including giraffes, eland, bison, elephants, rhino, zebra, ostrich, and antelope, wandering free over hundreds of acres. There's also a petting zoo and an amusement area that includes paddleboats, a boat ride, and an old-time carousel.

You'll use your own vehicle to drive through the preserve; the car cannot have broken windows. Convertibles and other inappropriate vehicles must be exchanged for available rental cars. In 2001 rental rates were a reasonable $6 for ninety minutes.

The park is located on Lion Country Safari Road, Loxahatchee, eighteen miles west of West Palm Beach off Exit 99 of the Florida Turnpike. Loxahatchee is about 175 miles from Orlando. For information, call ☎ (561) 793-1084 or consult 💻 www.lioncountry safari.com. Open every day 9:30 A.M. to 5:30 P.M. Admission: adult, $15.50; child (3–9), $10.50; senior (65 and older), $10.50.

Silver Springs. Silver Springs has been drawing visitors to its natural beauties since the early 1800s. In the 1860s steamboats explored the area. In 1878 Silver Springs became famous for the invention of glass-bottom boats for display of underwater wonders. Six of the original Tarzan movies were filmed at Silver Springs in the 1930s and 1940s; *The Yearling*, starring Gregory Peck and Jane Wyman, was filmed there in 1946. And more than one hundred episodes of the "Sea Hunt" television series, starring Lloyd Bridges, were filmed at Silver Springs from 1958 to 1961.

Divers have mapped and explored what is said to be the largest spring system in the world, the source of up to two billion gallons of water daily. Discoveries at the site have included fossilized mastodon teeth dating back ten thousand years, a giant ground sloth claw, and a mammoth tooth from the Pleistocene period. In addition, several species of troglobitic life, including crayfish, have been found.

Panther Prowl features rare Florida panthers and their close relative, the eastern cougar, in an outdoor habitat of trees, caves, and ponds.

The **World of Bears** attraction may be the only place in Florida where guests can see majestic grizzly and Kodiak bears, plus three other ursine species. Recent new arrivals include a pair of Asiatic black bears and two Sun bears from Southeast Asia.

And the **Big Gator Lagoon** added a half-acre cypress swamp habitat with more than two dozen of Florida's largest alligators, adding to the extensive collection at the park. Another exhibit showcases a white American alligator, one of only seventeen known specimens in the world.

Visitors can cruise on glass-bottom boats on a tour that explores seven natural formations, including **Mammoth Spring**, the world's largest artesian limestone spring. Creatures in the nearly pure spring include alligators, turtles, garfish, and largemouth bass. Along the riverbanks are great blue heron, cormorants, ibis, egrets, raccoons, and river otters.

The **Jeep Safari** takes passengers on a four-wheel-drive vehicle into a jungle that is home to free-roaming wildlife, including African waterbucks, two-toed sloths, Brazilian tapirs, and four species of deer. The highlight of the safari is a trip through a three-foot-deep pit teeming with alligators.

The **Lost River Voyage** explores an untouched cypress jungle, a glimpse of wild Florida as it was thousands of years ago. At Cypress Point you may be lucky enough to see Sonek, believed to be the world's largest American alligator.

From about Thanksgiving to New Year's Eve, Silver Springs celebrates with a Festival of Lights, a central Florida version of a winter wonderland. Apropos of nothing else, the park is also the home of **A Touch of Garlits**, a museum of antique and racecars honoring famed drag racer Don "Big Daddy" Garlits.

Located in Silver Springs, about seventy-two miles from Orlando; take exit 69 off I-75 to S.R. 40 East. Silver Springs is open every day 10 A.M. to 5 P.M., with extended hours in the summer and on holidays. Admission in 2001: general, $31.95; visitors under forty-eight inches tall, $22.95; senior, $28.95. For information, call ☎ (352) 236-2121 or consult 💻 www.silversprings.com.

A glass-bottom boat explores Silver Springs
Courtesy Orlando/Orange County Convention & Visitor Bureau

Adjacent to Silver Springs is the **Wild Waters** water park, which offers nine water flumes, including the **Twin Twister**, a pair of sixty-foot flumes for two-person inner tubes, the **Tornado** water ride, and the 450,000-gallon **Wave Pool**. The Lazy Bones River sends guests on a slow tour of an eight-hundred-foot jungle waterway, and **Cool Kids Cove** children's play area, a version of an 1800s riverboat with water cannons, net cage bridges, water slides, and more.

The water park is open spring through early fall. Call for operating schedules. Prices in 2001 were general admission, $22.95 plus tax; visitors under forty-eight inches tall, $19.95. For information, call ☎ (352) 236-2121 or consult 🖳 www.wildwaterspark.com.

Valiant Air Command Warbird Air Museum. Historic displays of aircraft and aviation memorabilia from World War I, World War II, Korea, and Vietnam. Adult, $9; senior, $8; child (3–12), $5. Open daily 10 A.M. to 6 P.M. 6600 Tico Road, Titusville near the Kennedy Space Center. ☎ (407) 268-1941. 🖳 www.vacwar birds.org.

Weeki Wachee Spring. Mermaids abound at this old water park on the Gulf Coast. Presentations include an underwater show, *Little Pocahontas Meets the Little Mermaid*, as well as a Wilderness River Cruise, a Birds of Prey Show, and a petting zoo. Adults, $15.95; seniors, 10 percent discount; children (3–10), $11.95. North of Tampa on U.S. 19 at the intersection with S.R. 50. ☎ (352) 597-0360 or ☎ (877) 469-3354. 🖳 www.weekiwachee.com.

Next to Weeki Wachee Spring is the **Buccaneer Bay** water park, open from April to early September.

Chapter 24
Shopping

To heck with mice, sharks, and whales—for some folks, the ultimate Orlando recreational activity is . . . shopping. And the millions of visitors to the entertainment attractions of Orlando have become a tremendous lure to retailers.

Bring an empty suitcase with you and leave time for some of the shopping adventures listed here.

192 Flea Market. ☎ (407) 396-4555. 4301 West Vine Street (I-192) in Kissimmee. A full-time, free admission market with as many as four hundred dealer booths under one roof. Disney souvenirs, jewelry, crafts, clothing, and more. Open daily from 9 A.M. to 6 P.M.

Altamonte Mall. ☎ (407) 830-4400. North of Orlando, east of I-4 on S.R. 436 in Altamonte Springs. Burdine's, JC Penney, The Gap, Cache, The Limited, Sears, and more than 175 specialty shops. Open Monday through Saturday from 10 A.M. to 9 P.M., and Sunday from 11 A.M. to 6 P.M.

Belz Factory Outlet World. ☎ (407) 354-0126. 💻 www.belz.com/factory/locations/orlando. Located at the north end of International Drive, past Kirkman Road. A huge collection of factory outlet shops, with more than 170 companies represented in two enclosed malls and four shopping centers, all within walking distance of each other. Manufacturers include L'eggs/Hanes/Bali, Maidenform, Totes, Polly Flinders, Bally, Bass, Stride-Rite, Mikasa, Adolfo II, Anne Klein, Geoffrey Beene, Jordache, Leslie Fay, Levi Strauss, Van Heusen, Oshkosh B'Gosh, Capezio, Dexter, Corning, Burlington Brands, Guess Jeans, London Fog, Danskin, Londontown, Harvé Bernard, and Young Generations. Open Monday through Saturday 10 A.M. to 9 P.M. and Sunday from 10 A.M. to 6 P.M.

The Florida Mall. ☎ (407) 851-6255. Intersection of Sand Lake Road (S.R. 482) and South Orange Blossom Trail (Highway 441). Dillard's, Gayfers, JC Penney, Saks Fifth Avenue, Sears, and two hundred specialty shops. Open daily from 10 A.M. to 9:30 P.M., and Sunday from 11 A.M. to 6 P.M.

International Designer Outlet. ☎ (407) 354-0300. International Drive near Belz Factory Outlet. A collection of upscale clothing and accessory stores, including Ann Taylor, Dansk, Saks Fifth Avenue, Anne Klein, Liz Claiborne, Jones NY, and Coach.

Kissimmee Manufacturer's Outlet Mall. ☎ (407) 396-8900. 💻 www.floridaoutlets.com. I-192 near Kissimmee. Shops include American Tourister, Casual's Unlimited, Fieldcrest Cannon, Geoffrey Beene Company, Nike Factory Store, Olde Times, Publishers Outlet, Tommy Hilfiger, Totes Factory Store, Van Heusen, and Westport Limited. Open Monday to Saturday 10 A.M. to 9 P.M., Sunday 11 A.M. to 5 P.M.

Mercado. ☎ (407) 345-9337. 💻 www.themercado.com. 8445 International Drive. A small but interesting collection of shops and eateries. Just as Disney's creative roller coaster packaging makes Space Mountain an above-average ride, the unusual Mercado "package" makes this mall a different sort of shopping experience.

Mercado includes more than sixty specialty shops, including Kandlestix, Pet Palace, Krazy Kites, House of Ireland, Earth Matters (wildlife and marinelife clothing and accessories for the conservation-minded), and The Magic Shop.

Restaurants include Damon's—The Place for Ribs, Charlie's Lobster House, Bergamo's Italian Restaurant, The Butcher Shop Steakhouse, and the Blazing Pianos Red Hot Rock 'n' Roll Piano Bar. There's also Cricketers Arms, an English pub. In the International Food Court you'll also find The Greek Place, Wok 'n Roll, Sabor Latino, the All-American Grill, Gino's Pizza, Fiesta, The Sandwich Gallery, Chicken Magic, and Le Gelateria Molto.

At night the grounds and shops are alight with twinkling lights, and free entertainment is presented in the courtyard.

Shops open from 10 A.M. to 10 P.M. daily, until 11 P.M. in season; restaurants and bars close later.

Pointe Orlando Entertainment Center. ☎ (407) 248-2838. 💻 www.pointeorlandofl.com. International Drive at Universal Boulevard.

A sprawling retail and entertainment center that features more than sixty shops, a twenty-screen movie multiplex, an Imax theater, and seven restaurants, across International Drive from the Orange County Convention Center. The two anchors of the mall are a huge FAO Schwarz retail toy store, designed to look like an upside-down toy box with toys scattered around the perimeter, and WonderWorks, designed to look like a three-story upside-down mansion that landed atop a brick warehouse. Do you get the point?

You'll also find the Muvico Pointe 21 Theaters with an Imax 3-D theater, plus shops such as Gap and Gap Kids, Banana Republic, Abercrombie & Fitch, Victoria's Secret, B. Dalton Booksellers, Speedo, Bath & Body, Express, Biker's Image, and Image Leather.

You'll have to pay to park in the parking garage, although the ticket can be validated for free parking with purchase of a movie ticket or food and beverage at one of the participating restaurants.

Pointe Orlando shops are open every day from 10 A.M. to 10 P.M., and until 11 P.M. on Friday and Saturday. Many restaurants and bars stay open later.

Part VIII
Tampa

Chapter 25
Busch Gardens Tampa Bay, Adventure Island, Florida Aquarium, Museum of Science and Industry

Busch Gardens Tampa Bay opened as a hospitality center for the Anheuser-Busch brewery in Tampa in 1959, showcasing a collection of exotic birds and some of the Busch family's collection of African animals.

In 1971, when the era of Florida as theme park began, the company began a massive expansion of Busch Gardens.

Today the park is like stepping onto the African veldt—albeit a veldt with a sky ride above and a passel of outrageous roller coasters on the horizon.

Visitors can enter into the veldt on **Rhino Rally**, an off-road safari among elephants, white rhinos, antelope, alligators, cape buffalo, warthogs, and other exotic African species. Another recent manmade thrill is **Gwazi**, a mammoth double-track wooden roller coaster. It joins recent expansions, including **The Edge of Africa** up-close animal safari and the spectacular **Montu** coaster in the Egypt area of the park.

Busch Gardens is a welcome getaway from the concrete of Walt Disney World and environs, drawing three million visitors a year to its 355 acres, home to more than 2,800 animals. The brewery that was the original reason for Busch Gardens Tampa closed at the end of 1995; part of that land at the heart of the park was used for the Gwazi coaster.

The map of Florida looks so huge to many visitors that the thought of a drive from Orlando to Tampa seems like an all day drive; it's not. Measured from the intersection of I-4 and I-192, Tampa Bay is an easy seventy miles, at 65 miles per hour to the gates of SeaWorld, about seventy-five minutes.

Although it is only about seventy miles away, Tampa Bay is on the other coast of Florida and sometimes in a different weather pattern than Orlando.

MUST-SEES

Rhino Rally
(the world's first safari-coaster)

Gwazi
(double-trouble wooden coaster)

Moroccan Palace Theater
(ice show fans)

Akbar's Adventure Tours
(up-close and simulated)

Montu
(the latest steel roller coaster)

Myombe Reserve: The Great Ape Domain

Serengeti Safari
(a real African safari, in Florida)

The Edge of Africa

The Scorpion
(a steel coaster ever so slightly less intense than Kumba)

Kumba
(ever so slightly less intense than Montu)

Congo River Rapids

Stanley Falls Log Flume

Tanganyika Tidal Wave

One March day we left Orlando in heavy rain and arrived to find the sun blazing in Tampa.

The busiest times of the year are similar to those of the Orlando attractions: June to Labor Day and spring and Easter breaks. Other times of the year bring large crowds of foreign visitors, including planeloads from South America and Brazil.

Lines, though, rarely are anywhere as long as those you'll find at Walt Disney World or Universal Studios Florida during peak summer and holiday periods.

Operating hours are 9:30 A.M. until 6 P.M. Extended hours into the evening are offered in summer and over selected holiday periods.

Busch Entertainment Corporation operates parks including Busch Gardens in Tampa and Williamsburg, Virginia; SeaWorld in Orlando, San Antonio, and San Diego; Adventure Island in Tampa; and the Sesame Place theme park in Langhorne, Pennsylvania.

From Orlando: Take I-4 West about sixty miles to Tampa. Exit at I-75 North and find the Fowler Avenue off-ramp (Exit 54). From there, follow signs to the park.

Leave the Driving to Them

Orlando visitors can catch a ride to the park on the **Busch Gardens Shuttle Express**. Round-trip bus tickets in 2001 were just $5.

You can board the Shuttle Express at SeaWorld Orlando, the Mercado Shopping Village, Lake Buena Vista Factory Outlet Mall, Universal Studios, and Kissimmee Old Town Shopping Village.

Pickup times range from 8 to 10:15 A.M., with shuttles returning from Busch Gardens to Orlando locations at 5, 6, and 8 P.M.

The Busch Gardens Shuttle Express also services some forty hotel locations in the Central Florida area in conjunction with Orlando Flex Ticket transportation routes.

For information, reservations, and schedules call ☎ (800) 511-2450.

Busch Gardens Tampa Bay Tickets

Not including 7 percent tax. Prices were in effect in mid-2001 and are subject to change.

	Adults	Children
Single-Day Ticket	$47.95	$38.95 (3–9)
Busch Gardens/Adventure Island Combo One day at each park	$59.95	$49.95
Busch Gardens Tampa Bay/SeaWorld Florida Value Ticket One day each at Busch Gardens Tampa Bay and SeaWorld Florida in Orlando	$78.95	$63.95
5-Park Orlando FlexTicket Unlimited admission to Universal Studios Florida, Universal Studios Islands of Adventure, SeaWorld Florida, Wet 'n Wild, Busch Gardens Tampa Bay. Valid fourteen consecutive days.	$196.95	$157.95
Busch Gardens Tampa Bay Silver Passport Valid for twelve months. Includes parking.	$84.95	$74.95
Busch Gardens/Adventure Island Silver Passport Valid for twelve months. Includes parking.	$114.95	$114.95
Busch Gardens/SeaWorld Orlando Silver Passport Valid for twelve months at both parks. Includes parking.	$124.95	$109.95
Busch Gardens/Adventure Island/SeaWorld Orlando Silver Passport Valid for twelve months at all three parks. Includes parking.	$154.95	$139.95

Power Trip for Summer and Holiday Periods

Begin your Busch Gardens tour by studying the schedule of entertainment you will be handed at the gate; depending on the time of year, some major shows like the ice extravaganza at the **Moroccan Palace Theater** are presented many times during the day, while other entertainments may be scheduled only once or twice. Adjust your Power Trip to include any must-see shows.

The new **Rhino Rally** off-road safari will likely be the leading attraction for many guests; head there first. The lines will be shorter and many wild animals are more active in the cooler morning anyway.

Second on the list for most thrill-seekers is the **Gwazi** double-track roller coaster, followed closely by **Montu** in Egypt, and **Kumba** in the Congo. You can count on lengthy lines at all three of these attractions in the heart of the day. Go early or around dinnertime to make the most of your time.

While you're in Kumba's neighborhood, check out **The Congo River Rapids.** On the occasional chilly day you might want to store a dry sweatshirt in a locker before you ride. Now try the relatively biteless (but still intimidating) **Python** roller-twister-coaster. When you're through, the majestic tigers on **Claw Island** will probably seem tame, but they're certainly worth a visit. Of the two other water rides, **Stanley Falls** may be more fun but the **Tanganyika Tidal Wave** is more dramatic. What the heck: ride 'em both.

Animal lovers will want to arrive early at **The Edge of Africa** to experience a close-up encounter with hippos, lions, giraffes, and more.

For a different type of thrill consider signing up early in the day for one of the **Serengeti Safari** truck tours into the animal preserve.

If you are not in the mood for an immediate upside-down rattle and roll, you can instead start the day by bearing right from the entrance toward Crown Colony to visit the wacky **Akbar's Adventure Tours** simulator adventure. Once you return to Florida, backtrack to the **Skyride** to view the Serengeti Plain from above.

When you've accomplished all of your goals, take a leisurely circuit of the park on the **Trans-Veldt Railroad.**

Busch Gardens Attractions

Rhino Rally

There are real safaris in Africa, and theme-park safaris in Florida. And there are water rides and roller coasters just about anywhere you could toss a guidebook.

Animal expert Jack Hanna introduces the Rhino Rally vehicles
Photo courtesy of Busch Gardens

But only at Busch Gardens Tampa Bay will you find Rhino Rally, a safari/water ride/coaster. There was nothing else like Rhino Rally when it opened in 2001 within the Serengeti Plain.

From the international Rally Plaza, seventeen guests at a time board a special version of a Land Rover for a journey into the midst of white rhinoceroses, elephants, Cape buffalo, Nile crocodiles, zebra, antelope, warthogs, flamingos, wildebeests, gazelle, and other species. So far, what we've got here is a version of the Kilimanjaro Safari at Disney's Animal Kingdom. But it goes way on from there.

After a tour through the preserve—you'll see different animals at different times of the day and weather conditions—the truck begins to cross a pontoon bridge across a raging whitewater river. Suddenly the bridge breaks loose, sending the truck down the river, through a canyon, and under a waterfall.

The one-of-a-kind ride uses a roller-coaster-like track hidden beneath the water, transporting the truck back to the plaza. In some ways the ride is derived from SeaWorld Orlando's Journey to Atlantis, another unique entertainment that combines a roller coaster with a flume ride. Rhino Rally can take about 1,600 guests per hour.

WOW Gwazi

In African legend, or at least African theme-park legend, Gwazi is a fierce creature possessed of a lion's body and a tiger's head.

At Busch Gardens Tampa Bay, the Lion and Tiger chase each other for a mile and a half, heading right at each other on six "fly-by" maneuvers in which they come within just feet of each other at crossing speeds of near 100 miles per hour. We're talking about a roller coaster, of course, and this is a truly amazing ride.

The double-track wooden coaster has two different sets of rails. Gwazi Tiger has a section of slalom track, more like a bobsled than a wooden coaster. Gwazi Lion's highlight is a nearly continuous series of spirals.

As the two trains crest at the top of the ninety-foot lift hills, both drops are on a "stingline," allowing riders to see the opposite train charging straight at them. At the last possible moment, the trains veer to the side. In the fourth of six fly-bys each train arcs at a fifty-one-degree angle; the fifth fly-by delivers an extended weightless stretch on a parabola of track.

The loading station for Gwazi

Photo courtesy Busch Gardens

Top speed for the coaster is a zippy 50 miles per hour; when the two trains head at each other, engineers consider them moving at a "crossing" or "closing" speed of 100 miles per hour. Though the wooden coaster follows an old concept, constructed out of more than 1.25 million board feet of lumber and more than two million bolted connections, modern technology is also applied. Computer sensors attached to both tracks monitor Gwazi's trains, regulating their spacing along nearly seven thousand feet of track. The computer also manages the braking systems, a far cry from the days when an operator had to physically pull a huge hand brake to slow down a train at the station.

Morocco

A re-creation of the exotic city of Marrakesh, featuring unusual architecture and demonstrations of Moroccan crafts, snake charmers, the Mystic Sheiks of Morocco marching band, and the Sounds of Steel, a five-man steel drum band.

WOW Moroccan Palace Theater

World Rhythms on Ice took to the ice for a run of several years in this 1,200-seat arena. The show includes skaters displaying the costumes and cultures of many parts of the world, including Germany, England, Brazil, and the United States. Former Olympians from Canada and Russia are among the cast.

Midday performances fill up within twenty minutes of show time. The half-hour show features fourteen skaters and two vocalists.

Marrakesh Theater

In 2001 the daily show was *Moroccan Roll*, a singing and dancing show with a Middle Eastern flavor. Check the daily schedule for performance times.

Serious shoppers may enjoy a visit to the brass store just past the ticket booths; an artisan/importer from Morocco offers an impressive display. And, if you like to pay to carry someone else's corporate slogan or ad campaign, check out the **Rabat Label** store, where you can buy just about any article of clothing or sporting equipment with one or another Anheuser-Busch logo on it.

Egypt

WOW Akbar's Adventure Tours

Hold on to your hats—and your wallets—when you embark upon the wacky journey led by comedian Martin Short, starring as a shady Egyptian tour guide hanging on to a shoestring travel business. His newest product is a simulated journey across Egypt, which he desperately hopes will save his business from repossession by Stanford "Don't call me Stan" Wharton (played by comedian Eugene Levy).

Equipped with his brother Omar's home movies, Akbar embarks on his greatest venture ever.

Visitors waiting to board the simulator will see posters depicting some of the awesome attractions of the tour . . . and they won't be able to avoid noticing the very humble means by which Akbar proposes to take them there. Before boarding you'll meet Akbar himself, the "world's greatest tour guide."

In a preshow film, Akbar takes us into his workshop, where his possessions are being removed by Stanford Wharton. After a bit of friendly persuasion by his "baby" brothers Corky and Chip, Stanford reluctantly agrees to give Akbar one more chance at success with his homemade simulator.

And then you'll be face-to-face with the simulator: homemade may be too kind a description. Perhaps "nouveau dump" would be a bit more accurate. But Akbar promises that no misfortune could possibly befall anyone on the maiden voyage. You believe him, right?

The journey begins on camelback, jostling through a bustling marketplace as merchants and pedestrians dive for safety. Weaving and banking just above the desert surface, the simulator, now a biplane, struggles up into the sky to reveal a perilously close encounter with the ancient pyramids. From there it is on to the Sphinx, and this time it's not a near-collision: let's just say that the big cat receives a long-overdue face-lift.

Once the simulator regains control, it's on to the excavation of the forbidden tomb, riding on an out-of-control mine train. The train somehow gets on the wrong track and ends up in a spooky, skull-filled chamber. The monstrous guardian of the chamber expresses its displeasure with Akbar's intrusion by sending the visitors hurtling through a vortex and out of control . . .

Did you expect anything less?

Akbar's Adventure is located just outside the gates to Egypt, the former home of the Questor simulator. There are two simulator cabins, each seating fifty-nine guests. The total length of the show is about six minutes, which gives an hourly capacity of about 1,416 passengers.

All kidding aside, the simulators themselves are very high-tech, with each cabin hydraulically powered to move in six directions—pitch, roll, yaw, heave, surge, and sway. The audiovisual system is based on an eight-channel laser video-disc surround system.

WOW Montu

The world's largest inverted steel roller coaster soars across nearly four thousand feet of track and includes three first-of-a-kind elements:

- The "Immelman," an inverse loop named after a German stunt pilot
- The world's largest vertical loop on an inverted coaster, at 104 feet
- Two vertical loops slanted at forty-five-degree angles, known as a "batwing." Coaster experts say these are the wildest stretches.

Montu is named after a hawk-like Sun God worshiped by ancient Egyptians at Thebes.

As the trains leave the loading station, they drop toward a pond that is home to several live crocodiles. Other elements include a camelback maneuver that delivers three seconds of weightlessness, sweeping arcs crossing over and under the tracks of the Transveldt Railway, and a corkscrew finale.

There are three trains made up of eight cars, each of which holds four passengers across for a total of thirty-two riders per train. The cars hang from the

Upside-down on Montu
Photo courtesy of Busch Gardens Tampa Bay

top and swing out from side to side; the foot platforms drop out when the train departs, leaving feet dangling below the car; at one point the swooping cars dive as close as eighteen inches above the ground. The tracks dive into three Egyptian-theme tunnels below ground.

Peaking at speeds in excess of 60 miles per hour, Montu reaches a maximum G-force of 3.85 at certain points during the three-minute trip. Riders must be at least fifty-two inches tall.

The approach to the loading area for the ride is through a portal in a spectacular fifty-five-foot-tall wall decorated with hand-carved hieroglyphs.

Visitors to Egypt can also tour a six-room replica of King Tutankhamen's tomb as it looked when it was first discovered by archeologist Howard Carter in the early 1920s. Young visitors will be able to dig through a sand pit with buried artifacts of the ancient culture.

The area also includes shopping bazaars for the older visitors. Items for sale at the **Golden Scarab** and **Treasures of the Nile** shops include hand-blown glass and cartouche painting on scrolls.

Transveldt Railroad

The train offers some of the best close-up views of the animals on the Serengeti Plain between the Nairobi and Congo stations. Other portions of the track offer a tourist's-eye view of the back sides of the Python and Scorpion roller coasters.

The train is a three-quarter-scale replica of an African steam engine and cars; the engine is an unusual combination of energy sources, using propane gas to boil water for steam that powers an electric generator for the wheels.

Nairobi

WOW Myombe Reserve: The Great Ape Domain

An animal habitat featuring six lowland gorillas and eight common chimpanzees in a tropical forest setting. Gorillas include Lash, an eighteen-year-old, 330-pound silverback male who was hand-raised by surrogates at the Cincinnati Zoo after his mother died. Also resident is a social group of five gorillas on a long-term breeding loan from Emory University in Atlanta.

Visitors enter the three-acre habitat through dense foliage to a clearing that has a glass wall where they can observe the chimps; passing through a bamboo thicket, guests come upon the gorillas at the base of a mountain between waterfalls in a simulated tropical rain forest. (On cool days boulders near the viewing areas are heated to draw the animals near.) There are chimp nests scattered in the trees; some are as much as seventy feet off the ground.

At each turn in the reserve, you will see educational displays that tell you about the lives of the gorillas, and how humans are threatening their natural environment. Some things you'll learn: a young female uses blades of grass and stems to extract termites, a chimp delicacy; chimps, who eat mostly fruit, use plants for medicinal purposes to kill parasites, fungi, and viruses; before chimps were observed using tools it was assumed that humans were the only ones to do so.

Vanishing gorillas. Gorillas, the largest living primates, are seriously endangered or in some cases on the brink of extinction in the tropical forests, woodlands, and mountain regions of Africa. Most threatened is the mountain gorilla subspecies; perhaps fewer than 450 remain.

Aldabra Tortoise Habitat

Opposite the train station, you'll find a collection of gigantic tortoises, including the Aldabra tortoise, often found on Aldabra Island in the Indian Ocean. Brought back from near extinction, Aldabras often weigh as much as six hundred pounds when mature, and are now seen in large groups wallowing in mud or shallow lagoons.

In the same area you may also see an African Spurred Tortoise, Africa's largest land tortoises. They span the continent along the southern fringe of the Sahara Desert to the Red Sea.

WOW Serengeti Safari

I enjoy roller coasters well enough, but for me the real thrill at Busch Gardens Tampa Bay is a very special tour available to only a handful of visitors each day: the Serengeti Safari.

Several times a day, as many as twenty visitors clamber on board an open flatbed truck for a one-hour visit behind the fences of the sixty-acre **Serengeti Plain**, with close-up views of giraffes, zebras, hippopotamuses, and other animals. A park guide accompanies visitors on the truck.

It's a fabulous opportunity for camera buffs and animal lovers of all ages. On one trip, a herd of giraffes ambled over to our truck to snack on apples, with a few friendly nips at hats and jackets; into the middle of the giraffes came a group of nearsighted ostriches that pecked at anything within reach. A good time was had by all, including the animals; several of the giraffes loped along behind the truck to bid us goodbye.

Only four to six truck tours are conducted each day; in 2001 the charge was $29.99 per person. There is a twenty-guest limit per truck and no children under age five are allowed. Depending on the time of year the thirty-minute safaris go out three to five times per day. You can book a trip at the **Edge of Africa** gift shop near the entrance when you arrive; you can also prebook a place on the 11:15 A.M. safari by calling ☎ (813) 984-4073.

Animals. In this area you can get as close as you can to some of the animals, with some special treats for the children. You'll find an unusually attractive **Petting Zoo**, but don't overlook the **Nairobi Station Animal Nursery**, home to Busch Gardens' newest and littlest arrivals including tiny birds, alligators, and snakes, set in a replica of an African hospital of yesteryear. The clinic includes operating rooms; X-ray, laboratory, and recovery areas; and brooder rooms for birds.

The **Elephant Wash** is just what it sounds like: ponderous pachyderms stand still for showers several times a day; nearby is a small enclosure where guests can climb onto a seat on the back of an elephant for a short ride.

Crown Colony

The Skyride

An open cable-car ride from the Crown Colony to the Congo and back, passing above the Serengeti Plain and then deep into deepest, darkest amusement park land with good views of the Scorpion and the Congo River Rapids. A lovely way to see the park on a lovely day; when it is not lovely the ride can be a bit chilly, and it is shut down in high winds and inclement weather.

Clydesdale Hamlet

Some of Anheuser-Busch's famous corporate symbols can be visited in their stables here. The largest adults can be as large as six feet at the shoulder and weigh about a ton.

Serengeti Plain

The largest open area of the park, an eighty-acre natural setting that features more than eight hundred animals in free-roaming herds of camels, elephants, zebra, giraffes, chimpanzees, rhino, Cape buffalo, gazelles, greater kudus, and hippos. The Transveldt Railroad circles the Plain, while the Skyride passes overhead. The park's newest attraction, **Rhino Rally**, ventures into the plain.

WOW The Edge of Africa

In the largest animal expansion in the park's history, guests to The Edge of Africa venture forth on a safari in search of hippopotamuses, giraffes, lions, baboons, meerkats, crocodiles, hyenas, and more. The area makes use of moats and other hidden barriers to preserve the appearance of the wild.

The trek into the fifteen-acre compound begins with an exploration of the remains of an old fishing village, a riverine habitat where hippos, baboons, and various species of fish coexist. A glass window allows up-close observations of hippos from above and below the surface of a pool; hippos, born underwater, ordinarily stay beneath the surface for three to five minutes but can remain submerged for as long as thirty minutes.

As the excursion continues you'll come to a Masai village, where members of the nomadic African tribe have vacated one of their many temporary homes; the reason for the hasty exit becomes apparent when you discover the lions and hyenas that have taken over the village.

Among rock outcroppings and giant termite mounds, expeditioners will also discover species such as vultures and meerkats in areas offering distant views of the Serengeti Plain.

Roaming safari guides and naturalists offer guests educational facts about the various animals and regions.

Look for the visitor's information center posting the day's animal sightings and diets. As you move into the area, watch for sleeping lions in one of the abandoned safari vehicles parked in the compound; lions spend as much as eighteen hours a day relaxing. In the wild they would spend their waking time hunting; at Busch Gardens they receive catered meals of about seven pounds of raw meat several times per week. (The much smaller hyena, along with the lion, one of the most feared hunters in the jungle, eats as much as one hundred pounds of food—including animal bones—per week.)

Timbuktu

WOW The Scorpion

It goes up to the top of its tower, then down and to the left at 55 miles per hour before entering a full 360-degree loop into a series of corkscrew descents that put you on your side. The Scorpion is by most accounts in the middle between Python and Kumba on the wildness meter.

Parental Guidance: The exit to the ride is in a different area from the entrance. You must be at least forty-two inches tall to ride.

Dolphins of the Deep Show

Bud and Mich (sounds vaguely commercial, doesn't it?), with their sea lion sidekick and their trainers, demonstrate their speed and agility in an amusing show at the Dolphin Theater.

In front of Dolphins of the Deep Theater, be sure to locate the **Floss Silked Tree**. Native to South America, in late fall the leaves shed and large showy flowers appear. At the peak of color, the canopy is a mass of pink orchid blossoms. When flowering is over, pear-shaped fruits appear that explode when they are ripe, sending a silky cotton material floating to the ground.

Carousel Caravan. A most unusual merry-go-round, featuring desert camels and Arabian horses.

The Phoenix. A dry boat ride that gives new meaning to the term *rock 'n' roll*. The platform moves forward and then backward with increasing power until riders make a complete pass up and over the top a few times. This is a bigger and wilder version of the amusement park pirate ship ride.

Other rides here include the **Sandstorm**, an aerial whip; the **Crazy Camel**; a collection of children's rides; an arcade; and a group of carnival games.

Congo

WOW Kumba

Kumba means "roar" in a Congo dialect. It might have been a better idea to call it "aiyeeeee!" or some other such scream. Kumba is one of the largest and fastest steel roller coasters in the country, reaching speeds in excess of 60 miles per hour and putting as much as 3.75 Gs on the bodies of its lucky riders.

The coaster includes several unusual elements, including a diving loop, which plunges riders into a loop from a height of 110 feet; a camelback, a maneuver that creates three seconds of weightlessness while spiraling 360 degrees; a 108-foot vertical loop, the world's largest; a cobra roll that turns passengers upside down as they twist around a spectator bridge; and more ordinary super-coaster thrills, including an oblique loop, a vertical spiral, and a double corkscrew-shaped twist.

But the ride itself is even wilder than its description—longer and with more twists and turns than three or four ordinary coasters put together. Riders are securely locked into place with an overhead harness and are seated four across. The outside seats give the best view—that is, if you are able or willing to turn your head while moving.

But before I scare you off, consider the fact that Kumba's roar is much worse than its bite. You are moving so fast that you hardly realize that you are on your head or your side or your back. And if it makes you feel any better, know that my then-nine-year-old daughter led the family onto the ride one morning; she rode it once with me and her big brother, a second time with her brother, and a third time by herself when we all insisted on a rest.

The ride is very nicely integrated into the bushes and trees of the park, with many of the dips and turns hidden in the landscaping. You can walk beneath much of the track, too, which offers a great view for spectators and bragging rights to successful riders.

You must be at least fifty-two inches tall to ride and in good physical condition. Did I mention that I started that day with two Dramamine tablets?

The Python

Only at a park like Busch Gardens would a roller coaster like the Python have to settle for second-class status behind Montu and Kumba. The Python includes wicked twists and turns and a 360-degree double spiral, and cars reach speeds of more than 50 miles per hour. All that said, the Python is a very short ride; you'll be back at the loading station before your heart has returned from your throat.

If you're a little uncertain about your roller coaster credentials, you may want to try your stomach at Python, then move on to Scorpion, and then make it all the way to Kumba, and finally to Montu.

Riders must be at least forty-eight inches tall.

WOW Congo River Rapids

Riders sit in a twelve-passenger circular air raft and are let loose on a churning whitewater trip in an artificial river with rapids, logs, and other boats in the way. We'd tell you to sit at the back of the boat to avoid getting soaked, but the darned thing keeps turning around.

The ride won't get your heart pounding quite as fast as one of the flume trips, but it's still a lot of fun and cooling on a hot day. Riders have to be at least thirty-eight inches tall, or at least two years old and in the company of an adult.

A Congo River Rapids raft approaches a geyser

On the bridge that overlooks the rapids beneath the Kumba track there are coin-operated water cannons that can be aimed at rafts below. Put a quarter into the **Congo Water Blasters** and add a little extra water to the raft riders passing by.

Other rides in this area include **Ubanga-Banga Bumper Cars**, the **Monstrous Mamba** octopus ride, and more kiddie rides.

Claw Island

In a valley below a pedestrian bridge is a hideaway where you can get as close as you may ever want to a rare white Bengal tiger.

Stanleyville

WOW Stanley Falls Log Flume

Over the edge of a forty-three-foot plastic cliff in a hollowed-out log. Lines build at midday; visit early or late in the day to avoid long waits.

WOW Tanganyika Tidal Wave

Boats depart regularly for a pleasant little cruise through lush, tropical foliage. Sounds relaxing . . . that is, until your twenty-passenger boat plunges over the edge to fall fifty-five feet into a splash pool. The result is a huge wave—really huge—that wets the passengers but can really soak observers standing in the wrong place on the walkway below.

For an excellent view of the tidal wave, climb the bridge and stand within the glass-walled tunnel. If you are riding, the back of the boat gets wet the least. You must be at least forty-two inches tall to ride.

A few years back the park added a habitat for a white rhino by the name of Timmy. His home can only be seen by guests sailing by high in the air on the Tanganyika Tidal Wave.

Land of the Dragons

Busch Gardens' children's play area is built around a shaded three-story tree house. The Land of the Dragons is home to Dumphrey, a friendly imaginary beast. Kids are invited to explore the winding stairways and mysterious towers of the tree house. The area also includes a children's theater, slides, a rope climb, a ball crawl, and a gentle waterfall. The rides area includes a mini-sized Ferris wheel, a flume ride, and a dragon carousel.

Bird Gardens

The oldest area of the park, built in the shadow of the original brewery in 1959. The lush foliage includes nearly two thousand exotic birds and birds of prey, representing 218 species and including one of the largest managed flocks of Caribbean flamingos.

Some of the park's most famous species are seen here. Eagles on display near the old brewery site include golden and American bald eagles. The koala habitat also includes Dama wallabies and rose-breasted cockatoos.

The park's Chilean Flamingos ordinarily live in large colonies on brackish lagoons in South America. Their bent bills are fringed at the edges and when held upside-down in the water filter out mud and retain shrimp and algae.

Koala Display. A series of educational exhibits leads up to the home of the park's koalas, among the most unusual animals at Busch Gardens. You'll glide past the glass cages on a moving sidewalk; at the end you can also climb up some stairs to a stationary viewing area. Koalas are marsupials, unusual mammals with a pouch that covers the mammary glands on the abdomen. In the Americas the only current species of marsupial is the opossum.

Lory Landing. Bird-watching soars to new heights at Busch Gardens' aviary, featuring more than seventy-five colorful and unusual tropical birds from around the world. The environment is designed as if it were a deserted island with waterfalls, floral landscapes, vine-covered trellises, and ponds. It is the home to lorikeets, hornbills, parrots, avocets, touracos, and other brilliantly colored species.

In a large free-flight area visitors become human perches as lorikeets land on arms, shoulders, and heads to feed on nectar (sold for a nominal fee).

Closer to the aviary's entrance, separate enclosures offer views of several types of endangered parrots, including thick-bills, red-tailed black cockatoos, hyacinth macaws, and hawk-headed parrots.

Amateur bird-watchers will find feathered facts and artifacts such as eggs tucked into surrounding trees, as well as species identification signs and notes describing threats to the species' native habitats.

Busch Gardens Bird Show. Several performances each day of a show that includes macaws, cockatoos, and birds of prey in free-flight.

Lizard Habitat. A showcase for Asian water monitors, crocodile monitors, rhinoceros iguanas, and green iguanas from regions that include Indonesia, South America, and the Caribbean.

Hospitality House. The patio nearby fronts on a small pond, patrolled by a flock of geese; it's one of our favorite places for a break from the sun and crowds. Free samples of Anheuser-Busch beer are offered, along with a simple sandwich-and-pizza menu. A musical variety show including ragtime jazz piano is presented on a small stage.

Special Programs

Busch Gardens offers a variety of educational programs; check with the park for a schedule. Among the offerings is **Zoo Camp**, five different weeklong summer camp programs for children from kindergarten through ninth grade.

Eating Your Way Through Busch Gardens Tampa Bay

Morocco

Boujad Bakery. An exotic place to grab a bit of breakfast or a sweet at any time of the day. Check out the gigantic blueberry and other types of muffins; also sold are impressive turnovers and pastries for $2 to $3 each.

Zagora Cafe. An exotic outdoor bazaar setting for un-exotic burgers, onion rings, and turkey sandwich platters, priced about $7.

Key

= Fast food

= Pub

= Full-service restaurant

Congo

Vivi Storehouse. Near the Python coaster, this restaurant is open in the peak season only from 11:45 A.M. to 4 P.M. Offerings include sandwich platters for about $6, as well as chicken fajitas.

Crown Colony

Crown Colony House. A lovely 240-seat restaurant with spectacular views of the Serengeti Plain from its glass-walled **Veldt Room**. Another interesting location is the **Library**, stocked with antique books and a collection of photographs from colonial days in Africa. A piano player entertains during meals.

Featured is Crown Colony's Famous Family-Style Chicken Dinner: platters of batter-dipped chicken, coleslaw, soft yeast rolls, dressing, mashed potatoes and gravy, garden vegetables, and cranberry relish. The fare is a reasonable $9.25 per person; diners twelve and younger are billed a reasonable $3.95. The

Serious shoppers only. Busch Gardens offers a plan for visitors who want a quick shopping spree at one of the shops just inside its gates. Buy your ticket, go forth and shop, and be back at the Guest Relations booth within thirty minutes and you will be given a refund of your ticket. (You'll have to pay for parking, though.) We're told that some visitors make a mad dash from the gate to the Smokehouse restaurant for take-out ribs or chicken.

same platter can be ordered with batter-fried fish instead of chicken. Other items include broiled grouper.

There are only about a dozen tables next to the windows in the Veldt Room, and they go fast. No reservations are accepted.

The least crowded times to visit are before noon, and from 4 to 5:30 P.M.; each day a throng heads for the restaurant about 12:15 P.M. when the midday ice show lets out.

Timbuktu

Das Festhaus. The ceiling is an attractive blue-and-white striped tent. In the center of the large 1,200-seat hall is a bandstand, home of the **Bavarian Colony Band and Dancers** who present the ***International Show***. The show makes note of the early German settlers in Africa who made their home in Timbuktu. Also seen on the stage is the ***Festival of Nations Show***, which features music and performances from around the world.

Offerings include corned beef sandwiches and a German sampler platter, each for about $6. There are also spaghetti platters and cannelloni for about the same price. A range of Anheuser-Busch beers is offered.

Stanleyville

Stanleyville Smokehouse. Slow-smoked chicken, beef brisket, and pork ribs, served with french fries and coleslaw. Prices range from about $5 to $9. Grab a bunch of napkins and prepare for a tasty mess.

Bazaar Cafe. Barbecue beef sandwich platters and salads.

Bird Gardens

Hospitality House. Pepperoni and Chef's Combo pizzas, at $3 to $4 per slice. Tampa sandwiches—salami, turkey, cheese, and salad on a roll—sell for about $5.50. Free samples of Anheuser-Busch beers for adults.

Adventure Island

Although the tidal wave and rafting expeditions at Busch Gardens are guaranteed to dampen your hairdo, if you want to get really wet, you may want to head around the corner to Adventure Island.

The twenty-two-acre water park, also owned by Busch Entertainment, offers giant speed slides, body flumes, diving platforms, inner tube slides, a wave pool, water games, a white sand beach, and volleyball courts.

The **Wahoo Run** tunnel raft ride sends five riders down six stories and more than six hundred feet of unforeseen drenching twists, drops, back-to-back curves and turns. The thrill slide has a unique tunnel design that careens riders through alternating daylight and darkness and four waterfall curtains. The rafts are propelled by more than ten thousand gallons of flowing water per minute in a nine-foot-diameter tube.

Aruba Tuba is a "tubular" slide that twists in and around and below Calypso Coaster; the ride can be enjoyed by solo riders or two at a time.

Calypso Coaster is a spiraling snake-like ride down an open flume in an inner tube or raft for two. **Rambling Bayou** is a slow float along a winding river around bends, under bridges, and through a man-made rain forest.

Caribbean Corkscrew takes riders from a four-story tower down a fully enclosed, twisting translucent tube. **Water Moccasin** is a triple-tube water slide that cascades riders downward and through a spiral before dumping them in a pool.

Adventure Island Tickets

Prices were in effect in mid-2001 and are subject to change. They do not include 7 percent tax

Adult 1-day	$25.95
Child (3–9) 1-day	$23.95

Busch Gardens/ Adventure Island Combo

1 day at each park

Adult	$59.95
Child (3–9)	$49.95

Tampa Typhoon is a free-fall body slide that drops from a height of seventy-six feet before it levels out in a slick trough. **Gulf Scream** is a speed slide in which riders can go as fast as 25 miles per hour down a 210-foot slide.

Everglides takes riders down a steep seventy-two-foot double slide on water sleds that hydroplane up to one hundred feet over a splash pool; a lift system carries the sleds back to the top of the slide platform. **Runaway Rapids** is a thirty-four-foot-high artificial mountain that features five separate curving and twisting water flumes as long as three hundred feet.

Wahoo Run at Adventure Island

Photo courtesy of Busch Gardens Tampa

Paradise Lagoon is a nine-thousand-square-foot swimming pool fed by waterfalls; built into the surrounding cliffs are twenty-foot-high diving platforms, a cable drop, a cannonball slide, and tube slides. Stretching overhead across the pool is a hand-over-hand rope walk. The **Endless Surf** is a half-acre pool that mechanically produces three- to five-foot waves for body and rubber raft surfing.

Splash Attack is a huge water playground that offers squirt guns, waterfalls, slides, and a huge bucket that dumps water.

The addition of heating for the outdoor pools now permits the park to be open from Valentine's Day through October; at the beginning and end of the season the park is open on weekends only.

WOW The Florida Aquarium

Florida was here long before the Mouse, and one of the most spectacular collections of creatures that have an aquatic link can be found at the Florida Aquarium along downtown Tampa's waterfront.

Alligator hatchlings, roseate spoonbills, river otters, mangrove forests, coral reefs, and thousands of fish are among the exhibits awaiting visitors.

The Florida water story begins at the **Florida Wetlands Gallery**, which features nearly fifty juvenile American alligators, river otters, and great horned owls. The **Florida Bays and Beaches Gallery** has a display that includes bonnethead sharks, Southern stingrays, flounder, and bighead sea robins; at the **Florida Bay Bottoms** gallery creatures include spiny lobsters.

The heart of the Florida Aquarium is its **Coral Reefs Gallery**, an unusual glimpse into a habitat ordinarily only explored by divers. The design simulates a sixty-foot dive from shallow water reefs to deeper, darker waters. At the top of a walking tour, visitors discover a variety of corals populated by grouper, moray eel, and parrotfish. From there is a descent through the reef face into an underwater coral cave with viewing windows.

And finally there is an underwater theater facing a stunning forty-three-foot-wide, panoramic window. There you'll see coral colonies silhouetted by beams of sunlight from the surface, with brightly colored fishes and wandering sharks. Several times a day, divers descend into the tank, sometimes conducting question-and-answer sessions by radio with viewers on the other side of the window.

Tickets in 2001 were $12.95 for adults, $7.95 for children (3–12), and $11.95 for seniors (50 and older). For information, call ☎ (813) 273-4000 or consult 💻 www.flaquarium.net.

WOW The Museum of Science and Industry (MOSI)

The amazing, expanding Museum of Science and Industry in Tampa has tripled in size to become the largest science center in the Southeast. Permanent exhibits include **The Amazing You** where you can tour the human body in all its complexity from DNA to cells to organs to individuals; the ***Challenger* Learning Center**, a living memorial to the crew of the shuttle orbiter *Challenger*, with a replica of a space vehicle and mission control; the **BioWorks Butterfly Garden**; and a flight simulator.

A permanent exhibit showcases a pair of seventy-five-foot-long diplodocus skeletons guarding the lobby. The skeletons were from remains found in Wyoming. The dinosaurs were believed to weigh about twenty tons when they flourished in the western United States during the Jurassic period. *Diplodocus carnegii* were named in honor of industrialist Andrew Carnegie who funded the expedition that recovered the first specimens in 1901.

Diplodocus means "double beam," referring to the chevron-shaped vertebrae in the creature's tail.

The **Imax Dome Theater** presents a changing series of big-screen films.

MOSI is located at 4801 East Fowler Avenue, one mile north of Busch Gardens Tampa. For information, call ☎ (800) 995-6674 or ☎ (813) 987-6000, or consult 💻 www.mosi.org.

Admission prices to the museum in 2001 were $13 for adults, $9 for children (2–13), and $11 for seniors (50 and older).

BUSCH GARDENS

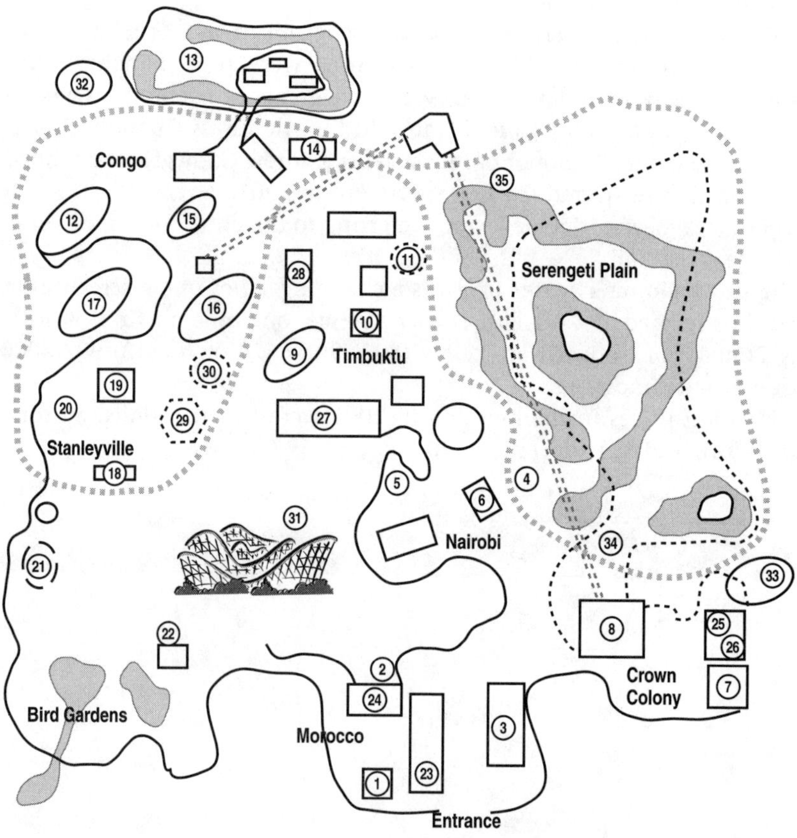

1. Marrakesh Theater
2. Sultan's Tent
3. Moroccan Palace Theater
4. Aldabra Tortoise Habitat
5. Myombe Reserve: The Great Ape Domain
6. Train Station
7. Akbar's Adventure Tours
8. Skyride and Monorail Station
9. The Scorpion
10. Carousel Caravan
11. The Phoenix
12. The Python
13. Congo River Rapids
14. Congo Station Transveldt Railroad
15. Claw Island
16. Stanley Falls Log Flume
17. Tanganyika Tidal Wave
18. Stanleyville Station Transveldt Railroad
19. Stanleyville Theater
20. Zambezi Theater
21. Land of the Dragons
22. Hospitality House
23. Boujad Bakery
24. Zagora Cafe
25. Crown Colony House
26. Anheuser Busch Hospitality Center
27. Das Festhaus
28. Oasis
29. Stanleyville Smokehouse
30. Bazaar Cafe
31. Gwazi
32. Kumba
33. Montu
34. The Edge of Africa
35. Rhino Rally

Special Offers to *Econoguide* Readers

Look to your left, look to your right. One of you three people on vacation is paying the regular price for airfare, hotels, meals, and shopping. One is paying premium price for a less-than-first-rate package. And one is paying a deeply discounted special rate.

Which one would you rather be?

In this book you've learned about strategies to obtain the lowest prices on airfare, the best times to take a trip, and ideas on how to negotiate just about every element of travel.

And now, we're happy to present a special section of discount coupons for *Econoguide* readers.

All of the offers represent real savings. Be sure to read the coupons carefully, though, because of exclusions during holiday periods and other fine print.

The author and publisher of this book do not endorse any of the businesses whose coupons appear here, and the presence of a coupon in this section does not in any way affect the author's opinions expressed in this book.

econoguide '02

$3.00 OFF 2-Day Ticket

Enjoy two days of unlimited park-to-park access to both Universal Studios® and Islands of Adventure℠ theme parks!

UNIVERSAL Orlando® RESORT

Two Amazing Theme Parks, Non-Stop Nightlife, and World-Class On-Site Resorts.

Not valid with any other discount or offer. Must present at time of purchase. Discount good for up to 6 tickets. Offer valid through 12/31/02.

$3.00 OFF CityWalk Party Pass℠

CityWalk® is Orlando's hottest spot for entertainment, where you'll find such exciting clubs and restaurants as Jimmy Buffett's® Margaritaville®, Pat O'Brien's®, Emeril's® Restaurant Orlando, and the world's largest Hard Rock Cafe®. Home to the best of the best in live music, casual and fine dining, dancing, shopping, movies and more, CityWalk has it all!

Admission to CityWalk is FREE! As the sun goes down, CityWalk's restaurants and nightclubs start pulsing to the beat of live entertainment, and some individual cover charges go into effect (hours vary). So the best way to experience it ALL is with the CityWalk Party Pass, offering one night of ALL-CLUB ACCESS* for one low price. It's Orlando's best entertainment value!

Not valid with any other discount or offer. Must present at time of purchase. Discount good for up to 6 passes. Offer valid through 12/30/02.

*One-night access only. Restrictions apply. Not valid for separately ticketed concerts and special events. Some venues require 21 or older for admission. Proof of ID may be required.

econoguide '02

ADVENTURE EXPRESS

SeaWorld
ADVENTURE PARK
Orlando

$5.00 Off

See the best of SeaWorld with Adventure Express!

Adventure Express is a 6-hour exclusive adventure and includes front-of-the-line access to rides, reserved seats at select shows, animal interaction and feeding opportunities and an expert guide to help make your day a great adventure. Sign up at the information counter.

$1.00 OFF

Behind-the-Scenes Tours

Present this coupon at the Information Counter inside SeaWorld Orlando and receive $1 off a **Behind-the-Scenes Tour**. Choose from *To the Rescue*, *Predators* and *Polar Expedition*—or take all three! These one-hour adventures are filled with animal interactions, adventure and fun!

SeaWorld
ADVENTURE PARK
Orlando

ADVENTURE EXPRESS

Sign up at the Information Counter inside SeaWorld Orlando or call **800-406-2244** for advance reservations. Discount valid for up to six people. Not valid with any other offer. Tour availability and components subject to change. Park admission is not included and is required. Expires 12/31/02.

SeaWorld
ADVENTURE PARK
Orlando

Behind-the-Scenes Tours

Discount valid for up to six people. Not valid with any other offer. Tour availability and components subject to change. Park admission not included and is required. Expires 12/31/02.

SeaWorld
ADVENTURE PARK
Orlando

SHAMU

$5.00 Off Adult & Junior Luau Admission

Aloha POLYNESIAN LUAU

Our nightly South Seas extravaganza, Aloha Polynesian Luau, is the most unique dinner show in Central Florida! While you're entertained by our authentic Polynesian dance revue, you'll enjoy a multi-course, family style banquet of island delicacies. Don't miss this tropical getaway that's not far away.

SeaWorld
ADVENTURE PARK
Orlando

SeaWorld
ADVENTURE PARK
Orlando

Orlando's highest, longest, fastest, and only floorless coaster!

Aloha

POLYNESIAN LUAU

Limit six guests per certificate. Reservations required. Inquire at Information Center or call (407) 351-3600. Offer not valid with other discounts. Present certificate before bill is totaled. Redeemable only at time of Luau attendance. Luau price separate from park admission. Park admission not required. Photocopies not accepted. Seating begins at 6:30 p.m. Operating hours and prices subject to change without notice. Valid through 12/31/02 only.

SeaWorld
ADVENTURE PARK
Orlando

$2.00 Off Admission

KRAKEN℠

Limit six guests per certificate. Reservations not valid with other discounts, special events or on purchase of multi-park/multi-visit passes or tickets. Present certificates at Front Gate before bill is totaled. Redeemable only at time of ticket purchase. Photocopies not accepted. Operating hours and general admission price subject to change without notice. Certificate has no cash value. Valid through 12/31/02.

SeaWorld
ADVENTURE PARK
Orlando

PLU 4354/4353

Bring this coupon to the Pointe*Orlando Guest Services Desk for your FREE Coupon Book full of excellent savings

International Drive across from the Convention Center
(407) 248-2838

Open 10 A.M. daily
www.pointeorlandofl.com

FL02-32 Expires 12/30/02

Pointe*Orlando

Over 60 shops and seven restaurants including FAO Schwarz, Banana Republic, Victoria's Secret, Dan Marino's Town Tavern, AIX Armani Exchange, and Yankee Candle

---

Buy one regular admission, get one FREE

A flying and working museum specializing in the display and restoration of WWII aircraft. Knowledgeable guides. T-6 Warbird flights available through Warbird Adventures, Inc. adjacent to the museum

Open daily

231 North Hoagland Boulevard, (south off Highway 192). Kissimmee, Florida.
(407) 933-1942 www.warbirdmuseum.com

FL02-35 Expires 12/31/02

Tom Reilly's

Warbird Restoration Museum

HRN REBATE COUPON

HOTEL RESERVATIONS NETWORK

(800) 964-6835
www.hoteldiscount.com

Major Cities - Rooms for Soldout Dates - Special Rates

UP TO $50

$10 REBATE with 2-Night Booking
$20 REBATE with 4-Night Booking
$30 REBATE with 5-Night Booking
$50 REBATE with 7-Night Booking

UP TO $50

Name: ____________________

Booking Number: ______________ Hotel: ____________________

FL02-34 Dates of Stay: ________________ See reverse side for rules.

COUPON

Do you like to travel? Don't just dream about it. You've earned it.

Receive $50 or $100 off your next cruise or vacation*

**minimum purchase required. Coupon expires 12/31/02*

Donna Zabel, Destination & Travel Specialist
168 Lake Terrace Drive, Munroe Falls, OH 44262
PH/Fax: (330) 686-0401 E-Mail: dz@ald.net
Website: www.dreammaker.org

DREAM MAKER DESTINATIONS
RESEARCH TO REALITY!

FL02-09

HRN REBATE COUPON

Coupon Rules:

UP TO $50

1. Must return this coupon to receive rebate.
2. Coupon expires 12/31/02. **3.** Rebate mailed after check-out.
4. Coupons non-combinable. **5.** Not retroactive.
6. After check-out, send this coupon with self-addressed stamped envelope to: **HRN 8140 Walnut Hill Lane, Suite 203, Dallas, TX 75231.**
7. Rebate check mailed within 2–3 weeks.
8. One rebate per customer.

5% bonus discount!

travel*store*: www.travel-store.com

(800) 826-3119

5% off based on TravelStore's best vacation package or discounted cruise price with minimum purchase of $499 per person. Not combinable with other discount coupons. Not valid on airline tickets only. Must complete brief travel questionnaire to receive certificate.

Expires 12/31/02

CST#2002736-10

FK02-33

Brentwood Beverly Hills Santa Monica Los Angeles Malibu Palos Verdes Westlake

---

Experience Polynesian Islanders Review at the world famous Mai-Kai Restaurant and Show Club. See beautiful maidens and agile warriors perform native dances of the South Pacific. It's an authentic, flower-filled, thrilling show—highlighted by the dramatic Samoan Fire-Knife Dance. Group rate and packages available.

2 for 1 Show Charge

Maximum of six (6) people. Not valid on Saturdays or holidays. Not valid with any other offer. Non-transferable. No refund value. Void if altered.

3599 North Federal Highway, Fort Lauderdale, FL
(954) 563-3272

Expires 12/31/02

FL02-31

DO THE ZOO

SAVE SAVE SAVE SAVE

$1 OFF regular adult admission

(321) 254-9453

Not valid with other discounts or special events.
Limit 6 guests per coupon.

Exit 73 off I-95. 8225 North Wickham Road, Melbourne, FL
Near Cocoa Beach and Port Canaveral

Regular adult $7 Senior $6 Children 2–12 $5 Under 2 FREE

BREVARD ZOO™

Expires 12/31/02

FL02-01

Boggy Creek Airboat Rides

Experience the Central Florida Everglades

U.S. Coast Guard-Approved

$2.00 Off each adult

On day trips only. Not valid with any discounts or coupons.• Minutes from Central Florida attractions • 5 Different areas of wetlands • Speeds up to 45 mph • Restaurant and gift shop • Beautiful half-hour tours

Open 9 A.M. 'til 5:30 P.M.—7 days a week.
1-hour nighttime alligator hunts available.

407-344-9550 www.bcairboats.com

Expires 12/31/02

FL02-16

Ripley's
Believe It or Not!®

ORLANDO ODDITORIUM

8201 International Drive, (407) 363-4418

Present this coupon for

$2 Off each admission

Limit 6 people per coupon.
Not valid with other discounts.
All trademarks are owned by Ripley Entertainment Inc.

AECO-CECO

FL02-07

Expires 12/31/02

$5 off general admission

Limit six guests per coupon.
Not valid with other discounts or on the purchase of multi-visit passes or special ticket events.
Operating hours and general admission prices subject to change without notice.

(863) 324-2111

www.cypressgardens.com

CYPRESS GARDENS℠
WINTER HAVEN, FLORIDA
Florida's First Theme Park • Est. 1936

Located between Tampa and Orlando, off US27 just 22 miles south of I-4.

FL02-37

#1205

Expires 12/31/02

Buy one admission and get second of equal or lesser value free

Not valid with other offers or discounts

Skull Kingdom
5933 American Way, Orlando, FL 32819
At International Drive across from Wet 'n Wild

SKULL KINGDOM™
A Haunted Family Attraction

FL02-05

Expires 12/31/02

SeaEscape®
to a Ship Full of Fun!℠

RESERVATIONS:
3045 North Federal Hwy., Lndmk #7
Fort Lauderdale, FL 33306
(954) 453-3333
(877) SEA-ESCAPE
www.seaescape.com
Ask for code "C5"

YOU ARE ENTITLED TO

$5* OFF A SeaEscape PARTY CRUISE

Sailing From Port Everglades, Ft. Lauderdale
Day & Evening Party Cruises • 13 times a week
Fabulous Buffet • Spa • Live Entertainment
Las Vegas–Style Casino Action on a Big Ship

*NOT VALID ON SATURDAY NIGHT OR HOLIDAYS.
TAXES NOT INCLUDED. RESTRICTIONS APPLY.
OFFERS CANNOT BE COMBINED. CAPACITY CONTROLLED.
SHIP'S REGISTRY: BAHAMAS. SYMBOL: SEPI
Expires 12/31/02

FL02-17

Full Casino Action

Sailing from ports all over Florida and Myrtle Beach, S.C.!

SunCruz CASINO FLORIDA

- *Free shuttle*
- *Buffet*
- *Entertainment*
- *Table games & slots*

(800) 474-DICE

Buy $10 in slot tokens. Get $5 in tokens free

Visit our locations: Hollywood, Port Canaveral, Daytona Beach, Clearwater, John's Pass, T.I., Fort Myers, and Jacksonville

Expires 12/30/02

FL02-19

BUY 1 TICKET
AT REG. PRICE

GET 1/3 OFF 2nd TICKET
2nd TICKET MUST BE OF EQUAL VALUE OR LESS WITH COUPON
VALID THROUGH 12/31/02

SAWGRASS RECREATION PARK
(954) 389-0202
AIRBOAT TOURS

INCLUDED IN AIRBOAT TOUR:
- INDIAN VILLAGE (18th CENTURY)
- ALLIGATOR & REPTILE EXHIBIT
- BIRDS OF PREY EXHIBIT
- ALL TOURS ARE NARRATED

1-888-4-AIRBOAT

Sawgrass Recreation Park
P.O. Box 291620
Fort Lauderdale, FL 33329
(954) 389-0202
(900) 457-0788

Expires 12/31/02

FL02-15

$2.00 OFF

DAYTONA USA
THE ULTIMATE MOTORSPORTS ATTRACTION
Official Attraction Of NASCAR

DAYTONA USA
The Ultimate Motorsports Attraction

Located at
Daytona International Speedway

Coupon Good For:
$2.00 off on DAYTONA USA and Speedway Tour, for up to 6 guests.
Must present coupon at time of visitation to DAYTONA USA.
Offer not valid in conjunction with other coupon or discount.
Offer valid through December 31, 2002

CODE: ECONOGUIDE

FL02-10

The Mercado World Marketplace
$200 Savings Passport Book

Redeem this coupon in our International Visitor's Center for a coupon book worth $200 in savings at The Mercado.

The Mercado is the home of a world-class attraction: Titanic—The Exhibition, plus six award-winning restaurants, 60 specialty shops, free nightly entertainment, an authentic British pub, visitor's services, and International Drive's only international food court

THE MERCADO

Open daily
from 10 A.M. until 2 A.M.

8445 International Drive
Orlando, FL 32819
(407) 345-9337

FL02-08

Expires 12/31/02

$5 OFF

Enjoy eco dining on the St. John's River.
Sailing daily for lunch and dinner cruises.
Conveniently located between Daytona and Orlando.
Experience the history, wildlife, and beauty while cruising on Central Florida's finest rivership.
Fully climate controlled with full service staff.

Call for reservations (800) 423-7401 or (407) 321-5091

American River Cruises
presents
The Rivership Romance
433 N. Palmetto Ave.
Sanford, FL 32771

FL02-02

"Econoguide" restrictions apply

Expires 12/31/02

FL02-22

Samsonite®
Company Stores

10% OFF
your entire purchase

Not valid on Kodak, Hasbro, or Safety First
Not valid with any other coupon offer

Expires 12/31/02

MurderWatch
Mystery Dinner Theatre

AT WALT DISNEY WORLD VILLAGE
GROSVENOR
RESORT

$4.00 Off per person (up to 6 in party)

For reservations, phone (407) 827-6534.
Not valid with other coupons or discounts.

1850 Hotel Plaza Boulevard, Lake Buena Vista, FL 32830-2202
Expires 12/31/02

FL02-40

econoguide '02

Treasure Chest Quest Game Show

AT WALT DISNEY WORLD VILLAGE
GROSVENOR RESORT

$3.00 Off per person (up to 6 in party)

For reservations, phone (407) 827-6534.
Not valid with other coupons or discounts.

Treasure Chest Quest© Game Show

1850 Hotel Plaza Boulevard, Lake Buena Vista, FL 32830-2202

Expires 12/31/02

FL02-41

Sleuths Mystery Dinner Show

You Solve the Crime!

$4 Off per person

Up to 6 people

Tickets must be purchased at door.
Not valid with any other offer.

Sleuths Mystery Dinner Shows

7508 Universal Blvd. (behind Wet 'n Wild), Orlando, FL 32819

For reservations, call (407) 363-1985, (800) 393-1985 (USA)

Expires 12/30/02

FL02-06

Miniature Golf
Buy One Get One Free

Coupon cannot be used with other coupons or discounts.
Located across from the 192 Flea Market.
Located between markers 14 and 15.
Hole-n-one prizes given out daily.

Open 9:00 A.M. to 11:30 P.M.

PIRATE'S ISLAND ADVENTURE GOLF

Pirates Island, 4330 W. Highway 192, Kissimmee, FL 34746, (407) 396-4660

Expires 12/31/02

FL02-14

Largest selection of new, used, custom logo, and personalized golf balls. Huge savings

10% off first order

www.golfballs.com
(800) 37-BALLS

(Maximum discount is $20)

golfballs.com
1.800.37.BALLS

FL02-03

Expires 12/31/02

Promo code EG301

econoguide '02

$20 off

based on vacation package with minimum purchase of $500. Not valid on airline tickets

Danny Travel Inc.
310E 46th Street #6W
New York, NY 10017

Danny Travel Inc.
www.dannytravel.com
(212) 557-1009
(800) 565-8553

FL02-21

Expires 12/31/02

Miniature Golf
Buy One Get One Free

Coupon cannot be used with other coupons or discounts.
Located next to Old Town, behind Red Lobster.
Located between markers 9 and 10.
Hole-n-one prizes given out daily.

Open 9:00 A.M. to 11:30 P.M.

Pirates Cove, 2845 Fla. Plaza Blvd., Kissimmee, FL 34746, (407) 396-7484

Pirate's Cove®

FL02-13

Expires 12/31/02

Golf Shoes Plus

Golf shoes, walking shoes, and street shoes

Mention ECONOGUIDE #1001 for a ***10% discount*** on any one pair of shoes

www.golfshoesplus.com

PRO'S EDGE

FL02-23

Expires 12/31/02

Golf Shoes Plus

30% to 50% off everything in stock

SHOES • GLOVES • SOCKS • ALL ACCESSORIES

Nike, FootJoy, Etonic, Reebok. More name brands available

2704 Stickney Point Road, Sarasota, FL 34231
(941) 925-4733

www.golfshoesplus.com

PRO'S EDGE

FL02-24

Expires 12/31/02

Golf Shoes Plus

$5 off any pair of shoes up to $75, and $10 off any pair of shoes over $75. Also 20% off any accessories.

Golf shoes and walking shoes (Footjoy, Etonics, Nike, and Adidas) and accessories

1850 Boyscout Drive, Suite #111, Ft. Myers, FL 33907
(941) 278-3331 www.golfshoesplus.com

PRO'S EDGE

FL02-25

Expires 12/31/02

Pro's Edge

The Big $moke Golf Clubs

Mention ECONOGUIDE #1002
for a ***25% discount***
on one club *or* one complete set
of 1, 3, 5, & 7 wood, any flex available.

www.thebigsmoke.com

PRO'S EDGE

FL02-26

Expires 12/31/02

Magnetic Therapy Sales Specialist

Discount for mail order
25% off one product

Call for brochure or information on magnetic support products (knee tube, elbow tube, back support, inner soles, head and wrist bands), magnetic bracelets, and jewelry

1850 Boyscout Dr., Suite #209, Ft. Myers, FL 33907
(888) 883-0813 or (941) 278-5503
www.magnetictherapysales.com

PRO'S EDGE

FL02-27

Expires 12/31/02

Golden Link Motel

LOW SEASON
$29.95 to $39.95
1/3–2/4, 4/29–6/16,
8/21–12/23

HIGH SEASON
$39.95 to $49.95
2/5–4/28,
6/17–8/20

(Excludes holidays and special events)

Located on beautiful Lake Cecile. Only four minutes from Walt Disney World. Satellite TV. King size beds. Heated pool. Water and jet ski.

Please present this ad at check-in. Reservations suggested.
Located at the Intersection of Hwy. 192 and S.R. 535.
4914 W. Irlo Bronson Hwy., Kissimmee, FL 32746, (407) 396-0555, (800) 654-3957
Expires 12/31/02

FL02-11

econoguide '02

Wynfield Inn–Main Gate

(Four miles from Walt Disney World)

50% Discount on rack rates

Scheduled shuttle to Disney theme parks. Free coffee and tea in lobby 24 hours. Close to shopping and restaurants. 1–4 persons per room, swimming pool, non-smoking rooms available.

Wynfield Inn–Main Gate
5335 West Irlo Bronson Hwy., Kissimmee, FL 34746
(800) 346-1551, (407) 396-2121

Based on availability, no other discounts apply.

Expires 12/25/02

FL02-29

Wynfield INN MAIN GATE

www.wynfieldinns.com

Wynfield Inn–Westwood

(SeaWorld—International Drive Area)

50% Discount on rack rates

Scheduled shuttle to Disney World
I-Drive Trolley picks up every 15 minutes in front of Westwood property. In-room coffeemakers

Wynfield Inn–Westwood, 6263 Westwood Blvd., Orlando, FL 32821
(800) 346-1551 (407) 345-8000

Space availability, no other discounts apply.

Expires 12/31/02

FL02-20

Wynfield INN WESTWOOD

www.wynfieldinns.com
wynfieldin@aol.com

$29.95 for 1–4 persons

(1/4–2/10, 4/23–6/8, 8/20–12/14)

$39.95 for 1–4 persons

(2/11–4/22, 6/9–8/19)

Minutes from Disney World, swimming pool.
Free refrigerator and microwave in all rooms.
Free morning coffee. Two extra-long double beds or a king bed.
Smoking or nonsmoking rooms. Limited availability.
Rates subject to change during holidays and special events.

801 East Vine St. (Hwy. 192), Kissimmee, Florida
Reservations: (800) 780-7617 or (407) 846-1935 Fax: (407) 846-7225

Expires 12/31/02

FL02-36

FLAMINGO INN

AAA 2 Diamond Rating

Better than the big names, at lower cost

www.flamingoinn.com

Caribbean Villas Vacation Condos

Just minutes from Walt Disney World, Orlando, Florida

Sleeps Six	Sleeps Eight
2 Bedroom/2 Bath	3 Bedroom/2 Bath
Off-peak $65 per night	Off-peak $85 per night
Peak $85 per night	Peak $105 per night

Published Rack Rates $99–$160 per night. Minimum stay requirements apply. Subject to Availability—Tax additional. Not valid during Holiday Periods or Special Events. Advance reservations suggested. Present coupon upon arrival.

2003 Trinidad Court, Kissimmee, Florida 34741
Reservations: (800) 327-4730
www.flvacationvillas.com

FL02-12

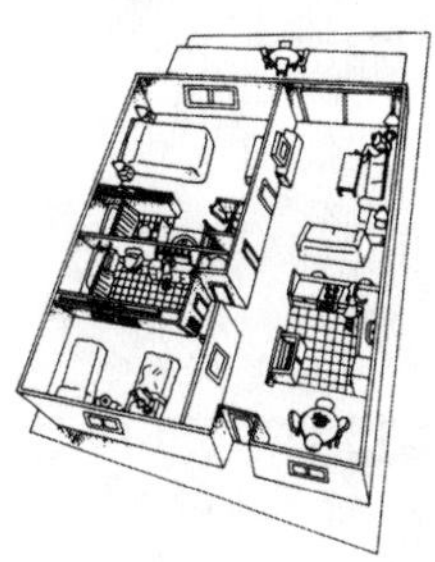

Caribbean Villas

Expires 12/31/02

econoguide '02

econoguide '02

Quick-Find Index to Attractions

(See also the detailed Contents)